Odilo Globocnik,
Hitler's Man in the East

D1610278

To my mother, Helena Krepinska-Poprzeczna, and my half sister, Zofia Krepinska-Rurka, both of Skierbieszow, 17 kilometers northeast of Zamosc. They were victims of the Globocnik and von Mohrenschildt–initiated Zamosc Lands ethnic cleansing action of 1942–43 that saw the launching of *Generalplan Ost* upon Polish lands by Hitler and Himmler, the Third Reich's most ardent Eastern Dreamers.

Odilo Globocnik, Hitler's Man in the East

JOSEPH POPRZECZNY

McFarland & Company, Inc., Publishers
Jefferson, North Carolina, and London

LIBRARY OF CONGRESS CATALOGUING-IN-PUBLICATION DATA

Poprzeczny, Joseph.
  Odilo Globocnik, Hitler's man in the East / Joseph Poprzeczny.
  p.   cm.
  Includes bibliographical references and index.

  ISBN-13: 978-0-7864-1625-7
  softcover : 50# alkaline paper ∞

  1. Globocnik, Odilo, 1904–1945.   2. Holocaust, Jewish
(1939–1945)— Poland.   3. Waffen-SS — Officers — Biography.
4. Nazis — Austria — Biography.   5. War criminals — Biography.
6. Slovenia — Biography.   I. Title.
DS135.P6P62   2004
364.15'1'092 — dc22   2003024603

British Library cataloguing data are available

Cover photographs: (top) Odilo Globocnik, second from right in Lublin's
Old Town Quarter, 1943 *(Yad Veshem Film and Photo Archive); (bottom)*
Odilo Globocnik *(US Embassy Office Berlin, Berlin Document Center)*

Manufactured in the United States of America

*McFarland & Company, Inc., Publishers
  Box 611, Jefferson, North Carolina 28640
  www.mcfarlandpub.com*

Acknowledgments

Work on this study received crucial assistance from several historians, researchers and experts, and Irmgard Rickheim, who was engaged to Odilo Globocnik from mid–1941 until late 1942; she provided personal information, as well as previously unpublished photographs. Also helpful were Michael Tregenza of London, and lately of Lublin, who has conducted groundbreaking research and published many new findings on Globocnik's central role as head of *Aktion Reinhardt*, including pioneering work on aspects of Globocnik's Belzec killing center; Professor Maurice Williams of Okanagan University College, Kelowna, British Columbia, Canada, an internationally recognized expert on Austrian National Socialism, its far-reaching impact on Slovenia, and Globocnik's longtime and important Nazi Party associate Dr. Friedrich Rainer; Erwin Lerner, New York playwright with productions off-Broadway, whose international contacts and researches on Globocnik have resulted in his acquiring a large array of previously unknown sources, including especially Georg Wippern's two postwar court statements; Siegfried Pucher, the author of Globocnik's only biography by the year 2003, which is in German and arose from Pucher's academic thesis, who provided information and advice in addition to that biography; Dr. Alfred Elste of Villach, Austria, for providing a copy of a Globocnik-signed wartime album that set out the blueprint for the Germanization (*Eindeutschung*) of Poland's Zamosc Lands (*Zamojszczyzna*), a pivotal World War II document showing precisely how the first steps in the Germanization of this region were to be undertaken; Dr. Berndt Rieger, formerly of Wolfsberg, Austria, and lately of Bamberg,

Germany, especially for his assistance in providing his findings on the largely forgotten but crucially important Carinthian, Reinhold von Mohrenschildt, and this SS man's Baltic ancestry; Ales Brecelj of Trieste, who discovered early original sources on Globocnik and the Globocnik family in Trieste and made these and other findings freely available; Helmut Wabnig and Dirk Lorek, for translating Siegfried Pucher's thesis; Professor Larry V. Thompson of the U.S. Naval Academy, Annapolis, Maryland, and Dr. Peter R. Black, senior historian, Center for Advanced Holocaust Studies, U.S. Holocaust Memorial Museum, Washington, D.C., who both provided early English-language versions of their biographical essays on Friedrich-Wilhelm Kruger and Odilo Globocnik, respectively, that were to be published in German; Michael T. Allen of the Georgia Institute of Technology, who drew my attention to several crucial issues, including clandestine moves against Globocnik in Berlin, and who provided copies of an early chapter from a manuscript for my use; Stephen Tyas of London, who located several previously unknown documents that had been recently declassified on Globocnik and his Lublin years and held by the Public Records Office, Kew; Robin O'Neil, whose work on the Jewish Holocaust in Eastern Galicia necessarily considered Globocnik's murderous activities, in great depth (he also provided a copy of Globocnik's 1941 New Year's card); the late Brigadier Guy Wheeler of Somerset, who provided a detailed account of Globocnik's capture and death; Marian Pawlowski of Sobieszyn, for historical and other details about this village; Arthur Radley of Holland Park Avenue, London, for providing a copy of Alexander Ramsay's handwritten report of his capture and identification of Globocnik; Simon Withers of Holland Park Avenue, London, for promptly acquiring several important sources; Peter de Lotz, London bookseller and expert military bibliographer, and Gitta Sereny, for alerting me to Michael Tregenza's existence and whereabouts; Dr. Leon Popek of Lublin, for his assistance in acquiring several key documents held in the Lublin National Archives; cartographer Michael Pepperday of the University of Western Australia for his maps, compiled at such short notice; Martin Saxon, for his assistance in checking so many aspects of the final manuscript; Tom Rovis-Hermann for his expert assistance, especially in preparing the Rickheim photographs; Greg and Annalise Derfel, for their assistance in translating and explaining documents in Globocnik's SS file; Marek Zimowski for his patience, precision, and care in translating Stanislaw Piotrowski's important but largely forgotten 1949 study of the thieving aspects of Globocnik's administration of *Aktion Reinhardt;* and last but certainly not least, my wife, Carolyn, who was there and helped every step of the way both as a researcher and wise and insightful adviser.

Contents

Introduction

"He [Hitler] is surrounded not by friends but by accomplices, depraved and vicious creatures or blind and brutal instruments."
— Otto Strasser (1940)

Adolf Hitler's and *Reichsführer-SS* Heinrich Himmler's most vicious wartime accomplice, *SS-Brigadeführer* (Brigadier-General) Odilo Globocnik, although dying in the spring of 1945, was a genocidal killer who is virtually forgotten, including, strangely, by most Israelis and Poles. And this despite having been one of the most bestial murderers of Jews and Poles that the 20th century was to produce. He was intricately involved in the planning and administration of the mass killing of at least 1.5 million and perhaps as many as two million people in three specially constructed but out-of-the-way killing centers — Treblinka, Sobibor, and Belzec — erected in occupied Poland to exterminate Jews. Globocnik and Rudolf Höss, commandant of that other "terminal station," the huge Auschwitz-Birkenau killing center and concentration camp in Poland's Upper Silesia, can rightly be named as having been among the first industrial-style mass killers in human history. Yet it is difficult to find much written about Globocnik, most especially in the English-speaking world, and even less about his ancestry, his early life and later political career, and most important of all, his nearly four years in the southeastern Polish provincial city of Lublin, where he was the central figure in the 20th century's major genocide, the Holocaust. He was also on the road to becom-

1

ing the pre-eminent demographic or ethnic cleanser in history, not just of the 20th century, having refined plans to expel into Western Siberia over 100 million Poles, Russians, Ukrainians, Belarusans and Balts. Globocnik's nearly four years as head of the Himmler-controlled SS and the police in Lublin far exceeded in bloody magnitude the much written about and horrifying Reign of Terror that Arras lawyer, Maximilien Robespierre (1758–94), and his bloodthirsty Jacobins inflicted upon late 18th century Paris and Revolutionary France.

Globocnik was not merely a tyrant. Like his bloodthirsty ideological mentor and superior, the German Reich's *Führer*, Adolf Hitler, he betrayed his fatherland, Austria, and went on to command a number of criminal agencies in occupied Poland and later in northern Italy that employed large numbers of Austrians, thereby even further blackening his country's, as well as Germany's, name. Hand in hand with his German and Austrian staffers and many hundreds of Ukrainians who were involved as auxiliaries in the genocide of the Jews as well as in the ethnic cleansing of Poles living in the occupation region Berlin had designated Lublin District, beginning with that district's historic Zamosc Lands, they together wreaked bloody havoc. Globocnik was able to cooperate with the Ukrainian Nationalists because they were allied with Berlin and were seeking to create, with German assistance, a purely Ukrainian ethnic enclave that included Poland's historic Zamosc Lands. This racially pure enclave was seen as the beginning of a Greater Ukraine that would emerge after Hitler's conquest of Stalin's huge Red Army of Workers and Peasants. The significance of the Zamosc Lands was therefore that these two Axis allies, German Nazis and their Ukrainian ideological *confreres,* who were loyal to the wartime Poland-based Fascist Organization of Ukrainian Nationalists, both saw this segment of Globocnik's district as the first block in their bids to create an expanded Greater Reich and a fascist-style Greater Ukraine respectively. [1]

Globocnik had earlier conspired with Hitler to destroy Austria's independence, thereby helping to take Hitler closer to his primary political goal of territorially unifying all the Germanic peoples of Central Europe, the so-called *Anschluss.* That goal, however, was to be only the precursor to Hitler's primary wartime aim of acquiring, by military conquest, extensive tracts across all of Eastern Europe so that these conquered lands could be settled by Germanic people. The Slavs — Poles, Russians, Ukrainians, Belarusans, and Czechs — and most Balts were to have been forcibly expelled into Western Siberia following the defeat of the Red Army. Globocnik was also to have had a preeminent role in this subsequent or wartime Hitlerite aim as an ethnic cleanser of all the inhabitants of Poland and Western or European Russia, including Ukraine. He therefore conspired with Himmler, who conspired with Hitler, in all of the Third Reich's major demographic resettlement programs, as well as with the later internationally well-known Adolf Eichmann, in Hitler's top-secret program of killing all European Jews, codenamed *Aktion Reinhardt.* Just 10 months after *Reinhardt* was secretly commenced, on Himmler's orders, Globocnik launched on 28 November 1942, across Poland's Zamosc Lands, Hitler's other and far more ambitious demographic program, the now largely forgotten top-secret *Generalplan Ost,* which, as its first stage, envisaged the deportation of up to 21 million ethnic Poles into Western Siberia.

Globocnik's nearly four years of non-stop murderous and policing activities in occupied Poland, from his various Lublin-based offices, therefore included participation in both the *Reinhardt* or Jewish genocide and the launching of the ethnic cleansing of an entire Slavic nation, Poland, as part of the *Generalplan.* Both actions — *Reinhardt* and the ethnic cleansing of the Zamosc

Odilo Globocnik. This is the photograph held in Globocnik's SS file. (U.S. Embassy Office Berlin, Berlin Document Center)

Lands — were precursors to the purging of all those deemed to be non-Germanic from the entire East, from all the lands between Berlin and the Ural Mountains, well in excess of 100 million Russians, Ukrainians, Belarusans, Poles, Czechs, Jews, and Balts.

If Josef Stalin's Red Army had collapsed and been defeated — as Hitler initially so confidently predicted would happen — during 1941, or 1942, or even early 1943, Globocnik would have been ideally placed in Lublin to have taken charge of the ethnic cleansing not only of all of Poland but the entire European or Western segment of Stalin's Soviet Union, which, to Hitler and his paladins, was simply the East. And, if that had come to pass, Globocnik would have surpassed even Stalin as a deporter of humans into desolate Western Siberia. No one else was so well situated to have undertaken these truly unprecedented demographic ventures which German National Socialism sought to advance Hitler's and Himmler's dream of a racially pure people having adequate territory in which to dwell and prosper forever.

Odilo Globocnik, who hailed from Austria's southern, or Slovene, fringe of Carinthia, during the latter part of 1941 and throughout 1942 and early 1943, was therefore literally on the brink of a career that would have propelled him into becoming history's worst mass murderer. His crimes would have been far greater than those of Stalin. Only vast quantities of British and American military equipment, shipped to the Soviet Union via the North Sea and the Persian Gulf, and the Red Army's enormous manpower resources and that army's suicidal fighting ability blocked Globocnik from ascending to such dizzy criminal heights. Significantly, not even the controversial British author David Irving, who has persistently contended that Adolf Hitler was unaware of the Jewish Holocaust (*Aktion Reinhardt*), has sought to minimize Globocnik's murderous record and culpability in this regard.

In light of all this, it is puzzling, indeed, that Globocnik, for nearly half a century, failed to attract significant attention of mainstream Israeli, Western European, and American historians. Fortunately, this was not the case in Poland, where the first generation of postwar historians, men like Stanislaw Piotrowski and Czeslaw Madajczyk, Artur Eisenbach, and Zygmunt Mankowski, did not share in this myopia. All stressed in their writings Globocnik's pivotal role in *Reinhardt* or the forgotten, in the Western world at least, *Generalplan,* Himmler's blueprint to expel some 100 million Slavs into Western Siberia, so that all the Slavic lands between Berlin and the Ural Mountain chain could be re-populated with those classified as Aryans, Germans, Dutch, Danes, Norwegians, some Belgians, Austrians, and *Volksdeutsche*—that is, people of German ethnic background who had either settled in the New World or across Eastern Europe in earlier times.[2] For this they should be commended, for, as a result of their writings and teaching, subsequent Polish historians have continued to give Globocnik and his truly incredible list of crimes and plans for further crimes the attention he and they truly warrant.

How could the central murderous figure of *Aktion Reinhardt* not have attracted a biographer for so long, or at least a detailed analysis of his murderous Lublin days? Was he perhaps not as significant as the writings of those in Poland had suggested? I only gradually — over most of 1985 and all of 1986 — became aware of the existence of this disparity in knowledge and research focus upon Globocnik and the pivotal *Generalplan* between what were still known as the Eastern and Western blocs. Initially I was baffled. Why was it that this senior SS man, his role in *Reinhardt,* and his launching of the *Generalplan* upon the Zamosc Lands seemed to be relatively extensively written about and discussed in Poland, while in the West only *Reinhardt* was considered — and in a large and growing body of excellent books and articles — while *Reinhardt's* chief executive officer, Odilo Globocnik, and the *Generalplan* that he actually launched, were virtually ignored? This was certainly difficult to comprehend, for it seemed to be topsy-turvy. All my experiences until then had been that the reverse was invariably the case — censorship was an Eastern Bloc phenomenon; freedom of thought and expression were inherently Western values and ones that were practiced. How could it therefore be that Globocnik was hardly heard of in the West? How could it thus be that I could only find a handful — and a tiny one at that — of generally cursory references to the *Generalplan*, with most of these actually carried in officially-sanctioned English-language Polish publications? How had both Globocnik and the *Generalplan* slipped past Western historians almost completely unnoticed? Was the *Generalplan* perhaps a carefully constructed or exaggerated Communist fabrication, therefore not deserving scholarly research? Both Warsaw and Moscow, I well knew, had, since the late 1940s, regularly launched baseless and deceitful propaganda campaigns about a range of politically and ideologically motivated issues. I was always skeptical of anything either government did in this regard. Moreover, both the leftist totalitarian parties that headed governance of Poland and the Soviet Union had vested interests in exposing, to the maximum, what Hitlerism and Nazism had done and what they meant to them and their people. This, no doubt, partly explained the existence of so much published and censored literature on both these issues that were hardly ever raised or heard of in the West. But even despite such a far from noble motive to highlight Globocnik and the *Generalplan*, if this in fact applied, I could not help but conclude that the outcome of the work of the four Polish historians mentioned above was in no way diminished. The fact was that the more one inquired, the more evident it became that Western historians of Nazism had been remiss on Globocnik and Hitler's and Himmler's *Generalplan*. The first, and one of the best, references I found to Globocnik and this plan, though without actually naming the plan, was written by senior SS man Rudolf Höss, Commandant of Auschwitz-Birkenau, in his important autobiography: "He [Globocnik] worked out fantastic plans for a series of strongpoints stretching to the Urals."[3] So, inquisitive Western readers were in the somewhat absurd position for many years of having to rely on one of the 20th century's major industrial-style mass killers for information about the other major 20th century industrial-style mass killer. Moreover, the *Generalplan* was certainly not a Communist attempt to hornswoggle Western historians.

Another who also deserves commendation for his dedication and outstanding research achievements is British historian Michael Tregenza, a German and a Polish speaker, and an expert on many unknown and little-known aspects of Globocnik's murderous Lublin years. Tregenza had actually settled in Lublin to conduct his private researches on *Reinhardt* and Globocnik.

Three others that I discovered must be commended for having cast light upon important World War II blank spots involving Globocnik and his

"Carinthian Mafia." Two of them were young Carinthian historians, Siegfried Pucher and Dr. Alfred Elste, who had published in German. The third was an Australian-born Canadian, Maurice Williams, who had published in English, German and Italian on aspects of Globocnik's early political activism and later career. By the late 1990s, these three had published important works on Globocnik and several of his key associates, including that other little-known Carinthian, Dr. Friedrich Rainer, a man who was so central in Globocnik's life and career, and who was even to be at Globocnik's side when he died.

Well before the beginning of the 21st century, therefore, inquisitive Polish readers were able to satisfy their curiosity about Globocnik. By the late 1990s, German readers could do likewise, thanks to Siegfried Pucher's and Alfred Elste's researches and writings. However, the huge international English-reading public, as late as 2003, was still without a published account and general assessment of Globocnik's life and his many wartime behind-the-front criminal deeds and activities, directed primarily against civilians: men, women, and children.

I hope that this study helps satisfy any curiosity that may still exist in the West so long after Hitler's defeat of May 1945, the same month that Globocnik died, and that this biography propels others to investigate more closely the many remaining aspects of Globocnik's incredibly destructive 41-year-long life, as well as the roles of all those who worked with and for him in Klagenfurt, Vienna, Lublin, and Trieste, before and during the war.

Finally, toward the end of my long period of initial bewilderment — between 1985 and 1987 — about Globocnik's failure to attract substantial historians' attention, I met leading Israeli historian Yisrael Gutman, a Holocaust expert and a survivor of the Warsaw Ghetto, which senior Globocnik staffer and co-conspirator *SS-Sturmbannführer* Hermann Höfle helped clear. Gutman was also a participant in that ghetto's doomed uprising, and thus an unequivocal enemy of and combatant against Globocnik. Naturally I asked about the absence of a Globocnik biography, the lack of detailed analyses, or even basic inquisitiveness, and the absence of any comprehensive articles on Globocnik in the still-growing body of Holocaust literature. Why had no one in the West, including especially Israel, ever bothered embarking on such scholarly projects about Globocnik? His answer, certainly thoughtful and sincere: "Possibly because there had never been a process, a trial." He may well be correct. We are unlikely ever to know. Certainly Adolf Eichmann and Ernst Kaltenbrunner were tried, and both, as well as being executed, have attracted considerable scholarly attention. However, if that was the reason for Globocnik being treated like a blank spot, it did not, to me at least, excuse this oversight by historians who, thankfully, do not need to wait for lawyers to pave the way for them.

By then, however, I had already resolved to launch my own investigations, during which I had the good fortune of both meeting and being in regular contact with so many excellent Eastern and Western historians, researchers, librarians, archivists, and people who were simply keen to help, all of whom believed Odilo Globocnik's life should receive scrutiny.

I

Ancestry and Early Life

More than half a century after Odilo Globocnik (1904–1945), one of Hitler's major accomplices, died in an exquisite part of southern alpine Austria, not far north of his birthplace of Trieste, he had not attracted an English-language biography. Although passing references, some of them even moderately detailed, could be found in several specialist books and journals on this murderer of more than 1.5 million people, by far most of them Jews — the exact figure is unlikely ever to be known — his life and background had inexplicably failed to capture the imaginations or curiosity of the first and second generation of postwar German, Jewish, Polish, or English-speaking biographers, including especially those who specialized in researching the Jewish Holocaust, in which Globocnik was a pivotal as well as central figure.[1] Interestingly, when another 20th century tyrant who had murdered about the same number of people as Globocnik, Khmer Rouge leader Pol Pot, died more than two decades after launching a genocidal onslaught against his people, his death attracted worldwide media attention.[2]

That said, the one thing of which we can be certain about Odilo Globocnik is that he was not a Reich German. Whether he should be considered an Austrian, like Adolf Hitler, is a moot point. According to investigations conducted by Carinthian historian Siegfried Pucher and Trieste-based historical researcher Ales Brecelj, it appears Globocnik can best be described, ethnically speaking, as part-Slovene and possibly part-Banat German, whose family acquired Austrian citizenship — probably automatically — after the collapse of the Austro-Hungarian Empire in 1918. (See Map 1.) However, we cannot be

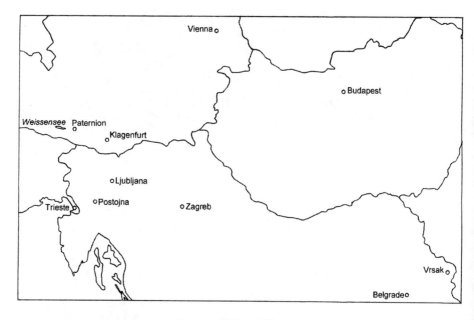

Map 1. Globocnik's roots.

absolutely certain he was part-Banat German, for he may have had Magyar or even some other part-ethnic ancestry that was not German. The British historian Dennison Rusinow has, for instance, claimed that the former was, in fact, the case: "*SS-Gruppenführer* Odilo Globocnik ... was born in Trieste of a Slovene father and Magyar mother and lived there until he too moved to Carinthia in 1923."[3]

However, to further confuse this not insignificant issue, we find that another historian has attributed yet another ancestry to Globocnik, which is probably incorrect, claiming that he was "The son of an Austrian Croatian family of petty officials and a builder by profession..."[4]

Moreover, Italian historian Susan Zuccotti has made a claim similar to Rusinow's in her study of Italy's Jewish Holocaust, which was largely implemented by Globocnik from his birthplace of Trieste after Il Duce Benito Mussolini's demise in Rome in mid–1943, making Trieste a major focal point of these southern European mass killings: "Globocnik's father was a Slav and his mother a Hungarian. His family settled in Klagenfurt, Austria, in 1923."[5]

These conflicting views on his ancestry are further reinforced by Peter Black of the Center for Advanced Holocaust Studies at the Washington-based U.S. Holocaust Memorial Museum:

> Globocnik was born to Austro-Slovene parents on 21 April 1904 in multinational Trieste, then the principal seaport of the Habsburg Monarchy. A Habsburg

cavalry lieutenant and later a senior postal official, his father died of tuberculosis during his adolescence, after which the wife, herself born in the Hungarian Voivodina, settled in Klagenfurt. Though both parents bore Slavic names (the mother's maiden name was Petschinka), Globocnik could claim at least partial German ancestry — both grandmothers bore German names.[6]

Hungarian ancestry is also attributed to Globocnik's mother by Gallan Fogar, one-time secretary of the Resistance Archives in Trieste: "He was born in Trieste in 1904 and lived in this city until the collapse of the Austro-Hungarian regime. His father was Slovenian, his mother Hungarian."[7]

An American intelligence biographical report, prepared for the U.S. War Crimes Office, in part backed the above claims by stating, under the heading, "Family History," that Globocnik "is of Slavonic antecedents. Nazi ideologies seem to prevail in his whole family ... At one time his whole family were arrested including his old mother."[8]

If the latter contention of Nazi ideology pervading his family is correct it may well go some way to explaining why Globocnik's mother was present in Lublin during part of the time that he headed *Aktion Reinhardt*. Could his mother's outlook and attitude toward Jews perhaps have been a significant factor in their subsequent extermination? Unfortunately this point has been impossible to confirm, but it cannot be discounted. That said, however, the moot point on the question of his ancestry is whether his mother was of German ethnic origin, a *Volksdeutsche*, or a southern Slav — a Slovene — like Globocnik's father, or a Magyar, something that it appears now to be impossible to definitively establish. Irrespective of which of these ethnic combinations is correct, we can safely say that Globocnik was an enculturated or Germanized part-southern Slav, most likely part-Slovene, but certainly not a Reich German nor even an ethnic Germanic Austrian. Another reason for saying this is that the region from where his mother hailed, the Banat, which is adjacent to Transylvania, was ethnically extremely diverse. At least some Slovenes had settled there, as well as a not insignificant number of Jews. The English travel and children's book and spy thriller writer, Bernard Newman, has written: "... all other ethnic complications pale beside the social tangle of the Banat."[9] Describing a pre-war bicycle tour he made through the Banat (the word means "frontier province"), Newman wrote:

> I recall one incredible morning when I road through a succession of seven villages; they were inhabited by Magyars, Germans, Czechs, Serbs, Rumanians, Slovaks — and French! The Tower of Babel was a comparative holiday — Maria Theresa, who was responsible for many remarkable schemes of colonization in the Balkans, took in hand the reclamation of the province [from the Turks]. From all corners of the Austrian empire settlers were invited, with special privileges: they came also from Bavaria, the Rhine provinces and Alsace. Added to the surviving remnants of the original population, they made up an ethnic

medley of a complexity unknown even in the Balkans. The seven I have mentioned by no means exhaust the races of the Banat: there are smatterings of Croats, Slovenes, Italians, Spaniards, Gypsies, and others, and plenty of Jews.[10]

Newman's account certainly shows this region, from where Globocnik's mother hailed, to have been an ethnically complex one. In addition, University of Ljubljana (Slovenia) historian Fran Zwitter has made several pertinent observations about the place or standing of Slovenes within the Germanic Habsburg Empire, which, even if they do not explain the Globocnik family's ethnic status and background during the later part of the 19th century and the immediate–Great War years, certainly highlight the complex nature of Germanic-Slovene relations. During these times, Zwitter argues, Slovenes were without what may be called an upper class or cultural upper strata, intelligentsia, or intellectual elite.

> The Slovenes formed the bulk of the agrarian population in the areas which they inhabited. There were almost no agrarian settlements in this territory in which other languages were spoken. On the other hand, nearly all the upper classes — the nobility, the more affluent bourgeoisie, the newly-created bureaucracy, the professional people, and the intellectuals — belonged to other ethnic groups. In most instances they were German. These classes regarded themselves and were generally looked upon as socially and culturally superior to the Slovenian peasants; consequently they readily assimilated the Slovenes who were ascending the social ladder.[11]

These points seem relevant to the Globocniks, for the father was a government official — a member of "the newly-created bureaucracy" — and was most certainly ascending the social ladder, for he was not a peasant farmer in a largely peasant society. If, in such a family, the mother was strong-willed, or someone who firmly favored the German language and culture, then the move by that family toward becoming Germanized or so enculturated was assured, and relatively quickly so. Such enculturation was also, no doubt, quite welcomed; indeed, it was probably actively sought by the Globocniks. Zwitter also points out that a feature of those inhabiting the lands surrounding present-day Slovenia was the "lack of coincidence between ethnic and administrative boundaries." Rather than living within the Austro-Hungarian Empire in a single province, the Slovenes formed "a significant percentage of the population of each of more than a half dozen different administrative subdivisions of the Austrian Empire," with about half living in provinces in which there was a non-Slovene majority.[12] This meant that those Slovenes who moved away from traditional agricultural occupations invariably had greater contact with non-Slovenes in their newly-found professional, if not daily,

lives. Such an experience would no doubt have tended to encourage enculturation, including departure from at least their mother tongue, and eventually away from other uniquely Slovenian sensibilities and outlooks.
Interestingly, and despite this, a provincial English newspaper, in an article
in mid–1938, when Globocnik was 34 years old but already one of the most
powerful men in Nazi Austria, and on the way to becoming precisely that in
the soon-to-be conquered and occupied Poland, claimed that his ancestry was
neither German nor Austrian: "The new Governor of Vienna, for instance,
Globotchnigg, is a Slovene from Carinthia."[13]

Was this journalist's informant attempting to put Globocnik down? Was
this informant attempting to drive some sort of wedge into the ranks of the
then quarrelsome and bitterly divided Austrian Nazis? Or was he or she simply well-informed or else just making the obvious point that the name Globocnik was not German, just as Sikorski, and Pilsudski, for that matter, are also
not German surnames? Whatever the case, the point seems noteworthy that
a man who was to emerge to become Hitler's major wartime mass killer and
who aspired to become a great exterminator of Slavs was neither a Reich German, nor an ethnic German.

Siegfried Pucher's investigations show that Globocnik's father, Franz,
was a postal service employee, while his mother, Anna Petschinka (the name
was also spelled "Pescinka"), was from a middle-class family background in
the Banat, suggesting enculturation into German culture by both his parents,
from both the maternal and paternal sides of his families. Ales Brecelj also
identifies the name Petschinka, which, like the name Globocnik, is of Slovene
origin, so it was the ethnic ancestry on both parental sides, with the encul-
turating phenomenon identified by Zwitter being further confirmed. The
paternal side of Globocnik's family came from Neumarkt (Nowy Trg), a German enclave in Oberkrain, Slovenia. Puchers, who has traced its origins to
the mid–1700s, says that the name, initially written "Globotschnigg" or
"Globotschnitsch," is of Slovene origin and means "from the lower valley."
Sometime during the middle of the 19th century the name reverted to the
Slovene style, probably because that was the way a priest wrote it in church
records. Globocnik's mother, Anna, was from another Balkans region, but one
that also had a long and close association with German culture.

> Anna Petschinka came from a family of officials from Werschetz (Vrsak) in the
> Banat district. Allegations in literature that she originated from a peasant fam-
> ily are contradicted by her short autobiography, by Globocnik's *SS-Erbgesund-*
> *heitsfragebogen* and by the statements from contemporaries: "As the daughter
> of a judicial adviser, the marriage was quite consistent with an officer's station."[14]

Globocnik's father, Franz, was born in 1870, the same year as his mother,
so both were aged 34 when their only son, Odilo, was born. Because of lim-

ited financial resources, Franz was unable to buy himself out of the Austro-Hungarian Army, even if he had wanted to, and remained a reserve officer while employed as a postal official in Trieste. Franz and Anna were married on 24 October 1898, near Postojna, 35 kilometers northeast of Trieste and about the same distance southwest of Ljubljana, in present-day Slovenia, known since the 1820s for its unique cave network, the Postojnaska Jama. Odilo's grandfather, Franz Johann, was a secondary school teacher in Laibach (Ljubljana), Slovenia's capital; his great-grandfather, Rochus, was a Neumarkt physician and had served in the war against Napoleon Bonaparte in 1809 in an auxiliary capacity. This ancestry suggests that the Globocniks had probably opted for Germanization well ahead of Franz marrying Anna. After having defeated the Habsburgs, Napoleon forced Vienna to cede parts of Carinthia, Carniola, Gorz, Istria, Friuli, and Dalmatia, from which the French leader created the Illyrian Provinces of France, a predominantly Slovene territory. This early Globocnik family political stand against France, then an ascendant European power, cannot be ignored and probably gives a hint as to why the young Odilo was prone to side or identify with Germanism rather than being attracted to another ethnic group, namely the Slovenes, or even some other southern Slavic loyalty.

Brecelj's findings largely confirm the above and include details about the young Globocnik's siblings as well as his father's military service. He says that Franz had participated in the Great War on the Russian Front where he was wounded, and was discharged as a captain from the Habsburgian cavalry. This claim is flatly contradicted by Siegfried Pucher, who claims a stomach defect prevented Franz from going to war.[15] He died on 1 December 1919, aged less than 50, a little more than a year after the war ended, when his son was aged just 15, coincidentally, the same age at which Adolf Hitler lost his father. Brecelj concurs with Pucher's findings on Globocnik's mother, who he said was the daughter of a Wilhelm, and that she was born in Werschetz (Vrsak) the major city in the ethnically diverse Banat region, which was then in the Hungarian segment of the dualistic Austro-Hungarian Empire. This may explain claims of a part-Hungarian ancestry for Globocnik by some. But Brecelj adds that another factor, one also highlighted by Peter Black earlier, permits Globocnik to lay claim to German ancestry: Both his grandmothers were of German origin.

It is also perhaps noteworthy that both his paternal father and grandfather had given names that were German-sounding or written in the German style, and that this side of the family hailed from what Siegfried Pucher describes as a "German enclave" in Slovenia. Perhaps this was due to a strong attraction to Germanism or perhaps it was a coincidence. Living in a German enclave does not, of course, necessarily mean one is a German, though it most certainly seems to indicate something about one's sentiments. Here

Zwitter's point about the Slovenian propensity to adopt German customs and traditions readily is therefore pertinent. Perhaps Bernard Newman's claim that "The Tower of Babel was a comparative holiday," when considering Europe's Banat region, was far more correct than even Newman realized.

Birth and death registration searches by Brecelj uncovered the following details on Globocnik and his siblings: Odilo, Franz's and Anna's third child, was named Odilo Lothar Ludovicus; and was baptized on 19 July 1904, in the Trieste Catholic Church of San Vivanni Decollato. Lothar is not an uncommon Germanic name, probably because there were several famous Lothars who were kings of the Franks, an ancient Germanic tribe. The choice of names appears to be partly explained by the name of Odilo's godfather, Ludovicus Hvllerl, whose wife, Elisa, was Globocnik's godmother, both undoubtedly being close family friends, perhaps even relatives. The first Globocnik child, Hildegardris, was born in Trieste in late January 1900, but died on 20 April the same year. The second, Lidia Matilde Milena, was born on 8 August 1901. She was followed by Odilo on 21 April 1904, the only son, and their fourth, Henrica (Erika) Maria, was born on 21 August 1909. The Globocniks lived in Trieste at Via della Caserma No. 9, which in the 1990s was Via 30 Ottobre. It seems fair to refer to the family as being middle class loyal Austro-Hungarian citizens who were neither purely Austrians, Slovenians, nor Hungarians, but, to use Newman's turn-of-phrase, probably a medley of these ethnic backgrounds, with a strong or overriding propensity to identify with the ascendant German culture across the northern Adriatic region, and in Odilo's, and probably his mother's, case, a strong antithesis toward the Slovenes, and perhaps also Jews early in his life. Whether this antithesis was extended to Russians and Serbs, both enemies of Austro-Hungary during the Great War, we do not know.

By, or in, 1923, when Globocnik was 19, the family was well established in Klagenfurt, which, ironically, was a significant Slovene enclave within a markedly diminished Austria that was now without a multi-national, that is, largely Slavic, empire. We cannot be sure that the family departed Trieste that year, as Susan Zuccotti confidently states, since the last available or known reference to their being residents of the former Austro-Hungarian Adriatic port city was in 1915. Ales Brecelj's published remarks on this point are worth noting: "According to some sources the family moved to Klagenfurt at the outbreak of World War I in 1914. According to the 1935 data of the Prefecture of Trieste the move took place in 1923."[16]

There is, unfortunately, a gap of nine years here, and if Brecelj, who conducted his research in Trieste, is correct, it is probable that the year of their move will never be established with certainty. Little therefore appears to be known of the Globocnik family's road north to inland Klagenfurt, a city that after the Great War was even claimed by Slovenia, by then a part of the new

Kingdom of Yugoslavia. Nor is the reason for this city, with its sizeable Slovene minority, being chosen by the family known. Indeed, Siegfried Pucher, who comes from southern Austria and was able to interview several people who had known the young Globocnik, refers to the period 1915 to 1923, which encompasses the move from Trieste to Klagenfurt, as "the poorly researched years," suggesting we are probably unlikely ever to get answers to an array of interesting questions about this family whose single male offspring was to have such a destructive impact on so many Jews, Poles, and even Russians. Siegfried Pucher also refers to a claim that Franz was alleged to have been a deserter, but this allegation was denied to him by a military source. It is possible the Globocniks' move north or inland was made because Italy acquired Trieste after Europe's post–Great War settlement, whereas Carinthia remained within the diminished postwar Austrian republic, even if certain southern Slavic political activists, including fighting groups, challenged Austria's possession of at least parts of this contested southern Alpine province. Interestingly, a plebiscite was held to decide the Klagenfurt region's fate. We know that statistically speaking a Trieste family identifying with Austro-German culture and sensibilities was certainly not in the majority in this port city during the early 20th century. The 1910 Austrian census showed this Adriatic city's population stood at just over 220,000, and of these, Italians made up nearly 120,000, while Croats and Slovenes together slightly exceeded 50,000. Those classified as "others," primarily Austrians, stood at about 50,000. Eleven years later, in 1921, around the time the Globocniks departed for Klagenfurt, plus or minus a few years, the numbers of those classified as "others" had slumped to below 40,000, meaning that what can be called the Great War decade, 1911 to 1921, including Odilo's mid-teens, show the city's Austro-German minority having fallen by some 20 percent, while the Italian component had markedly risen. (The 1921 census was conducted by Italian, not Austrian, authorities, so distortions favoring the Italians were certainly likely to some extent.) When this region was in Austria's hands, nationality was gauged by the language in common or daily use in a particular home, that is, the *Umgangssprache*. This tended to favor the Austrians in the same way that preference for the use of English by certain Indians, Pakistanis, and Sri Lankans at the time of the British Raj could have boosted the number of British at a census, even though a segment of those counted as British were definitely not ethnically Celtic or Anglo-Saxons.

These latter points are telling in that the Globocniks were probably classified in the 1910 census with "others," considering themselves to be Austrians or even Austro-Germans — we know their *Umgangssprache* was German even though at least one and perhaps both parents could be regarded as Slovenes. Franz's links with the Habsburg military establishment would probably have reinforced this opting for the German language, the *lingua franca* of the barracks. If the departure to Klagenfurt was a deliberate or conscious one, as opposed to a mere employment transfer or some similar reason, then the Globocniks' identification with Germanism was able to be accommodated by simply moving out of a predominantly Italian city in an Italianized region. Moreover, Trieste's environs, the adjacent smaller towns and villages, were largely Slovene dominated. An option for those wishing to identify with Germanism was to do precisely what the Globocniks and up to about 10,000 "others" had done between 1910 and 1921, that is, simply to depart so as to dwell in an Austrian or German-speaking urban center, Klagenfurt, even though Slovenes formed a significant component within it. In Adriatic Trieste the German language was associated with the ruling elite and the dominant power based in Vienna, while Slovene was the language of the laborers, suggesting that anyone wishing to be upwardly mobile could be expected to identify with the former. A postal official was certainly not in an altogether lowly occupation, but rather, lower middle class, and the wife of such a postal clerk and official could regard herself as having socially outranked a woman whose Slovene husband worked, say, on Trieste's wharves. To add to such occupational considerations, deliberate use of the German language in the home would have helped reinforce one's feeling of upward social mobility and social standing. American historian Arthur J. May's study of the Habsburgs during the Great War gives backing to this point, when he writes, "The language spoken in the city was overwhelmingly Italian, with Slovene the tongue, in the main, of newly come proletarians."[17]

Another historian, Thomas Barker, has offered a different perspective on Carinthia's Slovenes in the years just prior to and immediately after the Great War. He has pointed out that the Klagenfurt basin, about one fifth territorially of Carinthia, was a linguistically mixed region and had nearly 80 percent Slovenes, whereas across all of Carinthia Slovene speakers made up only about 20 percent. Klagenfurt, where the Globocnik's settled, was thus very much a Slovene enclave, so that the Globocnik family's move from Trieste was not necessarily a major communal break. Austria's 1910 census showed that Carinthia had about 66,500 Slovene speakers, yet there were nearly 100,000 people of Slovene origin, so there was a high probability of a Slovene showing a marked preference to be regarded, if not as an Austrian, then certainly not as a Slovene, the very thing we know Globocnik's parents did, with Odilo understandably following suit.[18] The Globocniks were therefore far from an unusual Adriatic family. Moreover, many Carinthian Slovenes went even further, for they backed such personal decisions — that of not adhering to their language and opting instead to identify with Austrian cultural and other sensibilities — in the ballot box. Voting returns in an October 1920 League of Nations-sponsored plebiscite to determine whether Carinthia's southeastern sector should be incorporated into Austria or the newly-created Kingdom of the Serbs, Croats, and Slovenes showed that a high proportion of the Slovenes preferred the former, that is, ethnic Slovenes voted for southern Carinthia not to be merged into Slovenia, which was by then part of the new southern Slav nation. Notwithstanding all this, the little available evidence suggests that the young Odilo was, if anything, a thoroughly satisfactory child, at least until his teens — around the time of his father's death — after which he showed signs of becoming something of a rascal. Moreover, from that relatively early age he followed in his parents' footsteps by ever increasingly identifying with one of the dominant European nationalisms of the 20th century, namely the Germanic ideology, out of which Hitler's National Socialism grew.

Although Globocnik spoke Italian, Trieste's overwhelmingly spoken language, in his youth, the language used in the Globocnik home was German, something his parents appear to have strictly enforced, or desired of their children. There is no reason to believe that his friends or political allies regarded him as anything other than an Austrian, or if not that, then certainly as a thoroughly assimilated Austrian. There is nothing to suggest that ethnic Austrians or Germans in the SS, or any other German or National Socialist agency with which he was to be intimately associated in later life, sniggered at his name or considered him anything other than a German or Austro-German. He was not so unusual in this regard, for even a smattering of traditional Polish-sounding names can be found among those in the German military and the SS, with the best known, even if hyphenated, being that of Erich von dem Bach-Zelewski, which many postwar Polish writers tended to write with the second or Polish segment deleted. Either individual Polish historians could not bring themselves to write the Polish segment, or else, which is likely, postwar censors deliberately removed the Zelewski segment. SS man Bach, after all, had murdered many Poles, including during the Warsaw Uprising of 1944, on behalf of Hitler's and Himmler's extreme variant of Germanism. Conversely, a smattering of traditional German names could be found in the large Polish Underground, the *Armia Krajowa*, which as the war years passed, increasingly combated the ruthless German occupant.

During the Great War the young Globocnik moved from an elementary to a military school in Sankt Pölten, which is near Vienna, suggesting his father considered the Habsburg military favorably and wished to see his only son proudly follow in his footsteps. At Sankt Pölten, originally a Roman settlement, he had been described by superiors as "talented, very diligent with very decent and well seen behavior" and "showing perfect adaptation," Siegfried Pucher reports.[19] Dr. Black describes these early years as follows:

> After six years of Volksschule in Trieste, young Globocnik entered the *Militar-Unter-Realschule* in St. Pölten in 1914. The dissolution of the Habsburg state in the wake of World War I necessitated a career switch; in 1919 he enters the

Höhere Staatsgewerbeschule in Klagenfurt, where he studied construction engineering until 1923 without obtaining a certificate.[20]

Siegfried Pucher writes that Globocnik was regarded as a "serious, willing, reliable, cheerful, assiduous and polite" youth, a not dissimilar assessment that was applied to the young Adolf Hitler. However, the defeat of Germany-Prussia and Austro-Hungary in November 1918 put an end to this career option, so in 1919, the year his father died, the 15-year-old now Carinthian commenced attendance at a higher vocation school for mechanical engineering. Although a military career was therefore his first choice, we do not know if his inability to pursue it was a disappointment that lasted for much or, indeed, most of his life. Nothing up to entering the Klagenfurt-based vocational school can now be identified with any degree of certainty as having been the cause of his later unprecedented viciousness.[21] While there he was twice threatened with expulsion, suggesting he became troublesome by about the age of 16, 17, or 18. The year 1920, when he was just 16, was in all likelihood the turning point in his general world, and perhaps also social, outlook. Dr. Black's point that he left the Klagenfurt institution without formal qualifications appears to confirm a lack of academic direction and purpose. What were the other things on his mind?

An insightful political assessment of the Trieste, Kuestenland, and Carinthia regions, among others of late and post–Habsburgian Austria, by the American historian Bruce Pauley, may well be pertinent in relation to the lower-middle class Globocnik family, which came to include an ailing civil servant and veteran breadwinner, and whose wife, later widow, was politically committed to Germanism to the point of being arrested for her devotion. All this seems pertinent in the development of their only son, Odilo, whose ideological commitment and subsequent activism from 1923 to 1945 was so important in the history of the Hitler Movement. Professor Pauley points out that Austrian Nazism's founder was George Ritter von Schonerer (1842–1921), who, like Hitler, used the title, *Führer*. Schonerer, like Hitler, was a violent anti-Semite and adherent of Pan-Germanism. More pertinent is the fact that Schonerer's followers tended to hail from the middle and lower-middle classes, which encountered Jews in various occupations that grew out of the steadily industrializing Habsburg lands, as well as in universities and the new urban professions.

The role of direct forerunner of the Austrian Nazi party belongs not to Schonerer's Pan-German Party but instead to the German Workers' Party. Founded in 1903, it was one of many parties that profited from the nationalistic clash of German and Czech workers in Bohemia. Even after the party enlarged its name in May 1918 to German National Socialist Workers' Party (NSDAP), it continued to appeal to a lower-middle class population consisting of government employees such as railway workers, artisans, academically trained professionals, and after World War I, veterans. Other civil servants hard hit by inflation or among the 25,000 pensioned off in the austerity measures of Federal Chancellor Ignaz Seipel, joined the DNSAP in late 1922 or early 1923. *Geographically, most of the membership was concentrated, especially before the [First World] war, in ethnically mixed provinces like Bohemia, Moravia, Austrian Silesia, Styria, Carinthia, Trieste Carniola and Kuestenland* [emphasis added].[22]

Because the Globocnik family so snugly fits the above general stereotype, it is difficult to resist concluding that its only son was very much a product of the contemporary ideological, sociological, and filial forces and influences that Pauley has highlighted for regions that comprised outer Austria, in three of which Globocnik and his family lived. Furthermore, there is no evidence to suggest that the Globocnik family showed any sympathy toward or interest in Austria's other, and until 1938, far more significant political groups: the Social Democratic Workers' Party and the Christian Social Party, which "had been founded about 1890 and consistently attracted about 75 percent of the vote in parliamentary elections between 1919 and 1930."[23] Politically and ideologically speaking, the Globocniks almost certainly belonged to that other 25 percent. If Pauley's overview of political inclinations and outlooks indeed applies to the Globocniks, who hailed from Trieste, the Kuestenland, and Carinthia, then the origin of their son's Nazism stemmed not from any sudden appeal to belated Hitlerism, but rather from other longstanding beliefs, perhaps even von Schonerer's teachings, outlooks that had emerged during imperial Austria's latter years. However, because nothing written has survived to confirm this idea, unfortunately it must remain simply conjecture.

In the years after the young Odilo's basic education was completed, a new and increasingly violent young man began to emerge. Those searching for the origins of his evil will have difficulty finding it in his boyhood, with the possible exception of him being threatened with expulsion from school, certainly not a propitious sign. Siegfried Pucher has interviewed all those who are ever likely to be quizzed about these times, and the picture that has emerged is not entirely unfavorable to this future genocidal killer. The sister of Globocnik's first fiancée, who knew him during the 1920s and 1930s, claimed he could be good-hearted though he was not a convivial individual, and it would be wrong to regard him as popular. Interestingly he met the Michner sisters — daughters of the nationalistic and widely admired Emil Michner, at Café Lerch on Heumarkt Square, Klagenfurt. His favorite adjutant in Lublin was Ernst Lerch, whose father, the café's owner, like Michner, was an ardent German nationalist. Lerch was to know all Globocnik's murderous wartime secrets. The young Odilo tended to be extremely self-reliant, was known to arrange dances, and in these situations was friendly to those women who were without a male partner, suggesting that a kind or sympathetic streak existed. Frau Michner said he showed no sign or hint of his later brutal proclivities, though he had a tendency to talk and talk about political and ideological issues to his obviously tolerant and patient fiancée, Grete Michner. The young Odilo had a knack of leaving a good impression with elderly women, though this did not extend to what may well have been his future mother-in-law, Frau Michner. Another acquaintance, whom Siegfried Pucher did not identify, someone younger than Odilo, said he was not an outstanding figure but was nevertheless friendly and was known to bring gifts to his employer's children, suggesting he either made small personal sacrifices or else was not as badly off as may be assumed. However, he tended to be silent on the topic of his father, as if he was ashamed of an aspect of his military career. But as the 1930s progressed he proceeded to combine his social climbing with political or party activities. It appears that throughout his adult life he was if not a moderately heavy then at least a solid drinker, but his alcoholic consumption might in fact not have altered his character. This was the case until his Lublin years, when he underwent a major mental breakdown that may have been partly brought on by drink and some other emotional stresses apart from his mass murdering.[24] Here it must be remembered that he was undoubtedly under enormous pressure from Heinrich Himmler and senior members of Hitler's Chancellery to murder millions of Jews, and as quickly as possible, and to commence expelling tens of thousands of Poles from their homes, especially from the Zamosc Lands region just southeast of Lublin so as to launch the top-secret *Generalplan Ost*. No matter how strong-willed any man may be, these two, in many ways quite unprecedented, orders would undoubtedly have placed enormous pressure upon anyone's conscience, and this could easily have had physical, as well as mental, repercussions.

Both during and after World War II, considerable confusion existed over Globocnik's professional or employment qualifications. Some writers described him as a builder, others as an architect, and others still as an engineer. One historian has even demoted him to the level of a simple bricklayer.[25] Globocnik initially described himself as a building technician, a building contractor, or master builder. However, in the latter part of his destructive 46-month stay in Lublin he referred to himself as an engineer, which is quite inaccurate and suggests, if not an inferiority complex, then misplaced ambition, and status climbing by deception, with the latter characteristic by then an integral part of his daily life. His association with another Himmler favorite, Doctor of Engineering Hans, sometimes referred to as Heinz, Kammler, also a cruel SS man briefly involved in Lublin, may have prompted this. It is generally agreed that Globocnik, from 1920 to 1923, was poorer than would have been the case had his father lived. He apparently became something of a mummy's boy and found part-time jobs to earn extra money, in all likelihood by trading in building supplies. To refer to him in this way does not mean he was soft or a weakling, but rather that he maintained a close ongoing contact with his mother, and she certainly mothered him greatly, to the point of actually going to live from late 1941 to possibly well into 1942 in Lublin where he was busy murdering Poles and Jews, though mainly the latter. This might be a strange thing to do even under ordinary circumstances, but to have been there while her son was killing on a mass scale is strange indeed. Globocnik's attachment to his mother, and vice-versa, remained a feature of his entire life. Her influence upon him may in fact have been secretly sinister: She may have been seen as a kindly lady by outsiders but within the family circle was known to be something quite different. His handwritten curriculum vitae which has survived in his SS file, as well as claiming he spent a total of 65 weeks in jail, claims his mother was also incarcerated. Whether this was the case it is difficult to say, but she would almost certainly have been at least interviewed if not interrogated by police during his clandestine years.[26] The handwritten note also claims that in 1935 he faced high treason charges. We can only surmise what may have happened had his father lived well into the 1920s when Austria, like Bavaria, was a center of extremist political activity, especially of the right-wing variant. Perhaps the hand and advice of a wise and respected father was what Globocnik in his late teens needed, rather than the company of hotheaded ideologically motivated border fighters. Globocnik claimed that he had fought Slovene irredentists during the early 1920s who regarded the picturesque Klagenfurt basin as rightfully belonging to Slovenia.[27] This anti-Slovenian passion or regional loyalty lasted right up to the last month of his life, May 1945, when he fled Trieste and briefly and secretly wandered around Klagenfurt with futile plans to defend Carinthia from Yugoslav partisans, who, during World War II, were Communist-led and controlled.

This opposition to the Slovenes involved Globocnik in some bitter ethnic fighting around Grafenstein and Bleiburg, in southern Carinthia, perhaps as a member of an SA unit, with his life and death enemies being strangely like some of his paternal ancestors. The Yugoslavs were attempting to incorporate a substantial slice of southeastern or Alpine Austria, which included the Klagenfurt Valley of Carinthia, into the newly-created Slavic state, the Kingdom of the Serbs, Croats, and Slovenes.

> What really compelled Austrians of all persuasions to take up arms, however, was the invasion of Carinthia by irregular bands of Yugoslavs. The successful defense of the province eventually provided a *Heimwehr* legend, but, because of this early Carinthian *Heimatschutz* not only cooperated with the *Volkswehr* but also included many workers in its ranks, nearly a year passed before a clearly partisan, bourgeois organization was firmly established in Carinthia.[28]

These fighting efforts gave birth to the above-mentioned deeply patriotic *Heimwehr* (Home Guard), and similar guards emerged in the Tyrol, to combat the Italians, and also in Styria. The *Heimwehr*, as the 1920s proceeded, became an increasingly extreme nationalistic right-wing organization, and it became difficult to determine if the loyalties of its members were to the future authoritarian corporatist Dollfuss Government or to German National Socialism, as led by the western Austrian at large, Adolf Hitler. Pucher writes, "For his brave behavior in the fights for Kaernten he was awarded the Cross of Kaernten. During the time of the preparations for the plebiscite in Kaernten Globocnik acted as 'illegal propagandist,' setting up placards calling for the German case in the area behind the demarcation line, occupied by Sokoln" [Yugoslav irregular units.][29]

Historian C. Earl Edmondson points out that the *Heimwehr* "received encouragement and support from like-minded agitators in Bavaria and Hungary who were not content with their triumphs at home"; this aid consisted of smuggled weapons as well as money, two essential ingredients for victory. "Because of German support for the anti-Yugoslavian propaganda in 1919, the Carinthian rightists maintained close ties with Bavarian organizations through 1923."[30]

The link to Bavaria, where Adolf Hitler was at this very time emerging as a significant southern German ideological Pan-German activist and from where Heinrich Himmler hailed, should not be overlooked as a possibly important one in Globocnik's rise as a National Socialist, though, of course, he was by now already a committed ideological seeker due to strong commitments within his family, especially, it seems, his determined mother's, and his association with Emil Michner. The border between Weimar Germany and Austria was not as impervious as may be assumed. There were German speakers on both sides and sentiments as well as other cultural traits were similar. For instance, Oron J. Hale, in his study of the Nazi press, points out that Hitler's party newspaper, *Völkischer Beobachter*, circulated not only in Bavaria but well beyond its provincial borders, even beyond Germany, and most especially, in Austria. "Rightist and strongly racial in its direction, the paper served during this period [1919–23] as a general organ of the *völkisch* movement in Southern Germany and in the Austrian and Sudetenland areas."[31]

However, doubt remains about Globocnik's actual involvement in these quite bitter border skirmishes. Siegfried Pucher cites a source that alleges that Globocnik's name fails to appear "in the completely preserved lists about persons awarded the Cross of Kaernten."[32] It was not unusual, though, for young fighters to be involved in this ethnic conflict. Even a battalion of students from Graz University volunteered to fight this far south. These students were led by Hans Albin Rauter, who, like Globocnik, went on to become a Higher SS and police chief, based in wartime Holland, being junior there only to that other important Austrian, and a Globocnik comrade, Artur Seyss-Inquart.[33] Another expert on Austria and Slovenia, Canadian historian Maurice Williams, doubts if Globocnik really earned these fighting credentials, claiming they were, if not non-existent, then at least exaggerated. It is possible, however, that Globocnik gave some minor amount of assistance to some Austrian resisters, and as time passed he was to embellish his role in the way fishermen's tales inevitably see the size of the caught fish growing each time the story is retold. Notwithstanding this, by 1922, when aged just 18, Globocnik had already joined the Austrian National Socialists or NSDAP (A), which should not be confused with the party Adolf Hitler had revived in Bavaria and infused with a newly-found nationalistic zeal and racial and blood theories that were to become the basis of later German demographic policies implemented both within Germany and occupied Poland.[34]

Another factor that cannot be denied is that it was during the early 1920s, as he was completing his education and entering the workforce, that Globocnik became politically active in other ways. His activism included a growing passionate attachment to Germanism which evolved into hatred of Jews as well as Slavs, three emerging tendencies that led him inexorably to a position as head of the SS and the police in Lublin, where he was able to lead a bitter unilaterally declared genocidal war against both the ethnic groups he hated. The impact on Globocnik of these early years, with his claimed involvement in ethnic border skirmishing against Slovenes, as will be seen, is well described and analyzed by the Slovene historian Tone Ferenc, who also shows conclusively that Globocnik mixed with a group of Carinthian ethnographic researchers who had a deep influence on his outlook toward non-Germans. The step toward eventual population cleansing of Poles from his Lublin seat of power was therefore not such a large one following his alleged involvement in border fighting against Slovenes during his youth in Klagenfurt, or Celovec, as Slovene irredentists refer to it. As for his murderous treatment of the Jews of Lublin, this was an extension of his inhumane Vienna period, when he was the capital's *Gauleiter*, during which time over 100,000 Jews emigrated — fled is perhaps the more appropriate term — under duress, to the four corners of the world.

What appears to have happened to Globocnik between 1920 and 1923, the concluding years of his formal education, was thus a confluence of several crucial events: He was without a father, he was not rich, he became involved in nationalistic movements, which included street marching, and he had become an admirer of a border fighter, Emil Michner. The latter relationship either directly or indirectly led to a romantic association with one of Michner's daughters, Grete, that resulted in a long engagement, but not marriage. This marital complication resulted in considerable disputation with the Michner family while Globocnik was the top police officer in occupied

Poland's Lublin District and he ended up paying out a substantial sum of money for reneging. All these deeply emotional encounters were experienced by a teenager without a father over a period of just 30 to 40 crucial months.

On leaving the *Höhere Staatsgewerbeschule* in Klagenfurt in 1923, Globocnik gained employment in the KÄWAG (Electricity Distribution Company of Carinthia; *Kärntner Wasserkraftwerke* AG) building power stations and ancillary facilities. He obtained this position with Emil Michner's assistance because his prospective father-in-law had spoken to the then mayor of Klagenfurt on his behalf. Significantly, he initially worked in the Frantschach area north of Wolfsberg. Globocnik left Klagenfurt in 1924 and was basically away working as a construction contractor on power station projects for some six years, so did not return permanently until 1930.[35] It was probably during these years that Globocnik made friends with Paul Gasser, from Wolfsberg, 50 kilometers northeast of Klagenfurt. Gasser was a Nazi activist who established Globocnik's department and administration in Lublin in late 1939. Globocnik returned to Klagenfurt so that he could become a master builder with a number of city-based construction companies, work he carried out until 1933, the year Hitler won power by cleverly manipulating affairs around two out-of-touch elder statesmen, Chancellor Paul von Hindenburg and Franz von Papen, in Berlin.[36]

Clearly, Globocnik was extremely fortunate to have met, in or around 1922, Herr Emil Michner, the retired first lieutenant, who was widely admired around Klagenfurt for having been an "*Abwehrkämpfer*," and had confronted the Slovenians and perhaps other southern Slavs in the post–World War I contest for southern and even central Carinthia. By now Globocnik was also a member of the extreme nationalistic as well as anti-Semitic student fraternities *Markomannia* and *Teutonia*, which had emerged on the political scene around 1920. One of the more memorable features of his long engagement was to be that Grete had to endure long political lectures from the increasingly obsessive young and increasingly politically-oriented Carinthian. Peter Black describes Globocnik's early political activism: "In 1918, at the age of 14, he joined one of the numerous *Heimwehr* units hastily established to defend the Klagenfurt Basin against incursions of South Slav troops. After the Austro-Yugoslav border was determined by plebiscite in October 1920, Globocnik transferred to the Carinthian *Sturmabteilungen* (SA) of the NSDAP."[37]

Also noteworthy is the fact that the pivotal and undoubtedly highly patriotic Michner association proved advantageous in another respect, for this older patron helped make arrangements for Globocnik to sit an examination as part of his building industry qualifications while serving an early jail term because of his illegal NSDAP (A) activities. As a result of its illegality, this political group quickly adopted what can only be described as the cloak-and-dagger techniques of an underground organization or secret society. It resembled in many ways the party that Vladimir Lenin had imposed upon the Soviets or Old Bolsheviks, with secret cells, passwords, men operating and living underground for extended periods, codenames, and secret houses. Such an environment inevitably came to affect Globocnik's personality and outlook. And all this activity was ultimately motivated by a burning desire to gain national executive power so as to transform the society in which they lived, something Globocnik shared with his ideological compatriots in Germany who manned the Hitler Movement then emerging.

II

A Carinthian Becomes a
Viennese Pro-Hitler Activist

Parallel to Globocnik's construction industry career were his clandestine political escapades and activities that prompted Siegfried Pucher to refer to these times, between 1923 and 1936, as his "Dark Years." Dark here does not imply nothing is known of them, but rather that he lived a life that came increasingly to involve subterfuge and conspiracy. Life came to revolve more and more around undercover work and clandestine activities. During these 13 interwar years, Globocnik ceased being a student and became an underground activist, an international courier, a conspirator, and in all likelihood a terrorist. He had ongoing contacts with one of Nazi Germany's most sinister political figures, Reinhard Heydrich, and even the growing German National Socialist Workers Party's (NSDAP) *Führer*, an older Austrian who made his political career in Germany, Adolf Hitler. Most important of all, however, was the fact that he joined in 1934 Heinrich Himmler's emerging elite corps, the SS, the ideological driving force or cutting edge of Nazism, especially following the invasion of the Soviet Union in mid–1941, when Himmler, with whom Globocnik had developed and maintained exceptionally close contacts, was able to begin implementing the Nazi Party's major aim and intention, the Germanization (*Eindeutschung*), or as Hitler and Globocnik were to call it, the "re-Germanization" of the East, with its dual requirements of permanently ridding these lands of Slavs and Jews. The activities of the SS, more than any other wing of Hitler's National Socialist movement, distinguished Germany's eastern conquests and expansions during World War I and World War II. Globocnik for this reason appears to have been deliberately stationed by Himmler and Hitler in the most easterly city of German-occupied Poland, the General Gouvernement, Lublin. This city became an important base, with Lodz (Litzmannstadt), where another SS man, Hermann Alois Krumey, was based, in the campaign to rid the Polish lands of all ethnic Poles, a policy that was intensified concurrently with the far better known program that came to be called *Aktion Reinhardt* in 1942, aimed at ridding not just the Reich but Europe of all Jews.

Hitler's Bavarian-based party became gradually established in Austria in the late 1920s, primarily under the leadership of a dogged character, Major Hubert Klausner, who was a close associate of Globocnik's. Klausner was another ardent Carinthian, and a man with whom Globocnik was to have close and abiding contact.

Globocnik joined the national socialist movement by formally joining the National Socialist German Workers Party in 1930. In the same year, during the Great Depression, he managed to find a position with Rapatz, a Klagenfurt construction company. Beginning in that year Klagenfurt's well-known Café Lerch emerged, or re-emerged, as a congregating center for the new generation of depression era nationalistic activists. Initially Globocnik was a party worker, a *Gaubetriebszellenpropagandaleiter*, primarily involved in handing out and distributing party leaflets and other printed propaganda, a leg man. In 1931 he met a local Klagenfurt lawyer, Dr. Friedrich Rainer, in the office of the then *Gauleiter* of this region, Hubert Klausner. This was the beginning of a lifelong association that played a key, indeed crucial, role in Hitler acquiring Austria seven years later. Both men were uncompromising ideologues. By 1933 Globocnik was the local or provincial *Gauleiter*, having earlier been the deputy, and was rising steadily to senior rank.

In 1933 Globocnik was first incarcerated for his activities with the Nazis. He was arrested in August for attempting to contact imprisoned Nazis held in Klagenfurt's police jail. A subsequent arrest was for possession of explosives stored on an employer's property. The National Socialist electoral performance in Germany and Hitler's skillful January 1933 manipulations that were to see him emerge as chancellor appear to have been a turning point in Globocnik's life, and we now see him leaving behind his building industry career to embark full-time on political and clandestine activities. It is likely, however, that his years with KÄWAG had sharpened his skills of authority, and this assisted him in his political wheeling and dealing at the crucial rank-and-file level. Though he became a manager or organizer of men, he was never a truly skillful one. Financial management was certainly not one of his fortes, but that did not hinder his progress within the SS, though he came close to being severely punished.

Sometime during 1934 he re-established his acquaintance with the younger Ernst Lerch, whom he had known as a boy in Lerch's father's Klagenfurt café, and the two worked jointly as conspirators. They adopted the codename for their Carinthian-based conspiratorial group or fraternity, the "Kohlmaier family," with Lerch being known as "Luise" and Globocnik as "Mr King."[1] This name may well be a sign of his deep ambition, his drive to get to the top. Globocnik claimed that between 1933 and 1936 he faced high treason charges, which included sentences totaling 65 weeks imprisonment, though he served less than a year.[2] These clashes with the law meant Wild West-style wanted posters that carried his name and police mug-shot adorned walls across Kärnten. The clashes also meant that a new and determined individual had begun to emerge. A six-month jail term in 1935 resulted from a police raid on Dr. Rainer's office, during which police found a list of names, including Globocnik's. They arrested him nine days later in his Vienna apartment on Wiedner Hauptstrasse 59. The sentence was to have been for eight months, but he was released two months early because of an amnesty.

> According to the existing criminal files it can be confirmed that several legal actions were brought against him, but the precise number and the counts of indictment cannot be determined for sure. According to the list compiled by the *Staatspolizeistelle* [State Police Branch] Klagenfurt, Globocnik received the following sentences due to illegal activities for the NSDAP.
> On 17 September 1933, 6 weeks/42 days.
> On 13 November 1933, 4 weeks/28 days.
> On 12 December 1934, 6 months/183 days.
> On 29 August 1935, 6 months/182 days.
> Due to a common amnesty Globocnik did not have to spend the last 70 days in prison in the last sentence. The document mentions further that a warrant for high treason according to paragraph 58 St. G., implying 18 months imprisonment was issued.[3]

We learn from the Munich-based National Socialist Party's newspaper, *Völkischer Beobachter*, of 21 April 1938, which commemorated Globocnik's 34th birthday, under the headline, "A Birthday Boy," that while the party was banned he had "five high treason law suits" filed against him and had served "more than one year" in prison. "Also his whole family, including his very aged mother, were arrested."[4] The article went on to refer to his "silent performance," no doubt alluding to his international undercover work, with his longtime friend, Dr. Friedrich Rainer, and associate Dr. Artur Seyss-Inquart, and there is mention of how this trio "had played a decisive role of leadership in the political development which made possible the 12th March 1938" (Germany's takeover of Austria, the *Anschluss*). At one point during this politically hectic period, Globocnik found himself at large while most other senior party members were behind bars.

In 1934 he joined the SS and soon became one of the principal Nazi leaders in Austria. During that time he frequently visited his birthplace, Trieste, and some other places in Italy's northeast, and occasionally in the then lower (Sji) Austria (South Tyrol, Alto Adige) areas. During 1934 he and his co-conspirators used the Klagenfurt townhouse of the wealthy von Mohrenschildt family as a meeting venue. This ducal family had previously lived on the Carinthian-Slovenian border, but had been forced to flee north during the bitter and bloody 1918–1920 ethnic struggles, a family response that may well have hardened the young Reinhold von Mohrenschildt's wartime views toward the Poles of the Zamosc Lands during the war. Earlier, at the turn of the century, the Mohrenschildts had departed Estonia, probably because of the Czarist government's russification policy; they had thus moved twice in about 30 years because of Slavic encroachment, something that Hitler and Himmler attempted, during 1941–44, to reverse by forcibly Germanizing the so-called East, a policy in which both Globocnik and von Mohrenschildt played pivotal roles. With Globocnik's mother hailing from the Banat, which by the 1930s was very much a German settlement enclave surrounded by Slavs, it can be seen that the Mohrenschildts and Globocniks had something else in common, something that proved important in the 1940s when both found themselves in Lublin as senior SS demographic planners and policymakers. Both, by then, had access to research and other information from a Globocnik-created and directed research institute in this Polish city.

Although Globocnik was not directly involved in the bloody July 1934 coup attempt that resulted in the murder of Austria's diminutive Chancellor Engelbert Dollfuss — who bled to death in his chancellery — he helped some of the murderers by arranging their escape to the Reich, via Yugoslavia. He was thus an accomplice after the fact in a murder. After this assassination the Nazis, primarily members of the SA, launched several minor uprisings that all failed. One of these was by the Wolfsberg Group, in the Lavant Valley, situated in eastern Carinthia. After two days, however, the army drove these SA insurgents out and they fled across the mountains into Slovenia, where they were interned but were later retrieved by Hitler in the ships *Sierra Cordova* and *Deutschland*, and taken via the Adriatic to Bremen. The departure of the SA men meant that younger party members like Globocnik now moved to the forefront of the Carinthian or the Klausner Clique, which was set to become such an important factor in interwar Austrian political history. Globocnik, after 1934, turned to working as a courier and intelligence operative. This entailed employing female agents and using several export companies based in northern Italy as cover to smuggle sizeable quantities of funds from the Reich into Austria in exchange for information. This internationalist aspect of his career was apparently highly valued by Major Klausner, for whom Globocnik was now a senior and top operative, and it was also admired

by Heydrich. This work was a crucial stepping-stone for the young, enthusiastic Carinthian in being able to emerge within the ranks of the party's winning faction during the *Anschluss* of 1938.

During these so-called "Dark Years," Globocnik at times based himself
by the lakeside village of Krumpendorf, just eight kilometers from Klagenfurt, where Grete Michner and her father lived. Moreover, a German citizen
named Grafe allowed Globocnik use of his villa during winter months, and
this became a clandestine party cell precinct. On 1 September 1934, Globocnik had entered the SS with the I.D. number 292,776; this calculated and
careerist move was followed by increasingly regular contacts with the SS and
the *Sicherheitsdienst* (*SD*), Heydrich's intelligence arm within the Reich. It also
meant regular visits to Munich, the city that gave birth to Hitler's party.
Globocnik, with Dr. Rainer, now gradually began moving onto the Austrian
national stage, and eventually moved to Vienna to live and work, probably
in early 1936 or perhaps late 1935.

During 1935, Globocnik and Dr. Rainer used the office of Rainer's employer as a clandestine headquarters. Also during that year, for a time, Globocnik actually headed the regional party, not from Vienna but from across the
border in Budapest. However, he made secret trips back to the capital, stay-
ing with von Mohrenschildt in student quarters, a favor he returned to von
Mohrenschildt who, for a time, lived in Globocnik's Lublin SS mansion on
Wieniawska (*Ostlandstrasse*) Street. Never satisfied with just being on the run,
he recruited students to the Nazi cause, and even signed up both Mohrenschildt's sisters. His Vienna visits included meetings with Seyss-Inquart. Trips
to Munich, the southern and initial capital of the NSDAP, were also not
uncommon. Trieste-based Slovene researcher Ales Brecelj has summarized
this shadowy period in Globocnik's political career:

> The police brought this to the attention of the Italian authorities, which placed
> him on the list of foreigners who should be kept under surveillance when vis-
> iting Italy. Thus, for instance, for the year 1934 (in July the Nazis staged an
> abortive *putsch* in Vienna at which time they murdered Chancellor Engelbert
> Dollfuss) the data in the government archives in Rome show that Globocnik
> traveled twelve times from the airport in Venice to Munich and back. A record
> also exists of his travels to Italy by train, particularly through the border cross-
> ings between Austria and Italy and Yugoslavia until 1937.[5]

The six years from 1934 to 1939 therefore saw Globocnik steadily rising
toward the upper echelons of the SS and thus toward the administration and
control of criminal and inhuman demographic campaigns against civilians,
especially Jews, and also Poles. Although naturally unaware of it during the
early stages of this six-year phase, Globocnik was now on the road to becoming one of the 20th century's major mass murderers, robbers, and population

cleansers — as a loyal servant of Heinrich Himmler, who, with Hitler and Stalin, to name two others, sit at the peak of this murderous and destructive league.

This budding Austrian right-wing extremist also possessed what can only be described as a rather cheeky or disrespectful streak. While working as a building contractor and being involved in the construction of a seminary, he gave the local bishop a guided tour, by vehicle, during which the senior cleric was unknowingly sitting directly above several packages of explosives that were to be used in violent activities, not building work. Perhaps because he was known to be have been involved in such deeds, Globocnik is reputed some years later of having murdered by bombing a Jewish jeweler in Vienna. The Polish lawyer and historian Stanislaw Piotrowski, who attended the Nuremberg trials as a member of the Polish delegation and became the first to highlight Globocnik's wartime or Lublin crimes, refers to bombings by Globocnik in a brief 1949 assessment of him as a plunderer of Jewish treasures: "Odilo Globocnik was born in Austria and was rewarded for throwing bombs at Jewish shops. After the annexation of Austria by the Reich he became *Gauleiter* of Vienna."[6]

Much confusion exists about the killing of this jeweler, with many published references claiming Globocnik was the culprit, something Siegfried Pucher does not discount but casts some doubt upon. However, the Czech journalist, Walter Tschuppik, who published a booklet in London during the war on Berlin's much-feared Fifth Column activities, has claimed, or at least strongly insinuated, that Globocnik did murder this Jewish jeweler. Writing about the years just prior to the *Anschluss*, Tschuppik said:

> Dr Seyss-Inquart issued false passports to Austria's worst enemies, murderers and terrorists who many years previously had been sentenced to death by the Austrian courts but who had managed to escape to Germany. Men, against whom warrants had been issued and who were under sentence of death for brutal murders, suddenly appeared in the streets of Vienna, Graz and Innsbruck. The police were unable to raise a hand against them.
>
> If one of the police recognized such a man and said to him: "You are Herr Globotschnigg, the murderer of Futterweiss the jeweler," he would take a brand new passport from his pocket, saying: "You have made a mistake. I am Herr Müller. I have no idea who Herr Globotschnigg is."
>
> Late at night, in a back room of Hotel Regina, Dr Seyss-Inquart would meet the murderer Globotschnigg, who called himself Müller, and several other men of similar character.[7]

According to Siegfried Pucher (who shows the jeweler's surname as Futterweit), documentary evidence implicating Globocnik in this violent killing could not be found, leading him to argue that if such a grave crime had occurred a record would have existed in police files. This may be true, but still not explained is why Tschuppik used Globocnik, or at least his uncommon

non-Germanic surname, as the example to illustrate Seyss-Inquart's duplic-
itous behavior. Was it coincidence or just a random selection to make a point?
Or was it because Globocnik had become a senior member among those creating the new order in Austria? Unfortunately, we are unlikely ever to know.
However, Globocnik appears to have had a reputation of resorting to use of
explosives, and emerged as a committed and violent anti-Semite as well as
anti-Slavic. In light of this reputation and the fact that he had been involved
in the heavy construction sector in mountainous areas, he was certainly familiar with the destructive power of dynamite. Did he use this explosive to terrorize those he designated as enemies? It is difficult not to believe that he did.
Nor have others been hesitant in coming forth to point the finger at this purposive Carinthian. It is also worth remembering that Globocnik became in
May 1938 Vienna's *Gauleiter,* the most powerful post in Austria's capital,
where power to remove documents was within his grasp. Siegfried Pucher has
listed several examples of such accusations, including one by Eugen Kogon,
the author of probably the most important early book on the Nazi concentration camp system. Kogon was a German who had been interned and who
played an important role in the compiling of the immediate postwar Buchenwald Report.[8] Siegfried Pucher says that Kogon's version was reproduced in
the U.S. *Eighth Army News* on 9 July 1945, describing Globocnik's deeds:
"During the Nazi terrorism of 1933 he [Globocnik] hurled a bomb into a jeweler's shop at Futterweit, killing the proprietor and a customer. He was caught
and sent to prison, but was released by the amnesty of 1936."[9]

On the basis of information from another publication cited by Siegfried
Pucher, it is claimed that: "On June 12, 1933 — a bomb was thrown into a
shop of the Jewish jeweler Norbert Futterweit in Meidlung, [and] the proprietor was killed in the event. Moser does not mention the name Globocnik."[10]

The Kogon claim, which he published immediately after his liberation
from Buchenwald concentration camp at war's end, stated:

> The Lublin Distrikt was the stamping ground of SS Lieutenant-General
> Globocnig [sic], an Austrian who, following the murder of a Jewish jeweler in
> Vienna in 1933, had fled to Nazi Germany and in 1938 had returned to Vienna
> as *Gauleiter.* A year later he was involved in a huge foreign-exchange scandal.
> Public prosecution, however, was quashed and Globocnig was shifted to the
> SS.[11]

Apart from Siegfried Pucher's certainly not-to-be-ignored qualifications
for Globocnik, as descriptions of this incident were reproduced, the story
altered with the jeweler's name being spelled differently. A point not out of
place here is that Globocnik, while in Vienna working as an activist, may not
have actually thrown the bomb in question but planned or inspired a method

of killing that was not unfamiliar because of his long association with explosives easily acquired while a building industry employee in out-of-the-way parts of mountainous Carinthia. This resulted in rumors, though no actual evidence, that he was the killer, which he may not have been. By late 1936 and 1937 Globocnik was no longer a low-ranking party member but in the Carinthian party's upper echelons, so it is certainly not unlikely for him to be the planner of bombings and other political activities designed to inspire terror, something that was not unusual across Austria at that time. As gossip and rumor spread, Globocnik's planning or inspiration of a killing may have been changed to a claim that he was the actual perpetrator. Kogon suggests that he was away from Austria for a full five years, which is simply incorrect. Though a roving activist who moved through Italy, Germany, Hungary, and perhaps even Switzerland, he was not away from his fatherland for such a long period. Despite this serious error of fact, what is noteworthy here is Kogon's background. He was born in Munich in 1903 and studied in Munich, Florence, and Vienna, where he worked until 1934 as a writer, editor and business manager. "Immediately after the Germans marched into Austria, during the very night of March 11–12, 1938 he [Kogon] was finally arrested as one of the first opponents of the regime."[12]

If nothing else, Kogon before the outbreak of the war was a marked Vienna resident, and was in a position to know of Globocnik's reputation and *modus operandi*, for he was in Austria, indeed, Vienna, while his ideological enemy was active and about to become even better known. Nevertheless, until more conclusive documentary evidence can be provided, even Globocnik must be given the benefit of the doubt regarding any guilt for the death of the jeweler.

One of Globocnik's important Vienna contacts now was the Carinthian Reinhold von Mohrenschildt, who was studying economics in the capital. In Vienna Globocnik set about building an underground *SD* network. But life was not all work. We know that he and Rainer regularly drank together in cafés. Both attended the February 1936 Winter Olympics held at Garmisch-Partenkirchen in the Bavarian Alps, which Hitler also attended as *Führer*, though no evidence exists that they met their leader on this auspicious occasion. But they were relatively close to their much-admired leader. Nazi propagandists hailed this international sporting extravaganza as a huge success, since it had attracted 500,000 spectators. However, the enormous number of German troops present cast a shadow over the entire contest. Less pleasing for Berlin was the fact that this fourth Winter Olympics had sparked controversy over the Hitler Government's policies toward and campaigns against Germany's relatively small Jewish minority. Berlin consequently came under considerable pressure from the International Olympic Committee. One outcome that would no doubt have displeased Globocnik and Rainer was the fact that Rudolf Ball, the Jewish star of the German ice hockey team, and who had been the best player in Germany's 1932 bronze-winning side, was reluctantly invited back from voluntary exile in France to lead Germany. Ball was the only Jew in the German side and was included as a token gesture.

Dollfuss's brutal July 1934 assassination had also meant something else for Globocnik. This rightist bloody grab for power resulted in Hitler personally entering an agreement by treaty with successor Chancellor Schuschnigg which, on the face of it, appeared that Berlin had resolved to abide by a purist self-determination approach in German-Austrian relations. This agreement confused many Austrian Nazis, for its wording was completely out of step with their preconceptions. Hitler slowly came to realize this, as some, especially those associated with the SA wing of the movement, continued to be determined to launch further violent bids to snatch power. Because Hitler did not wish to see such an adventurist approach continuing at this time, he decided to make direct personal contact with his Austrian followers and that meant calling upon his two loyal Carinthians.

> He summoned two of their leaders, Rainer and Globocznigg, to make his position clear. The two Austrian Nazis arrived at the Obersalzberg on July 16, 1936. Rainer's account reveals their disappointment that they received no praise for their daily fight in the *Führer's* cause. On the contrary Hitler let fly at them, explaining in icy terms why he had concluded the Agreement.[13]

At this important meeting Hitler made it abundantly clear that he had other fish to fry. His army still needed building up and certain foreign policy considerations had to be attended. Moreover, Italy, which was at one with France and Great Britain on the perennial *Anschluss* issue, remained nervous about an expanded Reich as a northern neighbor. Interestingly, Hitler, while speaking to the two, suddenly walked over to the huge window in his exquisite mountain retreat that looked north toward Salzburg, and said: "Yet I am the loyal Eckard of Austria; here I stand, and I shall never desert you."[14] A truer word he never spoke, and on that note the two young couriers returned overland and convened a conference at Anis, near Salzburg, on 17 July, to explain to the party faithful inside Austria the *Führer's* party line.

It is worth stressing that the NSDAP (A), although older than its Bavarian and Hitler-led ideological cousin, had developed exceptionally strong dependent ideological and clandestine links with Berlin. However, in March 1938, when moves were set in train by Hitler to annex Austria, it was his trusted German follower, Hermann Göring, who pushed for the drive to occupy Austria. At the last minute Hitler had weakened and he had lost his cool, requiring Göring's dogged determination to push the takeover through. But well before that takeover, intricate financial links had been established between the two parties, with the Austrians being the indisputable mendicants.

There also existed a willingness on the part of many Austrians to fall in line with instructions from Munich — the German party's base — and later Berlin. This, as much as anything, facilitated the *Anschluss*.[15] Maurice Williams provides an insightful description of the complex financial relationships that extended into the area of relief and welfare for Austrian Nazis, who had encountered tough times because of their political and ideological commitment to the trans-national *völkisch* cause centered on Berlin and Munich.

> The continuous German management of Austrian affairs was amply demonstrated by the relief work undertaken by the party after the 1934 *putsch*. Reich Nazis had set up a vast hierarchy and a far-ranging organization to care for those Austrians who had fled, and for National Socialists, their families, and their sympathizers who had remained in the country. On August 3, [1934] Hitler had established the relief Work for Austrian Fugitives and Dependants (*Hilfswerk*) under SS-leader Alfred Rodenbuecher. This officer had the sole responsibility for all Austrian questions, including the dissolution of the existing Nazi headquarters in Munich. By the summer of 1936 Rodenbuecher had had a Berlin staff of 260 and had distributed financial assistance of 20 million *Reichsmarks* (RM) per year.[16]

This assessment demonstrates, among other things, that Hitler's many and varied followers and advisers were a real match for that other financially adept and ingenious German, Willi Münzenberg, who, at the same time, created similar clandestine financial networks across Western Europe for Stalin's formidable Comintern.[17] German, meaning Nazi, funds at this time flowed through a variety of secret channels, including front organizations and banks in Poland, Switzerland, Czechoslovakia, and Hungary. Also used were German companies with branches in Vienna or elsewhere in Austria.

Despite all the disputation and squabbling within the Austrian Nazi movement, Globocnik was able to emerge in early 1938 within the ranks of the winning faction of the clique-ridden Austrian party. One of the reasons for this was his association with the much underestimated fellow Carinthian, Dr. Rainer, who, by 1937, had helped devise, among other things, a two-track strategy to give that party the best chance of becoming the only political force in Austria. Within this Rainer-devised strategy Globocnik played an important role, and two experts on this period, Radomir Luza and Maurice Williams, credit him with single-mindedness. Globocnik was not working in an easy-go-lucky political environment. Far from it. Between 1928 and 1938, the decade before Austria's incorporation into Hitler's Reich, the party underwent a series of traumatic factional upheavals, including leadership changes; a failed coup attempt in 1934, during which a chancellor was left to bleed to death in the nation's chancellery; a stop-start approach by Hitler to admitting whether or not he really controlled things; bitter regional disputes; ongoing arrests and jailings of senior and lower level apparatchiks; and rank-and-file confusion over what may be required of them. Were they to embark on a violent takeover as Hitler had attempted in Munich in November 1923, when the army blocked him, or was the tactic to be along the lines that had led to Hitler's rise in Berlin in January 1933? Few Austrian party members knew which of these approaches was best or likely to be adopted. There was confusion and dithering. In the midst of all this no thought appears to have been given by the party's divided leadership groups — neither by the contending Captain Josef Leopold or the Klausner group — to the specific nature of the relationship being sought with the Reich, and with Hitler, who, although a western Austrian, was now in power in Berlin. Radomir Luza, quoting Leopold Tavs, states: "Because there was hardly time to work out ready-made formulas in the middle of battle. Ultimately, all aimed at some kind of settlement along the lines of the status of Bavaria in the Bismarckian Reich in 1871."[18]

However, the status of Bavaria was precisely what Hitler never envisaged. He was a centralist as well as a totalitarian. It was not a coincidence that he had included a chapter in his famous 1924 book, *Mein Kampf,* titled "Federalism as a Mask." Hitler and his top four party colleagues, all Germans — Göring, Göbbels, Himmler, and Hess — wanted nothing less than a centrally controlled state with themselves at the top pulling all, not just some of, the strings. This, moreover, was why Hitler and his associates promoted the notion of *Gleichschaltung* (coordination), which placed them in the position of being the puppeteers, not puppets, of the needs and desires of differing regions or interests. They were not federalists. *Gleichschaltung* meant that loyalists like Globocnik and Rainer were there to do as ordered, something that both did with utter loyalty before and during the war, even when this meant murdering on a mass scale, expelling and forcibly transferring people from their homes. Both became population cleansers, and all the historical evidence suggests that they would have carried out such tasks on an even larger scale if Hitler's Reich had won the war.

In Austria's last two years of independence, 1936 and 1937, the fractured local Nazi Party was led by retired Captain Josef Leopold, a man who adopted what one writer has called the gradualist as opposed to activist approach. Globocnik, although aligned with Klausner and Rainer, joined this move. In July 1936, immediately after the agreement between Berlin and Vienna, Captain Leopold founded the Committee of Seven, which, although a front organization, was able to gain Schuschnigg's recognition, since Captain Leopold was prepared to negotiate with the government. More important here was the fact that Globocnik was one of the seven, not as a Carinthian official but as the Vienna district leader, showing how far this provincial activist had come since 1930.[19]

Professor Williams says that the decision to take a gradualist path at first worked well for Captain Leopold. He seemed to be on the same wavelength as the self-centered coordinator, Hitler, who had deliberately trodden that path in Germany between 1926 and 1933, following his encounter with Bavarian law and a period in jail. Such a path, moreover, had eventually led to victory for Hitler, and it allowed Captain Leopold to re-establish his authority within his faction-ridden party.[20] He followed this by fighting off the ever-growing challenge of Klausner, that other dogged Carinthian, who was eventually forced to resign as a *Gauleiter*. Captain Leopold, the SA man, cooperated with Franz von Papen, Hitler's ambassador in Vienna, and he briefly dealt amicably with Schuschnigg, even negotiating the long-awaited legalisation of the party. In the Austria he envisaged, the National Socialists would no longer be regarded as mere traitors. He even adhered to the view that an *Anschluss* between the German nations of Central Europe was no longer an issue once the German people came to accept things for what they were. But Austrian politics, like the weather over Central Europe, was unpredictable, and for Captain Leopold the unexpected now occurred, for Schuschnigg gradually discontinued speaking to him and failed to fulfill most government promises. The failure of Captain Leopold's domestic peace ploy meant backers fell away, and, to make matters worse, Schuschnigg's police struck the party's national office — the so-called Helferstorferstrasse Raid — and found compromising material that further led to Captain Leopold's decline in standing because of his blatant carelessness. However, according to Radomir Luza, Captain Leopold and his followers — Globocnik not being one of them — were simply incapable of grasping the need for a more sophisticated style of politics, that is, the need to adopt a gradual transformationist approach rather than to plot and plan for an eventual putsch, which they envisaged. They "...never fully subscribed to the new gradualist approach. The SA spirit of tavern brawls and street fighting was alien to an understanding of the instrumentalities of the new politics."[21]

But one man who was capable of grasping this need, and the opportunity, because of the vacuum at the top, was none other than Dr. Rainer, and with him came Carinthians Klausner and Globocnik. Major Klausner, now a retired officer on half-pay, was a Hitler confidant — a crucially important relationship — and the *Führer* held him responsible for all illegal activities inside coveted Austria. Rainer emerges at this point as something of a distant puppeteer, for he devised the dual approach of cultivating an illegal party that was complemented by having a "legal person" safely and strategically ensconced at the top. That man was the softly-spoken Viennese lawyer, Artur Seyss-Inquart, with whom Schuschnigg was prepared to deal, and who went on to rule wartime Holland and be hanged after the war as a major war criminal. Bolshevik hero Vladimir Lenin has long been hailed by political theorists for devising the notion of the Bolsheviks being the "vanguard of the proletariat," but Rainer has never attracted acclamation for his contribution, the making of a cunning middle-class lawyer the "vanguard of German Volkdom" inside Austria. Significantly, it was Rainer who did this, not Globocnik, who, in many respects, had more in common with Captain Leopold's group. There is little doubt that despite his propensity for violence, Globocnik was shrewd enough to remain close and loyal to his long-time Carinthian contacts. That helped save his career more than once within the Hitler movement as well as within Himmler's SS. Rainer no doubt looked after his old party chum again and again until the day of Globocnik's death, which Rainer witnessed. The two were that close. They chattered, they plotted, they drank together. They sometimes traveled and went on excursions together, and had much time to contemplate each other's views and assessments.

> In the following weeks as Seyss-Inquart, supported and encouraged by Rainer, moved from one success to the next, the circle of moderates [the Carinthians and Seyss] grew while the faction following Leopold declined. The *Landesleiter* [Leopold] himself insured that the split would be permanent. In September [1937] he severed ties with Rainer because of disloyalty and opposition. Later he called Seyss-Inquart's associates traitors, scoundrels, and blackmailers, and went so far as to expel Globocnik from the party. In the process alienating others, Leopold also issued orders that forbade party members from associating with the German ambassador, Franz von Papen, and Wilhelm Keppler (Hitler's special liaison to Austria) as well as Seyss-Inquart.[22]

This episode ended, and not coincidentally, for Captain Leopold, with Hitler ordering him to go to Germany where he was reprimanded and even told to leave Austria altogether. People in both capitals were now rolling up their sleeves for a final showdown, which was going to arrive sooner rather than later. By the time Hitler had ordered Schuschnigg to his Bavarian mountain retreat just south of Salzburg, in February 1938, all was in place for that dramatic finale which shook European foreign offices. The apparently unsuspecting Austrian chancellor was largely surrounded by political enemies. Schuschnigg, who fully appreciated the nature and style of his enemies, had, since the 1936 agreement with Hitler, become accustomed to compromising and giving in, even though his police and secret service were keeping him abreast of certain crucial clandestine developments around him. But he did not realize that his foreign minister, Guido Schmidt, was one of the many sinister traitors in his camp. Pan-Germanism had many variants, including one stressing loyalty to the Hitler strain. The English newspaper, *The Daily Herald,* reported some two months after the *Anschluss* that Schmidt had received a job that paid the equivalent of 40,000 British pounds as general manager of the Hirtenberger Patronen-Fabrik, the "greatest Austrian ammunition factory."[23] That was his reward. Though treacherous, his position was certainly to be far more comfortable than that of Schuschnigg, who was placed under house arrest and later languished for four years in Dachau concentration camp. Others were not so fortunate, having lost their lives at the hands of Hitler's followers. Many met such a fate. According to one student of Nazism's Fifth Column techniques, the key element of the emergence of the new German-Austrian relationship can be traced back to Hitler's by now infamous secret policeman and SS man, Reinhard Heydrich, who worked primarily with two key Austrians, Linz lawyer Ernst Kaltenbrunner and the former Klagenfurt-based builder and construction worker Odilo Globocnik, who was by 1938 well and truly a Vienna resident. Through this successful Austrian duo the sinister secret service chief, Heydrich,

> ...quietly and unobtrusively built up a Nazi Fifth Column, which penetrated into almost every sphere of Austrian life. High government officials, important industrialists, members of the Austrian secret service, well-known professional men, and even the private secretary of Chancellor Schuschnigg himself— all were agents of Heydrich's *SD*.[24]

Heydrich's work in infiltrating the camps of his designated enemies must surely be considered one of the most successful such operations of the 20th century. A Dollfuss biographer, in a study of the *Anschluss,* described this aspect of these scene-setting months of Austria's finale as follows:

> The only parts of this complicated double game which emerged clearly to Schuschnigg at the time were, of course, the threatening reference to those 'ten million Germans along our borders' and the appointment of a new Nazi *Gauleiter* for Vienna. *The fact that Klausner's reorganized illegal party network inside Austria seemed to be built on the SS (Kaltenbrunner, Rainer, Globocnig [sic]) rather than on the SA of Captain Leopold and his cronies did nothing to reassure the Chancellor.* By 1938 the *Reichsführer* of the SS, Heinrich Himmler, and his henchmen like Heydrich, were already figures that caused a shiver in any anti–Nazi breast. It was Himmler who had received Seyss-Inquart when the latter flew to Berlin on February 16, 'for consultations'. One wonders what the muddled Austrian Catholic and the ice-cold German heathen made of each other as they discussed police methods [emphasis added].[25]

Another identity to emerge as a significant Viennese figure during these tumultuous weeks was another Globocnik associate, the western Austrian or Salzburg art historian Kajetan Mühlmann, whom one writer has described as "arguably the single most prodigious art plunderer in the history of human civilization."[26] Mühlmann had aligned himself with the influential but devious Seyss-Inquart group in the capital, a clique that managed at times to be referred to as "moderates," despite playing such a deceptive stalking role in assisting Hitler to acquire Austria.

> It is significant that Mühlmann and Globocnik became friends: first, because of the implications for the Austrian Nazi Party prior to the *Anschluss,* with

Mühlmann's emergence as an effective mediator in the intra-party feuds; second, because this relationship continued during the war when both were active in Poland in the General Gouvernement (the part of Poland not incorporated into the Reich or ceded to the Soviets in 1939).[27]

Mühlmann, like Globocnik, had a dark, even criminal side, leading him to the wilful deprivation of others' liberty. Although he had formally joined the NSDAP only in April 1938, and quickly went on to become an *SS-Oberführer*, he, in fact, had maintained a close and long association with the banned Austrian National Socialists. During the years it was banned, 1933–38, Mühlmann also worked as an undercover agent for Heydrich if he was not actually a formal clandestine *SD* member. Although arrested in 1935, he managed to avert attention from himself. "Despite this experience, Mühlmann's association with the Austrian Nazi Party remained sufficiently concealed to enable him to work as a seemingly independent front man or liaison during the period of Nazi prohibition."[28]

The opportune moment to "surface" came, of course, with the lead-up to the *Anschluss*, so Mühlmann naturally came out into the light, emerging temporarily even as Austria's state secretary for fine arts in the short-lived Seyss-Inquart cabinet.

Mühlmann's significance up until the outbreak of the war, after which he was basically a grand master art thief, was that he had family links to Hermann Göring, and worked as a key undercover operative and informer for Reinhard Heydrich, like Globocnik and Kaltenbrunner. This was a lucky combination of Berlin superiors, because Göring and Himmler by then had teamed up and were working closely over these years, Mühlmann's work being basically for the same Berlin political ends. This is the way Radomir Luza assesses Mühlmann:

> The Carinthian group [Globocnik and Rainer] worked closely with Kaltenbrunner and the *SD*. Also the circle around Seyss-Inquart was tied to the SS. Another influential SS member, Dr Kajetan Mühlmann, a friend of Seyss-Inquart, used his connections to Hermann Göring to obtain necessary background material useful to the Rainer-Seyss-Inquart line. Göring and Himmler — not Konstantin von Neurath and Papen — took over control of events in Austria.[29]

Ernst Kaltenbrunner's biographer, Peter Black, puts this point somewhat similarly:

> Rainer was not only concerned about making contact with the Austrian government via Seyss-Inquart; he also wanted Berlin to endorse his and Seyss-Inquart's efforts. To achieve this, he depended on the embryonic Austrian *SD*, through which he maintained contact with Himmler, Heydrich, and Göring. The liaison contacts were a small group of students who formed an *SD* cell at

the University of Vienna; Kajetan Mühlmann, an art historian who had good relations with Göring and Heydrich; and Ernst Kaltenbrunner, who linked Rainer to Himmler and Heydrich.[30]

In addition, Mühlmann was a courier for Hitler to his famous southern mountain retreat, Berchtesgaden. In the weeks immediately prior to Chancellor Schuschnigg's sudden decision to call a nationwide plebiscite — his way of seeking legitimacy against Hitler's mounting and increasingly intolerable pressures for unification or annexation — Mühlmann was a major conduit carrying crucial information to Hitler as the *Führer* sat overlooking Salzburg, Mühlmann's home city.

After the *Anschluss*, Mühlmann began acquiring — expropriating — highly prized art works owned primarily by Jews and eventually by other designated enemies. This was the period of so-called "wild Aryanization," the phase during which Globocnik, as *Gauleiter* of Vienna, came undone and was severely reprimanded by his Berlin superiors for misappropriating funds. Austria during the second half of 1938 and much of 1939 saw tens of thousands of these ideologically targeted people leaving for destinations such as Australia, South Africa, Canada, Irish Free State, and New Zealand.[31] Mühlmann went on to repeat his gargantuan plundering activities in occupied Poland and also in the Netherlands until about 1943. In Professor Luza's words, in an understatement if ever there was one, "In the fall of 1939 he took charge of art objects in the occupied territories."[32] Although Mühlmann and Globocnik were ideological allies, it is worth stressing that Globocnik was quite at ease with someone who was an obviously well-educated person, just as he was undoubtedly comfortable with his other Carinthian pals, the educated activists, Dr. Friedrich Rainer and Reinhold von Mohrenschildt. This point is made to caution against viewing Globocnik as merely a street rowdy or thug — though the latter he no doubt was — for he undoubtedly also had an interest, and an abiding one, in ideas, if only National Socialist ones, and Pan-German programs, which, it must be said, had their own complexity and sophistication, relying on quasi-historical, archaeological, and linguistic theories and contentions. It should not be forgotten that Globocnik created his own research institute in Lublin, and we know he sought to develop contacts with eminent personages with academic qualifications, including the famous geopolitical theorist, Karl Haushofer, who had earlier befriended both Rudolf Hess and Adolf Hitler. His approach to politics was therefore not simply to beat, rob, bash, and dynamite the enemy. Globocnik, as will be seen later, also worked toward longer term goals, things which eventually included, first and foremost, the ethnic cleansing of the East — Poland, Ukraine, Belarus, European Russia, and the Baltic — of Jews and Slavs, so that these lands, which Nazi ideologues claimed had been usurped by the Slavs from the Goths a millennium earlier, would become a new expanded vast Greater Germanic homeland. This, incidentally, was the outlook that Mühlmann also adamantly held to, something he even enunciated in his jointly authored wartime publication, released in Krakow in 1940 and published by the office of Governor-General Dr. Hans Frank.

> The *Ostmark* [Austria], the Sudetenland, Eastern Silesia, the region of the river Weichsel [Vistula River in central Poland]—many names characterize a piece of German history from an inner consistency *that affects us all deeply*. [Emphasis added.] German history in the East: that is the fulfillment of a thousand year old struggle and fight of Germanic life-energy.... Securing German living space (*Lebensraum*) is the task. Achieving it through German spirit and culture is the result. Already centuries ago (this region) was settled and secured by our Germanic ancestors.[33]

That this strongly held view that reunification of Upper or Eastern Silesia, Austria, the Sudetenland, and central Poland with Hitler's Reich affected certain people deeply is crucial to understanding the wartime work for the SS of men like Globocnik, Rainer, Mühlmann, and their many friends, colleagues, and associates, men on Globocnik's staff like Paul Gasser, who preceded the later ever-present Ernst Lerch, and Sepp Nemetz, Gustav Hanelt, and Dr. Franz Stanglica. The last two were the senior personnel of Globocnik's Lublin-based research institute, which was working on plans to Germanize all of occupied Poland, Ukraine, Belarus, and European Russia. This institute appears to have been based on a style of work undertaken in southern Austria by several pre-war Globocnik acquaintances, including Dr. Helmut Carstanjen, Anton Dorfmeister, and Alois Maier-Kaibitsch, who will be considered later. These three in particular were important officials based in Graz and Klagenfurt from where they subsequently directed moves for the Germanization of northern Slovenia. In the case of another who will be later considered, Reinhold von Mohrenschildt, the Baltic lands, once settled by pioneering Germans, among them his ancestors, had a similar emotional appeal, and this acted as motivation for his ethnic cleansing wartime work in occupied Poland.

For Mühlmann the SS's presence in occupied Poland, the subsequent widespread removal of cultural artifacts, and the clearly implied or ethnic cleansing of its citizenry—Jews, eventually by extermination, and Poles primarily by expulsion—were simply the beginnings of the historical squaring-off process to become known as the "re-Germanizing" of these lands: "re-Germanization" because these ideologues believed that the East had once been Germanic, and had been usurped many centuries ago by incoming Slavs. That was precisely the way Globocnik viewed occupied Poland, and why he went on to jointly direct the exterminationist and expulsionist policies for Hitler and Himmler during his murderous Lublin period of nearly four years. In light of this, it is difficult not to conclude that all these Austrian SS men had been influenced by a knowledge of the fact that Austria's Great Empress Maria Theresa and her son Emperor Joseph II, following the Treaty of Passarowitz/Pozarevac of 1718, had been involved in large-scale settling of Europeans across the Balkans that for several centuries had been controlled by the Turkish or Ottoman Empire. This is what the English travel writer Bernard Newman had noted during his travels through the Banat region — Globocnik's mother's homeland. Both Austrian monarchs had played a key role in "re-Europeanizing" large tracts of the Balkan region. This Austrian legacy may even explain Hitler's decision to view so favorably ethnic cleansing policies undertaken by his government throughout World War II, especially by members of Himmler's SS. "Interestingly, too, is [Friedrich] Heer's argument in *Der Glaube des Adolf Hitler, Anatomie einer politischen Religiosität, 1968,* that Hitler was influenced by the Austrian emperor Joseph II as much as, if not more than, the Prussian Frederick the Great."[34]

III

The *Anschluss*: March–April 1938

During the second week of March 1938, Globocnik was one of a relatively small number of in-the-know actively treasonous Austrians who played a key role in assisting Adolf Hitler gain control of Austria, Hitler's former homeland. These internationally tense days, which markedly shook Europe, were the climax of moves that commenced at least in 1918–19, when Britain and France blocked the creation of a single Germanic Central European power, based on Germany-Prussia as well as Austria — in many ways the *Mitteleuropa* that activists within both these nations, which had been loyal allies throughout the long Great War, had been propounding since the late 19th century. Crucial after that conflict, and for the next two decades, was the fact that Italy, a belated Great War ally of Great Britain and France, looked toward the retention of a separate or independent Austria, despite what many Austrian and German activists desired. Among those who sought unification were Germany's Austrian-born chancellor, Adolf Hitler, and the Austrian Nazi Party's leadership, which, by late 1937, was dominated by three Carinthians, namely Rainer, Globocnik, and Klausner and the local SS chief, Ernst Kaltenbrunner, a lawyer, like Rainer, from Linz, in western Austria. Pan-Germanism, however, was a sentiment that not only Nazis of the German or Austrian variants sought: It was a far more broadly based sentiment.

The single event that finally propelled Hitler toward the takeover was Schuschnigg's unexpected announcement of a plebiscite that was designed to confirm Austria's independence from Hitler and Berlin. This surprise playing of a democratic or electoral card came out of the blue, for Austria was essentially a weak, depressed, and authoritarian corporate state that had failed to recover from or adjust to the loss of its multi-national empire and military power, which also included a sizeable navy. Politically speaking Austria was split into irreconcilable groups, with the National Socialists more loyal to Berlin than Vienna. Another reason was that Hitler had himself proposed such a plebiscite at least once, showing that one need not be a democrat to resort to a managed or guidable democratic technique or ploy. Political suppression of both the extreme left and right, and even Austria's social democrats, toward whom Schuschnigg had shown no warmth whatsoever, was resorted to in Austria. Schuschnigg's administration oversaw a type of guided patriotism through a front organization known as the Fatherland Front. Longtime extremists like Klausner, Globocnik, and Rainer had contributed markedly to this tense state of affairs, as did Hitler from across the border by his constant pressure, bullying, and intimidation through infiltration, radio and newspaper campaigns, and pamphleteering, techniques later resorted to against Poland, and the channeling of a lot of money to his ideological friends and followers. Globocnik played a not insignificant role in all of this. By early March, hard-on-the-heels of the 12 February 1938 Schuschnigg-Hitler meeting in Hitler's Bavarian mountain retreat adjacent to Salzburg, Schuschnigg, a Tyrolese, felt he could no longer withstand the obsessive Hitler, a lowland western Austrian, and his local and equally obsessive disciples and camp followers, so the long-ignored Austrian people were turned to in a quest to gain legitimacy.

Also significant was Germany's Austrian-born *Führer*'s newly found sense of confidence that arose from the fact that Rome was moving away from alignment with Paris and London as the 1930s progressed, since Italy's bombastic Benito Mussolini was hell-bent on creating a neo–Roman Mediterranean and North African Empire extending to the shores of the Indian and Atlantic Oceans, something the French and the British, with African colonial and other possessions and therefore interests in this region, increasingly and understandably resisted.

> Mussolini at first opposed the nazification of Austria because he feared that it would enable Hitler to extend his influence over the Balkans. Thus it was that in 1934 he averted a Nazi coup in Vienna by bringing Italian troops to the Brenner Pass. A year later, at Stresa, Great Britain, France, and Italy signed a resolution supporting Austrian independence.[1]

Hitler, as slowly became evident, but only to some, was also intent on acquiring vast territories to create, if not an empire, then a huge extensive unitary state, a Greater Germanic Reich, one extending east to the Ural Mountains from Central Europe. Hitler and his advisers soon noted Mussolini's imperial desires, so the *Führer* gradually and shrewdly coaxed *Il Duce*—a man whom he had admired since the early 1920s — away from opposition toward an *Anschluss* in Central Europe, and thus away from Stresa commitment or resolution. The first and most obvious victim of the new axis or partnership between these two totalitarian men, each wanting an empire — one to his east, the other to Europe's south — was the deeply divided Austria of Schuschnigg, within which various shades of Pan-Germanism competed and co-existed, and not only among those who were well-disposed toward the *Führer*. As time passed, Mussolini's Italy also intentionally moved toward an active policy of challenging Great Britain and France in many of their Middle Eastern imperial possessions, areas adjacent to Italy's planned path of North African expansion. The crucial factor, however, was that Rome's challenge not only threatened their colonial grip but also markedly weakened their bargaining position in Central Europe, which was slowly being dominated by concern over Hitler's Germany. One expert on Anglo-French relations in the 1930s has described the bind in which London and Paris now found themselves:

> France, the second greatest colonial power, faced challenges in her North African territories, in Mandated Syria and in Indo-China. There were insurrections in Syria in 1925 and 1936. A joint Franco-Spanish expedition was required in 1926 to crush the rebellion of the Moroccan leader, Abd-el-Krim. France had to transfer abroad a third of her military strength. Britain's main anxieties were Egypt and India. After 1929 unrest in India tied down substantial forces. In the same year an Arab revolt against Jewish immigrants broke out in Palestine, then under British Mandate. The bulk of the regular army was posted to Palestine. *In the late 1930s Italian propaganda was active in the Middle East, inciting Arab nationalism against British and French rule. This running fight against nationalist revolt was a constant drain on the energies and resources of the two leading colonial powers* [emphasis added].[2]

Hitlerian Berlin benefitted greatly from this Italian-inspired instigation against the two major Western powers, and just as Germany was moving toward rearming. Even so, Hitler had taken a risk with Italy, according to his longtime interpreter, Dr. Paul Schmidt, who revealed after the war that the *Führer* in his telegram to Mussolini — "*Duce*, I shall never forget this." — insisted on honoring that claim to his dying day.[3] Great Britain's response, in the tradition that came to be known as appeasement, had been to work for a détente with Mussolini, something that prompted the then British foreign minister, Anthony Eden, who had championed Ethiopia's cause against Italian aggression, to resign his post in February 1939, on the eve of the *Anschluss*. That move made way for the less resilient Halifax to move into Eden's crucial position until 1940. Moreover, Eden's resignation failed to have any impact upon the outlook of British Prime Minister Neville Chamberlain toward continental Europe's two emerging dictators. Most accounts of these complex times that saw the coercive unification of Germany and Austria suggest that

Schuschnigg set out being confident of attracting approximately 70 percent of the electorate in a nationwide plebiscite. His decision to arrange a plebiscite appears to have had approval. Where he seems to have lacked a consensus was due to his choice of printing the affirmative ballots, which carried the word "*Ja*," whereas the "*Nein*" ballots were expected to be provided by voters. Furthermore, the voting age was raised to 24 years, and voting was not as had traditionally occurred in, say, Australia, where the secret ballot was pioneered (following the influence of the British Chartists), to the extent that this form of secret voting became known worldwide as "the Australian Ballot." Clearly, defenders of the *status quo* were wary of the fact that Nazism appealed to younger people.[4]

Even so, the consensus appears to be that Schuschnigg's case was on a winning cycle, even though the fight was not to be altogether open, fair, and just. On his side were the Christian and other labor movements, the Catholic and the Protestant Churches, and a range of other institutions, including even the illegal Communist Party. Hitler and his local Nazis were therefore confronted with a sizeable, if loosely knit and certainly not united, front. Though we will never know, what seems to be a tenable assessment of the electoral climate was made during a belated conversation between Italy's Foreign Minister Count Galeazzo Ciano and a British ambassador. On 12 March, Ciano, defending the Italian stance that developments in Austria were a "bygone affair," said there was nothing Italy could have done, since she could not "force the people to be independent if they do not wish to be so." Ciano saw the so-called Austrian revolution as a *fait accompli*, one that had been carried out with enthusiasm not only in Alpine regions such as Graz and Innsbruck, but also in Vienna. He viewed the *Anschluss* as akin to *Il Duce's* famous 1921 March on Rome, an assessment that may not be too far off target, since both *Il Duce* and men like Globocnik subverted a political order through threats. Britain's ambassador, however, balked at his assessment, saying that only 30 percent of Austrians "were really Nazi supporters and without outside aid [the] *coup* would never have taken place." But the count disagreed, claiming that those in the minority "were enthusiastic, well organized and young," whereas the majority "were much older men without any strong views and divided amongst themselves."[5] This assessment is also difficult to dispute. One of Austria's leading but now forgotten anti-Nazis, the admirable if not politically astute pundit, *Frau* Irene Harand, author of the book, *His Struggle: An Answer to Hitler*, as well as proprietress of the weekly newspaper, *Gerechtigkeit* ("Justice"), wrote as late as 8 March 1938 from London: "Pessimists are making somber forecasts, declaring that the Nazis will advance. I don't consider this possible as the real power in Austria rests in the hands of our Government headed by Chancellor Dr Schuschnigg —*Behind Schuschnigg stands the overwhelming majority of the Austrian people*" (emphasis added).[6]

Others who agreed with the 70 percent pro–Schuschnigg figure pointed out that it was not uniform across Austria, with Carinthia only likely to be about 60 percent and Styria just 50 percent. However, crucial "guidance" and pressure from across the border by Austria's smaller, leaner, and generally younger political "hares," Globocnik most certainly one of them, helped to out-maneuver quickly the larger group of Austrian "tortoises," bringing a quick end to the nation's sovereignty. The man who could take most credit was not Hitler but his crony, Hermann Göring, who took decisive steps, which, interestingly, involved even Globocnik. Ciano's 1938 response stood in stark contrast to Italy's stand just four years earlier, when Dollfuss was so brutally murdered by Nazis who had stormed his chancellery. In that case Mussolini, on learning of that *putsch,* had immediately ordered his army to advance toward the famous Brenner Pass and the Carinthian border region. This act of self interest and loyalty to Dollfuss had largely arisen because of Dollfuss's 1933 Easter visit to Rome, where the two had agreed an independent Austria was needed.

> On the second day of the Easter visit, Mussolini had set the diplomatic tone by drinking to the "future of the Austrian Republic" at a banquet in the Austrian Chancellor's honor. By the end of Dollfuss's Whitsun trip, public reference was already being made to the possibility of a triple association between Italy, Austria and Hungary, while, in secret, Mussolini was even giving certain military assurances to his guest.[7]

With this in mind, subsequent moves by Hitler must be assessed as having been extremely astute, especially with respect to Mussolini. When the 1934 murder of Dollfuss finally came, German intelligence agents alerted Berlin that Italian units based near Brenner Pass were being issued battle ammunition. Nor had Mussolini confined himself to the military sphere, for back in Rome he met with Britain's and France's ambassadors to devise a united front. Berlin's re-emergence as the "light on the hill" for Austrian Nazis was not, however, something new and unexpected by the late 1930s. Both Ciano and the British ambassador were correct about the cult of youth and external assistance coming together to constitute the winning formula. Germany, even during most of World War I, had maintained controlling contacts over Vienna, a state of affairs that continued even when Hitler was denying that the Reich had ulterior motives. Throughout the '30s the Reich was a base for assistance to Nazis who commonly fled Austria in search of aid and sustenance. The Reich was also the base for a network of aid stations or semi-clandestine offices situated in Munich, Hamburg, and Berlin, more evidence that a big brother existed who may one day act.

A measure of Austrian dependency was the fact that Germany had become home for some 25,000 Austrian political fugitives and disgruntled and often over ambitious activists who, after the *Anschluss,* formed the Austrian Legion. Although Globocnik was still a relatively minor figure, and not a policy-maker, in Hitler's first significant move to change the shape of Europe, this 34-year-old Carinthian nevertheless played a not insignificant supporting role between 9 and 15 March, 1938, when Austria was merged into the Third Reich. That penultimate week also served to propel him to become within four years the key exterminator of Jews, the worst such exterminator in European history, and a cleanser of Slavs, with the Poles being the first targeted, from Globocnik's headquarters in provincial Lublin.

Day 1, Wednesday, 9 March

Six days earlier, Schuschnigg had decided that a plebiscite advancing a proposal "For an Austria free and German, independent and social, Christian and united," would be held on 13 March. On 9 March, he and his foreign minister, Guido Schmidt, broke the news to the upper echelons of government and their colleagues in the pro-government Fatherland Front and quickly launched a hasty "*Ja*" campaign. Notwithstanding this, news of the decision was already out, in large part because the Nazis, some of them even tea ladies, had either pilfered discarded paper placed in wastepaper baskets, or had learned of the plan otherwise and passed it up their party's all-pervasive network of agents. Even so, Hitler and those within the Austrian Nazi Party's senior ranks in Berlin were, surprisingly, still caught off-guard by the announcement. After a long telephone conversation between Hitler and Göring, the *Führer* ordered that Germany should prepare for military action. Globocnik and Rainer, who had heard of the plebiscite the previous day, with Rainer actually telephoning the news to Berlin, drove by hired car toward Vienna's city center. After years of underground activity, both were now free to step into the open as political activists. They had been Vienna-based covert activists since early 1937, since the establishment of the *Volkspolitische Referate* (Racial Political Councils), which were headed by Walter Pembauer. Schuschnigg's political meanderings had resulted in Pembauer acceding to the formation of the RPCs on condition that the Nazis operate within the government-controlled Fatherland Front. Quizzing Pembauer that day were Nazi leaders, Major Klausner and also Dr. Hugo Jury, an old party member. Soon after, Globocnik and Rainer also arrived, and the four finally decided to visit their undercover colleague, Dr. Seyss-Inquart, and tell him to protest Schuschnigg's unexpected move. But Seyss felt he could not follow such orders. Since he was still a minister, he regarded himself as being bound by the rules of Cabinet solidarity: He could not provide information to his co-conspirators, not overtly at least. This troubled character therefore had to devise a devious method of being dishonorable and at the same time somehow placating his conscience. To do this he handed his party pals a "the carbon copy of his letter to Schuschnigg," giving them the necessary information to pass on to Berlin.[8]

Shortly after they had left Seyss, Rainer telephoned Berlin to speak to Hitler's Austrian affairs expert, Wilhelm Keppler, a descendant of the great scientist of that name and a model and wealthy Nazi industrialist, who had recently visited Vienna and compiled a long optimistic report on the southern Nazis. Keppler went to meet Hitler to bring him up-to-date with developments. Shortly after this Globocnik left for Berlin with a letter that contained everything that was to be reported to Hitler. Despite all this hurried movement and telephoning, Keppler was ordered to return to Vienna to make another assessment. News of the proposed plebiscite also sparked frantic activity across the political spectrum, in cafés, homes, and most important of all, on street corners and the streets, with lorry loads of supporters (Fatherland Fronters) and opponents (Nazis) driving around. Walls and street pillars were being plastered with posters. Austria was approaching its third major turning point of the 20th century—the previous two being declaration of war in August 1914, followed by loss of empire four years later. Somehow all three seemed related. Schuschnigg had already moved toward creating an informal pact with the Socialists, the so-called illegal Left. Among all the uncertainty something resembling a democratic milieu was set to descend upon the land. Austria's Nazis were in a quandary largely because they had come to rely so heavily on instructions and guidance from Berlin, but this had not been forthcoming. Rainer and Klausner drove to a secret location in central Vienna from where they intended communicating with their *Gauleiters* and other regional activists. The message they dispatched told these followers that the plebiscite was to be opposed, and as further plans unfolded these would be communicated, since neither had any ideas beyond that. What they were in fact waiting for was Globocnik to return from Berlin, since he was in the Reich Chancellery acting as their "political postman."[9]

Day 2, Thursday, 10 March

For Globocnik this was undoubtedly, up to this point in his life, his most important day. Keppler, who had now returned from Vienna, was in the Reich Chancellery where he had to wait three hours to see his *Führer,* and, "...while waiting in the ante-room, he had observed Odilo Globocznigg, the Austrian Nazi Party's representative, being shown in to see Hitler. 'Globus' had been in Berlin for twenty-four hours. Only now could Hitler make use of him again as a tool in the furtherance of his plans."[10]

Hitler appears to have decided to call upon his longtime Austrian contact man because he had concluded that the efforts of his diplomats, Papen and Stein, had failed to bear the fruit that the *Führer* desired. The new tactic was therefore to play the Austrian Nazi Party card, that is, to have his devout followers commence full-scale political action. As a result, Globocnik was told to advise Seyss-Inquart that the latter would soon receive detailed instructions. That Hitler had Globocnik undertake such a crucially important mission shows that the *Führer* held him in high regard. Soon after, Keppler was also handed a letter. His was from the "Head of the Central Security Office of the *Reichsführer-SS*," and he was addressed as "*SS-Gruppenführer* Wilhelm Keppler."

> Secret III 224/! Az. 1790/38
> Subject: Organization plan for the Movement in Austria and situation report
> Priority: None
> The attached organization plan for the movement in Austria and situation report is sent with the request that the contents be noted. Signed by the Head of the Central Security Office for Chief of Military Intelligence by order of Dr Filbert, *SS-Hauptsturmführer.*

The enclosure contained the following details: Major Hubert Klausner was to be the leader of the Austrian Nazi Movement; Globocnik and Rainer were to rank equally with Klausner, with the three forming a troika heading a leadership council that included the *Führerstamme* (*Führer* Clans), political cells based on occupational or along guild lines. Farmers were thus to be headed by an engineer, Anton Reinthaller; workers by Sepp Nemetz; the *Mannschaft*, or other ranks, came under First Lieutenant Hans Lukesch; youth under Hans Schoas; the SS under Ernst Kaltenbrunner; and the *Volkshilfe*, or People's auxiliaries, under Franz Langoth. Dr. Hugo Jury, who headed the *Volksdeutsche Arbeitstelle*, the German-national labor authority, was also councillor for racial-political and constitutional affairs, and Dr. Artur Seyss-Inquart was listed as minister of security and the interior.[11]

Globocnik returned to Vienna that afternoon, by special flight. He was met by Rainer, who immediately took him to the Hotel Regina. There the two faced Klausner and were told that Hitler "had granted the Austrian Party complete freedom of actions." Their next task was to meet Seyss-Inquart. However,

> ...the "Carinthian Mafia" considered it inopportune to inform their official linkman [Seyss] with the government of this development. So Seyss was only able to note that his Party colleagues betrayed little interest when he told them he had been discussing possibilities of a Black-Brown coalition with Schuschnigg. They answered him by indicating that Berlin rejected the plebiscite and telling him that the following morning a messenger would be coming who would hand Seyss the necessary instructions.[12]

Significantly, Rainer addressed members of the Party, SS and SA, telling them "to prepare for major engagements." Other crucial developments on that second day that did not directly involve the "Carinthian Mafia" included the chief of Austria's clandestine SS, Ernst Kaltenbrunner, arriving in Vienna, where he immediately went into hiding, and clashes breaking out in several cities between Nazis and backers of an independent Austria.

Day 3, Friday, 11 March

On this Friday, Schuschnigg, whose office and state administration, secret service, and even military establishments were thoroughly penetrated by Berlin's agents, publicly capitulated to Hitler in a bid to save Austria from invasion. The plucky Tyrolian who lost his position as Austria's chancellor later this day revealed this to the citizenry in a sullen tone during a radio address: "...and so in this hour I bid farewell to the Austrian people with a German word and wish from the heart: God protect Austria."[13]

Austria's army was advised that should a German invasion occur, it was not to "withdraw without resistance." Berlin's aim, in Hitler's words, was "a peaceful entry, welcomed by the population." Friday commenced with the Austrian government blocking from distribution several newspapers carrying pro-Berlin articles with Dr. Jury's by-line. The day also saw Germany mobilizing for an invasion, and several people alerted Schuschnigg that failure to call off Sunday's plebiscite would mean invasion. Globocnik, Rainer, and Klausner had remained in the Regina Hotel from the previous evening. At about noon Seyss-Inquart, after meeting Schuschnigg, met this Carinthian group and read to them Hitler's letter that called for abandonment of the plebiscite by 2 P.M. that day. After they discussed its contents, they devised a plan of action. It included deciding that if the demand was not acceded to, then Hans Fischböck and Dr. Jury, two national ministers, would resign. Seyss-Inquart then put this demand to paper.[14]

All the senior conspirators were briefed on the outcome of the crucial meeting between Chancellor Schuschnigg and Seyss-Inquart and Edmund Glaise-Horstenau, the military historian and ardent Pan-German at the Nazi Party's Vienna headquarters. Those to be briefed were Klausner, Rainer, Globocnik, Jury, Fischböck, and Mühlmann, the art historian.[15]

Schuschnigg was already close to buckling by 2 P.M., and after a second ultimatum he had resigned from office. Rainer had sent Globocnik to the chancellery some time late in the afternoon to act as go-between, since a new chancellor had not emerged. Mühlmann, the sinister art critic, accompanied Globocnik to the chancellery so as to be at hand in case Globocnik suddenly required a courier, since pressure was being put on Schuschnigg to cancel the plebiscite that Hitler so adamantly opposed.

In the Hall of Columns the Austrian Nazis, Globocznigg and Mühlmann, had appeared on the scene. Mühlmann went to Glaise-Horstenau and asked him about all the to-ing and fro-ing and inquired how things stood. Glaise: "He's a dead duck already." Mühlmann, amazed: "Who?" Glaise: "Schuschnigg. He's capitulated already. I kept saying to him: Don't hold your plebiscite. Now he's a dead duck."[16]

Amidst all this, diplomatic moves were in train among London, Paris, Berlin, and other capitals, and the German military was preparing to move against Austria. Vienna's streets saw rival groups and gangs on the move aboard trucks and other vehicles. Globocnik was not among these, however, for he was at the very heart of things. Rainer and he then made plans to go to the German Legation and report on the situation. Globocnik was dispatching information after Seyss-Inquart's assessments to Berlin. There was also concern that the many thousands of members of the Austrian Legion would suddenly begin descending upon Vienna, something that was not wanted at this early stage.[17]

At 5 P.M., Globocnik telephoned Hitler's longtime pal, Hermann Göring, the key Berlin player behind the *Anschluss* move, whom Globocnik told of the situation in Vienna. But the conversation was futile because Globocnik was in error on a series of matters, most important of all being that Schuschnigg was set to stand aside for a National Socialist group. Part of the Globocnik-Göring conversation went as follows, with Göring assuring Globocnik that Austria's National Socialists would be taken care of, something that did not occur in the way that these Austrians anticipated:

OG: I have to report further, that the SA and SS have already been detailed to act as auxiliary police.
HG: The demand must also be made that the Party is to be legalized with immediate effect.
OG: *Jawohl!* That will be put in order!
HG: With all its organizations, SA, SS, Hitler Youth.
OG: *Jawohl!* Herr *Generalfeldmarschall!* The only thing we would ask is that the formations that are presently in emigration do not come in for the meantime ... (but only) after the ballot is over.
HG: ...what kind of ballot are you wanting to hold?
OG: Well, he [Seyss-Inquart] says that the program that will be laid out will be carried through by Hitler.
HG: ...and as regards the referendum, somebody will come down and tell you what sort of referendum will be held ... What did Seyss-Inquart mean when he said that the German-Austrian relationship has to be put onto a new basis?
OG: Well, he means that Austria's independence remains, you see, but that otherwise everything is regulated on National Socialist principles.
HG: Ha, that will all take care of itself...[18]

Globocnik was also told that Keppler was set to arrive in Vienna and would bring the names of those to be included in the new Cabinet, and that

Fischböck was to be minister for trade and commerce; Kaltenbrunner was to take charge of security, and Lieutenant-Field-Marshall Eugen Beyer would be in charge of the armed forces. Seyss-Inquart was to temporarily oversee foreign affairs, and Franz Hueber, Göring's brother-in-law, was to become justice minister. But all this had been premature because Globocnik's reporting to Göring was incorrect. President Miklas, who was casting around for a new chancellor, had still not accepted Schuschnigg's resignation. Rainer and Globocnik belatedly learned of the hold-up only on returning to the chancellery, and were thus forced to admit to Keppler, who was now in Vienna, that a Seyss-Inquart government was still not in existence. This lead to Göring telling Keppler by telephone that power simply had to be seized. Both Rainer and Globocnik agreed with this hard-line option. But it never came to that, because Schuschnigg finally stood down and made his radio address to the nation, ending with the words: "God protect Austria." The speech was delivered at 7:50 P.M., and at precisely 8:18 P.M., Seyss-Inquart sat before a microphone and broadcast that he was still interior minister, but nothing more, and went on to urge the maintenance of law and order. He said resistance to the German army was "out of the question." Seyss-Inquart was in fact deceiving the public, for when President Miklas accepted Schuschnigg's resignation he had also relieved all ministers and state secretaries of their offices. At this time Globocnik was inside the chancellery, where he sprang into action by taking calls from all over Austria from those heading the disparate SA and SS units who wished to know precisely what to do.

> He was ready with instructions: they were to do nothing. The previous administration would be replaced by new men. In between whiles Globocznigg [sic] telephoned Party leaders in the provinces or sent telegrams. He did this almost always in the name of Seyss-Inquart and at the expense of the Austrian government.[19]

At 8:45 P.M. Hitler issued Directive Number Two, which gave the go-ahead for the invasion: "To avoid further bloodshed in Austrian towns the German armed forces will march into Austria on 12.3 in accordance with Directive Number One. I expect no effort to be spared to ensure the aims laid down are achieved as swiftly as possible."[20]

The major significance of Rainer and Globocnik later that day had been, among other things, the guiding of the seizure of power out in the provinces, a not insignificant achievement. Back in the chancellery, Rainer, after the two radio broadcasts and with Seyss-Inquart and Keppler present, took to a typewriter and began drawing up names for a ministry, relying, of course, on the suggestions Göring had made late in the afternoon. The list, with several changes, was finally ready at midnight and carried several names that even President Miklas did not associate with National Socialism. Neither Globocnik,

Rainer, nor Klausner was named, nor was an emerging fourth significant Carinthian, Reinhold von Mohrenschildt, included. Like Globocnik, he eventually found himself in Lublin and other parts of Eastern Europe working on demographic matters. By now, however, the horses had bolted, and not only in Vienna, but across the entire country, and Globocnik was the first to know. Nazis from across Austria were advising Globocnik of their victories. Whenever Globocnik received a call from an official loyal to the government, he lied by saying he was an official representative without alerting Seyss-Inquart of this. Later, however, he said to Seyss-Inquart: "You know. I've seized power for you, and took the part of the government, but I didn't tell you anything, because you would have been against it."[21]

What Globocnik learned was that in Linz, following demonstrations, the swastika flag rose over the town hall and that the SA and SS had occupied "the taxation offices, the customs and excise offices, both railway stations, the Workers' Chamber, the District Governor's office and the fatherland Front building." In Graz, the city's main square was filled by some 70,000 people, after which National Socialists took over the city's and province's main premises. Villach saw the SS and SA take power, as did Innsbruck.[22] General Wilhelm Zehner, Schuschnigg's defense chief, became the first victim of National Socialist punishment. He was shot in his apartment the next day, in treatment similar to that parceled out by Hitler during the Night of the Long Knives on 30 June 1934, when nearly 200 leading German Nazis perished. The historian Paul Hoffman pointed out that in Austria's Alpine provinces, in particular Styria and Carinthia, schools, government offices, police and army barracks, were all being taken over by National Socialists with the swastika rising high above these public premises. Vienna followed with tumultuous applause by huge crowds, with the police letting matters take their course. A form of mass or communal hysteria had taken over, and Odilo Globocnik was very much responsible for this mood, having done so much to lay its basis.[23] Although President Miklas had not officially approved the new government at midnight, the end of Schuschnigg's administration had arrived. "The question was whether the Austrian National Socialists, having won power with Berlin's help, could defend it against the lust for annexation of the German Reich."[24]

At 5:00 P.M., Göring had told Globocnik such things as Austria's independence would take care of themselves. But as the next day unfolded Globocnik found no reason to feel more confident about seeing Austrian independence realized.

Day 4, Saturday, 12 March

This point was driven home to both at 3 A.M., when Globocnik and Rainer, with Klausner and Kaltenbrunner, ventured to Vienna's Aspern airport to welcome *Reichsführer-SS* Heinrich Himmler, who was flying in from Munich. Himmler landed at 4:30 A.M., and within a few minutes was whisked off while Globocnik and Rainer found themselves stranded for over an hour. Berlin's armed forces continued pouring across the border; political opponents began to be rounded up, Jewish businesses were raided and ransacked; threatened opponents of the new order resigned senior positions, and others fled Austria fearing incarceration in a concentration camp. Thousands of others went incognito to friends' and acquaintances' homes. Himmler, who had left his two loyal followers stranded, began work by removing State Secretary Dr. Michael Skubl from Seyss-Inquart's government. Adolf Hitler entered the town of Braunau, his birthplace. The town's National Socialist Party leader said to him, "My *Führer!* The great honor has fallen to me to be the first to greet you on the soil of your homeland." The *Führer* replied, "No power in the world will tear this country from me now."[25] These were emotional times, indeed, with most prone to use highly emotional language. At 7:30 P.M. the *Führer* entered the Linz Town Hall, where Seyss-Inquart and tumultuous applause welcomed him.

Saturday also saw Mühlmann adopting the role of a kidnapper when he, with "two young SS-men with pistols in their belts," appeared uninvited at the home of Theodor Hornbostel, the political director of the Austrian Foreign Office, by now a designated enemy of unified National Socialism. "Mühlmann announced that Hornbostel was under house arrest and was not to use the telephone. At that moment the telephone rang. Mühlmann picked it up. The Netherlands Embassy was inquiring after Hornbostel's health. 'Dr Hornbostel is very well,' said Mühlmann."[26] The caller could not have realized then that within three years Mühlmann would be involved in plundering, for the Reich, some of Holland's finest art works.

Day 5, Sunday, 13 March

Kaltenbrunner replaced Dr. Michael Skubl and took over the security portfolio. Klausner also joined the Cabinet as minister for political education, giving the Cabinet an unmistakable National Socialist tinge. But Globocnik and Rainer remained out in the cold. At noon a new and important figure, Josef Bürckel, the *Gauleiter* of the Saar-Palatinate, passed a document signed by Hitler to a senior press officer in Vienna advising that he was in fact the center of power in the city. That document said that *Gauleiter* Bürckel of Saar-Palatinate had been handed the task of reorganizing the National Socialist Party in Austria. Bürckel was made provisional head of the National Socialist Party of Austria and had been instructed to make preparations for a plebiscite. It concluded by stating that Bürckel had been empowered to fulfill this mission.[27] The Seyss-Inquart Cabinet met soon after lunch to discuss a solitary item on the agenda — passage of the *Anschluss* law.

Day 6, Monday, 14 March

Hitler began his historic journey by road from Linz to Vienna, and his cavalcade was joined by Seyss-Inquart just outside the capital. Most people were elated. The savior was about to arrive. Soon after reaching a joyous Vienna, Hitler came out and stood on the balcony of the Hotel Imperial to address the huge and ecstatic crowd. Among other things, Hitler referred to the takeover of Austria as an historical turning point. He added that whatever happened in the future, no one would be permitted to "ever again divide the German Reich."[28]

Unity had been achieved and Odilo Globocnik could take pride in his contribution to the widespread joy and elation. True, without him it would have happened. He was not a central figure. But he had fulfilled his role with ardor and with loyalty. He could rightly say he had been an important and historic German.

Day 7, Tuesday, 15 March

Hitler addressed the people of Vienna in the Heldenplatz from the Hofburg's balcony. This exhilarating event was followed by a parade with a fly-past involving hundreds of aircraft. Hitler left for Germany by air, and wept while looking down at Austria. "All this is German soil now," he was heard to say. Soon afterwards another Austrian, another Adolf, Adolf Eichmann, who was to play an important role in supplying Jewish victims for Globocnik's killing centers of Treblinka, Sobibor, and Belzec in occupied Poland, arrived in Vienna to launch the expulsion of Jews. Unlike Globocnik, Eichmann was not the executive officer overseeing the actual mass killings, but rather, a central Reich coordinating official who ensured Jews were transported, generally by train, to Globocnik's and other killing centers. Eichmann, who visited Globocnik in Lublin several times, therefore complemented the Lublin SS and police chief in the coming wartime genocide, and both were therefore close to Himmler and Heydrich, even if not in daily contact with them.

Twenty-six days later, on 10 April, 99.73 per cent of Austrians voted "Yes" in a plebiscite for incorporation into the Third Reich. One of the eventual outcomes of that vote was that many ambitious and fanatical Austrians — Globocnik, Rainer, von Mohrenschildt, Muhlmann, Lerch, Paul Gasser, and

Nemetz, to name only some — would find themselves in key posts in occupied Poland within just two years, working as loyal servants of Hitler and Himmler, with the most senior of these being the Carinthian, Odilo Globocnik, a man who gained the power of life and death over more than two million people.

IV

Gauleiter of Vienna: 28 May 1938 to 30 January 1939

Appointment

We know of one pertinent and embarrassing incident involving Globocnik that seemed ominous for his hopes to carve out a career within Hitler's expanding Reich, as opposed to being only a minor figure upon the Austrian stage. This occurred when Globocnik and Rainer found themselves left high and dry at Vienna's Aspern airport on Himmler's arrival from Berlin. And there was also Göring's barely noticed quip during his 11 March telephone conversation with Globocnik, claiming all would "take care of itself" with respect to the manner in which Austria would be treated once acquired by Berlin's National Socialist ruling clique. But both incidents were part of a wider misunderstanding on the part of most Austrian National Socialists about their role and place within Hitler's New Order, something Maurice Williams has described:

> Austrian Nazis readily accepted the guidance and ideology of Hitler, but they expected to control their country, developing Nazi principles in Austria as they saw best — not as others dictated. These delusions, not conspicuously challenged until the 1938 *Anschluss*, led to widespread disillusion when the realities of power surfaced. In March 1938, German Nazis absorbed the party just as they absorbed the country.[1]

Bruce Pauley's assessment of this immediate post-*Anschluss* period in his pioneering study of Austrian Nazis is similar, with Austria's senior Nazis quickly realizing after 12 March that many of them counted for little. Himmler, for instance, quickly dumped Seyss-Inquart's head of security, Dr. Michael Skubl, replacing him with Ernst Kaltenbrunner.

> What little regard Himmler had for Odilo Globocnik and Friedrich Rainer was revealed when the two Austrians, who had come to the airport to greet the *Reichsführer*, were left standing with no means to return to the city. So discouraged were Globocnik and Rainer that a few days later they, along with Major Klausner, flew to Berlin to persuade Hitler that they had played an important role in the takeover of Austria....[2]

Globocnik's and Rainer's old Carinthian friend, Major Klausner, later became education minister, while Dr. Jury, Anton Reinthaller and Franz Hueber also gained ministerial posts. Rainer and Globocnik, on the other hand, were overlooked, initially at least. Alfred Frauenfeld was even banned from returning to Vienna. Pauley's point about the exclusion of Frauenfeld, who was known to be a popular figure, might explain why Globocnik was eventually chosen to be Vienna's *Gauleiter*, because he was seen as an obedient servant and someone without a local power base. This may also explain Hitler's later reluctance to dismiss Globocnik from the post of *Gauleiter* of Vienna when so many wanted to see him go because of his incompetence and unpopularity. After 15 March, Globocnik, to put it bluntly, suddenly went from being a relatively big fish in a small pond — Carinthia and Vienna — to being a small fish in a far bigger pond — namely, the Third Reich, which now included Austria. This slide into virtual insignificance and no influence could have resulted in him, and Rainer, for that matter, simply fading away into the relative obscurity or the lower ranks of the growing number of bureaucracies that were now being created across incorporated Austria, especially through the efforts and edicts of Heinrich Himmler and Josef Bürckel; both Germans, of course. Understandably, neither of these ambitious Carinthians wanted such an outcome. Not only had both been loyal National Socialists for nearly a decade, but they had also done much to facilitate the takeover of Austria by Berlin even if they, like so many other Austrian Nazis, misunderstood or never fully appreciated the nature of Berlin's ultimate goals or *modus operandi*. What was therefore quickly required by each was to boost their size and weight, politically and bureaucratically speaking, within the new and larger pond, something they quickly did. Austria's new order required as much, if not more, self-help and assistance from others as the old Austria. According to Siegfried Pucher, Globocnik actually approached Himmler and Heydrich just before the Hitler plebiscite of 10 April and discussed his desire to become *Gauleiter* of Vienna, the post he gained in late May. That approach even

involved depositing a list of candidate names for the top jobs with these two
SS superiors. Before this happened, however, Globocnik managed to have
himself hired as the NSDAP's inspector for Austria, with the rank of a *Standartenführer.* This appointment took effect on 12 March, the same day that
another close Carinthian conspirator, Reinhold von Mohrenschildt, joined
both the SS and the NSDAP. Significantly, von Mohrenschildt's appointment
was made either from Himmler's office or at Himmler's direction. At the same
time, Klausner became Bürckel's deputy, while Rainer became a Bürckel
departmental head and was made responsible for the preparation of the referendum or *Auschluss* plebiscite.[3] The main reason for their gravitation toward
Bürckel appears to have been because the Carinthian troika had been in contact with this Hitler "Mr. Fix-it" since 1936.

The next milestone in Globocnik's career came on 22 May 1938, more
than two months later. Three days later *The Times* of London carried a brief
article headlined: "Administration of Austria — Redistribution of Provinces,"
which reported that for administrative reasons Austria was to be divided into
seven *Gaue,* centrally-controlled administrative units, creating jobs for that
number of *Gauleiters.* The seven *Gaue,* and their heads:

> 1. Vienna, extending from the town of Fischeramend to Wiener Neustadt,
> where it will border on Styria; *Gauleiter,* **Herr Odilo Globotschnigg.**
> 2. Lower Danube, including the southern part of Upper Austria, and a part
> of Burgenland; *Gauleiter,* Dr Hugo Jury.
> 3. Upper Danube, consisting of the northern part of Upper Austria and the
> northern part of Lower Austria; *Gauleiter,* Herr Karl Eigruber.
> 4. Styria, including part of the Burgenland; *Gauleiter,* Herr Siegfried Uiber-
> reither.
> 5. Tyrol; *Gauleiter,* Herr Franz Hofer.
> 6. Salzburg; *Gauleiter* **Dr Friedrich Rainer.**
> 7. Carinthia; *Gauleiter,* **Major Hubert Klausner.**[4]

The Third Reich, of which Austria had now become an integral part,
was to have 43 *Gaue* by 1942, so each member of the once clandestine troika
had done well for himself, even if somewhat belatedly. Moreover, one of the
index cards in Globocnik's SS-file states that during 1938 he even served as
a member of the *Reichstag.* Whether he attended these extravagant gatherings
is not known. In addition, an American Office of Strategic Services biographical report on him claimed he was one of 109 new members to be
"elected" to the *Reichstag.*[5] But Globocnik's climb to the top — becoming a
bigger fish in the far larger pond — had not come about without struggle.
Siegfried Pucher and others have found evidence of considerable scrambling
for these top Austrian posts, especially for the prized Vienna *Gau,* which
Globocnik won, but managed to hold only briefly. No doubt his longstanding SS links and his association with the *SD* were important, probably crucial,

contributing factors. Five of the seven new *Gauleiters* were SS members. Sieg-fried Pucher says that until about the time of Austria's plebiscite, two other candidates were favored for the plumb Vienna post. The first was the Danziger, Albert Forster—*Gauleiter* of Danzig-West Prussia—whose name was being promoted by a Christian Opdenhoff, the party's senior personnel manager, who had been dispatched from Berlin to Vienna by Rudolf Hess, Hitler's number two man. The other was the popular but luckless Viennese, Alfred Frauenfeld. Globocnik's name surfaced on 9 April, and Bürckel's personal assistant, Karl Barth, appears to have backed him for the prestigious Vienna post.[6] Globocnik, the man from the provinces, took up the capital's new and powerful position on 28 May, or less than three months after Austria was incorporated into the Third Reich. Historian Evan Burr Bukey describes the administrative bedlam at the upper levels well. He said that on 11 March the SA leader Franz Lahr moved into Vienna's city hall as mayor. However, 48 hours later Lahr was sacked by a Hermann Neubacher, an associate of Seyss-Inquart, hardly conduct of a tranquil and stable order. "Several days later émigré *Gauleiter* Alfred Frauenfeld, popular among the party faithful, returned to a hero's welcome, but he was quickly hustled out of town."[7]

At this point Christian Opdenhoff moved in to try to find the right per-son for this major city's top job. He weighed the requirements, and although not overtly opposed to Frauenfeld taking up the position, concluded that a Reich German was probably what was needed, so began giving serious con-sideration to bringing in Danzig's *Gauleiter*, Albert Forster. But things proved to be more complicated.

> The problem was that Bürckel had other ideas. The *Reich* commissioner wanted a man strong enough to contain Seyss-Inquart but sufficiently malleable to con-trol. When Odilo Globocnik insinuated himself into the contest, Bürckel jumped at the chance. On 23 May Hitler appointed the Carinthian adventurer *Gauleiter* of Greater Vienna. It was a disastrous mistake.[8]

Vienna's First *Gauleiter*

On taking office Globocnik immediately saw his task as that of ensur-ing that the NSDAP became Vienna's sole power center, and he appears to have set the end of November 1938 as his target date for that to be achieved, giving himself a six-month deadline, but he found himself ignominiously out of the job in less than eight months. Opposition to party principles was one of the matters that was to be deliberately eradicated: He was a hard-liner as well as an impatient enthusiast. Notwithstanding all these intentions, wide-spread dissent persisted.

Herr Globocnik, recently appointed *Gauleiter* (Governor) for the province of Vienna, referred in a speech published today to criticism and discontent within the Nazi Party, of which there have been many reports in Vienna lately. He was addressing a rally of Brown shirts.

They could see in retrospect how ungrateful the majority of people were, he said. Almost everyone in Austria was longing for salvation — that is to say, political and in some cases, physical liberty. He went on: "Today we have won them this liberty, but I say now there is far more criticism than is necessary or justified. It seems to be much easier to gain power than to keep it."

He concluded: "He who shows himself incapable of maintaining that power must resign. His own incapability does not justify him in criticizing our work and, therefore, paralyzing it."[9]

Turning to the inevitable question of Austria's, and in particular Vienna's, Jewish minority, members of which were being rapidly expelled from the capital as well as from across the rest of the country by Adolf Eichmann's efficient Central Office for Jewish Emigration, Globocnik announced: "We shall not shrink from the strongest measures to solve the Jewish problem if the interests of our people demand it. Even stronger action will be taken against Aryans who still buy in Jewish shops or do business with Jews."[10]

Globocnik also strongly and publicly promoted anti-Semitism to the population at large:

In his early tenure as *Gauleiter*, Globocnik espoused Nazi anti–Jewish philosophy: "I will not recoil from radical interventions for the solution of Jewish questions." Later that same year he opened Vienna's first anti-Semitic political exhibition, which was attended by 10,000 visitors on the first day. Prominent at the exhibition and received enthusiastically by the public was the film, "The Eternal Jew."[11]

In October Himmler ordered all Austrian Jews to be concentrated in Vienna, a precursor to the much larger concentration of Poland's Jews, primarily within large urban ghettos, during October of the following year.

According to an internal memo of the *SD's* Jewish section, Eichmann discussed the transfer of an estimated 10,000 Jews still living outside the capital with Odilo Globocnik, the *Gauleiter* of Lower Danube [sic], and himself set out on October 26 to tour the Austrian provinces in order to inform the SD chief in each region "that with the help of the Gestapo stations, they advise the Jews either to leave the country by 15/12/1939 or to move to Vienna by 31/10/1938 (probably an error for 31/12/38)."[12]

On the role of churches, Globocnik, a Catholic, like Hitler and Himmler, said that their clergy must confine themselves to the task of pastoral care. It is safe to assume that this meant he would not tolerate the Church's involvement in political and ideological issues, which became the exclusive prerogative of the party. He then announced his "next seven tasks," which included, among other matters, the party evolving not into a rigid but a receptive organization, the development of teamwork, employers meeting with employees, and job creation.[13]

This totalitarian program shows that Globocnik was a party loyalist through and through, and a man who had a rather unsophisticated, tightly structured, and simplistic view of life and humanity. He certainly appears to have been an enthusiast, someone whom Gilbert and Sullivan could easily have ridiculed in an operetta, to the point where an audience would have had considerable delight laughing at the serious-minded two-bit player before them, no doubt in uniform, carrying an abundance of medals and bray. A series of contemporary foreign press reports from these days reveals that as well as getting himself into strife with Bürckel over a range of rather peripheral issues, he continued behaving in other areas in his by now established semi-operatic style. For instance, London's *Daily Telegraph* of 14 June 1938, less than a month after he took up the Vienna post, reported that Globocnik was urging the public to exercise in a manner not dissimilar to that later seen all over China under Chairman Mao Zedong, especially during the so-called Great Proletarian Cultural Revolution, which drew so heavily from Mao's early 1940s Yenan Days of ardent ideological fervor and the promotion of ideological purity. In light of this it is difficult not to believe that Globocnik would have felt at home being a Maoist cadre. The *Daily Telegraph* article, headlined "Vienna Nazis to Join Leader in Exercises," reported:

> All the leading Nazi officials in Vienna are to join Herr Globocnik, leader of the Vienna Nazis, *in physical jerks and early morning sports twice a week in future.* [Emphasis added.]
> Herr Globocnik himself made this announcement in a speech to 6000 Nazi officials in the Vienna City Hall.
> Executive officials were told that the general orders of the week would be given out at these early morning gatherings. Military training would be given as required.
> In his speech, Herr Globocnik protested against the ingratitude of "the majority of mankind," in this instance clearly meaning Austria. Nearly all, he said, has obtained the freedom they had long for during the last three months and there was much more criticism than was necessary or justified.
> "It was always easier to acquire power than to use it and maintain it," he went on.
> "Anybody who could not rise to the occasion must resign. But incapacity was no excuse for criticizing a successor and retarding or paralyzing the efforts of the responsible executive."[14]

Soon after, the same newspaper reported that Vienna's new *Gauleiter* had appealed to the city's men and women to enroll in the anti-aircraft service.

Herr Globocnik begins his exhortation by stating that Vienna, as a mighty guardian of culture, a Danube port, and the commercial gate to the South-east of Europe, will have a very important position in the future in the German Reich. For this reason it is the National Socialist duty of every Vienna man and woman to share in defending it.

Everyone in Vienna who loves the *Führer*, his own city and his family, it is emphasized, must recognize that he must help to protect Vienna against air attack.[15]

Nor did their new *Gauleiter* show respect for old institutions and sensibilities about the bloody fate of the nation's once popular chancellor, Engelbert Dollfuss. The onetime Catholic, who was baptized in Trieste, had absolutely no compunction in criticizing his former church. When Vienna Cardinal Innitzer's palace was stormed in mid–October, 1938, Globocnik's answer to official Church protests was that this had occurred because of "the actions of certain black circles"— with black, in this context, presumably meaning conservative or traditional Catholics. This was an early example of a victim being blamed for others' thuggery, and a sign of Globocnik's perverted assessment of a situation. Portraying the victim as the culprit was something Globocnik repeated over the coming years. Like the Jews, Catholicism came under a broad attack, and this included press campaigns: "Anti-Catholic propaganda continues. The clergy and the religious are accused of being politically hostile to the regime and morally corrupt. On the second page of the Viennese edition of the *Völkischer Beobachter* there is almost every day an anti-clerical article."[16]

Non-Jewish owners of firms were first ordered to dismiss Jewish employees within a fortnight; this was followed by an order, issued on 23 June by Globocnik, calling upon Jewish-owned firms to follow suit. This campaign was overseen by some 5,000 minor bureaucrats, including block and cell leaders. Globocnik's circular publicizing this order stated:

Every Jewish employee must be removed from Jewish firms within 14 days. Discharge without notice and without compensation is possible on the basis of Law of May 21, 1938, concerning contracts. This law provides that the claims for compensation in place of notice will be permitted only in accordance with equity, because the Court may refer to an administrative board for the settlement of equity claims, which may be filed. The board in turn may give a verdict in accordance with political necessity. This announcement must be brought to the attention of individual firms through the presentation of this letter. A written acknowledgement will be given by the firms.[17]

On 2 August 1938, as part of the increasingly vicious campaign against the Jews, Globocnik officially opened an exhibition at Vienna's North-west Station titled The Eternal Jew.[18] As the winter of 1938 approached, with the outright robbery of property and a growing number of cases of violence against individual Jews, even Globocnik is recorded as having had second thoughts, prompting him to say, "a series of events occurred that alienated the public."[19] Clearly, he was by mid-1938 involved in a self-declared war against all opponents of National Socialism; Jews, Catholics, especially the clergy, and even foreigners such as the Czechs. In July that year Globocnik appeared before a 20,000-strong crowd, in a highly tasteless extravaganza that commemorated the death of a number of deceased Nazis. According to one press report:

> Memorial celebrations were held today in a number of places in Austria where Nazis lost their lives in July and August 1934 by the hand of the executioner or in open fighting.... In Vienna the chief event of the day was the unveiling of the large tablet on the Governor's Palace, formerly the Chancellery, to commemorate the raid in which Dr Dollfuss was murdered. The tablet has been placed on the wall immediately under the window of the room in which the Chancellor was twice shot and allowed to die of his wounds. The inscription read:
> 154 German men of the 89th Stormtroop *Standart* entered here on July 25, 1934, and seven found death at the hands of the executioner....
> Dr. Seyss-Inquart, the Governor, formally accepted the tablet after it had been unveiled by the Nazi leader of Vienna, Herr Globocnik, and many speeches were delivered commemorating those who have died and those who risked their lives for the sake of Great Germany. Thousands of medallions were sold among the crowd with the inscription, "Eternal remains the fame of the deeds of the dead, July 25, 1934–38."[20]

The Austrian wing of the NSDAP staged several such spectacles soon after the pandemonium arising from the *Anschluss*. According to one Berlin newspaper of 19 June 1938, the fifth anniversary celebrations for the outlawing of the NSDAP were held on a square named Hero's Place. The article was, not surprisingly, headlined "The Fighting Was Not in Vain."

> Vienna's streets had an abundance of flags flying. Bürckel appeared on the balcony overlooking the Palace as did Seyss-Inquart, Dr Jury, and Globocnik. With these political figures stood Vienna's mayor, Reschny, and the Army was represented by General Kienitz. Globocnik spoke to the assembled throng on the suffering and victory of the party's pioneering members. There was a people's march and *Gauleiter* Globocnik took the salute.[21]

First hints of internecine party strife also surfaced in June, within a month of Globocnik's taking office. The British newspaper, *The Yorkshire Post*, carried a brief but surprisingly detailed summation of National Socialism's first 100 days in Austria. The writer claimed that the population had voted 99.75 percent for the Hitler group in April's plebiscite because Austrians "could not bear any longer the general feeling of instability which had frustrated every effort of the Schuschnigg regime."[22] Despite the resounding pro-Berlin nation-wide vote and a desire to get on with matters, a utopia had certainly not arrived, and it was still far away, according to *The Yorkshire Post's* correspondent: "The Austrian Nazi Party is no longer an organized, well-disciplined force, if it ever was. Every position, every job, is fiercely contested by rival factions, groups, cliques and individuals. Herr Bürckel was appointed because six Austrian Nazi leaders had filed their rival claims with the *Führer's* secretariat."[23]

There seems little doubt that these words were both accurate and apt, even in relation to Globocnik getting his top job. The report went on:

> The new provincial Governors and party leaders are scarcely known to the rank and file and the Reich authorities have seen to it that men from outside are appointed to most provinces.
>
> The new Governor of Vienna, for instance, Globotchnigg is a Slovene from Carinthia. The peculiar organization of the Nazi party favors the formation of rival factions. The picked shock troops of the *Führer*, the Black Guard [i.e. the SS] regard the Brownshirts as a proletarian mob. The Austrian Legion, 25,000 tough fighters, who had to flee from Schuschnigg's Austria, consider themselves as the flower of the Austrian party. Then there are the so-called Old Fighters of the party and the political wire-pullers of the old Civil Service. All want jobs, money, and promotion....
>
> Within the party, propaganda is now mainly directed against the governor, Herr Bürckel. The radical faction is led by Globotchnigg, the new leader and governor of Vienna, who hopes to succeed Bürckel. The latter's job is to keep Austria going and make Nazi rule in Austria a success. He is therefore trying to stop wholesale and outright confiscation of Jewish property and businesses which has ruined business in Vienna already, and endeavors to curb eager party authorities whose constant interfering in everyday economic life is causing great resentment.[24]

London's *Daily Telegraph* reported in July 1938 that Globocnik had gone to the extent of publicly alluding to dissent within party ranks. This report said the party had conducted 52 special district meetings, four of which were actually attended by Globocnik, to discuss strife within its restless ranks. At one of these gatherings Globocnik was reported as having said:

> When we have succeeded in bringing back to industry those poor devils whose hostility to us has been caused only by their lack of employment, and when all the factory chimneys in Vienna are smoking, when we have mastered the specter of unemployment, the last of our opponents will relinquish his hostility and join with us.
>
> But I warn you against those people who immediately after March 11 declared themselves with us without conviction. They sympathized with the Reds when these were in power and cheered the green *Heimwehr* when Starhemberg for a time was master of the situation.

Now that brown is fashionable they change their color again and perhaps hope soon to make another change. We want to keep away from these people altogether and set no value upon their co-operation.

But we do value the co-operation of every compatriot who is honestly in sympathy with us and our efforts.[25]

Globocnik's Viennese Financial Shenanigans and Dismissal

Irrespective of Globocnik's political and ideological exhortations and his conflicts, his job scrambling and maneuvers against party opponents, foreigners, Catholics, and Jews, his major problem arose from none of these, but rather from the manner in which he handled money: public and party funds as Vienna's inaugural *Gauleiter*. Problems and inquiries stemming from the mishandling of these funds while Globocnik was in Vienna resurfaced while he was in Lublin. Because of this he turned to Himmler for backing and assistance, further indebting him to Himmler. At this time he sought Himmler's protection against the calculating and formidable investigative skills of the *Führer*'s longtime Munich confidant and friend, the NSDAP's pedantic treasurer, Franz Xaver Schwartz (1875–1947), who, according to one of Hitler's earliest German biographers, Konrad Heiden, took money "from the *Gauleiters* with an iron fist."[26] One slip during Schwartz's drawn-out and inconclusive investigations may have meant Globocnik being arrested, charged, tried, and perhaps even executed if the findings had been unfavorable. Although it is difficult to determine from Globocnik's SS file precisely what he did with these funds, it is also difficult not to conclude that Globocnik came dangerously close to being charged and punished severely. Neither the Party nor the SS was averse to killing its own over financial misdealing. Globocnik's Lublin fiancée, Irmgard Rickheim, certainly believes that Himmler had quite extraordinary powers over her partner, which cannot be simply put down to one seeing the other as a savior, though there was also an element of that. Rickheim has recalled that she felt that the extra element stemmed from something in Globocnik's Vienna days.[27] Globocnik's relationship with Himmler was in all likelihood a complex mixture of admiration, gratitude, fear, blind loyalty, and a desire to please, at all times. What all this seems to suggest is that Himmler had a pliant, almost blackmailed, agent in Lublin to carry out his extermination of Jews and murder of ethnic Poles during the crucial years of 1942 and 1943. Being on the wrong side of Schwartz, and having, at the same time, to rely on Himmler for assistance was an unenviable position to find oneself in. Both Schwartz and Himmler were longtime Hitler cronies, with the former having been described as follows:

This plump, bald man remained one of Hitler's "old comrades" and a member of his close circle. With Max Amann he helped cover up the scandal of Geli Raubal's [Hitler's niece] death. As treasurer, he had control of membership subscriptions, so all figures of membership came from his office and were probably falsified to fit his accounts. Under his control all enrolment to the party was suspended in May 1933, when there were a million and a half applications outstanding. In 1945 he burnt all Party financial documents in the Munich Brown House.[28]

This deliberate act of destruction of records, among other things, means that the few fragmentary pieces of information dealing with Globocnik's encounter with the powerful Schwartz can probably never be cross-checked, since Schwartz's notes and other details pertaining to Globocnik were most likely destroyed at this time. Globocnik's financial shenanigans during the second half of 1938 are not easy to understand fully for several other reasons, the main one being that we do not have all the precise details, and, thanks to Himmler, Schwartz was, if not thwarted, then at least slowly coaxed into agreeing to finally drop his investigations of this matter in 1943. Globocnik's SS file contains what seems to be a summary of a single report. But to further complicate matters, three typed versions of this report exist, with all being slightly different, though essentially the same. This suggests that Globocnik was forwarding explanations to Berlin, not to Schwartz, and refining points of explanation, with someone in Berlin overseeing this exercise in belated deception. It also suggests that this unidentified figure or someone else was unhappy with each version, and that Globocnik was consequently further refining his explanation. But we cannot even be certain of that. Whatever the reason, Globocnik was taking Schwartz's demands for an explanation of his financial activities in Vienna seriously and was refining his report to the party's treasurer. One of the reports was signed and two are dated, 4 March 1941, showing that Globocnik was having strife over his short-lived days as Vienna's *Gauleiter* nearly two years after his ignominious and hurried departure from that post. These three drafts allow us to conclude safely that the amount of money at stake was over 650,000 *Reichsmarks* (RM), and this when the salary of a skilled German (*Facharbeiter*) in Schleswig-Holstein stood at 400RM a month with food and lodgings free. A sum of 50,000RM had also been paid to the Vienna Skating Club. Globocnik justified this by claiming that the club's rink was a world class and famous venue, and that he, as *Gauleiter,* wished to ensure it remained operational. Prior to this Jews had headed it, so the finances were withdrawn. When the presumably new organizers asked for assistance, Globocnik said he acquired these funds outside the budget. "I didn't want the party to put in its own funds."[29]

Another 420,000RM was associated with something called a "settlement fund." Globocnik claimed this had been in order, but it was a transaction that he could not disclose. He had, however, supervised this fund's management and stated that during the Aryanization campaign in Vienna many mistakes had been made—a contention bathed in crocodile tears, no doubt. Aryanization was, of course, the forcible removal of Jews, and to a lesser extent other political adversaries, from jobs and their professions, and it also involved their forcible expulsion from apartments and even Austria itself. When people are expelled from a country or city, then real estate remains, and those in positions of power have access to such assets to do with what they will. The chiefs of Aryanization gained money and property, and quite large amounts, and in a short period. One crucial outcome of this experience for Globocnik was that when he came to head up *Aktion Reinhardt* in early 1942, he no doubt immediately realized that there would be loot, and lots of it, to be acquired, stored, and taken account of for his superiors in the Berlin-based *Reichsbank* or wherever else it was to be directed, and this proved to be the case. Several other smaller gifts were also uncovered, with one to a pawnbroker, and another to a journalists' association because of a scheduled visit by overseas journalists to Vienna. In light of Globocnik's control over substantial assets, one gains the impression that the issues being referred to were only peripheral to Globocnik's other monetary dealings. Though the lack of precise data about these transactions does not allow for a judgment to be made, there can be little doubt that Vienna's inaugural *Gauleiter* was, at best, an unorthodox financial manager, so much so that his methods and practices made the party's dogged and competent treasurer immediately suspicious. Schwartz for some time wanted to press ahead with a no-holds-barred investigation into this Austrian party comrade. Siegfried Pucher's assessment of Globocnik's financial maneuverings is set within the context of the policy of Aryanizing Austria and Vienna. He rightly concludes that so-called Aryanization simply meant public larceny or looting, with large quantities of money and assets directed into the Vienna *Gau's* accountants. Globocnik understandably saw all this money and treasure as the vehicle through which he could fund his ambitious program for Vienna, with "short cuts," meaning little or no auditing or accountability, the order of the day. "He therefore risked financial adventures and by late summer 1938 the 'district of Vienna faced bankruptcy.'"[30]

During these months of widespread mass robbery, Globocnik created the Property Circulation Office, which specialized in acquiring real and other assets, including enterprises, most of which were directed —"siphoned-off"— to party members and political favorites. In addition to the expropriation of apartments, enterprises, furniture and other household fixtures, even art works were taken from the targeted Jewish community. Expropriations went on for many months, with the whole process justified on grounds that it was designed to modernize and rationalize the economy. Added to this, and compounding

the large-scale public larceny, was the fact that Vienna's governance, under
the new order, lacked proper accounting procedures and financial checks and
balances to ensure prudent practices. One wonders how proper auditing could
exist under these criminal circumstances. Viennese-born historian Karl
Stadler, who emigrated to England soon after the *Anschluss*, to get away from
Vienna's Globocnikian order, describes the immediate post-takeover changes
as follows:

> ...Austria was turned into a Land of Germany and Josef Bürckel, who had
> engineered the triumphant return of the Saar to Germany in 1935, was dis-
> patched to Vienna as Hitler's emissary. His special powers were a foretaste of
> things to come: in addition to being answerable to Hitler alone, which enabled
> him to exclude Reich Ministries from all direct contact with Austria, he was
> also in charge of the extensive purges of the administration and of public life
> in general of all non-Nazi and anti-Nazi elements, which completed the process
> of Nazification within a few weeks. This policy, combined with the arrests of
> thousands of political opponents, the public display of cruelty and brute force,
> and a powerful propaganda campaign, produced that feeling of helpless aban-
> don and chilling fear which led to the affirmative vote of 99.7 percent of the
> electorate, and Bürckel's appointment as 'Reich Commissar for the Reunification
> of Austria with the Reich' was Hitler's reward for work well done. Even though
> the majority of the seven *Gauleiters* were Austrians, it was the German party
> machine which controlled the NSDAP in Austria, and hordes of German
> administrators, managers, and civil servants were now in charge of affairs in
> every sphere of public life and of the economy....[31]

Globocnik prospered and rose to Vienna's highest position under this
new centralized order where accountability was thrown to the wind. The Bürckel era was one in which most party-appointed administrators had a great
deal of leeway and discretion. Little wonder the slap-dash Globocnik went
off on his own adventurous, money juggling and larcenous way. However, he
was quickly found to be wanting, both on grounds of inability to administer and, closely associated with this, his inappropriate methods of dealing
with party and other funds. Special accounts were created and so-called
trustees appointed to hold and administer the loot stolen from the targeted
Jews. A not surprising outcome of this expropriating hiatus was that many
people who had never before considered joining the party suddenly found an
incentive to do so, for party members were being favored in acquiring publicly stolen assets and gaining access to housing and other valued services, including jobs. Globocnik seems to have taken to this type of criminal paternalist
milieu very naturally, even if only temporarily. So well was he adapted to the
new "rules" that he had to be disciplined, held back, told to be more dis-
cerning, and careful. Little wonder that one German official communicated
the following assessment of Vienna's inaugural *Gauleiter* to the Reich Treasury:

> The *Gauleiter*, party comrade Globocnik, differs distinctly from all *Gauleiters* in the *Ostmark*. He basically cares for everything. Administrative matters seem to find his peculiar attention. He tries to regulate membership in a way which suits him. Also concerning membership fees, salaries and so on he has his own opinion, which he tries to put into action in every respect ... I can indeed say that I always have to fight with *Gauleiter* Globocnik — a fresh-and-merry fight. After having dressed him down thoroughly several times, he seems to see reasonably clearly once again....[32]

The optimistic note on which this memorandum concluded was, however, quite premature, for Globocnik's *modus operandi* did not alter. Only his complete removal from the post of *Gauleiter* of Vienna would ever fully resolve this. Globocnik's SS file shows that he was initially contacted about his financial shenanigans in January 1940 — a year after he had departed Vienna — and that he was asked to provide information about his handling of finances while *Gauleiter*. A letter dated only, I. 1940, from Himmler's chief of staff, Dr. Rudolf Brandt, said, "The *Reichsführer-SS* asked you to be sent all the documents on the auditors report in which you were not exonerated and you asked the *Reichsführer-SS* to get Treasury to get you exonerated."[33]

Although no reply to this high-level Berlin request exists, the investigations were obviously continuing, because in December the same year Globocnik wrote a blunt letter to *Parteigenosse* (party member) Franz Müller, located in room 15 Parliament House, Vienna. Müller was in fact an auditor, a man who was working either for or with the formidable party treasurer, Franz Xaver Schwartz. By now Globocnik was, of course, in Lublin as the SS and police chief, and the ploy he chose to utilize was to play for time and claim he was too busy to meet this auditor's needs:

> I have received your letter of 9th this month and inform you that I have given instruction for you to be sent the revised reports unanswered. Even if I had a great deal of time to work on them I greatly regret that an ultimatum was given to me in such a brisk manner and it is not easy from Lublin to get together evidence and documents from Vienna and Klagenfurt. In addition, it has not been possible for me to get away from here more than once in five months. The general work overload compels me to give priority to the most important things. *Heil* Hitler.[34]

Globocnik obviously believed that this haughty approach would bring things to a halt, at least for some time. In the following month he wrote directly to Himmler offering an explanation for his financial problems. He claimed that following the *Anschluss* administration had been difficult and that Bürckel had forbidden the then treasurer to do anything. "As *Gauleiter* I had to battle through financially as I never received funds," claimed Globocnik.[35] He resorted to claiming he was short of money and was therefore unable to fulfill his duties.

The blunt letter to Müller was deemed unsatisfactory, because there is a copy of a letter to Schwartz in Globocnik's SS file, dated 20 February 1941, signed only "Ihr" and stamped "*Stab Reichführer-SS*" (Himmler's headquarters), which may have been from Himmler's chief of personal staff, *SS-Gruppenführer* Karl Wolff. In it the author alluded to the letter to Müller and repeated that Globocnik was unable to leave Lublin because he (in fact, Jewish slave labor) was busy constructing anti-tank ditches and resettling some 30,000 so-called Chelm Germans out of his district. It is likely that carrying out this population transfer of these ethnic Germans also involved his Carinthian pal, Reinhold von Mohrenschildt, though no evidence has been found confirming this. The unknown author of this letter asked Schwartz that Globocnik's "behavior be judged mildly." Schwartz was also told that Globocnik was due to have a vacation over the summer of 1941 during which time he would be "able to explain it all." The author stated that he did not believe Globocnik was dishonest, but that he had been involved in "not quite correct behavior."[36] The letter therefore set about toning down any preconceptions that may have surfaced about Himmler's man in the East.

The following month, on 3 March, Globocnik wrote to Schwartz claiming that he had at all times acted with the noblest intentions, and he sought to be exonerated. This letter is clear evidence of the standing and power Schwartz had within party circles, for Globocnik advised him that he "wanted this behind me." Globocnik added that he regretted that Schwartz did not think well of him and went on to repeat that he had been busy and was under great pressure of work. The tone of the letter, however, was unmistakably well mannered, in stark contrast to that sent to Müller in Vienna.[37]

The pressure must have been getting to Globocnik, since he wrote to Karl Wolff beseeching him for assistance. Wolff received a copy of the letter to Schwartz and was advised that Globocnik had spoken to Himmler about his predicament. "I have only one wish and it is to be free of the Vienna histories," Globocnik concluded.[38] Never a truer word was spoken. But things were at least moving favorably for Globocnik, because Himmler had written to Schwartz on 6 March advising that he appreciated the treasurer's opinions but advised that he was "sure we would now get a satisfactory result." By early 1941 Globocnik was therefore further in debt to Himmler. But his decision to seek his SS superior's assistance bore fruit, for in June 1941, the month of the invasion of the Soviet Union, Schwartz finally relented. In a two-page letter to Himmler, he stated that he had been more than lenient toward Globocnik. However, he let it be known that he believed that during Globocnik's Vienna days black money existed. Schwartz, the long-time former Munich municipal accountant, had obviously been most reluctant to let the matter rest without a successful resolution. "If I look back at it now I see it all in a different light but I have no intention of reopening it," Schwartz assured Himmler.[39] For Globocnik this ordeal had been a very close shave, indeed. If he had pocketed public or party money, he had gotten away with it.

The English *Catholic Herald* briefly reported Globocnik's Vienna demise, highlighting it in a March issue under the headline "Real Reason of Vienna Purge — Vienna Paper Makes Daily Attack on Catholics."

> With the Nazi governor of Vienna, Herr Globocnik, almost all the leading men in the Vienna Nazi organization have been fired. Reports that they have been sent to a concentration camp are emphatically denied by the new *Gaulieter* of Vienna, Herr Bürckel, who in all his speeches *insists on the necessity of honesty and reliability and denounces corruption in public life.*
> *Obviously one of the reasons for the "purge" was such corruption* [emphasis added].[40]

Clearly, Globocnik had quickly come to see the Vienna *Gau* as more or less his personal fiefdom, and was unwilling to accept interference or oversight by Schwartz's emerging network of German auditors and agents. These authoritarians responded by hounding him for his first two years in Lublin, until the summer of 1941. But funds from so-called Aryanization, and the failure to accept budgetary and expenditure oversights, were just the beginning. Globocnik appears to have also devised several fundraising ventures associated with party memberships, sale of cheap imitation badges being one. In addition, he had also moved into a property and a business venture, with that move also becoming the target of investigations, and one which also found the *Gauleiter's modus operandi* to be wanting. The move into business was an almost fatal error, since Schwartz had kept the party running since the early 1920s solely with income from party subscriptions, certainly no mean feat, and he became curious about funds emanating from beyond that source. Any other money, such as gifts from large donors, industry, or the like, was seen as "cream on top of the cake," that is, not to be expected or relied upon, and something Schwartz viewed with great suspicion. There is no reason to believe that Schwartz's decision to pursue Globocnik was anything more than his utterly scrupulous manner in treating financial matters. Schwartz's pivotal role in the growth of Hitler's party has never been adequately studied or assessed. His efforts to bring Globocnik to book, or at least have him explain himself, was not, for instance, a conspiracy to ensure obedience or some such other motive. Globocnik was a fanatic, a man who had at least been suspected of killing by use of explosives, so he needed little cajoling toward a criminal direction. He was already a criminal on the day he became Vienna's *Gauleiter*. Moreover, he had served time in prison, so his outlook on life and behavior was hardly that of a middle-class gentleman.

Clearly, by Christmas 1938 Globocnik had shown himself to many to be the loose cannon on the deck of a far from well-managed ship of state, *Gau* Vienna. The Church, some Catholics within the NSDAP, and others, began pushing harder, even if behind the scenes, for his removal. Many, no doubt, were still bitter about his having outmaneuvered their favorite, Frauenfeld, for the job. Hitler was even alerted to problems in the city where he had once lived and studied, so he probably commenced looking toward a replacement, even if somewhat reluctantly. But it needed no lesser a figure than Hermann Göring — if not the third then the fourth most powerful man in the Reich — to convince the *Führer* at last that Globocnik simply had to go. To combat this growing pressure, Globocnik shrewdly turned to the *Führer's* trusted deputy, Rudolf Hess, but even this ploy was unable to help as disunity within party ranks, rather than diminishing, was seen to be on the rise. Hess later alluded to these tense days when the son of one of his mentors, Heinz Haushofer, complained in a letter of certain injustices perpetrated by National Socialism. According to the English writer David Irving, Hess replied to the young Heinz by stating, "You know full well how I do my utmost to intercede wherever I am told of individual cases of undesirable effects."[41] Irving went on:

> He [Hess] mentioned the case of the SS official Odilo Globocnig [sic], accused of massive corruption. Hess had instituted an investigation and the corruption charges had been found to have been exaggerated, but Hess had still obtained Globocnig's [sic] dismissal from office (*he* [Globocnik] *later headed the mass-extermination operations in the East*) [emphasis added].[42]

Globocnik's departure from Vienna appears to have caused little grief, with the British journalist Paul Bretherton writing in London's *Daily Mail* of 23 February 1939, and probably describing an aspect of the sacking as accurately as anyone: "Herr Globocnik *was a great enthusiast* without much leadership, and it is said of him that 'he ought to have been in with either Seyss-Inquart or Bürckel, but to have fallen out with both was hopeless!'" [Emphasis added][43]

So, on 30 January 1939, the nearly 35-year-old longtime Klagenfurt activist, the helper in the *Anschluss*, the Hitler contact man, the incompetent administrator, ignominiously left his powerful and prestigious Vienna post. Globocnik's demise was to some extent caused by the fact that he was a "wild Aryanizer," meaning a plunderer of goods and assets that had been sequestered from the growing number of Jews being expelled from Vienna throughout 1938 by Adolf Eichmann. Globocnik was, during these heady days, part of a group that was involved in such behavior whose activities had been drawn to Berlin's attention. Those activities had even attracted calls for reports detailing the Vienna *Gau's* financial position, and such calls reached Globocnik as early as 6 December 1938. However, as Globocnik was prone to do, he missed that deadline to supply answers, and found himself being called to Berlin for talks with Hess. It was this encounter which the Deputy *Führer* referred to in his letter to the young Haushofer. That meeting was, of course, a show-down, so Globocnik's 1938 Christmas break was undoubtedly an uncomfortable one. Globocnik, however, turned to the man who would dominate the rest of his life until the spring of 1945, Heinrich Himmler, his SS superior. Two days before Christmas he wrote to the *Reichsführer-SS* thanking him for sending him several books. However, he missed another deadline in January, and this appears to have thoroughly outraged Göring, who by now was determined to see Globocnik's removal no matter what. Göring then confronted Hitler, who at first wavered. But the matter was finally resolved after a lengthy meeting between Hitler and Göring in Göring's office.[44] Although Globocnik's letter to Himmler therefore failed to stop his removal from the Vienna post, it was instrumental in saving him from a fate that would in all likelihood have been far worse. Had he been without a powerful patron in Berlin, he may have faced charges, jailing, or something even worse, there and then. As stated earlier, the SS was known to execute those involved in criminal activities. Rather than vanish into some lowly party position or even into the SS, Globocnik was to now be propelled upwards by briefly joining Himmler's staff.

In early 1939, Himmler was on the brink of embarking on a drive to fulfill a series of German National Socialist Workers' Party dreams that drew on the teachings and writings of men such as Max Sering, Adolf Bartels, Heinrich von Class, Alexander Tille, Otto Amman, Alfred Ploetz, and Wilhelm Schallmeyer, backers of expulsionist policies as well as exterminationist ones, to be done on a massive scale, especially in Poland, where Globocnik was directed.[45] Himmler's SS eventually employed a range of men to help ensure his demographic cleansing dreams and aspirations were fulfilled, including SS Professor Konrad Meyer-Hetling, Hermann Krumey, Adolf Eichmann, Christian Wirth, and Gustav Hanelt. However, Odilo Globocnik was arguably the most important of these in the realization of the drive to rid Europe of Jews and to remove ethnic Poles and later other Slavs from Central and Eastern Europe. This, indeed, was their reason for going to war. A February edition of the newspaper *Neue Zürcher Zeitung* carried a brief report on the removal in Vienna, headlined "Globocnik Lost his Job and the Austrian Nazis are Disappointed." It claimed Globocnik's wishes could not be fulfilled, and that Bürckel had a stronger will and discipline. Bürckel's "hard hand" was said to be required in this difficult post.[46] This article may have been prematurely published, for a letter carrying the same date, 2 February 1939, from Himmler's chief-of-staff, *SS-Gruppenführer* Karl Wolff, to Schmitt of the same rank, and also stationed in Berlin, which advised that Himmler had asked him (Wolff) to telephone Bürckel, and with his agreement, to publish the following announcement in the press: "*SS-Oberführer* Globocnik will be transferred from February 1st 1939 from tasks in the Danube District to join the staff of the *Reichsführer-SS.*"[47]

Bürckel acceded to Wolff's request and, because Globocnik was in line for three to four weeks' leave, he was not due to arrive in Berlin until late February. So, almost exactly eight months after being so dramatically promoted in Austria, he moved north to the *Altreich*, Germany, from where he would be sent into action against Poland in September, and on 9 November would emerge as the *SS-und Polizeiführer* of occupied Poland's Lublin District, with the enviable senior rank of *SS-Brigadeführer*, and all of this as if his Vienna days had never occurred. Moreover, three years to the day, 9 November 1942, Globocnik was promoted to the rank of *SS-Gruppenführer* (major-general), three weeks before he launched the Zamosc Lands cleansing action and less than 10 months after the Wannsee Conference had given the go-ahead for what came to be known as *Aktion Reinhardt*. Did the undesirable aspects of Globocnik's hectic, "wild," and eventful Vienna days qualify, rather than disqualify, him for the work ahead in occupied Poland? If we are to believe his Lublin fiancée, Irmgard Rickheim, and there is no reason not to, perhaps the problems of Globocnik's Vienna days gave Himmler even greater sway and power over the obedient as well as purposive Carinthian. By early November 1939, Himmler had himself also been promoted by Hitler by being elevated to the ominous-sounding post of Reich Commissioner for the Strengthening of Germandom (*RKFDV*). Adolf Hitler had created this new post which gave the *Reichsführer-SS* absolute powers over all demographic affairs, that is, mass expulsions, settlement, and resettlement, deportation of Germans and non-Germans alike. Earlier ardent German nationalists had written or recommended such options, but it took Himmler only slightly more than a month after Poland's conquest to have powers conferred upon him to do precisely what these advocates had promoted. Significantly, Globocnik, with his new and powerful Lublin post, was, like other *SS-und Polizeiführers* in the General Gouvernement, to have bestowed upon him all of Himmler's *RKFDV* powers. But before this elevation of the failed and disgraced Vienna *Gauleiter* could be effected, he was required to undergo specialist military training, because first Poland, and thus the Lublin region, had to be conquered.

The Making of a Soldier: Military Training

Globocnik's nine-month interlude between departing Vienna and arriving in Lublin was not entirely uneventful. True, it no longer involved political activity, including conspiracy. These months are best viewed as an interlude in his life, a transition phase, away from conspiracy toward policing and administration, with widespread destruction of life as the end goal. According to documents in his SS file, he was primarily involved in military training over this period, and was thus initially stationed in Berlin. One of these documents shows that he was even advised to take three weeks' holiday by the sea during this unexpected interlude. He spent three months training with the *SS-Standarte "Der Führer*," after which he was transferred to *SS-Standarte "Germania,"* either in Hamburg or its environs. His training was undertaken between 1 March and 3 June, and involved serving in a single group and in company activities during which time he was deemed to have been eager, mentally active, and a man who showed understanding and the will to achieve. The examiners judged him to be an above average and very satisfactory combat student, after which he was promoted to *SS-Rottenführer* (Corporal).

During this period he underwent a comprehensive medical test, one normally undertaken by pilots. The test disclosed the following: Globocnik's lung capacity was 4,400 cubic centimeters; he was 176cm tall; had a heart with no abnormalities; blood pressure, 120/70 when resting, 130/70 after exercise, falling to 115/70 after three minutes. Various heart pulse rates were also recorded. Interestingly, both this and a subsequent test were taken in Vienna, with the second of them leading an SS and army doctor to report that his patient suffered from nervous sleeplessness. But no other problems were found. His more than 350-page SS file discloses several other interesting characteristics, including that he claimed to be of German descent (*"Ich bin Deutscher..."*); an Aryan, and not a member of a freemasons' lodge or any similar secret society. This claim to being German is, of course, untrue, because Globocnik was a Slovene on his father's side, and possibly also on his mother's side, and thus at least of part Slavic ancestry. According to a letter dated 13 September 1939, he indicated his wish to be called an engineer, and he alerted the staff office that he had acquired the medal of Remembrance for Sudetenland (*Sudeten-Erinnerungsmedaille*). One of his personnel cards shows he had joined the NSDAP in 1930 (No. 429,939), the SS in 1934 (No. 292,776), and at one time his address had been 11 Kostlergasse, Vienna. The file contains a letter dated 23 December 1938 from Globocnik to Himmler, in which the former thanked his superior for forwarding several publications from, perhaps even written by, a Dr. Hermann Gmelin, and Globocnik assured Himmler that he would study them.[48]

Himmler appears to have been something of a proselytizer with Globocnik, exchanging books or else providing them to his now up-and-coming young Carinthian. Here was one of the Reich's major demographic theorists, Himmler, advising one of his underlings to study certain ideological tracts. A week before Poland was invaded, Himmler had given Globocnik his Death's Head Ring (*Totenkopfring-SS*), a significant milestone in an SS man's life and career. Receipt of the ring is important for another reason, for Globocnik wrote to Himmler's personal staff thanking the *Reichsführer-SS* for this obviously prized gift. That handwritten letter, dated 10 October 1939, shows that Globocnik served with 1st Battalion 1st Company (Field Post 3299) during the Polish Campaign. "Since 19 August I have been on the move as I have been participating in the Polish Campaign, meaning the letter has only reached me today," he wrote.[49]

At least one Polish historian has a different opinion on these days, saying Globocnik was in jail, presumably because of his corrupt Vienna practices, claiming that Globocnik had been incarcerated in a Breslau prison during the period prior to the outbreak of war. However, no evidence has been found to support such a claim. Vienna's misdemeanors, far from hindering Globocnik's career, only redirected it, to Lublin, where he was to elevate himself as a mass murderer.[50] There was something about the way he conducted himself in Vienna that appealed to Himmler, who wanted a man who was both utterly loyal and not afraid of unilateral actions against those who may be technically his superiors, like those in the soon-to-be-created civil administration of occupied Poland, which Himmler himself ignored and urged Globocnik to do likewise. By early 1939, Himmler had become adept at bureaucratic wrangling, and far from expecting less of it in his life knew there would be more, especially once new lands had been conquered across the East. He probably therefore realized that his life, dedicated to fulfilling his racial desires — expulsion of Jews and Slavs and the settlement of Germans in their place — would involve many bureaucratic rows and imbroglios with men like occupied central Poland's general-governor, Dr. Hans Frank, Hitler's former lawyer. As things transpired, the selection of Odilo Globocnik was the perfect choice for such purposes. Put candidly, Himmler made Vienna's loss his gain.

V

Lublin District's *SS- und Polizeiführer*: 9 November 1939 to 17 September 1943

Lublin District's 2.4 million people were to have *SS-Brigadeführer* Odilo Globocnik imposed upon them for the first 47 months, or two thirds of the European war. Lublin's population in 1939 stood at 122,000 people, including 42,830 Jews. Lublin was not a new Polish city for it had been settled since at least the 12th century. Like so many other European cities, it had experienced its fair share of calamitous times. The Globocnik years were at least as turbulent as many of the city's harsh experiences. In the 12th century the then township, which was situated on the trade route to Ruthenia, was even fortified. During the 13th century Lublin was destroyed several times due to invasions of the Tartars, the Ruthenians, and the Jadvingians, a Lithuanian people. In 1550 Lublin's total population stood at 840 people, so it was a sizeable town but well below city status. This figure rose to 1,200 in half a century, and its population stood at only 1,725 residents in 1765; population growth had been extremely slow. During Europe's tumultuous Napoleonic era, Lublin could boast in 1806 a population of 4,105 residents, of whom nearly 3,000 were Jews, or almost 75 percent. It is therefore fair to say that Lublin at this time could not be regarded as an ethnic Polish city, but rather, a Jewish one. However, the Jewish portion had fallen to almost half by 1827, when the city's total population stood at 13,475, with the Jewish component being 6,795. As the turn of the century approached, in 1897, the same ratio existed. The city's total population was 46,301, and the Jewish component was 23,586. It was only in the 20th century that the non–Jewish share commenced to rise significantly: In 1921, when the total was 94,412, the Jewish segment was 37,337, and in 1931, when the city's total population was 96,608 people, Jews made up nearly 39,000.

Globocnik, the fanatically dedicated National Socialist, SS man, anti-Semite, and a man with a record of, if not hatred of Slavs, even though being of partial Slavic ancestry, then nearly lifelong deep contempt for them, arrived early in November to take over from the *Wehrmacht's* administration. Lublin's 42,380 Jewish residents and nearly 80,000 Poles could not have had a less welcomed SS man, though no SS man could possibly have been welcome considering the previous 12 years of intense indoctrination by members of this Himmler organization. Globocnik, however, was a particularly unfortunate choice from Lublin's perspective. The nearly four years of his tyranny and terror were undoubtedly among this city's and region's most extreme, challenged

Odilo Globocnik, second from right, with other uniformed personnel and one civilian, probably in Lublin's Old Town Quarter, 1943. (Yad Veshem Film and Photo Archive)

only by the period when it was briefly occupied by the Swedes, the so-called Deluge, during the 17th century. Globocnik was, in the words of the wartime Polish Exile Government's major historical analyst and German affairs adviser, Jozef Winiewicz, like a Germanic Margrave of old, a man with a mission to destroy the Poles and other occupiers of the Vistula River valley and the valleys of its tributaries. To him, like earlier Germanic Margraves, the Slavs and Jews stood in the way of German eastern territorial and racially purist demographic ambitions. He was not in Lublin simply to administer. Globocnik's historic predecessors, as far as Winiewicz was concerned, were Margrave Gero, Albert the Bear, Henry the Lion, and Barbarossa, all of whom struck terror into the hearts of Slavs of old. But Globocnik was to be far more destructive that any of these.[1]

Lublin District Not Lithuania

Although too much should not be made of it, Globocnik could have become Himmler's senior SS and police officer in Lithuania rather than in what was soon to be designated Lublin District (See Map 2), had territorial issues with the Soviet Union been finalized differently immediately after Poland's rapid defeat. The reason for this quirk of history was that under the 23 August 1939 Molotov-Ribbentrop Pact, which paved the way for World War II — Hitler invading Poland just eight days later and Stalin occupying eastern Poland 25 days after that date — Lublin province (*wojewodztwo*) had initially been assigned to the Soviet "sphere of interest," while Lithuania was to have come within Berlin's orbit. Most significantly, it was Hitler who asked to have the dividing line changed following Poland's collapse, according to former United States State Department consultant, Herbert Feis.[2] Consequently, under the terms of a second or refining treaty, finalized on 28 September 1939 — when precise borders, as opposed to mere "spheres of influence" were determined — most of Lithuania was reallocated to the Soviet Union while the Lublin District was moved over to Germany on payment by the Soviet Union of "the amount of $7,500,000 gold dollars, the equivalent of 31,500,000 German marks."[3] Relevant here is that it was Hitler who moved, although belatedly, to acquire defeated Poland's Lublin province, whose western perimeter was quickly brought into play as a possible Jewish Reservation — a rural out-of-the-way ghetto — and Globocnik, within a matter of weeks, was assigned to become this district's senior SS and police officer. The circumstantial evidence would appear to be that Lublin was earmarked early for some special or possible demographic purpose. Hitler appears to have intended acquiring the Lublin lands as a Berlin-controlled region, for during a secret address to his generals delivered on 22 August 1939, he had said, *inter alia,*

Map 2. General Gouvernement (Poland) and the Zamosc Lands

that "The new method of conducting war corresponds to the new draft of the frontiers — one continuous rampart from Reval, Lublin and Kosice to the mouth of the Danube. The rest will be awarded to the Russians. Ribbentrop has instructions to make every offer and to accept every demand."[4]

The later renegotiated articles of the 23 August secret Hitler-Stalin Protocol read:

> *Article I.* In the event of the territorial-political reorganization of the districts making up the Baltic States (Finland, Estonia, Latvia, Lithuania), the northern border of Lithuania is simultaneously the border of the spheres of influence of Germany and the USSR. The interests of Lithuania with respect of the Vilnius district are recognized by both sides.
>
> *Article II.* In the event of a territorial-political reorganization of the districts making up the Polish Republic, the border of the spheres of interest of Germany and the USSR will run approximately along the Pissa, Narew, Vistula and San Rivers.
>
> The question of whether it is in the [signatories] mutual interest to preserve the independent Polish *State and what the borders of that state will be ascertained conclusively only in the course of future political development.*
>
> *In any event both governments will resolve this matter through friendly mutual agreement* [emphasis added].[5]

This initial arrangement was altered at Hitler's behest with the exchange of Lithuania, then within the German "sphere of interest," for the Lublin area, as follows:

> Point 1 of the secret supplementary protocol signed on 23 August 1939, is changed so that the territory of the Lithuanian state is included in the sphere of interest of the USSR because, on the other side, Lublin voivodship and parts of Warsaw voivodship are included in the sphere of interest of Germany (see map accompanying the Treaty on Friendship and the Border between the USSR and Germany, signed today). As soon as the Government of the USSR takes special measures on Lithuanian territory to protect its interests, the present German-Lithuanian border, with the object of making it a natural and simple border, will be adjusted so that the Lithuanian territory that lies south-west of the line shown on the map goes to Germany.[6]

The fact that the city of Lublin became the organizational hub or the SS's nerve center for the planning of the extermination of so many European Jews, after February 1942, and that Lublin District was selected as the launching pad for *Generalplan Ost* after November 1942, may have been a coincidence. But that may not have been altogether the case. The region may have been chosen quite early, by Hitler himself, as a possible demographic *Sonderlaboratorium*—a venue for some imminent demographic plans and policies. The fact that there was a Lublin Jewish Reservation created so early seems significant. For Globocnik to have been stationed there suggests he was seen to be the right, pliant, and obedient person when it came to undertaking such special demographic "experimentation." He was seen as the SS man with the necessary qualities to undertake and guide any such "experiments." True, it is difficult to say with any degree of confidence precisely what Hitler's puzzling phrase, "The new method of conducting war corresponds to the new draft of the frontiers," meant precisely. But notwithstanding that, it seems reasonably clear that Hitler saw Lublin and its environs as being out on "the frontier," and thus well situated for conducting some form of "experimentation," well away from Western Europe, and largely out of sight. Perhaps Lithuania, closer to Moscow, was seen to be inappropriate for such activities. Lublin, on the other hand, was on the edge of the long sought after black earth fields of Ukraine, which had such an appeal to so many Nazis. It is against such a background of vague considerations and Hitler's deliberate, if belated, move to acquire this Polish region, that it is valuable to view Globocnik's appointment to Lublin.

The best-selling monumental book by American correspondent and author William Shirer, *The Rise and Fall of the Third Reich*, briefly alludes to the belated switch in control of Lithuania and Lublin District by Europe's two totalitarian powers. Shirer writes that 10 days after Soviet forces had commenced occupying eastern Poland, that is, on 27 September, Ribbentrop had flown to Moscow to refine the parameters of the dismantling of Poland and its three smaller northeastern Baltic neighbors (Estonia, Latvia and Lithuania), "by means of a friendly agreement." On Ribbentrop's arrival in Moscow a German diplomat handed him two telegrams just received from Berlin, drawing attention to the fact that Moscow had already begun exerting pressure on the most northerly of these neighbors, Estonia, by demanding that its government allow the basing of two Red Army divisions and an air force brigade within this tiny Baltic state's territory. Hitler responded by ordering the evacuation of some 86,000 *Volksdeutsche* from Estonia and adjacent Latvia.

> Before the day was up he [Hitler] *was also giving up Lithuania*, on Germany's north-eastern border, which according to the secret clauses of the Moscow Pact, belonged to the Reich's sphere.
> Stalin had presented the Germans two choices in the meetings with Ribbentrop, which began at 10 P.M. on 27 September and lasted until 1am. They were, as he [Stalin] had suggested to [Reich ambassador] Schulenburg on the 25th: acceptance of the original line of demarcation in Poland along the Pissa, Narew, Vistula and San Rivers, with Germany getting Lithuania; or yielding Lithuania to Russia in *return for more Polish territory (the province of Lublin and the lands to the east of Warsaw)* which would give the Germans almost all of the Polish people [emphasis added].[7]

Shirer goes on to state that Stalin had strongly urged Ribbentrop to yield to the second option, that is, that Moscow acquire Lithuania and forsake the

Lublin region. Shirer says: "Ribbentrop in a long telegram to Hitler filed at 4am on 28 September put it up to Hitler, who agreed."[8] This would appear to contradict the claim by Herbert Feis, who, although not giving the source of his contention that it was Hitler who pushed to acquire the Lublin region, prepared his study using documentary evidence rather than what he was told at the time, which Shirer, as a correspondent, necessarily relied upon so often. Unfortunately, Ribbentrop's memoirs, written while he awaited execution, fail to give a clear answer to this issue. Writing about his September 1939 visit to Moscow, he said:

> It again became apparent what tough bargainers the Russians were in obtaining their diplomatic aims, for Stalin and Molotov, *while waiving claims to the Lublin region of Poland,* made a new claim which conflicted with our agreement the preceding August; now they also wanted to include Lithuania in their sphere of influence. As the Russians stubbornly insisted on this I telephoned the *Führer* from the Kremlin. He rang me back a little later to say, with some misgivings, I sensed, that he agreed to Russia including Lithuania in her sphere of influence. He added: "I want to establish quite firm and close relations." When I reported these words to Stalin he said laconically: "Hitler knows his business" [emphasis added].[9]

Ribbentrop's phrase "while waiving claims to the Lublin region of Poland" appears to suggest that it could have been the German side that sought this area, with Stalin concurring, and suggesting Lithuania become his in return. That the German side was surprised that Stalin expected territory for territory is amazing and difficult to believe. Perhaps they felt that territory could be gained for goods involved in the trade component of the negotiations. Stalin was a tough wheeler and dealer, a man who, as well as practicing purging of opponents, and demographic or ethnic cleansing, also practiced *realpolitik.*

Shirer's succinct account, which recognized the belated Lublin acquisition by Berlin, also fails to reveal that the Lithuanian-Lublin territorial exchange included a substantial cash equivalent consideration. Both the August and September territorial deals meant that Europe's post–Great War order, as created at Versailles in 1919–20, and in the absence of both Germany (which was simply punished) and a new Red Russia, was finally being fully and completely dismantled, with Hitler moving to acquire lands that extended even farther east than Bismarck's Prussia had once controlled, while Stalin was recouping most of the lands once held by Czarist Russia. These were lands which his predecessor, Vladimir Lenin, had effectively lost to new independent nations whose very existence was sanctioned at Versailles. It is also interesting that the August Pact was signed by senior German and Soviet officials while they stood beneath a photograph of Vladimir Lenin. There was no longer to be room for Wilsonian notions of national self-determination, and the man who best described the long-held hidden intention of both totalitarian powers to do precisely this was Bolshevism's founder and Stalin's often-ingenious predecessor, Lenin himself, who said in 1920, "Germany wants revenge, and we want revolution. For the moment our interests are the same, but when our ways part, they will be our most ferocious and greatest enemy. Time will tell whether a German hegemony or a Communist federation is to arise out of the ruins of Europe."[10]

Though Lenin's statement can only be described as brilliantly prescient, not even he could have imagined in 1920 that within about a decade of his uttering these words, a new consolidated political force, based on old German *völkisch* notions, whose origins dated back to the previous century, would appear with powerful representatives in Berlin, for whom mere hegemony over Eastern Europe was not the aim. Adolf Hitler's *völkisch* movement sought far more, namely, the removal and murder of *all* Jews, and the removal of all Slavs (i.e. eastward expulsion) from all Greater Germanic Reich-controlled lands which the Reich's leadership was determined to conquer militarily, *right up to the western face of the Ural Mountain range*, with the newly-acquired lands to be settled *only by Germans*. This was Hitlerism and Himmlerism, at its crudest and simplest, and Germany's primary reason for waging World War II in the European theatre. For this dream to be realized after military conquest had been effected, men like Globocnik, a bloody ethnic cleanser, were essential: They were going to put these long-held German, *völkisch* dreams into reality. At the end of a successful eastern war, Hitler's and Himmler's senior SS men like Globocnik would therefore have been involved in establishing across Western Siberia a network of Slavic *Bantustans*.

This trio of aims was to become Globocnik's three missions while in Lublin: extermination of all Jews; expulsion of all Poles and Slavs; and settlement of Germans upon Lublin District, beginning with the Zamosc Lands, followed by the remainder of the General Gouvernement, and subsequently, following the conquest of Stalin's Red Army, upon all of Western Russia, including Ukraine and the Baltic Lands. What had happened in Germany between Lenin's 1920 statement and shortly before Hitler in January 1933 gained executive power over Germany was that revenge for the so-called Versailles Diktat had been largely displaced by an increasingly well-thought-out format of ideas which revolved around a belief in the need to acquire the vast expanses of the East by the emergent Reich. The East which so preoccupied Nazis included many tiny enclaves and regions which had been settled by German communities over several previous centuries; this included Germans in a handful of villages in Poland's Zamosc Lands, which had come under Globocnik's control in November 1939 when he was made SS and police chief of Lublin District. These non–Slavic communities, whether integrated or unintegrated into the societies within which these people lived, were regarded by men like Globocnik and his SS superiors and academically trained researchers as "lost German blood," lost, that is, to the greater Germanic community (*Volk*) that centered on the Reich that Adolf Hitler headed. Globocnik's wartime bailiwick, his base for the implementation of this long-term German National Socialist and SS planning, as well as his unprecedented genocidal activities, was therefore to be Lublin, the General Gouvernement's most easterly city, which the Hitler Reich only belatedly acquired from Stalin under the Soviet German Boundary and Friendship Treaty. That treaty also covered strategic commodity — oil and grain — deals to ensure that Berlin was largely able to deflect the impact of Britain's naval blockade. It was followed, over the succeeding months, by a series of other treaties which saw people defined by Berlin as being Germans, but living within Stalin's sphere of control, being moved west into the German sphere, with most of these newcomers settled in pre-war western Poland (Warthe Land). But the August 1939 treaty was finally dishonored on 22 July 1941, when the Soviet Union was invaded, with the Lublin District serving as one of the major springboards for this most ambitious of Hitler's military actions, putting Germany on the road to recovering what *völkisch* proselytizers had claimed in thousands of booklets, pamphlets, and lectures over previous decades, were long-lost Germanic lands.

> The Nazi Party, as it emerged between 1930 and 1933, was really the conflux or fusion of those numerous "racial" or *völkisch* movements which had sprung up, largely by secession from the Conservative camp, under the leadership of such men as Count Reventlow, von Graef, Wulle, "Knuppel" Kunze, Ludendorff, and others. Between 1925 and 1932 most of these political sects came to join forces with their largest competitor, the Hitler movement. These movements were strongly influenced by and closely linked with the much older Pan-German Movement.[11]

It is valuable and instructive to view Globocnik's increasing dedication to the cause of the Germanic ideology, violent or aggressive Pan-Germanism, during the years 1930 to 1933, as this conflux or fusion took place on the national stage. His work in Lublin between 1939 and 1943 is best understood in the context of Hitler's eastern goals of ethnic cleansing, in whatever way, of those regarded as "aliens," and the settling of Germans in their place. Globocnik was crucial to this undertaking and was, by far, Hitler's and Himmler's most important and destructive eastern agent in the fulfillment of these aims. This was his significance.

Globocnik's Lublin District Executive Powers, Responsibilities, and Staff

Odilo Globocnik reached Lublin in the second week of November, with his appointment to this ethnically mixed eastern Polish city being announced on the 9th, to head up the SS and the district's police. There he led a thoroughly ideologized racial fraternity that was formidably armed and whose men had access to back-up police and militarized units, including the *Wehrmacht.*[12] Lublin was officially handed over to civil administration on 1 November, even though civilian officials, especially from the German Labor Office (*Arbeitsamt*) had begun arriving there during the previous month.

> On 9 November, Odilo Globocnik was made Chief of Police and SS in the district. His appointment marked the beginning of a constant wave of terror against the local population — arrests, confiscations, beatings, and executions. The main victims were the Polish intelligentsia, who were regarded by the Germans as a dangerous element that could lead a resistance movement against them. Globocnik, who was a close associate of Himmler, and himself of a cruel nature, achieved a special status in the Nazi hierarchy.[13]

In subsequent months, indeed for almost the next four years, Globocnik steadily acquired a large number of additional responsibilities, and by mid–1941, when Hitler invaded the Soviet Union, he was the absolute ruler of Lublin District, challenged, half-heartedly only, by the civil governor, Ernst Zörner (sometimes also referred to as Emil), a long-time acquaintance of

Odilo Globocnik's Lublin mansion. (Courtesy of Irmgard Rickheim)

A rear view of Globocnik playing 9-pin bowling (*Kegel*) in his specially built lane alongside his Lublin mansion. Max Cichotski (aka Runhof) in the foreground. (Courtesy Irmgard Rickheim)

Adolf Hilter's and Josef Goebbels's, who reached Lublin in March 1940, but with whom Globocnik quarreled bitterly over the next three years. The Lublin District's governorship was temporarily held by *SS-Oberführer* Friedrich Schmidt, who had taken over from the *Wehrmacht* on 29 October 1939 when the area was still under military administration.[14] Schmidt had left Lublin by March 1940. English historian Robin O'Neil sees this early appointment of Schmidt, followed by Globocnik less than a fortnight later, as evidence of Himmler getting in ahead of the German civilian administration and thus as an early sign of future SS intentions for this region, a contention with which it is difficult to disagree.

> The Himmler-Heydrich Executive, seizing their opportunity before the civil administration could obtain a foothold, stamped their claim to eastern Poland by placing their personnel in positions of strength. The arrival of *SS-Brigade-führer* Odilo Globocnik in Lublin with Himmler's authority behind him was a signal to the General Gouvernement that the SS were taking charge and had their own political agenda.[15]

Zörner, who remained in Lublin until April 1943, had served as mayor of Dresden, and in June 1937 rumors suddenly surfaced throughout that city that he had attempted suicide by shooting.[16] It is relevant here to know that Zörner, an early member of the NSDAP, from Brunswick, and the man responsible for Hitler gaining German citizenship, at no stage received any form of assistance from Hitler in his drawn-out and bitter conflicts with Globocnik, who increasingly encroached upon Zörner's powers and responsibilities. This is a measure of Hitler's priorities — assistance in gaining German citizenship did not take precedence over what Globocnik and the SS were doing! But having all that power failed to satisfy Globocnik, for the moves against Zörner covered up something even more sinister and ambitious. It is entirely likely that Globocnik was not simply nipping at Zörner's authority to ensure his, and Himmler's, will was done, but rather that he was actually involved in a far larger power grab. Globocnik's goal was to take control of all spheres of power across the entire General Gouvernement. The aim was to attain the post of chief of the NSDAP for all of occupied Poland, and from this commanding political height, with his police powers, to do anything that he and Himmler desired. Moreover, in March 1942, when General-Governor Dr. Hans Frank called for Globocnik's resignation, following on-going objections about his behavior by Zörner, Himmler went so far as to suggest that Zörner be sacked and that Globocnik be made the governor of Lublin District.[17] A central or integral policy of Globocnik in such a position would have been to remove by expulsion all unwanted Poles — a dream of the German nationalistic imperial political right since well before the turn of the century — from the General Gouvernement, including the so-called Warthe Land, Silesia, Danzig-West Preussen, and later, eastern Poland. Though this may sound fanciful, it will be seen that where Globocnik stood in relation to racial and demographic plans and policies, such as the extermination of Poland's entire Jewish population and his launching of a program of expulsion of ethnic Poles, both these programs were simply the opening gambit of moves to remove completely Poles from lands that made up all pre-war Poland. Furthermore, by Christmas 1942, Globocnik was well on the way to achieving this, having at last launched the clearance of the Zamosc Lands. Zörner, understandably, thought Globocnik was plotting a *coup d'etat* against him, and this suspicion was not altogether off target. At minimum Globocnik's power grab from Hans Frank and Ernst Zörner took place through demographic policies. Power over who lived and stayed in a particular region was ultimate power.

On his arrival in Lublin, Globocnik was already armed with the power of life and death over everyone in or even passing through this recently acquired district: Pole, Jew, and Ukrainian. By the time he left he had, in various ways, murdered no fewer than 1.5 million Jews, most of these transported into the General Gouvernement from other parts of Europe to be exterminated in specially constructed out-of-the-way killing compounds, as well as several tens of thousands of Poles. Two of his large killing compounds were situated within this district — Belzec and Sobibor — while the third, Treblinka, was outside the district, to its north, mid-way between the larger cities of Warsaw and Bialystok, both with large Jewish ghettos, so Treblinka was well situated to easily transport these inhabitants for quick killing.

In addition to being the head of local SS units and being the district's chief police officer, Globocnik also headed, from mid-1942, the NSDAP, being its *Distriktsstadtsführer*, the equivalent of a *Gauleiter* in the Reich, and another exceptionally powerful position. He also represented Himmler in his capacity of *Reichskommissar für der Festigung deutschen Volkstums (RKFDV)* — the powerful Reich Commissioner for the Strengthening of Germandom; the *Volksdeutsche Mittelstelle (VoMi)* — German Racial Assistance Office; and was also placed in charge of *Rasse-und Siedlungshauptamt (RuSHA)*—Race and Settlement Office. These last three positions gave him total power in the crucial demographic planning and policy areas that were to be launched with full force on 28 November 1942 with the removal early that day of some 110,000 Polish peasants from their homes and land in the village of Skierbieszow. That expulsion, however, was simply the first of many intended across Russia, Ukraine, Belarus, and the Baltic Lands. By then, of course, the extermination of Lublin District's Jews was well underway; there was little that Globocnik did not control in this district under the title of demographic affairs. Little wonder Zörner felt impotent and eventually resigned and withdrew from the scene. Planning and related moves associated with the Zamosc Lands action, however, had in fact begun a year earlier, in November 1941, five months after the invasion of the Soviet Union. Globocnik had also come to control the *Selbstschutz* (Self-Defense Units), which were manned primarily by *Volksdeutsche*, many hailing from Lublin District itself, and over which he sought to exercise complete and personal control. Having local *Volksdeutsche* in his pay gave him access to an enormous amount of first-hand local information.[18] This type of knowledge was further augmented through local and other Ukrainians who came under the control of Globocnik through the aegis of the Krakow-based and pro-German Ukrainian Central Committee, which had paid officials based in Lublin and its district's major centers, including many villages. The Lublin District had a significant Ukrainian minority, and Ukrainian town officials were seen as "men of trust" who were part of a complex network of spies and informers working against the majority ethnic Poles. Precisely what such agents did in relation to Jewish affairs has never been researched. Globocnik was also secretly designated chief executive officer of what later became known as *Aktion Reinhardt* in early 1942. It is not surprising, therefore, that Globocnik felt at ease ignoring the policies and exhortations of the nominal superior of Lublin District, its governor, Ernst Zörner.

In addition to these eight powerful ideological, policing, demographic, and extermination positions, Globocnik steadily acquired a dozen or more powerful economic and business posts, making him Lublin's economic czar, and showing conclusively that his Vienna days' financial shenanigans hadn't been a barrier to promotion to levels far beyond the average person's wildest dreams. Many of these posts simply arose from his SS racial and demographic work, which, as stated above, was envisaged as extending well into the Soviet Union. Lublin was seen, especially by Himmler, as the logical center for such yet-to-be-launched "eastern work" because it was the General Gouvernement's most easterly city, Warsaw being too far north and in the center, while Krakow, which was the occupation capital, was too far south and west. Globocnik's additional dozen derived positions were:

1. *Deutsche Ausrustüngswerke GmbH, (DAW)* ; German Armament Works Ltd.
2. *Ost-Industrie GmbH, (Osti)* East Industry Ltd.
3. *SS-Standesabteilung-u Standartkommandaten,* (SS-Garrison. Administration of SS-Garrison Commando's Office) and its offices.
4. *SS-Ausbildungslager Trawniki,* (SS-Training Camp, Trawniki).
5. *Arbeitslager,* Labor Camps — Poniatowa, Budzyn and Krasnik.
6. *Bekleidungslager-u der Truppenwirtschaftslager der Waffen-SS, (Waffen-*SS Clothing Depot and Troop Economic Office).
7. *Zentralkrankenrevier mit SS-Zahnstation,* (Central Hospital with SS Dental Depot).
8. *Zentralkauteilung des Waffen-SS-u Polizei Lublin,* (Central Construction Office of the *Waffen-SS* and Police, Lublin).
9. *SS-Benleitung Zamosc,* (SS Construction Office, Zamosc).
10. *Die SS-Betriebsgruppe Wirtschaft,* (SS-Economic Operations — SS-Farms).
11. *SS-Sonderkommando — Dirlewanger.*
12. *Die Siedler-Wirtschaftsgemeinschaft, Zamosc,* (Settlers' Economic Aid Association, Zamosc).[19]

This gargantuan Globocnikian economic, business, welfare, and killing empire, which employed tens of thousands of prisoners, a large proportion of them Jews, (Poles were predominantly producers of the food as peasant farmers, so they were spread across the district's hundreds of villages and were subjected to heavy contingent demands), and, after mid–1941, many thousands of Soviet prisoners-of-war, grew out of Globocnik's absolutist monopoly power over the Lublin District's citizenry and Berlin's plans, the origins of which dated back at least to World War I, to exploit the East and transform it into a German area of settlement.

Although we cannot be absolutely certain of the dates that all of his various individual staffers appeared on the Lublin killing scene, or when they left, much is known of many of Globocnik's key men thanks to the investigative work conducted many years after the war by the Ludwigsburg *Zentrale Stelle* and several historians, not least the British historian Michael Tregenza, who settled in Lublin in the early 1990s to conduct ongoing research, especially on *Aktion Reinhardt*, the Belzec killing center, and on the former Stuttgart detective, Christian Wirth.[20] The first, and in many ways the most important of the staffers, was Ernst Lerch, a Klagenfurt waiter and later café owner, a man from the same city as Globocnik. Lerch was 10 years younger than his Carinthian superior and was well known to him during his Carinthian underground days. Lerch, an *SS-Sturbannführer*, was one of the five members of Globocnik's inner staff (*Engerer Stab*). He was Globocnik's most trusted confidante and a man who knew everything that his superior was doing and planning. The closeness of this relationship can be gauged by the fact that it was Lerch who was sent to ask a female member of another later Globocnik inner circle staffer if she was perhaps favorably disposed toward marrying the *SS-Brigadeführer*. The other inner staff members were: *Sturmbannführers* Hans Maubach, Sepp Nemetz, Hermann Höfle, and Paul Gasser. There was also Max Cichotski, who later adopted the surname Runhof, a *Hilter-Jugend Gefolgschaftsführer*, who, with Maubach, was the other non–Austrian among these five. Maubach hailed from Hagen, Westphalia, while Cichotski was from northern Poland, and despite his Polish-sounding name, was a *Volksdeutsche* and a passionately pro-German one at that. Cichotski's name is spelled variously, including von Czichotzki and Cichotzki, none of which seem to have pleased him. His disposition toward Germanism is shown by the fact that toward the end of the war, probably in 1944, he changed it to Runhof, a surname that belonged to one of his German ancestors. Despite this he was tracked down 16 years later in Wiesbaden by German investigating officials, and he provided a lengthy and at times revealing statement about various aspects of his Globocnikian Lublin days. He also briefly gave evidence in an Austrian court against Lerch, but the case was never concluded.

Globocnik was responsible for the whole Jewish "resettlements" [ghettoization, death through labor, and extermination] in Lublin Distrikt. These "resettlements" began in 1940 and ended in 1943. He was also responsible for the resettlements of Volhynian, Bessarabia, Banat and Rumanian Germans. How many resettlement operations and anti-partisan operations were carried out by him between 1940 and 1943 is not known. There were, however, a great many Jewish operations. The "resettlements" of the Jews was carried out from 1940 by Globocnik with vigor. In 1940 a large part of the fit male Jews from the four Distrikts of the Generalgouvernement [Lublin, Warsaw, Radom and Krakow] were sent to Belzec and its vicinity. The overall leadership of their construction project was taken over shortly afterwards by the SS-officer Hermann Dolp, who had been demoted in rank from SS-*Sturmbannführer* to SS-*Standartenführer* and transferred to Lublin as punishment. Dolp had the commandant of various *Konzetrationlagers* in the Reich. For the Jewish operations Globocnik had a *staff which had been placed at his disposal by the KdF [Führer's Chancellery] (Reichsleiter Bouhler and SA-Oberführer Blankenburg). This staff was led by a certain SS-Sturmbannführer Christian Wirth. Globocnik's closest staff consisted of the SS-Sturmbannführers: Ernst Lerch, Hans Maubach, Sepp Nemetz, Hermann Höfle, and the above mentioned Christian Wirth* [emphasis added].[21]

Eight Major Lublin Globocnikians

Ernst Lerch, Ever Loyal Disciple

Lerch reached Lublin probably in the summer of 1940 and quickly headed up Globocnik's Jewish Affairs Department, which had been created in December 1939. He succeeded its inaugural chief, Dr. Karl Hofbauer. Lerch was born in Klagenfurt on 19 November 1914, and was younger than his Klagenfurt superior by nearly a decade. He was in Lublin with his wife and a child until September 1943, when he joined the more than 400-strong Globocnik group that drove south to Trieste. Lerch has been described as a man with a genuinely friendly disposition, someone who was at ease with strangers and friends. This no doubt suited him in his chosen career of being a waiter and later a café proprietor. A spin-off of his occupation was that he was the type of person who was orderly, organized, and thorough, all qualities that were needed when work began on murdering tens of hundreds of thousands of Jews and the deportation of tens of thousands of Poles. He was just the sort of man that Globocnik needed. Lerch entered the SS the same year as Globocnik, 1934. Understandably, then, the famous Vienna-based Nazi hunter, Simon Wiesenthal, did not overlook Lerch in his writings, even though the entry is surprisingly brief.

> SS-*Sturmbannführer* Ernst Lerch, Globocnik's ADC and for a time his chief of staff, is a colorful personality. In 1932 he was a waiter in Paris and there, in a

German club, came into contact with Nazis. In 1934 he returned to his native Klagenfurt and joined the illegal SS. As he made a little money he was in a position to open a cafe, which became a meeting place for Carinthian illegal Nazis. This is how he made the acquaintance of Franz Kutschera, [aka Classen], Ernst Kaltenbrunner and, more particularly Odilo Globocnik.[22]

Lerch went on to become an *Obergruppenführer* in 1936, experiencing rapid promotion while an Austrian political illegal. Two years later he moved to the Reich, where he became an *SS-Hauptsturmführer* in the Reich Security Directorate in Berlin. According to his initial British interrogation report, he was educated in Klagenfurt and briefly studied at the *Hochschule für Welthandel* in Vienna. "From 1931 to 1934 he worked as a waiter in various hotels in Switzerland, France and Hungary to learn the hotel trade. From 1934 until the *Anschluss* he was employed in the café of his father in Klagenfurt."[23]

This report said that Lerch had been a member of the illegal Nazi Party and the highly secretive *SD* since 1936. The *Anschluss* brought him promotion, to the rank of an *SS-Hauptsturmführer,* and he became an *SD Leiter,* a post he resigned from in July 1938. He was called up into the army in December that year. Lerch claimed to have been involved in the Polish campaign as a signals corporal and, like Globocnik, probably saw action. But he was careful

Ernst Lerch in party attire, including party hat. (Courtesy Irmgard Rickheim)

not to mention to his postwar British interrogators his nearly four Lublin years. At this point his report shows he told blatant lies, and not surprisingly so because he was one of the key participants in the crime of genocide. Like so many others with a Lublin or Globocnikian past, he claimed to have been a member of the *Waffen* (Fighting) *SS*.

> ...in 1940 he was temporarily released and employed with the *Fremdenverkehrsverband* Kaernten in connection with the resettlement of German hotel proprietors from South Tyrol. In September 1941 he joined the *Waffen-SS* and was appointed *Rasse und Seidlungsführer* at the Generalgouvernement in Cracow. In 1942 he was promoted *Sturmbannführer* and *in September 1943 he became a member of the staff of the Höherer SS-und Polizeiführer Adriatisches Kuestenland in Trieste.* The source held simultaneously the appointments of Adjutant to *SS-Gruppenführer* Globocnik, *Leiter der Arbeitsgemeinschaft für Fremdvölkische Verbaende* (dealing with the administration and political supervision of Cossack and Chetnik Formations) and that of a *Kampfgruppenführer* in charge of anti-partisan operations [emphasis added].[24]

When he came to giving an account of his nearly four years in Lublin with his wife and child, the tormenting and killing of hundreds of thousands of people, he told the British he was instead in Klagenfurt and Krakow and went on to claim he had met Globocnik only in September 1943, the very month the two in fact left Lublin together for Trieste. He had erased Lublin from his past. Clearly he knew he had much to hide, not least the fact that he had directed Globocnik's Jewish Affairs Department, and therefore had been Dr. Karl Hofbauer's successor.[25] In Berlin before the war he married a Gestapo employee, and Globocnik was one of his marriage ceremony witnesses. This may help explain the fact that Lerch approached, on behalf of his superior, Hans Maubach's secretary, Irmgard Rickheim, to ask if she was perhaps interested in marrying Globocnik. If nothing else, that shows how exceptionally close Lerch and Globocnik were. Lerch rose to the position of head of Globocnik's office, replacing Sepp Nemetz, who, in turn, had taken over from *SS-Obersturmführer* Paul Gasser, a close friend of Globocnik's, but one about whom little is known. Gasser (1904–1941?) hailed from Wolfsberg, and may have been a participant in the fateful Wolfsberg Group's short-lived 1934 eastern Carinthian uprising, mentioned above. Globocnik appears to have struck up a friendship with Gasser during the early 1920s, while he was based in northern Wolfsberg as an employee of KÄWAG. Globocnik may have even been a member of the Wolfsberg Group while stationed in this provincial town. Gasser was a member of the Globocnik group that reached Lublin early in November 1939, and served as his personal aide until late 1940, for about a year, when the two suddenly fell out. His significance is therefore that he helped lay the basis of Globocnik's Order in Lublin District. According to Dr. Berndt Rieger, Gasser's wartime fate has not been conclusively established, but it is believed that after the two Carinthians fell out, Gasser was keen to leave Lublin and volunteered for the Russian front in the summer of 1941, where he was a casualty within the first weeks of service.[26] Lerch's long-lasting relationship with Globocnik had a number of extremely secretive aspects, most of which are unlikely ever to be fully explained or unraveled. A case in point is that he had access to Globocnik's direct radio communications facility, giving him independent contact with Berlin, further evidence that he was something of an *eminence grise* as well as a close confidant who shared many, if not all, of Globocnik's darkest and most evil and murderous secrets. Wiesenthal also claimed Lerch "had been entrusted, by Globocnik's letter of 15 May 1941, with the department of Jewish affairs for the [Lublin] region."[27]

After the war Lerch managed to avoid full legal retribution for his murderous Lublin activities until 15 May 1972, when he finally faced trial. But three days after the trial commenced it was suspended to be indefinitely adjourned. It never resumed.

> Like Höfle — and indeed like nearly all Nazis in virtually all their trials — Lerch denied everything: he had done nothing and he had known nothing; besides it must be a case of mistaken identity.... All important evidence incriminating Lerch was only read out: the witness Runhof [aka Max Cichotski] stated that Lerch was, after Globocnik, the second highest SS officer and as such of course directly involved in all the actions of his superior.[28]

Wiesenthal, in 1971, intervened with Austria's Ministry of Justice in an effort to move proceedings against Lerch.

> Legally Lerch's vital contribution to mass murder was assessed as "remote accessory to murder," because in the view of the authorities Lerch had "only" been a so-called desk murderer. This figment, however, collapsed when one of Lerch's subordinates, the SS leader Hermann Worthoff, senior police officer and chief of the Gestapo in Lublin, stated in evidence during a trial in Germany that Lerch, as ranking officer, had overseen the liquidation of thousands of Jews from the Majdan-Tatarski ghetto in a wood near Krepiece.[29]

Lerch, the convivial and diplomatic *eminence grise*, may have developed influential contacts in postwar Austria, allowing him to block any attempt to bring him to book, even when at the wire. As late as 1997, the year he died, two researchers said of him and his two even more sinister Austrian colleagues: "Odilo Globocnik, Hans [sic] Höfle, and Ernst Lerch, the leaders of the *Aktion Reinhardt*, [were] responsible for the killing of 1.8 million Jews in the death camps in East Poland in 1942 and 1943."[30]

The two researchers went on to highlight the vast disparity between the way war criminals were treated in West Germany and Austria. In the former, a series of well-publicized trials were witnessed during the 1960s and 1970s, whereas in Austria "the past has been dealt with only by a very small circle of critical researchers."[31] Turning again to the quite obviously influential Klagenfurt café proprietor, they wrote:

> In Austria, however, there was no "large trial" at that time. Of the few proceedings that took place *some ended with incomprehensible acquittals:*
> Two days into the trial the prosecuting attorney dropped the charges against Ernst Lerch. Lerch was Odilo Globocnik's adjutant at the time of the *Aktion Reinhardt* mass murders. He was responsible for the killings of hundreds of partisans in and near Trieste as well [emphasis added].[32]

One of the "incomprehensible acquittals" was the Lerch trial, and until the relevant documents, which are probably held in certain Austrian party political, legal, and perhaps even police archives, are accessed and objectively analyzed, all that can be said with any degree of certainty is that Lerch was one of the 20th century's most destructive behind-the-scenes operatives. His skills appear to have been revived after the war, after bluffing his way past skilled British military interrogators; he went to his death in 1997 without ever having to pay the ultimate price for his enormous genocidal Lublin crimes. Notwithstanding this, the British held him for some time in Wolfsberg, from where he escaped and hid out between 1947 and 1950, after which he was able to arrange being de–Nazified. But it appears he was sentenced to a two-year term that was deferred because of his Wolfsberg internment. Lerch, a shadowy character, to say the least, certainly deserves far greater study and analysis, and such investigations could well reveal that he might have been even more significant in Lublin than Globocnik or Wirth, as a behind-the-scenes planner and coordinator.

Hans Maubach, Adjutant

Maubach, who hailed from Hagen, reached Lublin on 7 January 1940, in the company of his Berlin secretary Irmgard Rickheim and the temporary governor of Lublin District, SS man Friedrich Schmidt, who had taken up his position in October but left Lublin by March 1940. Later, Maubach's wife, Charlotte, who many believed was perhaps Jewish, also came to live in Lublin. Charlotte Maubach worked as a photographic cataloguer. Jewish workers with much pre-war photographic experience, carried out the development of photographs in her presence. Whether Charlotte did in fact have Jewish ancestry is not known. But if she did and her Jewish prisoner photographic co-workers also believed this was the case, then they experienced a most bizarre episode before eventually being murdered. Schmidt's term in Lublin was brief, because he was replaced by Ernst Zörner, the man who had

arranged German citizenship for Adolf Hitler soon after the end of World
War I. Maubach probably joined Globocnik's staff in 1941, having first worked
for Zörner's civilian government, as the officer-in-charge of military and other
vehicles, according to Rickheim. In Berlin he had been employed in Ribbentrop's Foreign Ministry, having joined the ministry in about 1936. While there
he oversaw youth matters, arranging excursions for foreign youth groups to
the Reich, as well as for German youth to other countries. He employed Rickheim after they met while she was working as a secretary in the *Hitler-Jugend's*
Berlin headquarters during 1938. They drove to Lublin, via Krakow, with
Schmidt, leaving Berlin on 5 January 1940. Maubach and Globocnik later
fell out, and Maubach left Lublin in September or perhaps October 1941,
about a year before Rickheim returned to Berlin after Globocnik had broken
off their liaison, though, as will be described later, under some duress.
Maubach's house, opposite Globocnik's mansion on Wieniawska Street (*Ostlandstrasse*), came to be used by Globocnik's mother, sister, and niece. Maubach, who, like Nemetz, fell out of favor with Globocnik, was pushed off to
become a member of the *Waffen-SS*, in the *Leibstandarte* Adolf Hitler, a fate
similar to that of several members of Globocnik's staff. Maubach met Globocnik once more after having left Lublin, but that was for just two hours, in
Trieste, in 1945. Maubach also spent time working for the infamous Leonardo
Conti, Reich Health Leader and head of the Department of Health in the
Interior Ministry, where Maubach founded the German Sauna Club.

Sepp Nemetz, Viennese Pal

As with Paul Gasser, little is known of Nemetz, also an Austrian. Of the
five inner staffers he was the oldest, in his late thirties when war broke out.
Nemetz had been a close pal of Globocnik's in Austria, and the two may have
spent time in jail together. According to the Israeli researcher, Tuviah Friedmann, Nemetz was born in Vienna on 25 April 1901. In Lublin he was accompanied by a female companion, probably with the name Benes, who apparently
was not his wife. He was involved as an underground activist in pre–*Anschluss*
Austria. His name surfaced in a secret letter sent by Himmler to Hitler's special emissary to Austria, Wilhelm Keppler, titled: "Organization plan for the
Movement in Austria and Situation Report." An enclosure showed Nemetz
to be head of one the networks of secret *Führer* Clans (*Führerstamme*), which
were responsible to Major Hubert Klausner, Rainer, and Globocnik. Nemetz
was at the head of what was called the workers' clan, suggesting he had been
involved in the industrial wing of the Austrian underground. Other so-called
clans oversaw farmers, youth, and people's auxiliaries, suggesting the word
was used to mean cell or guild.[33] Nemetz therefore stood outside the Austrian leadership group, which was largely Carinthian-dominated, but he was

closely associated with it. After Globocnik became *Gauleiter* of Vienna, Nemetz emerged in a significant party position, that of *Gau* inspector. In this position he was overseer of all the party's associated organizations duties, which included handling general political complaints from members. He also had the power to pardon those charged for misdemeanors. Nemetz was removed from this position soon after Globocnik lost his position of *Gauleiter*, suggesting that he had gained the position in a "jobs for the boys" maneuver. Like so many other former pals, Globocnik broke with him during his Lublin years. It would be most unlikely if Nemetz was not involved in one way or another in some of Globocnik's financial schemes and misbehavior.

Hermann Julius Höfle, Mass Killer and Ghetto Cleanser

Of the inner staffers, Höfle, Globocnik's chief-of-staff, was the one who probably traveled most widely across occupied Poland and was most often away from Lublin. He was later described as "an officer for special tasks." After Christian Wirth he was undoubtedly the most sinister and powerful in the Globocnik "court of killers." Statements made by Adolf Eichmann to Israeli police interrogators revealed that it was Höfle who demonstrated gassing equipment to Eichmann. Höfle was involved in the first "resettlements" of Jews to the Belzec killing center from within the General Gouvernement. Höfle's two secretaries were Hanna Fuhrmann, a Dresdener, and Berta Gottschall. Höfle's deputy was Helmut Pohl, a lieutenant who was born in Klagenfurt on 27 September 1901, and thus significantly, another Carinthian. Pohl was to be Globocnik's chief contact man for *Aktion Reinhardt*, and was based in the Julius Schreck Barracks (*Schreckkaserne*) with Höfle, from which he assisted in organizing the daily Jewish transports to Globocnik's three major extermination camps, the so-called "terminal stations."[34] Julius Schreck was a onetime member of an immediate post–World War I Red Army group in Germany, and later a longtime chauffeur of Hitler's. Hitler relied greatly on him and several others like him who also had shadowy pasts. Many of these men were ever-present with Hitler after he gained power in 1933, prompting the Nazi Party's sometimes iconoclastic press officer, Ernst "Putzi" Hanfstaengl, who later fled to the United States where he become a White House adviser on Nazism, to dub Schreck as a member of Hitler's "Chauffeureska"— the tightly-knit group of Bavarians surrounding and controlling access to their fanatical *Führer*. Julius Schreck was no doubt in the mind of another leftist and former Hitler colleague, Otto Strasser, when he wrote his apt one-liner on that motorized entourage: "He [Hitler] is surrounded not by friends but by accomplices, depraved and vicious creatures or blind and brutal instruments."[35]

According to Georg Michalsen, Höfle lived on site, that is, within the Julius Schreck Barracks.

The staff building was a three story-house. On the ground floor — immediately by the entrance — there was the transport squad. On the first floor — on one side — there was the administration, accounts and archive (documents) offices. Here, the chief-of-staff also had a room and an ante-room. On the second floor there was located the personnel department. Here Hermann Höfle also had his living quarters in one room.[36]

Born in Salzburg on 19 June 1911, Höfle joined the NSDAP on 1 August 1933, with party number 307,469, having become a member of the Austrian Nazi Party three years earlier. As well as being a trained mechanic, he had been a Salzburg taxi driver, and at one point even owned a taxi company. Höfle went on to join the SS and during the latter part of 1935 until January 1936, served time in a Salzburg police prison. A year later he headed *Sturmbann* 1/76, an organizational unit of the SS. Although a notoriously bad speller, he was judged to be honest, with a good intellectual grasp of matters, and a man with a strong will. He had briefly served in Sudetenland before the war, and after the conquest of Poland — 10 December 1939 until 1 September 1940 — he served either in the *Selbstschutz* in Nowy Sacz, southern Poland, or the *SD*; it is not clear which, but probably the latter. Beginning 1 November 1940, he served as an overseer of Jewish work camps associated with the Bug-Graben (Bug-Moat), a network of huge anti-tank ditches and tank traps southeast of Lublin, near Belzec, in the vicinity of where Globocnik's first major killing center of that name was erected in late 1941. This trench network was Globocnik's idea, and attracted scorn and criticism from military men because of its impracticality and futility. It is difficult to believe, however, that it was not inspired by someone senior to Globocnik, perhaps even Hitler himself, for the *Führer* had spoken before the outbreak of war of Lublin being a linchpin border outpost. Globocnik thought highly of Höfle, seeing him as someone who performed all his assignments in an impeccable way, and as someone who was suited to all the tasks given to him. Höfle was married and had four children. He is reported to have lost twins, an event that prompted him to believe that this was a form of punishment for his genocidal deeds against thousands of Jewish children whom he had sent to their deaths in one or another of Globocnik's killing centers. "This is the punishment for the children of Warsaw!," he is reported to have said at his children's graveside.[37] By late 1942, he had emerged as a divisional leader of *Aktion Reinhardt*, holding the rank of *SS-Hauptsturmführer*. One of his major tasks during this time was the clearing of the Bialystok and Warsaw Ghettos by transporting their inhabitants into the Treblinka and Belzec killing centers, especially the former. From his office within the Julius Schreck Barracks, Höfle initiated the moves to recruit several hundred so-called Soviet or Red Army prisoners-of-war, most of whom were Ukrainian captives, to become guards at the killing centers. These men were given a choice — die in their prisoner-of-war wire compounds or agree to work for their captors. The Julius Schreck Barracks also became the headquarters after late November 1942 for the Zamosc Lands cleansing action with Reinhold von Mohrenschildt in charge. The Ukrainians were trained at the Trawniki Camps, 40 kilometers southeast of Lublin. Their ranks included some men from the Baltic States, and some were even of ethnic German background. Höfle's other duties during the *Aktion Reinhardt* operation included overseeing collection of clothing and footwear of murdered Jews. Globocnik's other friend, Georg Wippern, as will be described below, was assigned at this time to the duty of collating the cash, bullion, and jewelry removed from Jews shortly before their deaths by gassing. Globocnik thought highly enough of Höfle to consider him for a post of leader of one of his 36 proposed major SS and police strongpoints to be located across European Russia, with Höfle to be in charge of one situated in Tiflis, Georgia. The strongpoints were the key component, the building blocks, of *Generalplan Ost*. After Globocnik pulled out of Lublin in September 1943, Höfle stayed on for some time. One of the tasks he completed in early November 1943 was the infamous Harvest Festival massacres (*Aktion Erntefest*) of some 42,000 Jews.[38]

> This operation was prepared and organized by Kruger and Globocnik. The preparations were carried out under the very strictest secrecy and apart from the two above named, the only others who were "in the picture" were [Jakob] Sporrenberg [Globocnik's Lublin successor], *Stubaf* Höfle, *Hptm* [Werner] Wehrheim and the *KdS Stubaf* Dr. Puetz.
>
> A great number of troopers were concentrated in Lublin consisting mainly of SS and Police troops. They came from various districts, such as Kattowitz, Krakow, Debica, Radom, etc. Their arrival early in November 1943 was timed in a way that they would arrive not before the eve of the action. [Hans] Offermann [a Globocnik adjutant who remained in Lublin after Globocnik's departure for Trieste] estimates that the approximate number of troops in Lublin at that time was 5000, all of them under Sporrenberg's command, for the purpose of this action. The pretext for the troop concentration was given out as a large scale fight against partisans.[39]

The above account, by Globocnik staffer Johann Offermann, aligns with another written soon after the war by the Polish historian and lawyer who was a member of Poland's Nuremberg team, Stanislaw Piotrowski. Piotrowski contended that Himmler gave the order to kill the remaining Jews of Lublin District, well over 40,000 of them, as early as August 1943, because of mounting fears that the belated 2 August uprising in Treblinka had sparked. But another uprising in the Sobibor killing center on 14 October broke out, and this led Himmler to believe that there existed a district-wide conspiratorial network.

The order was given via Friedrich-Wilhelm Kruger in Krakow, who called Globocnik's designated replacement, Jakob Sporrenberg, to Krakow. During the meeting Kruger read out Himmler's order:

To the Higher Commander SS and Police *Obergruppenführer* General in Krakow.
The Jewish problem in Lublin Distrikt has grown to extremely dangerous proportions. This matter must be solved once and for all. I order the Odilo Globocnik Unit to fulfil this matter. I hereby call the HSPF (*Ost*) and the SSPF in Lublin to give the unit all possible assistance. Heinrich Himmler.[40]

Himmler had also said:

"...form a special cordon of 2000 soldiers from units of a *Waffen-SS* Brigade" and Globocnik was to return to Lublin to oversee it. Apparently 150 Polish prisoners-of-war were included in the killings. These were held in a camp on Lipowa Street, Lublin. Sporrenberg inquired telegraphically about what should be done with them [the Poles] and Himmler replied "no exemptions."[41]

There were in Lublin and its immediate environs, according to Sporrenberg's calculations, 13,000 Jews, with a further 14,000 at the Poniatowa camp west of Lublin — some sources place this number as high as 18,000 — and 12,000 at Trawniki, southeast of Lublin. All those in work camps in and around Lublin perished either at Majdanek, on a huge shooting field near this camp, well away from the main road, or near the other camps. These, Globocnik's and Höfle's last victims in Poland, had survived *Aktion Reinhardt* because they were stationed in the various outer Lublin District work camps; Trawniki (10,000 prisoners); Poniatowa (18,000); and Majdanek, while several thousand more were in a number of smaller work camps, including Lipowa, which probably had on the order of 3,000 men. Polish historian Jozef Marszalek claims that all those held at Poniatowa were executed. According to Marszalek's account of this gruesome episode, in which Höfle was a central player:

Beginning from the autumn of 1943 executions by shooting were resumed in Majdanek as the basic form of mass executions. This period was — so to say — "inaugurated" by the executions of 3 November, the largest in the history of Majdanek and other concentration camps when 18,000 prisoners of Jewish extraction were killed. This murder of the remnants of the Jewish population incarcerated in the camps of the Lublin region was code-named *Erntefest* (Harvest Festival).[42]

German authorities during the autumn months of 1943 had become alarmed because of the Warsaw Ghetto Uprisings as well as similar Jewish resistance in Bialystok ghetto and rebellions in two of Globocnik's death camps,

Sobibor and Treblinka. Sporrenberg, after his capture in Oslo in 1945, was adamant that *Aktion Erntefest* was ordered by his predecessor, Globocnik, which was probably the case. On this English historian Robin O'Neil writes:

> When Globocnik was transferred to Trieste he was replaced by one of Himmler's most trusted police *führers*, SS-*Gruppenführer* Jakob Sporrenberg. Before Sporrenberg left for his new appointment in Lublin, Himmler had warned him not to concern himself with the Jewish Question as this was in the hands of Globocnik, and for the foreseeable future would remain so. In the course of a long and detailed talk on policy, Himmler ordered him to concentrate his efforts to look after the German settlers in Lublin, and that he expected the entire district to be Germanised by the end of 1944. Himmler also ordered him to build fortifications along the Bug River and along the 1941 Russo-German border. In fact, Sporrenberg was advised to occupy himself but on no account become involved in Jewish matters.[43]

The fact that Höfle conducted or oversaw the massive November killings with such brutal efficiency strongly suggests Globocnik was involved, though Sporrenberg cannot evade responsibility, for he was, by then, the senior SS and police chief of Lublin District. It is simply too difficult to believe that the senior SS man of a district would or could be unaware of the arrival of 5,000 troops in his area of command, even if he had not actually initiated that huge movement of men. Moreover, Friedrich-Wilhelm Kruger had read the Himmler order to him, so he knew a killing action was scheduled. That would hardly have perturbed Sporrenberg, who by then was one of Hitler's most hardened SS men. It is interesting to note the British interrogator's views with respect to Sporrenberg's role in relation to, if not in, *Aktion Erntefest*:

> ...[E]ven if the main burden of the work of killing 42,000 innocent human beings rested on Globocnik and his henchmen, such a task could not have been carried out by a mere handful of men in 14 hours. Sporrenberg admits that he obtained no reports from his commanders after the action and he would not, in fact, know, if these men participated in the actual killing or not. But they certainly assisted inasmuch as they brought the victims to their place of execution and then provided guards to see that none would expect their fate and that the action would not be interrupted from outside. To this, Sporrenberg himself had given detailed orders and the troops used for this purpose were under his sole command.[44]

After departing Lublin, Höfle briefly worked as commander of a guard battalion at Sachsenhausen concentration camp in the Reich, followed by time in the Netherlands and even Brussels, but rejoined Globocnik in Trieste. Rudolf Höss, commandant of the Auschwitz-Birkenau killing center, claimed Höfle was briefly at Oranienburg concentration camp where he was refused permission to take charge, but Höss is probably confused, and meant

Sachsenhausen.[45] Like Globocnik, Höfle committed suicide, but not until 21 August 1962, when in Vienna during pre-trial detention, perhaps suggesting that he was without the political pull of his onetime compatriot, the Carinthian *restaurateur*, Ernst Lerch. Of Höfle's Lublin days Wiesenthal wrote:

> Trained at the officers' school in Dachau, he first commanded a few smaller forced-labour camps and in the later summer of 1942 was dispatched to Warsaw. But the list of his crimes started even before Operation Reinhardt. From the office of the SS police chief of Lublin he conducted the "expatriation" of Jews from Mielec and Rzeszow prior to being responsible, from Lublin, for the deportation of 310,000 Jews from Warsaw to Treblinka, Sobibor, Belzec and Majdanek. When he was chief of staff of Operation Reinhardt the number of dead he was responsible for exceeded the two million mark. *In the hierarchy of the Nazi crime syndicate he ranks equal with Globocnik, immediately below Adolf Eichmann* [emphasis added].[46]

Höfle learned in 1948 that the Polish Communist Government had launched a search for him to have him extradited to face trial in Poland. He reacted to this alarming news by immediately turning to his Bavarian SS pals, who helped relocate him to Italy, where he lived until late 1950 or early 1951. Soon after returning to Austria, in March 1951, he made an unauthorized attempt to enter West Germany, but was arrested. Rather than hiding his true identity he told the court his correct name and said he was being sought by the Poles, who, he feared, wished to kidnap him. The following month he received West German identification papers, and was permitted to become a Bavarian resident. Notwithstanding all this good fortune and his efforts to go unnoticed, he came to the attention of the American Counter Intelligence Corp (CIC), as a possible informant on the activities of extreme right-wing groups and former SS men. At the time, the U.S. Army was interested in such people as well as Communists. Before hiring him, however, the Army placed him under surveillance for a time, after which he was called in for a discussion. Initially he resisted these overtures, but changed his mind and agreed to become a low-level agent.

A CIC assessment of Höfle, dated February 1954, was inaccurate largely because of bureaucratic incompetence or outright lethargy, probably both, but perhaps deliberately so.

> Subject is punctual, militant in action, truthful and trusting in persons only after his trustworthiness has been proven. Subject has been found to be most appreciative and courteous.... Based on information received from subject, he can be evaluated as fairly reliable at this time. Subject is considered "usually reliable" insofar as party activity of the SS and Gestapo is concerned. It is pointed out, however, in the majority of cases that subject must be asked specific questions during meetings because he is prone to minimize an occurrence or event rather than to magnify it.[47]

Höfle told his CIC controllers that he had served in the *Waffen-SS*, a story so many senior *Aktion Reinhardt* killers tended to spin, suggesting they probably jointly decided on this line. He further embellished this tale by claiming that he had fought partisans in Russia, so it was well tailored for the then Cold War atmosphere in Germany. He also claimed to be involved in "security work" in Poland. What remains mystifying is why the CIC failed to call up his SS file, which had been captured, along with every other SS members' file, by the U.S. military at the end of the war. If this had been done, all Höfle's lies would have been exposed. The CIC was also aware that the Polish (Communist) government was seeking Höfle, with Poland by then a loyal ally of the Soviet Union. His undercover name was to be Hans Hartman, and he drew a stipend of DM100 per month. But he was only a short term CIC informant, employed for only five months. At minimum, American bureaucratic lethargy was the reason for Höfle being able to avoid apprehension throughout the early 1950s. Added to this, in all likelihood, was an understandably widespread feeling among Americans of deep contempt for Communism, and thus disregard for quite legitimate Polish efforts to bring him to justice. It would be close to another decade before Höfle was apprehended to answer for his numerous wartime crimes. Höfle was thus a man who gained much from World War II, and extra years of freedom from the Cold War. As will be seen below, researchers, journalists, and others steadily learned during the 1960s and subsequent decades that certain American agencies that were involved in combating Soviet penetration of Western Europe at times employed people with SS backgrounds. This practice led at least one American group, based in California, to allege in the 1990s that Globocnik had been hidden away by the United States, an allegation that has no truth in it whatsoever.

Associated with Höfle's killing work in Lublin and described as "an officer for special tasks" was Amon Leopold Göth. He was transferred to southern Poland, where he commanded the concentration camp, Plaszow, near Krakow. Göth, unlike most others on Globocnik's inner staff, was brought to justice and tried after the war by Polish authorities. He was executed in Krakow on 13 September 1946, a fate that had also awaited Höfle in Poland, but that he managed to evade through lies, cunning, and guile.

Max Cichotski (aka Runhof), Loyal Outsider

Max Cichotski's surname is derived from the Polish word, "cicho," which means low voice, softly, silent. Strangely, it appears his personality was somewhat in tune with his name. He was not bombastic. He had, if not an aloof personality, then at least a rather withdrawn one. Of all Globocnik's assistants or adjutants he appears to have been the least assertive. Yet, he was the only member of Globocnik's staff who, apparently willingly, gave evidence: Behaving contrary to what his Polish name implied, he did not remain silent, unlike other more formerly assertive war criminals.

Because Cichotski spoke Polish fluently, Globocnik was able to use him as an interpreter and, at times, his driver. During most of his time in Lublin, Cichotski was single, but became romantically involved and proved to be a welcomed provider because of the abundance of goods that he could so easily acquire as a member of Lublin's new ruling racial elite, the racial nomenclatura. Like Lerch and Michalsen, he followed Globocnik to Trieste in September 1943. After the war Cichotski was captured and interned by the Soviets, returning to live in West Germany only in 1947, the year Höfle left Germany for Italy. But Cichotski now used the name Runhof, which he had adopted during the latter part of the war. However, he did not gain official permission to use that new name until 1958. Some time later he remarried. It was Cichotski whom Globocnik designated to escort his former fiancée, Irmgard Rickheim, when she was driven back to her home city of Berlin with several containers of chattels in late 1942. Cichotski applied to join the SS, having had a career for several years as a leader with the *Hitler-Jugend*. Cichotski met Maubach in Munich, either in 1947 or 1948, and Maubach indicated that he was seriously considering leaving Germany to settle probably in either Norway or Sweden. Whether such a decision was being considered because of Maubach's Lublin experience is not known, and whether his intention, and presumably also Charlotte Maubach's, to leave postwar Germany was fulfilled is also not known.

Cichotski gave a detailed statement in response to a Wiesbaden subpoena, issued by a special commission, the Office of the Hessian Criminal Investigation Department, dated 15 September 1961. According to the statement, he was born on 25 March 1916, and attended school at Lechowe and later at Bydgoszcz (Bromberg), in Poland's agriculturally productive northern Kujawy region. His father had been a farmer but had died when Cichotski was aged 20, after which he became an apprentice interior decorator and attended art and craft school, pursuing contemplative disciplines. Cichotski was active in the scouting movement and worked with ethnic Germans in northern Poland as well as Pomerania. As a Polish citizen, he was drafted into the Polish army for two years, and just before Poland was invaded in September 1939 he was called up. He deserted by not answering the call to arms, and fled to the Reich, via Danzig (Gdansk) and Konigsberg, making his way to an uncle, a co-owner of a Berlin interior decorating company. The young fugitive found work for which he was qualified. Because Poland was quickly defeated in September 1939, he was never charged for desertion. A chance meeting with an *SS-Obersturmführer* Horst Ranke resulted in Cichotski gaining a foreign office position as a Reich youth leader. It was Ranke, who was either based in or had lived in Lodz (Litzmannstadt), who told Cichotski that he could gain work in Lublin. The crucial fact here may have been Cichotski's fluency in Polish, since all Germans in the General Gouvernement were being consolidated in designated areas and suburbs of Polish cities or across western Poland, and not all spoke German. Cichotski claimed he wore his *Hitler Jugend* uniform, not an SS uniform, while he was one of Globocnik's adjutants, and this affectation may have alienated him somewhat from those in the SS and Globocnik's inner circle. Between early 1940 and about May 1942, he worked as an *Oberscharführer* of the *Hitler-Jugend*, having the Lublin, Hrubieszow, and Chelm areas as his bailiwick. While in Chelm, during the spring of 1942, he was offered the post of adjutant to Globocnik. It is possible that Cichotski, during these years, worked as an interpreter with Ukrainians who spoke Polish, since they were partners of the Germans and had been set against ethnic Poles. Maubach, who had also been involved in youth affairs within the Foreign Ministry in Berlin before the outbreak of war, may have been instrumental in this change in duties, though this is conjecture. Cichotski held his Lublin position until September 1943, when he and Globocnik's *Aktion Reinhardt* team drove south to Trieste.

No evidence appears to exist linking Cichotski directly to *Aktion Reinhardt* but he was definitely involved, and at a senior level, in the Zamosc Lands expulsion, perhaps because of his association with *Hitler-Jugend* cadres in various newly-occupied former Polish villages. An unsigned August 1943 document exists which carries a comprehensive list of all the resettled or cleansed villages and other or associated Polish rural settlements. Copies of that document went to, among others, Globocnik; Cichotski (though his name was spelled "Ciechotzky" in the reproduction); Lerch, as the *RKFDV* representative; Dunkel; Gustav Hanelt; Construction Commissioner Richard Thomalla; Georg Michalsen; and Hermann Höfle. Cichotski, in other words, was in significant SS company, deemed one needing to be notified of aspects of the Germanization process being undertaken across the Zamosc Lands. This strongly suggests that he would have been involved in similar adjunct work had *Generalplan Ost* been implemented fully across Ukraine, Belarus, and Russia, as intended. The introduction to that memorandum reads:

> Between November/December 1942 and July 1943 Germans colonized by the Zamosc County, and the adjacent shire of Szczebrzeszyn; Bilgoraj country and the shire of Miaczyn; Hrubieszow County (according to Polish topographical descriptions), 107 villages, 46 colonies, and 60 hamlets.
>
> Because there is no German equivalent for the Polish terms "colony" and "hamlet" from now on all such settlements will be referred to as villages. All these listed in the table below shall henceforth be called villages by the SS Police *Führer* and the commissioner of the Reich Commission for the Strengthening of Germandom.

There are altogether 126 German villages, which form 11 major regional villages. From now on there will only be reference made to 126 villages in Zamosc County.[48]

The memorandum shows conclusively that none of its recipients could claim ignorance of the fact that a vast region-wide expulsion campaign had been effected against Polish peasants, and that Germans of varying backgrounds were being settled in their place. The disparity between the 126 figure and the total of 213 settlements (villages, colonies, and hamlets in Polish parlance) under whatever name meant that 87 of these had simply been eliminated, that is, probably destroyed, literally. Unfortunately, this memorandum, which advises of changes to nomenclatura, fails to tell us in what capacity Cichotski served in at this time. But the fact that his name was included indicates he most certainly had some form of senior level involvement. Cichotski was therefore relevant. As will be seen below, he was fully aware of Himmler's and Globocnik's paramount interest in creating SS and police strongpoints in the East, but first across the Lublin District. It is therefore safe to conclude that he had a good grasp of Nazi and SS demographic planning and ideology, like von Mohrenschildt, and was helping to implement it, at least in relation to the Slavs, in this case specifically the Poles, if not the extermination of the Jews.

Cichotski remained in Trieste as Globocnik's personal adjutant until August 1944, when he claims he was drafted into the *Waffen-SS's* 3rd Communications Regiment in the Death's Head Division. The move to the *Waffen-SS* led to his service on the Hungarian Front, and his capture at Saatz, Czechoslovakia, by Soviet troops. He became a Soviet prisoner-of-war for 18 months, working in Upper Silesia's Hindenburg mines. How he managed to be released is not known, but he claimed to have reached Munich, where friends from Lodz (Litzmannstadt) assisted him. Cichotski revealed in his Wiesbaden Court statement that he had, in 1947 or 1948, met Maubach in Munich. Maubach was then living in Augsburg, and at different times he had also met Höfle, who was working in Munich, first in a scrap metal yard and later in a glass factory, before Höfle fled to Italy to ensure that agents of the Polish government did not capture him. Höfle told Cichotski that Ernst Lerch was still alive, and that Reinhold von Mohrenschildt was also still living. He also discovered that Globocnik's long-time personal private secretary, Mimi Trsek, was living in Vienna. Interestingly, therefore, some members of Globocnik's Lublin team kept in contact, if only irregularly and on an *ad hoc* basis, and they inquired about each other's whereabouts and fate. According to Cichotski, Himmler had visited Lublin three times, not just once as is generally believed, always in the company of an *Obersturmbannführer* Grothmann, that is, his military adjutant. This number of alleged visits is markedly below that cited by several other senior SS men after the war. Cichotski's Wiesbaden statement says:

> Q. What were the reasons for Himmler's and [Karl] Wolff's visits?
> A. I assumed Himmler came to speak about the establishment of the [SS and Police] Strongpoints in the East. With his visits I had to do everything to make him comfortable. I was not there for discussions. When Wolff came he also did so to discuss the Strongpoints. I know he went to some of these places when in Lublin.[49]

The Wiesbaden interrogation then moved on to inquire how Wirth had met Globocnik. Cichotski recalled that both *Aktion Reinhardt* executive officers had spent about three to four months together — he did not name those months — and that "all Globocnik's commanders were asked to come for discussions, which Wirth attended." Cichotski named these commanders as Kientrup, Georg Wippern, Johannes Müller, and Ernst Lerch, with a *Sturmbannführer* Magill also probably present. He said he had tried to attend these meetings, but was excluded by "someone close to Globocnik." That someone, he believed, was Lerch, who, he said, jealously guarded Globocnik's direct line to Himmler. Once, in his capacity as an occasional chauffeur, Cichotski drove Globocnik to a camp outside Lublin, on Cholmer Strasse, where Lerch was waiting to receive his superior. The two spent 45 minutes inside the camp, with Cichotski not being permitted to join them.

> Q. When did you hear of the Belzec and Sobibor camps?
> A. In connection with Belzec and Sobibor we only spoke of work camps. During a Himmler visit we got the order to collect a commando to escort Himmler to Sobibor. When Globocnik drove to Belzec or Sobibor we also had an escort. For the escorts Kientrup was responsible for this and we called this Hunting...?[50]

Although Cichotski denied any knowledge of what was actually going on inside both the Belzec and Sobibor killing centers, he was exceptionally well informed about other matters. For instance, when quizzed about Globocnik's little-known but major mental breakdown, he went into considerable detail, since he had been closely involved with Globocnik during this embarrassing and seemingly perilous ordeal.

> A. It must have been in the spring of 1943. One day Globocnik left his office in the evening without his cap and coat. Sometime later he appeared in Wippern's flat from where I was called. I met him and he was completely oblivious to events around him (*Geisesabwesenden*). Only some hours later was he able to leave the house. Wippern had already mentioned to me that Globocnik had suffered a nervous breakdown. When I went back with Globocnik to his office I tried to find out what had really happened. He always said everything was

terrible and I should not ask him further. Then he begged me that if he should not survive that I should look after his mother and sister.

Q. Do you remember Professor [Wilhelm] Pfannenstiel?

A. Pfannenstiel was announced by Himmler's adjutant that he would come from Berlin. In this connection I received the order that I should accommodate Pfannenstiel in Globocnik's house. I told Globocnik about my order and he said Pfannenstiel should be accommodated in a guesthouse. When he arrived, Pfannenstiel, after dinner, had a long talk with Globocnik near the fireplace where they remained undisturbed.

Q. Which members of Globocnik's staff mainly dealt with expulsions?

A. Globocnik had so-called special command units. The leaders were Höfle, Michalsen and Claasen. These often came to Globocnik to report on their progress. I remember when Höfle came from Warsaw and Michalsen from Bialystok. All the internal things went to Lerch who knew everything. I never attended these talks.[51]

Pfannenstiel, about whom more will be said later, was undoubtedly on a crucially important confidential errand on behalf of Himmler, since the *Reichsführer-SS's* man on a mission to kill Jews and cleanse Slavs in the East had suddenly weakened by having an unexpected breakdown, and this before both eastern missions that Hitler had assigned to Himmler — extermination of the Jews and expulsion of the Poles — had been completed. Unfortunately, there is no reference to the breakdown in Globocnik's SS file, so we can say nothing more of it with any degree of certainty. It may have been brought on by heavy drinking, but it may also have been caused by something far more serious, such as pangs of conscience or related matters, such as a dashed love affair. We will probably never know. It is important to remember that Globocnik, by the spring of 1943, had killed some 1.5 million Jews, and was well on the way to completing the clearance of the Zamosc Lands of its Polish peasant farmers. But there were many other problems, most of which we know only a little about, so can only raise them and say little more. First and foremost, by May 1943, Globocnik's mother was, or had recently been, in Lublin for an extended period. What was Anna Globocnik's view of or role in relation to her son's life of mass murderer of Jews? Did she know the full extent of his duties? He was undoubtedly very close to her, something even Himmler realized. If she approved of his murderous ways, then surely he would have had doubts about the standing and character of his loving mother. If not, then he was hiding a deep, dark, murderous secret from someone he loved and cherished. Also, he had, by then, lost his fiancée, Irmgard Rickheim. Rickheim has claimed she was unaware of his *Aktion Reinhardt* activities, suggesting that neither his mother nor his fiancée knew what was really happening beyond Lublin. All the evidence is that he deeply and passionately loved this much younger Berliner. She was probably the only woman he had ever truly and passionately loved. They had lived together in Lublin for several months and had been sexually intimate throughout that period. But Rickheim had left Lublin due to a conspiracy that was, possibly, perpetrated and taken advantage of by people close to him, if not by Himmler himself, as will be considered later. Perhaps even his mother was involved, and he may have discovered, or at least suspected, this. And finally, by May 1943, the Reich's military fortunes, especially on the crucial Eastern Front, were being dramatically reversed, and it was now time to begin considering the likelihood of the Reich's defeat, and all that would mean to men close to Himmler. Thoughts may have even turned to a day of reckoning in an Allied or a postwar German court, along the lines attempted, under Allied pressure, in Weimar Germany during 1919–20. Added to all this were the mounting problems of fighting Polish peasant and other guerillas across the Zamosc Lands, who were doggedly fighting back and killing German soldiers as well as settled German farmers. Perhaps this had prompted second thoughts about the wisdom of launching that cleansing action, something many had warned against and that some had even sought to bring to an end. Globocnik was also a plotter and a schemer, so he undoubtedly had many other worries and concerns. It would have been surprising if someone at the center of so much murderous machinating and goings-on had not at some stage broken down mentally.

Interestingly, in light of Cichotski's revelation, in July 1943, very soon after Globocnik's breakdown, only one Polish Underground newspaper (*Samo Obronia*) carried a report claiming Globocnik had been the subject of an assassination attempt that was allegedly perpetrated by Germans.[52] It seems most likely that the rumor and gossip about the breakdown were the origins of that report, with whisperings that the mental disorder had stemmed from an attempt on Globocnik's life. And finally, Rickheim has disclosed that Globocnik was a regular consumer of pills to either pep himself up or calm himself down; she does not know which. He was, then, secretly consuming medication for some complaint, real or imagined. Rickheim said that when Globocnik sat down to undertake a bout of evening work with certain staffers in his mansion, he would first resort to these pills. Those involved in typing for Globocnik were his secretary Mimi Trsek, who in 1943 was 25 years old, a police civil servant called Kobler, and another called Weber.

> Q. Who was the administrator of secret matters?
> A. It was Lerch.
> Q. Did the office of Globocnik have radio and telecommunications?
> A. Our telegrams passed through the Governor's telecommunication network and some through the Security Police. Our office had one teleprinter and the responsible staff. The staff were Nemetz, Höfle, and Lerch. Working on these were SS and Police signals personnel. I don't know who they were.
> Q. Who took a telegram after working hours?
> A. I would take it and pass it on to Lerch and Globocnik.

Q. Was there in these telegrams information on Jews?
A. These were sealed envelopes and I did not have the right to open them.[53]

Georg Wippern, Keeper of the Vault

Georg Wippern was a central figure in the organized process of robbing Globocnik's Jewish victims: He gathered and processed the loot taken from them as they faced death. He was born on 26 May 1909, in Hildesheim, and in the early 1960s was living in Jaegersburg, District of Homberg/Saar Eichelscheider Strasse 61. He was still in his early thirties while based in Lublin. After the war he was a customs inspector in Saarbrücken, a career not far removed from his wartime Lublin duties where he oversaw the processing and forwarding of valuables (bullion) and goods to Berlin, and some, it seems, also to Krakow. In Lublin, of course, he dealt in stolen property, whereas after the war it was with legitimate trade.

Like so many of Globocnik's staffers, Wippern was located by the West German or Bonn government's war crimes investigators in the early 1960s, after the capture and interrogation of Adolf Eichmann, when Germany's state and federal governments combined to launch wide-ranging investigations into the murderous and thieving activities of the SS men based in, among other places, Lublin. These investigations, coordinated by the specially created *Zentrale Stelle der Landesjustizverwaltungen* based in Ludwigsburg, north of Stuttgart, quickly and inevitably came to focus a substantial portion of their time and effort upon the central role of Lublin within Hitler's and Himmler's secret genocidal activities, which Globocnik headed.

Wippern was for some time closer to Globocnik than all his other staffers, with the exception of Lerch. He was in charge of smelting precious metal artifacts and the tallying of currency, bullion, and other valuables, including gems, pearls, and diamonds, taken from victims, primarily Jews. His sorting and processing unit was known as *Abteilung Reinhardt* and *Abteilung IVa*. Assigned to Wippern were two senior men, *SS-Unterscharführers* Eichholz and Dorl. Although they worked at different times, they had assigned to them between 20 and 30 Jews who were involved in sorting and storing the high-value possessions removed from hundreds of thousands of Jewish families who had been railed in from many parts of Poland and Western and Eastern Europe by Eichmann and his assistant, Franz Novak. Wippern, however, was directly responsible to *SS-Obergruppenführer* Oswald Pohl in Berlin, nominally at least. He also had assigned to him trained banking personnel — *SS-Obersturmführer* Huber, *SS-Oberscharführers* Teichelmann and Rzepa, and an *SS-Unterscharführer* Pflanzer — because the sorting and classifying work had simply overtaken his staff. These men, who may not have been in Lublin at the same time, were involved in registering all valuables and their storage in a specially built steel strong room from whence much of the loot was moved by truck to the *SS-WVHA (Wirtschaftsverwaltungshauptamt)*, in Berlin, after which it was transferred to the *Reichsbank*. Wirth had also placed Wippern in overall charge of a facility called the Used Materials Administration Deport of the SS Administration Office. Wippern's first postwar court statement set out his duties and gives an insight into how he came to acquire this position:

> As I have already stated at an earlier examination especially by the public pros-ecutor of Hamburg, I as *Sturmbannführer* was leader of the SS-Garrison admin-istration in Lublin. In this capacity it was my duty to be responsible for the *Waffen-SS* units in Lublin Distrikt, generally speaking, for the troop admin-istration as well as caring for troop units passing through; articles of clothing, board and lodging payment. I was under the authority of the *Wirtschafstver-waltungshauptamt* [Central Economic Administration Office] of the *Waffen-SS* in Berlin (headed by Oswald Pohl). In 1942, the exact time I cannot give, the so-called housekeeper administrator in Krakow was switched from *SS-Stan-dartenführer* Schellin. Furthermore, I reported to the SS and Police Leader Globocnik because tasks were added, as for example the Settlers Economic Community in Zamosc and one of the *Reichführer's* representative for estab-lishing SS and Police Strongpoints in the New Eastern Territory, which was headed by Globocnik. Furthermore, I was made responsible for the adminis-tration of various business firms in Lublin Distrikt. In all those establishments I only had administrative functions.[54]

Wippern, for reasons unknown, but perhaps because he was so close to Globocnik, was considered significant enough by Governor General Dr. Frank to meet separately in Lublin. Frank, during his May 1942 visit to this largely SS-controlled city, went out of his way to meet Wippern in hospital. Wip-pern was in hospital because he had apparently been badly wounded.[55] Details of his injury are unknown, and it is also not known if it was sustained while he was with Globocnik during the alleged ambush aimed at assassinating Globocnik.[56] An SS man of not particularly high rank, like Wippern, receiv-ing a visit from occupied Poland's general-governor seems to be an unusual occurrence. Whether Frank did it because of some clandestine financial links between himself or one of his departments and the close Globocnik friend remains unknown. But it is probably significant that some of the loot Wip-pern processed was in some way directed to an SS officer in Krakow, for a time an *SS-Standartenführer* Schellin. Whether Frank was aware of this and precisely what was being done with that flow of valuables to Krakow also remains unknown. Wippern certainly had access to considerable amounts of stolen cash, bullion, and jewelry, so it is not incorrect to consider him one of the 20th century's biggest larcenists. But to go beyond that is guesswork.

Wippern's first court statement outlines in some detail how he came to be the SS's Lublin-based "Keeper of the Vault" and the conduit for dispatching and disposing of the loot taken from murdered Jews to Berlin, and some to Krakow.

In this context I want to mention that in the beginning I had nothing to do with jewelry and valuables. But then I was asked to come to Pohl in Berlin, who from then on put me in charge for the registration and delivery of valuables and jewelry. On this occasion I learned that they were Jewish property. Because of that I wanted to refuse handling this task, but finally in a fierce battle of words was referred by Pohl to the Brüning Emergency Decree from the year 1932. According to the [Heinrich] Brüning Emergency Decree where there was given an order that non-registered foreign currency and precious metals were due for confiscation. Enforcement of this law was an obligation of the Reich's finance authorities. At this meeting I heard for the first time the name Wirth. Because Wirth initially delivered the confiscated jewelry and valuables in a disorderly condition at the *Reichsbank* in Berlin, now this work should be done by me, nothing but as a purely administration specialist. In this context I refer to the statements which I made at the Public Prosecutor's Office in Hamburg. According to this, Wirth was obliged to deliver the valuables to me. This way I came to know Wirth. I want to emphasize that those jewels and valuables delivered to me not only came from extermination camps but also from SS and Police Leaders in Warsaw and other places.[57]

On 1 December 1962 Wippern, signed another statement for the Public Prosecutor's Office at the Munich District Court. This was obtained as part of the investigations into the activities of Josef Oberhauser, one of Christian Wirth's chief aides, and a man who had spent nearly 10 months at the Belzec killing center, and had the blood of many hundreds of thousands of people on his hands. Like the others, Oberhauser was recruited from the Euthanasia Program, having being a corpse burner at three of this program's killing "hospitals." Oberhauser was also in charge of the Ukrainian Guard, men who were a crucial element in the Jewish extermination program being directed by Globocnik from Lublin, and who had been recruited from Soviet prisoner-of-war compounds. Oberhauser was tried in Munich in 1965, and was sentenced to four years six months "for the crime of acting as an accessory in the common murder of 300,000 people."[58] Wippern, as pointed out, was the key man in charge of collecting and collating valuables, as well as all the smelting of platinum, silver, and gold that had been sequestered from condemned Jews as they were about to be murdered. Because so many of the not less than 1.5 million victims were from outside the Lublin Distrikt, one of the major items Wippern collected was foreign currency — notes and coins — from a wide variety of countries. Wippern's statement reads:

In my capacity as leader of the SS-garrison administration Lublin I received in spring 1942 from the leader of the main economic administration [Oswald] Pohl in Berlin the order to take charge of and sort out all jewelry, valuables and foreign currency and other money confiscated from Jews and to maintain their correct delivery. Accumulated jewelry and valuables, as well as foreign currency was delivered to the central economic administration, and the *Reichsbank* in Berlin, on receipt. Jewelry was melted down if the design was not of special value and then delivered to the *Reichsbank* as gold bars. The same happened with silver. Local currency (Polish Zloty) was transferred by my office at Emissions Bank in Lublin to an account at the *Reichsbank* in Berlin.

I neither had power of disposition of these transferred objects nor over the proceeds derived from them. For that I was threatened with capital punishment. The transport of confiscated goods to my office was done using locked and sealed suitcases. After these suitcases arrived, receipt was confirmed by number without referring to their content. They were broken open (there were no keys for opening them at my office) and their contents was sorted and recorded in an account book. Safekeeping at my office was done with a special safe, a vault, with two different locks. This was to ensure that the safe could only be opened in the presence of two persons. Until delivery was made to my department there were no assurances because exact bookkeeping and checking of the confiscated objects was not maintained. This was because there was no enclosed inventory list with the individual suitcases. I could not have known in advance if there were smaller or larger boxes. I wish to say that the bearers could have easily replaced larger cases with smaller ones, especially since my office only confirmed delivery of a certain number of suitcases. With this in mind, when I am confronted with accusations, I already had the order from Pohl to register and deliver confiscated goods. The delivery of such objects was directed to Berlin by use of couriers, so according to my orders and in my view there were underhand practices. If I'd known this at the time I can give an assurance that I would have immediately informed the *Wirtschaftsverwaltungshauptamt* in Berlin.[59]

It is possible, as Wippern stated here, that he was threatened with death, perhaps by Globocnik in Lublin, while in charge of the *Aktion Reinhardt* loot. The threat, if made by Globocnik, no doubt arose from the fact that certain people in authority in Berlin and Lublin either believed, suspected, or realized that some of it that was destined for Wippern's department, the *Abteilung Reinhardt* and *Abteilung IVa*, was being stolen. That Wippern highlighted the weaknesses in the processing procedures and in the conveying of the loot shows how much this issue concerned him at the time and that it was still at the forefront of his mind nearly two decades after the *Aktion Reinhardt* crime was perpetrated. His court statement went on:

> I know with certainty that *Waffen-SS* members working in the extermination camps as well as the remaining personnel did not receive their salaries from my department. Furthermore, I know with certainty, that *Waffen-SS* members on my payroll did not receive a special grant at Christmas, nor did they get a previously determined special vacation.[60]

Although it is difficult to determine precisely why Wippern made the above comment, it is likely that he did so to distance himself from the actual

killing of Jews, as opposed to processing the loot taken from them. Wippern
undoubtedly thought long and hard before putting pen to paper, and understandably so. Processing and smelting stolen valuables, he may have calculated, was certainly not a capital crime. He may have believed that it was
unlikely that he would be punished for such wartime deeds in occupied
Poland. However, if he was identified as perhaps being Globocnik's paymas-
ter of *Aktion Reinhardt* personnel, then that was an entirely different matter.
That could easily have raised his level of complicity and culpability.

> Furthermore, I remember that I had repeatedly participated at meetings at the
> office of SS Police leader, Lublin, [Odilo Globocnik]. I remember for sure that
> Wirth had also attended those meetings several times. There were, at times,
> office leader conferences, where all office leaders of SS and police took part.
> The subjects of the official conference topic discussions I do not remember in
> particular, but mostly they dealt with general garrison or security matters.
>   Special topics were always discussed in closed circles, because they were sub-
> ject to official secrecy and also could not be of interest to other departments.
> I can say here with certainty that at the department leader meetings, where I
> was present, questions regarding *Action Reinhardt* were not dealt with. That
> applies especially to internal matters.[61]

Wippern here is surprisingly candid in stating that he attended what can
fairly be described as planning meetings with Globocnik, though he was careful to state that he could not recall what was discussed, except, of course, by
claiming the issues were "general garrison or security matters," seemingly innocuous procedural affairs. Here he is undoubtedly distancing himself from
Aktion Reinhardt meetings or discussions, which inevitably included at least
Globocnik, Wirth, Höfle, Lerch and Michalsen, to name some. At meetings
that Wippern claimed he attended, "questions regarding *Aktion Reinhardt*
were not dealt with," he deliberately added.

Wippern concluded this statement by saying that he was familiar with
the names Oberhauser and Hackenholt, the second being Globocnik's gassing
expert, though he did not know either man, and therefore could not recognize them in photographs. This may be true, for Wippern was based in Lublin,
whereas they were generally away from that city, at one of Globocnik's killing
centers. Wippern did, however, admit to knowing Georg Michalsen, describing him as someone "of sturdy build and thick set." Although it is most
unlikely that Wippern was unaware of the murders being perpetrated in Globocnik's killing centers, he appears to have been careful not to become involved
in this side of *Aktion Reinhardt*. But there is good reason to believe that he,
Globocnik's and Himmler's "keeper of the vault" in Lublin, was not satisfied
that all loot being taken from Jews arriving at Belzec, at least, was reaching
him.

In December 1942 *Sturmbannführer* Wippern at the Lublin *SS-Standortverwaltung* [garrison administration] sent his chief accountant, *SS-Unterscharführer* Wilhelm Schwarzkopf, to Belzec to deal with the camp commandant. Commandant Hering, however, told him on arrival that he did not need any "snoopers" there. Schwarzkopf then waited in Belzec for two weeks without being able to gain entry to the camp. During this time Wippern himself turned up in Belzec on several occasions, but quickly left again each time.[62]

Finally, Wippern's work was part of a wider robbing operation. Himmler had ordered all his Higher *SS-und Polizeiführers* in the Eastern Territories on 12 August 1942 to send all precious metals and other valuables to the *SS-WVHA* for distribution to appropriate authorities, primarily the *Reichsbank*. Globocnik sent an interim report to Himmler in February 1943 on amounts collected that will be considered in Chapter XII and XIII. His subsequent communication — the signing-off report prepared — which he did with Wippern and Rzepa, was dated 15 December 1943 and sent to Himmler from Trieste.

Wippern joined Globocnik's Vienna friend, Kajetan Mühlmann, the plunderer of Poland's art, as one of the war's biggest thieves.

Reinhold von Mohrenschildt, Roving Eastern Ethnic Cleanser

This Carinthian deserves special attention because of his expertise in the management of demographic issues other than extermination. Reinhold von Mohrenschildt was the son of a wealthy Carinthian ducal family that had quietly backed the illegally operating Austrian Nazis in Klagenfurt and surrounds throughout much of the 1930s. Von Mohrenschildt played a key role in Carinthia's political realignment during Austria's crucial pre–*Anschluss* days.[63] Both he and his sisters were members of the *SD*, a clandestine Nazi family if ever there was one. In all likelihood, he was Globocnik's closest and most knowledgeable adviser on population cleansing in Lublin. For a time, while serving as an SS man in Poland, he even lived with Globocnik in his Lublin mansion on Wieniawska Street (*Ostlandstrasse*). However, this arrangement ended when Globocnik's fiancée, Berliner and former Maubach secretary, Irmgard Rickheim, moved into the mansion in the summer of 1941. Precisely why this friendship became so close is unknown, whether it was because he was a "von," or that the two had known each other so well in Carinthia, or because of their dedication to an ideology and its resultant demographic Pan-German commitments that so appealed to Hitler and Himmler. It was probably a blend of all these reasons. In Lublin, von Mohrenschildt assisted Globocnik in the strengthening of Germandom matters. He was directly involved in the transfer of eastern, mainly from Wolyn (Volhynia), ethnic Germans, west following the 3 November 1939 German-Soviet transfer treaty that resulted in over 100,000 such *Volksdeutsche* being moved from there as well as Galicia and the Narew District for settlement across tracts of western Poland, which had been incorporated into the Reich the previous month. During this period von Mohrenschildt was a commanding officer of a cavalry unit of the 2nd *Totenkopf Reiterregiment*, which was involved in protecting these settlers as they moved across central Poland. Such protection was required because Polish partisans, already dubbed "bandits," were a threat. Such duties also meant that he was only intermittently in Lublin, already an emerging SS and demographic planning center by early 1941. His *RKFDV* work arose from the fact that he was serving on the staff of Werner Lorenz, head of the SS's *Volksdeutsche Mittelstelle (VoMi)*.[64] Mohrenschildt was an assistant to Lorenz, and held executive powers in Lorenz's galaxy of varied demographic wartime duties. As a result, he found himself, off and on, in Lublin for extended or briefer periods. An appreciation of his roving demographic duties as a senior Lorenz staffer can be gleaned from a brief extract of a description of Lorenz's wartime duties.

> During World War II it [*VoMi*] had a considerable role in the transportation and "resettlement" of Germans in Poland, the Baltic States and the USSR to the Greater Reich. At the same time it sought to Germanize Poles and other foreign nationals who came under its protection.... The *VoMi* was eventually merged to form the Reich Office of the Consolidation of German Nationhood [*RKFDV*]. As head of the resettlement staff of the *RKFDV* and in charge of the International Relations Division of the SS Central Department, Lorenz was the chief executive in Himmler's drive to absorb racial Germans into the Reich and extend SS power in the occupied territories.[65]

This biographical entry is flawed to the extent that it ignores the fact that *VoMi*, *RuSHA*, and *RKFDV* commando units — meaning von Mohrenschildt, the roving, almost itinerant, demographic expert — were also intricately involved in the expulsion of non-Germans, that is, ethnic Poles, from various designated regions of occupied Poland, eventually including the Zamosc Lands. Von Mohrenschildt's direct participation and therefore inevitable insider's knowledge of the SS's overall eastern demographic activities, especially between early 1940 and the autumn of 1943, were therefore quite unchallengeable. If there was anyone who knew what the Hitler-Himmler eastern demographic plans and methods were, then that person was undoubtedly *SS-Hauptsturmführer* Reinhold von Mohrenschildt. Those insights meant his irregular Lublin stopovers ensured Globocnik's work was in line with the SS's wider scheme of things. Relevant here, however, is the fact that he also participated in the planning and the actual expulsion of the 110,000 Polish peasant farmers from the Zamosc Lands after 28 November 1942 — the actual launching of *Generalplan Ost*. In this regard von Mohrenschildt is unfortunate, because he spent much of the rest of his postwar life denying he was in any way implicated in criminal activities. Significantly, Globocnik had appointed him his deputy for this important new population cleansing operation, and based him in Lublin's Julius Schreck Barracks, from where the day-to-day detailed planning, administration, and coordination of *Aktion Reinhardt* was conducted by Christian Wirth and Hermann Höfle and their secret extermination teams, drawn primarily from Hitler's postponed euthanasia program. Another of Globocnik's team, Johann Offermann, who was directly associated with *Aktion Reinhardt*, and who remained in Lublin after his superior left for Trieste, stressed the secrecy of those involved in this huge killing operation. Globocnik was responsible for the evacuation and transfer of all Jews in the Lublin District movements which had already begun in 1940 and ended in late 1943.

According to the British interrogation report of Offermann:

> To carry out these movements and pogroms Globocnik used a unit which was placed under his command supplied by Hitler's *Reichskanzlei* (*Reichsleiter* Bouhler). The unit was commanded by *Stubaf* Christian Wirth. The personnel of this unit (it is not known whether they were SS) lived in complete isolation and never mixed with others. They were not on the strength [staff] of the SSPf. [Globocnik]. Offermann thinks that the only people who can give further information on this unit are the *SS-Sturmbannführer* Hans Maubach, Sepp Nemetz, Hermann Höfle and Ernst Lerch, who were very close friends of Globocnik's.[66]

We know von Mohrenschildt was involved in undertaking the Zamosc Lands expulsion action because he is named in a lengthy letter signed by Globocnik, which gave this ethnic cleansing project the go-ahead.[67] However, he absolved himself of any involvement, claiming in a three-page statement recorded in Klagenfurt on 24 May 1971 that he was an assistant to the *RKFDV* and Lorenz, and that he had left Lublin before these expulsions had been launched, a most unsatisfactory explanation, to say the least.[68] Von Mohrenschildt was questioned several times by the authorities in Klagenfurt when trials of other SS men occurred in Germany, but only as a witness, not defendant. In light of Globocnik's 22 November 1942 letter naming him the second-in-command of this large ethnic cleansing action, his postwar claims cannot be believed. Like Globocnik, he has managed to evade the gaze of postwar historians. He was certainly a relatively senior SS member and one who calls for greater investigation into his wartime activities in occupied Poland.

In von Mohrenschildt's case there is value in considering his family background in some detail, because it appears to tell us something about his motivations and involvement in SS demographic issues. The family's burial plot in Wolfsberg, Carinthia, dates back only to 1879. Reinhold was born on 8 November 1915, and died on 2 November 1990. He was born at *Schloss*

Leifling, a castle in southern Carinthia, within this province's Slovenian-speaking zone. The family, which had earlier relocated from an Estonian area, thus chose to live in a mixed German-Slovene region of Europe rather than one that was being steadily Russified. His father Erich was born in 1879, but not in Carinthia. Erich's father, also Reinhold, had sold the family's Estonian-based estate, known as *Kreuzhof,* in March 1887 to a Baron Stackelberg for 90,000 rubles, after which he migrated to Carinthia. Probably relevant here is the fact that by the end of the 19th century concern was mounting over the fate of the Baltic Germans among German nationalists inside Germany. For instance, in 1912, after the von Mohrenschildts had departed from present-day Estonia for Carinthia, the president and driving force of the powerful Pan-German League, Heinrich von Class, who advocated annexation of large tracts of traditional western and northern Polish lands and the pushing back of Russia markedly farther east, did not ignore these isolated and distant northeastern Baltic German folk groups. "[von Class] as editor of the Berlin *Deutsche Zeitung,* writing under the pseudonym Daniel Frymann, warned the Baltic Germans in Russia that Germany *could not help them,* and he even went so far as to envision the [1939–40] Hitlerite policy of repatriation of German minorities from abroad." [Emphasis added][69]

Russification of Estonia had already commenced by the 1880s and continued gathering pace thereafter. This may have been the reason the von Mohrenschildts moved after this family's more than 200-year-long stay in this Baltic area. In the face of such Russification some Germans nevertheless remained while others emigrated, a phenomenon that again occurred after World War II when Great Britain, France, Belgium, and Portugal saw the return of their expatriate "Whites" from the various outposts of their maritime empires, including especially Asia and Africa. The Germans and Germany or Prussia simply witnessed this trend earlier, and the Mohrenschildts were early participants in this phenomenon. Such a family experience would probably have affected succeeding members of expatriate families, men like the younger Reinhold for instance. Such a family background and the writings of von Class/Frymann make it logical to conclude that in light of Reinhold von Mohrenschildt's wartime and SS career, and his demographic activities, he and members of his family were ardent von Class disciples, like so many others in the NSDAP and SS.

The von Mohrenschildts are remembered in Carinthia as an established family of adventurers of the Baltic *Deutschordensritter* (league of warriors), having settled in Kurland at least by the 17th century. Erich was born in Reval, Estland, while his wife, Vally Freiin von Stromberg, was born in Angern, Kurland. The young Reinhold, future SS man, was in all likelihood thus infused with an emotional attachment from early childhood to the Baltic area, a region that appealed so magnetically to so many nationalistic German eastern

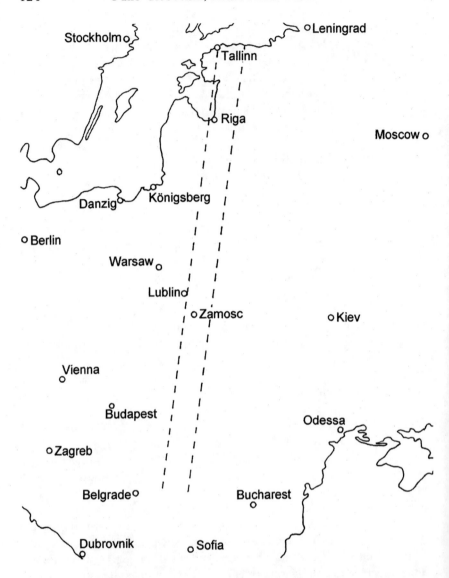

Map 3. The Globocnik-von Mohrenschildt Germanic settlement "wall."

dreamers, especially by the early 20th century. This is relevant here because the Germanization of the Zamosc Lands was to have been the first step in the creation of a Germanic settled belt of land, a demographic settlement "wall," that linked the long-established German communities of Transylvania (adjacent the Banat region from where Globocnik's mother hailed) and the Baltic region, as far north as Estonia (from where the Mohrenschildts came)—both regions long-settled by German communities — via the Zamosc Lands and thus Lublin District which these two SS men were on the brink of Germanizing.[70] For this reason, this settlement project can be fairly called the Globocnik-von Mohrenschildt Demographic "Wall" (see Map 3.) Across this "wall" of settlement a series of SS and police strongpoints — settlement areas, like the Zamosc Lands region — would have been established by initially expelling those living there and settling Germans in their place. As time passed German land acquisition and settlement would have spread from these strongpoints until the entire wall was occupied by Germans, after which another similar wall to the east of its predecessor would have been commenced. This process of creeping toward the Ural Mountains was expected to continue for 25 years. At the end of that time the entire East was expected to be Germanized, with the displaced Slavs having been "transferred," that is, expelled, into Western Siberia, east of the Ural Mountains. These were the broad tenets of *Generalplan Ost.*

In the von Mohrenschildt family's case there may have been the added factor of deep regret for having left their relatively vast ancestral lands for Carinthia. It is possible, indeed likely, that Reinhold would have viewed the German occupation of the Baltic area after June 1941 — following Hitler's invasion of Russia — as simply the takeover of the East over which Germans once held sway, and were seen as having introduced civilization, progress, and enlightenment many centuries earlier. Far from seeing that invasion as any sort of criminal act or as an act of aggression, the German military takeover of these lands would have inspired a feeling that Hitler and Himmler had simply demonstrated that a form of historical "justice" actually existed, even if it had taken so many decades to manifest itself.

In light of this it is instructive to recount Reinhold's ancestry, for it demonstrates the likely emotional attachment this ethnic cleanser and SS man understandably had toward the Baltic lands, even though he was raised in southern Austria. The family's Baltic founder was Johann Kock or Koch (born 1680), either of Danish or German descent. Koch served as "*Ratsherr*" (town councillor) and "*Stadtkammerer*" (town committee member) in Reval (now Tallin, Estonia), and was raised to noble rank on 20 September 1650, under Swedish aegis. The honorary name was originally "Morenskold," which German speakers wrote as "Mohrenschildt." The family's incorporation to Estonian knighthood status was registered on 14 February 1746, under the aegis of Russia, since it ruled Estonia from 1710. Koch's descendents were Hans George and Berend Johann (1758–1817). The former held estates known as Mahkull and Fahna, and the latter's were Kreuzhof, Hattokull, and Tammik. Reinhold's family line sprung from the Berend line. By the middle of the 18th century, there were eight Estonian families with the name Mohrenschildt. These families owned 12 estates. Berend's offspring were: son, Berend (died

1831); grandson, Reinhold von Mohrenschildt (1831–1905)— it was this Reinhold who relocated the family to Carinthia; great grandson, Erich (1879–1943); and great great grandson, Reinhold (1915–1990), the man who served intermittently in Lublin and on Werner Lorenz's staff as a member of the SS. Reinhold named his son Berend, and his daughter, Ebba. She married Count Christoph von Habsburg in 1973. The Mohrenschildts were associated through marriage with the Maydells, an even older German eastern family named in documents dating back to the 14th century. This link was through the union of Berend Otto Johann Baron von Baydell (1793–1870) and Leontine von Mohrenschildt (1812–1890), who is the aunt of George de Mohrenschildt.[71] There seems little doubt that von Mohrenschildt was a catalyst when in Lublin explaining, urging and outlining to his longtime friend Odilo the need for the cleansing of Slavs and Jews from the entire East.

In early 1934, well before the *Anschluss*, the young activist Reinhold commenced studying diplomacy and economics in Vienna and later briefly worked as a secretary for another significant Carinthian and long-time political colleague, Dr. Friedrich Rainer. He had joined the SS on 12 March 1938, the same day he formally joined the NSDAP. Eleven months later, in late August 1939, he moved to Berlin to be with his *Waffen-SS* regiment, with the rank of *Obersturmführer*. In the Reich's capital he also rose to become a *Sonderführer* within the Foreign Office, so had something in common with Hans Maubach, also a Foreign Office employee before moving to Lublin in early 1940 in the company of Globocnik's future fiancée, Irmgard Rickheim. Von Mohrenschildt's work as a *Diplomatenaustausch* appears to have involved a brief tour of duty in Danzig (Gdansk), by then a Germanized city under *Gauleiter* Albert Forster, who for a time had been considered as a possible Vienna *Gauleiter*. In October 1939 he was already involved in assisting in the return of ethnic Germans from pre-war Polish Wolyn (Volhynia) for settlement in western Poland, because Wolyn had come under Soviet control due to the terms of the Ribbentrop-Molotov Pact. In the summer of 1940, after the successful Western Campaign against France, Belgium, and Holland, the British and even Polish units, he was briefly stationed in Paris, followed by time in Holland, where he worked as a *Fachführer für Landwirtschaft*—an agronomical expert. From late 1940 until the invasion of the Soviet Union in July 1941, he may for a brief period have worked on his father's Carinthian estate. We cannot be sure of this. Von Mohrenschildt appears to have used his father's estate as an alibi in court depositions after the war to distance himself from certain embarrassing activities in various parts of eastern and Baltic Europe where he was involved in ethnic cleansing and both voluntary and enforced resettlement activities.

Following the Soviet invasion he was stationed in Riga, Latvia, as a *Fachführer*, and he even claimed to have seen action on the outskirts of Leningrad in early 1942. His claim that he left for Carinthia in late 1942, probably October, does not align with the facts, for he is named in Globocnik's cleansing go-ahead order as being the second-in-command for the Zamosc Lands expulsion action, launched on 28 November that year. By obfuscating this period in postwar records, which incidentally several other senior Globocnik staffers, including Lerch, Höfle, and Michalsen, also did, he casts grave suspicion upon himself. Many members of the Globocnikian Lublin "Mafia" claimed not to be in Lublin and its environs in that crucial year, some denying they were ever there. Nor is this ploy of distancing themselves from Lublin entirely surprising considering what had occurred there. Lublin was the capital city of the Jewish Holocaust, and the unrecognized center from which the top-secret *Generalplan Ost* was launched, marking the beginnings of the Final Solution of the Slavic Question. According to von Mohrenschildt, he first reported to work for Globocnik in Trieste in September 1943 the month that Globocnik reached his birthplace on the shores of the Adriatic, following his genocidal Lublin years. This is simply untrue, for he had served several tours of duty in Lublin, something he, like other Globocnikians, would undoubtedly have preferred to forget. We have Rickheim's and Max Cichotski's word that von Mohrenschildt was in Lublin with Globocnik, and not just as a brief visitor. Moreover, he is named by Globocnik on the latter's order to cleanse the Zamosc Lands of Polish peasant farmers. It was in Klagenfurt, von Mohrenschildt claimed, that he worked with Globocnik until the end of the war as an *RKFDV* employee. Denial or obfuscation about Lublin simply raises grave suspicions about any SS man's past. British radio interceptors encountered at least one message to von Mohrenschildt, though this dealt with the time soon after his Lublin period.

> To: *SS-Hstuf* von Mohrenschildt, Gassometergasse 8, Klagenfurt.
> From: *SS-Hstuf* Horn, Ostministerium.
> Re: SSD SS Pol.fhr Lublin Nr 78 of 5 December 1943.
> Please inform *SS-Gruppenführer* Globocnik immediately that *SS-Sturmbannführer* Wippern in Arolsen and I will meet him in Berlin on Tuesday, 7th Dec. 1943. Meeting remains scheduled for 8th and 12th. Exact proposed date from Berlin on 7th Dec 1943.[72]

Von Mohrenschildt, at this late stage, had become the man allegedly in charge of the Mail and Passport Office of the *Waffen-SS* for Italy, but was based in Klagenfurt, where he claims to have remained until war's end. The fact that he was being contacted about a meeting with Wippern, Globocnik's Lublin loot processor, is relevant, showing how trusted he was and indicating his level of awareness of matters in Lublin. Elsewhere he had claimed he had earlier worked for the *RKFDV*, and was responsible for the closure of its Oberkrain office, which consisted of nearly 300 workers. Leaving this latter duty aside, it is interesting that it was he who was contacted on behalf of Globocnik by what was probably the Dr. Horn who had served with Globocnik on the board of Ost Industries (*Osti*), the SS company that acquired many millions of dollars worth of Jewish capital assets and employed thousands of Jewish slave laborers. This suggests that even if von Mohrenschildt was not directly involved in acquisition of that loot, he may have been involved in its administration or at least assessment, transfer, and perhaps even storage. If that was the case, he was complicitous in a major, indeed, unprecedented felony that arose from the crime of genocide. This single message, unfortunately, does not permit us to draw any further conclusion. That the meeting referred to involved Wippern, Globocnik's other close Lublin pal, and the man in charge of smelting stolen Jewish gold and other treasures, and packaging and processing all other loot — diamonds, pearls, and foreign currency — certainly makes it significant. Placing an SS man with economics qualifications and with a wartime working history that focused upon demographic affairs suddenly into passport control and mail duties is a strange appointment. Whether Globocnik had an ulterior motive such as ensuring that von Mohrenschildt would have oversight over the transfer of valuables is simply not known, but cannot be discounted.

After the war, von Mohrenschildt was interned as a Nazi by the British not far from his home, at the Wolfsberg former prisoner-of-war camp, and was accused by the Austrian People's Court in 1948 of atrocities committed in the border region of northern Italy, indicating that his time in Lublin remained successfully hidden or downplayed in the immediate postwar years and well beyond. But this accusation never came to trial.

> In the spring of 1944, Mohrenschildt and a SD-man by the name of Patterer, and a couple of other SS-men, drove up to the Ploecken Pass, a border mountain pass linking Carinthia and Italy. This group drove into the village of Timau, picked up civilians at random, put them on trucks and took them to Paluzza, where they underwent severe questioning and beatings. The town of Paluzza was searched with SS-guards breaking into houses, looting and arresting more civilians. Next they got on to trucks and went on to the town of Paularo, where they repeated the above. What happened was that apparently quite a number of Italian civilians died during these proceedings. In the evening on the same day, the SS-guards, led by Mohrenschildt and Patterer, returned to the Carinthian side, their trucks loaded with stolen goods. Another trip of this kind in the spring was said to have resulted in eight or 10 deaths, and involved women, children and aged people at a place called Promos in the Alps.[73]

Although von Mohrenschildt's wartime record was not as bestial and inhumane as Globocnik's, Wirth's, and Höfle's — all three were mass murderers on a grand scale — he was nevertheless an ardent National Socialist involved in population cleansing on a massive scale and the administration of slavery.

He faced investigations, but not trials, in 1963 and again in 1971. The outcome of all his legal processes is unknown.[74] Because von Mohrenschildt traveled extensively as a roving ethnic cleanser, he was able to claim, after the war, that he was in places other than those where known mass crime had been committed. He was also able to portray himself as something of a social welfare worker — which he most definitely *was not*— by highlighting that he had been involved in re-settling eastern Germans. The relocation of eastern Germans westward, from lands acquired by Stalin in 1939, was part of a wider movement of people, and included expelling many Poles and Jews out of western Poland (Warthe Land) so that the German settlers had land and housing to take over.

We know Globocnik's ancestors, on his maternal side, hailed from the old German enclave of Banat, Werschetz (Vrsak), close to Transylvania, while the Mohrenschildts came from the Baltic region, from what is today Estonia. We also know that both these Carinthians directed the Zamosc Lands cleansing action to make this region the first Germanic settlement "island" in the General Gouvernement, and planned to go on to create a demographic "wall" of German settlement linking the Baltic region and Transylvania. Was this a coincidence or was it something these two pre-war Carinthian pals, while together in Lublin, privately plotted as senior population cleansing planners and executors? All this was done from within the Julius Schreck Barracks where the murderous *Aktion Reinhardt* was concurrently being directed. There seems little doubt that as well as launching the construction of this Germanic "wall" of settlement, these two Carinthians had set out to link their respective "ancestral" lands — Banat/Transylvania and Estonia, the Black and the Baltic Seas — with a wide belt of German farming communities. This uncanny and megalomaniacal dimension to the Zamosc Lands expulsion cannot be discounted as mere fantasy.

Georg Michalsen: "Dull Witted and Ignorant" Apparatchik and Ghetto Cleanser

Michalsen, like Cichotski (Runhof), had changed his name during the war to one that appeared or sounded German. Before the war he was known as Michalczyk or Mikalczyk, a Polish-sounding name. He was from Oppeln, Lower Silesia, having been born in Wendrien in 1917. When West German war crimes investigators closed in on him in 1961, as they did on most of the other Globocnikians, he was living in Hamburg with his wife and 18-year-old daughter. He was reported in the press at that time as saying: "During the war I was a soldier and sometimes I worked in administration." The second part of this claim was, strictly speaking, correct, but it was certainly not the whole truth. Whether he was ever a fighting soldier is unknown. Michalsen had been an accountant in Oppeln and joined the SS in 1932, before Globocnik. He became close to his powerful superior and, like Lerch and Höfle, was with Globocnik when they were captured by British soldiers in southern Austria early on 31 May 1945. Both Lerch and Michalsen were interrogated by the British, and both were careful to avoid referring ever to having been in Lublin. According to the initial report of his interrogation by the British, he was born on 13 September 1906, which differed from a later published date, and had attended elementary and secondary school.

> He then became a controller clerk of housing in Oppeln. At the outbreak of war he was called up to the Army, but was reclaimed by his employer as a key man. In November 1939 he was called up to the *Waffen-SS* and a few months later took a course for administrative officers of the *Waffen-SS*. In April 1944, [sic] after a period of sickness, he was sent to Tomassow, Macedonia, to recruit *Volksdeutsche* for Police and *Waffen-SS* formations. He later served two years in the Baltic region, as SS Admin Offr. In September 1943 he was posted to the staff of the *Höhere SS-und Polizeiführer Adriatisches Kuestenland* and put in charge of Abt II (Personnel). He held this appointment until his arrest.[75]

Like Lerch, Michalsen therefore claimed to be in the *Waffen-SS*, the fighting arm of the SS, as opposed to the far more notorious wing that was involved in so much "administration" in which he actually served while in Lublin. This false claim may have been conjured up by both these mass murderers, because Cichotski appears to have moved into the *Waffen-SS* from Trieste, though we cannot be absolutely certain of that either. However, as the war became more desperate for Berlin, a steady flow of manpower was moved out of bureaucratic functions and "administration" into the fighting or *Waffen* formations.

Willy Natke: Batman

According to one of Globocnik's batmen, Willy Natke, his superior was a brute who would not hesitate killing his own subordinates. On the question of Globocnik's lifestyle in his Lublin or Wieniawska Street mansion, Natke said it was extravagant. Average daily consumption of the household included about two dozen eggs, 1.5 to two kilograms of butter, vast amounts of coffee of the roasted and raw variety, and an abundance of champagne, wine, and spirits. He said alcoholic stocks reached the thousands of bottles. Little wonder Irmgard Rickheim occasionally remarked on Globocnik's excessive weight. Life in Lublin at the top of the racial nomenclatura was one of extravagant consumption.

> One might say that every evening drinking-bouts took place where the best stuff was being awarded to his clique. Alone the consumption of champagne

amounted to about 40 bottles on this standard booze-up. At least two or three times a week still larger soaks took place. To gain favor of high and higher personalities in government, the party and the *Reichsführung-SS*, they were continuously provided with large amounts of ham, bacon, meat, butter and other fatty things. In the same way those were supplied with first, leather, coats, boots, textiles of all kinds, genuine rugs, curtains, décor textiles and so on.[76]

Natke's statement also tells us that Globocnik had a secret account, perhaps with a bank, perhaps just a set of books, it is not clear which, that carried the quaint name, "Ordinario," perhaps harking back to something in Globocnik's days in Italy when he was a clandestine Nazi courier. The Lublin-based Emmissions Bank was a significant financial institution, but whether it was utilized by Globocnik for personal clandestine purposes is not known. The "Ordinario" account to which Natke refers may have been an official one associated with transfers to Oswald Pohl in Berlin and involving Georg Wippern.

Lorenz Hackenholt: The Gassing Expert

Another key, indeed indispensable, member of Globocnik's *Aktion Reinhardt* killing team, though someone with whom Globocnik had only limited contact, was *SS-Hauptscharführer* Lorenz Hackenholt. He oversaw construction and maintenance of the gas chambers used to murder most of the 1.5 or so million Jews over the course of about 18 months — March 1942 until around August 1943 — at Belzec, Sobibor, and Treblinka. Hackenholt, a bricklayer — a trade not far removed from Globocnik's pre-war occupation — came from Gelsenkirchen/Ruhr, and was 27 years old when he reached Lublin. Like that of Franz Stangl, his road to a brief career as an exterminationist was via the secret Hitler Chancellery-directed euthanasia program code named "T4," or the Charitable Foundation for Institutional Care (*Gemeinnützige Stiftung für Anstaltspflege*). "T4" was responsible for the deaths of tens of thousands of Germans who had been classified mentally or chronically ill. These people were murdered at six locations that were out-of-the way castles or mansions. Hackenholt was recruited into the T4 killing program out of the SS, which he had joined in early 1934, the same year as Globocnik. After two years military service, he joined the *SS-Totenkopf Standarte* (Death's Head Regiment) and in November 1939, the month Globocnik reached Lublin, he moved to Berlin for "special duty," involvement in T4 killings. Before this he had served at Sachsenhausen concentration camp as a guard and driver. Hackenholt was interviewed by *SS-Standartenführer* Viktor Brack, a member of the Main Office II in Hitler's Chancellery, and Brack's deputy, SA-*Oberführer* Werner Blankenburg, the two key figures who oversaw Globocnik's Jewish killing program during 1942 and 1943 from a comfortable Berlin office. Hackenholt saw duty in each of the T-4's six euthanasia centers, working as a bus driver and as what was called a "disinfector/burner," unloading corpses from gas chambers and assisting in their cremation.

Hackenholt reached Lublin in late 1941, probably September, and very quickly become involved in gassings for the yet-to-be launched *Aktion Reinhardt*. His early duties included working at an experimental gas chamber at Belzec, formerly the venue of Globocnik's "Otto Line" camp complex. Postwar West German and Bavarian *Lande* governmental investigation disclosed that he had been quickly assigned to work with Christian Wirth. Michael Tregenza describes this early experimental phase, that is, in the months just prior to the launching of *Aktion Reinhardt*, and the association between these two major mass killers. Tregenza tells of Wirth putting Hackenholt, a man with mechanical aptitude, in charge of the camp's garage and vehicles. In addition to such skills, Hackenholt was an inventive individual, one who was on the lookout for his ideas to be realized. Very quickly he moved from using an old hut as a gas chamber to converting a postal van into a mobile gas chamber, using the engine's exhaust gas as the killing agent. It appears that the first victims were a number of retarded and disabled from the surrounding region. It is not known if these unfortunates were Poles or Jews. Clearly, Wirth had found a man whom he could use. The next phase in Hackenholt's work was experimentation with different types of killing gases. Tregenza says that among the first Jewish victims were about 150 laborers who were brought in from nearby towns to undertake construction work. They were killed with Zyklon B, a hydrocyanic acid-based pesticide that had been obtained from military units.

> Further experiments using CO gas from steel cylinders, the same method used in the "T4" killing centers in the Reich, were also carried out on Jews from the *Durchgangsghettos* (transit ghettos) at Izbica and Piaski on the road between Belzec and Lublin. These experimental victims, brought to the camp in several railway goods wagons, were very probably Jewish mental patients deported from the Reich. One SS-NCO commented about these experiments conducted by commandant Wirth:
>
> Belzec was the laboratory … he tried everything imaginable there. In Belzec, Wirth tested the basics of the extermination machinery right through with his men.
>
> Finally, and to some extent influenced by Hackenholt's gassing van, the engine exhaust fumes from a Soviet tank were decided upon as the most suitable and economic means for the mass murder of Jews. Former SS-NCO Hans Girtig, who served in Belzec with Hackenholt, told officers from [the Munich-based] *Sonderkommission* III/a about this gassing installation in the camp:
>
> Hackenholt had installed the engine, this was explained to us at a duty conference … I know for certain that in the beginning Wirth and Hackenholt, and later Hackenholt alone, that is, with the help of Ukrainians, operated the gassing engine.[77]

Like most other *Aktion Reinhardt* operatives, Hackenholt was eventually transferred to Trieste, but he reached the Adriatic coastal region some time after his two superiors, Globocnik and Wirth. In Trieste they established three special SS and police divisions that were designated [EK]R-I which was based in Trieste; [EK]R-II, based in Fiume (now Rijeka in Croatia); and [EK]R-III in Udine. Wirth, who operated from a disused rice mill in the suburb of San Sabba, was placed in charge of all three. As in Lublin District, his main task was to find and apprehend Jews and, of course, to take over their property and other valuables. This work was given the codename *Einsatz [-Kommando] R* (Operation R).[78]

Hackenholt was attached to the EKR-I unit and based in the San Sabba rice mill, which served both as a transit camp for Italian Jews to be dispatched either to Auschwitz-Birkenau or other northern destinations, as well as a killing center. Cremations and executions ceased at San Sabba in the spring of 1944, on Globocnik's orders; it was operational for less than nine months, about half the time of the *Aktion Reinhardt* killing centers, though used for other purposes until April 1945. The three Adriatic EKR units were converted into anti-partisan fighting squads, a duty they were involved in for almost one year. For his Lublin District killing centers *Aktion Reinhardt* work, Hackenholt was awarded the Iron Cross II Class.[79] Although Josef Oberhauser, Hans Girtig, and Heinrich Gley claimed Hackenholt was killed in fighting near Trieste, Tregenza casts doubt on their claim, suggesting that Hackenholt may have survived the war and like Lerch, Höfle, and Wippern, Globocnik's main loot counter, was never brought to justice. "In 1945, Hackenholt contacted his wife in Berlin through an intermediary, in 1946 two former SS-NCO's from the Sobibor extermination camp met him in West Germany, and in 1947 his brother believed he saw him not far from their home in Gelsenkirchen/Ruhr."[80]

And Some Other Globocnikians...

The second level of Globocnik staffers included three significant men, all *Sturmbannführers,* like Michalsen: Herbert Ulbrich, Kurt Claasen (aka Kutschera until 1939), and Amon Leopold Göth. Göth, who was born in Vienna, and was hanged by the Poles on 13 September 1946 in Krakow, had been for some time in charge of the Plaszow concentration camp just east of Krakow, which was made famous years later in the Hollywood film, *Schindler's List.* These men were designated as *Personlicher Referent,* that is, officials in charge of special tasks, who reported only to their Lublin superior. Another aide was Globocnik's driver, Franz Eigner, also Viennese, who, although certainly not as close as Lerch, was undoubtedly well-informed, at least of generalities, such as the precise location of certain killing centers, matters discussed during private conversations inside his automobile, and personal proclivities of his superior. An indication of the disparity between Globocnik's first circle of staffers, men like Lerch, Maubach, Nemetz, Höfle, Cichotski, and von Mohrenschildt, and the next level is the fact that Rickheim said she knew all the former well, especially Maubach, her employer since 1938, but could not recall Michalsen, Wippern, Claasen, Ulbrich, or Göth. Another noteworthy feature of Globocnik's staff is that responsibilities tended to overlap: Any of these men could be and were assigned to "special tasks," which may have included overseeing the clearance of a particular ghetto, arranging transport, or overseeing an industrial work camp enterprise. Duties were in a state of constant flux. Nemetz, Michalsen, and Claasen, as well as the ever-present Lerch, at some stage all headed Clearance Commandos, deporting Jews from ghettos in the way von Mohrenschildt was most certainly involved in the clearance of the Zamosc Lands of ethnic Polish peasant farmers after November 1942. Some in the second rank were involved in factory and other management using forced labor. Lublin, as it was being built up as an SS eastern center became a significant venue for processing and manufacturing of military goods, and had workshops involved in ammunition box manufacturing and boot and military clothing repair. There were other characters worth naming, too, including Willi Scheper and Sepp Slany, with the first managing living quarters, and Slany in charge of food procurement. Slany was also linked to Höfle in the clearance of the Bialystok Ghetto.

Globocnik's staff, after these senior staffers, included nearly 40 additional middle rank men who held specialist positions, but their relationship with Globocnik varied from relatively close to probably simply cordial, and being at a distance. The man who was the most significant in relation to the Germanization of the Lublin District and Berlin's top-secret *Generalplan Ost* was Gustav Hanelt, an *SS-Hauptsturmführer*, with links to the SS's Race and Settlement Office (*RuSHA*). He headed Globocnik's Lublin-based Research Center for Eastern Settlement (*Forschungsstelle für Ostunterkunfte*).[81] This center, as mentioned earlier, was involved in laying out plans for the largest population cleansing action in history — the removal of all Poles, Ukrainians, Russians, Belarusans, and eventually even many Balts from their traditional lands and forcibly relocating them into Western Siberia. *Generalplan Ost*, although launched by the Zamosc Lands action in November 1942, faltered by August 1943, and was then discontinued and never re-launched. Several SS men described this crucially important but largely ignored research center after the war. Although none, unfortunately, went into the detail desired, one, *SS-Sturmbannführer* Albert Franke-Gricksch, conveyed its significance and the sheer magnitude of the demographic cleansing being envisaged by Globocnik and his planners had the Soviet Red Army been conquered during, say,

1942 or even early 1943, in the way that the Polish, French, and British armies were overcome in 1939 and 1940 respectively. Franke-Gricksch visited Lublin in May 1943. This Berlin-based *SS-Sturmbannführer* was an assistant to the head of the RSHA's personnel division, Maximilian von Herff, and a man who had briefly served as an SS police officer in Russia in late 1942, at about the time that the Zamosc Lands expulsion action was launched as the first step in the implementation of *Generalplan Ost* to cleanse initially the entire General Gouvernement of all ethnic Poles. On his return to Berlin, Franke-Gricksch compiled a lengthy report on his trip through the General Gouvernement, which included Lublin. He had made a brief stopover at what he called the SS-Barracks in Lublin's central quarter, where Globocnik's Research Center for Eastern Settlement was based, with its drawing and photographic rooms, library, publishing and cartographic divisions, as well as models of settlements envisaged across all of pre-war Poland, Russia, and Ukraine. That report, in part, reads:

> In the late hours of the afternoon we go and inspect SS Barracks in Lublin, and we are being shown round by SS Gpf Globocnik. In these Barracks the ideological planning for the reconstruction and colonization of the General Gouvernement takes place. It is gratifying to see the whole work in this sphere is planned to every detail and people will be resettled only after this planning has been completed. This detailed planning makes it possible to occupy thousands of settlements in a few weeks and to effect the whole resettlement, which means deportation of the Polish population and the settling of German farmers without great difficulty. The work of the SS in the sphere of preparing this resettlement is considerable. We see that the planning of the German settlements is thought out to the smallest detail, all the sanitary arrangements, canalization, electric light, water, economic problems are being worked out by young experts. The entire decoration of the cottages is considered, halls for festivals are planned, etc. The preparation extends even to the personal life of the settlers. A form of life is being tried out in these settlements in small proportion, *which is the final object of the SS organization for the whole of the German nation in the future.* We realize with joy that this huge work which is being planned and carried out under such difficult circumstances is not only theoretical but it has become a reality in the Eastern sphere. *For the first time we can understand the whole colonization plan of the Reichsführer.* One can see how he is building up a big belt of German settlements against the masses of the Slav nations. It is proved by statistics how much German blood can be saved out of the Polish people and these problems of the Eastern sphere are being scrutinized with German scientific thoroughness. It is delightful to sit together with these young men of the SS, who have University education, who, despite their sharp criticism, fully recognize the big mission of the German nation in the Eastern sphere. It is a pity that a great part of these men are disappointed by an entirely wrong policy with regard to personnel questions. Skilled engineers and tradesmen, experts on building and canalization run around with the rank of private and this alone gives them the feeling that the very work is welcome but ultimately not appreciated. SS Gpf Herff gets detailed information on all

these matters and promises to have these things altered. *After this very interest-ing inspection of the SS Barracks, which gave us for the first time a clear picture of the situation of the German in the Eastern sphere*, we attended a social function arranged by the SS Gpf Globocnik, General Moser, (Brigf), and his staff [em-phases added].[82]

Beyond Globocnik's inner staffers were more than two dozen more dis-tant ones, including George Wippern, described above, who were also cru-cially important in supporting his powers.

Key Staffers in Globocnik's Lublin District-Based Business Empire

German Armament Works (*Deutsche Ausrüstungswerke*) Lublin: Saw-mill — Pulawy: Horst Riedel. *Ost-Industrie GmbH* — Lublin: Dr. Max Horn. SS: Georg Wippern. (**Sub-Divisions:** Clothing Distribution: ? Zimmermann. SS-Landed Estates: Unknown. Training Camp — Trawniki: Karl Streibel. Work Camp — Trawniki: Franz Bartetzko. Work Camp — Poniatowa: Un-known. Work Camp — Budzyn [Aircraft Factory Works — Heinkel] Willi Franz. Clothing Storehouse — Lublin: ? Obermeyer.) Garrison Commander Office (Local Supervisory Authority): Eimann, Lange. *Troop Supply Depot of the* Waffen-SS*, Lublin:* Schraufstetter, Meister, Von Pistor, Kullman, Bruch-mann. *Research Center for Settlement of the East:* Gustav Hanelt, Werner Schri-ever. *SS-Garrison Barracks:* Werner Schriever. *Reich Commission for the Strengthening of Germandom* — *In Lublin:* Hartmut Pfeiffer; *In Zamosc:* Adolf Bareuther and Werner. *Ethnic German Communication. Hitler-Youth officer:* von Seltman and Klemens. *Race and Settlement Office:* Diehl and Rietz. *Cen-tral Infirmatory, maternity, optics, pharmacy, and orthopedic* — *work station:* Dr. Heinz Posetzchlack. *SS dental surgery:* Dr. Dieter Mahler. *SS-Construction:* Naumann; *Construction in Lublin:* Grothe; *Construction in Zamosc:* Richard Thomalla. *Estate Management (SS-Gute):* Dunkel. *SS Special Commando:* Dr Oskar Dirlewanger. *SWG (Settlers' Economic Association). Supervisory Board:* Globocnik, Herbert Naumann, Dr. Klaus, Dr. Becker.[83]

Tuviah Friedmann, referred to earlier, in his Globocnik Report named 20 senior staffers, all Austrians, who were also stationed in Lublin. Of these Lerch, von Mohrenschildt, Eigner (Globocnik's chauffeur), and Nemetz are referred to above. A sizeable number of the others hailed from Klagenfurt, but most were from Vienna. Globocnik largely cocooned himself within a Klagenfurt-Viennese cohort that also included: Hans Bohunsky, born 28 June 1922 in Bad Voeslau near Vienna, who had been in charge of the Trawniki camp near Lublin; Anton Doeltl, (b. 9 October 1918, Vienna); Ottmar Egger

(b. 13 June 1912, Klagenfurt); Benedikt Farkas (b. 21 September 1909, Vienna); Karl Hellesberger (b. 16 March 1907, Klagenfurt); Franz Hoedl (b. 1 August 1907, Aschbach on the Donau); Dr. Karl Hofbauer (b. 2 May 1911, Villach); Viktor Knorr (b. 7 May 1907, Vienna); Helmut Pohl (b. 27 September 1909, Klagenfurt); Josef Raich (b. 22 December 1910, Korneuburg near Vienna); Karl Rupp (b. 7 July 1912, Vienna); Alois Rzepa (b. 17 February 1908, Schrema/Niederdonau), who was cashier in charge of all loot, with Georg Wippern, taken from living and dead Jews under the secret *Aktion Reinhardt* program; Rudolf Schleissner (b. 14 March 1906, Klagenfurt); Lothar von Seltmann (b. 12 January 1917, Vienna), in charge of ethnic German communication, a great enthusiast for settling ethnic Germans in the Zamosc Lands during 1942 and 1943, and, no doubt, later, far beyond; Dr. Franz Stanglica (b. 27 May 1909, Vienna), precinct manager of Globocnik's Research Center of Eastern Settlement (*Forschungsstelle für Ostunterkunfte*), where he doubled as the librarian, archivist, and officer-in-charge of cartographic resources, and thus a key player in drawing up plans to Germanize first the Zamosc Lands, followed by the entire Lublin District, then the remainder of General Gouvernement, and finally all lands up to the Ural Mountains if the opportunity arose; Walter von Wanka (b. 19 February 1908, Vienna); and finally, Karl Wukowits (b. 19 September 1909, Klagenfurt). Globocnik was older than all his Austrian staffers by between about two and, in Bohunsky's case, nearly 18 years.[84]

Although Globocnik had a proclivity to terminate friendships suddenly and without warning—with Gasser, Nemetz, and Maubach, for instance— for reasons we do not know, Auschwitz-Birkenau's commandant, Rudolf Höss, claimed that his staffers remained exceptionally loyal to him. Both observations can, of course, be correct, meaning that with some individuals he maintained long-term friendships while with others he simply terminated an association for reasons only known to him. Höss, a seemingly good judge of situations and associations, described the situation well.

> Globocnik's staff was nothing less than a collection of misfits. But they nevertheless managed to make themselves indispensable and liked by him, which was not very difficult considering his poor knowledge of human nature. When their misdeeds had to be covered up, Globocnik gave them his help, both out of good nature and so that his own intrigues would not come to light.[85]

SIPO-SD (Security Police and Security Service) and the *Ordnungspolizei* (the Order Police)

Globocnik's work in Lublin was many facetted. As stated earlier, he was also in charge of policing and security in the most general sense as *der SS-und*

Polizeiführer for Lublin District. But the Security Police and Security Service (*Sipo-SD*) branch did not come solely under his jurisdiction, and the fact that he was left not fully controlling these secret police units, if anything, contributed to his eventual downfall, because he appears to have made enemies within their ranks. The existence of overlapping responsibility or dual loyalties is revealed in a report compiled by the British after the war, following interrogation of Johann Offermann, also one of Globocnik's adjutants.

> The SSuPF of the districts were subordinate to the Generalgouverneur Dr Frank; in matters relating to security they were responsible to the *Staatssekretaer fuer das Sicherheitswesen SS O'Fuh u.* Gen. d. Po. Kruger, and his successor Koppe. He was the territorial or zone commander for all SS and Police with the exception of the *Sipo-SD*. It must be added that the SSuPF was responsible for the security and thus the safety of the district. In addition, he represented the RFSS [Himmler] in the capacity of the *Reichskommissar fuer die Festigung des deutschen Volkstums* and his *Volksdeutsche Mittelstelle* and the *Führer des Rassen. u. Siedlungswesen* [sic].[86]

The impact of Globocnik's unpopularity within certain police and security circles upon his own career should not be exaggerated, for he retained Himmler's trust and assistance throughout his Lublin days. If it did have an impact, its contribution was only marginal, since Globocnik remained in charge of the SS in Lublin until mid–September 1943. Historian Peter Black says of his policing powers:

> As SS and police leader Globocnik *supervised* the personnel of the German security police (Gestapo and Criminal Police), security service (*Sicherheitsdienst—SD*) and the personnel of the German order police (*Ordnungspolizei*). The order police was further divided into municipal (*Schutzpolizei*) and rural (Gendarmerie) sections which controlled the Polish police force and Ukrainian auxiliary police units in Lublin. These agencies were also responsible to their central offices in Berlin, the Reich Central Office for Security and the Order Police Main Office. *Globocnik exercised complete and personal control only over the Selbstschutz and his own personal staff* [emphases added].[87]

Globocnik therefore only "supervised" the Gestapo, Criminal Police, *Sipo-SD*, and the personnel of the *Ordnungspolizei*; shared control with Berlin of the *Schutzpolizei* and *Gendarmerie*, and only had complete control of the *Selbstschutz*, or his district's indigenous German units. That said, however, Globocnik was inclined to keep a close oversight on areas not fully under his jurisdiction. He was a perennial dabbler, someone who interfered persistently and constantly and in as many matters as he deemed relevant and possible or within his reach. This should be kept in mind when thinking of him only in a supervisory role.

The Order Police or *Orpo* were split into two wings: The first had a network of territorial police stations across the district; the second was made up of operational units. A week after Globocnik reached Lublin, 16 November 1939, their duties were specified in an order of the General Gouvernement's *Orpo* commander, which stated that the "responsibility for the organization and function of the police stations lay with the gendarmerie commander of the Distrikt." During the last two years of the occupation there were between 150 and 170 such stations across Globocnik's district.

> The units of the Order Police, frequently referred to as "*Truppenpolizei*," formed a separate branch and were divided into platoons, companies, battalions and regiments. They were subordinated entirely to the *Orpo* Commander and their aim was to suppress the underground movement and guarding duties. The composition and distribution of those forces was subject to frequent alterations but over the years they grew steadily in strength, so that in the spring of 1944 the police units amounted to about a dozen battalions (excluding police stations).[88]

Those in the police stations were involved in the normal duties of any police force, but the growing numbers of battalions under the *Orpo* umbrella fought against the steadily expanding Polish Resistance Movement.

Globocnik also had the power to call upon Ukrainian police units, which he and von Mohrenschildt certainly did during the Zamosc Lands expulsion action of 1942–43. The *Selbstschutz* was initially headed by *SS-Standartenführer* Walter Gunst who moved to establish this new force during Globocnik's first week in Lublin. The first Lublin District *Volksdeutsche* enlisted on 23 November 1939, and most of the personnel were men of German ancestry from the District, recruited from within the ranks of the district's 30,000 *Volksdeutsche*. Globocnik was even to have an English-born German on his policing staff, a man called Rheindorf, who had a Birmingham accent.

> English-born commander of *Polizeiregiment* 25 in Lublin, which formed Globocnik's and Himmler's bodyguard detachment when he visited Lublin Distrikt, was Konrad Rheindorf. He was born in Birmingham in 1896. His father owned a bicycle shop. Konrad returned to the Fatherland in 1934 at the age of 38. Because he was in hospital in Lublin when the Red Army liberated the city he ended up in the Gulag until 1956 but returned to Germany after the amnesty of that year.[89]

The fact that Globocnik had such limited or supervisory control and overlapping responsibility over these segments of the district's police led to disputation. One of the district's early permanent heads of *Sipo-SD* was Walter Huppenkothen, who held these positions between February 1940 and July 1941, after which he was transferred to the Gestapo in Berlin. He claimed that although he took his orders from Krakow, locally he was "also subordinate to the SS and Police Chief for the Lublin Distrikt."

I made Globocnik's personal acquaintance after my transfer to Lublin. My official relationship with him was very strained. Although he had no professional knowledge of police matters, *he continually gave instructions, which clashed with the pertinent directives I was given, and with which I could not comply for Security Policy reasons.* Globocnik, having therefore repeatedly complained about me, and as unpleasant arguments had arisen, in which my superiors supported me or my department. *When I objected he would refer to special powers and special assistance from Himmler with whom he kept up a regular personal correspondence* [emphases added].[90]

After the war Huppenkothen returned to civilian life to work as a clerk in Mannheim. Significantly, although Globocnik was chummy with Huppenkothen's successor, Johannes Müller, even that liaison eventually soured. Müller stayed in Lublin until October, 1943, one month after Globocnik's departure. Huppenkothen's postwar statement shows that even though Globocnik lacked total or *de jure* power over *Sipo-SD*, this mattered little to him because he simply ignored this fact and went on to do what he desired. He held *de facto* control. And there is no reason to disbelieve this assertion of Huppenkothen's that Globocnik held "special powers and special assistance from Himmler," who, after all, headed all the Reich's policing agencies. Globocnik simply went over Huppenkothen's head.

Contrary to Peter Black's view, a Polish expert on German policing in the district, Bronislaw Wroblewski, says both policing agencies were simply subordinated to the SS and police leader. *SS-Sturmbannführer* Dr. Alfred Haselberg, who arrived in Lublin on 15 November 1939, about a week after Globocnik, and left a month or so later, established *Sipo-SD*. Haselberg's administrative structure had, in August 1940, six major operational departments: administrations (Julius Cramer); *SD* (Dr Heinz Buchardt); internal politics A. (Lothar Hoffman); internal politics B. (Alois Fischotter); intelligence (Heinz Noa); Criminal Directorate (Hans Kleyer). By 1940, when the agencies were under Huppenkothen's control, branches had also been established in Biala Podlaska (under a man called Glett); Chelm (Kruger); Radzyn (Fritz Fischer); and Zamosc (Bohlmann). In addition, offices of a Criminal Commissariat were also located in these centers, as well as in Bilgoraj, Hrubieszow, Krasnystaw, Krasnik, Pulawy, and Tomaszow-Lubelski. Most of these also had border outposts linked to *Sipo-SD*, meaning a broad penetration of non-ghettoized Polish society existed, with not all personnel centralized in Lublin. *Sipo-SD* were in charge of security, and therefore also had a network of jails and detention centers in which suspects were held for interrogation and relocated to other forms of incarceration.[91]

One of their major tasks was to combat the Polish Underground, which meant finding and creating informers by using whatever methods proved productive, namely, blackmail, threat of incarceration, punishment of family members, and the like. Also not to be ignored in this regard was Lublin District's sizable Ukrainian minority, which was linked via a formalized association with the Krakow-based Ukrainian Central Committee that was created and financed by the Gestapo. Many Ukrainians, like many local and other *Volksdeutsche*, were fluent Polish speakers, a not insignificant asset. In addition there was nothing except conscience stopping an ethnic Pole from committing an act of treachery against a neighbor or others. Globocnik's police forces and their networks had no end of ways and means of fulfilling their essential functions. As will be seen, the police had as their major prison what was known as *Zamek Lubleski* (Lublin Castle) through which some 40,000 prisoners were processed between October 1939 and 22 July 1944, that is, in 57 months or 1,700 days. Of this huge number of inmates, and over such a short period, 4,500 were executed while another 4,700 were unaccounted for, meaning one in five perished. But another 2,200 died in the Zamek during interrogations or died in custody, taking the loss rate to well over one in four. The loss rate was in fact far higher, because once arrested and processed, prisoners were deported to concentration or other camps, of which there was an abundance in Globocnik's district. Those in this category numbered 18,600, and of these 3600 later died.[92] Involuntary involvement — namely arrest and interrogation — by *Sipo-SD* was therefore a dangerous and naturally unwelcome fate to befall a member of any family. Also not to be ignored is the fact that Polish, Ukrainian, and Jewish police services existed, the latter within the ghettos. The last *Sipo-SD* chief was Dr. Karl Putz, a lawyer who had held the same post during 1942 and much of 1943 in Wolyn (Volhynia) Province, adjacent and to the east of Lublin District. He left in July 1944 when German forces withdrew ahead of the advancing Red Army.

As if all this was not enough, both Globocnik and the occupation forces in general had one last layer to ensure their security over a largely disarmed but slowly arming — through the Polish Underground — population. Backing up all these police formations was the German army, the *Wehrmacht*. It, like Globocnik's policing arms, participated in a range of suppressive actions and in some of these actually played a leading role. Army units were also at times used to convey the arrested population to Globocnik's varied detention centers. Lublin District formed one of the army's five Main Field Commands, giving Globocnik the army to fall back upon, if all else failed. A general uprising was simply out of the question, and the Polish Underground fully appreciated this. It was for this reason that the Poles had developed a strategy of planning for an uprising in the distant future, when the German occupation and its terror *apparat* was adjudged to be collapsing, that is, when it was on the brink of being toppled by force exerted from beyond the nation. The major Polish Underground fighting arm was the *Armia Krajowa* (AK) and it differed with the tiny Communist *Armia Ludowa* (AL) which promoted, at

Moscow's behest, the idea of fighting now. Nevertheless, when Globocnik and von Mohrenschildt launched the Zamosc Lands cleansing action, the AK's stand was reversed, since both it and the *Bataliony Chopskie* (BCh), Peasant Battalions, a significant force across Lublin District, launched what has come to be known as the Zamosc Uprising, and the AL joined in. The German army countered this uprising by launching a series of search and destroy operations.

The primary field command in Lublin was subdivided territorially and based in various major towns, with larger units called garrison commands and smaller ones local command posts. The army's units were primarily involved in guarding communications routes and military premises. This, in part, explains why the *Wehrmacht* became involved in the Zamosc Lands uprising launched by BCh and AK units against the forced evictions of peasant farmers across this region. The local commander, Major-General Hjalmar Moser, had at his disposal to help carry out his task about a dozen battalions. Clearly, Globocnik's Gulag was never under any threat of being toppled, either by German civilian administrators or by Polish partisan forces that were slowly readying themselves for such an overthrow once the Reich was set to be defeated by the Allies. Neither the AK nor the BCh's local or national commands even envisaged some suicidal bid to defeat the enormously powerful occupation forces of the General Gouvernement and its component districts.

Finally, Globocnik's role as overall head of *Aktion Reinhardt* and his links to *Sipo-SD* were further reinforced through intermittent personal contact with a specialist police training academy situated in southern Poland's Tatra Mountain region at Bad Rabka (a German name). Historian Robin O'Neil, who has focused on the Jewish genocide across Galicia, the region southeast of Globocnik's Lublin District, points out that this out-of-the-way police academy was established soon after Poland was occupied, well before Heydrich convened the Wannsee Conference in Berlin to give the go-ahead for the Jewish genocide. The *Sipo-SD* academy had initially been based at the Polish ski resort town of Zakopane, but in July 1940 was relocated to nearby Bad Rabka. Before the war this township had been a health resort situated on both sides of the Raba River, about midway between Krakow and Zakopane. O'Neil describes Globocnik's association with this important academy as follows:

> Globocnik also integrated the close-by [to Lublin] Trawniki Training Establishment, the central training camp for Ukrainian-Soviet guard auxiliaries. He was also able to call on the expertise of the highly trained personnel from the *Sipo-SD* Academy at Bad Rabka. All these support units were integrated into the system and when the time was opportune, were drawn together to expedite *Aktion Reinhardt*.... In late 1941 and well into 1943 there was a close liaison between Lublin *Aktion Reinhardt* officers and the Rabka *SD* Academy. There

was constant exchange of personnel either by the "Jewish experts" from both establishments engaged on lecturing and practical demonstrations at each venue. *Globocnik and Höfle often lectured at the Academy* to mid and senior *SD* management whereas [*SS-Obersturmführer* Dr. Karl Eberhard] Schongarth with his specialist team of *SD* staff visited Lublin [emphasis added].[93]

VI

The First Solution

As already indicated, a series of early 20th century German nationalistic propagandists, men like Adolf Bartels and Heinrich von Class, and even the late 19th century ultra nationalist and promoter of German eastern expansion, Paul de Lagarde, had advocated that both Jews and Poles could or should be removed en masse to regions well away from Germany's eastern borderlands. The annexed lands were seen as areas worthy of incorporating into Germany to be settled by Germans. It is noteworthy that such ideas of population expulsion and transfer were even propounded by Prussia's dominant and most famous 19th century chancellor, Otto von Bismarck, who, during an 1883 meeting with a Prince Chlodwig Hohenlohe, spoke of Prussia having "to restore Poland on the Dvina and Dneiper"—well inside the boundaries of contemporary Czarist Russia—if Prussia and Russia ever found themselves at war.[1] Bismarck, a man with a noted contempt for Catholics as well as his eastern Polish neighbors, most of whom were Catholics, had even effected an expulsion of several tens of thousands of Poles into central, or Russian, Poland from regions that were in his day known as Pomerania and Poznania, and part of Prussia. But he was not alone in holding such views, nor were the Poles the only targeted people. Adolf Bartels, a poet, historical novelist, and professor of German literature and member of the *Deutschevölk-isher* Movement, in 1914 spoke of compulsorily removing Jews to Ottoman-controlled territory, namely Palestine, which later Zionist thinkers emulated, though in their case such movements by individuals were voluntary. In light of such regular surfacing and re-surfacing of a nascent Germanic apartheid and expulsionist tradition, which so deeply influenced SS thinkers, especially those at its highest levels, it is not surprising that in the early victorious months of Hitler's war SS figures like Reinhard Heydrich and Heinrich Himmler, especially, and party ideologue Alfred Roseberg, promptly set about creating a reservation — a place away from the Reich proper — for Jews. This entity was to be located in a relatively isolated part of occupied Poland, one within what became Globocnik's Lublin District. This so-called Lublin Reservation was to have been around the towns of Nisko/Zarzecze on the River San, in Radom District, and nearby Zarzecze, which is just inside Lublin District. The desire for apartheid was so strong in Heydrich's case that just one day after Berlin had acquired the Lublin area from the Soviet Union, 28 September 1939, he began alluding to a "Reichs-Ghetto" within this District. At this stage Globocnik had not been assigned to be Lublin District's senior SS man and police chief. Moreover, the early provisional Jewish relocation plans referred to settling five million European Jews within this rural "Reichs-Ghetto."[2]

The location around which this entity was to have been constructed, near Nisko/Zarzecze, which in Polish means "low," resembled the generally low-lying and swampy areas surround Auschwitz-Birkenau, where many tens of thousands of Polish and other inmates were later forced to drain adjacent lands. The General Gouvernement was essentially a landlocked Polish reservation, ruled by a dual Austro-German bureaucracy made up of an SS Police arm and a civilian one. Eastern Poland, that half of the nation that had been traded off by Hitler to the Soviet Union, was to be Bolshevized. From there many members of the ethnic Polish demographic component were deported by Stalin's NKVD into Siberia and Kazakhstan, while ethnic Poles in northern and western Poland, which were formally annexed by the Reich with Upper Silesia in October 1939, were to be deported into central Poland. This would render the General Gouvernement, roughly a quarter of the area of pre-war Poland, for a time a Polish reservation, while the planned five million strong Jewish "Reichs-Ghetto" within the Polish reservation would be an even smaller, tiny entity. Both "reservations," however, were economically unviable.

Whether the short-lived Lublin or Jewish Reservation was originally seen as an end in itself, with the SS seeing it becoming a permanent and exclusive Jewish locale, like a White supremacist South African bantustan, or whether it was to be a halfway house to extermination or some other fate later remains a moot point. Considering the later drawing up of *Generalplan Ost*, it is safe to conclude that it was to have been only a halfway house with further eastward expulsions in store for these five or so million Jews. The one thing that we can be certain about, however, is that those living and working within this short-lived attempt to create an exclusively Jewish non-urban area, a *Jüdisches Reservat*, or *Judenvorstaat*, not a *Judenstaat*, could at a later date have easily been moved further east or elsewhere.

Most who have written about this early little-known interim National Socialist demographic creation to be located, initially at least, along the western perimeter of Globocnik's Lublin District, generally date its origin to a speech of 7 February 1939, given by the NSDAP's Baltic German ideologist Alfred Rosenberg to a group of foreign diplomats and international press corps members; exposing the idea drew Western attention.

> Thus only one question remains to be solved: which territory are the democracies willing to provide for the purpose of settling all the Jews. This territory must be suitable to take some 15 million Jews. For this purpose the Jewish millionaires and multi-millionaires all over the world would have to place their means at the disposal of, for instance, the bureau of the Evian Conference.... In the event of millions of Jews settling, elementary humanity towards Jewry demands that they should not be left to themselves, but every colony would be under the supervision of an administration trained in police work.... With regard to such settlement, there is no question of the establishment of a Jewish State, but only the establishment of a Jewish reservation.[3]

Six months earlier Rosenberg's article, "Whither the Jews," appeared in the party's official newspaper, *Völkischer Beobachter.*

At this time another idea of perhaps deporting Jews to the island of Madagascar also existed. Its origins, however, are far more difficult to determine. A German, Egon von Wingheue, published a pamphlet as early as 1931 in which he argued that Jews could be settled there. Himmler alluded to this island in 1934 and even a Polish fact-finding delegation had visited Madagascar in 1937 to assess if it could accept Jewish settlers, showing the idea was not simply a German or SS one. Madagascar had even attracted the attention of the Japanese as a potential settlement outpost of so-called surplus population, so this French colonial island held a strange mystique to a variety of people, not only senior Nazis. In 1938 South Africa's then Defense Minister Oswald Pirow had been invited to meet Hitler to discuss, among other things, settling German Jews in Madagascar, British Guinea, in South America, or in the former German African colony of Tanganyika. Pirow appears to have raised the question of an Anglo-American syndicate providing needed loan funds to bankroll Jewish settlement in Africa.[4]

Rosenberg played what can only be described as an early and crucial role in the formulation of the reservation plans. We know that he discussed it with Hitler at least once. Just after the outbreak of war between Germany and Britain, on 3 September 1939, Rosenberg met Hitler to advise of his concern at this unexpected, indeed undesired, development. Just 20 days later Rosenberg received a postcard from a British spy who had developed a close relationship with him and other senior Nazis, suggesting that Rosenberg and the spy should meet in Montreux, Switzerland. Rosenberg alerted Hitler about this; Rosenberg's English-language biographer describes the Hitler meeting:

"Six days later Hitler received Rosenberg to discuss the project *but spent most of the time describing his plans for conquered Poland and for creating a Jewish reservation, into which the Jews from the Reich, as well as from Poland should be driven*" (emphasis added).[5]

Considerable weight can be placed on this information, because Cecil's source is Rosenberg's published diary — a contemporaneous source — from the entry of 29 September 1939. The background to these moves to create a reservation within central Poland included first and foremost an overwhelming desire by the Reich's leadership to quickly remove all Jews from Germany and Austria, where the SS's Jewish affairs expert, Adolf Eichmann, was having considerably more success that his SS counterparts in Germany. Eichmann had effected quite substantial deportations — lifesaving ones as things transpired — through his Vienna-based Office of Jewish Emigration that he had established in August 1938, and in the *Protektorat* (Bohemia-Moravia), where he located a branch of the Vienna office. Globocnik had cooperated with Eichmann while he was Vienna's *Gauleiter*. Lying beyond all these possible non-European destinations, however, was more than half a century of fringe writings and propaganda by a range of German pamphleteers who focused upon the East as a final destination or resting place, for Jews and Poles alike. Another relevant element was the fact that following the German occupation of western and central Poland in September and October, 1939, another two or so million extra Jews had come under Berlin's, and thus the SS's, control. Only the last of these developments initially impacted on Globocnik's duties as newly appointed *SS-und Polizeiführer* of the most easterly district of occupied Poland. Significantly, the pie-in-the-sky Madagascar Plan had been the subject of discussions between the German Youth Leader Baldur von Schirach and the British Government as early as 1937. Also noteworthy was the fact that Berlin had participated in a major conference on refugees in 1938 in the southern French lakeside town of Evian-les-Bains, where resettlement of Reich or German and Austrian Jews was canvassed by international delegates. Moreover, after November 1938, the month of the pivotal widespread and violent attacks on Jewish premises and other property across the Reich, Hitler's minister of economics and president of the *Reichsbank*, Hjalmar Schacht, and Reich Ministry of Finance's state secretary, Hans Fishboeck, had attempted to devise a formula to arrange the funding of Jewish emigration. This effort involved George Rublee, director of the Intergovernment Committee of Refugees, which had been established at Evian. Like the other Reich apartheid blueprints being bandied about at this time, this one also came to naught, largely because Schacht fell out of favor with Berlin's power elite, and was removed from his posts by Hitler.

In early October 1939, Eichmann had convened a conference in Berlin, one which Jewish leaders from Germany, Austria and Czechoslovakia attended.

There he announced that an "autonomous zone" was to be created in the Lublin region. At the same time, he called upon these leaders to provide information about potential refugees. The Eichmann conference proceedings were then officially disseminated to the press and German diplomatic outposts, through the party's propaganda channels, and by radio.[6] As late as May 1940, Himmler was to please Dr. Hans Frank by advising him in a memorandum that he still foresaw the possibility of large-scale Jewish migration to Africa, something Hitler had agreed with; thus the Polish or Lublin reservation, which was within Dr. Frank's area of administration, was off the agenda.

Late in November 1939, Globocnik's former Vienna ally, Artur Seyss-Inquart, now deputy to General-Governor Dr. Frank, ventured to Lublin to alert the SS chief of developments concerning the Jews. After this meeting he, Globocnik, and Friedrich Schmidt, the temporary SS governor of Lublin District, visited the designated region on the district's western perimeter and gave it the thumbs up. Dr. Hans Frank, soon after, issued this statement at a conference: "We want half to three-quarters of all the Jews being located east of the Vistula River. These Jews will be squeezed in wherever possible. Included will be all the Jews of the Reich, Vienna, and from elsewhere. The Jews in the Reich are not needed by us. There will be no one else beyond the Vistula line."[7]

Although Dr. Frank cooperated with this scheme, he remained lukewarm about it, complaining at times about the fact that he was being asked to take more Jews into what he saw as "his" General Gouvernement. Despite such complaints, at other times, and on his own volition, he dispatched Jews into Lublin District. A considerable amount of uncertainty and backsliding existed all around, even while the Lublin reservation scheme was being hailed, promoted, and talked about, even if half-heartedly. On 12 March 1940, for instance, Himmler said: "German colonists east of the Vistula River will have to leave this region since this area had been declared a Jewish Reservation."[8] Even as late as March 1940, Globocnik was on the way to becoming an SS-Germanic "Pharaoh" figure of a "Reichs-Ghetto." At this stage it seems there were plans to move some five million European Jews into this region, and move out up to three million Poles, Ukrainians, and even German colonists — such as the Chelm Germans — living there. Another interesting development was the emergence of the idea that Jews being located there would be involved in constructing what was being called the "eastern rampart." It was also planned to erect four huge work camps with many affiliated establishments to house these people. From there they would be forced to work, as later happened to so many inmates of varying nationalities at Auschwitz-Birkenau and other SS-controlled work centers. The then supreme commander of the Land Army in Poland was told that 2.5 million Jews were to be involved in the work related to strengthening this "eastern rampart." This suggests that the five million Jews expected in the tiny Lublin Reservation were to become largely outdoor workers, toilers, not unlike the tens of thousands who actually built the pyramids. The rampart idea was, in all likelihood, the origin of Globocnik's scheme to construct huge anti-tank ditches around Belzec, along the Reich and Soviet border where many thousands of Jews would be forced to toil.[9]

News of the *Reservat* received some press coverage on 12 November 1939 in the *Luxemburger Wort*—a month after Eichmann had a meeting in Berlin with Jewish leaders, and just about the time that Globocnik reached Lublin, followed by *The Times* of London carrying an article on 16 December. Both reports referred to 45,000 Jewish men, women, and children arriving from Cieszyn, Katowice in Silesia, Bogumin, Moravska Ostrava, Prague, Pilzno, and other towns from Bohemia-Moravia (the *Protektorat*), Vienna, incorporated Danzig-West-Preussen, and Posen-Warthegau (western Poland). "Under the supervision of men of the SS Deathshead Corps, the Jews are compelled to work at road building, draining marshes and rebuilding the damaged villages. There is compulsory labor service for men up to the age of seventy and for women to fifty-five."[10]

News of this was even broadcast into Poland, either by German or perhaps even British radio. The Zamosc Lands' best-known wartime medical practitioner and a chronicler and diarist of the occupation years, Dr. Zygmunt Klukowski, living in Szczebrzeszyn, just to the west of Zamosc, wrote in his 7 December 1939 diary entry: "In our town, amongst the intelligentsia, there was considerable unease about news received by radio, that a portion of the Lublin region, including the part in which we live, was to be allocated to Jews from Germany and Austria, and we are to be transferred from here into the depths of Germany. Nice prospect indeed!"[11]

Klukowski appears to have been aware of the idea of the lands in Lublin District being used as some sort of Jewish reservation some five weeks earlier, at least on 1 November, because that day's diary entry says:

> Through Szczebrzeszyn, more and more Jews are traveling. Some are riding on horse-drawn wagons, but mostly they go on foot. Men, women, and children, with all their possessions, are going east. They have been expatriated from western Polish regions, they are maybe going past the Bug [river] to Soviet Russian occupation areas, or maybe they will stay in the Lublin region, *which is supposed to be reserved as a temporary settlement for Jews* [emphasis added].[12]

The American reporter Oswald Garrison Villard wrote in a December 1939 issue of *The Spectator:*

> With practically no publication of the plan in the German newspapers, Adolf Hitler is going ahead with the creation of a so-called Jewish state, located in

Poland, near Nisko on the San, south-west of Lublin. A stretch of land, about fifty by sixty miles in area, has been set aside. It is enclosed by a barbed-wire fence, and only the Jews will be allowed to live therein. Into this small territory are to be crammed no fewer than 1,945,00 Jews.[13]

Use of a figure exactly 55,000 short of two million — thus not rounded off upwards, which would have been quite legitimate — is puzzling and suggests Villard was probably writing from notes that carried tables supplied by his informant(s) which totaled exactly 1,945,000. This is a possibility, and the totals may have been of Jews from the Greater Reich — Germany, Austria, the *Protektorat*, annexed western Poland, and perhaps a number of large central Polish ghettos, indicating that Berlin's initial intention was in fact to create a single large Jewish rural reservation instead of an urban ghetto "archipelago" as occurred across Poland and, after the invasion of the Soviet Union, even further east. This, of course, is a guess, but not an unreasonable one. We know, for instance, that the huge Lodz (Litzmannstadt) ghetto, which was within the Warthe Land, located on land incorporated into the Reich in October 1939, was initially viewed as a temporary creation. The Lodz region's *Regierungspräsident*, Friedrich Uebelhoer, wrote on 10 December 1939: "The creation of the [Lodz] ghetto is of course *only a transition measure*. I shall determine at what time and with what means the ghetto and thereby also the city of Lodz will be cleansed of Jews [emphasis added]."[14]

Unfortunately, we do not know if Uebelhoer's reference to cleansing this ghetto meant deporting all its inhabitants to the Lublin Reservation. We also know that *Gauleiter* Arthur Greiser of Warthe Land had created this ghetto not as a long-term place of abode, but rather as a temporary measure. He believed that by forcing Lodz's (Litzmannstadt's) Jews into a ghetto it would be easier to slowly strip them of their wealth — currency or loot — by forcing them to spend it on food, after which "they will be expelled *over the border* [emphasis added]."[15] True, Greiser said nothing more than "over the border," not to a *Reservat*, but he may have been referring to a reservation rather than to one or more General Gouvernement urban ghettos.

In late 1940, therefore, the *Warthegau* [western Poland] Nazis had to decide *what to do with a ghetto that none of them had expected would still be in existence at that time.* Since Berlin still expected the Jewish question to be solved through expulsion *and refused officially to acknowledge that these plans had collapsed,* local authorities were left to cope as best they could [emphasis added].[16]

Nazi authorities in other areas were quite probably similarly disappointed, since the possibility of deporting several million European Jews to Madagascar, British Guinea, Rhodesia, or even east to the Lublin Reservation, or deeper inside a conquered Soviet Union, soon after it was invaded, were no longer options. The few contemporary Western press reports on the Lublin Reservation referred to above had apparently relied on information from several Jewish fugitives, with one of these probably the journalist S. Moldawer, who had managed to reach Palestine, via Lublin, some time before March 1940.

These press reports, though it could not have been known at the time, showed that the Nisko/Zarzecze or Lublin project clearly had the potential to become a huge concentration camp complex, one that could have easily rivaled the soon to be planned and built Auschwitz-Birkenau of Silesia, though it would have been called a "Reichs-Ghetto" or *Reservat*. This was something that Villard, though he naturally did not realize it, had the foresight to state in 1939, when he wrote that the reservation was "not a Jewish state, but a most horrible concentration camp, which can certainly become nothing else than a habitation of death."[17] Prescient words indeed. In January 1940, Reinhard Heydrich, in Berlin, claimed there were already 78,000 Jews on the reservation, with plans to boost this number to 400,000 during that year. So, although well short of the nearly two million quoted by Villard, the intention was for a sizeable number eventually to be located along the western perimeter of Globocnik's Lublin District. But nothing of the sort happened. Whether this was because of early and bitter resistance of General-Governor Dr. Frank to accepting more Jews into what he saw as an already overcrowded "Polish reservation," which he was administering for Hitler, or whether the Western press accounts affected Berlin's planning by shaming the senior Germans, we do not know. For whatever reasons, in April 1940, Globocnik's Krakow-based SS superior, Friedrich-Wilhelm Kruger, issued a directive saying the reservation plan had finally been discontinued. Earlier, at the end of March, Himmler had issued a similar order. Philip Friedman, director of the Bibliographical Division of the Joint Commission of Yad Vashem in Jerusalem and YIVO Institute for Jewish Research, New York, an authority on Nazi persecution, could enlighten us no further with his conclusion on the termination decision:

> What brought this sudden reversal of policy? We can only offer conjectures to answer this question since there are no documents available why the previous policy was altered. The following causes might possibly account for this change: (1) as a result of the overcrowding and miserable living conditions a typhus epidemic developed in the area; (2) the Germans needed all their means of transportation for the invasion of Norway and Western Europe which they were preparing and they could not, therefore, undertake any large scale transport of Jews; (3) the invasion of the Soviet Union (Plan Barbarossa) was already in its preparatory stages and the Nazis realized that it was not desirable to have a compact mass of Jews on the Russian-Polish border; (4) the possible effect of sharp conflict between Globocnik and the civil administration.[18]

This did not mean, however, that Globocnik had failed to continue development as an SS-Germanic Pharaoh-figure of Lublin District. He became precisely that, but more bloodthirsty than any Pharaoh had been. The chief difference was that his district would never become an exclusively Jewish enclave, a "Reichs-Ghetto," but a mixed Jewish-Polish district with a German or SS policing and killing strata in control, and alongside it a cooperating Ukrainian group.

More likely, though none of Friedman's suggested reasons should be discounted, was the early emergence of Globocnik as the preeminent industrial czar and "labor minister" of the Lublin District. He was obsessed with ensuring that Jews and Poles worked, and that their work contributed to the war effort and other Reich causes. His work camps now began to grow in number and expand in size, and they eventually became incorporated into his two huge industrial conglomerates of *Deutsche Ausrüstungswerke GmbH* (*DAW*) (German Armament Works Ltd.); and *Ost-Industrie GmbH* (*Osti*) (East Industry Ltd.).

> Naturally, Globocnik did it all with the knowledge and consent of the highest authorities in Berlin, who were later to designate him for this mission [*Aktion Reinhardt*]. At a session on April 22, 1940, Globocnik proposed the plan of creating labor camps for Jews. Men and women were to be isolated from each other. They were to be set at digging trenches and other fortifications on the Polish-Russian border. Globocnik reported that he had already registered about 50,000 Jews for that purpose.[19]

Though the Western democracies, including the United States, Great Britain, and Australia, and a number of other nations, especially Caribbean and South American, received many thousands of German, Austrian, Bohemian, and Moravian Jews during the later 1930s, none of the other options or plans referred to above, except the early stages of the Lublin Reservation, were commenced, let alone partially realized. With respect to the large-scale departure of Jews from the Reich during the years 1933–39, the Western academic and media orthodoxy since about the 1960s has been that the world refused entry to the expanded pre–September 1939 Greater Reich's threatened Jews, thereby being culpable for their becoming victims of Hitler's and Himmler's, and Globocnik's, ravages, which in many cases meant being worked to death and later killed in Globocnik's Lublin District, if not its early reservation. The term most frequently used and so well popularized to describe this alleged Western complicity has been the encountering of "paper walls," bureaucratic blockades, in the form of denial of visas and passports. But in the late 1990s this orthodoxy unexpectedly encountered a formidable critic in University of Wales-Aberystwyth historian, William D. Rubinstein, who argued that nothing of the sort had occurred. Rubinstein set out the exact opposite case, showing that most of the expanded Reich's — German and Austrian — Jews were in fact largely rescued from Hitler and Himmler's increasingly violent SA and SS, even if many were only temporarily safe because they had reached only nearby nations that were soon occupied by the *Wehrmacht* and thus the SS. The sudden declarations of war in September 1939, the quick collapse of Poland, and the subsequent rapid westward expansion of German forces in the spring of 1940, should not overshadow the earlier response to Hitler in general and Eichmann and Globocnik in Vienna in particular. Rubinstein's iconoclastic view is as follows:

> Fully 72 percent of German Jewry escaped from Nazi Germany before emigration became impossible, including 83 percent of German Jewish children and youth. Given the general restrictions on all refugee migration (including non-Jewish refugees), which prevailed during the inter-war period throughout the world, the emigration of most German Jews not only did not represent failure on the part of the democracies, *but constituted one of the most successful and far-reaching programs of rescue of a beleaguered and persecuted people ever seen up to that time.* [Emphasis added.] Far from the doors of immigration being shut just before the gates went up forever with the outbreak of the war in 1939, more Reich Jews found safety abroad in the last year preceding the outbreak of the war than at any time before. What trapped the estimated 140,000 Jews still remaining in the pre–1933 boundaries of Germany, as well as those in Austria and Czechoslovakia in the enlarged Reich, was the outbreak of the war itself: but for the rather unexpected start of hostilities in September 1939, it seems very likely that virtually every single Jew in the Nazi Reich would have emigrated to safety within, say, another three years.[20]

Rubinstein's supporting statistics show that the Reich's, including the Saarland's, Jewish population in 1933 stood at 525,000. By 1941, when emigration from the expanded Reich — it included central and western Poland, Luxemburg, Alsace-Lorraine, and parts of Belgium — was simply out of the question, even to the United States upon which Hitler declared war on 11 December 1941, the Jews of Germany totaled just below 140,000. Most had therefore emigrated willingly or otherwise; that is, they had not been "paper wall" victims. Quite the contrary. When the remaining Jews of Bohemia-Moravia (the *Protektorat*) and Austria are added to the residual figure, since both regions were absorbed into the Greater German Reich in 1938–39, this figure rises to 185,000. It was primarily from these three national groups, according to one estimate, that some 78,000 Jews found themselves dispatched eastward, under the Nisko/Zarzecze plan, either in late 1939 or early 1940 into the Lublin Reservation.[21]

Under the Nisko/Zarzecze or Lublin Reservation Plan, the first group of deportees of 1,000 men came from Moravska Ostrava as a pioneer corps to prepare the area for the arrival of later deportees. But Dr. Hans Frank cancelled the plan in the spring of 1940 in part because of his objection to having more Jews sent into his area of jurisdiction. He was in fact anxious to rid the city of Krakow of Jews as soon as possible, and went on to do so by deporting many of them into Lublin District. This reversal forced Adolf Eichmann to launch an operation returning those set down at Nisko. At about the same time, the Jewish residents of the then-German Baltic city of Stettin were deported into the General Gouvernement. The Baltic Germans of Estonia and Latvia, earmarked for settlement in the port Stettin, were those "with seafaring jobs." Heydrich had ordered the Stettin deportations in January 1940, claiming their apartments were urgently needed, which may have been true, because *Volksdeutsche* from the Baltic nations were being withdrawn west following demographic deals with Moscow. This action involved 1,300 Jews, and was a well-organized operation, carried out in a single night during the early hours of 13 February. The deportees reached Lublin, Globocnik's base, next day, and were then forced to march some 30 kilometers, an ordeal that took some 14 hours, with over 200 perishing. This harsh treatment of civilians, however, was just the beginning of an increasingly inhuman streak within the SS who took charge of this demographic sorting.

Differing theories and explanations for the reservation surfaced, even during the war, and from unexpected quarters. One of the more interesting was carried in what appears to be a book privately published in London by the author Francis Aldor. This intriguing book, which lacks a publication date but was probably released late in 1940, contains a lengthy and insightful section on the Lublin Reservation. Quoting just two extracts is perhaps adequate to characterize Aldor's assessment, which is almost certainly based on up-to-date intelligence, probably from Polish Exile Government circles in London which had obtained the information by clandestine radio communications or couriers from within occupied Poland.

> The conquest of Poland has given Hitler an opportunity to erect a prison-State for the Jewry he so fiercely detests. His is now in a position to play to an end this diabolical game with millions of Jews. Every human — or at least sane — person knows that the 5000 square miles of "Jewland" in the Government of Lublin is not sufficient to hold the two million Jews whom Hitler proposes to deport there, and to support them at any conceivable humane considerations.... Up to now more than 50,000 Jews have been deported to this area and have thereby been condemned to death by slow starvation.[22]

Further on Aldor writes:

> Very few details are allowed to leak out from the European "Devil's Island," but those that do leak out are horrible enough. Thus it is known that thousands of Jews, men, women, and children, who have been deported from western Poland, Sudetenland and the Reich itself, have had to travel hundreds of miles in cattle trucks and have been dumped in the snow covered fields on arrival in the Lublin area.... *Before the course of the war interferes with Hitler's*

plan, the Germans want to clear all Poles and Jews out of western Poland, all Jews out of central Poland, and all Poles out of the Lublin area [emphasis added].[23]

These early insightful comments of Aldor's, so succinctly put, suggest what Berlin was probably, even if only for a brief or intermediate period, bungling towards. It is worth keeping in mind that Globocnik was appointed *SS- und Polizeiführer* of Lublin District in early November 1939, precisely when such plans and options were being considered and were very much in a state of flux in Berlin. Was not perhaps Globocnik at this time earmarked to be a type of SS-Germanic "Pharaoh" of all the intended Jewish settlers of a "Reichs-Ghetto," a *Judenvorstaat* on the eastern perimeter of the General Gouvernement, or the Polish Reservation? It is perhaps not so surprising, then, that Lublin District, just two years later, became the center — both the coordinating and killing center — of what was named *Aktion Reinhardt*. That extermination program could quite easily have been located further east, in Galicien District or perhaps even Mogilev in Belarus, as one historian has suggested. But it was not.

Though Globocnik did not play a central role in initiating the Lublin Reservation, he was ready with follow-up plans to create work camps once it was discontinued for whatever reasons, and he would no doubt have had other ideas if the original master plan had proceeded. Globocnik was, instead, in the wings as the Nisko/Zarzecze or Lublin Reservation plan was evolving and ready to be put into action. There can be little doubt that if this part of occupied Poland had become a "Reichs-Ghetto" then he would have been its SS-Germanic "Pharaoh." He inspected the area where the reservation was located, and he followed up with efforts to construct the so-called eastern rampart, using Jewish labor, after the reservation idea was dropped. Rattling around during these early days of the war were a variety of ideas and contradictory moves and counter moves. This is understandable, because Hitler's Nazi Party and Himmler's SS, with their overriding and burning desire to create a racially pure Reich, had also inherited a range of Pan-Germanic views, which included an array of suggestions for deportation of Jews and Slavs. Palestine, Africa, and Madagascar were three hoped for destinations, the East was another. In the case of the Slavs, the wildernesses of Western Siberia were finally agreed upon within the SS's planning elite as the ultimate destination, and this was an integral component of *Generalplan Ost*. Hitler's 30 September Directive, for instance, stated that the new Reich-Soviet border through central Poland "will be constantly strengthened and built up as a line of military security towards the East." Globocnik followed this by moving, in early 1940, for the tank ditches — digging project, involving thousands of Jews in the Belzec area. Interestingly, an American expert on Germany and Austria contradicts this, claiming instead that Globocnik and Adolf Eichmann were in fact two main players in creating a Jewish settlement east of the Reich in this early phase of the war.

> A feature of the settlement plan *in its early stages was the creation of a Jewish Pale in the General Government of Poland* [emphasis added], and in 1940 Himmler had authorized an Austrian SS official named Odilo Globocnick [sic] to make plans for this and to maintain liaison with Adolf Eichmann, head of the *Reichsicherheitsamt* IV D, [sic] which handled the deportation of Jews from Germany.[24]

Unfortunately, sources for both these claims derive from the writings of the pathfinding historian of the Jewish Holocaust, Gerald Reitlinger, and specifically from a nonexistent chapter and page in Reitlinger's work. Thus we remain uncertain about the extent of Globocnik's involvement in these early phases of the creation of the Lublin Reservation.[25]

One of the most convincing, though far from comprehensive, explanations of this puzzling development is that given by the German historian, Christian Gerlach, who views it as one among many early demographic ventures that he categorizes as "utopian," which, although having little chance of success, nevertheless became a step along the way to the eventual decision to grasp at a cold blooded method of mass extermination by building compact barbed-wired compounds in out-of-the-way locations, and situated near railway lines where special teams, always out of sight, forced Jewish internees into gas chambers. Though the Lublin Reservation seems quite a long way away from this final approach, Gerlach says it, like the Madagascar Plan, had its place, with Globocnik playing a central executive role in both the work and the entire killing stages, if not the actual basic planning of the reservation.

> The National Socialists, with Hitler foremost among them, certainly entertained ideas about eliminating the Jews and indicated a willingness to put these ideas into practice well before 1941. But there is a difference between having ideas and intentions. The initial schemes for a "Final Solution" involved various plans for a forced migration. They were markedly destructive in character, with features such as slow annihilation through brutal living conditions and limits on reproduction. In a way, however, these plans were also utopian, principally because none of them, however seriously pursued, had any practical chance of being realized. *This was as true of the Madagascar plan as it was of the 1939–40 plan to deport Jews to the Lublin Distrikt. Destructive elements grew more pronounced in the plan to deport European Jews to conquered regions of the Soviet Union following a successful conclusion of the war there.* [Emphasis added.] Exactly how to go about exterminating the Jews became imaginable only little by little, even though a widespread readiness to do so had long existed. What was decisive for the actual realization of mass murder plans were the intermediate steps between the utopian emigration and extermination schemes, on the one hand, and liquidation programs that could be practically implemented, on the other.[26]

Significantly, in November 1939, Globocnik acquired from Lublin Distrikt's inaugural, even if only temporary, civil governor, SS man Friedrich Schmidt, the power to oversee "the systematic organization of all matters pertaining to the Jews of the district of Lublin."[27] Schmidt, as mentioned earlier, reached Lublin by automobile on 5 January 1940, in the company of Hans Maubach and Globocnik's future fiancée, Irmgard Rickheim; that trip for Schmidt was a return to Lublin. On acquiring these powers, Globocnik quickly created a special Division for Jewish Affairs headed by Dr. Karl Hofbauer, and later by his Klagenfurt friend, Ernst Lerch. This early acquisition of power over Jewish affairs appears to support Craig's contention that Globocnik was an early, if not significant, participant in the reservation plan. Although Rickheim is no longer certain, she recalled many years after the war that Schmidt's pre-war background was in the administration of concentration camps in the Reich; Schmidt's handing over of powers over Jewish affairs was simply one SS man giving that power to another SS man. Lublin District's civilian government had not, at that stage, been established. Schmidt's successor, Ernst Zörner, and his Jewish affairs consultant, Richard Turk, were soon quarreling with Globocnik and Karl Hofbauer. This early emergence of Globocnik as the "mover and shaker" in Lublin District's Jewish affairs area, particularly the mobilization for mass labor duties and projects, is described and insightfully assessed by historian Isaiah Trunk in his comprehensive study of the Nazi and SS-created Jewish Councils (*Judenrate*) of Eastern Europe.[28] Referring to the period around April 1940, Trunk writes:

> ...[T]he SS and police organs in the Government General, with Himmler's support, did not stop their efforts to secure authority for themselves over the Jewish population. These efforts were particularly evident in the Lublin Distrikt, where SS and Police Leader Odilo Globocnik, future chief of the murderous *Kommando Einsatz Reinhardt*, was in command.[29]

Friedrich-Wilhelm Kruger, Globocnik's nominal superior in the General Gouvernement, had gained from Dr. Hans Frank, as early as October 1939, the power to direct Jewish labor. As time passed, attempts were made to reverse this early SS acquisition, with Kruger resisting such moves, since that would have meant the downgrading of the SS, Globocnik, and, ultimately, Himmler. The dispute surrounding the question of who directed Jewish labor even came to involve the overall chief of the Security Police in all occupied Poland, Bruno Streckenbach, who lobbied for his units to have command of the Jewish population. Zörner, the Warsaw District governor, Ludwig Fischer, and Dr. Hans Frank, opposed this, wanting the civilian administration to be fully in charge. By June 1940 matters had moved in what can best be described as the Frank-Zörner direction, with Kruger seemingly ready to concede. Such decisions, however, had to be made known and realized at the district level.

...[T]he Lublin governor [Zörner] tried to convince Globocnik to submit to the new regulations in a broader interpretation that would give exclusive competence over Jewish labor to the civilian administration. But the negotiations with Globocnik were fruitless, since he had no intention of giving up his jurisdiction in this matter.[30]

In July, Dr. Karl Hofbauer demanded from the Labor Office 3,000 Jewish workers for the labor camp at Belzec. A week later a further 500 workers were sought. By now some 30,000 Jews were involved in building border fortifications. At this point a certain Hans Damrau, who was in charge of the Labor Office in Lublin, and therefore aligned with if not subordinated to Zörner, learned from Dr. Hans Frank that Dr. Hofbauer was to be removed from Jewish affairs, as was the SS.

Frank also informed Damrau that Jewish labor from Cracow district, and not from the Lublin Distrikt, would be used for building border fortifications. But Globocnik, certain of the backing of Himmler and his mighty SS apparatus, was not ready to give in. Without the knowledge of the local labor offices, he ordered the carrying out of raids on the Jewish population in the Lublin Distrikt to secure enough workers for SS labor camps then being established. Raids by the police took place on the nights of August 13–14, 1940 and December 11–12, 1941; and despite Globocnik's promises given to the chief of the Lublin labor department even persons with certificates testifying that they were employed by the Germans were picked up.[31]

This intensely antagonistic relationship persisted throughout 1940 and 1941, and involved unilateral SS-inspired press gang actions directed at the Jews of Lublin District. Globocnik by now had well and truly begun establishing his own network of work camps in and around Lublin — his Gulag — and had even "forced the Lublin Jewish Council to pay for maintenance, medical treatment, and other expenditure on behalf of the laborers."[32] Trunk points out that this antagonism was not limited to Jewish affairs.

Globocnik's absolutely uncompromising stance on the issue of Jewish affairs is significant with respect to his later genocidal work as head of *Aktion Reinhardt* because it was, so to speak, a bridge in that direction; a bridge between fantastic notions of eastward expulsion (the Lublin Reservation Plan and death-through-work approach) and extermination (*Aktion Reinhardt*). Trunk says that in early 1941, nearly a year before the senior officials of the civilian wing of the occupation government and some from Berlin met at Wannsee, Globocnik had let Zörner's chief of Jewish affairs, the hapless Richard Turk, know that he (Globocnik) had certainly not accepted that the civilian wing of government was in charge of "Jewish matters of a principle and political nature." Trunk writes: "...[H]e [Globocnik] let him [Turk] know that at Heydrich's request a special member of Globocnik's staff had been designated to handle Jewish affairs on behalf of the Security Police and *SD*, and *that all questions of principle or of a political nature should be cleared with this man*" (emphasis added).[33]

This advice to Zörner's man, Richard Turk, was given on 15 May 1941, about nine months before Heydrich convened the Wannsee Conference of January 1942, thereby formally advising that the all-clear had been given for the "Final Solution" in which Globocnik was to play the central administrative and coordinating role. Trunk, unfortunately, does not name the man who had been so designated to handle Jewish affairs for Globocnik. It was, in all likelihood, the ever-present Ernst Lerch, though it may have been Dr. Hofbauer. Whoever it was, the important point is that nearly a year before Wannsee was convened, a key member of Globocnik's staff had been given extraordinary powers over many tens of thousands of Jews, and Heydrich had cleared this appointment, suggesting that Himmler was probably the initiator. During all of 1940 and early 1941 Globocnik had resisted every effort by Dr. Hans Frank's various underlings to gain the ascendancy in this area. It seems likely, therefore, that Globocnik's sheer persistence and his obstinate approach to Jewish affairs meant that he continued catching the eye of officials in Berlin, namely Hitler, Himmler, and Heydrich, leading them to believe that he could help fulfill their desire to rid the Reich and its occupied lands

Globocnik's 1941 New Year card. (Courtesy Robin O'Neil)

of Jews once and for all. And ridding, in this context, and this time around, was to come to mean extermination, no longer mere expulsion eastward as the long-forgotten Lublin Reservation plan had entailed.

Finally, the scrapping of the Lublin Reservation plan did not mean deportations of Jews to the East had ceased. By the summer of 1940, according to a Warsaw Jewish Community report, Globocnik had 30 work camps. This number rose to 51 by early 1941, with the largest established in July 1940 at Belzec, where 30,000 or so Jews referred to earlier were forcibly put to work digging anti-tank ditches on what Globocnik saw as an Eastern Wall, at tasks not too different from those undertaken around Nisko/Zarzecze only a few months earlier. Although this project attracted severe criticism from some within the *Wehrmacht* who saw it as lacking military purpose, Globocnik was apparently quite proud of it. His 1941 New Year's Card sent to colleagues and superiors featured a number of small drawings on a map of Lublin District, and three men are shown digging in about where Belzec is situated, with a guard overseeing them (see illustration). The Belzec site became, in 1942, the Belzec killing center, on the southeastern side of the Globocnik district, strategically situated so that the Jews of Galicia could be easily brought in by rail. Globocnik showed, even if not immediately, that he was not satisfied with pie-in-the-sky projects like that at Nisko/Zarzecze on the western side of his district. He wanted work to have a purpose, one in which he strongly believed, even if senior military men did not. He was not content to see Jews sitting around ghettos until the war against the Soviets was won, after which they were to be deported to an even more distant *Jüdische Reservat*, either "on the Dvina and Dneiper," or deep in Western Siberia. Work throughout Lublin District, on projects Globocnik and his staffers designated as required, was the standard, but at great expense in health and life to the unfortunate laborers.

VII

Globocnik Moves to "Re-Germanize" Lublin District

Poland will be depopulated and then settled by Germans.... Who, after all, speaks today of the annihilation of the Armenians?
—Adolf Hitler, 22 August 1939

1. The Final Solution of the Jewish Question: Globocnik's *Aktion Reinhardt*

German National Socialism from its beginnings sought to create a unified and racially pure Germanic people or national community. Purity and unity for the Hitler group were far more important than socialism — the socialization of the means of production, distribution and exchange — which appears to have more greatly exercised the mind of ousted and murdered senior party member Gregor Strasser (1892–1934). "On 30 June 1934 he [Strasser] was arrested and murdered on Hitler's orders by the Gestapo, during the Night of the Long Knives. His death and that of the SA leader, Ernst Röhm, *symbolized the destruction of the Nazi left wing and the vague hopes for a second revolution in the direction of socialism*" (emphasis added).[1]

By definition non–Germanics were unwanted, which, in a practical sense, meant forced emigration, expulsion, deportation, resettlement, call it what one will, of all those people deemed to belong to unwanted groups. Extermination, by shooting or another method, such as gas or mass electrocutions — something Poles in wartime London were absolutely convinced was happening in occupied Poland from a very early stage of the occupation — or starvation, was therefore a major and new step to which reference is not readily found in early National Socialist or even *völkisch* literature or propaganda.[2] However, because silence could not be maintained, code words, or language anticipating George Orwell's Newspeak, were developed for use by those overseeing this killing program. Because racial purity was so paramount in Hitler's mind, Himmler, who shared this ambition as passionately, was able to maneuver himself into power over racial affairs, especially in occupied Poland where he had based Globocnik. Clearly, anyone close to and trusted by Himmler, such as Odilo Globocnik, was inevitably set to be drawn into working on racial and demographic issues. This was precisely Globocnik's career path once Poland was conquered, though, as pointed out earlier, if the Lublin Reservation had been successfully implemented he was ideally placed to have become an SS-Germanic "Pharaoh" ensuring several million Jews worked across his exclusively Jewish-inhabited district, a "Reichs-Ghetto."

Literature pertaining to the removal of unwanted groups spoke of deportation or expulsion, to Turkish-controlled Palestine for Jews, or somewhere far away in the East, South America, or Madagascar, and was to have affected several million Jews. The far graver decision for the removal by extermination of those defined as non–Germanic, non–Nordic, or non–Aryan, which was made by Hitler and his paladins late in 1941, is still not fully understood even more than half a century after the end of the war. German historian Christian Gerlach, referred to earlier, has pointed out that Hitler gave the all clear for deportation eastward of German Jews in mid–September, 1941. Four months later, Heydrich chaired the Wannsee Conference in Berlin that approved mass gassings in the Lublin District, therefore turning Globocnik loose to kill on a grand scale. Significantly, we know Globocnik visited Berlin toward the end of October 1941, just three months before the delayed Wannsee Conference.[3] This was a month after it was decided that Jews would be evacuated east, thus, a repeat, but on a far larger scale, of the ill-fated Lublin Reservation plan of 1939–40. It is important not to see these policies and emphasis in clear-cut terms, for the mass executions by firing squads — bloody exterminations — and by starvation — bloodless extermination — had already commenced across parts of the General Gouvernement as well as further east. Even so, Gerlach, writing in 1997, understandably stated:

> It is not clear if the German leadership actually intended to resettle Jews *as it had before* [emphasis added] or whether the phrase "sending the Jews to the East" had now become a code for murdering them.... During recent years surprising new revelations have emerged about activities of the SS in the Belarussian city of Mogilev. Jean-Claude Pressac has shown that in mid–November 1941

the Topf Company of Erfurt received a commission to construct a huge crematorium at Mogilev; the order came from Amt II of the SS Main Office for Budget and Building. On December 30, 1941, an oven with four cremation chambers was delivered and assembled. Three more ovens were available by August 1942 to be delivered to Mogilev and were then "diverted" to Auschwitz. The SS Building Administration of "Russia Center" already had paid most of the money for all of these ovens. Gotz Aly argued that the SS intended to ship some of the European Jews down the Pripet River and up the Dnieper to Mogilev and murder them there.[4]

Perhaps these most recent findings show that Mogilev in Belarus, not Lublin, or more correctly, Globocnik's Lublin District in Poland, was to have been, initially at least, designated as the center where European Jewry was to have perished en masse by a new form of bloodless killing via gas. Whatever the initial expulsion plans — and these arose from one of the foundation tenets of National Socialism of having a racially pure unified Germanic community: no Jews, Poles, or other Slavs — mass extermination was seemingly not yet considered, so Globocnik's role was not yet set out beyond that of working people to death.

The crucial, and initially unrelated, development that intervened was the longtime secret euthanasia program directed from Hitler's Chancellery, and headed by Philip Bouhler and Viktor Brack prior to 1942. It was the killing staffers of this secret program who provided Globocnik with a pool of already trained and experienced workers who undertook mass killing of Jews in his three isolated killing centers, the "terminal stations," two of them, Belzec and Sobibor, within his district, and the third, Treblinka, to the north of Lublin, on the railway line and roughly midway between Warsaw and Bialystok. The euthanasia program had been going on under a cloak of secrecy and tight supervision by several specialists within Hitler's Chancellery since 1939, but with its own Berlin headquarters at "T4," or Tiergartenstrasse 4. At its simplest, the top-secret extermination program that came to be called *Aktion Reinhardt* was therefore the merging, under Globocnik's control in Lublin, of what was initially intended to be undertaken at Mogilev, perhaps, by the men who had worked in German and Austrian sanitariums and hospitals gassing to death abnormal or otherwise incurable people. The euthanasia program's medical section was known as the Reich Association — Hospital and Nursing Establishments; Charitable Foundation for Institutional Care; and General Patient Transport Corporation, euphemisms for killing, and some 50,000 or more patients were killed by a workforce of just 450 personnel. Of these, only 94 were sent to Lublin at the turn of 1941–42, and these became the Globocnikian killers and supervisors of death with their Ukrainian auxiliaries.

Aktion Reinhardt was headquartered in Lublin, in the Julius Schreck Barracks on 1 August 1942, when the extermination of European as well as the

Lublin District's Jews was markedly accelerated. By the time these barracks in Lublin's central quarter were taken over, the three killing centers were fully operational and the euthanasia staff members were in place under Globocnik's control. In that month Belzec's commandant, the former Stuttgart detective who had a formidable and deserved reputation as someone who caught his man, Christian "The Terrible Christian" Wirth, became Inspekteur der SS-Sonderkommandos. Wirth had been an euthanasia program, or T4, employee. Hermann Höfle, Globocnik's chief-of-staff, became the administrative chief of Aktion Reinhardt, working alongside Wirth. Another key man, Josef Oberhauser, who became Wirth's aide, was placed in charge of the so-called Ukrainian guards, who were not all Ukrainians since they included a sprinkling of Russians, Latvians, and Lithuanians. A Willi Hausler took charge of basic administration, salaries, leave, and the like for these killers. The management was therefore tiny compared to the task and outcome. Very few people knew, even in Lublin, of the existence of this tiny set-aside group, because its members generally kept away from others. The story of the human cost of this murderous program has been told countless times. All that can really remain in dispute are the numbers of victims, and these tend to vary widely — Treblinka, 700,000 to 800,000; Sobibor, 250,000; and Belzec, 500,000: a total of no fewer than 1.5 million men, women, and children, including infants.[5] No evidence has ever shown that the Aktion Reinhardt staff was accurately counting its victims. There were no census takers or tabulators. By far the majority of those murdered were Jews, but a relatively small number, maybe even a few thousand, were ethnic Poles. The total figure does not include those Jews who died between November 1939, when Globocnik reached Lublin, and January 1942, when Belzec commenced its killings, nor are the deaths in Majdanek and those that occurred elsewhere in and around Globocnik's huge Gulag included, nor are the tens of thousands of Poles who perished under his various resettlement programs and other killings, especially the Sipo-SD's moves against the steadily more active Polish Underground and the later involvement by the Wehrmacht in that fight across the district's historic Zamosc Lands.

According to Michael Tregenza, Globocnik was to some extent the front man for both Wirth and Oswald Pohl, the head of SS-WVHA in Berlin, and these two men together had independent contacts with Himmler about which, in Wirth's case at least, unfortunately little is known.

> It's still not generally known just how close Wirth was to Himmler and what he could get from him by simple verbal requests — no red tape. It still seems extraordinary to me that during the couple of months Wirth had a temporary office in the Julius Schreck Barracks in Lublin, headed by Höfle, the majority of the staff there had no idea what his job was. Its staff were not allowed to use the SS canteen and had their meals in local restaurants, dressed in civilian clothing.[6]

Left to right: Georg Michalsen, Odilo Globocnik, Christian Wirth, Joseph Oberhauser, and Gottlieb Hering in Lublin. Man at far right, foreground, is
unidentified. (Courtesy Robin O'Neil)

To emphasize that Wirth and Himmler, in all likelihood, had a relationship that is largely unknown to other historians, Michael Tregenza continued:

> When Wirth discovered in 1942 that his youngest son — the favorite son — was
> on the Eastern Front with a *Waffen-SS* unit, he immediately requested that
> Himmler transfer him to a "safe" job elsewhere and he [the son] was immedi-
> ately sent to the U-boat pens in Le Havre, loading torpedoes. I shall never for-
> get this son, Kurt, telling me in Stuttgart in 1987 about the day he heard of
> his father's death in Istria. Apparently a full general (whose name regrettably
> he could not recall) came to see him personally at the pens and told him he
> could go home on compassionate leave. He declined — he was not very close
> to his mother — and instead went on a three-day "bender" in the bars of Le
> Havre (presumably from grief not joy!). *This kind of information — like that of
> Wirth's attempted suicide in 1918 — is not to be found in any document or archive*
> [emphasis added].[7]

Whether he was a front man or not, Globocnik's involvement in this
Aktion is indisputable, for we have many witnesses who have detailed this in
one way or another. These include Adolf Eichmann, Rudolf Höss, Joseph
Goebbels, Oswald Pohl, Viktor Brack, Wilhelm Pfannenstiel, Franz Stangl,

and Kurt Gerstein, seven of them members of the SS. What emerges is that Globocnik was under direct orders not merely from Himmler, but from the Reich's top National Socialist, an Austrian, Adolf Hitler, with whom Globocnik had enjoyed personal contact in the lead up to their other great first historic mission involving Austria, the *Anschluss*.

Adolf Eichmann: Supplier of Victims

Globocnik had a secretive relationship with Adolf Hitler, which helps explain why it took the personal intervention of Göring to get Globocnik sacked from his Vienna job in January 1939. Globocnik also worked closely for a time with Adolf Eichmann, who was found and kidnapped after the war by Israeli agents in Argentina and flown for trial to Jerusalem in May 1960, and later executed. During his interrogation by the Berlin-born Israeli policeman, Captain Avner Less, Eichmann, the Gestapo's chief Jewish Affairs expert, who initially worked in Vienna arranging the expulsion of Austrian Jews during 1938 and 1939, rightly portrayed Globocnik as the central figure in the Jewish genocide. He told Less he first realized all this after a conversation with Reinhard Heydrich, who had told him that if he, Eichmann, wished to learn about physical extermination of the Jews, then the best source to learn from was Berlin's man in Lublin. When Eichmann first mentioned Globocnik's name, Less had apparently never heard of him. Not even a German-born and leading Israeli law enforcement officer, who knew of *Aktion Reinhardt*, knew who Globocnik was a mere 15 years after the Holocaust. During the interrogation, when Eichmann and Less reached the issue of the Final Solution of the Jewish Question, Less asked if a document they were then discussing had been written before or after the outbreak of war. Eichmann replied:

> We can only be sure that it relates to the period when emigration [of Europe's Jews] had ceased to be possible and the more radical solution was resorted to. The war with the Soviet Union began in June 1941, I think. I believe it was two months later, or maybe three, [August-September 1941] that Heydrich sent for me. I reported. He said to me: "The *Führer*, well, emigration is...." He began with a little speech. And then: "The *Führer* has ordered physical extermination." *These were his words.* And as though wanting to test their effect on me he made a long pause, which was not at all his way. I can still remember that. In the first moment, I didn't grasp the implications, because he chose his words so carefully. But then I understood. I didn't say anything, what could I say? Because I'd never thought of a ... such a thing, of that sort of violent solution. And then he said to me: "*Eichmann, go and see Globocnik in Lublin*" [emphases added].[8]

At that point in Eichmann's long reply — when the name Globocnik was uttered — Less broke in, saying, "who," suggesting, perhaps, that even this senior Israeli police officer had not heard of the little-publicized Globocnik, a not altogether surprising fact, since Globocnik is little known among Western historians. Eichmann continued:

> Globocnik, the former *Gauleiter* of Vienna, was then head of the SS and the police in the Lublin Distrikt of the Government General. Anyway, Heydrich said: "Go and see Globocnik. *The Führer has already given him instructions.* [Emphasis added] Take a look and see how he's getting on with this program. I believe he's using Russian anti-tank trenches for exterminating Jews. As ordered, I went to Lublin, located the headquarters of SS and Police Commander Globocnik, and reported to the *Gruppenführer*. I told him Heydrich had sent me, because the *Führer* had ordered the physical extermination of the Jews.[9]

Eichmann met Globocnik another time in later 1942 or early 1943 at Treblinka, and was shown this killing center by Globocnik's adjutant, *SS-Sturmbannführer* Höfle.

Before concluding the Wannsee section of the interrogation, Less sought clarification that showed Globocnik had wasted no time in obeying the *Führer*'s instructions and had actually pre-empted them.

> LESS: I'm going to quote from your record of Heydrich's speech: "Emigration has now, with the *Führer*'s approval, been replaced by another solution, the evacuation of the Jews to the East. The present actions, however, must be viewed as mere expedience, but they offer a source of practical experience of the utmost importance with a view to the final solution to come." What does all that mean?
>
> EICHMANN: Since emigration was prohibited, *they were to be deported to the East.* [Emphasis added] This was the new — er — conception on behalf of which the conference of state secretaries was called.... The new conception that Himmler discussed with Göring, undoubtedly in Heydrich's presence.
>
> LESS: What is meant by "practical experience?"
>
> EICHMANN: The Wannsee Conference — we called it the Conference of State Secretaries — was held on January 20, 1942. Two months later, I was sent to see Globocnik. It is quite possible that the killing there had already begun.
>
> LESS: I see. So you think "practical experience" refers to the killing of the Jews, which had already begun? It's true that action teams were already at work at the time.
>
> EICHMANN: They started in.... Of course, there was killing.[10]

Hitler's behind-the-scenes involvement, as alleged by Eichmann, is further confirmed by Gerald Fleming, who has established that Globocnik had met Hitler after the outbreak of war, not only secretly during the mid–1930s before the *Anschluss*. Although we do not know what these two Austrians discussed, the fact that there was such a meeting between the *Führer* and the *Aktion Reinhardt* chief means it is reasonable to assume that the fate of Europe's Jews was at least raised. Why else would have they met? According to Fleming:

...we now know of Odilo Globocnik's visit to the New Reich Chancellery in Berlin, in 1942. Globocnik — "Globus" to his superiors and friends — was responsible, as the head of *Action Reinhardt*, for the extermination operations at Belzec, Sobibor, Treblinka, and Majdanek (Lublin) camps, functioning together with camp inspector Christian Wirth. On that visit Globocnik attended meetings without the officer who had accompanied him to the Chancellery.[11]

Moreover, Globocnik's adjutant Max Cichotski (aka Runhof) also disclosed, in a rather off-handed manner in his Wiesbaden court statement of 1961 that Globocnik had visited Hitler's headquarters. The question that prompted Cichotski to refer to a Hitler-Globocnik meeting, just in passing, and while *Aktion Reinhardt* was actually in progress, was that of the Jewish loot being collected in and around Lublin during these mass killings.

> Q. Do you know of the valuables of the Jews?
> A. *I like to mention what happened at the beginning of one evening when Odilo Globocnik was not there as he was at the Führer headquarters at Lotzow (East Prussia).* [Emphasis added] On this night a man called Blankenburg came from Berlin from the Chancellery — he came with a truck, which was full of suitcases and Blankenburg told me he had Odilo Globocnik's permission to store all the suitcases for safe keeping in the cellars. I didn't want to give permission and rang the *Führer* headquarters and Greitman said it is okay. I had to clear out a room in the cellar and a man, Natke, helped. Also two police ordnances worked for us and lots of cases were left in the cellars.[12]

Christian Gerlach, in an article tracing Hitler's involvement and the actual giving of the order to implement the extermination option — "the new — er — conception," to use Eichmann's words — the new solution, similarly refers to Globocnik actually meeting the *Führer*, though without giving the exact date: "News about the outcome of the meeting in Wannsee spread quickly. Heydrich gave Himmler a telephone report on the following day. Alfred Meyer reported to Rosenberg. Globocnik traveled to Berlin, probably on January 23. Hitler, too, seems to have been informed without delay."[13]

Gerlach's conclusion is remarkably similar to Fleming's claim that Globocnik had met Hitler "in 1942" and also to Cichotski's insider's revelation, and this applies equally to the claim by Eichmann to Less that Heydrich had told him to "Go and see Globocnik. The *Führer* has already given him instructions." Two scholarly analyses exist, then, contending that Hitler and Globocnik had actually met, concurring with one of Globocnik's staffers that they subsequently met, and Eichmann's claim — "The *Führer* has already given him instructions."

Rudolf Höss: Commandant of Auschwitz-Birkenau: Himmler's Other Major Industrial-Style Mass Killer

Auschwitz-Birkenau killing center's commandant Rudolf Höss made an official visit to Lublin, during which he met Globocnik. In his autobiography

Höss wrote: "He wanted to destroy every Jew in this [the East] area on the spot, except those whom he needed to work on 'his' police positions. He proposed to put all their property into a collecting center and utilize it for the SS."[14]

Globocnik's "police positions" refers to the SS and police strongpoints which formed the initial settlement colonies or centers, like the Germanized Zamosc Lands from which ethnic Poles were being forcibly expelled to make room for Germanic farmers. It was intended that the "police positions" would steadily expand in size as the Germanic colonists steadily acquired greater amounts of land, until the entire East had been fully Germanized and settled. And Höss's references to Jewish property being collected, that is, stolen, and "utilized ... for the SS," occurred to the extent that all the loot, money, bullion, precious stones, watches, and so on, were all collected, and what had not been pilfered was dispatched to the *Reichsbank* in Berlin to help finance the Reich's war effort. In the same pen sketch of Globocnik and his Lublin milieu, Höss wrote:

> He built labor camps for the prisoners, where he liked, without bothering in the least about [Oswald] Pohl or DII, for to him they were always "his" camps and "his" prisoners. In the same way he regarded Sobibor, Beczek [sic] and Treblinka as "his" extermination camps... While I spent my time arguing with Eichmann about slowing down the transports of Jews to Auschwitz, Globocnik was saying he could not get hold of enough. He wanted to be in the forefront with "his" extermination and "his" collection of valuables.... As his adviser on extermination, he had SA *Oberführer* Oldenburg, from the *Führer's* Chancellery, who before the war had devised methods of liquidating mental patients.... Among Globocnik's extermination centers, I saw Treblinka on the same tour of inspection.[15]

Joseph Goebbels: Hitler's Chief Reich Propagandist

Goebbels, who, with his family, was constantly near Hitler in Berlin, and was *Gauleiter* of the capital, Berlin, in his diary (27 March 1942) also unequivocally linked Globocnik to the extermination of the Jews. Goebbels was also clear-cut on who the ultimate driving force behind this genocide was.

> Starting with Lublin, the deportation of the Jews from the Government General to the East has been set in train. *It is a pretty barbarous business—one would not wish to go into details—and there are not many Jews left* [emphasis added]. I should think one could reckon that about 60 per cent of them have been liquidated and about 40 per cent taken for forced labor. The former *Gauleiter* of Vienna [Globocnik], who is in charge of the operation, is carrying it out with a good deal of circumspection, and his methods do not seem to be attracting much publicity.... One simply cannot be sentimental about these things.... The *Führer* is the moving spirit of this radical solution both in word and deed....[16]

Oswald Pohl: SS-Obergruppenführer— Chief of Wirtschaftsverwaltungshauptamt (WVHA)

Pohl was based in Berlin and had overall control of the business or economic aspects of the Reich's entire concentration camp system: He was the ultimate "accountant of death." He was therefore one of Himmler's most senior and trusted officers. Pohl was a co-director of *Osti* with Globocnik, and it has even been argued that he was in line to take over all of Globocnik's eastern responsibilities across Lublin District at some later date, to ensure Germanic settlement was conducted in an orderly, not "wild," or Globocnikian, manner. After the collapse of the Reich, he briefly hid out, but was arrested in May 1946, and was to be tried the following year by a United States military tribunal, which sentenced him to death. He was hanged in Landsberg Prison on 8 June 1951. During his incarceration before his trial, he prepared an affidavit for the U.S. Office of Chief of Counsel for War Crimes, which says in part:

> I knew *SS-Gruppenführer* Lt. Gen. of Police Globocnik personally and dealt with him in his capacity as Higher SS and Police Chief. He was the founder of the Lublin concentration camp [Majdanek]. On one occasion Globocnik spoke to me of the clearing of the Lublin area for settlement, and he mentioned the settlers' community he intended to found [Zamosc Lands ethnic cleansing action]. He was charged by Himmler with the job of carrying out the program against the Jews, known as *Action Reinhardt.*
> As far as I can remember *Aktion Reinhardt* was initiated in 1941 or 1942.[17]

Viktor Brack: Key Hitler Chancellery Euthanasia Linkman

One who described the origin of this new murderous chapter in Globocnik's life was Viktor Brack, who earlier oversaw the euthanasia program, T4, from within the confines of the *Führer's* Chancellery in Berlin, with Philip Bouhler, Franz Xaver Schwartz's old friend. Brack's sworn statement reads:

> In 1941, I received an oral order to discontinue the euthanasia program. I received this order either from Bouhler or from Dr [Karl] Brandt. In order to preserve the personnel relieved of these duties and to have the opportunity of starting a new euthanasia program after the war, Bouhler requested, I think after a conference with Himmler, that I send this personnel to Lublin and put it at the disposal of *SS-Brigadeführer* Globocnik. I then had the impression that these people were to be used in the extensive Jewish labor camps run by Globocnik. Later, however, at the end of 1942 or the beginning of 1943, *I found out that they were used to assist in the mass extermination of the Jews, which was then already common knowledge in the higher party circles* [emphasis added].[18]

At about this time the pace of *Aktion Reinhardt* was being markedly quickened. Eichmann's and Franz Novak's trains were generally running to schedule, and Globocnik's and Wirth's killing teams in the "terminal stations" were fully operational. In mid–1942, Brack wrote to Himmler, and again referred to Globocnik's role in this genocide:

> On the recommendation of *Reichsleiter* [Philip] Bouhler, I put my men at *Brigadeführer* Globocnik's disposal for the execution of his special tasks. Having received a further request from him I sent him more people…. *Brigadeführer* Globocnik has stated that the campaign against the Jews should be carried out as quickly as possible, as unforeseen difficulties might stop the campaign altogether and then we should be stuck in the middle of the road. You yourself, *Reichsführer*, some time ago drew my attention to the necessity of finishing this work quickly, if for no other reason than the necessity to mask it. In view of my own experience I now regard both attitudes, which after all have one and the same end in view, as all the more justified….[19]

Brack was not simply a desk-bound extermination planner, for he visited Lublin at least once, during which time he urged a quickening in the pace of *Aktion Reinhardt*. According to Christian Wirth's assistant, *SS-Untersturmführer* Josef Oberhauser, who was based in Belzec between about December 1941 and July/August 1942, Brack's visit was a surprise.

> At the beginning of May 1942 *SS-Oberführer* Brack from the *Führer's* Chancellery suddenly came to Lublin. With Globocnik he discussed resuming the extermination of the Jews. Globocnik said that he had too few people to carry out this program. Brack stated that the euthanasia program had stopped and that the people from "T4" would from now on be detailed to him on a regular basis so that the decisions taken at the Wannsee conference could be implemented.[20]

The overall coordination of *Aktion Reinhardt* from Hitler's Berlin Chancellery, although certainly implicating Hitler in this genocide, is not, of course, the same as being in possession of written evidence showing Hitler was definitely involved as its orchestrator. Several other points can be made, however, which make it much harder for anyone claiming Hitler was ignorant of Globocnik's Lublin activities to defend that point of view. First, we know Hitler and Globocnik knew each other well from the mid–1930s when Globocnik acted, with Friedrich Rainer, as a courier or messenger for and to the *Führer*, when Hitler was both in his southern German hideaway and in Berlin. We also know that Globocnik made trips to wartime Berlin, and one of his staffers, Cichotski (Runhof), has claimed the two had consulted in person while *Aktion Reinhardt* was in progress. It is most unlikely, therefore, that a pivotal Nazi demographic policy of this nature was not discussed by these two ardent anti-Semites. We also know that Himmler and Globocnik were close and that they consulted, if not regularly, then at least often on many policy directions and shifts during 1941 and 1942, the two pivotal years. This

Odilo Globocnik, Hitler's Man in the East

included at least one well-publicized visit by Himmler to Lublin. In addition, there is an unexpected and indirect piece of evidence that backs the view that a close Hitler-Globocnik liaison existed in relation to the Jewish genocide as well as the launching of *Generalplan Ost* to cleanse ethnic Poles from the Zamosc Lands. It emerges from work conducted by historian Werner Warmbrunn, in his analysis of the wartime Nazi occupation of the Netherlands, where Globocnik's counterpart, an *SS-und Polizeiführer* and also an Austrian, Hans Albin Rauter, was in overall charge, much as Globocnik was in overall charge of the Lublin District.

As in occupied Poland there existed in Rauter's case the question of who was specifically in overall charge of governance — the civilian administration or the SS. Rauter, like his SS counterpart in Lublin District, tended to act unilaterally, a pattern that all of Himmler's police leaders in occupied lands adopted. Warmbrunn describes this crucial issue as follows:

> Rauter's position was anomalous (as was not uncommon in the German hierarchy) since, in his capacity as SS and Police Leader, he received his orders directly from Himmler, although he was supposed to clear them with Seyss-Inquart. After the war, Rauter claimed that he was simply subordinate to Seyss-Inquart, *and that Hitler and Himmler told him so.... Others, including some of Rauter's subordinates, also believed that Rauter frequently had better access to Hitler, through Himmler, than Seyss-Inquart.* The latter could give orders to the police via Rauter, who would execute them if they were compatible with Himmler's directives. Actually, conflicts did occur, *which were resolved only after much discussion in The Hague and at the Führer's headquarters* [emphases added].[21]

It would be difficult to contend that the situation with Globocnik in Lublin was not identical. In light of the fact that the "Jewish Question" was so central to Hitler's and Himmler's ideological outlooks, dreams and aspirations, especially its final "solution," and also that the East and the fate of the East's non-Germanic inhabitants, plus the fate of Germans as settlers, were the basic purpose of the invasion of Poland and later the Soviet Union, it is most unlikely that Hitler did not, at least through Himmler, but at a number of crucial times, man-to-man with Globocnik, take particular interest in Globocnik's activities in relation to both the Jewish and Polish demographic outcomes. If Hitler's headquarters had become involved with Rauter's actions and disputes in the Netherlands, a country looked upon favorably by the *Führer,* then it was far more likely that the *Führer* did likewise vis-à-vis Lublin and Globocnik, whose work had an extra special place in Hitler's mind.

Wilhelm Pfannenstiel: Roving Professor and Hygiene Expert

Medical practitioner and academic Wilhelm Pfannenstiel, professor ordinarius of hygiene at the University of Marburg/Lahn and director of its

Institute of Hygiene, was an important witness for several reasons, not least because he was assigned in 1943 to take care of Globocnik following his major mental breakdown. Pfannenstiel, who was also a *Standartenführer* in the *Waffen-SS*, claimed to have first visited Lublin late in 1942, about the time that the Zamosc Lands' peasant population was set to be forcibly removed from homes and farmlets. He was in Lublin allegedly to assess hygiene conditions and to combat epidemics.

> According to the available documentation, I was in the city of Lublin for the first time in August 1942. It was here that I met *SS-Gruppenführer* Globocnik for the first time. At the time there were plans to build a large concentration camp on the outskirts of the city of Lublin, capable of holding about 150,000 people.... I naturally had other assignments in the area around Lublin which were also related to sanitary measures.... When I asked about the execution of Jews I must confess that on 19 August 1942, I witnessed an execution of Jews at Belzec extermination camp. I would like to describe how I came to be there. During my conversations with *SS-Brigadeführer* Globocnik, he told me about the large spinning-mill that he had set up in Belzec. He also mentioned that work at this camp would considerably outstrip German production. When I asked where the spinning materials came from, he told me proudly that they had been taken from the Jews. *At this point he also mentioned the extermination actions against the Jews, who for the most part were killed at the camp of Belzec* [emphasis added].[22]

Michael Tregenza has reported on this August 1942 visit, during which Pfannenstiel was accompanied by *SS-Untersturmführer* Kurt Gerstein. Both men initially met Globocnik at his home on Wieniawska Street, where they had an evening meal. After the war Pfannenstiel said he had wished to see the Belzec camp, where Jews were killed and Wirth was in charge. He also claimed that Gerstein had been charged by Globocnik to disinfect the large heaps of clothing at this camp.[23] This clothing was part of Globocnik's loot, and was clearly seen to be needed, and not to be simply burned or otherwise destroyed or done away with. That explains why Gerstein was needed for oversight and advice on disinfection.

Franz Stangl: Euthanasia Program Worker and Camp Killer

One of the most senior of the 94 euthanasia staff dispatched to Lublin was Franz Stangl, who was promoted to commander of the Treblinka killing center soon after arriving. After his capture in Brazil in 1967, he described while in detention his first encounter with Globocnik: "There were 20 of us traveling together, all from the [Charitable] Foundation [for Institutional Care]. I was put in charge. Later I found out that three or four of them had known, but at the time they said nothing — they didn't let on."[24]

Stangl said he reported to SS headquarters, Lublin, the Julius Schreck

Barracks, which were by a park in which all the trees were in full bloom. After identifying himself he was taken to the park and told that the general wanted to meet him there.

> I came upon Globocnik sitting by himself on a bench about 10m away from — and with his back to — the building. There was a lovely view across lawns and trees to buildings far away. The general greeted me warmly. "Sit down," he said, patting the space next to him. "Tell me about yourself." He wanted to know all about my training in the police, my career, my family — everything. I realized that this was in the nature of a "test" to ascertain whether I was really suitable for whatever assignment I was to have.[25]

Stangl told his new superior of his links to the foundation. Globocnik referred to some setbacks the *Wehrmacht* had suffered on the Eastern Front, and that it had been decided "to open a number of supply camps from which the troops at the front would be re-equipped."[26] He told Stangl that one, called Sobibor, was being built. An aide was called and asked to bring the plans. When these arrived Globocnik spread them out on the bench between them.

> They showed a design for a camps: barracks, railway tracks, fences, gates. Some of the buildings — bunkers they were — were crossed out with red ink. "Don't worry about those," he said, "concentrate on getting the rest done first. It has been started but they've got Poles working there. It's going so slowly I think they must be asleep. What the place needs is someone to organize it properly and I think you are the man to do it."[27]

In all likelihood the red ink-marked bunker was the work being supervised by Globocnik's gassing expert, Lorenz Hackenholt. Stangl was told arrangements had been made for him to leave for Sobibor the next day to work closely with the surveyor, Baurath Moser. Stangl claimed that soon after arriving he was alerted to the existence of "a new brick building with three rooms, three meters by four ... it looked exactly like the gas chamber at Schloss Hartheim."[28] Work apparently proceeded slowly on Sobibor, and Globocnik sent a messenger who told Stangl that: "If these Jews don't work properly, just kill them off and we'll get others."[29] Work had in fact begun on Sobibor in February or March 1942, a month or so after the Wannsee Conference and "early in May, shortly after the arrival of the first *Lagerkommandant—SS-Obersturmführer* Franz Stangl — the first gassings took place of Jews from Lublin."[30] Not long after this, Stangl was transferred to take charge of Treblinka, replacing Dr. Irmfried Eberl, also a former euthanasia official. Two months before Sobibor opened its gates to victims, another former euthanasia officer, Christian Wirth, had managed to get the Belzec killing center fully operational.

Wirth, as pointed out above, was a major link between Globocnik in

Lublin and the *Führer* Chancellery, which was secretly in charge of *Aktion Rienhardt*. Belzec began rising in late 1941 or early 1942 on land where Globocnik had created a network of Jewish work camps in 1940. Those confined in the Belzec network had worked on Globocnik's fortifications along the then German-Soviet border. By late 1940, some 36 labor camps existed in the General Gouvernement, with most under Globocnik's control. Again, according to Michael Tregenza, this killing center was not the first to be erected near Belzec with the advent of *Aktion Reinhardt* in early 1942.

> Early in 1940, while Wirth was still at Grafeneck, a labor camp had been established in Belzec and, according to the report prepared by the Lublin Jewish Council dated May 29, 1940, the first inmates were some 100 Jewish "volunteers." A week later, the Nazi authorities organized a Belzec Committee, supposedly to deal with the administration, health requisites and finance necessary for the labor to be undertaken; the digging of a 6-kilometers-long anti-tank ditch near Belzec as part of the German-Soviet demarcation line. On August 14, 1940, following the intake of an additional 10,000 Jews from all over the General Gouvernement area, six sub-camps were opened: Belzec Dwor, Belzec Mlyn, Belzec Parowozownia, Cieszanow, Lipsko and Plazow. The initial financing of these camps was the responsibility of the 37 Jewish Committees in the Lublin region, but apparently only nine actually provided money.[31]

Here was Globocnik in full flight: thousands of Jews forced to undertake manual work on huge make-work projects and even to finance this mass construction. As time passed, more sub-camps were established. This activity may have even reminded him of his days working in the mountains of Carinthia on hydro projects, but now it was on a far grander and far larger scale, and for Hitler's Reich, which was destined to settle the entire East; the Belzec camp complex and the coming attempt to Germanize the Zamosc Lands just to the north being the first tangible steps. Globocnik's efforts in this area were to see some 35 camps operating by 1941. This huge allocation of manpower was code-named, "Otto Line," and was originally intended to construct some six kilometers of trenches, but that figure soon rose to 140 kilometers using slave laborers from 15 camps, while the remaining 20 held men involved in anti-flooding regulation work on rivers between the Vistula and Bug Rivers.[32]

It is worth highlighting again that Hitler had specifically referred to Lublin during his secret address of 22 August 1939 to his military commanders as being one of the linchpins in the newly created border between the Reich and the Soviet Union. Hitler's words on that day: "The new method of conducting war corresponds to the new draft of the frontiers — one continuous rampart from Reval, Lublin, and Kosice to the mouth of the Danube."[33]

A cursory reading of SS Professor Konrad Meyer-Hetling's proposals for the East shows that Globocnik had already initiated the planned massive projects in his area of command by early 1940.[34] The Belzec area is best likened to a pre-medieval slave worksite, or a slave-labor project from the Egypt of the Pharaohs. It was what Meyer-Hetling imagined for the entire East, all of Poland and the entire Western Soviet Union. The out-of-the-way Belzec region across which the work was being done was isolated, swampy, and unhygienic. Michael Tregenza says that Zamosc's Jews, with others, paid 63,755 zlotys in May 1940, as punishment for those who had failed to meet their designated compulsory labor levy requirement.

> The Zamosc Jewish Community publicly announced that those who failed to report for forced labor at the appointed time and place would be handed over to the German authorities for punishment. Where the Jewish ghetto Police were unable to find the person named, other members of the families were deported instead, including children.[35]

Here was Globocnik in action again, arranging community self-enforcement to carry out Reich projects. We do not know why and when the Belzec labor camp network ceased operating, but it did. Eichmann, who visited Belzec and saw the gas chambers in operation, revealed that Heydrich had told him that Globocnik was "using Russian anti-tank ditches for exterminating the Jews"[36] through work. Until the practice of burning corpses was adopted, victims were buried in large pits within the Belzec compound. Later, however, these bodies were dug up and also burned. Like Sobibor, isolated Belzec had a small railway station — a "terminal station" — and was on the Lublin to Lwow line, well suited for the new purpose Globocnik required after 1941. Some time after mid–1941, probably in July, Himmler verbally instructed him to set up extermination squads and death camps. Michael Tregenza says that Globocnik responded by dispatching in October an officer with a small SS group and Ukrainian militia unit to the southern part of Lublin District and the Belzec site was selected for the first killing center.[37] By now Wirth, one of the Reich's leading gassing experts, like Stangl, was in the district, so all was set to proceed with the mass extermination of European Jews.

Kurt Gerstein: The Tormented SS Mole

Death, widespread death, was something Globocnik, Wirth, Eichmann, Stangl, and even Brack somehow adjusted to as perpetrators, even though Globocnik eventually buckled under the pressure with a breakdown, but not until early 1943. But another SS man, Kurt Gerstein, who has also implicated Globocnik in the genocide, did not live easily with the knowledge that death was being so frivolously treated by a small number of vicious Germans and Austrians. Incredibly, this engineer and mining assessor managed to join the SS some years after having been arrested by the Gestapo for distributing religious literature. Unlike Brack, Wirth, and Stangl, he had no direct association with the euthanasia program, only an "outsider's" interest in it. According to one brief account of his life, "Gerstein managed in 1941 to join the Health Department of the SS, where few questions were asked about his past. His initial motive was to find the truth about the murder of mental patients in the euthanasia institutes such as Grafeneck and Hadamar."[38]

In May 1945, while in captivity, Gerstein wrote an eyewitness account "of the mass gassings of Jews and other 'undesirables'." In it he described how the Grafeneck and Hadamar murders had promptly left him with "but one desire to gain an insight into this whole machinery and then to shout it to the whole world." Between the early years of the war and his postwar incarceration, he met several religious and other people to whom he outlined what he had observed. These included the secretary of the Swedish Embassy in Berlin, Baron von Otter, during a train trip between Warsaw and Berlin. That meeting was followed by two more, this time in the Swedish Embassy. Gerstein also visited the papal embassy in Berlin, but was not listened to after advising he was not a serving soldier. "I then went to see hundreds of people whom I told my story, among them the legal adviser of the Catholic Bishop of Berlin, Dr Winter, whom I expressly requested to pass the information on to the Holy See."[39] After the war Gerstein's account was confirmed during a trial by several of his contacts, including Dr. Otto Dibelius, Protestant bishop of Berlin, and the Reverend Herbert Mochalski of St. Ann's Church, Berlin–Dahlem.

Globocnik was a man with whom Gerstein had some dealings. He accompanied both Gerstein and Professor Pfannenstiel to Belzec, where he arranged for the camp commander Josef Oberhauser, in Christian Wirth's absence, to show the group around. Gerstein's major biographer, the French journalist Pierre Joffroy, described Globocnik's instruction as follows:

> "Lieutenant," Globocnik had said in Lublin, "you have two tasks to perform. First, to examine the best means of decontaminating the huge quantities of garments, shoes and so forth which come out of our places. Secondly, and this is more important, to devise some better method of carrying out the operation. At present we're using the exhaust-gases from an old Russian Diesel engine, but that has got to be changed. It's much too slow. The *Führer* wants things to be speeded up. Prussic acid may be the answer."[40]

Globocnik treated *Aktion Reinhardt* with great care and caution, and let all know that he expected the same of them. His words: "A State secret, and not merely one of the most important but, we may honestly say, the most important of all. Any man who breathes a word of what he sees here is committing suicide. We shot two men only yesterday for gabbing."[41]

This secrecy was extended to all *Aktion Reinhardt* workers who signed a highly legalistic document, the wording of which Gerstein's biographer has reproduced:

> SS-*Hauptsturmführer* Höfle, head of the Operation *Reinhardt* section under the SS Chief of Police for the district of Lublin, has informed me in detail of my duties in connection with the following:
>   1. the absolute ban on disclosure of any information, verbally or in writing, to any person outside the Operation Reinhardt section, concerning the transfer of Jewish populations or the incidents that may ensue;
>   2. the "State secret" rating of this operation in accordance with Instruction V on the safeguarding of secret documents;
>   3. the special instructions affecting the administrative services of the SS Chief of Police of the Lublin Distrikt, particular emphasis being laid on the fact that these are to be considered "service orders" within the framework of "obligations and prohibitions" as laid down in Article 92 of the Penal Code of the Reich;
>   4. the absolute prohibition of photography in all camps concerned with Operation Reinhardt;
>   5. the interpretation of Articles 88 and 93 of the Penal Code as issued on 24 April 1934 and of the texts dated 3 May 1917 and 12 February 1920, concerning entry and the violation of secrecy by non-authorized persons;
>   6. Articles 139 (obligations to report) and 353 (violations of professional secrecy) of the Penal Code of the Reich.
>   I have taken note of these instructions and of the texts referred to, and I am fully aware of the obligations they impose on me. I undertake to execute faithfully to the best of my conscience and ability. I am aware that I shall remain pledged to secrecy even after I have left the Service.
>   Signed...[42]

2. The Final Solution of the Slavic Question: The Zamosc Lands Expulsions, the Globocnik-von Mohrenschildt Demographic "Wall" of Germanic Eastern Settlement, and *Generalplan Ost*

Ten calendar months and two days after the 20 January 1942 Wannsee Conference gave Globocnik the all-clear to construct his three Bug killing centers and to make them operational as quickly as possible to murder the Jews of Lublin District and any others dispatched to him Globocnik issued, on instruction from Himmler, an order for the ethnic cleansing of tens of thousands of Polish peasant farmers from the Zamosc Lands upon which one of those killing centers, Belzec, was located. The Polish villages were to be commandeered and ethnic Germans, primarily from regions around Rumania, immediately settled within them. Globocnik was now aggressively murdering Jews and expelling, ethnically cleansing, Poles. The months between

November 1942, when the Zamosc Lands expulsions commenced, and mid–September 1943, when Globocnik left Lublin for Trieste, formed the apex of his career as an SS man, for he was fulfilling dreams and programs that had been promoted by a long line of ardent late 19th and early 20th century Germanic nationalist extremists.[43]

Globocnik's order, dated 22 November 1943, for the ethnic cleansing of the Zamosc Lands reads in part:

I. The resettlement will be launched on 24–11–42.

II. Command: The action will be under my command. My permanent deputy will be *SS-Hauptsturmführer* [Reinhold] von Mohrenschildt. He resides in the Julius-Schreck Barracks, Lublin. My operational deputy is *SS-Obersturmführer* Bareuther. His office is in the working headquarters of the SS, which is based at 23 Lwowska Street, Zamosc.

III. Command of those undertaking the action: The general direction of this action is under *SS-Untersturmführer* Werner. During the resettlement he will have his field headquarters in Mokre. He will draw up all the lists of people to be uprooted [Poles] and those to be resettled [ethnic Germans].

IV. Transport: To *SS-Obersturmbannführer* Perthen, Chief of Operations, *Volksdeutsche Mittelstelle* (*VoMi*), in Lodz.

1. Rail transport between Lodz and the Mokre resettlement camp and from the resettlement camp in Chelm to Mokre is under your supervision. You will sign requisition agreements with EBD (the chief railway directory in Poznan). The transports, on agreed dates, will be as follows: 24, 30, XI, and 4, 12, 14, XII, 1942. Through the resettlement office in Lublin you will receive lists of the German settlers and according to our instructions you will arrange the transport with them. In your Mokre field headquarters the field commander will decide a day before their arrival the exact lists of settlers. You will also decide the precise address of each settler. On the day the settlers are taken to their destination Gendarme Lieutenant Wagner will take over care of the settlers from you.

2. To the Lieutenant of the *Gendarme* Wagner.

Each transport from the Mokre transit camp to the village of settlement is under the direction of Gendarme Lieutenant Wagner. You will attempt to arrange and deliver the transport and take command over the settlers column from the chief of the resettlement camp in Mokre and escort them to the intended village. On arrival at the village you will pass them over to the village director. Timing of the transport should be arranged so you arrive at a village between 11am and midday. You are responsible for the safety of the transport between Mokre and each village. The necessary forces should be requested from Captain Eder. Because we will be resettling about three villages daily during this action you should have about 150 village carts at your disposal. You should request these from Polish villages not intended for uprooting and from the county chief if necessary if there are not sufficient. The counter-signed receipts by you should be submitted to the chief of administration of the *RKFDV*.

V. Organization of the Resettlement:

1. The chief of the operational SS headquarters is also the chief of resettlement. For the supply and implementation of the action and the work of those who undertake it is the SS Zamosc, *Untersturmführer* Wiebe.

2. The resettlement district will be divided into six units each with a central village. These are: Skierbieszow, Zlojec, Szczebrzeszyn, Zamosc, Miaczyn, Komarow.

3. The chief of central villages and director of resettlement.

In charge of each central village is the director of resettlement (to whom the name lists will be provided separately). As the assistant he has the following co-workers.

a) *Hauptsturmführer* Clemens will be the political assistant, representing *VoMi*, and he will be responsible for introducing to the action the *National-sozialistische Volkswohlfahrt*, the Womens' Union, *Hitler Jugend*, and the *Bund Deutsche Mädel*.

b) *SS-Haupsturmführer* Thomalla: Chief of the Building Group. He will supply the people in charge of building groups and the Germans who will supervise Polish workers.

c) Dr *SS-Hauptsturmführer* Sickel is responsible for Health Affairs.

d) There will be a Gendarme outpost of six people and if necessary it will be reinforced by local village guards.

e) There will be a village inspector responsible to the government-appointed mayor.

f) The plenipotentiary of SWG (Resettlers' Agricultural Co-operatives) will be responsible to the main office of the SWG.

g) There will be a branch of the Womens' National Socialist Union.

h) The Mayor. The resettlement director, in consultation with the county aldermen, will nominate the mayor who is to be assisted by the existing secretary.

i) Agronomics: The resettlement director will receive agricultural instructions from the county chairman of village organizations.

4. The village and its chief. The villages and hamlets named below will belong to the central village of Skierbieszow. Sady (83 farmlets); Cieszyn (37 farmlets); Ilowiec (21 farmlets); Hajowniki (20 farmlets); Laziska (35 farmlets); Lipina Nowa (11 farmlets); Suchodebie (8 farmlets).

In addition, there are the villages of Huszczki (small and large).

The forthcoming district of the central village of Zlojec will comprise the Zlojec village as well as the villages of: Zlojec (65 farmlets); Stary Zamosc (40 farmlets); Zarudzie (21 farmlets); Podstary Zamosc kol. (22 farmlets); Wolka Zlojecka (27 farmlets); Nawoz (42 farmlets); Chomeciska Male (28 farmlets); Staw Noakowski kol (14 farmlets)....[44]

Globocnik's historic order went on in this vein, listing many more Zamosc Lands shires and villages, and although the action was to have been launched on 24 November, it did not begin until the morning of the 28th, when the central village of Skierbieszow was surrounded by several German police and militia units.

The significance of this little-known action was many fold, not least that the clearance of Polish peasant families of Skierbieszow was the actual beginning of the Germanization (*Eindeutschung*) of what the SS had constantly referred to simply as the East. The earlier, 1939–40, mass expulsions of Poles and Jews from western Poland (Warthe Land), largely by Hermann Alois

Krumey, were not part of this new and intensified drive to Germanize the East, but rather an attempt to boost the German population across that region. The Zamosc Lands expulsion was the opening gambit in the implementation of *Generalplan Ost*, the primary reason for Hitler embarking on the war. Also significant is the fact that it was Globocnik, already head of *Aktion Reinhardt*, who had been brought in by Himmler to carry out yet another major aspect of Nazi demographic policy, removal of Slavs, in this case Poles. Moreover, the fact that this action's headquarters were within the Julius-Schreck Barracks, from where Christian Wirth and Hermann Höfle secretly organized the mass killings of the so-called Final Solution of the Jewish Question, is also not insignificant. One of the few Western historians to have fully grasped the significance of this new and intensified phase in Globocnik's Lublin duties and Hitler's and Himmler's moves is the American scholar Michael Allen, who has written:

> ...[I]t deserves mention that the SS, believing in the racial superiority that underlay eastern settlement policy, also took charge of "cleansing" the east of those who did not qualify as "Aryan." *The first death camps and the first SS settlements arose simultaneously, at the same place, under the supervision of the same SS officers at Lublin, in Poland* [emphasis added].[45]

By late 1942, Odilo Globocnik therefore had the unique distinction of not only being *Aktion Reinhardt* chief, but also of having launched and taken overall command of the ethnic cleansing of Poles, and with the help of Ukrainians. The Ukrainians' day had not yet come, and was never to arrive because when the Zamosc Lands expulsions were halted in August 1943, so was *Generalplan Ost*, which had called for the removal of all Ukrainians, like Poles, Russians, Belarusans and Balts, into Western Siberia.

The nearly 300 Zamosc Lands village and hamlet expulsions continued until early August 1943, and these ongoing clearances were undertaken in two stages. The first was between November 1942 and March 1943, and affected some 120 villages, while the second, from June to August 1943, involved over 170 villages. A German "wall" of settlement was being planned and, according to Czeslaw Madajczyk, Germans who had settled in Palestine in the 19th century were even seen as likely settlers for the Crimean peninsula. In addition, he contends, that the resettlement of some three million Dutch as seen as part of this purpose, and it was for that reason that in July 1942 the Netherlandsche Oost Compagnie was organized.[46]

Also noteworthy here is the fact that a year earlier, November 1941— several months before *Aktion Reinhardt* had commenced — Globocnik's staff had launched a trial deportation campaign affecting six Zamosc Lands villages involving some 2,000 people. In these cases Poles were removed and Polish speakers who were believed to be descendants of late 18th century German immigrant farmers, from Germany's Palatinate region settled in this area by Austrian Emperor Joseph II, were consolidated into segregated villages. This was consolidation of Germandom in action before the extermination of the district's and other Jews had even begun, showing that this was quite a separate and perhaps more fundamental policy commitment.

Altogether, some 110,000 people dwelling within nearly 300 villages, hamlets, and colonies were affected. Being affected entailed internment in a transit camp — in Zamosc or Zwierzyniec — where children and parents were separated, undergoing racial classification since the SS believed some Zamosc Lands dwellers carried "lost German blood"; being dispatched as laborers to the Reich; or simply being deported out of the region. At least two trainloads of expellees were dispatched to Auschwitz-Birkenau. As the expulsions continued over a nine-month period, many of those uprooted from their homes were even incarcerated in Majdanek concentration camps. Moreover, in the summer of 1943 nearly 4,500 Polish children — children of the Zamosc Lands — were transported into the Reich — Germany and Austria — and to this day their fate remains a mystery.[47] Other children, those not regarded as racially desirable, were placed with elderly people on trains and dispatched during the winter of 1942–43 to various villages, primarily those in Warsaw's environs.

But there was another category — those who fled their villages to evade capture who became forest dwellers. Many of these simply left their homes, often with livestock, and lived for months on end in the forests of their region — with families in dugouts and other shelters far away from the array of SS and Ukrainian ethnic cleansing units. In some cases entire villages fled and subsequently systematically raided and terrorized the new occupants, whether Germans or Ukrainians. Within this group were many young men and women who helped boost the ranks of the local partisans, who launched a resistance campaign against this second Globocnik action. This region's major partisan group was the *Bataliony Chopskie*, or Peasant Battalions *BCh*, who were steadily augmented by members of the pro–London Government's *Armia Krajowa* (National Army), *AK*. But the situation was never clear-cut, because units of the Polish Communist Party's *Armia Ludowa* (People's Army), *AL*, steadily joined in and there were, initially, even a number of independent Soviet units. As time passed and the Eastern Front moved toward Lublin, the Soviet contribution was increased because of the use of insurgents, erroneously referred to throughout the war as partisans, by the Soviet Red Army. But this was more the case in 1944. By late 1943, the independently launched resistance was therefore subsumed into fighting linked to the advancing front. This local response by the *BCh* and *AK*, because it came over 18 months ahead of wartime Poland's most famous response to occupation, the Warsaw Uprising of 1944, has been called by some historians the Zamosc Uprising. This would seem to

be a valid description, because it not only involved attacks on German settlers and the torching of their newly acquired villages, once Polish homes, but
also a series of minor battles, the ambushing of German vehicles, and dismantling of railway lines. The German response was to counter by launching a series of village massacres, meaning a tit-for-tat conflict had arisen
because of Globocnik's attempts to become a pioneering Germanic colonizer.
Equally significant was the fact that the Zamosc Uprising was the first all-out
Polish Underground fighting response to the German occupation since the
collapse of Poland in September/October 1939. The fact that such a response
developed meant that villagers of this region — and the underground network
among them — had concluded they now had their backs to the wall, thereby
discarding the long-established and agreed upon Polish resistance policy of
not countering the enemy with force until it was felt the Reich was collapsing, as it had in November 1918, when Poles in various parts of the country
rose to seize power and create an independent Poland.

The Zamosc Lands expulsions should not be seen in isolation. Globocnik, whose mother hailed from the Banat region of the Balkans, near Transylvania, and von Mohrenschildt, whose 19th and pre–19th century ancestors
were from Estonia, together planned to link those regions via the Zamosc
Lands with a settlement belt of German farmers. For this reason it is fair to
envisage or portray the Zamosc Lands region as the first brick in this ethnic
German colonialist wall that these two Carinthians were seeking to construct.
By late 1942, western Poland had to a very limited extent been Germanized
by the settling of Baltic and other Germans and deportation of Poles and Jews
into the General Gouvernement. It is fair to view the cleansing actions across
western Poland as the creation of the Reich's first ethnic German wall of settlement, created in large measure by the work of *SS-Obersturmbannführer*
Hermann Alois Krumey, who will be considered below, and who was brought
in by Globocnik from his Lodz (Litzmannstadt) base to remove Globocnik's
Polish expellees from his region. Globocnik's next step, if the action had been
successful, would have been to extend this Germanization across the entire
Lublin District, and from there it would have broadened backwards into the
remainder of the General Gouvernement. Thereafter new similar Germanic
demographic walls would have been created ever-farther east toward the Ural
Mountain range, but not beyond, for Western Siberia was seen as eventually
becoming the homeland of the Slavs, Slavic-Land.

All this was dependent, of course, on the *Wehrmacht* succeeding in its
aim of destroying and scattering the Red Army no later than the summer of
1943, after which that army's captured and disarmed soldiers would have
either been used as slave laborers to help reconstruct the East, or they would
have been systematically expelled into Western Siberia. There is no better
source to back up this seemingly preposterous and truly fantastic claim than

Reinhard Heydrich himself, who, not coincidentally, had chaired the 20 January 1942 mass murder plan to exterminate the Jews, the Wannsee Conference.

On 2 October 1941, nine months before Heydrich was assassinated by a British-backed Czech and a Slovak agent in Prague, he outlined at a secret gathering in his Prague-based seat of power, Cernin Palace, the fate intended for the tens of millions of Slavs living across what was increasingly referred to in SS circles in Berlin, and occupied Poland, simply as the East. Heydrich's candid briefing speech was delivered just four days after he took up his new position as Deputy Reich *Protektor* of Bohemia and Moravia, suggesting that what he said that day was of crucial importance both to him and to his administration, and he wanted his senior personnel to be aware of it as soon as possible. Before he delivered this secret address, his state under-secretary, *SA-Brigadeführer* von Burgsdorff, said during introductory comments that those attending were obliged to treat what they were about to hear as strictly secret information. All the points made were of crucial importance for anyone wishing to understand and appreciate what was about to unfold.

Heydrich first reminded those present that the SS was manned by the shock troops of the party "in all affairs concerning the internal political security of the region and the protection of the National Socialist idea." This was no idle statement, for Berlin's ethnic cleansing actions, at least in Poland, were exclusively planned and executed by SS men and a myriad of SS or Himmler agencies, including academic research institutes, with the help of supporters of the Ukrainian Nationalist Organization, and the Ukrainian Central Committee, in the case of the cleansing of the Zamosc Lands. He next went on to stress that he was undertaking the work of his superior, Heinrich Himmler, who held the position of Reichskommissar for the Strengthening of Germandom (*RKFDV*). Heydrich stressed that the Reich's military occupation of "enormous expanses in Europe," both Western and Eastern, was to pave the way for a permanent state of affairs, another Final Solution. His exact words on this confident proclamation were: "We will make it clear that the occupation of this space will, in any case, not be transitional *but final in many regions*" (emphasis added).[48]

In other words, the colonizing intentions of the Reich's all-powerful Hitler-Himmler leadership group were also destined to include a Final Solution of the Slavic Problem. Clearly, men like Globocnik were therefore needed, more so in the future than in the recent past. Those invited to hear this top-secret address also learned that the Hitler-Himmler group looked favorably upon Norway, Holland, Flanders, Denmark, and Sweden, since the peoples of these nations were seen as racial or blood brothers. People of Germanic origin had in the main settled these nations, which Heydrich preferred to refer to as regions, he alleged: "…and which in some kind of manner, about this we must be clear here, will belong to us whether in the framework of a state federation, *Gau* or in some other way."[49]

He stressed that these so-called Germanic peoples inhabiting these north-western and northern European nations should be treated with tolerance and understanding:

> It is clear that we must find an entirely different way in which to treat those people from that used for peoples of other races, Slavs and similar peoples. The Germanic race must be gripped hard, justly, but must be led in a humane manner, in a similar manner as our people, if we want to keep them permanently in the Reich and want to merge them with us.[50]

But the Slavs, those predominantly inhabiting the East, would, under no circumstances, be treated as mildly. Referring to the nations of the East — Poland, the Baltic States, and the various Soviet republics, he said:

> These, therefore, are the regions where a German upper stratum must be established in a very clear form of leadership; following the military development *deep into Russia and far up to the Urals,* these regions are to serve us as a raw material base and their inhabitants as workers for great and cultural tasks, as helots, to put it very drastically. These are the regions which one actually handles *as if digging dikes around new land on the coast:* by drawing a defensive wall far away in the East composed of warrior farmers, so as to seal off the land against the storm floods of Asia, *and then to subdivide it with cross-walls, so as to gradually win this land for us,* by continuing at the fringe of Germany property, which is settled with German blood, *and steadily moving forwards, one German wall after another,* making it possible to advance towards the East the German settlement by Germans who are of German blood. *It is from this viewpoint that you must see all the tasks in the East, which we now have to fulfil* [emphases added.][51]

The great Nazi racial divide was between East and West, between all of Europe and Western Siberia, with the Ural Mountain chain the new and great racial as well as physical or topographical divide; those seen as belonging to the former were doomed, in a variety of ways, but ultimately by wholesale dispossession of their lands, by their forcible removal, deportation, expulsion, and resettlement, as Globocnik showed on the Zamosc Lands. Those to the west were — if designated Germanic — to partake in the benefits that flowed from the Reich's victories and its colonization and exploitation of the eastern lands. They were to be settled across the newly acquired East. The Jews were also not forgotten by Heydrich. They were seen as a group whose influence simply had to be removed from *all* the societies of Europe's so-called Germanic region — Norway, Holland, Flanders, Denmark, and Sweden — since they were contaminating these peoples and that entire western region. According to Heydrich, "They [the so-called Germanics] are people who as a result of bad political leadership and *the influence of the Jewry* are somehow crooked and who must firstly slowly be brought back to the basic elements of present-day thinking." (Emphasis added)[52]

The Zamosc Lands expulsions not only fit snugly into Heydrich's eastern view; those lands became the first to see this view applied. Although nearly all the wartime documentation on *Generalplan Ost* was deliberately destroyed shortly before Germany's defeat in May 1945, several researchers, including especially Czeslaw Madajczyk, have conducted protracted investigation to find evidence that gives greater insight into this plan's scale, dimensions, and details.

From Madajczyk's and a small number of others' work, we know that Himmler created in 1939 a special unit, IIIB, within his Reich Central Main Office in Berlin, to devise the broad parameters of how Slavs would be removed from all the lands between Berlin and the Ural Mountain range, followed by settlement on this vast territory of Germans. This unit was headed by Dr. Hans Ehlich, who revealed the existence of *Generalplan Ost* while giving evidence at Nuremberg. A Berlin-based research unit headed by Berlin geographer and SS man Konrad Meyer-Hetling largely undertook the settlement aspects. Meyer-Hetling was sub-contracted to prepare a broad plan of settlement. Ehlich's experts had drawn up a two-stage proposal, with the first called the *Kleine Planung* (Little or Small Plan), and the second, or more ambitious, the *Grosse Planung* (Big or Bigger Plan), looking several decades ahead. The Little Plan considered only the lands immediately adjacent Germany's eastern border, specifically, western Poland, which had been incorporated into the Reich in October 1939. The implementation of the *Kleine Planung* had involved expulsions of ethnic Poles and Jews, many of whom had reached Globocnik's Lublin District during 1939–40 as expellees. Polish historians Janusz Gumkowski and Kazimierz Leszczynski have described the existence of this dual stage planning in the following way:

> The ... *Kleine Planung* covered the immediate future. It was to be put into practice gradually as the Germans conquered the areas to the east of their pre-war borders. The individual stages of this "Little Plan" would then be worked out in greater detail. In this way the plan for Poland was drawn up at the end of November, 1939. The second part of the Plan, known as the *Grosse Planung*, dealt with objectives to be realized after the war was won. They were to be carried into effect gradually and relatively slowly over a period of 25 to 30 years. *Generalplan Ost* presented the Nazi Reich and the German people with gigantic tasks. It called for the gradual preparation of a vast area of Eastern Europe for settlement by Germans and eventual absorption into the Great 1000-Year Reich. This area covered territory stretching from the eastern borders of Germany more or less to a line running from Lake Ladoga in the north to the Black Sea into the region of the Crimea in the South. The 1000-year Reich was thus to absorb the whole of Poland, Czechoslovakia, the Baltic countries excepting

Finland, (for the moment) and a huge chunk of the Soviet Union—most of Russia, White Russia, the Ukraine and the whole of Crimea. According to the Plan, these areas were to be "Germanised" before being incorporated into the Reich.[53]

Himmler and Globocnik, however, were unable to wait until the war had been won before they became ethnic cleansers and Germanic colonizers. They were impatient, which explains why they launched the *Generalplan Ost* in a fashion that can only be considered to have been wildly premature. One probable reason for this was the fact that Globocnik had in 1941 created his own research unit, the *Forschungsstelle für Ostunterkunfte* (*FfO*) (Research Center for Eastern Settlement), in Lublin, whose researchers, led by SS-*Hauptsturmführer* Gustav Hanelt, set about devising all the necessary sub-plots of the Germanization of the East; for instance, SS and police strongpoints, from which land settlement by German farmers would spread, and settlement walls would be created.[54] Precisely how the *FfO*, the *Kleine*, and the *Grosse Planung*, and all the other work carried out by Dr. Ehlich's Berlin-based researchers, and Meyer-Hetling's settlement proposals or blueprints dovetailed is unclear. The explanation may be that this is best understood by noting Globocnik's longstanding proclivity for not waiting or taking heed of anyone at any time. Another possible reason is that all the documents and working papers of the *Generalplan Ost* were deliberately destroyed just before the war ended, and that was also the fate of the *FfO's* working plans and papers. But once Globocnik appeared on any scene, there was the inevitable pattern: rivalry, confusion, bitterness, and recrimination. He invariably sought to become the man who gave the lead, and that could even mean acting well ahead of what Berlin's researchers and theorists may have foreseen. Himmler must also take some blame for this, since in the summer of 1941 he visited Ukraine and the Baltic region, familiarizing himself with the cities of these regions. Nevertheless, the most likely link between Berlin's *Kleine Planung* and Globocnik's Lublin work was that the *Kleine Planung* was simply the Germanization of western Poland. The work was conducted in large measure by Hermann Alois Krumey from his Lodz (Litzmannstadt) base.

The *Grosse Planung,* on the other hand, applied all the intended SS and Pan-German demographic upheavals—expulsion of Slavs and Balts eastwards and the settling in their place of Germans—on lands beyond western Poland, an operation that began with Globocnik's forced Germanization of the Zamosc Lands, with the managerial and ideological assistance of his Carinthian crony Reinhold von Mohrenschildt. There was also the case of the Baltic region, one in which Himmler took particular interest, placing it nearly on a par with the Zamosc Lands. Himmler's special interest in the Baltic region is in part explained by the fact that several of the major Baltic cities, when still only towns, had been associated with the Northern German commercial agency known as the Hanseatic League as ports or trading outposts. Moreover, Himmler visited several of these cities during 1941; seeing their architecture and central-city plans convinced him that the East had in fact once been a Germanic zone of Europe in its entirety. To Himmler it was therefore not a matter of purifying pockets of the East by removing anyone classified as "aliens"—namely, Slavs and Balts. To him the Germanization of the Baltic and Slavic Lands of the East was in fact a matter of retrieving, regaining, or reclaiming what Himmler saw as having once been Germanic. It was thus a venture of removing the racial usurpers to what Heydrich called "deep into Russia and far up to the Urals." Globocnik fits snugly into this outlook and this impatience of Himmler's.

Having Reinhold von Mohrenschildt as the second-in-command in the clearance of the Zamosc Lands was important because, it must be recalled, he had participated in the removal of German minorities westward from the Soviet sphere of influence of the East as early as the turn of 1939 and 1940, following a series of population exchange agreements between Berlin and Moscow. Both Carinthians were like Himmler, desperate to see the Germanization of the entire Lublin District sooner, much sooner, rather than later. They wished to embark on ethnic cleansing before the Red Army's defeat. This was why they embarked in November 1942 on the creation of a belt or wall of German settlement that stretched north-south to link Transylvania with Estonia, with this wall passing through Lublin District, which was midway. This ambitious demographic project was in accordance with Heydrich's secret 2 October 1941 Prague or Cernin Palace speech as well as the *Grosse Planung*. It was in fact the launching of both. The facts that Globocnik's mother came from the Banat region of the Balkans, and von Mohrenschildt's ancestors from Estonia, only make this point more telling. This second Germanic wall of settlement could, if all went well, even be completed before men like Hermann Krumey could claim to have entirely Germanized the Reich's first demographic wall, which focused on Germanizing incorporated Western Poland, the Warthe Land, and was set down in the *Kleine Planung*. *Grosse Planung*, was, to use Heydrich's words, again aimed at settling Germans upon all the lands "deep into Russia and far up to the Urals."

As we know, however, Heydrich's, and thus Globocnik's and von Mohrenschildt's, eastern dreams went unrealized. The reasons were twofold. First, in January 1943, Hitler's Sixth Army was forced to surrender at Stalingrad, only two months after the Zamosc Lands expulsions were launched. Second, the local Polish Underground fought back, and doggedly.

As 1943 unfolded, news from the Eastern Front was never sanguine. In addition to an entire German army being captured by the Red Army, there were exceptionally high casualties being inflicted upon German forces. Reports about the fighting against the partisans of the Zamosc Lands were also far from encouraging. Added to this, Globocnik's bombastic style meant that officials of the Lublin District's civilian government were finding their work increasingly difficult to conduct. This resulted in growing pressure from the district's Governor Zörner and his officials for the removal of Globocnik. In the end they managed, with assistance from various quarters in Berlin, to have him removed to Trieste, somewhat along the lines he had been dispatched out of Vienna in January 1939. Linked to the unsatisfactory outcome of the military encounters with Soviet forces was the Red Army's use of long-range raiding parties that were generally, and incorrectly, referred to as Soviet partisans. In July 1943, the famous Soviet long-range raider, Sydir Kovpak, led a large mounted raid deep into pre-war Poland's eastern or Lwow region, destroying oil wells and railway lines. Czeslaw Madajczyk considers this to have had a pivotal impact upon those German authorities with the power to halt Globocnik's attempts at Germanizing the Zamosc Lands.

> It is likely that the August decision concerning the suspension of further deportations [of Polish peasants] was also influenced by Kovpaks' raid which had reached Galicia in July. In the opinion of Becker, the Police Commander of the General Gouvernement, the raid required a transfer to Galicia of the Police Forces concentrated in the Lublin region.[55]

Madajczyk continues: "On 5 August 1943 Governor [Richard] Wendler in Krakow categorically requested from Globocnik that the deportation operation for which railway wagons had already been ordered, should be stopped."[56]

Three days earlier, another great Himmler favorite, and an expert partisan fighter on the Russian Front, Erich von dem Bach-Zelewski, had become involved in the Zamosc Lands fiasco by trying to mediate among Globocnik, Wendler, and Frank. Either during these talks or even earlier, Bach-Zelewski had come to the view that for countermeasures against partisans to succeed, the expulsion of Poles simply had to cease. Wendler, Himmler's brother-in-law, was at this stage Governor of Lublin District, while Bach-Zelewski was a general of the Higher SS and Police Leader Corps, who had been responsible for anti-partisan warfare on the Eastern Front. To Bach-Zelewski, at least, an event like the deep Kovpak raid was certainly pertinent and meaningful, and this was undoubtedly made known to the *Reichsführer-SS*. There is little doubt that this raid would have been fully appreciated even in other German circles, since it meant penetration into the Lwow region, in lands that were in pre-war Poland, which was still well behind German lines. The fact that it took a brother-in-law, an expert of Bach-Zelewski's standing, and the Kovpak raid to begin shifting Himmler's thinking shows how important the Zamosc Lands action was to him, and is also a measure of his attachment to Globocnik's undertaking of this task. Moreover, by July 1943, in addition to the overall breakdown of order across the targeted Zamosc Lands, Globocnik and his forces had initiated a series of counter-partisan actions, each bigger and harsher than its predecessor. These included, in succession, a *Sonderaktion*, *Grossaktion*, and *Aktion Wehrwolf*, implemented in two stages, and *Sturmwind* I and II in 1944. All these actions occurred in just an eight-month period. The last two pacification actions involved several tens of thousands of German troops, who managed to force the Polish and other partisans into the huge wildernesses of Bilgoraj County, called Solska Puszcza. In this boggy and forested area, many brave partisans died. The need for these large-scale counter measures showed, among other things, that Globocnik's nominal superior in Krakow, Friedrich-Wilhelm Kruger, was simply unable to guarantee security across his area of jurisdiction, a most embarrassing admission. Little wonder he soon followed Globocnik out of the General Gouvernement. A succinct overall assessment of the Polish resistance of 1943 and 1944, the single most important problem that faced Himmler and Globocnik, is presented by the Polish historian Jerzy Markiewicz, the leading expert on the Zamosc Uprising and the Lublin District's partisan movement.

> The defeat of the German Army in the east [i.e. especially at Stalingrad and Kursk] and the increasing harassment behind the front line by the partisans meant that from the spring of 1943, the Germans began to lose control over the Zamosc Lands. It was not only the Poles who were uncertain of the day or the hour that death may come, but the Germans also began finding themselves in the same predicament. From the time when the AK and BCh took up open fighting against the Germans, that is, at the turn of 1942–43, and which was dubbed by the Germans, *The Zamosc Uprising, and particularly the Battles of Wojda, Zaboreczne, Roza, Dlugim Katem, and Lasowcami, the initiative, with each day, passed slowly but inexorably in the direction of the Polish armed organization.* [Emphasis added] After the June [1943] *Aktion 'Wehrwolf,'* culminating in the autumn, the upper hand moved steadily in the direction of Polish Underground armed groups.
>
> One is compelled to mention such actions as the taking of the Bilgoraj Prison by the AK on September 24, 1943, the takeover of Jozefow, and a further action against Bilgoraj Prison [in December 1943] culminating in the Battles in the Hrubieszow district by BCh "Rysia" and the AL's "Wiktora." One must also mention the armed struggle of the AK's 9th Regiment.
>
> Those actions proved the weakness of the occupying German forces and resulted in the entire district being liberated. The crucial fact was the existence of the huge forests of Solska Puszcza and Lasy [the forests of] Jozefow. Bilgoraj's forests were the place where the partisan units were able to base themselves. In the autumn of 1943 when the Germans opened the fight for these forests they met their match and by spring 1944 the partisans had the upper hand.
>
> In the spring of 1944 the Bilgoraj district was under the complete control of the partisans and German control was limited to the town of Bilgoraj and the village of Tarnogrod where the Army had a strong garrison.[57]

In addition, Ukrainian officials who were allied to the German occupation administrations — SS and civilian — now found that Globocnik's and their efforts to create an exclusively ethnic Ukrainian enclave along the eastern and southern perimeters of the Zamosc Lands had failed to ensure security for its settled people. They, like Germans and Poles, were being ambushed and killed. The so-called Zamosc Uprising included bloody internecine ethnic warfare, with involvement by Ukrainian, Polish — Communist and Nationalist — units. Globocnik had therefore simply visited bedlam and carnage upon these lands, not the neat German settled rural colony that he and his SS-planners planned with Himmler in 1941.

> On 4 and 5 August talks were held with Dr [Wolodymyr] Kubiiovych, leader of the Ukrainian Nationalists in the General Gouvernement. In view of the reprisals of the Polish resistance movement he demanded that the Ukrainians should be transferred to compact settlements and that the recently started deportations of Ukrainian peasants from the Hrubieszow *Kreis* should be stopped. Frank assured him that large scale police operations had been suspended and that he would discuss with him the matters in detail in the presence of the Lublin Governor Wendler. The discussion took place the next day. It had been decided that the Ukrainian settlers would be withdrawn from the endangered areas. Kubiiovych's suggestion concerning the exchange of the Polish and Ukrainian population to create ethnically uniform regions, had been rejected.[58]

3. The "Re-Germanization" of the East

The move to effect the complete removal of Jews by mass execution and Poles by mass expulsion from Lublin District was not an end in itself, but a necessary precondition for the settlement of Germanic peoples; Germans, Austrians, Danes, Dutch, and Scandinavians, as well as those who had become known as German "splinters" (*Volksdeutsche*), upon these newly cleansed farming lands. The last category consisted of people who had lived in German enclaves either in Poland, the Soviet Union, the Baltic Region, the Balkans, Bukovina, or adjacent regions. A report in *The Times* of London on 26 September 1942, two months before the expulsion of Poles began, shows this racial link to Norway. Filed by "our special correspondent" in Stockholm and headlined "Punitive Force Ambushed," it said:

> Two Norwegian quisling Ministers, Stang and Fredheim, are visiting Poland to inspect camps for young Norwegian farm laborers and study agricultural conditions in the Lublin region. That these conditions are far from normal is known by reports received here of a fight between Polish outlawed patriots and a German punitive expedition sent to three estates in the Lublin Distrikt under German control, where the Polish laborers are said to have set fire to buildings and committed other acts of sabotage.[59]

The details of this fight are less significant here than the fact that young Norwegian males were working in Globocnik's district as agricultural laborers, and that two Norwegian Government ministers were on an inspection tour and making an assessment. Clearly, some form of government-to-government relationship therefore existed. Reinhold von Mohrenschildt had been involved in bringing such people together and settling them in western Poland from late 1939 until 1941. This is precisely what was now to occur on the Zamosc Lands, with the main difference being that these incoming people were being moved east to settle, not west, as occurred while Berlin and Moscow were allied.

One outcome of that alliance was that western Poland, by 1942, had become the venue of a network of camps in which many of these German "splinters" were living, most of them in utter boredom and, increasingly, unrest. It was initially these *Volksdeutsche* that Globocnik turned toward to make his colonizers the new settlers. He looked to a long-forgotten ethnic cleanser, *SS-Obersturmbannführer* Hermann Alois Krumey (SS Number 310,441) who only came to the attention of war crimes investigators shortly before 1961, following evidence provided by one of his Berlin superiors, Adolf Eichmann.

Krumey's emergence in Poland as a man with power that involved forcible removal of people from their homes and farmlets came after April 1940, once German SS and police bureaucracies had set out to centralize and formalize their demographic plans and intentions for western Poland, namely, to create as quickly as possible the Reich's first demographic wall of settlement across the length and breadth of this western segment of pre-war Poland, the incorporated territories. Significantly, Hermann Alois Krumey was also responsible to Dr. Hans Ehlich, in that he attended conferences and briefing seminars dealing with issues that the Berlin-based Ehlich bureau was considering and researching.

After Eichmann's capture and interrogation, Krumey was quickly found and contacted and was required to make a statement. That telling statement says in part:

After I joined the SS, my former gymnastics association was dissolved; it was already being wound up. In November 1939, while serving in that position, I was called up by a red notice to report to the SS Head Office for Personnel. From there I was seconded to the Higher SS and Police Leader in Posen, effective immediately after my having been called up.... *My task was to organize the transport by rail required to carry out the compulsory transfer from the Warthe District of those Poles evicted from their farms by the District Commissioners.... The trains for which I received requests, I would in turn, request from the Posen Reich Railways Office, and later possibly from IVB4 [Adolf Eichmann] in the Head Office for Reich Security, and my duties also included negotiating with office in the Generalgouvernement about the destinations of the trains in the Generalgouvernement* [emphasis added].

When these compulsory transfers caused difficulties and unacceptable situations because, due to inadequate arrangements, the Poles evicted from their farms had insufficient accommodation and no work in the Warthe District, and crime was therefore increasing, a separate organization was set up in order to run this operation properly. The Central Office for Migration [*Umwander-erzentralstelle Litzmannstadt UWZ*] was set up for this purpose in Posen, under the Inspector of the Security Police and the Security Service. A branch office of this Central Office was set up in Litzmannstadt [Lodz].... When this field office became an office in its own right, I was appointed to head it. That was in the spring of 1940.

There were several field offices subordinate to my officers, as well as a transit camp in Litzmannstadt [Lodz]. The purpose of the office was to handle processing of the Poles on their way to the Generalgouvernement, after they had been evacuated by office controlled by the Reich Commission for the Strengthening of German Folkdom [*RKFDV*]. In the transit camps, those Polish families which had been identified by the Race and Resettlement Head Office as qualifying for Germanization, were sorted out, as well as those Poles whom the Labour Office took away to work in the Reich. The field office had already previously sought out those who had been evicted from their farms, but were ethnic Germans or Poles who professed to being German. There were guidelines to be followed on this. These persons selected by the field offices, and also during processing in the camp, were excluded from deportation to the Generalgouvernement. In the camps a statement of property was also drawn up for every Polish family to be resettled; these were collected by the Main Trustee Office East and — so it was said — were to be the basis for compensating those transferred compulsorily.[60]

Krumey was careful here to mention only the deportation of ethnic Poles, making no reference to Jews. This is understandable, because Adolf Eichmann was being tried by an Israeli court for the deportation of Jews to Globocnik's killing centers, and faced execution. What Krumey did to ethnic Poles was not being judged. He therefore sought to distance himself and his work from any reference to Jews; Poles were clearly another matter. But he was undoubtedly also involved in deporting Jews during these early months of the war, for Jews were also deported from western Poland into the General Gouvernement, including the Lublin District. Later, during the spring of 1944, Krumey was responsible, as a member of a special unit, a *Sonderkommando*, led by Eichmann, for arranging the transportation of about 350,000 Jews from Hungary to Auschwitz-Birkenau — the so-called "Crime within a Crime" — for mass extermination, so he was one of the Reich's leading transportation experts and ethnic cleansers. He had accompanied Eichmann to Budapest for this special task, primarily because of this expertise, refined over several years of experience in "cleansing" western Poland. During the first two years of the war, this region saw many *Volksdeutsche* — German "splinters" — brought in from other parts to live around Lodz (Litzmannstadt) in a network of camps. This also explains why Krumey was turned to, for he had Germans to settle, people who were able to inherit the Zamosc Lands, with the main agency involved in settling them, naturally, being Krumey's Central Office for

Migration (*Umwandererzentralstelle Litzmannstadt UWZ*), to which he referred in his statement. According to Polish historian Janina Kielbon, Krumey's involvement resulted in some 13,000 Germans — a relatively small number — taking up land in depopulated Polish Zamosc Lands villages. Their settlement, however, weakened Globocnik's position, because they were widely dispersed and could be relatively easily attacked by Polish partisans, and they were. As well as going to great lengths to defend them, an array of Nazi institutions were involved in assisting these colonists to help Germanize this region. Another important consideration in relation to Hermann Krumey was that he attended conferences in Berlin where the *Generalplan Ost* was discussed, assessed, and closely considered. He as much as Globocnik, with his close personal contact with Himmler and Reinhold von Mohrenschildt, was fully conversant with the direction of all the ethnic cleansing and exterminations that was going on across the General Gouvernement.

VIII

Globocnik's New Order

It is most unlikely that Globocnik was put into the Lublin District by Himmler as the holder of the top SS, police, party, and other racial and settlement positions without some early ulterior motive, some future or as yet foreseen plan or intention. Himmler, like Hitler, was a devious and calculating individual, as well as a politician who looked toward creating future options and possibilities that would pave the way to fulfilling his passionate ideological dream of seeing the East totally Germanized. In this regard, it is worth recalling that a month before Globocnik was nominated for the position on 9 November 1939, Himmler, the skilled intriguer and manipulator, was himself elevated by Hitler to become the Commissioner for the Strengthening of Germandom (*RKFDV*) (7 October 1939), suggesting the Lublin appointment of Globocnik may have been an early move to have the "right men in the right place" for future consequences of this demographic appointment by the *Führer*. All this was over and above the early moves by Berlin to establish in Globocnik's district an exclusively Jewish enclave, the so-called Lublin Reservation along the eastern perimeter of the General Gouvernement. It is noteworthy that Himmler almost missed getting the powerful *RKFDV* position and made a determined and successful-last minute bid to ensure he did, ahead of Werner Lorenz, von Mohrenschildt's eventual superior, suggesting he knew its powers and responsibilities, and wished to be in charge of these matters. According to historian Peter Black, there is no doubt about the link between early Reich aims that were as yet undefined and the strategic appointment of Globocnik to this most easterly administrative unit of the General Gouvernement.

195

After Germany annexed the Polish territory between the Vistula and Bug Rivers in exchange for Soviet demands on Lithuania in October 1939, Himmler looked towards this "Lublin Distrikt" as the focal point of his efforts to obtain for the SS complete control over the instruments of Nazi domination in Eastern Europe. From Lublin, the SS would remove the Poles, concentrate and ultimately murder the Polish Jews, *create space for German settlers, and "retrieve" wayward German blood by identifying and securing the partially Polonized ethnic German population of the district* [emphasis added].[1]

As well as importing a cohort of Austrian loyalists, including especially some Carinthian associates like Lerch and von Mohrenschildt, a longtime friend like Sepp Nemetz from Vienna, and a substantial number of secretaries and ancillary staff, Globocnik quickly moved to show what the new order meant. Family partners, and even children of his staffers, also moved north from Vienna and Klagenfurt, or east from the Reich, as in the case of Reich Germans like Maubach, and as time passed even Austrian prostitutes found their way to Lublin to service "their boys." Work, killing, looting, and illicit sex were all integral to life for Lublin SS men, and for an extended period. District Governor Ernst Zörner reached Lublin in March 1940, (remaining, despite some monumental differences with Globocnik, until April 1943), so Globocnik had those four months to familiarize himself with the region and his new post before his future bureaucratic rival, Zörner, appeared on the scene. On 13 December 1939, the district's then governor, SS man Friedrich Schmidt, announced that Globocnik would be in charge of matters in his absence, presumably while Schmidt was away in Berlin. Schmidt returned to Lublin in January 1940, with Hans Maubach and his secretary, Irmgard Rickheim, who later became engaged to Globocnik. Initially, Maubach worked for the civil government structure, not for Globocnik, according to Rickheim. This appears to indicate that Globocnik held overall power in the district between mid–December 1939, and early January 1940, and cooperated with Schmidt until March 1940, giving him a full five months to get on top of matters. The fact that two SS men — Globocnik and Schmidt — were in charge of Lublin District when this region was destined to become a Jewish reservation is surely not a coincidence.

The new order also very rapidly saw a splitting of paths in material terms between the occupants — Germans and Austrians — and the occupied — Jews and Poles. The two ethnic groups were rapidly pauperized and pushed and shoved into becoming a lumpen proletariat or slave class, while the incoming Austrians and Germans became the unmistakable "haves," and on an extravagant scale. Rickheim says that these times were ones of utter abundance. Shoes, fur coats, alcohol and the like, could be obtained by simply asking. "There was lots of drinking and smoking, all these things were cheap," she said.[2] Being a German or Austrian in the General Gouvernement was also, materially speaking, the ideal situation because it largely allowed one to avoid all the restrictions or rationing that were gradually being imposed upon those living in the Reich. As time passed, the bombing of the Reich's major cities and industrial centers was something those in Lublin heard about, but never experienced. The big changes for the occupants, again materially speaking, came after the Stalingrad debacle of January 1943. However, although Rickheim was no longer in Lublin by then, she said that the atmosphere and mood within German ranks had begun to change markedly some time earlier — when the trainloads of German wounded began passing through Lublin railway station for hospitals in the Reich or at sanitariums in occupied Poland, such as at Zakopane, the preeminent Polish skiing and summer resort (which, coincidentally, had an unexpected impact later upon Globocnik's private life and relationship with Himmler). These slow moving west-bound trains, which each carried hundreds of wounded young and older men, had a dimming effect upon the occupiers' morale, and greatly, if silently, cheered the Poles, showing again that one person's grief can be another's joy.

First and foremost, Poles and Jews were shown who was in charge. For the Poles this came with mass arrests of those deemed to be likely to lead a resistance movement — clerics, academics, teachers, former officers, and even journalists. For the Jews it was encroaching ghettoization, therefore isolation from civic life — or what remained of it — as well as economic life as known before September 1939. Unlike the World War I experience, when the German and Austrian military administration, predominantly the latter in and around Lublin, was light-handed in this region, that imposed in 1939 was a dual administration — civil and SS-police — with Globocnik at the head of the SS wing, whose ideology increasingly determined police behavior and planning. The difference between the two war experiences is perhaps best demonstrated by the fact that Austria in the later stages of the Great War even introduced teachers to some Polish villages around Zamosc, whereas after 1939 policies of social or educational betterment for the Slavs were not on the agenda.[3] Nor was the occupation simply an authoritarian exploitative form of governance along the lines that Erich von Ludendorff had instituted and stolidly maintained in Ober Ost Land — northeast Poland and the Baltic States — during the Great War.[4] The Lublin region's second Germanic occupation of the 20th century affected Pole and Jew markedly differently. In this regard, Globocnik was like his SS counterparts in occupied Poland's other four districts of Krakow, Warsaw, and Radom, and after August 1941, Galicia, which was taken from the Soviet Union and incorporated into the General Gouvernement. His immediate superior Higher SS and Police Leader (*Ost*) Friedrich-Wilhelm Kruger obeyed Himmler's instructions to the letter throughout the years he was in charge of all policing in the General Gouvernement. Kruger was a key organizer of the Jewish Holocaust and the press ganging of Poles to be dispatched as laborers to the Reich.

Undoubtedly the most noticeable difference in treatment of Poles and Jews was that the Jews were relatively quickly ghettoized, locked away in a settlement or segment within a city or town with the outside world being largely out of bounds. The district's two major ghettos or Jewish enclaves were in Lublin and Zamosc. Two important impositions on Poles were the introduction of strict rural contingents: Each peasant farmer was compelled to meet the requirements of the state in potatoes, pigs, or other stock, grain, milk, or other rural products. There was no evading this, for punishment could mean death, though it was generally internment in a work camp. The other burden was a harsh and permanent policing with violent reprisals against resistance, real or imagined. Again, although some Poles hid away firearms and other armaments, their use was not likely until well into the future. Clandestine resistance groups basically did little overt resisting during 1940 and 1941. There were some targeted assassinations of collaborating Ukrainian officials, especially in the Chelm region, which Ukrainian Nationalists saw as the seed of a future greater Ukraine. They wished to see Poles and Jews expelled from here, something German officialdom never agreed to, because this clashed with Germany's long-term demographic plans in the East. The following year, 1942, saw resistance emerging as a real and growing problem, especially after the Zamosc Lands expulsion action was launched, from December onward that year.

The district was sub-divided into 10 counties or *Kreishauptmannschaft*— Biala Podlaska, Bilgoraj, Chelm, Hrubieszow, Janow Lublelski, Krasnystaw, Lublin, Pulawy, Radzyn and Zamosc. The pre-war Polish county of Tomaszow-Lubelski had not been reconstituted, but was rather incorporated or subsumed for reasons that are not known. This point is relevant only in that under the German sub-division Poland's historic Zamosc Lands fell under three *Kreis*, whereas postwar Polish writings constantly refer to the expulsions of Poles from four counties, thus referring to the pre-war Polish administrative arrangement. Each *Kreis* was headed by a *Kreishauptmann* who oversaw a network of departments, with the most important being food supply and agriculture. The other divisions were: internal affairs, administration, personnel, economy, finance, enlightenment and propaganda, road construction, railroads, labor, forests, justice, and veterinary. Many hundreds of Reich and *Volksdeutsche* held these new powerful local positions, and, as will be seen, within their respective bailiwicks there was a network of prisoner-of-war camps, prisons, work camps, penal camps, transit camps, ghettos, and finally, in the cases of the Zamosc Lands and nearby Chelm County, an extermination camp in each, Belzec and Sobibor respectively. Poles experiencing difficulties with this county-level departmental network, whether as suspects for belonging to or being linked with the underground, or for failure to meet food quotas, were guaranteed an encounter with the appropriate police agency. With that said, it would be incorrect to believe that there was total and outright opposition to some of the German rural policies by peasant farmers. Many Polish peasant farmers appreciated the return to peace after October 1939, and the adoption of some form of orderly rural administration, something that had been lacking across most of what became Lublin District during the 1930s under Polish rule. The administration of Dr. Hans Frank sought quite vigorously to see rural parts of Poland becoming a productive force in the overall German scheme of things. That administration did not seek to see the Poles tormented to the point of inflaming resistance, which Globocnik and von Mohrenschildt did provoke after November 1942, by launching their ethnic cleansing of the Zamosc Lands with Himmler's concurrence.

IX

Lublin as a Germanic Eastern Outpost

"Lublin was SS." These were Irmgard Rickheim's words 56 years after she had left Lublin for Berlin, never to return. Lublin's central city park, Park Litewski, on the city's main commercial thoroughfare, Krakowskie Przedmiescie, was renamed Adolf Hitler Park. One building, the Julius Schreck Barracks, at Pieradzkiego 17, the former Stefan Batory College, had been renamed after Hitler's former chauffeur. This structure eventually housed the planning and other work known as *Aktion Reinhardt*, and it was from here that the Zamosc Lands cleansing action was also directed. This structure was, even if only briefly, the headquarters of *Generalplan Ost*. There was a *Reinhard Heydrich Strasse*, and even an *Ostlandstrasse*, the German name of the street Globocnik lived on, Wieniawska Street, hardly a coincidence, it would seem. For Lublin, the year 1939 marked the beginning of a new era, one that was to see the old order eradicated so as to never return (see Map 4.) Entire buildings, residential and administrative, were commandeered by the SS and German civil administrators. Poles and Jews were forcibly moved from their quarters, with tens of thousands assigned places of abode either in other parts of the city or else well beyond the city's limits, in distant rural townships, never to return. German replaced Polish and Yiddish in the streets, in shops, workshops, and bureaus. German flags and banners, and the black Swastika, were visible, draped from the facades of most large structures, generally hanging over main entrances. Occupation steadily began displaying all the signs

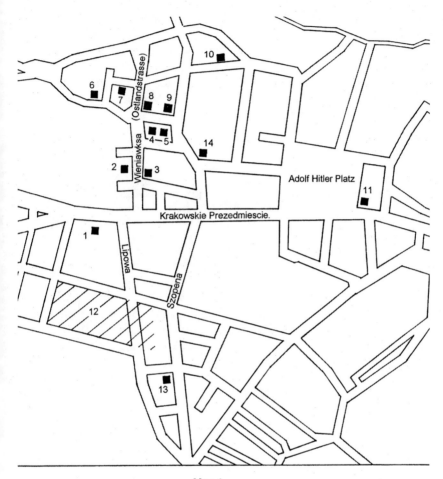

Map 4.

1. NSDAP House (Horst Wessel Str)
2. Globocnik's HQ – SSPF Lublin
3. Christian Wirth's Villa
4. SS Clubhouse
5. SS Brothel
6. SS-Polizeiregiment 25 Barracks
7. Globocnik's Villa
8. "Ullmannschenk" Bar
9. HQ Distrikt Governor (Ernst Zörner)

10. SS-Standortverwaltung – Lublin
    (Georg Wippern's and Globocnik's
    gold vault)
11. Goebbels Propaganda Department
12. Lipowa Street Labor Camp
13. Aktion Reinhardt warehouse
14. "Julius Schreck" Barracks, - Aktion
    Reinhardt HQ

Wartime Lublin

of displacement and replacement. This was not to be a temporary German stopover, as men like Heydrich constantly emphasized. The previous two interwar decades had seen the Great Depression of 1929–33; Lublin and its surrounding towns, villages, and settlements had not enjoyed a wave of economic prosperity. It is worth recalling in this regard that the Lublin area, along with other regions to its east, was amongst the poorest of pre-war Poland. Canadian historian and expert on Poland, William J. Rose, made this point well in 1939:

> The studies made in our day by the Poles of the needs, and the possibilities for improving their national economy, have resulted in the dividing of the country roughly into Poland A, Poland B, and Poland C. Strictly speaking the whole country falls into two parts, A and B. Region A includes almost everything west of the Vistula, and the foothills of the Carpathians with their timber, salt and oil. To Region B belongs everything else; the whole country east of the Middle Vistula…. Here there dwell 15 million people, *a great many of them at a bare subsistence level, but entertaining brave hopes for a better future* [emphasis added].[1]

Globocnik was in charge of a significant portion of what Rose described as Region B. But economic and social conditions for its inhabitants between late 1939 and the summer of 1944 became far worse. Demand for output in most manufactured or processed goods fell dramatically; those providing services faced another depression. Sustenance and survival were now chief objectives for most non-German families and individuals, even though there was a swing in relative benefits to village-dwelling food producers compared with urban dwellers. The war years witnessed the slow removal — by exchange — of valuables out of cities and larger towns into villages, because urban dwellers were forced to trade them for food. Consequently, valuables such as watches, jewelry, silver and other cutlery, and bric-a-brac steadily flowed from urban to rural peoples, a phenomenon that occurred across all the Polish lands.

All this was in stark contrast to what the Poles euphemistically refer to simply as the occupant, who was experiencing a material boom. Lublin, as well as being a garrison and administrative town, was by 1941 also put on the path to becoming a major supply center, especially after June 1941, with military and ordnance demand for the Eastern Front rising to ever greater heights. Most of this was done through the institution of work camps. A surprisingly large number of German companies set up agencies in Lublin, including, for example, Barth & Kohnenhamp, C. F. Corssen & Co., Deutsche Buchhandlung, F. Rover & Sohn, Schenker u. Co., Deutsche Gaststatte, Waagenfabrik "Ideal," and Landw. Maschineenfabrik. Lublin had well over 100 such companies, branches, or agencies, with most named *Chopinstrasse*, *Krakauerstrasse*, *Ostlandstrasse*, or *Bahnhofstrasse*. This caused an insatiable demand for slave laborers: Jewish especially, Polish, and even Soviet after mid–1941. On 26 January 1940, Globocnik finalized the city's boundaries to establish a zone for the administration and police. The limits of this German quarter were announced with relevant streets named, and the area soon became known as the police quarter, in part because it housed the most significant civilian administrative bureaus, as well as serving as the center of police and SS activity. In early March, Globocnik issued an edict declaring that labor service in the Reich was to be instituted, so that people could be dispatched out of Lublin District. The Order Police (*Ordnungspolizei*) took charge of this duty, and on 6 March it was announced that several work camps were to be created, and these came under this force's control. Their task was to detain anyone attempting to evade work duty in the Reich, which over the coming four years was to have an insatiable demand for foreign or eastern workers (*Ostarbeiter*). Press-ganging or state sponsored kidnapping became standard. Three weeks later another edict was issued, saying all weapons and military munitions must be handed in to the German authorities by 20 April. Those not doing so would face trial, but anyone reporting the whereabouts of such weapons was assured of receiving a monetary reward.

July 1940 saw two significant developments, one regarding the Jews, the other pertaining to settlement politics, which was designed to affect primarily the Poles. On 13 July, Lublin's *Judenrat* (Jewish Council) was told to create a special section that dealt with matters related to a work camp to be created at Belzec, south of Zamosc. Quick so-called "agreements" followed with respect to policing this camp, its administration, medical services, and sanitation. Doctors, engineers, kitchen quarters, a food supply department, and even a postal service were finalized. Borrowing from Eichmann's approach of funding the expulsion of Vienna's Jews in 1938–39, the Judenrat was forced to finance the camp, and another at nearby Tyszowce. The money was collected by the taxing of wealthier Jews. Tyszowce, which was established in the autumn of 1940, was liquidated in 1941. It was situated in the village of Tyszowce, and on average held 600 inmates, who worked to regulate the Huczwa River, a tributary of the Bug. Like so many other ghettos, it eventually experienced a typhus epidemic. At liquidation those interned within it were dismissed. Less dramatic but, as things transpired, also ominous was the fact that a Central Resettlement Agency commenced moving *Volksdeutsche* from the Lublin District to the Reich, mainly from the Chelm region. Globocnik was heavily involved in this transfer of what was expected to be some 30,000 people, for, as will be recalled, when he was contacted by the Viennese auditor, Franz Müller, about his days as the Austrian capital's *Gauleiter*, he claimed he was too busy because of this movement of ethnic Germans out of Lublin District. His crony Reinhold von Mohrenschildt was probably also heavily involved in this removal of Germans who had settled in the Chelm region since the 1860s. Years later the Josephine Germans who came to so interest Globocnik and his settlement researchers were seen as "lost German blood" that needed to be rescued. Although it was not possible to see this removal of people as a precursor of something as dramatic as the coming expulsions of Poles from the Zamosc Lands, it was in fact an early sign of a commitment to population cleansing. But the winter of 1940 brought a sizeable influx into Lublin of ethnic Poles and Jews from western Poland, where most of the Chelm Germans had been settled, which had been officially incorporated into the Reich in October 1939. Poles from Wolyn (Volhynia), the pre-war Polish province east of the Lublin District, also began moving into the district, something that further displeased local Ukrainian Nationalists, partners of Globocnik and the German civil administration, who adamantly contended that the Chelm region should be incorporated into a Greater Ukraine which they wanted to see emerge. Globocnik and his various demographic and settlement planners probably did not know that when Ukrainian Nationalists referred to the Chelm region — *Chelmszczyzna* — this actually included the Zamosc Lands that he and men like Gustav Hanelt and Dr. Franz Stanglica had firmly intended to make the first all–German rural enclave, and thereby launch *Generalplan Ost*. The Ukrainian Central Committee in Krakow took their right to the Zamosc Lands so seriously that they petitioned Dr. Hans Frank in April 1941 to help remove all Poles and Jews from this part of Poland so that a purely Ukrainian enclave could be created.

The year 1941 was to be far more eventful and rewarding for Globocnik, with Himmler making his crucial July visit. This trip included a stopover in and around Zamosc, which had already been targeted by some of Globocnik's academic demographic researchers in his Research Center for Eastern Settlement (*Forschungsstelle für Ostunterkunfte*) as a potential permanently Germanizable settlement zone. These planners, most of them university graduates, had during 1940 been visiting cemeteries, and city and church archives, looking for ancestral information — evidence of Germanic settlers — which they, in fact, found. They were also studying the writings of earlier researchers, including, especially those of a Dr. Kurt Lück, a native of Poznan, and although a *Volksdeutsche*, a Polish citizen. Dr. Lück had conducted extensive ethnographic research across the Lublin region before war broke out, and his investigations into long-settled German minorities acted as a catalyst for Globocnik and his planners, for they came to believe sincerely that this district already had the beginnings of Germandom. All that was needed now, they concluded, was to push their demographic process along by removing the unwanted "aliens": Poles and Jews.

Before the war Poznan had been the headquarters of an important German historical society, the *Historische Gesellschaft für die Provinz Posen*, which had as its director one of Hitler's early German friends, Hermann

Rauschning, who later dramatically broke with the *Führer*. Of greater significance was that one of this society's most energetic researchers was Kurt Lück, who, with a staff of collaborators supported by funds from Weimar and later Hitler's Germany, conducted ethnographic investigations across eastern parts of Poland, including broad-ranging research into the Germanic origins of individual families and even entire settlements and villages. Dr. Lück had for a time worked as an assistant to a German parliamentarian who sat in the Polish *Sejm* (Parliament). The results of Dr. Lück's main research project were published in *Deutsche Monatsheft* (German Monthly Journal) Poznan and Leipzig; the *Deutsche Wissenschaftliche Zeitschrift für Polen* (German Scientific Periodical for Poland), Poznan; and *Der Deutsche im Osten* (Germans in the East), Danzig (Gdansk).

In early 1940, Odilo Globocnik established his Lublin research center and began implementing his policy of expulsion and Germanization of Poles from the Zamosc Lands, Dr, Lück had published an article that listed a series of villages in the Lublin District, within which the Zamosc Lands lay. It appeared in the third edition of *Das General Gouvernement*, an attractive glossy journal released by Frank's occupation administration. Dr. Lück claimed that the inhabitants of these villages were of mixed German and Polish background, meaning, for men like Himmler and Globocnik, that there were indeterminable quantities of "lost German blood" to be found and retrieved nearby, almost on Globocnik's doorstep. These lost or racially submerged Germans were regarded by population cleansers like Himmler and Globocnik as hidden "splinters" of the main German community in the Reich, or carriers of "lost blood," and were seen as worthy of "saving" for the Reich German community or *Volk*, just like the more conspicuous "splinters" that had been transferred into western Poland from the Baltic States, eastern Poland, Bessarabia, Rumania, and the Soviet Union, during 1939 and 1940. Dr. Lück's writings and findings are therefore, in all likelihood, the origin of Globocnik's and von Mohrenschildt's Zamosc Lands expulsion campaign of 1942–43, launched on orders from Himmler.

It is not surprising that the planning for the wholesale Germanization and other preliminary demographic activities by those in the Lublin SS and police ranks, or more specifically, within Odilo Globocnik's Research Center for Eastern Settlement, headed by Gustav Hanelt of Holstein and the Viennese enthusiast Dr. Franz Stanglica, followed one of Dr. Lück's published village research lists. On this important point the wartime London-based Polish researcher, Jozef Winiewicz, also a pre-war resident of Poznan, wrote:

> Thus, in Dr. Lück's 'scientific' activities and in the inspiration which they gave to the ruthless and brutal methods of the Himmler security service we have a typical example of criminal distortion of science.... Kurt Lück has avoided

bearing responsibility for his activities: as a high officer of the SS he fell on the Eastern Front in 1942.[2]

Dr. Lück, who joined the SS and fought in the East, where he perished practicing what he preached, was aware that many people of German ethnic origin living in various parts of Poland, including central or Congress Poland and other eastern borderlands of Germany proper, had been steadily emigrating west, moving toward the urbanized and industrializing central and western lands of Germany. He knew this trend had commenced in the later 19th century. Significantly, he considered such a movement undesirable, an indication that he was an Eastern Dreamer, like so many others, including Hitler, Himmler, Globocnik, and von Mohrenschildt. Significantly, both Globocnik and von Mohrenschildt had ancestors who had either lived in German enclaves among Slavs — his mother hailing from Banat, near present-day Belgrade, while von Mohrenschildt's forebears had left Estonia for Carinthia before 1900. Globocnik, moreover, is believed to have fought against Yugoslavs, that is, Slovenes, who had attempted to incorporate Austrian Carinthia into the newly-created southern Slav nation, while the von Mohrenchildt family had to relocate itself away from southern Carinthia during those difficult times, the early 1920s. In his 1940 book, *Der Lebenskampf im Deutsch-Polnischen Grenzraum*, Dr. Lück wrote:

> We know very well that the final fate of our nation will be settled on our frontiers. We must learn from our mistakes in the nineteenth century. Our fatherland will not be able to regain its old German character if thousands of Germans migrate now, as they did then, to the west. Let us not deceive ourselves: this trend in the wrong direction still exists; this can be proved from many examples.[3]

The July 1941 Himmler visit to Lublin saw Berlin's stamp of approval placed on the plans to make Lublin the SS's city of the East, and to Germanize the entire district. Himmler wished to see Germans settling lands ever further east. Construction of Majdanek concentration camp was also given the all clear, and Globocnik was promoted to police general on 30 November.

Governor Ernst Zörner sought and gained Globocnik's backing for moves against illegal trading in January. By the end of the year Lublin's population stood at just over 133,000 people, with a huge 39,167 being children aged 15 or younger. Of this total, Poles made up 92,000; Jews, 40,000; and Ukrainians just 1,000; Reich Germans and *Volksdeutsche* numbered slightly fewer than 4,000.

The General Gouvernement had initially been considered a demographic dumping ground, one that was to be plundered and to provide labor — forced or otherwise — and an initial plan was worked out for Jews to be used as forced labor whenever and wherever possible. But this outlook was quickly altered for reasons that are still not entirely clear. It is worth remembering, however, that by March 1940, Dr. Hans Frank's administration's experts had devised a Germanic development master plan for the General Gouvernement, a sort of wartime reconstruction blueprint for the entire German occupied area. The Polish occupied lands were not to be simply left to vegetate, but would be moulded into a Germanized and developed region, and would eventually incorporate into the Reich, but without Poles, and most definitely without Jews, though their ultimate fate had not yet been decided. In many ways, much of this SS and civil government work was a continuation — even if far less humanely implemented — of the tradition that Erich von Ludendorff, Hitler's one-time friend, had begun in Ober Ost Land during 1915–18, with the added difference that extermination of the Jews was eventually adopted as a "solution" and the remaining Poles, in the interim, were to be used as labors. Poland, or the entire Vistula River valley region, was to take on a Germanic appearance. Lublin had a special role within this developing blueprint, because it was the most easterly of the General Gouvernement's major cities. Warsaw was too far north and Krakow, its seat of government, was too far south. Globocnik, whether by design or by accident, was therefore the best situated of all Himmler's Higher SS and police leaders. He was also the most loyal, the most enthusiastic, and the most indebted, the latter because of his Vienna days. At the same time, experts associated with Dr. Hans Ehlich within the SS's main office in Berlin were devising and refining *Generalplan Ost*, on the orders of and under the guidance of Himmler.

X

Globocnik's Lublin District "Gulag Archipelago"

Lublin District under Globocnik can rightly be regarded as one of Europe's major 20th century graveyards (Map 5.) The main reason Globocnik and his many and various policing agencies were able to kill as many victims as they did is that Globocnik established a Gulag along the lines of the one that Josef Stalin had created across much of the Soviet Union during and after the 1930s. Although it would be incorrect to see Globocnik as solely responsible for its creation, he was nevertheless the chief executive officer of the region which compiled this appalling and inhumane record.

The key physical components of this short-lived but murderously effective Gulag, concerning number of deaths and people displaced, were: 57 ghettos (*Jüdische Wohnbezirke*), with the Lublin ghetto by far the largest; 143 work camps, including 13 penal work camps; 27 prison camps plus three *Stalags* (319, 325, and 366/Z) and two *Durlags*; two killing centers — Sobibor and Belzec — with a third, Treblinka, situated in adjacent Warsaw District; one huge and expanding concentration camp, Majdanek, which also had mass gassing facilities, as well as Majdanek's six sub-camps; 17 transit camps; and finally, nine major prisons and 29 detention centers. All of this approached nearly 300 incarceration precincts of one kind or another, in which men, women, and even children were interned so they could be quickly killed by shooting, beating, or else by being dispatched to one of the three relatively new and nearby killing centers, or to Majdanek, to be gassed.

Map 5. Lublin Distrikt 1939–1944

These nearly 300 precincts made up Globocnik's Lublin District Gulag Archipelago.

In addition to such forms of violent death were added the perils of simply being an inmate of any of these precincts. Prisoners could be subjected to beatings or having to endure long cold winters dressed only in thin clothing, and existing in near starvation without essential medical services, and performing long hours of arduous work, usually outdoors, even during the winter. Finally, epidemics were especially prevalent in the district's nearly 60 ghettos. Moreover, it is fair to say that the thousands of Jews held in the Lublin District's network of ghettos were slowly starving to death before their eventual calculated mass murder, like their co-religionists in the other ghettos of the General Gouvernement. Starvation results in people moving more slowly, and it markedly impedes people's perception of reality, so a command group that is predisposed toward violence, and which has incarcerated such people, is likely to have further reason to hold them in disdain. All the available evidence is that Globocnik was already so disposed, especially to Jews but also to Poles, on arrival in Lublin. Ian Kershaw reports on Globocnik being prepared to see the Jews of the General Gouvernement dying en masse if they proved themselves unable to cope with the new SS Order that had been imposed: "The police chief of the Lublin District, Odilo Globocnik suggested that if the Jews coming to the General Government could not feed themselves, or be fed by other Jews, they should be left to starve."[1]

Prison Camps: Sub-Camps, Work Centers, Building Work Battalions

Globocnik's district was to have some 27 prison camps, most of them holding Soviet prisoners-of-war (POWs)—primarily Russians and Ukrainians, but also some Belarusans and a sprinkling of Lithuanians and other Balts; these compounds were hurriedly created after the invasion of Russia in June 1941. Although no evidence has been found to suggest they had come under Globocnik's direct control, they were nevertheless within his area of jurisdiction, and formed an integral part of his region's Gulag for a sustained period. According to one estimate, the years 1941–42 saw some 500,000 Soviet prisoners held in, initially, at least, as many as 35 such camps and their smaller affiliates, with the largest of them in Chelm, Biala Podlaski, Wlodawa, and Zamosc. In September 1941 alone, under an agreement with the *Wehrmacht,* 325,000 Soviet POWs were transferred to come under the control of the SS. All such incarceration centers had exceptionally high death rates, far higher than American, British, and Australian losses in Japanese prison camps, which were high in their own right, as well as large-scale executions. The attitude toward Soviet POWs was identical to that expressed by Globocnik toward Jews because the war in the East was a racial one, unlike in France and elsewhere in Western Europe. As one authority notes, "In camps on Polish territory, they [the Nazis] murdered at least 800,000 Soviet prisoners-of-war, as well as more than 22,000 Italian and about 15,000 French, British and American prisoners."[2]

Not all of this 800,000 died in Lublin District, of course, but, a great many did. Even if the 800,000 figure is an overestimate, and the actual figure was, say, 500,000, that remains an enormous number of POWs whose killing was a crime, with many of them murdered one way or another in Globocnik's Lublin District. This bloodied region was thus the last resting place of a large number of the total figures from all four nationalities. The Chelm camp, or *Stalag* 319, held officers as well as soldiers. In some documents it is referred to as *Stalag* 319A, and in November 1941 it held just over 21,500 POWs, while *Stalag* 319B at that time was holding nearly 28,000 POWs. *Stalag* 319 was built in July 1941, just a month after the Soviet Union was invaded, and it remained operational until April 1944, being utilized seven months after Globocnik had been transferred to the Adriatic region in September 1943. During 1941, its only inmates were Soviets. Hunger and epidemics resulted in many deaths. Prisoner numbers on 1 June 1942 stood at about 4,250, and were augmented that day by the arrival of a further 10,570. At the turn of 1942–43, its inmates even included Britains, Frenchmen, and Belgians. On 1 October 1942, it held 7,527 inmates, and among these, 6,229 were Soviets, including Russians, Ukrainians, and probably even a smattering of Baltic soldiers, all demoralized and hungry. The French segment totaled 1,144. The end of 1943 brought the arrival of Italians, because of Rome's withdrawal from the Axis with the Allied northerly advance following the successful North African campaign. It is often not realized that some 22,000 Italians, as German allies, had served on the Eastern Front, and they perished at the hands of the Nazis. On New Years Day, 1944, *Stalag* 319 held 22,615 POWs, and of these 2,163 were Italians. On 1 February 1944, it had nearly 24,950 Soviets removed from its compounds. The Chelm camp had been one of the largest such incarceration centers on occupied Polish lands. Nearby, at Borek Forrest, large mass executions of Soviet POWs were witnessed, with somewhere on the order of 90,000 men killed. The SS's eastern racial war was in full swing in Globocnik's district, though once again no evidence has been found linking him and his Lublin personal staff to these.[3]

The Polish Underground managed to acquire letters written by German soldiers stationed in this region or written in a variety of regions of occupied Poland, including Chelm Lubelski and Biala Podlaska, two locations that fell within Globocnik's control. An extract from a letter by a soldier based in the former said:

> You can understand that we don't bother much with the prisoners. If they have to stay here during the winter, half will die anyhow. Jewish prisoners are shot immediately and have first of all to dig their own graves. They are tied in groups of five so that they can fall together into a communal grave. There are between 300 and 400 executions daily.
> On October 1, [probably 1941] there were about 100,000 prisoners in an open

camp. They are completely unprotected and stumble in ditches. Some have a few rags, and some have straw. Twice daily they are given some kind of hot fluid and a quarter of loaf. Their hunger is so ravenous they even eat grass. There are between 60 and 70 deaths a day. (There were 6,000 deaths before October 1 in this camp.)[4]

The letter that originated from Lublin District's Biala Podlaska area said:

On Sunday I visited the Russian prisoner-of-war camp. I wanted to take photographs but just could not bring myself to do so. The squalid poverty and stark horrors are too much. There are between two and 300 deaths every night. It is not pleasant for us who have to guard them. They try constantly to escape, even throwing themselves wildly into the machine gun fire. They try to stone us. 600 Jews and partisans are segregated from the others and are guarded by the SS. The prisoners are dying of hunger, among them 13–15-year-olds. When we unloaded a transport of prisoners yesterday we found eight dead among the 4,000 and had to shoot a further 10 who tried to escape.[5]

Biala Podlaska was the site of *Stalag* 366/Z, which was affiliated with *Stalag* 366, and was situated in Siedlce. It became operational in August 1941, two months after the invasion of the Soviet Union was launched, and was evacuated in July 1944. Initially it held only Soviet POWs. On the night of 11–12 August 1941, an escape bid was mounted involving 121 POWs, of whom 37 were recaptured, with 23 killed and 23 wounded. Some 3,000 POWs perished in this camp. At the end of 1943, a group of Italian officers — backers of Marshall Badoglio, the man who had ousted *Il Duce* Benito Mussolini — were incarcerated in this camp. Many soon died of hunger and cold.[6]

The Zamosc-based camp for Soviet POWs was designated *Stalag* 325. It existed from July to December 1941, so was only briefly operational. In November it held about 8,300 POWs, and they lived out in the open. Hunger, a typhus epidemic, typhoid fever, and other serious illnesses prevailed. Little wonder that saw a prisoner uprising. But this only led to massive executions. POWs were also taken to camps in the town near Okrzei Street and placed into barracks. It is believed that between late 1941 and 1943, some 28,000 POWs were murdered at this site, which was to become the center of Globocnik's first Germanized zone in the General Gouvernement, the Zamosc Lands.[7] To the north, the Wlodawa camp for Soviet POWs was a wing of the Chelm-based Kommando *Stalag* 319, and it was operational between mid–1941 and 1944. It had barracks, and, in November 1941, held some 5,200 prisoners, with several thousand of these eventually being murdered.[8]

Some camps, like Lobaczew Duzy, were simply large transit or holding pens for Soviet POWs. Lobaczew Duzy, which held, on average, about 400 men, was established in August 1941, and liquidated relatively quickly, in March 1942. Another, at Terespol, was a work camp for Soviet POWs and was situated near a railway line. One Kalilow, was also a transit camp, or more correctly, a pen for Soviet POWs. Established shortly after the invasion of the Soviet Union, it was liquidated in December 1941. POWs lived beneath the open sky, dwelling in shallow holes — foxholes, American GIs would have called them. The internees died in large numbers due to disease and several waves of epidemics. Those still living were taken, in the early part of December 1941, from the railway station at Biala Podlaska in the direction of Deblin. Diggings after the war showed that there were some 13,000 bodies buried at Kalilow. The long-lived Rogoznica work camp came into existence in July 1940, and was liquidated on 15 March 1944. It consisted of barracks, and at first held Polish Jews, about 250 men. More Jews followed this group from Czechoslovakia. Later, Poles arrived and even Soviet POWs appeared. On average it held 400 prisoners, with about 2,000 inmates passing through its gates. They worked on tasks associated with the Krzna River project; the Krzna was a tributary of the Bug. A typhus and dysentery epidemic affected these men. Others were shot. Others still were taken to other locations, and partisans liberated some.[9]

In Lublin District's northern sector was the county town of Miedzyrzec Podlaski, which became the venue for three camps: a work camp and two separate compounds solely for Russian POWs. The first was built in 1940 to hold Polish Jews who worked in *Luftwaffe* labor teams. The first Russian compound was erected in October and November, 1941, and held about 200 POWs who worked on a large German landed estate, not unlike some that Globocnik instituted across his district. About 60 of these Russians died due to dysentery. The other Russian compound was built in June and July 1944, very late in Poland's occupation, and its prisoners worked at an ammunition dump. Sixty died of disease while the rest were shot.[10] Another such camp from this later stage of the war was situated at Suleje. It existed only during April through June 1944, well after Globocnik had moved out of Lublin, and it held some 280 Russian POWs who worked for the *Wehrmacht* constructing ammunition dumps and defensive bunkers. About 20 men escaped, and in the week that the Red Army arrived the remainder were taken to Miedzyrzec Podlaski and later to Siedlce. Radzyn Podlaski also held Soviets, and was linked to the Deblin camp, which came under the control of *Stalag* 307.[11]

Without doubt, the district's two most notorious camps were at Poniatowa and Trawniki, both locations for several different types of incarceration centers. The former was for Soviet POWs, and was built during 1941–42. It experienced a typhus epidemic and there were executions, beatings, and starvation; the death rate was exceptionally high, with the majority of the POWs perishing. The number who died or were killed stands at about 20,000. The notorious Trawniki site was the location of three such camps. The first was for Polish POWs, and had been built in late 1939, as part of the demobilization of the defeated Polish army. This was followed by erection of a transit camp for Soviet POWs that was created in mid–1941, when there were high mortality levels. Another was erected for building or construction workers in 1942. This was liquidated in 1943, and at the time it held only about 100 Poles, some of whom worked on the railroads, laying and repairing tracks.[12]

Lublin city, which was being deliberately Germanized, like Lodz (Litz-mannstadt), Krakow, and others, to become a major German eastern outpost, also held Soviet POWs. It is worth emphasizing that the city had 22 jails, ghettos, prisons, work camps, and other incarceration centers. In addition there was the huge Majdanek concentration camp on its eastern outskirts; Lublin was an SS-controlled city and a large incarceration center that eventually included seven work camps; six building team camps; a ghetto; an *SD* prison, The Zamek (Lublin Castle); a Gestapo prison; and three camps for Soviet POWs. The first of these was established in 1942 and held some 5,000 men who actually worked on erecting Majdanek. Many of these men died, and the survivors were later placed into Majdanek. Another camp was erected near the town toward the end of 1941. It was called the Tenth, with most POWs held in it perishing due to hunger and grave illnesses. The last was established in 1943–44 at 35 Nowy Swiat Road, with its inmates working at the city's tobacco establishment.[13]

The Jablon work camp also held Soviet POWs. It was erected at the turn of 1941–42, and its inmates worked in rural or farming jobs. Another smaller camp was located at Skrobow. Interestingly, it was also a hospital for Soviet POWs, and was established in the autumn and winter of 1941, and liquidated in March 1944. On average it held 3,000 prisoners, including even some women, whose origin is unknown. Approximately 7,000 POWs perished within its perimeter because of insufficient protection from the elements and a lack of care by their captors. When its hospital was liquidated, the prisoners were dispatched to an unknown destination.[14]

A segment of Konskowola was set aside as a work camp for POWs. It opened in October 1940, and its inmates worked in rural occupations for the Pulawy Institute and also unloaded railway cares arriving in that town. The camp at Antopol was a work sub-camp of a *Kommando* camp for Soviet POWs. It came into being in 1942 on the site of a farming estate. The average number of POWs stood at 600 to 700. These men mainly worked loading and unloading railroad cars at Naleczow and Sadurki. About 100 died, mostly due to hunger, and their bodies were buried in a nearby forest. Radawiec, west of Lublin, was also the site of a Soviet POW work camp, while a camp at Goscieradow was associated with Sandomierz's *Stalag* 359, and also held Soviet POWs. It was established in December 1941, at the height of winter, and its inmates worked as road laborers. Zwierzyniec's, which was located on the road linking Zamosc and Bilgoraj, had a section within it that held French POWs. It was linked with the Rawa Ruska Camp, or *Stalag* 325, had been built towards the end of 1941 and was operational until the spring of 1944.[15]

Zmudz was a wing of the Chelm POW camp for Soviets, that is, the notorious *Stalag* 319. It was established in 1941 and was operational until the autumn of 1943. POWs lived in barracks and worked in the forests and on road construction projects. Hunger, typhus, and dysentery epidemics resulted in many deaths, and there were also executions. One gravesite holds some 450 bodies. Extreme conditions were also to be the case with Hrubieszow, another sub-camp of *Stalag* 319. It was operational during 1943–44, but only held about 120 POWs, who were all executed. A transit camp for Soviet POWs was also located at Zulice between July and November, 1941. It held, on average, 1,000 men, with some 8,000 POWs passing through. As in so many other camps in Lublin District, men here were held under open sky. The one at Mikulin was established in the autumn of 1942, and on average held 3,000 men. POWs lived out in the open and in dugouts. Executions were common. With its liquidation, some of the inmates were killed while others were moved to Zamosc. Szewnia was simply a sub-camp for Soviets, and was built in the autumn of 1941; it lasted until the end of 1942.[16]

Finally, there were two special-purpose POW transit camps, the first at Zubowice, the other at Sielczyk. Zubowice held some 1,000 Soviets. Of these, about 100 died of hunger and a variety of illnesses. The others were executed. Sielczyk only operated from the summer of 1941 until December, holding, on average, 60,000 Soviet POWs. Some 100,000 men passed through this huge complex. There were no barracks and no kitchens. Inmates slept out in the open on the ground and in shallow dugouts. Hunger, typhus epidemics, and dysentery produced a high death rate, about 300 men daily. In addition, there were mass executions in nearby forests. The exact figure is not known, but the loss of life was approximately 10,000 to 17,000 prisoners. There was a mass breakout on 15 August 1941, with many throwing themselves at the wire fences. Some managed to break free. Others were killed during their desperate bid to escape. At the beginning of December 1941, the remainder were distributed among other camps. In August 1941, about 1,000 French officers were brought to the camp, with some perishing because of illnesses, but three groups managed to escape.[17]

Globocnik's Three "Terminal Stations": Treblinka, Sobibor, and Belzec

Treblinka, Sobibor, and Belzec formed the triple-legged centerpiece of Globocnik's relatively short-lived but highly effective killing empire. They made up the foundations of *Aktion Reinhardt*. Unlike Majdanek, situated on Lublin's eastern outskirts, and Auschwitz-Birkenau in Upper Silesia, the structures or compounds that made up these three camps were dismantled after their task of killing Lublin District's Jews and those railed in from other parts of Europe and Poland was completed. Moreover, Treblinka and Sobibor witnessed prisoner rebellions, and mass escape bids, which, although largely unsuccessful, prompted Himmler to liquidate hurriedly both killing compounds. The two uprisings were the reason for Himmler deciding to have executed over 40,000 Jewish skilled slave laborers based in work camps around Lublin during the infamous *Erntefest* massacre of November 1943, after Globocnik was already in Trieste, though he was in all likelihood involved even from as far away as the Adriatic arranging these killings. As described earlier, Hermann Höfle was the key organizer of this mass crime.

It is not necessary to describe each of the killing centers in detail, for an extensive body of literature has belatedly begun to emerge on each, even on Belzec, which has inexplicably been largely ignored by Holocaust historians, in the same way that Globocnik himself has been overlooked. To make the point that they were markedly different even from the dual purpose concentration camps and killing centers of Auschwitz-Birkenau and Majdanek, it is valuable to quote from Dutch historian Louis de Jong's writings on Sobibor;

> Unlike Auschwitz-Birkenau, which served as both concentration and extermination camp, Sobibor was simply an extermination camp, one of three *Vernichtungslager*— Belzec, Sobibor, Treblinka — set up in the spring of 1942 by the *SS-Sonderkommando des Einsatzstabs Reinhardt* (Special SS-Detachment of the *Reinhardt* Operational Staff). All three camps were guarded in the main by Ukrainian and Lithuanian volunteers. In Sobibor, as far as it is possible to tell, the guards were Ukrainian, dressed in brown uniforms with SS flashes on their collars — some 200 men altogether, commanded by "ethnic" Germans from the Ukraine. Sobibor also had a complement of 50 to 100 fully-fledged SS men.[18]

Entering one of these three out-of-the-way compounds by train meant one had literally and figuratively reached the end of the line. The radical right-wing British writer and publicist, David Irving, has euphemistically, but quite accurately, described these as "terminal stations," as was Auschwitz-Birkenau in Silesia. But unlike Treblinka, Sobibor, and Belzec, Auschwitz-Birkenau had the added dimension of also being a huge work camp, a mass prison, and a huge detention center. Because it was at the center of a network of over 50 sub-camps, it was in fact far larger than the huge fenced structure at Birkenau, situated on the outskirts of the onetime Austro-Hungarian railway junction town known as Auschwitz, or Oswiecim, in Polish. Once inside one of Globocnik's killing centers, victims were forced to walk through barbed wire corrals and to disrobe and enter a gas chamber naked where, after 30 odd minutes, many hundreds of people lay dead, with their bodies ready for removal for cremation or, in the early days, in some cases, burial. Before the people were gassed, all their worldly possessions were removed. Specially assigned Jewish work squads had initially buried the thousands of accumulating bodies at Belzec, but after some time this practice was discontinued, and the mounting numbers of bodies were burned. Loot taken from the victims, including lifetime savings, was eventually shipped to Lublin for processing by Georg Wippern's specialist sorting team. As will be described below, the acquisition of this loot was an integral part of *Aktion Reinhardt*. The few inmates who survived the three killing or extermination camps, or "terminal stations," some of them escapees, are one major source of information about the camp routines. In some cases German and Austrian personnel during postwar court hearings and pre-trial interrogations, and some ex–Soviet guards, have markedly augmented these accounts through unwilling disclosure. Because each of the three killing compounds was situated relatively close to the Bug River, Lublin District's eastern boundary, it is fair also to refer to them as Globocnik's Bug Killing Centers.

David Irving says that these killing centers were erected after long consideration on how Europe's Jews should be eliminated. This is true. Hitler, says Irving, felt Europe would eventually understand his hatred of Jews. Irving says Goebbels claimed at this time: "Somehow we must get rid of them if they are not to get rid of us." The word "rid" here is, of course, quite ambiguous. As explained above, it meant in the early phase of the war the construction of the ill-fated Lublin Reservation and urban ghettos, with the opportunity, perhaps, of eventually deporting the Jews overseas. If that was ever a possibility, which is doubtful, it rapidly faded away after early 1940. But over the two years of 1940 and 1941 the extermination option, with Globocnik at its center in Lublin, was steadily turned to by Hitler, Himmler, and Heydrich, with men like Globocnik, Wirth, and Höfle being willing and senior accomplices. "The precise mode of 'elimination' met with varying interpretations. Hitler's was unquestionably the authority behind the *expulsion* operations; on whose initiative the grim procedures at the terminal stations of this miserable exodus were adopted, was arguable." (Emphasis in original)[19]

Heydrich, Irving contends, told the Reich Ministries that Europe's 11 million Jews should be collected "in the East" until after victory, and then they could be removed en masse to a distant location like Madagascar.

> The actual operation proceeded differently. Starting in March and April [1942] European Jews were rounded up in occupied France, Holland and Belgium, and in the eager Nazi satellite Slovakia; for political reasons Hungary — which had nearly a million Jews — and Romania were not approached yet but were told that their Jewish "problems" would be left unresolved until the war was over. From Dr. Hans Frank's General Gouvernement of Poland too — beginning with the ghettos of Lublin — the Jews set out eastward *under the direction of one of the cruelest SS leaders, Brigadier Odilo Globocnik, the Trieste-born former Gauleiter of Vienna* [emphasis added].[20]

Irving further claimed that two documents shed light on precisely who was responsible for the eventually-selected extermination or killing path, that is, who made the fateful move away from expulsion to extermination, thereby giving Globocnik his unenviable place in history. The first of these is from a General Gouvernement cabinet meeting held in Krakow on 9 April 1942. At this gathering, Dr. Hans Frank insisted he was not responsible for disrupting work being carried out across the General Gouvernement by Jewish work teams and in ghetto workshops due to the elimination decision order. "The directive for the liquidation of the Jews comes from higher up," said Frank. Irving next refers to a letter of 26 June 1942 that revealed Himmler's concern that the liquidation process was too slow, and in danger of not being completed. Globocnik, in a letter to Himmler, wrote: "You yourself, *Reichsführer*, once mentioned that you felt the job should be done as quickly as possible if only for reasons of concealment."[21] Irving here is primarily interested in showing that the *Führer's* view or method of dealing with Europe's so-called Jewish problem — the first of Globocnik's eastern missions — differed from Himmler's and Globocnik's, in that the *Führer* sought *only expulsion,* that is, a fate also envisaged for all Slavs, and one promoted by a cohort of pre–World War I German propagandists and activists. Though Irving's ongoing disputes with so many other historians on this point — namely, his extraordinary claim that Hitler was unaware of the Jewish Genocide until 1943 — is beyond the scope of this study, his description of Globocnik's key role in it is nevertheless telling, accurate, and succinct.[22] Despite David Irving's proclivity for attempting to cordon off or sanitize Adolf Hitler — to prove his absolute and utter innocence vis-à-vis the Jewish Holocaust from direct responsibility, as opposed to backing mere expulsion, transfer or deportation eastward, that was to occur to Poles and other Slavs under the terms of *Generalplan Ost,* significantly Irving makes no such case for Himmler or Globocnik. Irving continues:

> In reality, Himmler was simultaneously throwing the murder machinery into top gear, while he was careful not to place responsibility for the massacre itself on Hitler in writing (Thus on July 28 he wrote to SS General Gottlieb Berger: "The occupied eastern territories" — meaning Poland — "are to be liberated of Jews. *The Führer has entrusted me with the execution of this arduous order.* Nobody can deprive me of this responsibility.") On July 19, three days after seeing Hitler, Himmler ordered the "resettlement" of the entire Jewish population of the Generalgouvernement to be completed by the last day of 1942 [emphasis added].[23]

Without Globocnik, long favored and looked after by the *Reichsführer-SS,* or someone of his ilk on his staff in Lublin, like Wirth or Höfle, this secretly-initiated genocide could not have proceeded. However, when assessing individual members of Globocnik's staff— Wirth, Höfle, Lerch, Michalsen, to name just four — it is difficult not to conclude that *Aktion Reinhardt* would undoubtedly have proceeded without him. All these were of the same ilk, genocidal killers. Nevertheless, many felt called, but only Globocnik was chosen.

Demolishing the three isolated killing compounds to conceal what had happened within these relatively isolated sites certainly proved to be an effective tactic, for when units of the formidable west bound Red Army passed them by in the summer of 1944, these locations had little, if any impact, if indeed they were even seen. This is in stark contrast to the impact of the more permanent Majdanek structure, which was moderately well publicized in the international press during 1944, in part because it was the first major concentration and death camp to be closely examined by an enemy of the Reich. In 1944, Moscow even released an English-language publication, *The Lublin Extermination Camp*, which was attributed to Constantine Simonov, who was billed as a "special correspondent of the *Krasnaya Zvezda*."[24] The pamphlet carried pictures and a two-page statement by the last German commander of the Lublin region, Lieutenant-General Hjalmar Moser, referred to earlier, who arrived there in November 1942.

> In that same summer of 1944, the Russians also overran three extermination camps: Belzec, Sobibor, and Treblinka; yet they made *no mention* of these camps in their own press and none appears in the Western press at the time.... Before the Russians arrived Jewish workers were sent to Belzec to clean out the burial pits and burn the bodies. The Russians occupied the area in mid–1944 *but perhaps did not immediately understand what had happened there....* [At Sobibor] all the permanent buildings were dynamited, large cranes excavated the burial pits, and the bodies were burned. To complete the concealment of the site, pine trees were planted where the camp had once been. As in the case of Belzec, *the Russians reported nothing* about Sobibor.... Whether the Russians discovered the full magnitude of the horror of the Treblinka extermination camp is unclear, but at least they did not release at that time any details that found their way into the Western press [emphases added].[25]

No mention was made of Globocnik's Treblinka, Sobibor, or Belzec, because all had been dismantled and all the permanent structures, including the gassing facilities, demolished.

Majdanek

Majdanek, or more properly, *Konzentrationslager*, then *Kriegsgefangenenlager SS Lublin*, and finally, from 1943 onward, *Konzentrationslager* Lublin, has been described as the cornerstone of Himmler's planned empire in the East. Himmler's order to build it was given during his important July 1941 visit to the city.

> Originally, then, the Lublin camp was to have been a concentration camp consisting [of] an extension of the then SS force labor camp in Lipowa Street. That

the camp was to be of that nature is evidenced by the fact that the Reich's Inspectorate for Concentration Camps (later called *Amstgruppe* D in the *WVHA*) participated in its organization and construction. However, the site of the proposed camp turned out to be inadequate, and on 22 September 1941, Heinz Kammler, head of Office II in *WVHA*, ordered work to commence immediately on the construction for 60,000 prisoners. Four days later, for the purposes of setting up a "camp for POWs" the governor of Lublin Ernst Zörner transferred some 270 hectares in the eastern part of the town to the SS. This included the district of Kosminek, and the grounds of the villages of Dziesiata, Abramowice and Kalinowka. Almost simultaneously, on September 27th, Kammler issued urgent orders for the construction of the camp in Lublin, which was to have been suitable for 50,000 POWs.[26]

The order by Himmler that to Germanize Lublin and Zamosc was the opening gambit in Germanizing the entire Lublin District, and thereafter the entire General Gouvernement west toward western Poland, which was being ably cleansed of Poles by Hermann Krumey. This in fact meant that Globocnik had received the all-clear to work on an opening stage of the Berlin-devised *Generalplan Ost*.

> During October and November 1941, the guidelines contained in the July program were rendered more specific. The detailed and expanded program of activity in this field was given the name Program Heinrich. It provided for the construction in Lublin of an SS base, which would constitute an economic support for SS posts in the occupied Soviet territories. It would consist, next to the SS housing district, of a Supply Works, a Clothing Works, a Supply Storehouse for the higher SS and police leader of South Russia (*Nachschublager des Hohren SS-und Polizeiführer Russland Sud*) as well as large workshops in the planned camp.[27]

To undertake this enormous Germanizing task, Globocnik thus had his area of jurisdiction extended into the pre-war Polish province of Wolyn (Volhynia), to the east of his Lublin District, putting him in charge of "constructing SS Police Strongpoints in the new eastern territories."[28] Here the word "eastern" meant not simply his Lublin District, but lands far beyond the Bug River — his district's eastern boundary — into pre-war eastern Poland, across Wolyn (Volhynia) Province and other former eastern Polish provinces and counties, then on into western and central Ukraine, north to Belarus and Russia, and even perhaps well into parts of the Caucasus. And this array of guidelines, orders, and revelations of colonizing blueprints were talked about by these two SS men as the powerful *Wehrmacht* was having incredible successes against the Red Army, successes that Hitler had fully anticipated. Lublin was understandably seen to be ideally situated to become Himmler's or the SS's springboard for bigger eastern ventures. The decision to build the huge Majdanek incarceration venue and killing center on Lublin's eastern outskirts was directly linked to plans to invade the Soviet Union so as to assist in the policy of steadily and progressively Germanizing the lands between the Reich's eastern border, which had been extended in October 1939 into central Poland, all the way to the Ural Mountains. Lublin was an ideal location for such a huge camp, because it could be used to assist in the Germanization of Lublin District first, the entire General Gouvernement second, and to play a role in an identical policy pursued further east. These policies will be considered more closely below, and it will be seen that among other things Majdanek was used during the expulsion of Polish peasants from the Zamosc Lands, especially in the later stages, that is, after mid–1943. Less well known is that Majdanek incorporated seven sub-camps, though most took on this formal association after Globocnik had left Lublin for Trieste. One of these sub-camps was even in Warsaw, another in nearby Radom, outside Lublin District, while two others were beyond the city of Lublin.

Majdanek's Sub-Camps

Unlike Himmler's and Oswald Pohl's other huge concentration camps in Germany and Austria and Auschwitz-Birkenau, which generally had many affiliates, Majdanek had just seven, and these only became linked to it late in the action. Another distinguishing feature, according to Jozef Marszalek, was that Majdanek did not supply workers to the sub-camps because they were adequately supplied with labor in their own right. Majdanek, for most of its existence, was thus a stand-alone concentration camp as well as a killing center.

Majdanek's first two sub-camps, Blizyn and Budzyn, or Krasnik-Budzyn, were situated within Lublin District, with the former being a sub-camp for men and women. In 1942, however, it became a POW camp for Soviets, and from March 1943 it was a work camp for Poles and Polish Jews. On average it had about 4,500 inmates, including Austrians, Germans, and Soviets. There were even about 1,000 women held within it. About 10,000 people passed through it. At first the prisoners worked in a rock quarry, then in shoe repair workshops, on tailoring tasks, metal works, and knitting and sorting of clothing, much of it for the Eastern Front. It became a sub-camp of Majdanek in February 1944, well after Globocnik had left Lublin. On 31 July 1944, Blizyn's inmates were moved to Auschwitz. Blizyn was initially linked to a Radom ghetto work camp, and the two were then administered jointly by Globocnik's counterpart in Radom District.

> In April 1943 the *Osti* company took over the workshops in both camps. After the company had been liquidated, they passed into the hands of the *DWA*, while the camps were subordinated to Majdanek.... The transformation of the camps into Majdanek sub-camps resulted in having the prisoners wear striped-cloth suits, in giving them the numbers of the Lublin camp, and in detailing

an SS staff to guard them. The liquidation of the Radom and Blizyn camps began towards the end of July 1944.[29]

Budzyn, or Krasnik-Budzyn, on the other hand, was a sub-camp only for men, and was established in the autumn of 1942 as a work camp for Polish Jews. It was located on the site of a former munitions factory. In the spring of 1943, it held some 3,000 men who worked for the Heinkel Aircraft Company; they were essential for maintenance of German air power over the Eastern Front. On 31 July 1944, its prisoners were dispatched to Auschwitz, further west into Silesia.[30] Budzyn's Jewish inmates were not executed during the belated *Erntefest,* or Harvest Festival, massacres of 3 November 1943 because they were desperately required by the Luftwaffe, which, at the time, was engaging the Soviets on the steadily collapsing Eastern Front. According to Polish historian Marek Chodakiewicz, Krasnik-Budzyn was also used in 1943 to intern about 4,500 Polish peasants of Janow-Lubelski County, which is just beyond the Zamosc Lands. These people were targeted for removal from their homes and farmlets.

> Between June 26 and July 13, 1943, a massive deportation campaign of the Christian Polish population was undertaken on the orders of *SS-Reichsführer* Himmler. Its object was to replace Poles with ethnic German and Ukrainians.... The campaign focused on the counties of the southern part of the District of Lublin. It was combined with the anti-partisan Operation Wehrwolf I and II (*Unternehmen Wehrwolf I and II*). In the County of Janow the southern and western parishes were targeted. According to Wehrmacht dispatches the police planned to deport most of the Polish population from the corridor along the Vistula and San Rivers. The operation there lasted from July 8 to 13. It was carried out by the so-called Stengel group composed of the SS, Order Police, gendarmerie, and the Ostlegionen. During the police sweep of the Parish of Jarocin alone, 205 farmsteads were burned, 142 peasants shot and 390 arrested. Altogether about 4500 people were seized and imprisoned in the concentration camp in [Krasnik-] Budzyn. At the end of July the offensive was called off by the civilian authorities because it brought the economy of the region to the brink of disaster and disrupted its administration. About 80 percent of the captives were released. The rest were sent to the concentration camps in Majdanek and Zwierzyniec, or dispatched to forced labor in Germany.[31]

Majdanek's third sub-camp, strangely, was located in Warsaw and known as "Gesiowka" because it was situated on Gesiej Street. It opened as a concentration camp on 19 July 1943, shortly before Globocnik left Lublin for Trieste, and its prisoners worked nearby in teams searching for jewelry and other valuables hidden in the ruins, cellars primarily, of the Warsaw Ghetto. These prisoners were later utilized to demolish buildings and to establish, of all things, a park. All were Jews, hailing from Austria, Belgium, France, Greece, Holland, Germany, and several other countries. However, it was only from

April 1944, that is, after Globocnik had reached Trieste, that Gesiowka formally became a sub-camp of Majdanek.[32] There was another camp, the fourth,
located in the provincial city of Radom, which was a sub-camp solely for
males. From August 1942 it was a work camp, and at the beginning of 1943
it was taken over by the SS police leader of Radom District. On average it
held 2,000 inmates, and on 17 January 1944, it became linked to Majdanek
concentration camp.[33] The fifth camp was an all-male unit located at Pulawy,
northwest of Lublin near the Vistula River, and was established as a Majdanek sub-camp in June 1943.[34]

Lublin itself was the venue of two camps that grew into large work establishments. One of the most significant was located at 7 Lipowa Street, and
had been established by Globocnik at the end of 1939. It was the first camp
in the Lublin District under the control of the SS. Lipowa Street employed
Jewish craftsmen who initially had to walk to work from their living quarters in Lublin's ghetto. But at the turn of 1940 and early 1941, some 2,500
Polish Jews moved in to live on the premises. From 3 November 1943 — after
the murder of these Jews — it became a sub-camp of Majdanek. A 500-strong
group of inmates from Majdanek was still located in Lipowa in 1944; it
included specialists and tradesmen, with some even being brought in from
other concentration camps. Lipowa had earlier been merged into the SS company, *DAW*. When Lublin was threatened by the Red Army's advance, all
POWs were moved west to Auschwitz, like those from Blizyn.[35]

Little has been recorded about the Lipowa camp, which became formally
linked with Majdanek in 1944, because most of its skilled Jewish workers perished either in one of Globocnik's killing centers as part of his *Aktion Reinhardt* genocidal killing program, or during the *Erntefest* massacre. However,
56 years after this little-known massacre, the camp's chief tailor, Jacob Frank,
published in the United States an account of his nearly four years as an in-
ternee. Frank, as well as having the extraordinary distinction of surviving this
ordeal, had the added one of actually giving evidence at the 1974 trial in
Hamburg against one of the camp's most inhumane commandants, *SS-Untersturmführer* Wolfgang Mohwinkel. Mark Lewis and Frank, in an account of
Frank's Lipowa Camp and other wartime experiences, have pointed out that
earlier writers had briefly mentioned or alluded to Lipowa, but had failed to
give this important work camp the attention it warranted.[36]

One of Frank's other minor claims to fame was that he actually made an
"iconographic, gray leather" coat for Globocnik, and thus had limited face-to-
face contact with the individual who had created Lipowa and was responsible
for the wretched lives its internees had to endure for so long. Lipowa Street
first came under the control of *SS-Standartenführer* Walter Gunst, who was
quickly followed by Ludolf von Alvensleben, a member of Lublin's *Selb-
stschutzführer* but who handed the day-to-day management of this important

camp to *SS-Obersturmbannführer* Dolp, who lasted in the post until June 1940.

> Starting in August 1940, the camp was commanded by the highly successful combination (in Nazi terms) of *SS-Untersturmführer* Horst Riedel and his adjutant *SS-Untersturmführer* Wolfgang Mohwinkel. Riedel concentrated on making business deals, which led to the economic success of the camp, while the "restless, arrogant and tireless" Mohwinkel implemented a brutal regime of discipline, including beatings, hangings and shootings.... In February and March 1941, the camp's business and economic planning were taken over by the German company *Deutsche Ausrüstungswerke* (German Supply Establishment) although in reality, this company was an SS subsidiary (or front) headed by Riedel and ultimately controlled by the notoriously corrupt *SS-Obergruppenführer* and Police Leader Odilo Globocnik. In November 1941, Globocnik relieved the business-savvy Riedel from his post, supposedly because of his arrogance, and the highly dedicated Mohwinkel took over as commandant until November 3, 1943; this is the date when all Jews in Lublin work camps were murdered in a mass execution, code-named the *Erntefest*, or "Harvest Festival."[37]

Just beyond Lublin city's perimeter was situated Majdanek's seventh sub-camp, which held both men and women. From 1941 onward it was purely a work camp. It was established on the site of aircraft workshops of Plagge and Laskiewicz, situated near Chelmska Road. Initially it held Polish women from The Zamek (Castle) prison, situated alongside Lublin's old or historic quarter. However, in the spring of 1942, these women were all relocated to Ravensbruck concentration camp in the Reich. After that the camp held Jewish women from Lublin and surrounding areas. After November 1942, it was transformed into a sub-camp of Majdanek. Held within it were some 3,000 female inmates and 1,200 inmates from Majdanek, who worked as sorters, packers, and railway car loaders of clothing and other goods acquired from Jewish victims of Globocnik's *Aktion Reinhardt* killings. The inmates also did other work, such as street paving. Later Jews even from Holland and Belgium were brought in to boost worker numbers.[38]

Ghettos

The Lublin ghetto was created in mid–1940. Between 10 and 12 March 1941, some 10,000 inmates were expelled from Lublin into the district's towns and townships, and their section of Lublin became the *Wehrmacht's* headquarters area preparatory to the eventual invasion of the Soviet Union. None of Lublin District's ghettos were as large as the two biggest in occupied Poland: that of Lodz (Litzmannstadt), with its 165,000 inmates, and Warsaw's, with about a third of a million people. Isaiah Trunk's monumental study of the endeavors of occupied Poland's major Jewish Councils' (*Judenrat*) efforts to grapple with forced ghettoization and isolation and the eventual mass extermination of their incarcerated inhabitants described this sizeable March 1941 evacuation, which, at a stroke, affected almost a tenth of the number of people victimized by the Zamosc Lands expulsion of 1942–1943.

> By order of the authorities, over 10,000 persons for whom no living quarters could be found within the small area assigned to the Lublin Ghetto were expelled to various small localities in the Lublin District. They became charges of the Jewish Council and were supplied with some cash before they wandered off to their assigned places. The financially pressed Council could not assist them and appealed to the ghetto inmates for donations. The minutes of the Council's meetings held on 16 March 1941 note that no more than 1500 zlotys could be allotted to these expelled persons out of Council funds. However, the Council delegated three doctors to practice in the localities assigned as places of residence. A substantial amount to help them (some 14,000 zlotys) came from Jewish Social Welfare in Cracow.[39]

On 24 March 1941, Globocnik's old rival, district Governor Ernst Zörner, ordered that some 30,000 people should be concentrated into another specified area. For some inmates this precinct was still not sealed off, but those without special passes (*Arbeitsschein*) were banned from leaving its confines. In January 1942, the ghetto was walled off. Another Zörner order, on 4 February 1942, split the ghetto into two sections, A and B, with "B" earmarked for those who worked for local German firms and the ghetto's administration.

Like other ghettos, and there were about 400 on the lands that comprised postwar Poland, Lublin's was administered by a *Judenrat* that had been created in late 1939. It came under the control of the Security Police (*Sipo*) through the Jewish Affairs section within the Gestapo (Referat IV B 4) in Berlin, and by Adolf Eichmann, the highly successful expeller of Austrian Jews during 1938 and 1939. From late 1941, interventions became increasingly burdensome, with searches, arrests, and executions routine. People's warm clothing was confiscated en masse. This expropriation of essential winter clothing was launched on Christmas Day, 1941, with inmates having until noon 28 December to hand in furs, coats, coverings, fur collars, and processed and unprocessed hides. That call netted 7,800 fur coats, 5,200 collars, about 700 sheepskin overcoats, over 1,200 men's and women's coats, gloves, caps, muffins, and hides. Not satisfied, Globocnik repeated the order, this time calling for the handing over of all wool and other clothing material. Five members of the *Judenrat* were assaulted and left standing wearing only socks on Lipowa Street. But the outcome was that 3,776 kilograms of wool was acquired. This expropriation was continued by Globocnik as part of *Aktion Reinhardt* as an integral element within the mass killing activities. Fuel was in desperately short supply, and this was particularly felt during the harsh winters of 1940–41 and 1941–42.

Congestion was the rule right across the ghetto, with people living in lofts and nooks and crannies. The death rate inevitably rose, epidemics broke out, and the ghetto's two hospitals could not accommodate all the sick. Zörner forbade Poles to have contact with this major Jewish quarter. As soon as the Belzec extermination camp — "terminal station" — was operational in early 1942, it commenced accepting Jews from all over the General Gouvernement. But the *Aktion Reinhardt* headquarters first targeted Lublin ghetto. On 8 March 1942, the security police stamped work cards of all those employed in German firms, the Jewish administrative arm, and anyone working in the hospitals. The ghetto's liquidation began on the night of 16–17 March 1942. Expelled from homes were men, women, and children. They were directed to the synagogue, and in the early morning those with the stamped cards were released, while the remaining 1,600 were dispatched to Belzec for extermination. Contrary to a widely held view that arose after the war, news of this and similar events did not remain unheard in the West during the war years. For example, in the following year, 1943, the American Federation of Polish Jews in the United States published *The Black Book of Polish Jewry*, with the following description of this ghetto's evacuation:

> In a statement at a press conference at the British Ministry of Information on July 9, 1942, Stanislaw Mikolajczyk, Vice-Premier of the Polish Government-in-Exile in London, gave the following information: "On the night of March 23–24, 1942, all the Jews in the district of Lublin were driven from their homes. The sick and the disabled were killed on the spot. 108 children, from 2 to 9-years old, were taken from a Jewish orphanage, led to the outskirts of the town, and murdered with their nurses. 2500 people were massacred that night; the remaining 26,000 Jews were removed to a concentration camp at Belzec and Trawniki.
>
> A report from the underground movement corroborates Mr Mikolajczyk's statement: "In March the city of Lublin was purged of its Jewish population. Again children and adults, the sick in the hospitals and numberless other inhabitants of the Ghetto were murdered. The number of victims in the Ghetto alone was over 2000. In addition, 25,000 Jews were taken from Lublin to an "unknown destination." Another 3000 were put in barracks in the Majdan Tatarski, a suburb of Lublin. There are no long any Jews in Lublin.[40]

In early March 1942, Jewish workers around Lublin were instructed to have their work permits stamped by Security Police (*Sipo*). On 17 March, Lublin's *Judenrat* was informed that Jews were to be deported. SS troops and locally based German and Ukrainian police units undertook this ghetto cleansing. Jews leaving the ghetto were processed by the inspection of work permits. Those in Ghetto A, with valid permits, were moved across to Ghetto B, and those without such permits were transferred to Ghetto A. At the same time, nearly 1,500 Jews were moved to the Maharshal Synagogue, from where they were eventually taken to railway cars destined for Globocnik's Belzec killing center on the southern extremities of Lublin District. A thoroughly methodical culling procedure had been devised.

> At first the transports left at night, but after a while they took place also in the daytime. Among those destined for extermination were also holders of valid work permits who had been rounded up by chance. The confused Jews wandered from street to street in the hope that they might be able to avoid deportation and gain another day of life.[41]

Many of those destined for deportation naturally sought refuge by hiding, but the ghetto was slowly searched house by house and block by block. Many were killed on the spot. Cleansed blocks were later searched again to ensure they were clear of Jews. From 24 March 1942 onward similar actions were conducted, that is, daily deportations to Belzec, each on average affecting about 1,400 people. In the course of just one week over 10,000 people had reached Belzec's gates to be murdered. The action briefly slowed, though on the outskirts of Lublin — at Majdan Tatarski — 320 children and orphanage personnel from Grodzkiej Street were shot, and three days later the liquidation of the hospitals commenced. Over 400 sick people were transported in heavy vehicles to a forest at Niemce, where they were murdered. Before launching later actions, membership of the *Judenrat* was reduced. New work cards were introduced with the letter "J" stamped, with those holding them earmarked to remain. On 31 March, the expulsion commenced again. On 14 April, expulsions of those without a work card were launched. The security police captured 4,000 people with these cards and removed them to a new ghetto, 3.5 kilometers away, near Majdan Tatarski.[42]

Lublin District's other major ghettos were at Chelm, Zamosc, Hrubieszow, Tomaszow-Lubelski, and Bilgoraj. Chelm's held the town's residents plus 2,000 Jews from Slovakia. Between 21 and 23 May, 1942, some 4,000 inmates were dispatched to nearby Sobibor killing center; 2,000 of them Polish Jews and 2,000 from Slovakia, and the sick and elderly. During this action a number of people were killed on the spot. The next transports were in July and August 1942, involving about 300 inmates; 27 and 28 October, involving 3,300 inmates, and others on 6 November 1942. Zamosc ghetto was opened in the spring of 1942 and liquidated in October the same year. It was located in the area known as New Settlement. Inmates from Kola, Wloclawek, Czestochowa, and from May 1942, Jews from the Reich and Czechoslovakia arrived, bringing the total to 9,000 inmates. Those assigned to labor duties worked on road construction gangs and the unloading and loading of railroad cars. In April 1942, 3,000 inmates were transported to Belzec. The next transport to that killing center was on 27 May 1942. Other's occurred on 11 August 1942 (about 600 people), and September 1942 (about 400 people). At the time of the ghetto's liquidation, 500 inmates were shot by the Nazis. The remaining

4,000 were dispatched to Izbica and later to Belzec. Izbica village is about midway between Zamosc and Kraznystaw, and was a predominantly Jewish settlement of some 6,000 people. During Globocnik's *Aktion Reinhardt* phase, its population at times was double that figure. Izbica was used as a sort of halfway house or stop-off depot for the Belzec and Sobibor killing centers. By October 1942, most of its Jewish internees, about 10,000 people, had been removed, and it became the site of a massacre of some 500 people. Some of those temporarily placed in Izbica were Jews from Vienna.

Bilgoraj ghetto became operational during 1941, and was liquidated relatively late in the war, in January 1943. Its inmates were from Bilgoraj itself and the surrounding county, as well as from Tarnogrod after November 1942. In March 1942, it housed 2,500 inmates. On 9 August, during October, and on 2 November, most were transported to the Belzec killing center. The remainder were shot on 7 January 1943. Hrubieszow ghetto's inmates were from across Hrubieszow County, with an additional 300 from Krakow. In May 1942 its population stood at 5,690. In June 1942 the entire population from the county was assembled — about 10,000 inmates. Between 2 and 10 June 1942, most were transported to the Sobibor "terminal station." About 500 were shot at the Jewish cemetery. The next transport of some 2,000 people as dispatched to the same extermination center in October 1942. A group of 200 remained to tidy the ghetto up, and were directed to the work camp at Budzyn in July and September, 1943. Tomaszow-Lubleski's ghetto was established in January 1942, and there were 1,450 inmates. On 25 February 1942, over 800 were directed to Cieszanow. The ghetto was liquidated on 25 May 1942. Cieszanow had been established in December 1941, and was liquidated in the spring of 1942. It held 817 inmates from Tomaszow-Lubelski and the surrounding region, and 500 from Mielc. Its numbers reached some 5,000, with males working on fortification projects. When it was liquidated, all inmates were sent to the Belzec extermination center.

In addition to these seven larger ghettos, there were an additional 50 in townships and larger villages. In most cases they held that town's or village's inhabitants, with these numbers being added to by those from their surrounding region. But many also held Jews from other countries and others part of Poland. In Tarnograd's case, Jews from Lodz (Litzmannstadt), Wloclawek, Kalisz, and 200 from Bilgoraj were brought in. In June 1942 it held 2,611 people. On 9 August 1942, a number were taken to the Belzec extermination camp, and at the time of its liquidation on 2 November 1942, the remainder were sent to Bilgoraj ghetto, and from there on 3 November 1942 to Belzec. Ulanow had just 500 inmates, a relatively tiny number, and was liquidated in October 1942, the month before the Zamosc Lands expulsions were launched, and a month during which a large number of the district's ghettos were liquidated. That of Komarow-Osada was opened during first half of 1942 and was liquidated on 10 November 1942. Its inhabitants were Jews from Lodz (Litzmannstadt), Wroclawek, Sierpca, and Zamosc, plus 400 from Czechoslovakia, a total of some 2,500 people. Those there were involved in tidying up work around Komarow. On 23 May 1942, a transport left for Belzec, and on liquidation the remainder were also sent to Belzec. Two other relatively large ghettos were Tyszowce and Grabowiec. Inmates in the former were from Lublin. In April 1942, there were 2,050 inmates. On 22 May 1942 a transport was sent to Belzec; the ghetto was liquidated in the autumn of 1942. Grabowiec's inmates were from nearby Hrubieszow County and from Krakow; its population stood at 2,026 inmates in May 1942. In the following month there was a 1,200-strong transport sent to Sobibor, with the remainder also being sent there at the time of liquidation in October 1942. The ghetto in Szczebrzeszyn, a relatively sizeable Zamosc Lands town, had Jews from Wroclaw (Breslau), Lodz (Litzmannstadt), and even some from Hungary, Czechoslovakia, and Rumania. Over 4,000 people passed through it. In 1941, some 40 people were executed. In May and August 1942, many of the inmates were dispatched to the Belzec extermination camp. During its liquidation on 21 October 1942, some were executed, while others were sent to nearby Izbica.[43]

This pattern was repeated across Globocnik's Lublin District throughout all of 1942 in the case of the remaining smaller ghettos, so it is truly extraordinary that Globocnik felt capable of launching the Zamosc Lands action against ethnic Poles that year. A significantly high number of the district's ghettos also had Jews from Krakow, the seat of power of Globocnik's rival General-Governor Dr. Frank, who so desired "his" city to be free of Jews. Many, including Krasnystaw's and Rejowiec's, had also received Jews from the Reich and from Czech lands, to name just two countries. Rejowiec had even received some Jews from Hungary. Nor were these ghettos that small. Kransnik's, for instance, held some 6,000 inmates, while that of Piaski had 7,000 people pass people through its gates. In Piaski's case, some 1,500 died during a typhus and cholera epidemic, a not uncommon occurrence at this time. Belzec and Sobibor were the main killing centers used, but Treblinka featured at times. In Opole Lublekie's case, inmates were initially sent to Bielsk Podlaski's ghetto and then on to Treblinka. One estimate has placed the number killed in Treblinka during 1942 alone at 45,100.[44] Although it would be incorrect to regard these ghettos as something uniquely Globocnikian, the point is that he fell in line with this preliminary form of administration and did so with verve and cruelty.

Prisons and Detention Jails

Zamek Lubelski, or Lublin Castle, which overlooks the city's historic old quarter, was the district's main jail —*Gefangnis der Sicherheitspolizei und des SD Lublin*—and was used by the *Sipo-SD*. It was instituted at the beginning of November 1939, at about the time of Globocnik's arrival in Lublin, and liquidated on 22 July 1944, when German forces fled west. Based at the Zamek were Globocnik's subordinates. Because the Zamek was his district's central jail, it held both men and women. Though its capacity was some 700 people, it in fact generally held up to 2,500, and on some occasions this rose to even 3,000 detainees. German documents show prisoner numbers during January 1944 were: Jan. 8th, 2,436 (women, 418); 14th, 2,304 (418); and 22nd, 2,336 (442). These levels and proportions remained until 20 July, when the jail held 2,124 inmates. Many of these were executed during the Zamek's last days. Records show that inmates were often dispatched to camps like Auschwitz, Majdanek, Sachsenhausen, and even Ravensbruck. Although Poles outnumbered others, even Polish Jews, Soviet citizens and even German Communists were held as detainees. Although mainly from across Lublin District, prisoners also came from other parts of Poland. It is impossible to give the exact number of prisoners who passed through the Zamek's gates, for estimates vary between 40,000 and 80,000, a huge range. Even if the smaller number was the case, little wonder that the jail gained such a horrifying reputation among the district's and city's citizenry, including within the ranks of the Polish Underground. One Polish study, which gives the jail's prisoner population at 40,000, says this figure broke down as follows: 18,600 deported to other camps, with 3,600 of these perishing within them; 4,500 executed by shooting or gassing; 2,200 dying during interrogations or in the Zamek; 10,000 released, escaped, or liberated; and 4,700 unaccounted for.[45]

Lublin Castle or Lublin's Fortress Prison was inquired about by the British who captured Globocnik's Lublin *SS-und Polizeiführer* successor, Jakob Sporrenberg, in Oslo. A summary of his interrogations, which in all likelihood refers to the later months of 1943, says:

> This prison, apart from being the German prison, was also the Polish town prison of Lublin. When Sporrenberg went to inspect it he was struck by the fact that a large number of inmates were Polish juveniles in their 12th, 13th, and 14th years, and it was explained to him that they were Polish "footpads." The overcrowding was alarming and when PW [Sporrenberg] saw the Commandant, *Ostuf* Dominik, a quiet *Justizsekretaer* from East Prussia, he demanded that something should be done about the congestion. PW states that this Commandant tried to make the very best of the unfortunate situation and that this was realized even by the Polish prisoners, and PW never heard any complaints of ill treatment or cruelty in the fortress.[46]

Another notorious, even if far smaller, precinct was the Gestapo's detention center in Lublin, known for obvious reasons as Pod Zegarem ("Beneath the Clock"), near the city's western end. Like the Zamek, it became operational in 1939, and was vacated with the German withdrawal in July 1944.

In its basement were a dozen tiny cells plus two darkened ones where suspects and detainees were held. Violent interrogations involving beatings were common. Like the Zamek, its main detainees were Poles. But Jews and Soviets were also interrogated there. Suspects were usually first interrogated at Pod Zegarem, after which they were taken to the Zamek. Shortly before these premises were evacuated on 19 July 1944, 138 political prisoners were shot there. Globocnik's district had another eight large jails, outer prisons that were somewhat evenly distributed across the region. In the north these were at Biala Podlaska, Lukow, and Parczew. In the south they were at Janow Lubelski, Bilgoraj, Krasnystaw, Zamosc, and Hrubieszow. In addition there were another 29 detention or interrogation centers (*areszty*), for a total of 37, which included Gestapo headquarters at Pod Zegarem.[47] As well as these, the district had a number of detention facilities that do not readily fall into the above categories. For instance, in the relatively large northern town of Biala Podlaska, the site of a *Stalag*, a ghetto, an *areszt*, and two standard work camps, were also two other facilities, namely a work camp, *Lager* "Vineta," and a so-called German Punishment Institution (*Deutsche Strafanstalt*).

The first of these was erected in 1941 and liquidated on 17 October 1942. It held some 3,000 Polish Jews who worked in metal workshops, and who undertook joinery work and were also involved in loading and unloading goods on railroad cars. Like so many of Lublin District's ghettos, this location was affected by a typhus epidemic, and shortly before its liquidation 40 inmates were executed. The *Deutsche Strafanstalt* was probably the first incarceration center to be opened in the district, in September 1939, and it was one of the last to be liquidated, during July 1944. This long-lasting center initially came under the administration of the police. But on 25 May 1940, it was acquired by the judicial authorities. The average number of inmates held stood at around 300 men and women, both Poles and Jews. A total of 8,000 people passed through it. Death sentences were passed by a special tribunal (*Sondergerichte*), from which prisoners were regularly sent to Majdanek and Zamek Lubelski. Interrogations were conducted by the Gestapo. In 1941, a work camp was established near the H.B. Raabego factory.[48]

Work Camps

Among the 143 work camps established across the district, 13 were known as penal work camps. Although most inmates were ethnic Poles, some were Jews from across the region. Trawniki, for instance, was a Building Service work camp that was erected in 1942 and liquidated in 1943. Its inmates were Poles, on average only about 100 men, who worked on railroads. Nearby, however, was another establishment, the *SS-Arbeitlager*, which was established in May

1942, and liquidated in November 1943. This one was situated in a sugar factory, and initially held Soviet POWs, but from the middle of 1942 its inmates were Poles, Russians, Ukrainians, Jews, and even, strangely, Austrians, Belgians, and Czechoslovaks. At its peak it held around 10,000 prisoners. Inmates labored in workshops that required skilled workers. There was also work done on digging peat. These camps experienced an epidemic during which the death rate was high. There were mass executions beyond the camps' confines in Dabrowie, Bork, and Lakach. Some 8,000 to 10,000 Jewish prisoners — the exact figure will never be known — were eventually shot at Trawniki.

Budzyn work camp was opened on 1 October 1942, and was liquidated 22 July 1944. Polish Jews were used here as laborers, working as carpenters and joiners. Another Budzyn work camp that was under the Building Service *Baudienst* (*Sluzby Budowlanej*) was opened in January 1943; its 200 or so inmates were Poles aged just 17 to 20 years on average. They were involved in metal-working tasks. The Kamienna Gora (Stone Mountain) camp opened in 1940, and was liquidated in 1942. It was located in a barracks; its inmates were Poles who had failed to meet agricultural targets, a common reason for incarceration of Polish peasant farmers. On average it held 300 prisoners who worked in the quarry. When it was liquidated, prisoners were simply released. Kapronie camp opened in May 1941, and was liquidated in August 1944, with inmates being held in a large barn. A camp at Dyle was established in December 1941, and liquidated a year later. It was made up of just four barracks in the village's center, and held Polish peasant farmers who had failed to meet requirements, as well as Polish Jews and Russians or Soviets. On average it held 250 prisoners, with a total of about 1,000 persons passing through its gate. Zamosc had three work camps, all holding Polish Jews. One held those who worked for the railways, another whose internees were required to work on building projects and the army's airfields, and the third on city repair and related duties.[49]

Transit or Ethnic Cleansing Camps

Globocnik's and von Mohrenschildt's two main camps used during the Zamosc Lands expulsion action were at Zwierzyniec and in Zamosc. The former had two sections, one for press-ganged workers destined to be sent to the Reich and the other the transit camp — *Umsiedlungslager*. Zwierzyniec, west of Zamosc, was established in 1940 and liquidated in 1944. It was made up of a series of barracks. In the beginning, civilians awaiting disbursement to the Reich as captured workers were held there. It also held suspects believed to be associated with the Polish Underground, primarily the *Armia Krajowa*. In the spring of 1942, 100 French prisoner laborers arrived to work on building projects, including road works. From December 1942 until the autumn of 1943, it was solely a transit camp for Polish peasant farmer families being expelled from the nearby counties of Tomaszow-Lubelski, Zamosc, and Bilgoraj. It held men, women, and a high proportion of children, with about 24,000 people passing through its gate. Selections were conducted, with the results used to determine where people would be dispatched, to Auschwitz, to Majdanek, or to be forced laborers. The elderly and children were dumped in numerous counties around Warsaw, including Garwolin, Siedlce, Minsk, and Lukow. At the time of the camp's liquidation, some of the inmates were dispatched to the Reich, while others went to Majdanek. The second, or the Zamosc camps (or more correctly *Zweigstelle Zamosc, UWZ Lager*), was operational from 27 November 1942 until 19 January 1944. Its inmates were held in 16 barracks that were separated by barbed wire. All came from Zamosc County. Between 28 November and 3 December 1942, it had housed nearly 10,000 inmates from 60 villages as part of the first phase of the Zamosc Lands action, which lasted from November 1942 until March 1943, and affected 116 villages and some 41,080 people.[50]

On arrival at Zamosc, internees were assessed and then registered (in barrack 2), after which they underwent a so-called racial selection examination (in barrack 3). Those included in Group I (German ancestry) and Group II (probable bearers of Germanic blood) were placed in barrack 7, and were quickly directed to Lodz (Litzmannstadt) to undergo a more detailed racial examination and to be sent on to the Reich to be Germanized. Those slotted into Groups III and IV were to be dispatched for work. Those below 14 and over 60 were placed into separate barracks, while the remainder were sent to the Reich to work. On 3 and 20 December, 1942, two transports took workers to the Reich. Children and elderly were placed in barrack 9a, 9b, 16 and 17, with the sick in barrack 12. Some from this barrack were sent to Oswiecim (Auschwitz-Birkenau). The barracks were not heated, windows were broken, and the structures were without flooring or sanitation. People slept on the ground. The worst conditions were in the horse barracks (9a, 9b, 16 and 17), where children and elderly were held. In barrack 16 some 700 people were detained, with some 1,700 to 2,000 passing through it, and there was an epidemic. On average between 15 and 30 children died daily, and between December 1942 and April 1943, 199 children died. From the beginning of December 1942, there were weekly transports departing, each carrying some 1,000 persons to Auschwitz or Berlin. Most went to Auschwitz, where the adults were killed by gassing and children by phenol injection. Others went to Majdanek. Children and those unfit to work were dispatched to Laskarzewa (9 December 1942); Siedlce (7 and 24 February 1943); Garwolin (30 January 1943, about 700 people); and Pilawy (February 1943, about 500): It appears some transports also were directed to Losic, Mord, Ceglow, Kaluszyn,

Parysew, and Mrozow. These train transports had unheated cars. On average, this camp held some 10,000 people, with many tens of thousands passing through it. The camp was under the control of the Zamosc branch of the Central Office for Migration from the outset, which was located in Lodz (Litzmannstadt) (*Umwandererzentralstelle Litzmannstadt UWZ*). This settling agency was directed by *SS-Obersturmbannführer* Hermann Krumey. The camp's director was *SS-Sturmbannführer* Hutte, while its commandant was the slow-witted *Unterscharführer* Artur Schutz, believed to be a former boxer. He held the position until 1943.

A third, though less significant transit camp (*Auffanglager*), Budzyn, was near Krasnik, and was opened in 1943 and shut down the following year. As mentioned, Budzyn was located in a factory.

> During 1943 transports arrived from the following places: 8-VII Zaklikowa, 9-VII Puszczy Solskiej, Woli Dereznianskiej and Ciosny, 10-VII Bodaczowa, and 11-VII Lazor. Gestapo personnel in the camp interrogated those brought in and some underwent torture and there were cases of prisoners being murdered. Two transports were dispatched to Graz [Austria] and others to Lublin Castle, Majdanek concentration camp and the Zwierzyniec concentration camp.[51]

These transit camps are significant because of their association with the Zamosc Lands cleansing action, the commencement of the Germanization of the entire East as called for under the terms of Himmler's top secret *Generalplan Ost*, launched just ten months after *Aktion Reinhardt*.

Transit camp Rogoznica (*Durchgangslager*) was established in 1942, and held workers brought in from Minsk and Smolensk. From Rogoznica they were taken for compulsory work in the Reich. Nearby Biala Podlaska was created two years earlier, in 1940, near the town of the same name, on a school site. Those held were peasant farmers who were later also moved to the Reich as compulsory workers. The larger center of Chelm also had a transit camp, which was established in 1940. Altogether some 10,000 uprooted peasant farmers, including entire families, passed through Chelm. In October 1940, 24 transports arrived with expelled people from Poland's Wielkopolska region, that is, western or incorporated Poland. The Rogoznica camp, which fell under the control of the border police (*Grenzpolizei*), presented particularly harsh conditions, including the outbreak of an epidemic, and there was the perennial problem of severe food shortages.[52] Uchanie was the venue of a small collection center and a transit camp that held only 224 people who were resettled on 23 February 1943, from the village of Pielaki.

Several short-term camps were established during the summer of 1943 to ensure the removal of Polish peasants from the Zamosc region as part of Globocnik's onslaught. The first was at Frampol, which was established in

June 1943, and liquidated in July the same year. On liquidation those interned were moved to camps at Zwierzyniec and Krasnik-Budzyn. The second was at Krynice, which also only operated in June and July, 1943. It held Poles who were resettled from Jeziernia. They were later transferred to Wierkowice in Krasnostaw district. Aleksandrow was established on 24 June 1943. It was located around a church, with about 3,000 people passing through, all of them Poles who were later transferred to Majdanek concentration camp. The last, Stary Majdan, came into being in June 1943, and held Ukrainians and Poles, with on average some 1,150 inmates. When it was liquidated, 94 people were murdered. The remainder were transferred to Majdanek.[53]

Bilgoraj and Harasiuki became sites for such camps, but during 1944, the year the district saw the Germans expelled by the Red Army. In Bilgoraj, a camp was established as late as April 1944, and liquidated three months later, when the area was liberated by Soviet units. This one mainly processed Poles, and from 9 to 14 June held about 4,000 people from the Bilgoraj region. Many were executed. The small Harasiuki camp was established on 10 June 1944. It held only Poles, and even then only 150 inmates were interned. Of these, 47 were executed. Another camp also existed at Puszcza Solska, a deep forest venue, through which some 8,000 peasant farmers passed. The district's southwestern township of Tarnogrod was the site of a camp that was also established in 1944 and liquidated in July the same year, after just two months. It was located on the town's market square, and was opened for the final phase of the pacification of the Zamosc Lands in 1943; it held only Poles, a number of whom were executed.

Lublin was the site of a large concentrated network of prisons and other detention centers, including the infamous Lublin Zamek, a large ghetto, nearby Majdanek, and a number of work camps. It also had two transit camps. The first was at 31 Krochmalna Street. It existed from mid–1940 until 1944. Its inmates were Poles, captured during round-ups launched as part of the pacification campaign across the Zamosc Lands during 1943. Those held were dispatched to the Reich to work. On average the camp held 500 internees. At the time of the 1943 Zamosc Lands pacification actions, the numbers were even larger. Lublin's second camp was also on Krochmalna Street, at number six. It also existed from 1940 until mid–1944. Inmates were Poles expelled during the course of the Zamosc Lands pacification action from the counties of Zamosc, Krasnik, Bilgoraj, and Pulawy. Those held, along with some Jews, were dispatched east to work in German occupied zones of the Soviet Union, a relatively rare occurrence. However, some of the internees were also sent to work in the Reich. There were, on average, around 2,000 inmates, and in Lublin they worked on municipal improvements and other menial tasks around the city.[54]

In addition to this enormous and constant movement of people into and out of camps, ghettos, and jails, Lublin District, which at the outset of war had 2.4 million inhabitants, was the recipient of a number of population influxes. It also lost inhabitants because of a range of demographic actions. During the entire occupation period, some 878,000 civilians are estimated to have entered the district, or 36.7 percent of its 1939 population. Of these, some 640,000 were Jews, 225,000 Poles, and there were also 13,000 Germans, people who were settled largely in the Zamosc Lands region by Globocnik and von Mohrenschildt. Nearly 260,000 people were removed from the district during the same period; 180,000 of these were Poles, with most of them being forced laborers sent to the Reich; 55,000 were Jews, and 24,500 were Germans, mainly from the Chelm region.[55]

The district's Jewish inhabitants were thus almost entirely eliminated, but in the case of the Poles, despite deportations like the Zamosc Lands, and ongoing expulsions as forced laborers into the Reich, their numbers actually rose, with the Ukrainians remaining at the pre-war level. The two main sources of the influx of Poles were those forcibly deported into the region in 1940 by Berlin, and other Poles who fled nearby Wolyn (Volhynia) because of ethnic warfare there launched by Ukrainian Nationalist killing gangs, especially in 1943 and 1944. Small numbers of Germans were removed from the Chelm area in 1940, and some ethnic Germans from Wolyn also briefly settled in the district that year. The next influx of Germans was in 1942 and 1943 during the ill-fated Zamosc Lands expulsions, when some 13,000 were brought in to help Germanize that region. But these, too, left in mid–1944, in the wake of the Red Army, followed soon after by the surviving Poles who wished to reclaim their land. Demographically speaking, the region underwent an enormous upheaval of movements in an extremely traumatic experience for which, in the main, one man was responsible. The year 1941 saw a virtual stagnation of these often unexpected inflows and outflows of civilians. That is not to say that the district had a respite, for after June that year, and certainly up until at least the turn of 1941–42, it became the venue for many tens of thousands of Soviet POWs, as described above. Some 443,000 people — 225,000 non-Jewish Poles and 200,000 Jews — were subjected to some form of displacement, being required to move from their original places of abode either to another part of the district or to a killing center, or a prison, work, or deportation camp.

> A significant influence was also exerted by the personality of the SS and Police leader, O. Globocnik, who shared the fascination of Hitler and Himmler for great conquests and displacements of population, and who enthusiastically undertook any operations in this sphere. A certain role too was played by the geographical position of the Lublin District which was to be the "beginning of the East," and which was to be depopulated on a large scale.[56]

XI

The Fate of Four
Globocnik Victims

"One death is a tragedy, but a million deaths is just a statistic."
(Attributed to Josef Stalin)

Because Globocnik did things on such a massive scale, one necessarily uses large numbers whenever referring to those his agencies killed, expelled from homes, jailed, or simply detained without due process. He was directly responsible for the murder of between 1.5 and two million Jews; the expulsion of at least 110,000 ethnic Poles — this figure may, however, be closer to 200,000 — and the jailing or internment of an unknown number, with perhaps 200,000 victims again being possible. No evidence exists of Globocnik himself actually killing a person; others did it on his orders. One problem with the constant reference to such large numbers is that these victims can easily become to any reader precisely that, mere numbers, nothing more. For this reason, this chapter focuses upon four of Globocnik's victims, three of whom survived their horrific ordeal and one of whom died, was murdered, in one of the killing centers, either in Belzec or Sobibor, it is not clear which. The four are Ernst Krombach, a German Jew and German citizen from Germany's industrialized Ruhr region, specifically the Essen area, whose family had not emigrated as did many tens of thousands of other German and Austrian Jews who were urged and cajoled by Nazi officials to do so during the 1930s; Jacob Frank, a Polish Jew who was born and raised in Lublin and was a citizen of Poland; and two ethnic Poles, Helena and Zofia Krepinska, mother and infant daughter, who were victims of Globocnik's Zamosc Lands ethnic cleansing action.

Information on Ernst Kromback comes solely from a transcript of a BBC radio program, "Long Train to Lublin," prepared and presented by University of Southampton historian Mark Roseman, and based on his research and findings. Details on Jacob Frank come from his autobiography, *Himmler's Jewish Tailor: The Story of Holocaust Survivor Jacob Frank*.[1] For the Krepinskas I acquired all the information independently in Poland and Australia, where both settled, Helena emigrating to Australia in 1950, her daughter Zofia emigrating from Poland in 1981. They were reunited 39 years after Globocnik's ethnic cleansing teams separated them in the Zamosc transit camp, following their removal from Skierbieszow village on 28 November 1942. Globocnik did not merely kill or dislodge numbers. His victims were people, and in a great number of cases they were even children or infants. Just as no distinction was made for Jewish World War I veterans who had fought for the Kaiser's Germany, no exception was made for infants and children. The secret mass death sentence handed down in January 1942 at the infamous Wannsee Conference was across-the-board, universal: no Jew was to be spared, with Odilo Globocnik hand-picked by Himmler to administer the entire campaign of extermination from Lublin.

1. Ernst Krombach: From the Ruhr by Train to Death, via Izbica, in a Globocnik Killing Center

According to Mark Roseman, Ernst Krombach was a "courageous, upright and handsome 21-year-old" from the Ruhr. From this heavily industrial region of the Reich and its environs, he and about 1,000 other Jews, including his family members, were congregated in late April 1942, and moved to Dusseldorf to await a train that would ship them to Lublin District. All the processing and planning was carried out by Adolf Eichmann's *IVB4* section of the *RSHA* in Berlin and Ruhr-based Gestapo officers. Krombach's father, David, had been a lawyer and an active member of his local Jewish community. Like so many male German Jews, Adolf Hitler and Globocnik's father included, the senior Krombach had risked his life for pre-Nazi Germany in World War I. He was a veteran, like Globocnik's father, and like Hitler.

The night before departing Dusseldorf railway station, all these Jewish Ruhr expellees were forced to sleep inside an out-of-the-way abattoir. The next day, 22 April 1942, this large group of civilians was compelled to walk to Dusseldorf station, a distance of some two kilometers. After several hours waiting, they boarded on Platform 1 a train that was designated DA52. According to

Roseman, this train had been used to transport Russian workers to the Reich, indicating that certain Reich trains were specifically used to shuttle some people east and others west, with Jews being boarded on the return or east-bound legs, at this time, destined for Globocnik's district and thus eventually one of his terminal stations. Documents that Roseman located in German archives showed that the train that carried the Krombach family had been designated for its west-bound journey, that is, when it brought Russian workers to the Reich, as RU7520. Shortly before departing Dusseldorf, eastward for Lublin District, via Hagen, on the afternoon of 22 April Ernst Krombach was able to dispatch a postcard carrying a brief message to his fiancée, Marianne Strauss. He managed to post another such card during his eastward journey across the Reich and Poland, and it is because of these brief letters that Roseman has been able to reconstruct both Krombach's journey and destination. One of the cards revealed that Ernst Krombach had learned that train DA52 was destined for Izbica, situated roughly midway between Lublin and Globocnik's Belzec killing center. Amazingly, Krombach had been able to post a third and final card from Izbica some three months after arrival there. In this last card he told his fiancée that this former village was, in 1942, a rural ghetto and was being used as a holding settlement from where Jews were being taken by train elsewhere. Naturally he did not name Belzec or Sobibor because he, like all the other German Jews at Izbica, did not know that their fate was to be killed in one of these two terminal stations. Izbica can therefore rightly be termed a "transit station."

Ernst Krombach's last postcard spoke of 14,000 Jews having been held at one time or another in Izbica. But during his stay, which lasted until at least August 1942, there were between two and three thousand held under extremely congested and brutal conditions. Roseman's good fortune of being able to find the Krombach postcards to his wartime fiancée was reinforced by the fact that he was also able to contact a Thomas Black, who was probably Izbica's only survivor. According to Black, Polish Jews had managed to learn of the fate of Izbica's inmates because some Poles had told them that the departing trains were going to Belzec, from which they later departed without people aboard. But the German Jews arriving in a steady stream at Izbica during the middle of 1942 were unaware of their imminent fate, Black said. We can be certain that the Krombachs all died soon after August 1942, shortly before Globocnik launched the ethnic cleansing of the Zamosc Lands.

2. Jacob Frank: From Lublin's 7 Lipowa Street Labor Camp, to Radom, and, via Auschwitz-Birkenau, to Natzweiler (Vaihingen), and Liberation in Dachau

Jacob Frank was nearly 28 years old when Globocnik reached the city of his birth, Lublin, to become its top occupation police officer and SS man.

Within six months, Frank found himself toiling in the first of Globocnik's major work camps, situated at 7 Lipowa Street, virtually in the center of Lublin, near the cemetery. This camp remained fully operational throughout calendar years 1940 through 1942, until November 1943, two months after Globocnik had left for Trieste, when its several thousand inmates were force marched to Majdanek concentration camp on Lublin's outskirts to be executed as part of the so-called *Erntefest* massacres which, saw over 40,000 Jews murdered across the entire district. Frank's account of his wartime years is a valuable source for several reasons, not least because he was in Lipowa camp from its beginning to virtually the end of its operational life. Furthermore, he was a native Lubliner, and thus observed all the developments and changes in Lipowa in a way that, say, a German or Austrian Jew arriving in 1941 or early 1942, would simply have been unable to do. In addition, Frank was the SS-designated supervisor of the camp's important tailoring division, and was in charge of some 475 workers, though not all were qualified tailors. As a result, he often had rather close encounters or contacts with senior SS men who oversaw the camp or certain of its working or production divisions. He even had a number of opportunities to observe Globocnik briefly from fairly close quarters. The Frank biography is an oral history, so has the disadvantage of relying almost solely upon memory and also, to an extent, upon postwar views and opinions derived from reading and other non-contemporary sources. Despite these drawbacks, because Frank was a mature man and a keen observer, his account of his drawn-out inhuman experience as a Lipowa inmate is of immense historical value in providing an insight into life within a harsh Globocnikian work camp, as well as in occupied Lublin. Most importantly, since so little has been written about the important Lipowa work camp, we can be confident that what Frank says is based on his experiences, not others' subsequent writings, views, and assessments. This more than anything makes this source valuable.

Like about 10,000 other Lublin region Jews, Frank decided, after consulting with family members, to escape to the Soviet-occupied sector of eastern Poland, and remained there, away from Lublin, for two and a half months, living with a Polish family he had known well before the war. But he finally decided that he would prefer to be with his family, which included parents, siblings, wife and two sons. Speaking in broken English, influenced by Yiddish grammatical structures, Frank described his fateful decision to return to Globocnik's Lublin: "I talked over with the people what they took me in, and I tell them I decided to go back to Poland on the German side to my family. They couldn't talk me out of this…. Later I found out that he was right — many, many years later.[2]

Prior to fleeing east, Frank had undergone a two-day registration ordeal, conducted by the SS. All of Lublin's male Jews, aged 12 to 60 years, were forcibly assembled for some 48 hours on the site that later become the Lipowa camp for this harsh and humiliating police action. Shortly after his return from his 10 week stay with his pre-war Polish acquaintances in Soviet-occupied eastern Poland, he and four other Lublin Jewish tailors were taken to SS headquarters where they were told in no uncertain terms to form a tailoring contingent for the SS. This may have been the beginning of Globocnik's move into business ventures. Frank was instructed at this time that he would become the leader of a tailoring workshop.[3]

At the same time, Lublin's SS-created *Judenrat* was formally advised by Globocnik's business-minded SS man, Horst Riedel, who commanded Lipowa camp for some time, that tailoring workshops were to be erected on a vast expanse of land that became the campsite. This order meant that Lublin's Jewish community had to first collect the necessary tools of trade, as well as provide the workforce to undertake this task, while the tailors, and later Jewish shoemakers, had to provide their own sewing machines, scissors, irons, needles, and other essential equipment to run Riedel's proposed workshops.[4]

Shortly afterwards, Frank learned from the head of the *Judenrat*, a Mr. Kestenberg, that the SS were calling for 100 tailors, with an order being issued to this effect. The order was eventually fulfilled by the threat of intervention by the Jewish police force, on orders from the SS. This was the Globocnikian method — orders having to be obeyed without delay, no matter how onerous or outrageous.[5]

Riedel gave Frank his daily order to go to SS headquarters to collect "the uniforms from the *Obergruppenführer* [sic] Globocnik and from the SS people what they are around him."[6] Frank was required to carry this out at 8 A.M. daily, with two other tailors. This group collected all uniforms that needed cleaning and pressing. At this time, however, members of the Lipowa tailoring workforce were still living with their families in Lublin Ghetto. Because Frank was a divisional supervisor, he had a special pass — one signed by Globocnik — which gave him considerable freedom of movement, as well as relatively close ongoing contacts with the new camp's SS commanders. Frank also lived under better conditions than his employees. He described Lipowa Camps as having either four or five separate blocks, with the perimeter being guarded by troops in towers and armed with machine guns.[7]

Frank's co-author, Mark Lewis, points out that the Lipowa campsite originally consisted of several horse stables. At the turn of 1939–40, however, a barbed wire fence enclosed it, with the guard towers added in March 1940. Riedel's assistant Wolfgang Mohwinkel, who became his successor, was an engineer and still in his 20s. He designed the camp, including its barrack layout. Sanitary conditions were atrocious, and the treatment of inmates grew steadily worse, and included beatings and executions, "with little pretext or no provocation on the part of prisoners."[8] Lipowa was sealed in late 1941, so

its craftsmen and other inmates were isolated from their families. After Lublin
Ghetto was liquidated in March–April 1942, they were left permanently isolated because their families had been removed and killed, either in Sobibor
or Belzec. Lipowa was an establishment that Globocnik was clearly proud of,
because he regularly showed its workshops to visiting Nazi dignitaries from
Berlin and elsewhere, including in the summer of 1941 to his superior, Heinrich Himmler. Frank recalls a 1942 inspection that involved Adolf Eichmann,
who was chaperoned by Globocnik, Maubach, Mohwinkel, Schramm, Klein,
Hantke, and the *Standartenführer* von Alvensleben.[9]

Frank said that most Lipowa inmates were in their 20s, and tended to
be markedly fitter and healthier than those in Globocnik's other camps, where
the age structure in all likelihood more closely reflected society at large. He
believed that because of this most could have survived until the Red Army
liberated Lublin in the summer of 1944, something they were denied because
of the horrific Höfle-managed and Globocnik-arranged *Erntefest* massacres.
But it was not Frank's age and physical fitness that saved him. He failed to
become an *Erntefest* victim because of his known reputation as a fine tailor,
one who sewed excellent leather coats. Just before these massacres began on
3 November 1943, Frank was transferred to a prison in Lublin, because
Globocnik, who had recently been transferred to Trieste, wished to have his
still unfinished leather coat completed. This lucky turn of events meant Frank
was deliberately removed from Lipowa to complete this task. In a bizarre way,
therefore, Globocnik's requirement — his desire to have a leather coat just like
Himmler's and other senior SS-men — actually saved Frank's life. This strange
incident also demonstrates that Globocnik retained contact with Lublin. Frank
makes no reference to completing the obviously prized coat, but we can
assume that it was eventually delivered to Globocnik in Trieste. It is worth
noting here that at the time of the *Erntefest* massacres, many Lublin SS men
"pulled out" individual Jews they wished to retain as their private servants,
as tailors or other skilled capacities. By late 1943, many members of Globocnik's SS staff had become thoroughly accustomed to having servants, not
unlike American slaveholders during much of the 19th century. One outcome
of this was that these Jewish servants either had their lives prolonged or, as
in Frank's case, actually saved.

A prison official or its commandant, it is not clear which, but a man
Frank recalls having the name Dominik, called up his new prisoner. Clearly,
and fortunately for Frank, the leather coat was a crucially important task and
had to be completed:

> After a few seconds he told me, "I have an order from the *Obergruppenführer*
> Globocnik to help you here, and here you are safe. But I have also a package,
> I'm sure that you have this upstairs. This is the coat for the *Obergruppenführer*,
> and we have here a shop with tailors. I set up place for you, and if you need

some help you tell me, and I'll give you all the help that you want from the other tailors what are there in the prison with you.[10]

Frank was led to believe that he would survive because he was needed. Shortly after, he was transferred to Radom, to the west of Lublin, having been excluded from the huge *Erntefest* killings.[11] This was either late June 1944, or perhaps early July, when all Lublin-based German military personnel and administrative officials were either retreating west toward Berlin, or else preparing to do so to avoid capture by the steadily advancing Red Army. This westward movement even included a small number of Jews, the handful who had survived this region's almost four Globocnikian years and thus the November massacres. Globocnik had by now been away from Lublin and in Trieste for over nine months, where he continued his war against the Jews as well as against Slovene, other Slav and even Italian partisans, all of whom were more often engaging Germany's increasingly besieged forces.

In Radom, with a dozen other prisoners, Frank was again incarcerated, this time in a work camp holding some 3,000 Jews: men, women, and children, all of whom had come from this town's ghetto. Radom camp's SS administration, according to Frank, was immeasurably more tolerant of prisoners than the officials in Lipowa. But because of the advancing Red Army, those held in Radom were moved west rather than left behind to be liberated.[12] According to Frank, all the inmates of the work camp were, in August 1944, forced to embark on a death march to Tomaszow-Lubelski. This must be mistaken, because that Zamosc Lands town is east of Radom, and had already been liberated by the Red Army in the previous month, if not in June. One can only conclude Frank meant to say Tomaszow-Mazowiecki, which is a sizeable town well west of Radom. Moreover, Tomaszow-Lubelski is about 250 kilometers southeast of Radom, whereas Frank refers to the march from Radom as being about 150 kilometers, roughly the distance between Radom and Tomaszow-Mazowiecki. At this time German military and other personnel were fleeing west, toward Tomaszow-Mazowiecki, not Tomaszow-Lubelski. The addition of the word "Lubelski" simply signifies within, or, of, the Lublin region, while Tomaszow-Mazowiecki means Tomaszow of the Mazowsze lands, the region surrounding Warsaw. In light of this, its fair to conclude that Frank, after more than half a century, was confused, and meant to say Tomaszow-Mazowiecki, not Tomaszow-Lubelski. The 1,700 to 1,800 survivors of this terrible ordeal spent three days in a deserted flour mill before being taken by rail to Auschwitz, where women and children were off-loaded while the remaining 1,000 to 1,100 male Jews were trained on further west to a sub-camp of Natzweiler camp. Natzweiler was in fact located in occupied France, but some of its sub-camps were not. These male prisoners were eventually split into three groups, with Frank's group being directed to a sub-camp called Natzweiler (Vaihingen), in the Stuttgart region.

In Natzweiler there was some war prisoners, prisoners from German descent
... socialists, communists, I don't know what nationalities, a couple hundred.
They had already there a kitchen with food, some water — they gave everybody
a portion of bread. The day was already over almost. They count us, and they
let us into the barracks. Just a bunk bed, no mattresses, not straw sacks, nothing.[13]

As will be seen below in relation to the fate of Helena Krepinska, in
August 1944 saw, trains carried Auschwitz's prisoners to other Natzweiler sub-
camps. Vaihingen's prisoners were assigned to work building a nearby underground ammunition or aeroplane factory, a *Bombenstelle*, or bomb-proof
facility, with the prisoners and workers split into working day and night shifts.
By the autumn of 1944, the work to locate German war production below
ground as a counter measure to Allied bombing had gained pace; prisoners
were crucial for this countermeasure. After being at Vaihingen until March
1945, Frank was again relocated, this time to Dachau, often seen as the mother
of all Himmler's camps, since it was established early in the Nazi era and so
many later camp commandants had been trained there. Dachau, like so many
other Reich-based camps, was liberated in May 1945.

3. Helena Krepinska: From Skierbieszow in the Zamosc Lands, via Auschwitz-Birkenau, to Escape from a Natzweiler Sub-Camp, Ebingen A.C., and Liberation in Lorraine (France)

One of Globocnik's Zamosc Lands expellees was 25-year-old Helena
Krepinska (nee Weclawik), who lived in the relatively large village of Skierbieszow, the seat of the municipality, 17 kilometers northeast of Zamosc. Krepinska was married and had a daughter, Zofia, aged just 18 months, when
Skierbieszow was targeted for Globocnik's and von Mohrenschildt's expulsion campaign in the early hours of 28 November 1942. Like many others in
Skierbieszow, she suspected well before that morning something horrible was
set to happen. Several nearby villages had been focal points for trial-run resettlement actions launched by Globocnik during November 1941, motivated in
all likelihood by the pre-war *Volksdeutsche* researcher, Dr. Kurt Lück, so there
was an abundance of rumors that the same fate was about to befall Skierbieszow. The first evidence that this fate would, indeed, visit this tiny rural
community came in the early hours of 28 November. An active partisan,
probably Jozef Smiech (code name "Ciag"), saw armed German units
approaching.

I was not asleep long because at about 2 A.M. my grandmother awoke me and pointed at lights along the road. Shortly after an armed soldier reached us and said four taxis had arrived and they were with mayor Harlosa. He was a *Volksdeutsche* who was a known exterminator of Poles. I immediately ordered an alarm and ordered the withdrawal of my platoon to Osiczynie. I stayed behind to pack the remaining supplies onto a cart. Within an hour I could see a long line of vehicle lights along the roadway. My God, what a large number of them are coming for us, I immediately thought. We'll all be caught, and with mothers and children. Like a bolt out of the sky the Germans dismounted and rapidly surrounded Skierbieszow and nearby Sady. I thought there were more than 300 of them.[14]

Perhaps another Polish partisan, though it may have been Smiech again, for the source is unclear, revealed in an article published soon after the war that the ongoing rumors of expulsion prompted many to believe they would be dispatched to the eastern side of the Bug River, into Wolyn (Volhynia) Province.

Already for several months people were asking about being resettled. In the Skierbieszow municipality consternation reigned. People thronged about asking each other — "What's going to happen?" — "What should be done?" — "What will be my fate?" — "I have small children, all will be dispatched." There were even some who claimed all would be expelled beyond the Bug River where we'd receive farmlets. But others claimed they would be resettling small landholders, with the larger ones being left alone. Various opinions circulated, claiming that there won't be a general resettlement but only a massive press-ganging of youth.[15]

Krepinska and her husband, Wladek, had heard such rumors, but became resigned to whatever fate would bring. There was, apart from that, nowhere else to go in the occupied and heavily policed Lublin District, especially if one had an infant child, as they did. The first sign that something was finally happening was when they heard cowbells being rung and rattled outside their cottage. The incessant din was accompanied by men yelling and dogs barking. Some of the 300 or so armed and uniformed men had descended upon the entire village. Strangers knocked on their door, on their windows, with even the walls being thumped or kicked. The couple was told, by screams and shouts, that they must assemble by the village school as quickly as possible. So, even before sunrise, they hurriedly and fearfully dressed, and with their 18-month-old daughter assembled where instructed by members of the uniformed contingents. By early afternoon most of Skierbieszow's residents were still near the school. Accompanying Krepinska was her widowed mother, Anna Weclawik, and mother-in-law, Aniela Krepinska. Fortunately, Krepinska's sister, Zofia Weclawik, who was five years her junior and after whom Helena had named her daughter, was away from Skierbieszow at the time, so evaded capture.

According to Zamosc Lands medical practitioner and clandestine wartime diarist, Dr. Zygmunt Klukowski, what was witnessed in Skierbieszow was repeated over the next nine or so months across this targeted region. It is not clear if the 300 or so men conducting Skierbieszow's expulsion actually included Ukrainians or Ukrainian units. If not, this was the exception, for Ukrainian units tended to be alongside German units during much of the Zamosc Lands cleansing action of November 1942 until July 1943.

> The inhabitants of the village were ordered to leave it without previous warning. Deportations were effected quite suddenly, in most cases early in the morning, between three and seven o'clock. Different German units arrived in cars, usually at night and closely surrounded the villages, part of them entered it. The units varied: the Gestapo, the SS, *Sonderdienst*, sometimes the *Wehrmacht*, the German settlers in the area (called "the black"), Ukrainians in the German service, and the local *Volksdeutsche*.... The population was driven to a common or a large square in front of the local community office, or church. The Germans shouted, pushed their victims, beat them with the butt-ends of rifles and with clubs, kicked and slapped them in their faces, set dogs on them and shot at those who resisted or made attempts to escape... The Germans inspected the assembled people and segregated them into groups. Workers employed in airfields, railways, sawmills, sugar factories or other plants were left; then farmhands were chosen for the new German settlers. In small towns the employees in the courts of justice, municipal office, post office, doctor, chemists and some specialists needed by the Germans were usually left. But sometimes doctors and chemists were also deported as was the case in Skierbieszow.[16]

Krepinska recalls that Skierbieszow's entire population was evacuated that day to nearby Zamosc, which had, near its old historic quarter, a readied transit camp that had earlier been used to hold Soviet prisoners-of-war. As the guarded villagers walked and drove aboard carts along the 17-kilometer Skierbieszow-Zamosc road, they noticed that Skierbieszow's new occupants, ethnic Germans from Rumania, Russia, and the Balkans, people who may have been assisted by Reinhold von Mohrenschildt two years earlier to leave their homes, were set to take over their dwellings. These generally swarthy strangers had already commenced dismantling the wooden framing the former owners had erected around their cottages to hold up compacted straw to help keep residences warmer during the winter. The forced evacuees also noticed that the swarthy strangers were discarding many of their possessions, especially personal decorations such as religious pictures, by throwing them out of doors and windows. No time was being wasted in occupying their newly acquired abodes.

Skierbieszow, by sunset, on 28 November 1942, was no longer a Polish village. Its fate that day was to be experienced by many other similar villages and hamlets across the Zamosc Lands. It was the first of nearly 300 Zamosc

Lands villages, hamlets and *kolonie*— settlements adjacent villages — to have its inhabitants totally or partially expelled.

In Zamosc, Krepinska and the others were marched into the newly trans- formed transit camp on Marshall Pilsudski Avenue, alongside Zamosc's his- toric market place. A plan of this camp shows it being a rectangular, double barbed-wired compound with a slight protrusion in the fence-line from the longer western side, giving it roughly the shape of the numeral seven. It had 21 barracks with numbers one to nine used as living quarters. The next three were designated as hospital and dispensary. The camp had four communal latrines. There was a large separate kitchen, and what was designed as a post office and a washroom quarter. At its entrance stood the commandant's home- stead and what was called the commandant's chancellery. Two stables and a jail were located outside the barbed wire compound.[17]

Inside, the internees were treated like prisoners or criminals. Dr. Klu- kowski has described life in the Zamosc transit camps:

> Shortly after their arrival the arrested were taken to a special commission, which divided them into four groups.... The "experts" in racial matters examined their hair, eyes, the shape of their skulls etc., searching for "German features"…. Medical inspection was made by Dr. Rembacz, who himself had been expelled from Skierbieszow and detained in the camp…. After the segregation into groups and a stay in the camp, which varied in length, the expelled people were deported to different places. Children and old people were dispatched by rail- way to the neighborhood of Warsaw. Men and women between 14 and 60, capable of work, were taken away to the Reich; they were employed there in factories, farms, etc. A part of the evicted population were carried with fami- lies and children to the Oswiecim [Auschwitz-Birkenau] concentration camp where the majority perished.[18]

Peoples' fates and fortunes varied markedly. For example, a group of Poles from the Zamosc Lands region reached the top-secret German V-1 and V-2 rocket testing Baltic site at Peenemünde in early August 1943. This facil- ity, because of the work being conducted, was attacked by a huge Royal Air Force bomber force on the night of 17–18 August, and many perished.

> The latest Polish arrivals at Peenemünde were the men of a transport between 100 and 200 strong from Zamosc, a town in the rich farming area of *Lubel- skiego* [Lublin Province] which had been chosen for "Germanization"— i.e. the Polish population was to be evicted to make way for an eventual all-German settlement. The *Lubelskiego* men arrived at Peenemünde about a week before the bombing.[19]

For Krepinska this compound was the first of four that she would have to call home until she luckily escaped from her captors in the autumn of 1944, when she was in distant Lorraine, France, which at the time was still an integral part of the Third Reich. During her 21 months in captivity, she was separated from her daughter, lost her husband and mother, both of whom died in Auschwitz-Birkenau, probably in January or February 1943, and spent thousands of hours working in damp swampy fields north, south, east, and west of the Auschwitz-Birkenau killing center.[20]

Zamosc's transit camp was one of four used by the Germans in their bid to Germanize the Zamosc Lands. The others were at Zwierzyniec, 40 kilometers east of Zamosc, Globocnik's Majdanek Concentration Camp on the outskirts of Lublin, and Budzyn, a Majdanek sub-camp, at nearby Krasnik.

Soon after reaching the transit camp she was joined by hundreds upon hundreds of villagers from other nearby villages. The Polish historian and expert on Majdanek concentration camp, Jozef Marszalek, describes Globocnik's and von Mohrenschildt's campaign as follows:

> ... the Zamosc region ... was to be colonized and turned into a "German protective wall" along the Bug River. The plans of the operation for dividing the deported population into four groups, two of which were to be Germanised, one sent for forced Labor in the Reich, and one confined in concentration camps. As during the first phase of the resettlement (November 27, 1942 to March 1943) Majdanek was still under construction, the transports of "undesirable element" i.e. persons suspected of being active in the resistance movement, were directed to Auschwitz. Only during the second phase (June and July 1943), combined with a pacification of the Zamosc region on the pretext of combating "gangs" (*Aktion Wehrwolf*), the apprehended population was deported in large numbers to the Lublin camp.[21]

Zamosc's transit camp, or *Zweigstelle Zamosc UWZ Lager*, was thus the Hermann Krumey establishment, and had formally come into existence just one day before Krepinska walked through its gate. It remained in use as a transit camp until 19 January 1944. After the Polish expellees were racially assessed, they were led to separate barracks. According to Dr. Klukowski, an SS man called Grunert was in charge of the segregation process, and was guided in this task by notations on files presented to him.

> Here Dantesque scenes occurred when parents were separated from the children. Grunert made the segregation on the basis of stamps and files. He beat and kicked the mothers who did not let the Germans take their children. The children were given to strangers, old disabled women. Children of parents from the intelligentsia were purposely transferred to old women from the countryside and vice versa. The old women received up to six children from 2 to 12 years.[22]

Evidence given by a Zamosc Lands teacher, Adam Skora, stated that each barrack had a separate locked enclosure, so it was impossible for parents to get a glimpse of their children. According to Skora, some women, children, and the elderly lived up to six weeks under these conditions.

Transports were prepared in the following way: after the files were completed people were driven to the open yard in the camp, usually early in the evening and lists of those to be deported next day were read. Since the transports were large this ceremony lasted until 7 A.M. All this time the old people, children and crippled lay on the snow. After the departure of each transport several dead bodies were taken from the yard.[23]

Since the camp was only a transit facility, its internees were marked for other destinations. The beginning of December saw two transports — each containing fewer than 1,000 prisoners — dispatched to Auschwitz-Birkenau and two others to Berlin. As stated, the camp stayed operational until January 1944, and during its last six months of operation, from about mid–1943, there were fewer than 200 detainees. But at its peak, around July 1943, it housed more than 12,000 prisoners. Its sister camp at Zwierzyniec had a far shorter life, being operational only during the spring and summer of 1943, and its internees tended to be detained for briefer periods, after which they were transferred to the Zamosc camp. According to Dr. Klukowski, on top of the appalling sanitary conditions, malnutrition and a range of diseases boosted the death rate. Prisoners during each morning and evening received coffee without milk or sugar, while at noon they received 140 grams of bread and transparent soup. Krepinska said this was the same basic ration allocation that was standard in Auschwitz.

Helena Krepinska was designated a political prisoner, even though she had never been involved in any form of political activity, either Polish or anti-German, yet she was designated to be sent to Auschwitz-Birkenau with her husband and mother. Her infant daughter was taken from her by the camp and racial authorities shortly before 10 December, but not before Krepinska had had a chance to write some details about her daughter and stitch them into the child's clothing so Zofia could be identified by anyone finding her. This decision would later prove crucial in locating the child, through the efforts of Krepinska's sister.

Soon after the trainload of children and their designated elderly guardians headed northwest toward Warsaw from Zamosc station, another of Hermann Krumey's trains was dispatched southwest, to the recently built concentration camp and killing center of Auschwitz-Birkenau. Krepinska arrived at Auschwitz railway station on 13 December 1942, from where she and the other expellees walked the last kilometer or so to the camp's now infamous death gate. When the 630-strong group arrived, this camp was still not directly connected to the town's rail network. Documents from the camp's archives show that soon after arrival Krepinska was tattooed on the left arm with the number 26,952.

The 13 December 1942 entry of Auschwitz Museum archivist and historian, Danuta Czech, reads:

The first RSHA transport arrives in Auschwitz from the camp of the so-called Central Resettlement Office (*Umwandererzentralstelle—UWZ*) in Zamosc with 314 Polish men and 318 Polish women. They have been deported within the framework of the plan to evacuate Poles from the region of Zamosc, which is planned as a settlement area for German colonists. On admission to the camp, the men and boys receive Nos. 82548–82859, 83910, and 83911; the women and girls receive Nos. 26810–27032, 27034–27038, and 27040–27129. The transport is composed of 644 people, 14 of whom were able to escape during the transport.[24]

Czech pointed out that the numbers 83910 and 83911 had been allocated to two boys aged eight and nine, "whose mothers wanted to keep the children with them and so passed them off as girls…. [T]hey first received Nos. 27033 and 27039 from the number series for women. This is discovered on December 17. Tadeusz Rycyk thereupon receives No. 83910 and Mieczyslaw Rycaj No. 83911. The two boys were killed with phenol injections on January 21, 1943."[25]

Her entry for the date on which they died reads:

SS Roll Call Leader Palitzsch brings two boys eight and nine years old from the Birkenau camp to the prisoners' infirmatory, Block 20. These are Mieczyslaw Rycaj (No. 83911) and Tadeusz Rycyk (No. 83910) who, on orders from Palitzsch, are killed the same day by phenol injections. The two boys come from the vicinity of Zamosc and had been deported with their mothers on December 13, 1942, with a transport to the camp.[26]

Another Zamosc transport arrived on 16 December. Czech's entry reads: "Poles evacuated from the region of Zamosc arrive with the second RSHA transport from the camp of the *UWZ*, 38 male and 48 female prisoners receive the Nos. 84441–84478, 27257–27274, and 27276–27305."[27]

The next entry dealing with the Zamosc region's expellees is for 5 February 1943, which was to be the third Zamosc transport. Unlike the previous two this one carried Jews as well as Poles.

A transport of Poles and Jews who have been evacuated from the Zamosc region has arrived with Special Train Po65, which departed from Zamosc on February 3, 1943, at 11am. Included are 1000 people. Following the selection 282 men, given Nos. 100096–100337, and 301 women, give Nos. 34289–34589, are admitted to the camp. The other 417 people are killed in the gas chambers.[28]

Because the 417 are not identified ethnically, it is not possible to say with any degree of certainty that the 1,000-person trainload had 417 Jews, as appears likely. All we can say is that by the third month of the Zamosc Lands expulsions, 1,644 people had been dispatched from this targeted region to Auschwitz-

Birkenau. Most were Poles with an unknown number of Jews, while 417 people were gassed virtually on arrival, two young boys were killed in January 1943, 14 had escaped on the way to the camp, and an unknown number had died of fatigue and hunger relatively quickly after arrival. Therefore, of the 110,000 or so people expelled from the region, well below 2,000 reached Auschwitz, or slightly over one per cent. Auschwitz-Birkenau, then, did not figure very highly in the disbursement of people from the Zamosc Lands region.

Early in 1943, probably March, but one cannot be certain since most of the documentation of the Auschwitz-Birkenau killing center did not survive the war, Krepinska was transferred to one of its sub-camps, Babice, located only a kilometer to the northeast of the huge Auschwitz-Birkenau complex, at the fork of the road to Katowitz and Krakow. Babice had been a Polish village until the SS commandeered it in April 1942, to convert it into a sub-camp. Some of its inhabitants had been expelled into the General Gouvernement; others were moved into the town of Auschwitz. Babice was emptied of residents at the same time as several other nearby villages, including Broszkowice, Budy, Harmeze, Rajsko, and Brzezinka (Birkenau)—between 7 and 12 April—had been similarly commandeered.[29]

As well as being a village, Babice had a large area of land around which the sub-camp was built, with the female prisoners being housed in the three-story school building. To the German administration it was known simply as "*Wirtschaftshof Babitz*," covered an area of nearly 750 hectares, and included 338 homesteads with a population of about 2,500.

By now Krepinska's mother and husband had died. Before reaching Babice, Krepinska had worked as a field laborer in the damp and swampy terrain around Auschwitz-Birkenau. This mainly involved carrying bricks from demolished houses in villages that were being dismantled all around the killing center. Bricks were in short supply, and were recycled for use in the construction of buildings within the killing center.

In Babice, Krepinska, with several hundred other female internees, continued a daily routine of digging drains, and planting and harvesting potatoes, beetroot, and rapeseed. She and other women were moved from the main camp to Babice early in 1943 to work under a scheme whereby the entire camp complex became and remained self-sufficient in food, and even produced surpluses. According to Danuta Czech's research, this program came under the control of a Dr. Joachim Caesar, an SS lieutenant colonel and an agricultural scientist, who in 1943 was aged 42.

A member of the Nazi Party and the SS (No. 74704), he became mayor of Holstein in 1933 and, from 1934 on, worked in the SS training office of the RSHA, which he later headed. In March 1942, Caesar was appointed head of all agricultural activities in Auschwitz, which gained prominence because of their importance to the war effort; Himmler followed these enterprises with particular interest. After the war, Dr. Caesar went into the laundry business and wasn't troubled by any investigations into his past until his death in 1974.[30]

Caesar was accompanied in Auschwitz-Birkenau by his wife, who also held a doctorate in chemistry, and the couple appear to have worked closely together. According to American historian Michael Allen, the huge camp was designed to include an industrial complex "for settlement development including the largest branch of the Experiment Section for Alimentation," which Caesar headed. Moreover, the camp became an "agricultural experiment station for the East."[31] What Caesar learned and developed here was to be further refined and modified as Germanic settlements were created farther east, after that region's conquest and settlement. By the time Krepinska and her relatives and husband arrived in early 1943, Auschwitz was thus already a huge and largely self-sufficient commune where people were tattooed, worked long hours, and died by gassing, with their bodies burned and buried. Whether because of her good health or her will power, Krepinska survived this ordeal until on 21 August 1944, when she and 1,000 or so other women — 500 of them Jews — were dispatched by rail to a sub-camp of the Alsace-based Natzweiler camp, known as Ebingen A.C. As Krepinska recalls this, along the way, somewhere in the Reich, perhaps Breslau (now Wroclaw), the 500 Jewish women, who were in separate cars, were detached. These Jewish women were probably needed to help clear bricks and rubble from the streets of Breslau because of aerial bombing by the Allies. The remainder, the 500 ethnic Poles, may have never actually reached Ebingen A.C. Krepinska does not know precisely where she finally ended up. All she recalls is that the group provided munitions workers for Lorraine, for just a few days, somewhere in the Thionville area. Czech's account of those departing the death camp differs somewhat from Krepinska's recollection, in that she makes no reference to the 500 Jewish women. But Krepinska remained adamant that these additional 500 women were on the journey for part of the trip. Czech writes:

> 500 female prisoners from the Women's Camp in Birkenau to Natzweiler in Alsace, the Ebingen A.C.
> 1000 prisoners are transferred from Natzweiler. They are Poles who were sent to Auschwitz after the outbreak of the Warsaw Uprising.[32]

Though not directly relevant to Globocnik's Zamosc Lands expulsion action, it is interesting to note that on the same day, 21 August 1944, as Krepinska departed Auschwitz for Lorraine, Czech reports that two male and 47 female prisoners reached Auschwitz "by order of the *Sipo-SD* for the Adriatic Coast, the region of Trieste, Fiume, and Pola-Istria...."[33] By then, Odilo

Globocnik's Lublin killing teams, although now some 1,000 kilometers from this death camp network in southeastern Poland, but administratively within the Third Reich, were still able to dispatch prisoners to it.

With the on-rush of the Western Allied armies, which had landed nearly two months earlier at Normandy, German military units were steadily falling back toward the Rhine and the Siegfried Line. After only a day's work in the Lorraine-based munitions factory, the Polish women prisoners were marched back toward the German border, and during an air attack on their column Krepinska and many others, including her friends Helena Noga and Ela Roszkiewicz, escaped into a forest and hid out in the Maginot Line. Later most of them managed to pass themselves off as civilians in nearby villages, with Krepinska working as a domestic aid for an aging farmer named Herder in the sometimes French, sometimes German, village of Kemplich.

4. Zofia Krepinska: From Skierbieszow via the Zamosc Transit Camp to Sobienie-Jeziory

Krepinska's daughter was found 40 kilometers southeast of Warsaw, 190 kilometers northwest of Zamosc, following a train trip. Similar journeys and separations were repeated many thousands of times by other children affected by Globocnik's Zamosc Lands cleansing action. Light is cast on 18-month-old Zofia Krepinska's fate in the following interview with the woman who informally adopted her, Mrs. Stanislawa Kowalska, who was then a widow living southeast of Warsaw, in Gora Kalwaria, near Sobienie-Jeziory.

Q: Where were you living during November and December, 1942?
A: At Sobienie-Jeziory.
Q: Where did you learn that there were transports with children?
A: A Mr. Antony Smerczynski said that a transport had arrived at Sobienie carrying children and adults. I immediately went to the place these children were and that was at the school. There were about 20 children and with them were adults or family guardians. Zofia was in the hands of a woman whose name I do not recall. This woman had with her two boys aged about six or seven years. They were possibly her grandchildren. She was also looking after Zofia. The lady said that a German who spoke Polish announced Zofia's name. This happened either at Skierbieszow or Zamosc. The lady said she had this child and the German said she should look after it.
Q: Had you heard of the Zamosc resettlement action?
A: When the children arrived only then did I learn that these were the children from the Zamosc area.
Q: Did you know to what destinations the transports were headed?
A: I heard from people that most transports went to Warsaw, but in our area they went to Deblin-Garwolin and Pilawa. Zofia came on the transport

to Pilawa, which is about 30 kilometers from Sobienie. This was about 20 December 1942. She was then 18 months old. The lady who had her said that she was the daughter of Helena Krepinska. She also told me how they had been transported in goods wagons. They were transported for about three weeks from station to station. Conditions were very difficult. People sat on each other and the sanitary conditions were bad. The transport was very big and at Pilawa they left about 20 children and 30 adults, that is, women.

Many people in Pilawa gave board and lodgings. The children without family members were taken to be raised. I heard that after the war families who survived took back their children. During the transporting that lady said they received food, but only marmalade and black bread. But when the transport stopped somewhere at a station, then locals brought food and water and passed it through small windows. They had to do it that way so the Germans wouldn't see. Some Germans may have seen but pretended they didn't see. The people were always thirsty.

Q: What did people say of the transports? What did they say of the buying of children?

A: I heard that when a transport arrived in Warsaw that people took children but did not buy them.

Q: At what time and with what thoughts did you go?

A: I went with the thought that I'll get someone to raise. This was in Sobienie. The Germans told some men from Sobienie to take horse-drawn wagons to Pilawa, about 30 kilometers away, to the railway station and bring back people from the transport. These were metal-wheeled wagons and it was 20 December 1942. And I went to the school.

Q: Did anyone die on that transport?

A: I heard from those with the transport that a large number of children and adults did die and that typhus broke out. The Germans threw the dead off the train. The people in those locations dug graves and buried them.

Q: What did you see when you reached the school?

A: When I arrived in the school there were adults and children who were sitting on the floor. I saw someone I knew, called Jan Szurbinski, and he was speaking with a woman who was holding Zofia in her arms. Zofia started to say "Mum" to me. I said to the lady that she should give her to me and in the first instance she said she did not know me. But Mr. Szurbinski said to her that she shouldn't be scared and that she should give Zofia to me and that she will be well-looked after. I took her home. At first I had to feed her, all the time she cried for food. After that I had to wash and powder her because she had wounds. She very quickly became attracted to us. In about a year Mrs. Krepinska's sister, Zofia, came to me and wanted to take Zofia away. But she was a young lady and I did not know how she could look after Zofia. So I said I wouldn't give her up but in that eventuality then only to her mother. During 1943 Zofia Weclawik came to Sobienie because she wanted to be close to Zofia [her niece] so she found work at nearby Gora Kalwaria as a gardener and from time to time visited Zofia and me.

Q: How did Zofia Weclawik find out that Zofia was with you?

A: The lady who gave up Zofia apparently wrote to Skierbieszow to her family saying she had Helena's daughter and they gave the information to Zofia (Weclawik). In this way she found out that Helena's daughter was with me at Sobienie.[34]

Q: After you took Zofia where did you live during the occupation?
A: Until the end of the war we were at Sobienie-Jeziory. In 1945, in November, we went to Gdansk. From 1942, when I took Zofia, I was a widow, and until 1944 I looked after her myself. In 1944 I remarried.[35]

Infant Zofia's aunt, Zofia Weclawik, as related above, had been away from Skierbieszow when her home village was surrounded by German *Völksdeutsche* and probably also Ukrainian ethnic cleansing units, so she found herself still relatively free, even if homeless. She wandered about, avoiding capture, for a fortnight or so, and eventually met a female relative of her niece's train trip guardian who had taken care of the child on that winter journey that ended at Sobienie, near Warsaw. This woman, a Janka Piotrowska, knew Zofia Weclawik was Krepinska's sister, since Piotrowska came from the nearby village of Dulnik, and said she had been told Zofia's niece was at Sobienie being cared for by a woman who wanted to have her. It was this fortuitous meeting that prompted Zofia Weclawik eventually to move to the Sobienie area and remain there for the remainder of the war. Before this move to Sobienie, however, Helena and her sister had seen each other briefly one last time. The day Krepinska was being railed from Zamosc to Auschwitz-Birkenau, Zofia was walking the streets of Zamosc and saw her sister, her mother, and relatives walking with others, under armed guard, to the Zamosc railway station.[36]

XII

Globocnik and Georg Wippern Ravage Jews' Homes and Businesses

Aktion Reinhardt did not solely focus on the physical extermination of Jews. It also sought to acquire all fixed and liquid assets of this doomed European ethnic and religious minority. In fact, the term *"Aktion Reinhardt"* was originally the codename for the seizure of Jewish wealth and property. However, this is complicated by the fact that this robbing of the victims was sometimes even referred to as *"Einsatz* R," with the word *Reinhardt* stemming not from Reinhard Heydrich's given name but from a Fritz Reinhardt, a senior Reich Finance Ministry official.[1] The code term *"Einsatz* R" was resurrected in late 1943 in Trieste, where Globocnik, now a *Höherer SS-und Polizeiführer,* continued his earlier persecution of Jews and broadened it to include non-Jewish opponents and partisans. As bizarre as it may sound, for a brief time in 1942 the robbing of the Jewish victims was also referred to as "Catholic Action" in some quarters in Lublin because the main depot for much loot at this time was in a building that had been erected before the war by the Catholic Action organization, at Chopin Strasse 27. Jewish factories and business establishments were simply commandeered, as were similar assets owned by some Poles. Expropriation was the rule. Globocnik also expropriated landed estates from members of both ethnic groups across his district, and these went on to become SS strongpoints within Lublin District. Residences and other similar fixed assets such as housing, warehouses, and the like were also forcibly acquired on a large scale, for use in whatever manner was deemed to be appropriate. The background to Globocnik's eventual murder of the Jews was therefore one that resembled the Bolshevization and socialization of the early Soviet Union by Lenin, Leon Trotsky, and Feliks Dzerzhinski, activities that prompted tens of thousands of generally penniless Russians to flee this early 1920s Red Revolution.

Less well known, however, is how liquid assets such as bullion, jewelry, pearls, and other valuables such as watches, fountain pens, spectacles, and currency (Polish, German, and foreign), was handled. Death in a killing center came relatively quickly, certainly within 48 hours of one's reaching its barbed wire confines, unless one was designated to be a *Kapo* or was directed to special tasks such as corpse disposal. Such duties, however, only affected a minority of Jews, and even these people were eventually killed. But most were simply done away with by gassing in Globocnik's three killing centers or "terminal stations," Treblinka, Sobibor, and Belzec, and also in Majdanek, well within 24 hours of entering. Lublin District was also the venue of a number of marches during which many thousands died or were killed; victims were also killed by firing squads.

What was crucial with respect to each of the "terminal stations" was the processing phase, for it was here that people were dispossessed of clothing and valuables. Many thousands of Jews across Lublin District were involved in processing and folding of clothing and polishing and repairing boots and shoes. A far smaller number were involved in removal, packing, and processing of bullion, jewelry, currency, and other high value objects, duties that Globocnik associate *SS-Sturmbannführer* Georg Wippern oversaw. Naturally none of this loot was allowed to be simply buried or otherwise destroyed. For a first-hand insight, it is best to turn to the report of *SS-Sturmbannführer* Albert Franke-Gricksch. He saw Globocnik's Research Center for Eastern Settlement (*Forschungsstelle für Ostunterkunfte*) in May 1943; this center was deeply involved in planning future Germanic eastward expansion and settlement under the direction of Gustav Hanelt, constituting the drawing up of the Final Solution of the Slavic Question. According to Gricksch's report to his Berlin superiors, he visited what he called the concentration camp and salvage dump in Lublin on the same day, although it is not clear if he means here the city of Lublin or the actual district.

> A great part of this depot has been switched over to war production. In the salvage depot, all things gained from the deportation of Jews are rendered useful by the Jews. The blankets and linen coming from Jewish households are being collected, cleaned and repaired or reformed into raw material for new production of cloth. This camp alone has delivered 1800 trucks of textiles for the last big drive of old material.... From Trawniki we traveled back to Lublin to inspect

> the special enterprise *Reinhardt. This branch has the task of realizing all mobile Jewish property in the Gouvernement Poland. It is astonishing what immense fortunes the Jews have collected in their ghetto and even ragged and vermin-infested dirty little Jews who look like beggars carry with them, when you strip their clothes off them, foreign currency, pieces of gold, diamonds and other valuables* [emphasis added].[2]

Globocnik was apparently quite proud of the loot sorting establishments that he controlled. Rudolf Höss, who was in charge of Auschwitz-Birkenau, has even described in his autobiography how Globocnik showed one of them off to a senior Berlin SS man, the chief of the SS personnel head office, *SS-Obergruppenführer* von Herff, suggesting that Globocnik's pride in "his" workshops was obviously discussed among other SS men.[3]

Nothing Franke-Gricksch wrote was as amazing as it may appear at first sight. Pre-war Poland was a pre- or non-welfare state, without universal medical care, and it never saw widespread use of life insurance or other forms of insurance, at least at the village and town levels, where such matters were hardly heard of. Banking was also a not overly-utilized service. The 1930s were years of widespread bank failures worldwide. Any individuals, including Jews, who tended to be small traders and craftsmen within the traditional or underdeveloped Polish economy, retained assets in the way that Gricksch has so succinctly, even if quite unsympathetically, described. There was no alternative.

> We wandered through the cellar of this "special enterprise" [*Reinhardt*] and we were reminded of the fairy tales of the "Arabian Nights." Whole boxes full of genuine pearls, cases full of diamonds, a basket full of pieces of gold and many cwts [hundred weights] of silver coins beside jewelry of every kind. In order to carry out a better realization of all these valuables the gold and silver are melted into bars. We inspected the melting process in the garden of the house. There was a small foundry where gold and silver are melted and then formed into bars and then delivered to the German National Bank on certain days.[4]

The cellar that Franke-Gricksch refers to was the workplace of Globocnik's close friend, *SS-Sturmbannführer* Georg Wippern, his comrade-in-arms, who was in charge of Lublin's Jablon Palace, situated not far from Globocnik's home and the venue of two huge steel safes. Globocnik established a new agency, *Abteilung IVa (Aktion Reinhardt)*, within the garrison administration (*SS-Standortverwaltung*), which was headed by Wippern, and located next to his headquarters on Pilsanski Avenue. Wippern's chief cashier was *SS-Oberscharführer* Alois Rzepa, who kept detailed accounts and tabulations of valuables that were received from the various killing centers where victims were dispossessed just prior to being killed by gassing. Rzepa worked closely with a team of bankers and accountants dispatched from Berlin, and Globocnik was in overall charge of this program of mass dispossession of murdered Jews.[5]

Wippern's staff included people who sorted cash, watches, and other valuables, and a 20-man Jewish work brigade was also employed as assistants to undertake the menial sorting and storing of valuables. Loot was delivered to Berlin. Michael Tregenza's findings indicate that two regular couriers, Erich Fettke and Philip Post, were supplied with special passes signed by Himmler which forbade anyone to open their luggage. And couriers from T4 also made similar loot collecting trips. But this system soon proved far from satisfactory. Many things quickly went missing, and late in 1942 procedures were altered. Tregenza's researches have shown that Oswald Pohl's division of the SS, the *SS-WVHA*, had issued instructions for the collection of all valuables plundered from the about-to-be-gassed Jews. One of the reasons for this directive was concern at the widespread pilfering by Globocnik's killing center officials, camp staff, and others in the chain of acquisition and processing of the plundered goods and valuables, that is, *Aktion Reinhardt* staff. Tregenza's findings have established that one of the countermeasures against pilfering, especially of gold, silver, and platinum, was the installation of two smelters which transformed these regal metals into ingots, something much more easily accounted for by tally clerks. These coke-fired smelters were located in the courtyard of *SS-Standortverwaltungsamt.*[6] Diamonds, jewels, watches, and other similar valuables obviously remained a policing problem, and one that was in all likelihood never satisfactorily solved.

Tregenza's investigations in Lublin have also uncovered the fact that in the basement of Wippern's premises was a specially built six by four-meter steel strongroom which could only be entered if one had two separate sets of keys. It was here that Lublin District's stolen treasure was held or temporarily deposited; it was a transit safe. But, as will be seen below, not all of it reached the *Reichsbank*, though most got to Berlin, being dispatched by Wippern's *Abteilung IVa* first "to the *SS-WVHA* in Berlin and then forwarded to the *Reichsbank.*"[7] According to Franke-Gricksch's report:

> "Special enterprise" *Reinhardt* has so far delivered 2500 kilos of gold, 20,000 kilos of silver, and six and a half kilos of platinum, 60,000,000 *Reichsmarks* in currency, 800,000 dollars in money and 144,000 dollars in gold. The huge quantity of diamonds and pearls can hardly be evaluated. The best proof of the repercussion this enterprise has on the international market is the quotations on the Swiss Stock Exchange and the effects on the international market in diamonds and brilliants. The prices have all gone down and Switzerland could not absorb any more diamonds, because our enterprise has swamped the market. In this respect alone, the "special enterprise" *Reinhardt* gives us the means for our political struggle and would have a decisive effect on the world market.[8]

The impact Franke-Gricksch was referring to was unlikely to have been solely due to *Aktion Reinhardt*'s loot. Similar outcomes were repeated in Auschwitz, and not all the bullion and other valuables necessarily came from Jews.

Apart from other valuables there are 60,000 watches, most of them double-cased watches and a huge quantity of other small valuables from tobacco and cigarette cases and gold fountain pens and silver bracelets, etc. In special work-shops all these treasures are sorted out and examined by specially trained Jews' jewelers, bank clerks, goldsmiths. If necessary the diamonds are broken out in order to separate them and use the metal in a different way. The wrist watches will be repaired, if necessary, and will be handed out to front-line troops. When one goes through the cellar of this special branch it appears like a secret trea-sure and you get a very different idea of all the things for which people have sacrificed their lives and forgotten, through them, the real issues.[9]

Finally, let us see what Oswald Pohl, the man at the center of the col-lection of all this loot from the dead, who was captured by the Americans in May 1946, and tried as a war criminal the following year and executed in 1951, revealed about this organized and massive program of larceny. His affidavit contains much that is worth quoting at some length on the question of this loot, for it tells us something of the procedures adopted when it reached Berlin.

Arrangements through which deliveries of concentration camp loot were to be delivered by the SS to the *Reichsbank* were directed by Himmler. Subsequently I contacted [Emil] Puhl on the question of delivery. These transactions were to be carried out in extreme secrecy.

Globocnik was in Berlin quite frequently because he was required to deposit valuables obtained through *Aktion Reinhardt* in the *Reichsbank* or in the Reich Main Treasury. Accompanied by Georg Loerner, August Frank and several oth-ers I visited the *Reichsbank* and we were shown the contents of the vaults by Emil Puhl. On this occasion Puhl made the statement: "Well, your things are among them." Further details concerning the delivery of the concentration camp loot to the *Reichsbank* were worked out by my subordinates and the reports were squared by special *Reichsbank* and *Amtsgruppen-A* personnel.

The first shipment of valuables of which I knew was made in the autumn of 1943. At this date there was no question as to the source of the material turned over to the *Reichsbank*. Generally speaking the loot realized from *Aktion Rein-hardt*, as I learned later from Globocnik's final report and Vogt's auditing reports, consisted of a great variety of personal items such as gold teeth, rings, jewelry and foreign currency. It was never doubted that this loot was taken from Jews exterminated in the concentration camps.

The gold jewelry and foreign currency was to be placed on deposit for the Reich in the *Reichsbank* for the benefit of the German Reich.

Clothing was distributed on Himmler's order to the NSV (National Social-ists Public Welfare) to other offices and to foreign workers in Germany. I knew about these things in my capacity as Chief of the *WVHA* which operated from Berlin.

In 1944, on Himmler's order, I conferred with Walter Funk with the purpose of obtaining for the *Waffen-SS* a larger quota of clothing on which occasion I was told to mention the surrender of old clothes from Lublin and Auschwitz. The old clothes belonging to the prisoners who had been exterminated were stored in Auschwitz and Lublin. They were delivered for utilization by *Gruppenführer* Georg Loerner.

Though Loerner never participated with the discussion I had with Globocnik, it is quite possible that Globocnik himself spoke to Loerner about textiles obtained from Action Reinhardt.

I sent *Sturmbannführer* Opperbock to Lublin so that he might take over the enterprises set up or acquired by Globocnik. These enterprises were co-ordinated into a new company, Ostindustrie (*Osti*) GmbH and placed under the command of Stab W of the *WVHA*.

Upon the completion of *Aktion Reinhardt* all the concerns and the complete economic part of this action, which consisted largely of carpentry shops, locksmiths' workshops, tailoring workshops, etc., were officially taken over by the *WVHA*.

I received a letter from Himmler expressing his thanks for my carrying out the economic side of *Aktion Reinhardt*. I am unable to approximate the value of the materials seized through *Aktion Reinhardt* because I had no criterion by which to judge the worth of all the loot. As I was told, fairly accurate accounts were kept of depositions of foreign currency to the *Reichsbank* or the Reich Treasury in the name of Max Heilieger, a fictitious person.[10]

SS Man Heinrich Gustav Wilhelm Wied's Revealing Lublin Investigations

As stated above, not all the loot reached official institutions in Berlin, or even Lublin for that matter. Lublin by late 1942 was the center of a great deal of corruption, larceny, and private wheeling and dealing. This is excellently revealed in the case of a German policeman who was arrested by the British on 21 July 1945, because he had been an SS member. This man, Heinrich Gustav Wilhelm Wied, was a well-educated and dedicated police officer, a man who believed in upholding the law. In American or Hollywood parlance, "he hated crooks," which meant he certainly had his work cut out for him in Lublin, where it would have been nearly impossible to have found an honest man, one not "on the take." Because the SS was declared at Nuremberg to be a criminal organization, it is easy to make the deduction that all its members were criminals. Wied shows that generalization to be erroneous. After completing his training, Wied, in July 1939, was placed in charge of the Fraud Department (*Betrugsdezernat*) in Dusseldorf, and later transferred into the *SD*, where he received intelligence training. But he returned to criminal investigating work in Dusseldorf in early 1942, after which he went to Berlin, undertaking similar investigations. He then assumed charge of the section that investigated Luftwaffe corruption, and later performed similar work in occupied Greece, then in St. Denis, near Paris, where he investigated "swindling in the supply of razor blades to the *Wehrmacht*. [He] later visited Warsaw where the Asid-Serum-Institute was charged with using eggs and alcohol supplied for research purposes in order to brew liquor."[11]

In his debriefing by the British, Wied touched on a case involving Lublin, where he had arrived in December 1943, nearly three months after Globocnik had departed for Trieste. Despite Globocnik's absence at this time, this issue is relevant because it involved individuals and agencies Globocnik had either employed or else had overseen. Wied apparently remained in Lublin until April 1944, working on this case. His debriefing report reads:

> *Bekleidungswerke* Lublin. Dec 43–April 44.
> This organization had been set up to collect and make use of property removed from prisoners entering the Kz [concentration camp] Lublin [Majdanek]. It also served *Arbeitslager* Pulawy and several other camps in the Lublin area.
> The "*Werk*" used three hangars on the disused Lublin airfield as warehouses and employed a staff of some 70 SS men. The responsible authority was the *Reichskanzlei* [Reich Chancellery], Berlin, Vosstrasse 4, which had created a special department called "*Gemeinnuetzige Stiftung fuer Anstaltspflege*" for the purpose.
> Wied established that this same 'Stiftung' was responsible for the liquidation of Jews in Kzs and the inmates of asylums etc. This activity bore the name "*Aktion Reinhardt*." The leading persons were *Ober Reg. Rat* Alpers, *Stubaf.* Wirth and *Hstuf.* [Gottlieb] Hering. The then police chief of Lublin *SS Gruf.* Globocznik [sic] was equally responsible.
> W's investigations in Lublin established that 18 SS men, mainly on the "*Bekleidungswerke*" staff, were guilty of corruption on a large scale. Through his investigations Wied had to combat deliberate obstruction from the higher *Stapo* leaders because they themselves were also deeply implicated. For example, the a/m Alpers intervened on behalf of one of the accused SS men in whose possession Wied had found a large quantity of obviously stolen jewelry and clothing etc. in that he declared that the accused had taken the articles WITH the authority of "*Stiftung*."
> The cases against the 18 accused were heard before the *SS u. Polizeigericht* Kassel. Sentences up to three years imprisonment were imposed but in several cases no verdict could be reached since the defendants were absent allegedly on front line service.
> The resentment against Wied's interference in this profitable "racket" in Lublin found expression in a variety of ways. On one occasion he found the tyres of his car slashed, on another occasion there was sugar in the petrol-tank.[12]

The ease with which the guilty escaped even SS "justice" in this case suggests high-level attempts to sabotage Wied's entire policing and investigative procedure, suggesting that members of Globocnik's Lublin hierarchy had high and influential connections. Given that over half a century has elapsed since these events, the whole truth is unlikely ever to come out fully, short of the discovery of a revealing diary of one of the thieves. But the most probable explanation is that the SS hierarchy intervened to save their own necks: that if the case was ever heard in a court, evidence would have come out about *Aktion Reinhardt*, and SS leaders, as high as Himmler and possibly even Hitler, would have been implicated by the documentary evidence. In short, the SS could not afford to allow the guilty to be found guilty, because those who were even guiltier could have logically been called to accounts. There simply could not be a court case. It is obvious that the best way out was to quash investigations as soon as possible.

Wied was most certainly not impressed by Wippern. His debriefing report identifies him as an "obstructionist." The entry in the British debriefing report is damning:

> The staff of the *Bekleidungswerke* Lublin came under the command of the *SS-Standortkommandant, Stubaf* Wippern. This man showed no inclination to support W. in his investigations, the probable reason being that he was too deeply involved in corruption himself. There was no check or record of property removed from prisoners. It was obvious from the lavish spending and extravagant living of the staff of both Kz and *Bekleidungswerke* that this must be their source of income.[13]

One should perhaps be reminded that all this was happening at the height of the war, when the Reich was fighting for its very existence.

More Evidence of a Pilfering and Corruption Pandemic Amongst the Globocnikians and Their Underlings

Michael Tregenza has concluded similarly with respect to widespread institutionalized pilfering, as well as the private acquisition of massive quantities of loot, that Globocnik oversaw a regime that can fairly be described as a kleptocracy. At Lublin's old airfield there were three hangars that had been converted into sorting or processing depots for the huge quantities of clothing, bedding, and other textiles from Globocnik's Jewish victims. According to Tregenza, some 2,000 prisoners, mainly women, worked here as sorters of all this loot; "There were also big crates into where were deposited the gold, silver, diamonds, pearls, gold watches, and other valuables. At the end of each day, up to six men were needed to carry each crate to the *Kommandantur*. A lot of wealth accumulated was pilfered daily by guards and prisoners alike."[14]

There was no precise documentation referring to the value of the consignments of valuables sent to the Reich from the old Lublin airfield; nor is there any record of the total value of gold, valuables, and cash collected at the depot. After the war, Josef Oberhauser, who worked in the *Kommandantur*, could only comment that "The unregistered jewelry and valuables from the individual death camps were delivered to the *SS-Standortverwaltung*, [garrison administration] whose head was Wippern. I had not the slightest thing to do with this."[15]

According to Michael Tregenza, Wippern emphatically denied "ever having utilized any of the Jewish loot for himself." Instead, he claimed that Globocnik had threatened him with death if he had ever done the contrary, a threat that is credible, indeed likely, in light of what others have said of Globocnik's proclivity to threaten people. But Tregenza disputes all this, saying Wippern had been quite dishonest in this postwar claim. He points out that Wippern had a reputation in Lublin as a racketeer, and that he, his wife, children, and their two daughters-in-law "also employed at the *SS-Standortverwaltung*" proudly displayed their extensive wardrobes: "Wippern was counted among the prominent around Globocnik, and at social gatherings both he and his wife wore expensive rings, usually encrusted with diamonds."[16]

The three hangars, which were about a mile or so from the main entrance to Majdanek concentration camp, and into which a railway track led to bring and take away loads of loot, were even out of bounds for the most senior SS men. Michael Tregenza relates the case of Globocnik's successor, Jakob Sporrenberg, reaching Lublin in August 1943, about a month before Globocnik's departure for Trieste. Himmler had told Sporrenberg not to become involved with Jewish affairs in Lublin, advice Sporrenberg appears to have failed to heed. Being determined to inspect aspects of Globocnik's Jewish Gulag, he eventually came upon the three hangars. At one stage Sporrenberg had attempted to enter the old Lublin airfield complex, which was still being overseen by Wirth. After the war, while in British hands, Sporrenberg descibed his encounter with a man "of great physical stature" who had a whip in his hand and how he, Sporrenberg, ostensibly the leading SS man in Lublin District, had objected to being treated thus.[17]

By the time Sporrenberg had reached Lublin, men like Wirth and his team had been there for approximately two years, and were totally familiar with all arbitrary procedures and personnel. Globocnik and his staffers had been there two years longer. They had literally become a law, if that is the appropriate word, unto themselves, with property, bullion, and especially life, being treated as if they were theirs to give or take, which they were. They could and did take all these things, whenever they pleased, and for granted. Sporrenberg's treatment shows just how hardened and murderous the Globocnik-Lerch-Wirth team, and all their hangers-on, had become. No one, not even Globocnik's replacement, was seen as having the right to oversee them. The corruption was so deep that nothing else but their discretion prevailed. And this could change day to day, hour to hour.

Another corrupt official was Johannes Müller, the man who after the war so accurately disclosed and described the role of Globocnik's Research Center for Eastern Settlement (*Forschungsstelle für Ostunterkunfte*). Müller, also a close friend of Globocnik's, was "a quite brutal and generally heartless man" who entertained lavishly — a 16-course meal for a visiting Chinese consul-general's dinner — and, like the Wipperns, collected, with his wife, valuable jewelry.

Even before the dogged and inquisitive Heinrich Wied arrived, word had reached Berlin that all was not in order in Lublin. A murderous ruling kleptocracy had emerged with Globocnik at its peak. Things had reached such a level that Himmler arranged for an investigation. An SS judge, *Obersturmführer* Konrad Morgen, transferred to the Criminal Police to undertake the task. The fact that such an appointment was made indicates that concern over corruption had even reached the ears of those at the highest level in Berlin, as it had in late 1938 about the Vienna *Gau* and its then inaugural *Gauleiter*, Globocnik. But Lublin was simply Vienna writ extremely large. Morgen was later to give evidence at Nuremberg, where he took the somewhat original tack of claiming the SS was innocent of slaughtering Jews, something he appears to have genuinely believed. His claim was based on his discovery that a secret group, *Aktion Reinhardt*, existed, and that it was in fact the guilty agency. He thus overlooked the fact that Globocnik, Lublin District's most senior SS man, was in charge, not to mention Globocnik's long association with Himmler on Jewish and Slavic settlement affairs. Morgen was simply naïve, incredibly naïve, to say the least. Notwithstanding this, Morgen's extensive and indeed thorough investigations and often bizarre discoveries make him a reliable and revealing witness of certain realities of daily life, habits, and procedures in and around Lublin, including, of course, the robbing of victims. And, like Sporrenberg, he eventually reached the infamous hangars at the Lublin airfield.

> It was a camp which held the belongings, or a part of the belongings of victims. Because of the extent of this — there were unheard of piles of watches stacked up there — I had to realize that something monstrous was going on there. I was also shown the valuables. I can say that I have never seen so much gold, especially foreign gold; I saw all kinds of money from all over the world collected together, as well as melted-down gold, whole ingots of gold.[18]

Max Runhof (Cichotski), in his 1961 statement made in Wiesbaden, recounted an incident which may indicate that private transfers of loot and gain involving even Globocnik were occurring. One night an individual by the name of Werner Blankenburg, one of the central Berlin figures coordinating and administering *Aktion Reinhardt*, reached Lublin and asked to store several crates in *Aktion Reinhardt*'s headquarters cellar. Blankenburg, was, of course, from the *Führer*'s Chancellery, working with *Reichsleiter* Bouhler. Rather than granting permission, Runhof contacted Globocnik, who was away at the *Führer*'s headquarters in Lotzen (Gizycko), to have this request cleared. But Runhof was indiscrete enough to quiz Blankenburg, a senior Reich Chancellery official, no less, about the contents of the crates, and was told that they

were "important items for the front."[19] When Runhof relayed this to Globocnik, Globocnik called it "nonsense, but that I should mind my own business."[20]

Soon after the mysterious cargo was removed by lorry to Berlin, and the
curious Runhof situated himself nearby to secretly watch the operation.

> During the loading I watched from behind a window and saw that one of the
> containers was damaged and the contents — items of gold — rolled over the
> ground. The items were gathered up and put back. This incident made it clear
> to me that these valuable items must have come from the persecution measures
> against the Jews.[21]

True, Runhof was not saying that Globocnik was necessarily "on the
take." But one does not need to go far to find someone who suspected as much.
SS man, professor, and medical practitioner, Dr. Pfannenstiel, who minis-
tered to Globocnik after he had his emotional breakdown during 1943, claimed
after the war that he believed his powerful former patient and one time col-
laborator in crime was corrupt. But Pfannenstiel chose his words extremely
carefully. "I had the impression that the whole thing was a 'private enterprise'
of Globocnik's. I was of the opinion therefore that Globocnik had feathered
his own nest with the whole thing, *and was its originator*" (emphasis added).[22]

We know, for instance, that Globocnik had the habit of giving expensive gifts to powerful people in Berlin, and to other key officials he saw as
being important or of use to him. His largess included expensive fur coats,
food, fine wines, French champagnes, and the like. Globocnik had access to
commercial or business enterprises with links in Western Europe, especially
Holland, which kept him supplied with luxury items such as fine wines and
champagne. There is another significant point in relation to all the pilfering
and high lifestyle of the Globocnikians and their underlings, which a participant at a 1980 conference on Nazi concentration camps, Felicia Karai, believed
had been overlookd: "Lastly, a comment concerning the SS men who served
in the concentration camps. For some reason the lecturers forgot to stress that
these men profited doubly from their positions: they avoided active service
at the front, and amassed large fortunes from booty and stolen goods."[23]

Although Werner Blankenburg was a high Berlin official, having succeeded Viktor Brack in Hitler's Chancellery, and may have been on official
business in Lublin, there appears to be no evidence of the signing and counter
signing of receipts and authorizations. Crates were broken and contents were
put back, it seems. Were the contents of each crate audited? Questions of this
nature cannot be answered so long after the war, but there is considerable
doubt over whether disciplined or prudent procedures were in place. It seems
that all along the line — between the robbing of victims, sorting, storing, and
delivering, first to Lublin and then to Berlin — there was room for removal

of the loot, and the likelihood even of involvement by Globocnik through side deals, whether with Werner Blankenburg or Georg Wippern. Anyone who has witnessed or has had explained the intricate checking procedures that exist in diamond and gold mining operations, mints, or casinos, would undoubtedly be amazed if asked to believe that the jointly run Lublin and Berlin *Aktion Reinhardt* operation was not fraught with huge loopholes that allowed at least some pilfering by the ever-present "sticky fingers." And there was a lot to plunder or skim off the top.

Efforts have been made to quantify the value of all property lost by Poland's Jewish minority. Economist Joseph Marcus has put the U.S. dollar value as at least $3.07 billion at the purchasing power of that dollar in Poland in 1938. The U.S. dollar's purchasing power in Poland was between 40 and 50 percent higher than in the United States, meaning the Marcus calculation of the "national wealth" of the Jewish minority on the eve of World War II was slightly below $US2.2 billion.[24] It is not being claimed that Globocnik's Lublin kleptocracy acquired that much; they certainly did not. That huge figure includes fixed assets such as housing, property, and capital goods. Or, as Artur Eisenbach so concisely summarized this huge material dimension:

> The property of the Jewish population in the occupied territories [western Poland] was confiscated by the Reich and taken over by the *Haupttreuhandstelle Ost* (HTO) as early as 1939–41. All the real estate of the Jews and most of their personal property were confiscated by the HTO at the time of their transfer to ghettos, that is by the middle of 1941. What remained was taken away during the mass deportations to death camps.
>
> In the General Gouvernement Globocnik's operational staff was given full authority over the Jewish populations as well as the right to Jewish property. The looted valuables were assembled in the "*Reinhardt*" headquarters in Lublin and accounts were kept by the SS and police commanders of various districts who plundered Jewish property in their area....
>
> The preliminary financial report *Reinhardt* 1, drawn up by Globocnik, covers the period April 1, 1942 to December 15, 1943. this is only an account of the articles and money taken from the Jews in the death camps and the various ghettos after deportation. It does not include the goods, raw materials, machines and factory installations which were partly taken over by the *Osti* SS company which was set up later.
>
> In the middle of July 1942, Globocnik organized in his general headquarters a central index of all the valuables acquired int he course of Operation *Reinhardt*. Apart from this central index, files were also kept in some camps, eg. Trawniki, Chelmno, Lublin (*Bekleidungswerke*) in accordance with the regulations issued by Globocnik on September 16, 1942. After the completion of the operation, Globocnik was to submit a detailed report to Pohl, chief of the *Wirtschaftsverwaltungshauptamt* (*WVHA*).[25]

XIII

Globocnik and Wippern
Exposed as Plunderers
of the Dead

The first postwar writer to fully draw attention to the financial and asset plundering, as opposed to only the killing side of *Aktion Reinhardt,* was the Polish lawyer and historian Stanislaw Piotrowski, who perhaps without realizing it was following in the footsteps of the dogged but forgotten SS police officer, Heinrich Gustav Wilhelm Wied, who had come under such an onslaught while investigating, in wartime Lublin, the Globocnikian kleptocracy. In 1956 Piotrowski released the first abridged volume of Dr. Hans Frank's Krakow office wartime diary — *Dziennik Hansa Franka (Sprawy Polskie przed Miedzynarodwym Trybunalem Wojennym w Norymberdze)* — which had proved to be so useful to Allied prosecutors at Nuremberg. Hardly noticed or recognized, however, was Piotrowski's small 1949 booklet, *Misja Odyla Globocnika: Sprawozdania o Wynikach Finansowych Zaglady Zydow w Polsce* (*The Mission of Odilo Globocnik: A Report on the Financial Outcome of the Extermination of Poland's Jews*). This 59-page commentary and analysis, written in a turgid 19th century Polish prose style, which may explain why it has been referred to only a handful of times by subsequent Jewish Holocaust and other researchers, is based on three crucial letters and two financial statements that surfaced at the immediate postwar Nuremberg Major War Crimes Trial. Piotrowski immediately saw the significance of these documents, which were correspondence between Himmler

and Globocnik and accompanied by two 1943 financial statements, constituting a signing off or financial accounting of *Aktion Reinhardt* by an executive
officer to his immediate superior. Specifically these documents were:

• A letter of 4 November 1943, from Globocnik, then in Trieste, reporting to Himmler. Attached was an appendix, a 3 February 1943 financial state-
ment (Hereafter, the Wippern Financial Statement) signed by Georg
Wippern, at that time still in Lublin.
   • A letter of 30 November 1943, from Himmler to Globocnik.
   • A letter of 5 January 1944, from Globocnik in Trieste to Himmler.
This had attached appendices, a 15 December 1943 financial statement (here-
after, the Wippern-Rzepa Financial Statement) from Globocnik, then in Tri-
este, which was signed by Georg Wippern, Alois Rzepa, and also Globocnik.
This was the final *Aktion Reinhardt* statement.[1]

Piotrowski refers to these letters and financial statements collectively as
"The Document," and his commentary discloses that he had deduced that a
number of other pertinent letters and attachments were obviously and unfortunately missing, either deliberately destroyed, or else lost or simply misplaced.
They were never found. According to Piotrowski, "The most important docu-
ment in the case of the persecution of Jews by Hitler's Government in Europe
was lodged at the International Military Tribunal at Nuremberg in the report of
Odilo Globocnik, *Gruppenführer* Lieutenant of Police, on the financial outcome
of the extermination of the Jews on the territory of the General Gouvernement."[2]
In the first letter, of 4 November 1943, to Himmler from Globocnik,
Globocnik claimed that in his opinion Lublin was "an extremely dangerous
Jewish center." This certainly suggests that Globocnik was involved, as some
claimed, at least in the planning stages of the November 1943 Harvest Festival massacres in which over 40,000 Jews were shot in just a few days. According to Piotrowski, Globocnik had backed his claim with evidence, but that
evidence, again unfortunately, is missing from the collection of documents.

Secondly, Globocnik said work carried out by Jewish slave labor was important.
It was achievements with very few Germans in control. And significant numbers of German manufactures became interested in the methods used. Furthermore, he wrote that he had passed the Jewish work camps over to Oswald
Pohl who was then in charge of concentration camps.
   Globocnik reminded Heinrich Himmler of his promise that for extraordinary
achievements in fulfilling this work would it be possible to have the Iron Cross
awarded. He asked for permission to lodge special application forms and added
that the second-in-command in Warsaw's *SS-und Polizeiführer* had received such
recognition for the liquidation of the Warsaw Ghetto, which was only a small
part of a larger task which was *Aktion Reinhardt*. Globocnik would be grateful to
Heinrich Himmler if he recognized the hard work of his subordinates.[3]

The accompanying Wippern Financial Statement of 3 February 1943 showed that the goods acquired from all Jewish victims had been valued at a total of 100,047,983.91 *Reichsmarks* (RM). Of this, 53,013,133.51RM was accounted for in three separate sub-totals — 15,931,722.01RM as cash in hand; 31,500,000RM had been delivered to an Economic Affairs officer in Krakow; and 5,581,411.50RM was delivered to the *SS-WVHA*, Oswald Pohl's division in Berlin. Thereafter the statement is sub-divided into five other categories: Foreign currency in notes, (1,452,904.65RM); Foreign Gold Coinage (843,802.75RM); Gold, Silver and Platinum (bullion that had probably been smelted by Wippern's Lublin smelting and storage unit), (5,353,943RM); Other Valuables (26,089,800RM); and Textiles (13,294,400RM). The category "Other Valuables" included a large variety of items which were each classified under general headings, such as 49kg of pearls, valued at 4,000,000RM; two theatre binoculars, valued at 100RM; 13,455 male pocket watches, valued at 269,100RM, and so on. The "Textiles" category had involved the use of 462 railroad cars to move these rags; 261 cars to move bedding feathers; and 317 cars for clothing and underclothing.

The Wippern Financial Statement was not, however, Globocnik's final accounting of his Lublin or *Aktion Reinhardt* booty. That information is contained in the Wippern-Rzepa Financial Statement that was also dispatched to Himmler in Berlin by Globocnik from Trieste. According to this statement, cash reserves were 17,470,796.66RM; the amount paid into the *Reichsbank* in Berlin in banknotes (*Reichsmarks*) and coinage was 3,979,523.50RM; the amount paid into the *Reichsbank* in Berlin as gold coins was 5,000,461.00RM; the amount dispatched to an Economic Affairs officer in Krakow, 50,416,181.37RM; the amount borrowed by SS enterprises, 8,218,878.35RM; and outlays on titles, 656,062.40RM; which totaled 85,741,903.28RM.[4]

This second statement showed that outgoings totaled 11,889,822.54RM, with this figure including 11,765,552.62RM paid to meet 40 percent of the cost of having Jews transported ("J-Transports") by rail to Globocnik's killing centers. In addition, the equivalent of 28,062.64RM is listed as having been found to be counterfeited Polish Zlotys, and 96,207.28RM as ration dues. The 11,889,822.54RM were deducted from the 85,741,903.28RM, and the remainder, 73,852,080.74RM, was called net or clear income.

As in the case of the Wippern Financial Statement, the subsequent Wippern-Rzepa Financial Statement of 15 December 1943 carried a breakdown of notes and coins of various nationalities, bullion, and other valuables. For instance, the haul of pearls was shown to be 114.20 kg, and valued at 6,000,000RM. Also listed are 15,883 gold rings with diamonds or other precious stones, watches, broaches, and diamonds; even 230 thermometers were noted. The statement then added the net income figure shown above to the value of five separate items placed under the heading, "General Computation."

These five items are: bullion (8,973,651.60RM); foreign banknotes (4,521,224.13RM); gold coins (1,736,554.12RM); precious metals and the rest (43,662,450.00RM); and textiles (46,000,000RM), giving a total of 178,745,960.59RM.[5]

Precisely what this figure on which Wippern, Rzepa and Globocnik signed off actually meant is difficult to say, for the layout or presentation of these accounts is unorthodox to say the least. Moreover, in light of the known evidence of widespread theft in Lublin, and what may have even been an organized stealing operation by senior SS men or a group of SS men — something Wied certainly believed existed — it is a wonder that any sort of statement was ever forthcoming and sent to Berlin by Globocnik. Yet we are dealing here with a man who, when the chips were down, felt compelled to seek Himmler's powerful backing to ensure that the Nazi Party's financial stickler and treasurer, Francis Xaver Schwartz, did not pursue him further to determine precisely all the financial shenanigans Globocnik had gotten up to during his brief Vienna days as *Gauleiter*. Could the Lublin days in matters of finance have been any different? Probably not. It is also worth remembering that Globocnik requested that his 15 December 1943 report to Himmler — the Wippern-Rzepa Financial Statement — although provisional, should be treated as a final reporting. He clearly did not wish to be hounded again, as he had been after his departure from Vienna in early 1939. Significantly, therefore, Piotrowski writes:

> Odilo Globocnik insisted that everything that was taken was delivered. *SS-Obersturmbannführer* Vogt executed an introduction control of all acquisitions that were taken up to 1.4.1943 and found everything in order. Further acquisitions demanded similar controls. Odilo Globocnik underlined that this introductory report should be counted as *final and that all-financial statements and documents should be destroyed* [emphasis added] but without further controls by the national treasury. In this direction there was agreement with the Reich Finance Ministry in line with the order to keep *Aktion Reinhardt* a secret.[6]

In the case of Lublin, however, there was the added gruesome factor that at least 1.5 million people had been systematically murdered and all their worldly possessions had been taken and tallied in a rather haphazard way. One is therefore compelled to conclude that the Wippern-Rzepa Financial Statement (perhaps it ought to be called the *Aktion Reinhardt* Statement), which Globocnik had signed with his two associates, really meant little if one is searching for a truly accurate tally of the value of loot acquired. Probably of greater interest are the various headings and breakdowns — banknotes, coinage, bullion, and the like — in this undoubtedly inaccurate statement, which give us an insight into the nature of the enormous quantities of valuables, cash, precious stones, and other personal possessions acquired from Globocnik's

Jewish victims. This loot necessarily excludes capital items such as industrial assets and real estate, which, as will be seen below, largely came under the control of another arm of Globocnik's administration. The major beneficiaries, after the various Lublin pilferers had taken what they wanted, were the railway network that was used to transport the Jews to Globocnik's various killing centers either to be killed or to work; the *SS-WVHA*, headed by Oswald Pohl, one of Globocnik's fellow directors of *Osti;* and the *Reichsbank*. Items such as watches, glasses, and utensils were directed to the army. Fabrics and textiles went to the Reich Ministry of Economics.

> Some of these items were dispatched to foreign workers in the Reich but a larger portion went on to be recycled. The best clothing was received by the *Volksdeutsche* on the *Reichsführer-SS* orders. Footwear was segregated by usage and sent to *Volksdeutsche* or to concentration camps for use as leather parts for wooden shoes.... Household items, if in good condition, could mostly be sent to German settlers in the General Gouvernement.[7]

Elsewhere Piotrowski wrote:

> Globocnik explained that he organized one central managerial organization, which encompassed all of the General Gouvernement, and included all acquisitions of *Aktion Reinhardt*. The SS's *WVHA* dispatched people for the tasks. Guidelines of the *Reichsführer-SS* were set out — his 26 September 1942 instruction and 9 December 1943, which directed how to use or what to do with the acquisitions. Movables that were collected were constantly dispatched to the *WVHA*, which dispersed them, sending them to the *Reichsbank* or Ministry of Finance or to different textile establishments.[8]

Piotrowski included a brief assessment of the organized pilfering of loot, in a short section titled "Misuse of *Aktion Reinhardt* Funds," that relied, appropriately, on none other than Heinrich Gustav Wilhelm Wied's findings and experiences in Lublin that have already been described.

> To discover the real total value of the loot acquired under *Aktion Reinhardt* would demand a separate study. One reason is that Globocnik himself admitted in his report that the valuations used were the lowest and with foreign currencies the pre-war exchange rates were used to calculate values. We must also recall that the two itemized reports of *Aktion Reinhardt* included only those goods handed across for official registration. Some evidence exists that Globocnik somewhat too quickly judged his workers as being honest when acquiring and processing stolen loot.
>
> We can say this because of evidence provided by Dr. Heinrich Wilhelm Wied, an *SS-Hauptsturmführer*, who gave evidence before the Commission for War Crimes. Wied worked for the RSHA in Berlin with the section dealing with corruption in the Army and SS organization. From December 1943 until April 1944 Wied led investigations in the "textile factory" in Lublin. Under that name existed a special SS undercover group of some 70 people who were actu-

ally managers of *Aktion Reinhardt*, also known as Globocnik's *Einheit*. Officially the "textile factory" was involved in collecting and distributing movable chattels taken from prisoners in the various camps in Lublin as well as work camps.

For this purpose they utilized three airport hangars which came under the direction and orders of the Reich Chancellery, and for this purpose a special department was created, called the Foundation for Welfare and Care for the Institute. According to Wied this Foundation was in fact used to kill the mentally ill in hospitals and also liquidated Jews.

The Foundation was directed by *Oberregierungsrat* Alpers, *SS-Sturmbannführer* Wirth, who headed Globocnik's group and went with him to Trieste, and SS-*Haumptsturmführer* Hering, assistant to Wirth and also Globocnik.

Wied found evidence that 18 people from the so-called factory were involved in large-scale abuse. Along the way he encountered a great deal of hindrance from the local Gestapo officials who were also implicated.

Alpers himself came to the rescue of one of the accused in whose house was found a large amount of jewelry, clothing, etc., claiming that the man was holding these items with the knowledge of the Foundation.

An SS and Police court in Kassel examined the case against the 18. In a few cases they could not reach a verdict because the defendants had apparently gone to the Front. In other cases the court handed down sentences up to three years.[9]

Ost-Industrie GmbH (Osti) East Industry Ltd.

If the Wippern and Wippern-Rzepa Financial Statements provide only limited insight into the amount stolen from Globocnik's Jewish victims under *Aktion Reinhardt,* the situation is far less satisfactory with respect to Globocnik's other role — as Lublin's industrial czar, that is, as director of the huge wartime industrial venture known as *Ost-Industrie GmbH*, or simply *Osti.* This budding industrial conglomerate, about which little more is known now than in the late 1940s, when Piotrowski wrote a brief analysis of it, is like *Aktion Reinhardt* in that it had its genesis in secrecy, and also in illegality because it had only "two investors who at the same time were directors" when the corporate law required more, a measure of the organization's secrecy.

Osti, which was registered in March 1943, was established with the aim of best using Jewish slave labor held in camps and was born in Berlin where it was registered in the office of lawyer, Dr. Wilhelm Schneider. The company's registration number was 169/43 and although based in Berlin it was permitted to have branches. *Osti* was to operate and create new manufacturing ventures, particularly textile, metal works, workshops, and to enter into partnerships with similar manufacturers. The firm had right to take decisions that would result in its growth and expansion. Its foundation capital was set at 100,000RM. Director minister Oswald Pohl was to be responsible for raising 75 percent of this sum and Georg Loerner, Engineer Diploma, for the remaining 25 percent. Initially they infused only 25 percent of their agreed amounts. At a sharehold-

ers meeting held on 19 November 1943 the executive board included:
Chairman: Oswald Pohl.
Acting-chairman: Franz [sic] Wilhelm Kruger (Krakow).
Dr. Ferdinand von Sammern Frankenegg (Warsaw).
Georg Loerner, dealer.[10]

Pohl was head of the SS's economic and concentration camp controlling arm, *SS-WVHA*; Kruger was head of the SS policing in the General Gouvernement; and Frankenegg headed the SS and Police in Warsaw. He, among other roles, was the author of the plan to "liquidate" the Warsaw Ghetto. Kruger and Frankenegg were replaced as company officials by one Schelling, an "economic officer" in Krakow, and Globocnik, who was registered as being from Berlin and billed as an "engineer," which he was not. The other Berliner was Dr. Max Horn, presented as a dealer, whereas he was in fact an *SS-Hauptsturmführer* in Globocnik's office. It was decided to wind-up *Osti* on 1 March 1944, and this feat was, amazingly, completed in just 21 days, with Dr. Horn nominated as the liquidator. An *SS-Unterscharführer,* Jan Sebastian Fischer, was ordered to conduct the audit, and it was done between 21 and 26 May 1944, in just five days. *Osti*, according to Piotrowski, was created "to manage the entire Jewish assets but excluding the cash, jewelry and clothing, and in particular it should distribute the Jewish labor force in the General Gouvernment to work for the Third Reich." In other words, it stripped Jews of all their assets, that is, valuables that they were unable to carry through the gates of Globocnik's killing centers and other camps. *Osti* generally took the valuables left behind by those taken to a killing center to be murdered, including fixed assets or capital items, workshops, machinery, supplies, and the like.

At a conference attended by Kruger on 1 June 1943, this illegally registered SS-firm was given three specific duties: to use Jewish slave labor across the General Gouvernement by already established manufacturers operating in conjunction with Jewish work camps; to take over manufacturers held by offices of the SS and Police; and to commandeer Jewish machinery and other capital. Consequently, it stole from Jewish owners a glass works near Warsaw, at Wolomin; a large peat deposits near Lublin; and it produced brushes, acquired large textile establishments, and even built steel works. Jewish labor was extensively utilized. The peat diggings at Dorochutczy utilized mechanical extraction methods, and this operation employed about 1,000 Jewish workers — male and female. One of its brush factories employed 1,800 Jewish workers. Clearly, then, when it was decided to murder over 40,000 skilled Jewish workers in and around Lublin in the Harvest Festival massacres, the end of *Osti* had certainly arrived, so it was liquidated by May the following year, with the decision to do so having been made before March.

From 1 July 1943 *Osti* took over industries managed by the SS and *Polizeiführer* in Radom [the district adjacent to Lublin District] which included clothing workshops, wood works, ammunition plants, peat works and quarries. Radom's labor camp employed about 6000 Jews. In 1943 the company paid the SS and *Polizeiführer* in the Radom Distrikt 1.60 Zlotys per worker per day. It extracted the revenue of the establishments in the Radom Distrikt.[11]

Globocnik, on the eve of his departure for Trieste, was therefore manager and director of a large European industrial conglomerate. And this on top of being a police chief and a mass murderer. He was an SS industrialist. There were, thankfully, few people like him. But of all those in the SS he was amongst the most powerful and most murderous and easily the wealthiest, as long as he was in favor with Himmler. In all likelihood only Oswald Pohl surpassed him in this regard. This financial side of Globocnik cannot be ignored, for one can be left with an image of just a killer and a population cleanser, whereas he was much more.

SS-Unterscharführer Fischer, who was given little time to carry out a liquidation audit on *Osti*, something similar to the request Globocnik received from Himmler with respect to *Aktion Reinhardt*, claimed he could not calculate how many machines and how much equipment had passed through the company's books. It is most unlikely that Fischer was actually expected to come up with anything resembling an accurate assessment. All that was sought was the actual formal liquidation. Fischer discovered, among other things, that Globocnik had purchased from Holland for his Lublin District establishments goods worth millions of *Reichsmarks*, thereby adding a multinational dimension to his otherwise secret wheeling and dealing.

XIV

Globocnik's Controversial
Lublin Love Affair

Odilo and Irmgard Before the
10 April 1942 Zakopane Note

Globocnik is believed to have had intimate sexual affairs with several women during his 46 months in Lublin, including with a Marianne Hillmann, who many appear to have maintained was half Jewish; a Frau Radischat; and a Frau Hamacher, who was a member of the *Bund Deutsche Mädel* (*BdM*), the Hitler women's movement. In addition, while in Lublin, he was involved in a complicated break-up with his longtime Klagenfurt sweetheart Grete Michner, whom he had planned to marry well before the outbreak of war, but had reneged. This prompted Grete's father, a longtime and hero of the teenaged Globocnik, and someone who had greatly assisted him, to go so far as to write and complain directly to Himmler about Globocnik. The change-of-mind cost Globocnik at least 15,000 *Reichsmarks*, probably more. Interestingly, the "buy-out" was put in place with the assistance of Globocnik's longtime party pal, Dr. Friedrich Rainer, who was at the time *Gauleiter* of Salzburg.

This is relevant because Globocnik's letter of 28 January 1941 to Himmler's then chief of personal staff, *SS-Gruppenführer* Karl Wolff, provides an insight into how seriously Globocnik took Himmler's involvement in his private or matrimonial affairs, and how concerned he was that Himmler thought properly of him, as if a stern father-son relationship existed. Globocnik's letter, which quotes extensively from a letter he had received from Rainer, says:

> Dear *Gruppenführer* Wolff!
> I have received the following letter from Friedrich Rainer:
> "The following I have written to Michner on 18.1.41.
> "Pg. Globocnik immediately agreed with me to contribute with reasonable limits to your financial relief. He could provide an amount which already has been once discussed, of 10,000RM right away.
> "The figures given by you exceed this amount considerably, although I cannot assume that you will want to state these amounts as claims because there does not seem to be a connection.
> "To complete that case satisfactorily clearly and finally I ask for information and if you would consider the amount of 10,000RM as sufficient or what amount you are considering, so that indemnification of your *Fraulein* daughter will be settled."
> Subsequently I received the following answer:
> "I confirm receipt of your esteemed writing from 18 of this month and notify that an amount of 15,999RM — that is about half of the liabilities resting on the property — seems appropriate to me. Attached are deposit slips for our postal savings bank account."
> I just happened to be in possession of the 15,000RM and paid them immediately. I ask you, *Gruppenführer*, to take note of this and hope that now the affair is finally settled, and that on the basis of this whole settlement the *Reichsführer* will be convinced that my action was correct and that I am not to be blamed for being objectionable.
> With hearty regards.
> And *Heil* Hitler!
> Odilo Globocnik.[1]

This issue had been in dispute since late 1939, for Himmler, in a letter to Rainer of 31 November that year, revealed that the angry Herr Michner had even written to Hitler's deputy, Rudolf Hess. Himmler had alerted Rainer of this and said that Globocnik ought to wind up the relationship properly. Also disclosed in Himmler's letter was the fact that Grete Michner had apparently behaved badly "towards Globocnik's mother who Globocnik is very fond of." What she had probably done was to tell Anna Globocnik precisely how she felt about her son's conduct toward her and his failure to marry, and probably went on to outline what this had cost her.

However, of all Globocnik's Lublin romantic affairs his most public liaison — the others in Lublin appear to have been if not clandestine then certainly rather discreet — was with Berlin-born Irmgard Rickheim, who, as stated earlier, had arrived in Lublin early in January 1940, coming as secretary to Hans Maubach, for whom she had briefly worked in the Reich Foreign

Office in Berlin after Maubach hired her from within youth leader Baldur von Schirach's *Hitler Jugend* headquarters.

But even this relationship did not result in marriage, for in early 1942 a letter was written to Heinrich Himmler in Berlin by an unknown person who claimed to be an *SS-Sturmbannführer*, complaining about Rickheim's conduct at an evening function in the southern Polish mountain resort town of Zakopane. This letter, or what can be called the Zakopane Note, and its consequences, will be considered in greater detail below.

Prior to the watershed Zakopane Note surfacing in Himmler's Berlin office, that is, the period between about June 1941 and April or May 1942, Rickheim's life with Globocnik was extremely comfortable, passionate, and loving, and certainly exceptionally privileged. Life as fiancée and lover in the police chief's Lublin mansion, materially speaking, was prosperous and idyllic, all that a woman and lover could ever dream about and hope for, in a material sense. There were at least three servants. Globocnik had the mansion completely refurbished, with extensive grey carpeting throughout and wooden paneling on the walls. One reason the remodeling was undertaken was that Globocnik saw his personal mansion as a transit residence that was likely to be fairly regularly used by none other than his great and powerful Berlin-based superior and mentor, Heinrich Himmler. The *Reichsführer-SS* had let his man in the East in on many very private secrets during their irregular discussions and contacts, and Himmler had especially alerted Globocnik of his eastern and racial aspirations. It was understandable, then, that Globocnik was set on making his Lublin home, which had more room than any single man may require, readily available. There Globocnik could have discovered first-hand what his leader thought and planned as they set out Germanizing the entire East over the coming expected victorious decades. When Himmler visited Globocnik in Lublin, secret servicemen first inspected the mansion meticulously to ensure no bombs had been placed inside so as to assassinate Himmler. The invasion of the Soviet Union meant many trips would be undertaken to the East, via Lublin, by the ever-active Himmler. Moreover, Lublin had been selected by Himmler to be propelled into becoming a major SS staging and supply post, for it was seen to be at the very western extremity of the East, an ideal launching pad. The conversations the two men held in the mansion were constantly prefixed throughout with each other's titles, Herr *Reichsführer* and Herr *Brigadeführer*, for rank was extremely important to both, says Rickheim. Discussions about non-Germans were prefixed throughout with terms like "the Jews" and "the Poles"—*Juden* and *Polen*—with both ethnic groups never receiving any positive regard.

Globocnik had access to fine foods and the best champagnes of Europe thanks to the commercial agencies of his growing business empire that extended beyond his district, with branches even in Western Europe, and especially, it seems, in Holland. Those working on the Reich's new eastern frontier — in the Lublin District — had to be provided with the best that Western Europe could offer. Alongside the mansion, against one side wall, a full-length enclosed single lane nine-pin bowling alley (*Kegel*) was constructed. This private bowling alley amounted to Globocnik copying Hitler, whose mountain residence in Obersalzberg, which Globocnik had visited, also had such a facility. Rickheim led the life so many Hollywood films have portrayed of a damsel in the ante-bellum Southern United States, but only more so. Moving from being a mere secretary stationed in Lublin to becoming Globocnik's fiancée was to move from an already relatively comfortable lifestyle to the

Irmgard Rickheim

standards of, say, a postwar Texas or Beverly Hills millionairess. Life in Lublin for her included parties and formal meals with senior SS men and their spouses; visits by leading SS figures from Berlin and other parts of the Reich, including Himmler at least once; regular horse riding excursions in the forests around Lublin; gardening; at least one trip to Austria, when she and Globocnik were chauffeur-driven in a Mercedes limousine, first to Salzburg to meet his longtime party pal *Gauleiter* Friedrich Rainer, and then on to Klagenfurt to meet her future mother-in-law, the dogged little white-haired Anna Globocnik. Just to sit in a Mercedes for most women of her age and at this time would have been a breathtaking experience. One memorable horse ride she recalled was made in the company of Globocnik, near, in all probability, the Lipowa work camp, that eventually held some 3,000 Jewish craftsmen and other workers. On the day that she and Globocnik rode by this camp, one of its Jewish workers confronted the *SS-Brigadeführer* on horseback, demanding that Globocnik shoot him, there and then! This man was angry, very angry, and repeated over and over, in a raised voice, his demand that he be shot, there and then. This never to be known and incredibly brave, or foolhardy, Jew was not shot, not there and then, anyway, but one can image the embarrassment of such an encounter in front of one's fiancée.

Brief trips to holiday resorts like Zakopane were also not out of the question. Even when Rickheim was later temporarily ensconced nearby, in a village

Hermann Höfle and Irmgard Rickheim during one of Globocnik's lavish Lublin parties, probably late 1941.

called Sobieszyn, where Globocnik had dispatched her in secret after the mysterious Zakopane Note surfaced, she lived in a mansion and had her horse and dog with her. She spent her Sobieszyn days riding in forest settings alongside the river and the region's massive manmade fish ponds, as well as simply relaxing, with boredom probably being her main problem. The time was, it should be remembered, the very height of the war in the East, when tens of thousands of Soviet troops were dying and as many Germans were being killed or maimed. This was, therefore, a far more preferable fate to that which many millions of other Germans were undergoing at this time, especially those living in the Ruhr and Berlin, which by now were accessible to Great Britain's Bomber Command. While in Sobieszyn, Globocnik visited her at least twice, with one of these get-togethers occurring at the same time as her mother was present, having come from Berlin.

Millions of German and Austrian girls would probably have given anything to experience the life Rickheim was leading in Lublin prior to the Zakopane Note of April 1942. She had moved into Globocnik's Lublin mansion in the summer of 1941, after his longtime Carinthian friend, *SS-Hauptsturmführer* Reinhold von Mohrenschildt, who dealt with *RKFDV* matters of demography and resettlement, had left to undertake duties unknown. An added advantage was that she ceased working. The Globocnik household was

Irmgard Rickheim standing between the horses she and Globocnik owned.

situated at the western end of Lublin's German or Police Quarter, Wieniawska Street or *Ostlandstrasse*. It was a two-story structure with large windows, and the roof at the rear was held up by large rectangular columns. During the day a single unarmed sentry stood on watch, but the mansion remained unguarded otherwise. On the same street was a nearby cavalry station.

The large and refurbished mansion tended to double as an office, since Globocnik's work-style was often to remain at home. He called staffers if he needed work done, and would dictate to his secretary, Mimi Trsek, in his residence. Trsek came over from the nearby office both during the day and sometimes in the evening. It was also the venue for senior officers going to and coming from the Eastern Front, who regularly stopped in. Meetings with senior staffers were also regularly held there, so it was probably the venue for some of Globocnik's most notorious orders, but which of his decisions we cannot know. It was also the site of his monthly staff parties where champagne flowed, literally freely. Those attending these extravaganzas, which were held on the ground floor in the main or great hall, first viewed a film, usually the latest brought in from Berlin. A screen was lowered, lights were turned off, and after the film it was time to party along. The great hall held a huge conference table, a large record player with a collection of Wagner discs, and a three-legged grand piano. The upstairs or first floor level had two smaller rooms, one of which Globocnik used by as a breakfast dining room beside his large bedroom. The second had been lived in by von Mohrenschildt, and later Rickheim used it for her belongings.

Two female servants and one male ensured the household functioned smoothly. Rickheim said both these women were Poles, though one may have been a *Volksdeutsche*, for she spoke German. Her given name was Charlotte, but she was called Lota. Globocnik also had a batman who took care of his clothes and other needs, including waking him at the given hour each morning. Lota and her assistant were in charge of the kitchen and household cleaning. Both women, according to Rickheim, seemed to like Globocnik. His batman was an SS man. Rickheim had access to or assistance from a Jewish seamstress, who came to the mansion to make her dresses and to take care of similar needs. She went shopping in downtown Lublin. Security or personal safety in the town was not a problem.

Rickheim recalls only one meeting with Himmler, during which she dined with the *Reichsführer*. She believes it was in September 1941, meaning she never met him during his crucial whirlwind July 1941 Lublin-Zamosc visit when he gave the all-clear for Lublin to be developed into an SS eastern outpost, and for the Zamosc Lands clearance and Germanization. At the end of that meal, Himmler ordered some carrots, almost as an afterthought. A servant went to the kitchen and soon after returned with a finely grated carrot on a small plate. Himmler reacted to this in a downright rude and ungrateful manner by scolding the servant for not bringing out peeled carrot sticks, which is what he preferred and had wanted in this case. Rather than simply explaining this to the servant, he instead created quite a scene, objecting, and making a general nuisance of himself, and thereby embarrassing all present. Rickheim insists that her very private view of Himmler even then was that he was a decidedly unimpressive individual, moody, pompous, and opinionated. But it was this man who had such an obvious overall grip over her fiancé and lover, and that was that. In this her position was like that of many employees whose employer or boss is disliked by a spouse, but the couple tolerate the situation to the point of inviting the disliked individual to their home for purely careerist reasons. The one difference in this case was that Globocnik at no stage ever expressed a critical word to her about his *Reichsführer*. Rickheim has also pointed out that Globocnik did not keep a personal diary, so if he had personal views on Himmler and others he did not write them down.

Globocnik's life and predisposition were not always serious-minded. Rickheim says that despite his historic record as one of the worst mass murderers of the 20th century, he nevertheless had a funny or cheeky side. An incident she recounted demonstrated this well. One day while speaking on the telephone to *SS-Gruppenführer* Friedrich-Wilhelm Kruger in Krakow, Globocnik was lying on the floor, with telephone receiver in hand. The conversation had its fair share of "*Jawohl's*" and "*Ja's*." But as he uttered each of these, Globocnik lying on the floor with his right leg with boot on pointing skywards, would move the foot at an angle, somewhat like a submarine periscope in unison with his replies. Thus he was bantering around with his immediate nominal superior, without Kruger realizing it, of course.

Globocnik also enjoyed a drink. He was somewhat overweight. He was not a flashy dresser. He had fetishes like retaining one old SS cap, even though it was very worn and battered. And he assured Rickheim: "*If it was not for this war then I would remove my SS jacket and hang it permanently on a nail on the wall.*" Perhaps this comment was not entirely untrue when one realizes that he was very much Himmler's man, a toady. Globocnik often claimed to her that he would have preferred being an engineer working in the Klagenfurt region, building bridges and other such mountain structures. This suggests he was something of a romantic with respect to his past, for when he was actually undertaking such work he let it, if not lapse, then at least take a back seat to his ongoing devious conspiratorial political work for the NSDAP, which was not only an illegal party then but linked to a foreign power, Germany, so he was increasingly treasonous. It is difficult to believe that Globocnik would have been content with living and working in out-of-the-way parts of Carinthia for the rest of his life.

Odilo and Irmgard After the 10 April 1942 Zakopane Note to Himmler

Because the Globocnik-Rickheim liaison was so unusually public, it may have become a target for a devious behind-the-scenes onslaught via what is probably best referred to simply as the Zakopane Note, an anonymous hate letter sent to Heinrich Himmler in Berlin.

Rickheim left Lublin permanently toward the end of 1942, probably in October, nearly a year before Globocnik's crowded convoy headed south for

Trieste with his *Aktion Reinhardt* killing team and most other staffers. But her farewell came only after she had spent some time, probably a couple of months, in relative isolation at Sobieszyn, a tiny and unusual Polish village some 60 kilometers northeast of Lublin, on the northern banks of the Wieprz River, just 12 kilometers from where it flows into the Vistula, roughly midway between Warsaw and Lublin. Globocnik had secretly placed her there under the care of an SS man named Hilse, a onetime farmer in the Reich who was in charge of an SS-commandeered mansion. Hilse was living in the manor house with his wife and young son.[2] It is likely that Globocnik arranged the move of his fiancée to a remote village through his rural business enterprises administrator, *SS-Sturmbannführer* Dunkel, who was in charge of all SS estates across Lublin District. He was responsible for the first genera-

Odilo Globocnik and Irmgard Rickheim near Lublin in 1941. This is the only known photograph of the two together.

tion of smaller so-called SS and police strongpoints that were designed to ensure a creeping trend of Germanization across the district, through settlement of German farmers. This type of Germanization had preceded the post-28 November 1942 large-scale settling of *Volksdeutsche* peasant farmers upon the Zamosc Lands, across southern Lublin District, that was accompanied by the uprooting of some 110,000 ethnic Polish peasant farmers and their families. Creating SS and police strongpoints on manors was certainly far easier, for it only required removal of a single Polish or Jewish owner and perhaps a few rural workers, and in the process acquiring relatively large tracts of land. Moreover, it did not spark a region-wide guerrilla war as the Zamosc Lands expulsion did, an outcome that led to Globocnik's removal from Lublin.

Globocnik's decision to dispatch secretly his lover to Sobieszyn village is interesting, and probably occurred in May 1942. The timing is probably fully explained by the fact that he was now under the gaze of his Berlin superior, Himmler. But there may be another reason. By then he was already in full murderous flight, killing a major portion of European Jewry. According to Alexander Donat, he was officially appointed head of *Aktion Reinhardt* late in April, at about the time that the Zakopane Note reached Himmler in Berlin.[3] Was his preoccupation with this mass crime perhaps the main reason for Rickheim being clandestinely dispatched out of Lublin to an out-of-the-way Polish village?

Sobieszyn was surrounded by exquisite larch forests and a huge network of large manmade ponds that had been used for carp breeding since 1926. For centuries this village and surrounding lands were owned either by the eminent Polish Sobieski, Zbaski, or Tarnowski families, with the Sobieskis selling out in 1648. Ironically, Poland's famous King Jan III Sobieski (1629–96) had played a critical role in ensuring that Austria's capital of Vienna did not undergo the same fate as Christian Constantinople had in 1458, being conquered and occupied by the Ottomans. Sobieski had dispatched his famous Polish cavalry units just in time to engage the southern Ottoman invaders on that city's outskirts in 1683. Now, 260 years later, in the early 1940s, a group of predominantly Austrian — Viennese and Carinthians mainly — occupiers ensconced in nearby Lublin were treating Poles far worse than the Turks had generally treated so-called infidels, by planning their expulsion into the vast wastelands of Western Siberia.

In the mid–1800s a large part of Sobieszyn's environs came under the control of August Kicki, and at the turn of the 19th and 20th centuries, during Poland's Russian Partition, it emerged as a significant agricultural educational and research center. In 1892, Antoni Sempolowski (1847–1936), an agronomist and a pioneer seed cultivation expert, established the Sobieszyn Agricultural Experimental Station. Prior to that he had been based in the Poznan region, which had fallen under the Prussian Partition. Subsequently an agricultural college specializing in development of seeds and plants was established. It was financed by a foundation created by the little-known civic-minded Polish philanthropist, Kajetan Jan Kanty Kicki (1803–78), son of August. This unusual village included a large estate with a small classical palace or mansion, built by the Tarnowskis in the early 1800s, and which had been extended by Kicki under the supervision of the Warsaw architect, Henryk Marconi. It was in this palatial residence that Rickheim was hidden out by Globocnik and Dunkel for several months.[4] evidence exists showing that a group of *Volksdeutsche* farmers from the Chelm region, most of whom were later removed from their homes by Globocnik and von Mohrenschildt to consolidate and strengthen German numbers in western Poland, had visited Sobieszyn during the early months of the war, probably on an educational or fact-finding excursion. Prior to Rickheim's arrival in the spring, in May or perhaps June of 1942, the palace was the residence of the Hilse family. Rickheim recalls her time there with her most vivid memory being the huge man-made carp lakes that had been constructed between the palace and Wieprz River after 1926.

After about eight or nine months of engagement, Rickheim had the misfortune of traveling, over a part of February and March 1942, when Globocnik was about to officially launch *Aktion Reinhardt*, to Poland's premier mountain ski resort town of Zakopane. Vladimir Lenin and his wife Nadhezda Krupskaya had lived there before the outbreak of the Great War, and the great Polish English-language writer Joseph Conrad had briefly lived there in 1914, just after that war broke out, before he was able to return to England through American diplomatic endeavors with the Habsburg Government in Vienna.

During World War II Zakopane had been transformed into a major German military rest and convalescence center for troops wounded on the Eastern Front. While there, Rickheim attended an evening sing-along gathering in a tavern or café, and was apparently observed by an unknown person who may have been working on behalf of a personal enemy of Globocnik, or who was in the pay of such an enemy. The culprit may have been Anna Globocnik or Mimi Trsek. Rickheim continues to believe that Globocnik's secretary, Mimi Trsek, who was also born in 1920, probably had a crush on Globocnik. Documentation of this point is unlikely ever to surface. Then again, the ill-disposed clandestine Zakopane observer of Rickheim may have been acting alone, with no contact with anyone in Lublin, or Berlin, for that matter.

Irmgard Rickheim with husky in Zakopane, February or March 1942.

For whatever reason, within two months of Rickheim's Zakopane sojourn, a letter carrying an indecipherable signature reached Himmler's Berlin office. It told of Rickheim's allegedly unacceptable but unspecified behavior at that very public evening's gathering while in the presence of a chaperone and Globocnik's niece. It is because a Globocnik-arranged chaperone and his niece were present at the very table in question that the allegations are difficult to believe even today. But despite that, all the evidence seems to point to Himmler believing the opposite.

Over the coming months this letter sparked a substantial number of inter-office memos, written in Berlin, and letters between Lublin and Berlin, with Rickheim herself eventually writing directly to the *Reichsführer-SS* from her new Berlin address, for, by late 1942, she was working in Dr. Josef Goebbels' Propaganda Ministry as a secretary to a Berlin radio news reader. In her letter she proclaimed complete innocence of whatever it was she was alleged to have done—"very bad manners in a public house and flirted"—during that February or March Zakopane evening in the presence of a chaperone and Globocnik's niece. Her misbehavior was never specified beyond those words. The worst one can say of her allegedly bad manners and flirting was that she perhaps spoke bluntly to a male party goer at an adjacent table and that had therefore upset him, or, and she denies this to this day, she may have kissed a wounded soldier or an airman on the cheek, or briefly put her arm around his neck or shoulder in sympathy and friendship. However, at the time she was suffering from dermatitis, so may have been quick-tempered or easily irritated, and someone, understandably, may have become quite upset at a young woman being offhanded or abrupt. However, she also denies having behaved in such a manner.

Globocnik had arranged for the Lublin-based German nurse, Emilie Thomas, to chaperone his fiancée to Zakopane. Thomas was certainly present at the controversial evening's function, for she was sitting at the same table as Rickheim. Thomas and Rickheim were not friends in Lublin, but Thomas subsequently prepared a written statement that she sent to Johannes Müller, Lublin's *Sipo-SD* chief, backing up Rickheim's claims of innocence and her version of events. Rickheim sent a copy of that statement to Himmler with her own letter of 25 November 1942. But no amount of pleading by either woman was about to ameliorate matters for Rickheim. The alleged incident certainly seems more bizarre because Globocnik's niece, Henny, then a 16-year-old, had accompanied both women and was actually present at the fateful evening's partying. But no evidence exists to suggest she in any way prompted any anonymous accusations.

There is, of course, the possibility that Globocnik's mother, Anna, and his trusted Viennese private secretary, Mimi Trsek, were involved clandestinely. Both women were on good terms in Lublin and both, Rickheim said, did not seem to like her. Trsek was a regular evening visitor to Anna Globocnik's home in Lublin, Rickheim said. This meant that Rickheim might have been up against not one but two separate and powerful alliances: Himmler and his personal assistant Dr. Rudolf Brandt, and Anna Globocnik and Mimi Trsek. Each appears to have felt strongly that the powerful 37-year-old SS man from Klagenfurt had chosen badly. An additional factor that was perhaps also not insignificant in relation to the Globocnik/Trsek alliance was that there existed an ongoing underlying rivalry between northern Germans and Austrians, a southern Germanic people. And here was Globocnik, a Germanized Slovene, choosing a German, not an Austrian *Fraulein*, to be his bride!

Rickheim was born in Berlin on 8 December 1920. She was one of two daughters, with her elder sister dying in 1936. Her mother, a beautician, had remarried during the war. The first Himmler heard of her was in a telegram from Globocnik dated 5 July 1941, in which the *Reichsführer-SS* was told the couple had been engaged and that Globocnik sought his permission to marry her. Lerch had been asked by Globocnik to approach the then 20-year-old Berliner to ask if she would agree to a marriage proposal. She indicated to Lerch that she would do so, and soon after, she and Globocnik went horse riding near Lublin and he put his case for marriage to her. Marriage was next raised some evenings later when the couple was in Hans Maubach's home for a social gathering. Globocnik waited for a moment of silence and then said: "Standby for an important announcement! Standby for an important announcement!" These words were identical to those used by Radio Berlin announcers whenever a major statement or warning was made across the Reich's airwaves and the airwaves of occupied lands; Globocnik had borrowed them for extra dramatic effect. He continued by saying that he and Miss Rickheim wished to announce their engagement. When asked about her extraordinary liaison some 57 years later Rickheim wrote:

> I just would like you to know that I was 19 years old when the war started and I was in Lublin with my employer from January 1940 until spring of 1942. During that time I had met the staff of Odilo Globocnik and him also. As a young girl I was not interested in O.G. since he was 16 years older than I was at that time. Mr. E. Lerch, who was his adjutant, arranged that O.G. approach me one day to ask for an engagement. I was flattered because some older girls from Austria were eager to get close to him. There was a lady from Austria who hated me; her name was Mimi Trsek. It could have been she who wrote some hate mail. I just don't know. Mimi Trsek also had O.G. mother on her side and both did not approve of my engagement with O.G.[5]

The Anna Globocnik/Trsek encounter took on significance from late 1941, when Anna was living in Lublin for an extended period, certainly until March or April 1942, but perhaps much longer. Anna was accompanied by her daughter, Erika, and Anna's 16-year-old granddaughter, Henny, who was the daughter of Anna's eldest daughter, Lidia Pomerantz, who had remained in Austria. Erika, who was married to a Baron with the added title of "von," also took her baby daughter, also called Erika, to Lublin. These relatives all lived just across the road from Odilo's mansion in which his fiancée was also living. Globocnik, from mid–1941, when he was about to launch *Aktion Reinhardt*, was therefore preparing to marry, and his white-haired diminutive but formidable Carinthian or part-German and part-Hungarian mother was living close by, in Hans and Charlotte Maubach's former house. His Viennese secretary, who got along well with Anna Globocnik, was also not well disposed toward the Berlin-born spouse-to-be. The situation so deteriorated that Rickheim even wrote a letter to Anna Globocnik pointing out that it was her son who had made the marriage proposal, not the other way around. Trsek, having been Globocnik's private secretary by the winter of 1941, had nearly two years experience in her Lublin secretarial job working for the district's top SS man and policeman, so she certainly had a complete understanding of preparing correspondence to Himmler, specifically, how it was to be addressed and the like, and she is likely to have also had an appreciation of Himmler's hard and fast opinions on womanhood and motherhood. Trsek undoubtedly also understood Brandt's role in such delicate matters. We do not know how well Brandt and Trsek got along. Jealousy, with the prompting of the mother of her employer, is certainly an understandable motive to move against the Berliner, who may have been seen to be socially climbing beyond her station by seeking to marry an *SS-Brigadeführer*. Rickheim certainly did not hail from a socially pedigreed Berlin family. If Rickheim's denials of bad manners are to be believed, then someone with sinister motives existed. But who it was is unlikely ever to be known.

Had Rickheim and Globocnik married, and had the Reich conquered the Soviet Union, as it had Poland in 1939 and so many other countries shortly after, then Rickheim stood to be the equivalent of an SS princess, eventually probably living in a huge and well-defended manor house somewhere in central Ukraine or western Russia, from where her SS husband would have issued orders for the construction of additional expanding SS and police strongpoints and other Germanic settlement projects, while he was planning and initiating more major regional population or ethnic cleansing actions along the lines of those on the Zamosc Lands. Globocnik would, in all likelihood, have been selected by Himmler to take permanent charge of the planned 36 SS and police strongpoints that were to be created across Russia, Belarus, Ukraine, the General Gouvernement, and even into the Caucuses, an integral part of *Generalplan Ost*. Seen from this materialistic perspective, Odilo Globocnik was most certainly worth catching. There would have been the occasional holidays or return trips to Berlin, and rest and recreation on the Black Sea or other exclusive SS-controlled and owned resorts, perhaps even

Zakopane, again. There would have been servants, banquets, and other lavish living. All this was preferable to being a secretary in Lublin.

Another interesting and noteworthy point is that Himmler had not, by early 1942, received a full racial reckoning or ancestry certification from Rickheim, the so-called *Ahnentafel*. This was something only people close to the couple or to Globocnik, and a few in the higher echelons of the SS in Berlin, could possibly have known about. Knowing this and understanding its significance would have been valuable information for someone wishing to thwart Globocnik's marriage intentions. Himmler and Brandt were certainly aware of it. Was anyone else? All SS men were expected to come forth with an *Ahnentafel* of their spouses before marriage was permitted. Failure to do so would have meant Himmler regarded Rickheim as not having met all the necessary racial requirements, so this would have made her suspect. Did she perhaps have Jewish blood flowing in her veins? This is not as outrageous a question as it may seem today, for Rickheim has since revealed that while making inquiries for her *Ahnentafel*, she discovered that her maternal great grandmother had the given name Rebecca, not a common German name, but one often ascribed by Jews to their daughters. Moreover, she had asked her mother about this surprise discovery; her mother said she knew absolutely nothing about Rebecca. Was the long-dead Rebecca Jewish? Rickheim said Himmler, in 1941, probably in July, had told her while dining in Globocnik's Lublin mansion that he wished to see her *Ahnentafel*, so it was in all likelihood something very much at the forefront of his mind whenever thinking of Globocnik and his unexpected marriage plans. Rickheim in her eighties still said that Himmler appeared to be somewhat hesitant about her because of her age — 16 years Globocnik's junior — and that she was not a senior person in the SS or the party structure, like the woman Globocnik later married, in October 1944, Lore Peterschinegg, who headed the Carinthian *Bund Deutsche Mädel*.[6] That wedding, not surprisingly, was a major social event in that wartime Austrian province, and one that Himmler approved. He even sent Globocnik a fine set of silver cutlery as a wedding gift. In addition, Globocnik had told Rickheim, in strict and loving confidence, that Himmler had earlier hinted to him, quite broadly, that perhaps he ought eventually to marry Germany's 1936 gold medal-winning Olympic discus thrower, Gisela Mauermayer, with whom Himmler appears to have had a strange fascination. Mauermayer's successful sporting career extended through to 1942, the year of Rickheim's marital woes, when she was still throwing the discus. In the early 1930s she was also a shot putter. Clearly a Globocnik and an Olympian liaison seemed to have appealed to Himmler far more than the one Globocnik had himself established; some of the scenes surrounding this whole imbroglio, both in Lublin and Berlin, had Shakespearean if not Gilbertian qualities. Himmler's private suggestion of Mauermayer as a possible bride would appear to indicate that he took a remarkably keen interest in Globocnik's welfare, and in a manner than extended far beyond merely having his top Lublin SS man under his thumb. Himmler was in all likelihood interested in offspring. The desire to see Globocnik linked matrimonially to Mauermayer may have been the origin of Rickheim's eventual problems that blocked her intended marriage to Globocnik, beginning so dramatically with the Zakopane Note in early 1942. Also, Himmler was aware of Globocnik's dashed liaison with the hapless Grete Michner, so probably had some firm views about his man's future.

In addition, it is worth noting that Himmler's views on various subjects beyond his obsessions with mass eastern rural settlement by Germanic peoples and Jews have been the subject of some inquiry. One such study has focused on Himmler's diaries from the years 1914–1916, 1919, and 1921, with entries for some months even in 1922 and 1924. All were found in 1945 by "an American intelligence officer stationed in Bavaria" who obtained them from a G.I. "who had found them while searching for souvenirs in Himmler's village at Gmund on the Tegernsee."[7] In the late 1950s, two scholars analyzed the diaries and concluded *inter alia* that Himmler held quite firm views about womanhood and the role of women in society and the family.

> Himmler's rigid convictions concerning sex sometimes appear as outright prudery. Twice, upon visiting art exhibitions, he was unfavorably impressed by works which struck him as indecent, and on another occasion the sight of a naked girl called forth this complaint: "Irmgard leaped out in the nude before going to bed. I do not approve of this at the age of three when one should teach the child modesty."[8]

Is the name Irmgard purely coincidental in this case? The authors went on to conclude that Himmler liked women but tended to adhere to rigid and stereotyped views of them and was rather patronizing in his outlook toward women during the years 1914–21. This was some two decades before one of his favorite and most important SS-men in the field had become romantically involved with a woman also named Irmgard, of whom the *Reichsführer* apparently did not entirely approve, if for no other reason than her age. She was, after all, living with her fiancé, and they were not yet married! To someone who retained a streak of "outright prudery," this arrangement would not have been acceptable. The diaries also reveal that when Himmler was 21 years old, he wrote a "formulation of his view of women," and he appears to have retained this outlook into 1942:

> A woman is loved by a man on three levels: as a dear child who has to be chided, perhaps even punished on account of her unreasonableness, and who is protected and taken care of just because she is tender and weak and because one loves her. Then as wife and a loyal, understandable comrade who fights life's battles alongside (the man), and stands everywhere by his side without hemming

in and fettering the man and his mind. And as goddess whose feet he must kiss, who gives him strength through her feminine wisdom and childlike, pure sanctity (which) does not weaken during the hardest struggles and bestows upon him in ideal hours the soul's most divine gift [*der Seele Gottlichstes*).[9]

When these personal and strangely idealistic lines are read alongside Himmler's letter of 30 August 1942 (see below) to Globocnik about Irmgard Rickheim, it is difficult not to conclude that this 24 November 1921 diary entry could easily have been penned in August 1941, or August 1942, for that matter. Even though the two sets of writings are separated by more than two decades, they have an uncanny similarity. Is it being fanciful to believe that perhaps Himmler initiated the sordid little behind-the-scenes campaign — the Zakopane Note — to demonize Rickheim, so she could be discretely removed from Lublin, as indeed she was? Hardly. Himmler, forever the conspirator and the dabbler, had many outrageous ideas, including especially toward Jews and Slavs. With respect to the former, how could one forget that he arranged to have them murdered by the millions, by none other than Globocnik? The Slavs, especially Poles, he arranged to have murdered by the tens of thousands, and had expelled about a million of them from their homes out of western Poland and the Zamosc Lands, with many of the crimes against Poles also perpetrated by Globocnik. That unenviable record, in light of his 30 August letter and 24 November 1921 diary entry, makes Himmler a suspect as the initiator of Irmgard Rickheim's Lublin troubles. Of one thing we can be certain: Globocnik, in early 1942, was crucially important to Himmler. Whether that importance extended to Himmler intruding deeper into his personal and sexual affairs, we do not know, but it is not out of the question.

Because there are so many unknown and unexplained aspects and other likely explanations associated with the Zakopane Note, that so dramatically terminated Rickheim's rise to prominence and perhaps even fame, it is impossible to be certain of the various likely machinations involved in Rickheim's fall. These intrigues are even more extraordinary when one realizes that the Lublin SS machinery of policing and suppression headed by Globocnik at precisely this time had been geared up for a massive genocide of Jews and shortly afterwards a pioneering population cleansing action directed at Polish peasants living upon the Zamosc Lands. Yet here were some of the main players of Nazidom, including Himmler and Dr. Brandt, men who literally held sway over millions of lives, dabbling in someone's private life. The matter would rightly be considered hilarious if it were not for its immense gravity. Never to be discounted, although again it can never be proved, is that a key player behind the scenes may have been the ever-present Ernst Lerch, though Rickheim does not believe this. After all, it was he who played the pivotal role in bringing Rickheim and Globocnik together, at the latter's request. He had entered her quarters and outlined what he had discussed in great privacy with Odilo. Maybe, for whatever, reason, Lerch, the constant and apparent servant, had decided, alone or with others, that Rickheim was not the woman for his nominal boss. Lerch's secret links with Berlin have never been investigated or explained, and, like some other details concerning Globocnik, are unlikely ever to be known.

The Zakopane Note surfaced on Himmler's desk in Berlin soon after 10 April 1942, when it was allegedly written with its indecipherable signature, claiming Rickheim's bad behavior. Seven months later, on 25 November, Rickheim wrote to Himmler from Berlin denying the note's allegations, and asking for the identity of the anonymous person who had made such a claim, something she would never receive. Furthermore, a series of letters in Globocnik's SS file show him to be what can only be described as most uncertain of himself and a complete underling. There is also a difficult-to-explain belated claim by Globocnik in a letter of 29 December 1942 to Dr. Brandt that an SS man had told his 16-year-old niece, Henny, in Zakopane, that he intended complaining to Himmler about Rickheim, something supported neither by Rickheim nor Thomas. The precise origin of this later claim is also impossible to determine. Moreover, a brief letter to Globocnik from Dr. Brandt, dated 19 December 1942, almost 10 months after the alleged incident came to notice, refers to the accuser, a *Sturmbannführer,* perhaps having been located. If that was in fact the case, then no evidence exists suggesting that he was interviewed. And Rickheim was certainly never told of this. Globocnik had raised his niece's belated claim after Rickheim had left Lublin to live in Berlin, in an apartment Globocnik had arranged, and by then the engagement was truly finished. Globocnik, by then, had obviously decided to lean toward what he believed was no doubt Himmler's preference, irrespective of his feelings toward Rickheim; career came ahead of his love. Although it is almost impossible to feel sympathy for a man who was directly responsible for so many murders, he undoubtedly deserves at least some pity. Here at last the full consequences of his years of obsequiousness toward Himmler were bearing bitter fruit.

By mid–1942, when Rickheim was in Sobieszyn, Globocnik's fate was irrevocably tied to the fate of Himmler. Their three "terminal stations" were venues of mass killings of Jews, and they were about to launch the cleansing of the Zamosc Lands as a first step in completely Germanizing Poland. Globocnik had come a long way since the *Anschluss,* in the spring of 1938, but always with Himmler's help and backing. He had been more or less honorably extricated from Vienna in January 1939, after which Himmler had defended him from a formidable onslaught by party treasurer Franz Xaver Schwartz, and that man's dogged and no doubt competent band of auditors; and he had been elevated to a high SS post in occupied Poland, all this by and due to Himmler. If the clash with Schwartz had turned out differently, Globocnik may have faced trial and perhaps a death sentence. For all this he had ruthlessly persecuted and crushed the more than two million Poles and some 250,000 Jews of his Lublin District; he had bitterly fought Governor General Dr. Frank and his delegate in Lublin, Ernst Zörner; and he was now murdering hundreds of thousands of Jews within his Bug Killing Centers and planning a major expulsion action against the Poles within the Zamosc Lands. Globocnik literally had nowhere to go except in the same murderous direction as Himmler. It is, in fact, little wonder that he had a mental breakdown in May 1943. What is surprising is that this breakdown had not come earlier. If Himmler (and Dr. Rudolf Brandt) disapproved of his marriage intentions, his choice of partner, then Globocnik could hardly openly disagree with them on that issue. It was simply politic to go along with his determined master's wishes, no matter how tangentially they were conveyed and no matter what his own feelings. Globocnik was a puppet, a kept man, despite the SS uniform that terrified so many, the stern look under that peaked cap, and all the other paraphernalia of that order.

Irrespective of all this, the one thing one can state with confidence is that if the Rickheim matter had reached a court of law in a nation where the rule of law and the rules of evidence prevailed, the accusations against her would never have stood up, if for no other reason than that the accuser would not only have been absent from proceedings but could not even be identified or found. Nevertheless, the most significant letters and memos pertaining to the Zakopane incident are worth reading, since they give insight into both Himmler and Globocnik, the two most important figures in relation to Lublin District and the East, though on an issue that is quite unrelated to the expulsion of Poles and the Jewish genocide. Nothing in these letters, or any others available, suggests involvement by Anna Globocnik or Mimi Trsek, or Himmler. Nor, for that matter, did the mystery accuser actually state precisely what it was that Rickheim's alleged misbehavior involved. The whole affair appears to have the makings of a concocted uproar, but one that grew to unbelievable, indeed bizarre and Byzantine, proportions. Whatever the truth of the matter, it tells us much about Himmler, his office, and his murderous Lublin weakling, Odilo Globocnik. Another man would have cast the whole trivial matter aside. After all, whose fiancée or wife, has not, at some stage, been curt to a stranger, and a stranger that may well have been rude or too forward anyway? And it is difficult to believe Rickheim had flirted in public, before the eyes of her Globocnik-appointed chaperone and his teenage niece. Globocnik, after Himmler's, Brandt's, and perhaps his mother's involvement, chose instead to cast aside the woman he had so passionately loved. It should be noted, however, that he met Rickheim in the presence of Rickheim's mother and stepfather in Berlin some time late in 1942, when he invited them all to an evening dinner, and this despite the fact that he had advised his Berlin superior in December that the engagement was over, something he never told Rickheim. She seems to have naively believed for some time afterwards, probably into early 1943, that even though they were apart — she in Berlin and he in Lublin — the engagement was perhaps still in effect. Globocnik had, however, arranged a Berlin apartment for her, a rare and difficult thing to do for a single person during wartime conditions, indicating some compassion and concern for a former lover. He had arranged for the apartment to be well furnished, and he had her chauffeured to Berlin by one of his trusted staffers, Max Cichotski (Runhof). Furthermore, he had arranged a secretarial position for her in Göbbels' Propaganda Ministry, as secretary to a radio newsreader, where she remained until after the defeat of besieged Berlin and thus the defeat of the Reich.

The historical significance of Globocnik's controversial love affair is related neither to the long list of potential suspects nor to Rickheim. It is, rather, that this correspondence commenced shortly after the Jewish Holocaust had begun, with Globocnik's three killing centers fully operational, and as planning for the Zamosc Lands expulsion actions was being finalized. That Globocnik, Himmler, Dr. Rudolf Brandt, and obviously many others, including Johannes Müller, both in Berlin and Lublin, were involved in what essentially seems to be nothing more than a petty brouhaha and without an identified accuser but with accusations obviously taken seriously reveals much about these perpetrators of one of the gravest crimes of the 20th century.

The Zakopane Note and Subsequent Correspondence[10]

The Zakopane Note

Berlin 10 April 1942. (Find out who the sender is).*

Reichsführer!

Some weeks ago I had the opportunity, during my stay in Zakopane, to meet the fiancée of the SS Leader of Lublin in a local tavern.

There was intolerable behavior by some guests on the table next to ours, which was occupied by some Air Force officer, and this included that of a girl who was with another lady and a young girl and some Air Force sergeants. However, I later discovered that she was the fiancée of *SS-Brigadeführer* Globotschnik [sic] who had the very bad manners in a public house and flirted. There was also the manner she had dressed and many guests took note and found it quite terrible.

Reichsführer. I know of the SS Police Leader of Lublin as a most able man, a great idealist and a valued person, and only purely in comradeship would I advise you of such standards of behavior, which in public created an impression that serves to undermine the entire SS and should be forbidden of anyone engaged to so high an SS leader.

SS-Sturmbannführer.

(Indecipherable signature).

* The words "Find out who the sender is" are a handwritten comment at the top of the letter in German.

Rickheim protests her innocence to Himmler and asks for her accuser's identity.

Irmgard Rickheim, Berlin. 25 November 1942. W8 Mauerstrasse 45. III Floor. 0.87.

Reichsführer!

I had the great honor and good fortune to be presented to you personally by my fiancé *SS-Gruppenführer* Globocnik in Lublin, during your September 1941 visit. I write today therefore to give you my full trust and ask you to assist me. Through my fiancé I've heard of a letter, which was addressed to you, *Reichsführer*, in which my honor was attacked in the lowest possible manner. This letter, whose writer remains unknown to me to this day, was sent in July of this year and is related to a farewell evening for wounded SS-personnel in the German Home in Zakopane during February/March of this year. I attended that evening on the invitation of a Captain of the Air Force together with a nursing sister, Emilie Thomas, who nurses in the Central Hospital of the SS in Lublin, as well as Henny Pomerantz, who is the niece of my fiancé. A copy of the happenings of this evening by Sister Emilie Thomas has been given to the commander of the *SD* in Lublin. I enclose it for your information. I attempted, through the commander of the *Sipo-SD* in Lublin, *SS-Obersturmbannführer* Müller, to obtain the address of the person who had sent that letter. I only know that he was a *Sturmbannführer* but it has been impossible for me to learn more. All my attempts until now have been in vain so the only thing I am able to now do is to approach you *Reichsführer*. I ask you now *Reichsführer* to give me the name of the writer. I have waited a long time and ask you *Reichsführer* to believe me that I would not have dared to take your time if I could envisage another possible way. *Reichsführer*, as a German girl and the fiancée of an SS-leader, I have to try with all my power to get myself rehabilitated and ask you *Reichsführer* to give me the name of the man so I can speak with him if that is at all possible.

Heil Hitler, Irmgard Rickheim.

An internal memo to the Chief of the SS-Personnel Department, *SS-Obergruppenführer* Schmitt from Dr. Rudolf Brandt

Dear O/gf.

Would it be possible to find out who the *SS-Sturmbannführer* who wrote the enclosed letter on 10 April 1942, addressed to the *Reichsführer*-SS could be?

An internal memo to the Chief of the SS Personnel Department, *SS-Obergruppenführer* Schmitt

> To compare the known signature so as to find the name of the writer of the letter was impossible. Looking at the carelessly written signature one can only assume that the person didn't want to give his real signature.

Rickheim's Globocnik-appointed nursing chaperone, Sister Emilie Thomas's letter to *Sipo-SD* Chief, Johannes Muller in Lublin

21 September 1942.

In February and March I spent a 14 day holiday in Zakopane in the company of Miss Rickheim, the fiancée of the SS and Police Leader Lublin and his niece Henny Pomerantz. During this time we met a captain of the Air Force who was also a *Sturmbannführer* of the SS and who was in the rest home for convalescence. During an evening of comradeship of the home for wounded soldiers the captain invited us to this German home. Together with Miss Rickheim and Henny Pomerantz we spent this evening at a table together with badly wounded soldiers and also sitting on this table were some Red Cross Sisters and women auxiliaries. The person who arranged this evening wanted the wounded soldiers who were going into a camp to spend an enjoyable evening with other people. As I am myself a sister in the main hospital of the SS with the SS Police Leader in Lublin it was not difficult for me to get into a happy mood and I asked Miss Rickheim very often that she should be happier and join in the fun. She was at this time being treated for dermatitis by Dr. Beck in Zakopane and did not have the right mood. At times the captain came to our table but after a short greeting he left and when we saw him later he was drunk. But we had the opportunity since Henny Pomerantz, who was collecting stamps, to get the address of the captain. During this evening Miss Rickheim was spoken to by an *SS-Unterscharführer* who heard from the captain that she was the fiancée of the *SS-Brigadeführer* Globocnik and the captain said he also knew him. The *SS-Unterscharführer* was happy to tell her that he knew *Brigadeführer* Globocnik from the *SS-Standarte "Germania"* as they both served in the Polish campaign. He was happy to tell Miss Rickheim what had happened during the campaign and asked her to send his greeting to the *Brigadeführer*. When we wanted to leave with Miss Rickheim and Henny Pomerantz our attention was focused on the now extremely drunk captain who had a fight with some soldier who had the Iron Cross, first and second class. We heard the words of the captain and he said he would not go to the front to get his bones broken and be shot at. We went over to him to say goodbye. Miss Rickheim always wanted to go home quickly and she was the first to say goodbye to this man and waited at the door and the captain spoke of it. We then went with Miss Rickheim to our quarters. As witnesses of this evening there are Paratroopers Sergeant Schindler and Sergeant Stein, who now belong to the school of disabled soldiers of the Air Force.

Emilie Thomas.

Undated letter from Dr. Rudolf Brandt

Dear *Brigadeführer*,

Enclosed please find a copy of a letter that we received some time ago. I have the original. I tried to find out if the SS-Sf because of his illegible signature could be identified. Perhaps you could advise what you think about it. I have not informed the *Reichsführer-SS* about this letter.

Obersturmbannführer. R.B.

Schmitt's telegram to Dr. Rudolf Brandt

Dear Brandt,

Regrettably, neither the Personnel Office nor the *SD*, as in the enclosed letter from [Bruno] Streckenbach shows, was it possible to find the name of the *SS-Sturmbannführer*.

SS-Obergruppenführer. Schmitt.

Memo to Globocnik, undated and unsigned

Further to my letter of 13 July addressed to you I can now inform you that intensive investigations by the SS Personnel Office, which as we had assumed in advance, we must now tell you that there was a result was negative. The signature could not be determined on the anonymous letter. We could find out nothing.

Himmler's letter to Globocnik regarding the outcome of the Zakopane incident advising that he break his engagement with Rickheim

I've read your letter of 30 August 1942 that was addressed to Dr. Brandt.

Please find out if your fiancée was indeed with other men who went into a café. If yes then break the engagement.

It has to be made clear that with the youth of your fiancée nothing can be excused because if a girl, and she is immature, she would, with the work you have ahead of you, and not having adequate time to take care of your wife, she would be a disappointment for you and constantly deceive. Your marriage instead of being a strength for you would therefore become a constant burden. And what is even worse you would always doubt if you had children if indeed they were really yours.

You can see someone else gave you the facts and told you about her. You can also see that this written warning has to be taken seriously.

I can only advise you to terminate the engagement. Friendly greetings.

Heil Hitler. H.H.

Letter from Dr. Rudolf Brandt to Globocnik, dated 19 December 1942

Dear *Gruppenführer,*

Today I briefed the *Reichsführer-SS* about the letter which Fraulein Irmgard Rickheim had sent to the *Reichsführer-SS* on the 25-11-42. The *Reichsführer-SS* would like, however, that the captain of the Luftwaffe who is also in the General-SS as a *Sturmbannführer* to be heard on this matter.

I would be grateful therefore if you would give me the address of the *SS-Sturmbannführer* (if I recall correctly they told me they had found out which *SS-Sturmbannführer* it concerned).

Friendly greetings. *Heil* Hitler.
R.B.

Letter to Irmgard Rickheim, at her Berlin address, 19 December 1942

Dear Fraulein Rickheim.

I would like to confirm to you today the receipt of your letter of 25-11-42 to the *Reichsführer-SS* and I could only briefly inform the *Reichsführer-SS* of the content of your letter and of the position of Sister Emilie Thomas.
I hope the still necessary determination will be at hand by the middle of January — the moment of the return of the *Reichsführer-SS* from various inspection travels on the front — so that you are then able to obtain news.

Heil Hitler.
R.B.

Letter to Dr. Rudolf Brandt from Globocnik of 29 December 1942

Just as your letter from 19 December arrived I wanted to send a letter to Fraulein Rickheim to inform her that our engagement was finished. I kept the letter as I don't know when the whole matter will be finalized and what I shall do. I was forced amongst other things to write this letter as I had read the letter of the *Reichsführer-SS* of the 11 September, approximately 20 times and I also asked my 16-year-old niece, who was in Zakopane, and had seen everything. She gave me the address of the air force captain. The address is Fotkalm Pisle Captain of the Air Force in Kaznitz on the River Elbe. It is in the Resinborga. He also thinks he is a leader of the SS and told my niece that he wanted to write a letter to the *Reichsführer-SS* about the way Miss Rickheim behaved. Dear Brandt, it is not very easy for me that the *Reichsführer-SS* has to deal with this matter. It would be better if this could be avoided and I had already taken his advice. Would you be so kind and tell me if I should write to this captain, if I should show Miss Rickheim my letter or not? I don't want to do anything, which would upset the *Reichsführer*. Please send me a reply as soon as possible.

Odilo Globocnik.

Globocnik certainly appears to have taken the Zakopane Note issue extremely seriously. In another letter to Brandt on 30 August 1942, he referred to another air force captain named Vogt who had apparently made a statement, but it is not clear to whom, or what it alleged or clarified. Rickheim's adamant stand against being maligned, the written support she was able to produce from her nursing companion, Emilie Thomas, and the fact that the letter accusing her was from an anonymous source casts grave doubt upon the credibility of allegations of misconduct. The case has all the characteristics of a set-up, and a rather amateurish one at that. Who was behind it is something that is unlikely to be uncovered — was it some secret female admirer of Globocnik's? Possibly. Was it his mother who did not like Rickheim? Possibly. Was it perhaps Heinrich Himmler? Also possibly. But then again, it may have been a fourth party, another enemy of Globocnik's. If that was the case, then each of the former may have been content with the outcome; Rickheim's departure from the scene came sometime around October 1942. Another possibility is that the anonymous informant was mistaken and had written about one of the other women present at the table, believing she was Globocnik's fiancée. We simply do not know, but surely it was not Emilie Thomas, or one of the other nurses or auxiliary women also at that table.

XV

Himmler and Globus:
A Double-Cross?

Recent research conducted by an American historian suggests that Himmler, certainly the most powerful man in the Third Reich when it came to demographic affairs and dealing with the key plank of the NSDAP, had apparently secretly decided that Globocnik was not the appropriate man for the resettlement and Germanization of the East. This view came to the attention of the author only at the end of his research on Globocnik's murderous role in Poland's Lublin District. Nevertheless, it is one that cannot be ignored, despite the evidence that Himmler fought doggedly throughout much of 1943 to ensure that Globocnik remained at the head of that district against adversaries like Dr. Hans Frank, his district governor, Ernst Zörner, and a battery of other opponents. At the same time, Himmler fought equally doggedly against the party's formidable treasurer, Francis Xaver Schwartz, to ensure that Globocnik was never charged for his, at minimum, questionable monetary dealings and other financial shenanigans in Vienna while its *Gauleiter* in 1938–39. Moreover, as pointed out earlier, Himmler (and Dr. Rudolf Brandt) had a peculiar fatherly oversight over Globocnik when it came to his marital plans and love life. Irmgard Rickheim is adamant that Globocnik was more like a Himmler servant, as if Himmler were blackmailing him. This, unfortunately, tells us only that Globocnik was basically a lap dog with respect to Himmler. But Himmler also used the tried and tested method of operating by laying the basis of some future policy, well ahead of the commencement

date, which usually entailed placing certain key people into particular positions so those people could be called upon at a much later date. Indeed, it
appears that Globocnik was based in Lublin in November 1939 for this very
reason with respect to Berlin's long term demographic policies, that is, *Generalplan Ost*, and probably also what came to be called *Aktion Reinhardt*, and
if not that, then administration of all the Jews of occupied Poland as head of
the planned Jewish Lublin Reservation.

According to Michael Allen, a leading expert on the SS's important
Wirtschaftsverwaltungshauptamt (*WVHA*) division, headed by Oswald Pohl,
Himmler had already laid the groundwork, by mid–1941, for the Germanization of the East to be undertaken not by Globocnik and the killing and
planning teams he had at his disposal, but rather by this huge commercial
arm of the SS. The *SS-WVHA's* powerful Berlin-based chief, Oswald Pohl,
had at his fingertips a range of expert engineers with experience in coordinating major construction projects — road and rail works, river regulation,
reforestation, canal construction, and the like — something Globocnik, despite
having been a building works site foreman in Carinthia, clearly lacked.
Globocnik also had a known record of mismanagement. But he was ambitious in the extreme, as the plans developed by his Research Center for Eastern Settlement (*Forschungsstelle für Ostunterkunfte*) so clearly show. Allen
contends in his novel and challenging findings that Himmler was accompanied by Pohl during his visit to Globocnik at the time of their Lublin and
Zamosc inspections in the summer of 1941. But behind the scenes many more
significant things were happening of which Globocnik was not fully abreast.

> Himmler seems to have avoided criticizing Globocnik directly — at least accord-
> ing to the written record that remains. He simply shifted responsibility for con-
> struction directly to Pohl's HAHB. [*Hauptamt Haushalt und Bauten*: Main
> Office for Budgets and Buildings.] Globocnik stayed on, nominally in control
> of the design and layout of settlements (though, *de facto*, Pohl's new chief of
> engineers began to take over this work as well). Globocnik also finished up some
> temporary construction already underway, but his influence diminished rapidly.
> In March of the coming year, [1943] Himmler removed him from the plan-
> ning of [SS and Police] Strongholds completely (at a time when the RKF[DV]
> announced plans to triple their number). This must have been a bitter blow,
> for settlement policy carried high prestige within the SS well into late 1942,
> and Globocnik's relationship which was to sour Pohl ever after.[1]

These are interesting observations and thought provoking conclusions,
ones that clearly cannot be ignored even though they appear to be contradicted
by the fact that by October 1942 Globocnik was laying out the entire plan of
action to remove tens of thousands of Polish peasants from the Zamosc Lands.
What is more, he was to direct this, in many ways pioneering, action with the
assistance of his longtime Carinthian SS pal, Reinhold von Mohrenschildt.

Globocnik was, at this stage — in the summer of 1941 — within about six months of being placed fully in charge of *Aktion Reinhardt*, and the killing of tens of thousands of Jews each week, a program that was also close to Himmler's heart. All this also raises the question of why Himmler made his few visits to Globocnik's Research Center for Eastern Settlement in Lublin. Was he simply culling Globocnik's — and therefore Gustav Hanelt's and Dr. Franz Stanglica's — ideas with the intention of giving Oswald Pohl the eventual glory to become the Third Reich's major settlement and resettlement czar? Again, according to Allen, Himmler and others associated with the *Reichsführer-SS* had made a conscious decision for the Germanization of the East to be undertaken by people other than Globocnik.

> Himmler had made a choice between two different styles of organization. By backing Pohl, he chose systematic, impersonal — that is modern — administrative hierarchy over Globocnik's personal initiative. Globocnik had essentially set about handcrafting the New Order. He had failed to master the modern means that SS rhetoric led him to admire, and, at best, he presided over the Lublin District more or less as a foreman would run one construction site. He had never juggled correspondence with national ministries and agencies that could accelerate large projects or cut them off completely in a hail of audits, property-rights inquiries, raw-materials vouchers, and permits. The RKF[DV] was talking about dispersing tens of billions of *Reichsmarks*, and as always when the scale of the SS's responsibilities multiplied, the demand for accountability and competence increased in step. Whereas Globocnik had focused on a small constellation of settlements surrounding Lublin, Pohl had in mind an organization that could purchase property in the East, order steel from the *Hermann-Göring-Werke* in Salzgitter, bricks and stone from the DESt at Sachsenhausen or Mauthausen, hammer out priority ratings and permits with ministries in Berlin, and mobilize the SS's available machinery, labor, and civil engineering corps within a matrix of closely calculated time schedule.[2]

Allen makes the truly original claim that the SS's huge concentration camp sector was already, at this crucial stage of the war, just after the invasion of the huge Soviet Union, in a position to back up and assist in the coming planned demographic challenges ahead; and in the reconstruction and settlement of the East by Germanic peoples through the construction of the SS and police strongpoints, which were to form the backbone or foundations of the eastern settlement program, that is, *Generalplan Ost*. This is consistent with the work that the Berlin geographer and SS consultant, Konrad Meyer-Hetling, had written for Himmler. It is also therefore not inconsistent with the early work undertaken by Berlin-based demographic planners under Dr. Hans Ehlich, who headed the IIIB Group at the SS's main security office of the Reich between 1940 and early 1945. Again, although the claim of the emergence of Pohl over Globocnik appears to be contradicted by the fact that it was Globocnik who launched and oversaw the Zamosc Lands expulsions,

and that Globocnik was destined to be moved further east to cleanse demographically all those lands inhabited by Slavs, Allen's findings that Globocnik was in the early stages at least of being "white anted" cannot be easily
discounted. If Allen has perhaps overstated his case, then Pohl, who was based
in Berlin, and closer to Himmler than Globocnik, was at least maneuvering
his *SS-WVHA* into new areas of far greater responsibility. What senior bureau-
crat anywhere does not wish to see his empire expanding? If, however, Himmler was in the early stages of double-crossing a loyal old Carinthian servant,
then he may have been acting on the basis of personal observations and several years of rumors and complaints about Globocnik, a man who tended to
take short cuts that upset SS colleagues and others. The Germanization of
the East was closer to Himmler's heart than anything else — so close that he
was involved in ordering the murder of eastern Jews and Red Army captives.
It is understandable that Himmler did not therefore wish to see this penultimate project of his life, the one he was going to be judged on as a great Germanic nation builder, bungled. Not by anyone. And Globocnik, despite being
such a successful killer, was something of a bungler. By late 1941, we know
that Himmler had three matters which may have cast some doubts in his
mind about Globocnik; first, he had failed in Vienna; second, that failure had
compelled Himmler to intercede for Globocnik against the powerful party
treasurer, Francis Xaver Schwartz; and finally, Globocnik had failed to take
his superior's advice and hints in his matrimonial plans — opting for Irmgard
Rickheim rather than making an attempt to form a liaison with Germany's
1936 gold medal-winning Olympic discus thrower, Gisela Mauermayer, as
Himmler had secretly hinted.

There may have also been other issues that gave Himmler second thoughts about his murderous Lublin-based underling. There was, for instance,
the clumsy manner in which Globocnik moved to construct the anti-tank
ditch defensive network near Belzec, something that was ridiculed by many,
and Himmler may have been aware of this. SS settlement of the East was such
an important, indeed, central policy, that Himmler could have understandably
decided to bring in professionals — the engineers and others who were close
to his trusted ally, Oswald Pohl — to undertake it. The intention may therefore have been to have had Globocnik simply based out in Ukraine or beyond,
undertaking the early stages of settlement policy, namely, the bloody removal
of Slavs (Ukrainians this time) and the putting down of so-called bandits,
something Globocnik was, if not adept at, then at least capable of doing as
shown to an extent in the Zamosc Lands and by the later brutal anti-partisan activities around Trieste. If nothing else, he was ruthless enough, so ruthless that it is difficult to name another SS man who can challenge him in this
regard.

In addition there were the facts that Pohl had caught Himmler's attention because of his undoubted organizational talents. Thus, Pohl in early 1934 became an SS-*Standartenführer* and Chief Administrative Officer in the Reich Main Security Office.

> In June 1939 he was appointed a Ministerial Director in the Reich Ministry of the Interior. In that same year he joined the "Circle of Friends of Heinrich Himmler"—a group of wealthy patrons drawn from the top echelons of industry, banking and insurance, who played a leading role in supplying *Waffen-SS* units with arms and uniforms during World War II, in return for certain practical advantages and honorary rank in the SS. Pohl himself reached the rank of SS-*Obergruppenführer* and from 1942 to 1945 was a General of the *Waffen-SS*. In 1942 he was appointed head of the SS-*Wirtschafts-und Verwaltungshauptamt* (or *WVHA*), which was the Economic and Administrative Main office of the SS. Its sphere covered all works projects for concentration camp inmates as well as the camps inspectorate—altogether a gigantic concern designed to squeeze the maximum use out of captive labor for the profit of the SS.[3]

Pohl oversaw the crucially important economic side of the entire SS or Himmler extermination machine, the pivotal Nazi concentration camp empire; he was senior to Globocnik, who was only the executive officer of the extermination wing of that empire in Lublin District, as important as that was. Pohl was the man at head office; Globocnik was out in the field, in a branch office. Although Globocnik was the main killer, the man directing mass murder, he was not in overall charge. Pohl's administrative skills, his proximity to power, and his far closer and longer association with Himmler suggest that he, not Globocnik, would have been best situated to become the ultimate overseer of the Germanization of the East—*Generalplan Ost*.

We need only compare Rudolf Höss's assessment of Globocnik with that of Oswald Pohl in Höss's 1947 book, written in Krakow, shortly before he was hanged by Polish authorities. Höss had known Pohl for over a decade, between 1934 and 1945, and had dealings with Globocnik in Lublin.

Of Globocnik he said that "He caused so much mischief [as *Gauleiter* of Vienna] ... that he soon had to be removed"; that "Globocnik was a pompous busy body..."; that "He was able to spin the most extraordinary yarns to Himmler"; and that

> Globocnik had wanted to create a large German settlement in "his territory." With this in mind, he chose the district around Zamosch [sic]. He promised the Reichsführer-SS that he would move 50,000 new German settlers there within a year, as a model for the large settlements, which it was intended to build later on in the far eastern districts [the entire western or European Soviet Union].... According to Höfle's description this resettlement organized by Globocnik must have been catastrophic.[4]

Of Pohl, Höss wrote, "Pohl's methods ... instill accuracy into the administration of the SS..."; and that "Pohl had already made plans for industrial

undertakings of great magnitude, which would put even the IG Farben Indus-
trie in the shade. *Pohl also had the necessary energy to bring these schemes to
completion*" (emphasis added). He also wrote:

> Pohl's main objective from the beginning, however, was gradually to make the
> SS financially independent of the State and Party, by means of its own busi-
> ness undertakings, and thus to guarantee the *Reichsführer-SS* the necessary free-
> dom of action in his planning. It was a task with a far-reaching objective, which
> Pohl was convinced could be accomplished and for which he labored unremit-
> tingly.[5]

Need one go on? Clearly, Globocnik was not in the same league as Pohl,
and it is most unlikely that Pohl and Himmler hadn't discussed their man in
the East when it came to considering the question of how best to ensure that
Generalplan Ost should and would be successfully implemented. In light of
Höss's assessment of Pohl, it is highly likely that a role was found here for
him, as Allen argues. But precisely what it was and how Globocnik was to
participate is not known, for it never came to that. Globocnik and Pohl had,
irrespective of their vastly different backgrounds, abilities, aptitudes, and
qualifications, cooperated quite closely between 1939 and 1943, during
Globocnik's destructive Lublin days, suggesting they could have continued
doing so with Globocnik stationed farther East cleansing Slavs, had Hitler's
military won out. What Globocnik was therefore probably never destined to
be was the man who actually reconstructed the East for the new Germanic
Order. He was, to state the obvious, a killer and a destroyer, not a creator.
And his two Berlin-based superiors seem to have been fully aware of this.

In addition, a scan of the work Globocnik carried out in Lublin shows
that Pohl was at all times if not close by then somewhere just in the background, overseeing, keeping an eye on things. It is likely that both Pohl and
Himmler deliberately ensured this to have been the case. Perhaps both even
had doubts about Globocnik's broader abilities. In many ways Globocnik was
something of an incompetent, a man who was unable to follow through on
the details. Pohl was a co-director of *Osti*; he was involved in overseeing Wippern's loot collecting and collation. Well into 1941, Globocnik still had the
question of his handling of party and other funds in Vienna in a far from satisfactory way hanging over his head. He seemed unable to manage his personal life — buying himself out of a love affair with Grete Michner, with
Himmler's involvement, and breaking with Irmgard Rickheim, again with
Himmler's involvement. And Himmler had also been drawn into the investigations of this issue of his Vienna days launched by party treasurer, Franz
Xaver Schwartz. As if that was not enough, Globocnik could hardly claim
having been victorious in his supervision of the Zamosc Lands ethnic clearance action. All these matters probably served as reminders to Himmler of

Globocnik's, at minimum, shortcomings. Even a superficial comparison of Pohl's and Globocnik's personal links with Himmler, followed by their actual qualifications and achievements, shows that Globocnik was not Pohl's equal. But none of this should be seen as necessarily disqualifying Globocnik from a senior SS position on the eastern borderlands of, say, Ukraine or Russia, leading fighting units to cleanse thousands of villages of their Slavic (Ukrainian and Russian) inhabitants in the way he had victimized Poles between November 1942 and August 1943 across the Zamosc Lands.

XVI

The Lublin District's Demographic Upheavals, 1939–1944

With the possible exceptions of the clearance of the starved Jewish populations of the huge Warsaw, Lodz (Litzmannstadt), and Bialystok ghettos during 1942–43, and the subsequent separate action of removal of all ethnic Poles from Warsaw after that city's August–September 1944 uprising, the region of the General Gouvernement which saw the greatest demographic upheaval was the Lublin District. Its southeastern corner, including the contested Zamosc Lands was particularly brutalized. This region, more than any other, constituted Globocnik's "killing fields," to use an emotive but most descriptive term coined to describe Pol Pot's genocide of the Cambodian peoples in the 1970s. Globocnik's third major killing center, Treblinka, was erected well to Lublin's north, in the occupation administration's Warsaw District, and significantly, was situated midway between Warsaw and Bialystok, making clearance of those two city's ghettos that much easier and cheaper. If Lublin was the Capital of the Jewish Holocaust, then it can also rightfully be accorded the title Capital of the Final Solution of the Slavic Question, which commenced with Globocnik's and von Mohrenschildt's launching of the clearance of the Zamosc Lands on 28 November 1942. It was, in fact, capital of both these so-called solutions, and those implementing them were essentially the same personnel, headed in both cases by Odilo Globocnik, with von Mohrenschildt being

Christian Wirth's equivalent with the ethnic Polish cleansing task. The Zamosc Lands expulsions were the opening gambit of Hitler's and Himmler's top-secret *Generalplan Ost*, which was worked on and refined within the SS's Berlin headquarters, the *Reichsicherheitshauptamt* (RSHA), from at least the early months of 1940. Related and associated work on the clearance of the Zamosc Lands of ethnic Poles and all lands farther east, namely the western segments of the Soviet Union, was conducted within Globocnik's long ignored Lublin-based Research Center for Eastern Settlement, which Himmler visited on at least one occasion.

1939 — October/December

The first groups of ethnic Poles to be forcibly settled within Lublin District arrived ahead of Globocnik, who had reached Lublin in early November 1939. These expellees commenced arriving the previous month, and hailed from Danzig (Gdansk), Gdynia, and Orlowo, each on the Baltic coast, the region that had come to be known before war broke out as "The Corridor," and which Berlin had earmarked for rapid Germanization, thereby demographically linking it and East Prussia with the *Alt Reich*. This process was to also see people of ethnic German origin reaching these Baltic cities from the soon to be Soviet-annexed Baltic countries of Estonia and Latvia, under a series of special treaties with Moscow. These incoming Baltic German evacuees acquired Polish homesteads and properties, as well as even vacated business premises. The initial Polish expellees from the Baltic coast were followed by others from the Warthe Land (western Poland) which had been incorporated into the Reich early in October 1939. During this period, several thousand Polish families were compelled to move into the Lublin District, with some managing to take up residence with relatives, even if distant ones. At the same time, Jews from these western parts of Poland also commenced arriving in Lublin District, just as many other Jews were reaching other parts of the General Gouvernement, namely its large number of ghettos, including Warsaw, Radom and Bialystok. Although it is difficult to give accurate figures of those reaching Globocnik's district during these closing winter months of 1939, the total number of Poles was probably on the order of 15,000, with about the same number of Jews. The Jewish deportations also included those involved in Berlin's attempts at this time to establish a Jewish inhabited so-called Lublin Reservation along the district's western perimeter, as discussed earlier. However, about 10,000 Lublin District Jews had fled east into Soviet-occupied eastern Poland during this early phase of the war. Eastern Poland had been annexed by Moscow in September 1939, so they had opted to live under Soviet control, though some eventually returned to German-occupied

Poland voluntarily. At the same time, about 2,500 people, mainly Lublin District Poles, were dispatched to work in the Reich, with some of them perhaps even going voluntarily. Up to about 30,000 Ukrainian Nationalists fled Soviet-occupied eastern Poland, with many of them settling in Lublin and Chelm, while others traveled as far east as Krakow, where the collaborationist Ukrainian Central Committee was to be based. This committee was headed by a Krakow academic who was half Polish and half Ukrainian, Wolodymyr Kubiiovych, and he and his committee members plotted, unsuccessfully, for some time for all Jews and Poles to expelled from parts of Lublin District that the Ukrainian Nationalists called *Zakerzons'kyi Kraj,* which included Chelm, Zamosc, Bilgoraj and a swathe of southern Poland, land that made up the extensive foothills of the Carpathian Mountains. Kubiiovych and the committee wished to transform this, with German assistance, into a pure Ukrainian enclave, from which the Greater Ukraine they imagined would arise. But such aspirations clashed with Himmler's and Globocnik's aspirations for Lublin District, so a *modus vivendi* was abided by under which the two cooperated. This accommodation lasted throughout the war because of the fighting with Stalin. These winter months of 1939 also saw the commencement of the arrest and jailing a steadily growing number of Poles, and some Ukrainians, despite the fact that the Ukrainian Nationalists allied themselves with Berlin.

All these initial and relatively small movements were in addition to the demobilization and racial or ethnic segregation of soldiers of the conquered Polish army. That process meant separating ethnic Poles, Jews, Ukrainians, and anyone regarded as *Volksdeutsche.* Although demographic sorting therefore commenced immediately after hostilities ceased, this was still occurring on a relatively small scale, with people moving in as well as out of the district. It would, of course, be incorrect to see all of these demographic movements as the outcome of initiatives of Globocnik and his increasingly inhumane staff, men who were to play dominant and pivotal roles in the constant demographic overhauling of this eastern district, culminating in the mass killings of Jews under *Aktion Reinhardt* of 1942–43, and the demographic cleansing of the Zamosc Lands of ethnic Poles. In both these cases Globocnik was acting on behalf of Heinrich Himmler. Early acquisition of forced workers for the Reich had been launched without the involvement of either man. The gathering and transferring of workers was being carried out by the Labor Office, which fell under the aegis of the civilian government, headed after March 1940 by Hitler's former friend, Ernst Zörner.

Over and above all these early demographic upheavals came the vicious *Aktion-AB (Ausserordentliche Befriedungsaktion),* an initial terror campaign that involved arresting between 2,000 and 3,000 people across all of Poland who were regarded as high risk potential resistance movement organizers, including doctors, lawyers, social and political activists, journalists, teachers, and members of the clergy. *Aktion A-B* continued throughout the first half of 1940, gradually becoming transformed into a general enforcement trend of acquisition of grain and other provisions from peasant and other farmers. Globocnik's Vienna colleague, Artur Seyss-Inquart, with his superior, Dr. Hans Frank, oversaw this early culling and killing of possible resistance leaders.

Late in 1939, Globocnik, on the suggestions of a man named Streckenback, who was in charge of the Security Police and *SD* for the entire General Gouvernement, had actually forced some Jews within Lublin District to go east, into Soviet-occupied eastern Poland. This early policy of outright expulsion involved death marches, with many of the Jewish expellees being killed along the way, and with survivors being forced to swim the cold Bug River, the demarcation line between the Soviet and German zones.[1] On Thursday, 30 November, all the Jews of Chelm were ordered to assemble on the town Market Square the next day.

> Next morning, when the eighteen hundred Jewish men of Chelm had assembled in the Market Square, they were surrounded by SS men and soldiers. There was also a detachment of machine guns. One of the officers spoke to the Jews. His words were simple and easy to grasp. "All Jewish men are to leave the town immediately!" Even a reason was given. They were told that they were responsible for the outbreak of war and were the greatest and most dangerous enemy of the otherwise powerful German Reich.[2]

The above account was published in England in the following year, 1940. Although its author, Francis Aldor, does not name any SS man, it is most likely that Globocnik was the actual instigator. He was, after all, the senior SS and police chief of Lublin District, within which Chelm was a major town. Each man had all his cash and identity papers confiscated before being marched out of Chelm beginning at noon. "They were heading for the town of Hrubieszow. The pace was terrific. Those who were not strong enough to keep up were urged on with blows."[3]

By the end of the first day many had been shot along the roadside. That evening the large group was forced to camp down in a field near Hrubieszow, and in the morning they were joined by the Jews of that town. Eventually they were marched to the Bug River, and the survivors were forced to swim across to the Soviet side, where they were ordered to swim back. Sentries on both sides fired at members of this large but rapidly diminishing group of Jews. One survivor of this horrific ordeal, Israel Mayer, managed to reach Budapest either in December 1939 or early 1940. According to Aldor, "Israel Mayer also relates that on his first day in Budapest, he picked up a German newspaper and there he found, in small type, the news that the German authorities had been forced to suppress a Jewish revolt in Chelm and Hrubieszow."[4]

1940

The first calendar year of Globocnik's tyrannical and increasingly bloody regime continued being marked by a series of demographic as well as harsh policing initiatives. Beginning in May there was a steady influx of ethnic Poles, under what was called the "*Wolynienaktion.*" By December 1940 some 35,000 people had arrived, with a further two transports arriving in January 1941, bringing the total figure up to some 37,000. These newcomers were simply placed on trains in Lodz (Litzmannstadt), carrying in each case some 1,000 people, and were dumped at railway stations in major Lublin District towns such as Zamosc, Krasnik, Szczebrzeszyn, Lubartow, Lukow, Izbica, Naleczow, and Lublin itself. During September and October, a further 28,365 Poles, under what was called the "*Cholmeraktion,*" were similarly dumped. These later expellees were also dispatched from Lodz, having been concentrated there from surrounding regions. A third such intake by the district, this time numbering just 5,553 people, were from the Zywiec County, in southern Upper Silesia, which was being actively Germanized. They reached the district during September, October, and December 1940, as part of a movement called the "*Saybusch Aktion.*" However, this last operation saw the arrival of only six transports, which reached Lublin, Lukow, Lubartow, Szczebrzeszyn, Naleczow, and Zwierzyniec. During eight months of 1940, Lublin District received 90 transports, or some 69,953 Poles, who hailed from lands that had been incorporated into the Reich.[5]

As in 1939, when some 2,500 people were dispatched to work in the Reich, this practice continued, with 46,303 people removed from Lublin District for this purpose. Although most were Poles, some were Ukrainians. This figure was the highest of the five calendar years of the war, exceeding by 3,000 those forcibly deported to the Reich during 1943, the year with the next highest total.

German occupation authorities decided shortly before September 1940 to remove *Volksdeutsche* from the entire General Gouvernement, which they estimated would mean removal of some 30,000 people to the west. This evacuation, called "Aktion Chelm," and not to be confused with the "*Cholmeraktion*" mentioned above, was conducted during the months of September, October, and November 1940, with around 24,500 people actually being removed, of which only 1,130 were children. All originated from the Lublin District's Chelm region. The first transport of 500 people reached Gniezno, near Poznan, on 4 October, and the last arrived at Smier on 27 November.

Most were farmers, and were settled around Poznan, with about 1,700 directed to Danzig (Gdansk). This transfer can be seen as part of the removal of Germans from Estonia and Latvia for settlement in the same Polish regions. The obvious benefit from Berlin's point of view was that it boosted German numbers in the incorporated territories, lands annexed from conquered Poland. All received homesteads, or else a workshop pertinent to their qualifications. In both cases, tools of trade were acquired by these German settlers, who displaced the Poles who had earlier been expelled eastward, some into Lublin District. The fact that only some 24,500 of what was believed to be a 30,000-strong German Chelm minority community was resettled at this time meant that approximately 5,000 remained in Poland. Some of these appear to have refused to leave their homes, while others obtained work within the occupation administration, either in the Zörner or perhaps even the Globocnik bureaucracies of Lublin District. Considerable pressure was exerted on these people so they would move west; this was a time-consuming exercise, with not all these people seeing the alleged benefits of relocating to where the new German authorities and agencies claimed they ought to live. Globocnik was certainly involved in this demographic relocation project and von Mohrenschildt may have been.

Finally, there were the Jews of Lublin and its environs, who, in early 1940, had just two more years of existence as an identifiable ethno-religious group before they were exterminated en masse by Globocnik's specially-convened killing team. Beginning in early 1940, these people were first ghettoized, and other Jews were relocated into Globocnik's District from other parts of the General Gouvernement and areas beyond. The first Jews from outside the district were specially selected for the ill-fated Lublin Reservation, which was to be located between the Vistula and Bug Rivers. This short-lived expulsionist and settlerist demographic experiment was discontinued after March 1940. This year saw Jewish numbers, which had been augmented in 1939 by about 15,000 people, boosted by probably a further 9,500. The first Jewish arrivals came in February, when 1,200 came from the German Baltic city of Stettin. They were housed at 7 Lipowa Street, site of Globocnik's major work camp in central Lublin. Subsequent arrivals were directed to Lublin's surrounding townships, where small ghettos were created. Many of these immigrants suffered frostbite during their eastward rail journey. Moreover, some 9,800 more Jews reached the district from adjacent Radom District during August and September.

This year also brought the first transports of Jewish prisoners-of-war arriving from *Stalags* in the Reich. These men were dispatched on Göring's orders. The erection of work camps in the region had actually commenced in late 1939. Heydrich intended for these camps to become holding centers with several hundred thousand prisoners; those interned would become involved in the construction of fortifications, the so-called eastern rampart. A number of camps were erected in Bilgoraj and Zamosc counties — there were 21 across the entire district by late 1940 — as well as at Belzec, which became the site of one of Globocnik's killing centers. Many of these prisoners also worked on the construction of a network of airfields, road works, river and stream regulation, and small bridge construction. The first group of 1,367 Jews arrived in February, followed by 1,857 between March and May. Many Jews during these early months were force-marched between locations, and some did not survive such cruel ordeals. Executions and beatings occurred. Another 1,550 prisoners arrived from *Stalag* IIB Hammerstein, western Pomerania, during October and November, and a further 800 came from Konigsberg, East Prussia, in October, bringing the total for the year to over 5,500. At the same time, Globocnik managed to boost his intake of Jewish workers following a meeting on 9 August 1940 with the Works Department of the General Gouvernement. Under this agreement, Jews were obtained from Radom and Warsaw Districts.[6]

The intake from Warsaw District was about 5,250 workers. In November and December began another forced settlement campaign — the bringing in of 5,436 Jews from Krakow, the General Gouvernement's capital. Most of those affected by this action, however, actually arrived during 1941, with only three transports being dispatched in 1940, involving some 1,000 people. The first group of 319 was located at Miedzyrzec Podlaski, the second of 265 in Lublin, and the third of 433 in Chelm. The intake of Jews during 1940 more than doubled that of the last three months of 1939. Jews continued to flee eastward into Soviet-occupied eastern Poland, with an estimated 4,000 departing during 1940. This was less than half the number that left in the last three months of 1939. Over and above this, the ill-fated Jewish Lublin Reservation experiment, based on a region along the district's western perimeter, was discontinued.

1941

The second calendar year of the occupation and of Globocnik in Lublin was the exceptional one, for it experienced few demographic upheavals apart from those associated with the use of the district to station huge numbers of German soldiers and material, especially during spring and summer months, to undertake the momentous invasion of the Soviet Union, launched on 22 June 1941, when southern German military units crossed the Bug River. Many members of this force were stationed all over Lublin District for the invasion of Ukraine proper. Those based in East Prussia were destined for the Baltic lands and the Leningrad region. Lublin historian Janina Kielbon has pointed out that although the first three months of 1941 saw an influx of Poles from the Reich, Jews from Vienna, some prisoners-of-war, and even people from the adjacent Warsaw District, after April this came to a complete halt. The reason for this was that this Globocnik-controlled district became a major launching pad for the planned invasion of the Soviet Union, Operation Barbarossa, especially for the acquisition of Ukraine and Crimea.[7]

In January, two shipments, numbering 1,000 Poles each, arrived in Zamosc and Krasnik as part of *"Wolynienaktion"* that had commenced in May 1940. This *Aktion* settled just over 37,000 Poles across Lublin District. During February and March another 6,960 Poles from western Poland arrived, with seven transports of about 1,000 people each. In the first three months of the year, another 8,960 ethnic Poles arrived from other parts of incorporated western Poland, being settled within Globocnik's district. This nearly 9,000-strong contingent was part of a 76,663-strong intake of Poles from western Poland arriving during 1940 and 1941, who comprised 3.4 percent of the district's population of 2.4 million people. Nearly 21,000 of these were settled in Chelm and its environs, an area that Ukrainian Nationalists, allies of Berlin, claimed was part of the Greater Ukraine they foresaw emerging after or even during the war against Bolshevism. The Chelm region had, of course, experienced the evacuation of some 24,500 ethnic Germans during the previous year. Lublin and its immediate environs saw some 11,000 Poles settled. The remaining 46,000 were spread relatively evenly over the district's remaining counties: Biala Podlaska, Bilgoraj, Hrubieszow, Janow Lubelski, Krasnystaw, Pulawy, Radzyn, and Zamosc. Nearly 13,500 people, most of them Poles, though some would no doubt have been Ukrainians, were removed to be laborers in the Reich, a significant reduction of the previous year's 46,300, but more than five times as many as over the last three months of 1939.

The intake of Jews also slumped significantly during 1941, with the total number arriving reaching just over 17,000. Of these, nearly 6,300 were from western Poland; about 1,500 were prisoner-of-war slave laborers used to work on various military and public works projects; 2,200 were from adjacent Warsaw District, 4,420 from Krakow, which General-Governor Dr. Frank was seeking to make *Judenfrei* (free of Jews), and nearly 3,000 from Globocnik's former bailiwick of Vienna, people whom Adolf Eichmann had failed to deport during 1938 and 1939.

That year's New Year's eve was more than six months after Hitler had invaded the Soviet Union and less than a month before the Wannsee Conference, when the so-called Final Solution of the Jewish Question would be formally decided upon. That decision did not exclude death through work, so that Lublin District also became an important center for large Jewish-manned work camps, as well as separate Polish-manned work camps. The Final Solution, and the decision to embark upon *Generalplan Ost,* also taken in 1941, were the two most momentous demographic or ethnic cleansing deci-sions made by Hitler, and both involved Globocnik: the first as head of *Aktion Reinhardt*, the second by launching the clearance of the Zamosc Lands just 10 months later, in November 1942. Both these programs lay at the very heart of Hitler's decision to go to war, so Globocnik's involvement in each shows his importance in the broader Nazi scheme of things. The decision, though not the actual order, to settle Germans upon the Zamosc Lands, and conse-quently forcibly remove Polish peasant farmers, was also in train after mid–1941, with a trial run associated with the invasion of the Soviet Union involving the expulsion of Poles from half a dozen villages in November. The Nazi Party's two most momentous demographic moves which involved Globocnik as the chief organizer were therefore decided upon during 1941 but launched in 1942, and both continued throughout 1943, the year Globocnik departed Lublin for Trieste.

1942

If 1941 was Himmler's and Globocnik's year of relative demographic inactivity, then 1942 was one of hyperactivity, for it witnessed unprecedented movements and mass killing of people across the entire district. It was also the first year of the Globocnik-led *Aktion Reinhardt*, during which time he killed about 40 percent of all the Jews he was to exterminate, approximately three quarters of a million people, and it brought the launching of the piv-otal Zamosc Lands expulsion action, the commencement of Hitler's and Himmler's top-secret *Generalplan Ost*. Soon after the beginning of 1942, the district commenced accepting a steady flow of trains carrying Jews from West-ern Europe, Galicia, and parts of the General Gouvernement, most of whom were destined for immediate extermination in one of Globocnik's two killing centers. Treblinka, in Warsaw District, was similarly active, with some of its victims also being Jews from Lublin District's northern counties, but most destined for its gas chambers were from the Warsaw and Bialystok ghettos. Those living in the district were transported into these three killing centers between March 1942 and August 1943, with Lublin ghetto being cleared from late March. "The Jews of Lublin were the first to be exterminated en masse as part of the *Reinhardt Operation*, headed by Odilo Globocnik."[8]

Nine months after *Aktion Reinhardt* was secretly launched, in Novem-ber 1942 began the expulsions of some 110,000 Polish peasant farmers from four of the district's southeastern counties of Zamosc, Hrubieszow, Bilgoraj, and Tomaszow-Lubelski. The two major stages of this action lasted until a month before Himmler finally transferred Globocnik as a Higher *SS-und Polizeiführer* to Trieste in September 1943. A total of 297 villages and hamlets had all or most of their ethnic Polish residents expelled, with many of the villages being commandeered by German settlers brought in primarily from camps in the Lodz (Litzmannstadt) region. Many of those inhabitants, *Volksdeutsche*, came from lands that had fallen under Soviet control in 1939 and 1940, so they had been living in those camps since then. The Zamosc Lands expulsions are important because this action was the model to be used for the Germanization of the entire East — Russia, Ukraine, Belarus, and the Baltic Lands, all the way to the Urals — if the German Army defeated Stalin's enormous, Western-supplied Red Army. During November and December 1942, 62 villages had their Polish inhabitants removed — 12 during November and 35 in December from Zamosc County, and 15 villages from Tomaszow-Lubelski County during December. The remaining 247 villages were cleared, entirely or in part, between January and August 1943, after which this cleansing action was ostensibly postponed. It was never to be relaunched because of the military impact of the debilitating and ominous defeats at Stalingrad and Kursk, battles fought well east of the Zamosc Lands, as well as the increasingly burdensome and effective Polish partisan resistance across this contested region, which lay between the Globocnik killing centers of Sobibor and Belzec.

The majority of Poles failed to evade capture by escaping into nearby forests, and were marched to two main transit camps, one in central Zamosc, the other in nearby Zwierzyniec, where they were racially processed into categories. Anyone classified as probably of so-called Aryan extraction was eventually moved for more detailed racial assessment in Lodz (Litzmannstadt). The remainder went to the Reich as forced laborers or, in two known cases, were transported to Auschwitz-Birkenau. Those classified as unfit for work because of age, and children below 14 years, were segregated. An unusual feature of Globocnik's cleansing and joint Germanization and Ukrainianization — for German military and police units were accompanied in this ethnic cleansing by Ukrainian police units — of the Zamosc Lands was the decision to settle elderly Poles and children in what were termed "rental villages" (*wsi rentowych*). These villages, generally commandeered from Jews who had earlier been forcibly removed, were located in Sokol and Siedlce counties of Warsaw District, to Lublin's north. Efforts were also made to acquire similar depopulated villages in nearby Radom District. Between December 1942 and February 1943, the freezing winter months, over 2,100 minors were removed from parents who had been interned in a transit camp in Zamosc, and 3,200 elderly people were disbursed beyond Lublin District.

On average during 1942 about 2,300 people each month, generally ethnic Poles but including some Ukrainians, were forcibly dispatched to the Reich to become industrial or rural laborers. In 1942, some 27,500 Lublin District inhabitants were taken west. However, some who had been captured and interned during the Zamosc Lands cleansing action, during December of 1942, are included in this figure. These apprehensions and expulsions continued during 1943 when the total number reached 43,000 press-ganged workers.

The killing of Lublin District's Jewish population, including those who came from this region and those who had for whatever reason been forced into it prior to about December 1941, began early in 1942. Generally the first step taken was the removal of those living in small centers — village and township ghettos — to places with easy access to railway transport. This process went on throughout much of 1942, across all the district's counties. Many of the larger centers were emptied of their longer-term residents to make room for those about to be brought in from the Czech and Moravian region, Slovakia, and the Reich — that is, Germany and Austria. A case in point was the concentrating, in April, of all Jews living in Hrubieszow County into just five major centers. It was not until October that the Jews in Krasnystaw County were concentrated in Izbica, a major transit camp. As this concentrating process commenced, in March, the first transports began carrying members of the district's indigenous Jewish population into the Belzec killing center. Sobibor started receiving victims in May. Between March and November 1942, Belzec received nearly 87,000 Lublin District Jews, commencing in March with 18,000 from the city of Lublin itself. These were followed by deportations out of most of the district's counties. Starting in May, these counties saw inhabitants of other Jewish centers also being directed to Belzec. This involved some 75,000 people; this killing precinct accepted a total of some 162,000 people from the district. Apart from 4,000 of these, who were taken from Izbica and Wlodawa to Sobibor during January, April, and June of 1943, all Lublin District's Jews perished in Belzec during 1942.

However, not all Lublin District-based Jews were killed in both these extermination camps. Some 25,000 in 1942 and a further 10,000 in 1943 were directed into Majdanek concentration camp, which also had gas chambers. One of these shipments included a huge intake of 12,000 people. With these additional transports into Majdanek, nearly 242,000 perished in the three Lublin District killing facilities.

The first influx of trains bringing Jews into the district for extermination brought people from the Reich's Czech Protectorate and Moravia. These numbered some 78,600, and were initially concentrated in the Theresienstadt concentration camp near Prague. Their deportations began in March, with the first two trainloads arriving at Izbica camp, just north of Zamosc, after a two-day journey. The Czech and Moravian expulsions into Lublin District lasted until June, and involved some 14,000 Jews in 14 separate trainloads. Lublin itself received four of these transports, while Izbica, Zamosc, and Majdanek camp each received two; one each went to Sobibor killing center, Trawniki work camp, Piaski, and Rejowiec. Concurrent with these transports a similar action involving 39,000 Slovakian Jews was launched. Slovakia was estimated to have had a Jewish population of some 88,000 people. This expulsion involved 38 transports, each generally carrying just over 1,000 people, and headed north toward Globocnik's killing domain. Their destinations were Sobibor (10 trainloads); Lublin (4); and Izbica (2). Other transports from this Slovakian expulsion were directed to destinations such as Rejowiec (5); Naleczow (5); Lubartow (3); Chelm (2); Pulawy (2); Lukow (2); Deblin (2); and Miedzyrzec Podlaski (1). Those classified as young and healthy were generally directed to work camps, which Globocnik was erecting as part of his huge and growing economic empire that included *Ost-Industrie GmbH* (*Osti*) to supply increasingly the SS's needs as well as those of the army, then battling the Red Army.

Over the spring of 1942 the remaining Jews of Vienna, some 6,000 people, were railed to Lublin District in six train transports. The Izbica camp received four of these, with one each to Sobibor and nearby Wlodawa. These human shipments were made during April, May, and June. The Viennese deportations generally originated from that city's Aspangbahnhof, one of Vienna's major railway stations. Before the war, Wlodawa had a Jewish population of 7,000 in a total population of 10,000. Men who were classified fit, some 1,500, were involved in forced labor on river regulation and drainage works. The Viennese intake was in addition to the 9000 Austrian Jews who had arrived during 1941 and early 1942. Just before these shipments began, on 3 March, Governor Zörner was notified that in excess of 19,000 German Jews were to be accepted. These people came from Berlin, Darmstadt, Dortmund, Dusseldorf, Frankfurt am Main, Kassel, Koblenz, Cologne, Lipsk, Munich, Nuremberg, Stuttgart, and Wurzburg. Nearly 4,000 of these Jews perished in Izbica and 3,000 in Sobibor, with another 2,000 in Majdanek, and over 1,700 in Trawniki; just over half were killed. As in the case of the Viennese Jews, those from these large German cities generally boarded trains under armed guard at their home city's main station.

March 1942 also began the transportation of the Jews from the pre-war Polish region of Galicia into Globocnik's district, namely the Belzec killing center. This region, known after August 1941 as Distrikt Galicien, had a pre-war population of 573,000 Jews, of whom 100,000 lived in Lwow, its major urban center. Their extermination had in fact commenced in late 1941 through pogroms aimed at eliminating the intelligentsia and other specialists, especially in Lwow, Tarnopol, Boryslaw, and Zlorzow. Mass executions were also witnessed in Brzezany, Buczacz, Stryj, and Zbaraz, so that by March some 100,00 in these larger towns were already dead. Between the second half of March and early December 1942, nearly 252,000 Galician Jews had been moved to Belzec, using 71 rail shipments. Thirteen of these arrived in March, involving 13,700 people; two in April (10,000); two in June (7,000); one in

July (5,000); 14 in August (80,000); 11 in September (55,000); 9 in October (34,000); 14 in November (36,000); and five in December (6,000). All the district's major cities and towns were dispatch points: Lwow, Rawa Ruska, Stanislawow, Stryj, Tarnopol, and Drohobycz.

The pattern of executions and mass killings of Jews during 1942 across Galicia also took place in Krakow District, west of Lublin, at this time. Although some of this district's Jews were directed to Auschwitz, nearly 130,000 reached Belzec between March and December, and some 8,300 were trained in from nearby Radom District — 5,000 from Zawichost and 3,330 from Sandomierz — to Treblinka. Others from Radom District were taken to Auschwitz.[9] Just over 45,000 Lublin District Jews perished in Treblinka between August and November 1942, most of them from ghettos in the district's northern townships and counties.

Many thousands of Jews were transported into Globocnik's district in 1942 for purposes other than execution. Globocnik had a growing need for skilled workers — he had begun in this year to emerge as an industrial czar — which is why internees on some of the trains reaching Lublin from various parts of Western Europe were subjected to processing, irrespective of their origins. The purpose was to find younger and healthy people. This was the reason for Himmler's 9 October 1942 order to concentrate all Jewish workers in camps near Warsaw and Lublin, so they could contribute to supplying the German army. These work camps came under the control of the SS. After the clearance of the Warsaw Ghetto between 22 July and 9 September 1942, a steady stream of Jews was directed toward Lublin and Globocnik's surrounding work camps. They were taken from 35,000 skilled workers who had remained in Warsaw ghetto. In the second half of 1942, some 5,000 had been moved into Lublin's environs, following several thousand earlier that year.

A complicating feature of the Zamosc Lands expulsions was that the Ukrainians who lived in mixed Polish-Ukrainian villages were, at this time, segregated so as to be settled within exclusively Ukrainian villages, primarily in Hrubieszow County, but also in parts of Bilgoraj and Tomaszow Counties. This policy was sought by the pro–German fascist Organization of Ukrainian Nationalists (OUN), and especially its Krakow-based Ukrainian Central Committee, headed by the half–Polish, half–Ukrainian academic geographer, Wolodymyr Kubiiovych, who with his colleagues wished to see these lands cleared of Poles because he contended the Zamosc Lands were part of their planned Greater Ukraine. Progress on this segregation and resettling into a specially designated or exclusive Ukrainian sector — Hrubieszow and Tomaszow counties — of the Zamosc Lands was regularly reported upon directly to officials in Berlin who had oversight on Ukrainian affairs.

The first group of Ukrainians to be moved in this way involved nearly 6,900 people who had lived throughout Zamosc County. All were transferred to nearby Hrubieszow County between 7 and 21 December 1942, while ethnic Germans commandeered the vacated, predominantly Polish, villages. Between 12 January and 6 March 1943, ethnic Poles were expelled from 64 more villages so these could be transformed into purely Ukrainian-owned settlements. Altogether, the initial transfer involved 2,424 Polish families (12,224 people), and 1,726 Ukrainian families (6,900 people). However, the Polish expulsions and the concurrent Ukrainian concentrating process sparked an ethnic partisan conflict that rapidly spread across the entire Zamosc Lands. This was in addition to the Polish Underground launching a resistance against German farmers and military units. By early 1943, the Poles were therefore fighting German settlers, their military units, Ukrainians, and their police and militia units. All sides lost people in the steadily escalating bitter and bloody ethnic warfare. Because its magnitude and bitterness, something neither Globocnik nor von Mohrenschildt appear to have anticipated, became so grave, Polish historians and the Germans at the time have called this wartime conflict the Zamosc Uprising, a not inaccurate description. The fact that many segments of this part of Lublin District were so heavily forested meant partisan warfare was possible. This is something Globocnik must be judged upon harshly, for he had unwisely selected this area for Germanization. By August 1943, a further 11,500 Ukrainians were moved about the Zamosc Lands because of policy changes that were in part due to mounting insecurity.

1943

The fourth calendar year of the war saw both the Zamosc Lands expulsions of ethnic Poles and the extermination of Jews continuing throughout the first eight months. Both actions — the latter launched in March and the former in November of the previous year — probably reached their zenith between March and July, during the summer of 1943, after which both were suddenly discontinued, largely because of the exigencies of war, especially along the steadily crumbling Eastern Front. Globocnik left Lublin in mid–September, because of the province-wide disruptions caused by his and von Mohrenschildt's Zamosc Lands expulsions, not his extermination of this district's Jews and the Jews from other countries and the General Gouvernement. For the Jewish killings he was later commended for having been a successful and diligent killing servant, even though he would undoubtedly have seen such an assessment as off the mark, since he had not managed to kill more, for he had literally run out of time. In a very real sense the Zamosc Uprising by the Polish resistance, by resulting in Globocnik's removal, must be seen as having perhaps saved some — if only a very few — Jewish lives, even though it was basically fought to stop Germans and Ukrainians from taking Polish lives and property.

The Zamosc Lands expulsions resulted in many thousands of Poles being interned and sent to the Reich as workers. In some cases entire families were dispatched. These human shipments were primarily from the Zamosc and Zwierzyniec transit camps, that were used to intern people caught in ethnically cleansed villages, as well as from camps in Lublin itself, with one of these being situated near Krochmalnej Street. During July and August, over 18,500 adults were dispatched as forced workers. Over the entire year this figure exceeded 43,000, which was more than 23 per cent of all Poles dispatched to the Reich out of wartime Lublin District. At the same time a steady flow of children, numbering 4,454, was dispatched to German and Austrian cities for adoption or some similar racially inspired fate.[10] These minors had been acquired during the Zamosc Lands expulsions and were categorized as being Germanizable. There were, in addition, 644 people — men, women, and children — who had been dispatched in December 1942 and February 1943 to Lodz (Litzmannstadt) for assessment to see if they could or ought to be Germanized. These children and adults were extracted from the Polish population because the SS adhered to a blood theory, and believed that "lost German blood" existed amongst Poles. This theory in the Zamosc Lands case was believed to have been given credence, as pointed out earlier, by the fact that SS researchers had discovered that Austria's Emperor Joseph II had actually settled German farmers around Zamosc during the 1780s, along the lines of his mother settling Europeans in various parts of the Balkans that had been taken from them by the steadily retreating Ottoman Empire.

Added to this, after July 1943 many thousands of these interned Polish peasant farmers commenced being released from Majdanek concentration camp — it had been used as a makeshift holding or detention center — while others began leaving other nearby detention camps. During mid–August, over 3,800 Poles, in three roughly equal shipments, were dispatched to the Pulawy area northwest of Lublin. These and others who began emerging from hiding from forest dugouts and nearby counties where they had fled Globocnik's ethnic cleansing action teams now generally wished to reclaim their homes and properties, something that further exacerbated the already brisk and murderous Polish-Ukrainian ethnic war across the entire southern segment of Lublin District.

However, as the Zamosc Lands expulsions wound down in the second half of 1943, Lublin District began to witness steadily growing numbers of Polish refugees entering from the east — from Poland's pre-war eastern province of Wolyn (Volhynia), as well as from parts of nearby Galicia — because of the bloody ethnic war going on there between Polish and Ukrainian fighting units. This "war within a war" had been launched the previous year by the Ukrainian-manned fascist fighting formations of the so-called *Ukrainska Povstanska Armiia* (UPA). This quite separate conflict, from the Polish standpoint, was even bloodier and more bitter than the Globocnik-inspired Zamosc Lands expulsion action, and the resultant Polish-Ukrainian internecine conflict there overflowed to be fought out primarily in Hrubieszow and Bilgoraj Counties. UPA's killing gangs in Wolyn and Galicia, unlike the joint German and Ukrainian police and militia units operating on the Zamosc Lands, were not simply deporting Poles. They were, instead, massacring them; men, women, and children, in their villages, homes, or wherever else the Poles could be caught. The main reason UPA had launched these massacres was to remove all Poles from Wolyn and Galicia in their bid to have a racially pure Greater Ukraine, of which the Zamosc Lands were to be a part.

The Polish-Ukrainian ethnic war thus became a major feature of life across the southern segments of Lublin District throughout much of 1943 and into 1944. Just as Globocnik's expulsions were about to be discontinued, tens of thousands of Polish refugees began reaching this contested area, which his expulsions had already transformed into a major fighting zone of the General Gouvernement. Just over 24,000 Poles registered with the Polish relief agency, *Rada Glowna Opiekuncza* (RGO), during 1943, all seeking assistance, with a further 21,700 registering during the early months of 1944. However, these nearly 46,000 registrations markedly understate the numbers of actual arrivals in Lublin District between about July 1943 and June 1944 from the even bloodier east, Wolyn and Galicia. According to Lublin historian Janina Kielbon, the figure was probably closer to 100,000, maybe even higher. By the time this wave of eastern Polish refugees had peaked, however, Globocnik had departed Lublin for Trieste.[11] As strange as it may sound, the fact that these Poles fled into Globocnik's district serves to show that what was happening beyond it was far worse and more terrifying.

Alongside all these expulsions, all the ethnic and partisan warfare, and the beginnings of a large eastward movement of Polish refugees, *Aktion Reinhardt* continued unabated, with Globocnik involved in the incredible state of affairs of expelling Poles, resettling and defending Ukrainians, settling Germans and defending them against Polish partisans, as well as exterminating incoming Jews. No other SS man can claim to have been involved in so much demographic upheaval and bloodshed of people of all ages. His nearest murderous rival, Rudolf Höss, the head of the better-known Auschwitz-Birkenau, was only managing extermination and large-scale death through forced work. Globocnik was involved in far more destruction.

Another huge intake of Jews came during the months of March and April. All these, 34,300 men, women, and children, were from Holland, from the Westerbork transit camp —*Polizeiliche Durchgangslager*— in Drente Province. Globocnik's SS and police equivalent in Holland was Hans Albin Rauter, who hailed from Graz and who had fought against Slovenes in Carinthia just after World War I, even though he was only a student at the time, a conflict

Globocnik wished to claim he had participated in. Although all these Dutch Jews were destined for Sobibor, there were selection stopovers in Lublin where those who were younger were often directed to work camps around Lublin and at Majdanek. March also brought four transports of 1,000 people each from France. In September and October, 13,000 more Jews were taken to Sobibor, all of whom were from the Reich Commissariat East, with nearly 3,000 from Lida and 5,000 from Minsk, thus from areas well to the northeast of Lublin. The other 5,000 were from Wilno, in what had been during the pre-war years north-eastern Poland, *Wilenszczyzna*.

A practice which had commenced in late 1942, that of transferring skilled Jewish workers from Warsaw and its environs to work in Globocnik's network of labor camps that were involved in war production around Lublin, continued throughout 1943. Some 15,000 such Jews were transferred during April and May to Poniatowa camps, west of Lublin, the site of the textile company, Walter Casper Toeboens. At the same time, several thousand were moved to the Trawniki camp southwest of Lublin, the venue of Fritz Schulz & Co., to work as furriers, brush makers, and tailors. Majdanek concentration camp also received 16,000 more Jews at this time, including 3,500 survivors from the Warsaw ghetto.

Although Treblinka was the center primarily used to kill the Jews of Bialystok and environs — whose population included some 350,000 Jews before June 1941, when it was under Soviet control — some of these were later transferred into the Lublin District. Not all the 350,000 were to perish, because many had fled this region and the city with Soviet forces that had occupied the area in September 1939. Some had managed even to flee east well after the Germans occupied the region. Extermination began in the Bialystok area in November 1942, the month that Globocnik and von Mohrenschildt launched the Zamosc Lands expulsion. This involved concentrating the region's Jews into five collection camps. Widespread murdering now began, followed by the removal of Jews to Treblinka as well as, strangely, distant Auschwitz-Birkenau. However, some of the last Jews of Bialystok were moved to Majdanek, and perished on Lublin's outskirts; Globocnik was primarily responsible for the destruction of this huge community, like so many others.

By the winter of 1943, nearly all of Lublin District's Jews had been exterminated, with the notable exception of about 42,000 skilled workers, craftsmen and specialists, compulsorily employed within Globocnik's *Deutsche Ausrüstungswerke GmbH (DAW)* and *Osti* industrial and manufacturing conglomerates at Trawniki, Poniatowa, and other minor nearby work camps. Many of these, although it is impossible to say how many, did not come from the Lublin region. They had, over the previous two years, been forcibly imported. All these specialists or skilled workers were shot during a series of ongoing executions at Majdanek in early November (*Aktion Erntefest*) and at

Trawniki and Poniatowa, after Globocnik had reached Trieste, though his involvement in this crime cannot be discounted.

Easily forgotten at this stage is the fate of the district's Germans. Those living in commandeered Polish villages — the pioneers of Hitler's and Himmler's *Generalplan Ost*—were defending themselves against sporadic and systematic Polish partisan actions. The district's various county (*Kreis*) administrators were now under constant threat of death by assassination or ambush, and were increasingly cautious and ever on the defensive. And the region's southern segments — Hrubieszow, Tomaszow, and Bilgoraj Counties — continued witnessing minor battles and ongoing skirmishes between Polish and Ukrainian partisan units as well as German military units. This year also brought a number of major military actions — search and destroy — by the German army.

1944

German rural settlers who had been brought into the district during 1942 and 1943 to commence Germanizing it, thereby reversed policies implemented during 1940, when the Chelm Germans were removed to the west. During 1944, however, the 1940 pattern of westward movement of Germans was repeated to ensure that the Germans settled during 1942 and 1943 were not captured by the rapidly advancing Soviet Red Army. Their withdrawal was also prompted by intensified local Polish partisan actions. With these evacuees went the 5,000 or so remaining Chelm Germans who had opted not to be settled in western Poland during 1940. All these people joined the enormous flow of Germans who were also fleeing from the Baltic regions, parts of northern Poland, East Prussia, and even many parts of the Balkans, including from Globocnik's mother's home region of Banat. All were moving back toward the Reich, including Austria. Germandom was now moving west, in the opposite direction to what Hitler and Himmler had so desired. This movement was in addition to the steadily retreating German armed forces. The city of Lublin was officially liberated by the Red Army on 24 July 1944. Majdanek concentration camp, which in October 1942 had acquired concrete gas chambers and had held over 300,000 prisoners altogether during its years of operation, was therefore also opened.[12] Other smaller demographic disturbances included ongoing reprisal attacks upon villages during German-directed anti-partisan actions. There continued the removal of peasants for failure to meet set quota levels for grain, meat, and dairy products, and there were also displacements during the construction of military and related facilities and prisoner and work camps.

Janina Kielbon has summarized the magnitude of the difficult-to-comprehend demographic upheaval within this comparatively small region of Poland, which, on the eve of the war, had a population of just 2.4 million people. She has estimated that some 870,000 civilians reached the region from late 1939 until the middle of 1944, or 36.7 percent of its indigenous pre-war population. This figure, according to Kielbon, was made up of, at minimum, 640,000 Jews, 225,000 Poles, and Globocnik's and von Mohren-schildt's 13,000 German colonists. However, nearly 260,000 people were expelled from the district. Among these were 180,000 Poles, 55,000 Jews and 24,500 Germans — those from Chelm and its immediate environs. Among those expelled, members of the ethnic Polish component were generally deported into the Reich to become forced workers, while among those brought in, most were Jews who were generally directed immediately to one of Globoc-nik's two extermination camps or an intermediate ghetto from where they were later deported to Sobibor, Belzec, or perhaps Majdanek or a major work camp.[13] Some, however, had been placed in ghettos before being taken to a killing center, while others were directed to work camps. If the 640,000 num-ber is added to the district's 200,000 Jewish residents, then Globocnik mur-dered in the district some 840,000 Jews, excluding those who perished in Treblinka, which was beyond the district. One should at all times be mind-ful that these figures are the best available estimates that Kielbon was able to reconstruct after assessing all available sources. To the best of our knowledge, careful tabulations were not made by anyone on Globocnik's staff. If they were, they have not been found. It is unlikely, therefore, that we will ever be able to find figures that are more satisfactory than Kielbon's published esti-mates. There will, however, be room for contradiction and disputes con-cerning the magnitude of Globocnik's killings and deportations.

A great many people were also murdered in numerous executions beyond Globocnik's designated killing precincts. Many died during death marches — something that affected Jews especially — and during the countermeasures against Polish partisans who fought German units involved in the Zamosc Lands expulsions. Reprisals against Polish villages were also not uncommon. Here again Kielbon presents an excellent and succinct assessment of such added killings:

> ...[W]e must remember that Jews were also lost in ghettos, work camps, and the countless executions, with the biggest number happening in 1942. In many cases there were mass executions. For example, on 13 July 1942, there were 1500 Jews shot at Jozefow Bilgorajski; on 17–19 August, 1700 Jews in Lomaze, 19 August 1942, about 400 Jews in Parczew, 22 September 1943, about 200 in Serokomla. The biggest execution took place on the 3 November 1943 within the framework of the *Erntefest*, where about 40,000 were killed in Majdanek, Poniatowa and Trawniki. According to Robert Browning's calculations just one unit, Police Battalion 101, which was brought into Lublin District for half of

1942, killed 38,000 Jews. And they undertook many mass executions and deportations into camps. Moreover, this was not the only such unit involved in the extermination of Jews. *To date no one has undertaken a calculation in order to discover just how many Jews were lost in the Lublin District due to harsh living conditions in the ghettos and in countless numbers of work camps. It is highly probable that the number may reach up to 100,000 people* [emphasis added].

We reach here then an important conclusion to begin the study of this issue. Most of the Jews, before their final deportations to the extermination camps, had been moved several times. The reason for this movement is well described by Artur Eisenbach, who wrote:

Reallocations were organized by the *Sipo-SD* over the intermediate stages so as to isolate the Jews, and thus to break their links with neighbors, in order that mass opposition was a complete impossibility. Also, the many encounters during the various stages of the war [with the authorities] were designed to leave the Jew without a basic feeling of security, which arises from family and home, or even a prison cell. Human feelings were to be degraded to mere panic and fear of hunger and death.[14]

The lot for indigenous and imported Jews of Lublin District, for whom this territory became the very last destination, is in line with Eisenbach's thesis. The so-called resettlement of the Jews was simply the first stage in their extermination, and this was achieved on the territory of the Lublin District, Globocnik-Land, which became "Europe's unique burial ground" in which the central criminal and organizer of Jewish deaths was Globocnik.[15]

This dual movement of Jews makes it that much more difficult for researchers to make hard and fast statements about the magnitude of Globocnik's crimes. But as a result of them, by the end of the occupation period there were virtually no Jews amongst the remnant Lublin District population — they had been exterminated. Nor was there a German minority — its members had either been resettled into western Poland (Warthe Land), or else Globocnik's 1942–43 German colonists whom he had settled upon the Zamosc Land had either fled or were evacuated in the summer of 1944. Some, of course, had been killed by Polish partisans since their arrival gave the Poles ready and often quite isolated targets to strike at in reprisal. Despite deportations and exterminations, the number of Poles actually increased over these five years, according to Kielbon's calculations, whereas the number of Ukrainians basically remained unchanged.[16]

Although Globocnik was certainly not responsible for every single onslaught upon his district's inhabitants, he was, more than anyone, the person who carries the greatest direct individual responsibility and therefore guilt. Some of those deported into his district arrived because of SS agencies beyond his control, others due to the German army's initiatives. His relatively small and secret *Aktion Reinhardt* killing teams, however, were solely responsible for all the murders in Belzec and Sobibor killing centers, as they were for the more significant and larger Treblinka killing camp north of Lublin District, midway between Warsaw and Bialystok. He also carries the blame for the deaths inside Majdanek concentration camp. He, with Governor Zörner, was responsible for creating across Lublin District the network of ghettos that housed Jews, in which many thousands of people perished due to starvation, cold, and lack of medical supplies. He was largely responsible for the region's network of harsh work camps, and the cruel removal of the Zamosc Lands' Polish peasant farmers, though his ethnic cleansing teams were assisted by Ukrainian policing units. For that, the various Ukrainian collaborating agencies associated with the Ukrainian Central Committee, headed by Wolodymyr Kubiiovych, must jointly share the guilt. In this ethnic cleansing action, Reinhold von Mohrenschildt and Gustav Hanelt must also be held partly responsible, the former because he was second-in-command to Globocnik, and Hanelt because of his work as director of the Lublin-based Research Center for Eastern Settlement, which, as its title suggests, meant he advised and researched demographic issues that assisted in and were to help hasten the hoped for total Germanization of Lublin District. Globocnik's units were in charge of the huge network of work camps that held Jewish and Polish prisoners, and his policing units must take full blame for most of the repressions, the killings of tens of thousands of civilians, and so many Soviet POWs interned throughout his district. Globocnik was thus far and away the most culpable of the Reich's many war criminals who embraced the Hitlerian dream of Germanizing the East. Globocnik himself believed he had killed two million Jews. Precisely how many Soviet prisoners of war perished within his district is not known, but it must surely have been many tens of thousands, and no fewer than 40,000 Poles perished directly because of his murderous 46 months in Lublin. Globocnik was therefore truly Hitler's most vicious killer, and one of the 20th century's worst.

XVII

Globocnik in Lublin:
A General Assessment

Most people's personalities are such that their moods and predispositions have a marked degree of variance; sometimes happy, sometimes sad, sometimes kind, others far less so, sometimes even unkind. And these variations can come and go within minutes, in some cases even within seconds. This is simply part of what more recent writers and commentators have dubbed the human condition, rather than using the far older adage, that all of us sin at least seven times a day. In Odilo Globocnik's case such disparities most certainly existed. He was, according to the accounts given by Irmgard Rickheim, during a long series of interviews over several years, kind and generous to her during their engagement, which lasted from May or June 1941 until around December the following year, when she had already returned to Berlin. Rickheim does not remember him losing his temper, or striking her or exhibiting some other such undesirable characteristic common in so many men. Certainly, dispatching her to the historic but out-of-the-way village of Sobieszyn was a rather strange thing to do. But this came when his fiancée and lover was being criticized by an anonymous source, causing strife with his superior, Himmler. Moreover, and this should not be overlooked, it was at about this time that Globocnik had taken full command of *Aktion Reinhardt*. Rickheim claimed throughout all interviews when *Aktion Reinhardt* was raised that she did not know it existed, and knew nothing of its implementation. That being the case, perhaps Globocnik's secret intention in dispatching her away from Lublin was, at least in part, prompted by his involvement in the early stages of this genocide of Europe's Jews for Himmler and Hitler. As unsatisfactory as it is, the fact of the matter is that we will never know precisely why he made this decision. It may have been for any number of reasons, including the presence in Lublin of his mother, Anna, who did not get along with Rickheim.

Globocnik appears to have loved his mother dearly, remaining exceptionally loyal to her, to the extent of even having had her, with several other family members, living near him in Lublin during at least part of the first year of the Jewish Holocaust, his single most monstrous crime. This bizarre aspect of his life must surely remain one of the great mysteries of this most destructive and monstrous man. His attachment to his mother was the strongest attachment of his life, far stronger, it would seem, than the short-lived 20-month romantic association with Rickheim.

He could be charming and friendly to his many Lublin acquaintances and work colleagues; he was at times a funnyman, someone who was willing to snub pomposity, and the like, even if only in private. But he was also opinionated, ignorant, pompous, bombastic, and extremely ruthless, cruel, cunning, calculating, and not slow to threaten even people relatively close to him. *Aktion Reinhardt* was top-secret, and there are several documented statements that indicate he threatened people who had "loose tongues." Another most unattractive characteristic was his propensity to break contact suddenly with long-time associates with whom he had been close, and for no apparent reason. And, of course, he perpetrated, and this is objectively speaking, some of the most evil behavior that European history has seen visited upon human kind, namely the mass murder of men, women, and even children, and the disposal of their bodies en masse by cremation or burial in mass graves. Europe has an abundance of contenders for the position of being the most evil, and Globocnik is certainly among those at the very top of that list. All this took place in great secrecy. For this reason, Alexander Ramsay's claim that Odilo Globocnik *was* "the worst man in the world," or words to that effect, is close to the mark, though at the time Ramsay made this comment — soon after the end of the war — Stalin and several of his equally evil politburo and other ideological comrades, with whom Stalin had initially teamed up in the 1930s to purge and re-purge their party and millions of perceived enemies, were still alive and still held power in Moscow. Rickheim, however, never contradicted Ramsay's assessment when it was put to her.

To the Jews, Globocnik was the most violent and the most destructive anti-Semite of all time. It is difficult to name another who surpasses him in this regard. Hitler? Himmler? Heydrich? Rudolf Höss? Adolf Eichmann? These men, with Globocnik, were all part of the same huge continent-wide murder program created to kill all European Jews. They were members of the same murderous gang, perpetrators of the same crime. The tragedy of German history is that these men held national executive powers. The first three were Globocnik's superiors. Höss, as the commandant of the huge concentration camp and killing center in Upper Silesia, Auschwitz-Birkenau, oversaw the killing of about a million people, mostly Jews but also many tens of thousands of Poles and those of many other nationalities. Globocnik's death tally was at least 50 percent higher than that of Höss. Hitler and Himmler were co-conspirators and architects of the program of forced removal of Jews, and later their extermination, whereas Eichmann was largely a central coordinator of both these policies. The Jews of Europe had never encountered anyone more destructive or worse than Odilo Globocnik, with the possible exception of Christian Wirth, but here again he, like the vicious Hermann Höfle, was a senior member of Globocnik's Jewish exterminating team. Both Globocnik and Wirth continued in the same vein when they reached Trieste in September 1943. But the fact that Globocnik was Wirth's nominal Lublin superior means he must be placed ahead of Wirth in degree of culpability, even if only marginally. Globocnik's Lublin District Gulag was not merely a vehicle for a well-organized short-lived pogrom. *Aktion Reinhardt* involved putting into place a highly organized network of ghettos across his district; other SS men did likewise in other parts of the General Gouvernement, as did other senior SS men elsewhere farther east. Wirth was only in charge of the latter stage of this system, that is, the killing centers, what David Irving so aptly called "terminal stations." Globocnik oversaw their construction and administration of the entire program from November 1939 until September 1943, and possibly for a number of months later. And then he wrote, in a cold-blooded manner, a series of letters to Himmler outlining and accounting for the loot he had removed from the approximately 1.5 million victims, as if this whole murderous affair was akin to a series of pirate raids on the high seas. It was also Globocnik who erected alongside the ghettos and elsewhere a network of work camps that were designed to be halfway stations toward totally annihilating through work all Jews over whom he managed to gain power. Men like Ernst Lerch, Hermann Höfle, and Georg Michalsen cleared these ghettos, and not only ghettos located within Globocnik's district, so that their hundreds of thousands of by now hungry, sick, and frail inmates could be moved to the three killing centers of Treblinka, Sobibor, and Belzec. Globocnik's Gulag, once its three killing centers were erected and operational, was designed to bring about annihilation far more suddenly for the Jews than the intended eventual destruction of the larger number of Poles and later all other Slavs, who first had to be culled to find "lost German blood" that was believed to be flowing through some of these people's veins, and then to be used as mass labor to help win the war and also to assist in Germanizing the East with Reich Germans and *Volksdeutsche*. Incredibly, Globocnik and a number of his culpable colleagues in crime appear to have assumed they could somehow cover up their massive crime of genocide. They seem to have believed that the disappearance of some two million men, women, and children would perhaps go unnoticed or not be inquired into at some later date. The only evidence we have of some hesitancy, or perhaps doubt, on his central role in all this is Rickheim's revelation that Globocnik at times claimed privately to her that "If it was not for this war then I would remove my SS jacket and hang it permanently on a nail on the wall." This was a colorful way of claiming that he really preferred the plowshare to the sword, something he never demonstrated in fact. Remember that Globocnik, from his teenage years, moved rapidly to become a political activist. But even if he had not made himself available, there were others who would have willingly filled his Lublin shoes; Wirth, Höfle and Michalsen, to name just three. And what of that other sinister Carinthian, Reinhold von Mohrenschildt? What, also, of that other one, Ernst Lerch? Even as late as 1943, there was still no shortage of candidates in Lublin for such ideological work.

To the Poles, Globocnik was yet another Germanic Margrave set on finally destroying them, by implementing a Final Solution, an *Endlösung*, first by their forcible removal from the lands of the valley of the Vistula and its tributaries, and their resettlement away from this area of Europe, where they had long been an agricultural and more recently increasingly urban, industrial, and commercial people, who, at times, had been cooperative with the Germanic peoples, often borrowing ideas and practices from them, and who were no worse neighbors than other Europeans or European nations. The Poles were fortunate that Globocnik and Himmler literally ran out of time to undertake any further expulsion actions, for it can be easily argued that the killing centers of Treblinka, Sobibor, and Belzec may have been turned over to eliminating them in the way so many Jews had been eliminated within these three isolated Bug River valley barbed wire and gas chamber equipped compounds. Sobibor and Belzec were well located for the extermination of Polish peasants living in southern and central Lublin District. Treblinka, on the other hand, could easily have been swung into use to exterminate the populace of the Lublin District's northern counties. Globocnik's departure for Trieste in September 1943, something many Germans in occupied Poland worked to bring about, and the fact that *Aktion Reinhardt* was hastily being wound down as he departed, was truly life-saving news for the Poles, and not only those in Globocnik's district but in the entire General Gouvernement. If Globocnik had enjoyed his way, he would have removed all the ethnic Poles living under German occupation to distant eastern locations. His murderous record vis-à-vis the Jews means that fate should not be discounted for the Poles. With respect to the Poles, the Hitler regime had several other ideologically committed men who, if not surpassing Globocnik, came close to equaling him in brutality. Artur Greiser in Poznan, who ruled the Warthe Land, that is, much of western Poland, was an exceptionally cruel individual, certainly far crueler and a far more enthusiastic follower of Himmler's thinking than Albert Forster, who ruled Danzig-West Preussen. Globocnik's superior in Krakow, Friedrich-Wilhelm Kruger, also challenges him for brutality. It should be remembered that Kruger was Himmler's major coordination officer in the elimination of the Jews of the General Gouvernement. Forster in Danzig (Gdansk) was marginally less intolerant. Occupied Poland had a long list of modern Germanic Margraves, including Hermann Krumey in Lodz (Litzmannstadt), who expelled, murdered, and dehumanized in a variety of other cruel and bestial ways several million ethnic Poles. In most respects, Globocnik was simply one of the monsters. Where he differed from the others was his special relationship with Himmler, and through the planning of men like Gustav Hanelt and Dr. Franz Stanglica in his Lublin-based Research Center for Eastern Settlement. Had things been different on the Eastern Front, Globocnik would in all probability have led a successful total and complete depopulating of Poles from all traditional Polish lands. That was certainly Himmler's and Globocnik's aim from at least mid–1941 onward, when their plans for the Germanization of the Zamosc Land began to take shape, especially within Globocnik's Lublin-based research center.

To the Germans, and this, of course, includes *Volksdeutsche*, this non-Reich German and senior SS man, who came from distant Carinthia like his ultimate superior Adolf Hitler and his paladins, dragged down Germany's historical reputation to an unimaginably low level. In addition, Globocnik dismally failed to Germanize the Lublin District, and more specifically the Zamosc Lands. In both cases the ethnic Germans he introduced as settlers had made hasty westward retreats by the summer of 1944, after holding the land he thought would be theirs forever for about 18 months, hardly two harvests! True, this was not entirely Globocnik's fault, because the withdrawals were made in the wake of an advancing, and, understandably, bitterly vengeful force, the Red Army and the Soviet secret police, the People's Commissariat of Internal Affairs (NKVD). But he must take some of the blame, since it was he who was so adamant that settlement of his district and this region was required in 1942 and 1943, not later when men like Dr. Hans Frank and Ernst Zörner believed it should commence. It should be stressed, however, that Frank and Zörner also yearned for the day when the General Gouvernement was settled entirely by Germanic people. Both were dedicated followers of Adolf Hitler, both having been close pre-war personal friends, and both shared Hitler's eastern hopes and aspirations for the Germans. Globocnik chose instead to go for the hasty path and to confront the Polish peasants of his district, that is, to move against the food producers. His motto was, effectively, Germanize now, no matter what the cost and no matter if it harms other crucial Axis wartime aims and essentials, such as the supplying of German forces fighting farther east. No evidence exists showing that he gave even minuscule consideration or thought to possible difficulties and consequences. He was, instead, hell-bent on Germanizing his entire district, then the General Gouvernement, and finally any other designated lands to the East, and as soon as possible. Nothing short of that was acceptable to him. He operated on the principle that everything would go according to plan, which it did not.

The Polish partisans of the Zamosc Lands, apart from threatening food supplies, also caused a not insignificant drain on Globocnik's police manpower, something that was in short supply across the entire General Gouvernement. Furthermore, Globocnik had a very special criminal relationship with Himmler, of that we can be sure. But rather than using and cultivating the association with shrewd advice that would significantly help ensure that Berlin's ultimate goal of becoming the capital of an expanded Greater Germanic Reich, from at least the Rhine in the west to the Urals in the east, and at the same time being without Jews, Poles, and all other Slavs, he opted to be a Himmler camp follower to the point of unending obsequiousness and uncritical obedience. He was a toady, something that made the policing and administration of his district far more onerous for all other German occupation officials at the district and county levels. Here his days as *Gauleiter* of Vienna, which included financial fraud, and his choice of Irmgard Rickheim as a marriage partner, played into Himmler's hands. Globocnik was, in his relationship to his superiors, nothing more than a complete and utter yesman for an evil cause, and his decision to be a pliant disciple contributed in its own small way to the conquest of the Reich.

XVIII

Back in Trieste:
September 1943 to April 1945

September 1943 was a tragic month for central and northern Italian Jews, as it was for Italian and Yugoslav, especially Slovene, partisans and other dissidents (or suspected dissidents) living in these northern Italian regions, for Globocnik and his T4 killing team had arrived in Trieste by road. Himmler had written to him on 13 September advising he was to be a higher, not just a lower, SS and police chief in the operational zone named Adriatic Coastal Land Zone, or simply Adriatic Coastal Zone, and that he was subordinated to High Commissioner *Gauleiter* Dr. Rainer and Army Group B superior, *SS-Obergruppenführer* Wolff, someone who had knowledge of Globocnik since at least his days of financial strife in Vienna during 1938. In July 1941, Himmler had elevated Globocnik to "plenipotentiary extraordinary for designing and constructing SS Police outposts in the eastern territories," a further expansion and broadening of his Lublin powers, enabling him both to expel Poles and settle Germans.[1] Interestingly, an SS headquarters entry in Globocnik's SS file stated that between 1 and 17 September 1943 he was, as well as SS and police chief in Lublin, the representative for the Reich for the resettlement of Poland's pre-war Wolyn (Volhynia) Province, as well as for the construction of SS and police strongpoints in the "new eastern districts" and "also the special taskforce Reinhardt."[2] When he had departed Lublin for Trieste, Globocnik was at the very peak of his power, on paper at least, with the authority and power to kill any Jew and expel any Pole from the Lublin District and adjacent Wolyn Province. His long-awaited removal from Lublin not only meant the ignominious demise of the Zamosc Lands expulsion action, but also *Generalplan Ost*. Globocnik's move south, to Europe's Adriatic region, was thus the end for Hitler and Himmler of ever seeing their eastern dreams realized. This turnaround can be officially and validly dated as 17 September 1943, some 20 months before both Nazi leaders, and Globocnik, committed suicide.

Globocnik's SS file also reveals the size of his new staff, for late in October 1943 he wrote to *SS-Gruppenführer* von Herff, the SS's head of personnel in Berlin, giving an accounting. His inner and police staff, he claimed, included 49 men. Those involved in *RKFDV* work made up a smaller number, standing at 16. But those attached to the *SS-Mannschaftshaus* were only marginally below his private staff of 42. Many of these men, and one woman, Gustav Hanelt's wife, had been involved in planning German settlement of the Lublin District and lands farther east, well inside Ukraine and Russia. Those linked to the Trawniki work camp stood at just three, with the Trawniki training camp being staffed by 26 men. There were seven interpreters and 10 other staff members linked to the *DAW* industrial conglomerate. Precisely why these people left Lublin at this time is not clear, beyond Globocnik's preference for more rather than fewer staffers. The total thus came to 153. There were a further 186 designated to various duties described as *SS* leaders of police, work groups, *VoMi, RKFDV, RuSHA,* SS and police strongpoints, and those linked to resettlement duties, bringing the total to 339. In addition, there were 92 men from the Chancellery of the *Führer* for *Aktion Reinhardt,* the Jewish extermination project, or a total of 431.[3] This last group, no doubt, included men like Stangl and Wirth, and took in a large number of the Ukrainians who had been auxiliaries in his three Bug killing centers.

In September Italy had unilaterally withdrawn from its alliance with Berlin. Notwithstanding that 100,000 German soldiers were stationed on its territory and with Western Allied armies landing at points on its south-western coast, Italy became a war theater with Germans occupying the north and central regions while the Allies quickly gained possession of the south, up to central Italy. By early October, the Trieste region had been virtually annexed by the Reich, despite Hitler's expressions of gratitude to Mussolini for not challenging the *Anschluss* in March 1938, an event in which Globocnik had played such a key role.[4] Italy's provinces of Friaul, Gorz, Trieste, Istrien, Fiume, Quamero, and Laibach were made a single administrative unit that came increasingly under tight German oversight, if not control. The by then thoroughly experienced and Globocnik-led T4 killing team and police apparatus that had left Lublin and reached Trieste on 23 September, largely intact, with its trained and experienced Ukrainian auxiliaries, quickly established what became a cruel and deadly police detention and killing center called La

Risiera di San Sabba (the Rice Mill). Globocnik's transfer to the *Adriatisches Kuestenland*, the Adriatic Coastal Land Zone, came not simply because of resistance to his Himmler-backed Zamosc Lands colonizing venture. That failure, due to steadily mounting Polish partisan actions and the resultant economic dislocation in that region, explains why he was moved out of Lublin, but fails to clarify why he was sent to the city of his birth. Just as the pressure within the General Gouvernement's civil administrative circles finally convinced many in Berlin that Globocnik simply had to go, a need for a man with a bloodied "iron fist" had arisen in northern Italy, and that was probably the reason he was directed to Trieste. Added to this was the fact that with Berlin's control of northern Italy came a desire to ensure the elimination of its Jewish population, and no one could surpass Globocnik's qualifications on that count. According to Siegfried Pucher, it was believed that an urgent need existed to build up the police forces in the region to overcome what were seen as "Italian deficiencies" in spite of orders from Mussolini on the elimination of Jews. Italians were seen to be lax, needing German and Austrian assistance for such a task.[5] Siegfried Pucher backs this contention by stressing that Globocnik's Lublin staff was transferred to Italy with him, not left in occupied Poland where such ethnic killings continued in a range of places, including Auschwitz-Birkenau. This conclusion is certainly difficult to argue with. Some Italians, Croats, and Slovenes were recruited to help in these policing tasks, but these people were generally seen as also being deficient. In addition, Cossacks and auxiliaries from the Caucuses augmented Globocnik's ranks. So, as in Lublin, he was well supported against any threats.

As the autumn of 1943 approached, Berlin decided to create two operations zones that stretched across northern Italy to ready the Reich for stalling the advancing Allied armies that were manned primarily by the British, Americans, New Zealanders, South Africans, as well as a significant number of Poles, led by the indefatigable Lt. General Wladyslaw Anders.[6] It was not realized then that these forces would only slowly gain the upper hand across the Italian peninsula. It was not until May 1945, the last month of the war, that Trieste was liberated, a full 19 months after the Allies' southern Italian landings that commenced in September 1943. On the 12th of that month, Hitler's compatriot and early 1920s ideological idol, the now deposed Mussolini, was daringly rescued, on the *Führer*'s orders, from an out-of-the-way hotel known as Gran Sasso d'Italia, high in the Abruzzi Apennines, where he had been interned. After this rescue by Viennese-born SS man, Otto "Scar face" Skorzeny, the former *Il Duce* re-emerged as leader of a northern Italian pro-German state, named the Social Republic, or Duce-Land. The establishment of the operations zone of *Alpenworland* was officially announced on 17 September, and that of the *Adriatisches Kuestenland* nearly one month later on 15 October, with the *Gauleiter* Franz Hofer, in Innsbruck, and *Gauleiter*

Friedrich Rainer in Klagenfurt placed in charge as their regions' respective supreme commissioners.[7]

However, on 10 September Hitler made a national broadcast from his headquarters, the first such broadcast in several months. He spoke of Italy's collapse, claiming it had been foreseen long ago. Mussolini's downfall had come on the night of 24–25 July 1943, when the Fascist Grand Council voted 19 to 7 for his removal. This was followed by King Victor Emmanuel III arresting Mussolini, and Marshall Badoglio taking his place. On 19 August, Badoglio had contacted U.S. General Dwight D. Eisenhower without the Germans being forewarned. As Hitler was so often prone to do, he immediately went on the attack in the broadcast, blaming a group of unidentified Italians who, he claimed, had been working for several years to break the relatively short-lived Berlin-Rome alliance. He then referred to King Emmanuel, Marshal Badoglio, General Roatta, and an unnamed foreign office representative, saying each had failed to inform their ally of Italy's withdrawal from the Pact of Steel. After delivering a brief potted history of the alliance since 1939, he described his long-standing hero, Mussolini, as "one of the most important men produced by contemporary times — the greatest son of the Italian land since the downfall of the ancient Roman Empire."[8] Although too much should not be made of it, this historical comparison is an indication of the long view Hitler held of national histories, seeing himself as a latter-day Germanic Margrave with a mission to acquire on behalf of the Germans vast tracts of eastern land. Hitler went on to describe Mussolini as his friend, and again criticized those responsible for bringing about Italy's capitulation. More pertinent, however, was the fact that midway in his address he warned that:

> The interests of national strategy of the German people are for us as sacred as they are binding. We all know that in this merciless struggle it is the desire of our enemies to destroy the defeated and give a chance to live only to the victorious. We are therefore willing to take, in cold determination, all those measures, both in general and detail, which we consider necessary to foil our enemies' hope.
>
> But there are also numerous honorable Italians who, in spite of everything, consider themselves indissolubly united with the struggle of the two nations. The defection of Italy means little from a military point of view since the struggle in this country was for months mainly borne by German forces.[9]

At the time of Mussolini's ignominious removal from power, there were stationed in Italy six German divisions comprising some 100,000 men. By October 1943, three months later, these had tripled to 18 divisions, or some 300,000 men, meaning Hitler's words were followed through with actions, and at a time when the tide had turned against the Reich on the Eastern Front. The entry of Globocnik and the T4 killing team into Trieste was part of this enormous build-up across northern and central Italy, and is best viewed as a re-run of the entry of the *Einsatzgruppen* into Poland in September 1939, and the Soviet Union in July 1941, except in Italy's case such men had many years of experience in mass murder and policing.

Hitler went on to claim Germany would never see peace seekers emerging from within its ranks as Italy had done, not realizing that the beginnings of such a resistance movement already existed around him, and that within 10 months an attempt would actually be made on his life. Interestingly, after that attempt he met Mussolini and escorted him around the bunker in East Prussia in which the German coup leaders had managed to set off a bomb almost at Hitler's feet. Germany, he stressed, was still secure and the enemy was able to "terrorize the German homeland" only from the air. At this point he alluded to "technical and organizational conditions," claiming these were being readied to counter even the threat from the air, here probably hinting at the development of rockets, such as the V-1s and V-2s, that were eventually launched against England and the Netherlands, and the rocket-propelled Messerschmitt-262 fighter that was turned against Allied bomber fleets late in the war. Germany had by then also developed wire-guided missiles. Hitler next moved to downgrade the Allied Italian landings.

> Tactical necessities may now compel us in this immense fateful battle to yield something occasionally on one front or another or to evade special threats. This, however, will never break *the steel ring*, forged by the German homeland and held by the heroism and blood of our soldiers which screens the Reich [emphasis added].[10]

Whether Hitler was alluding to people like Globocnik when referring to "the steel ring," that now had to replace the broken Pact of Steel, we do not know. If so, it was an appropriate allusion, for Globocnik's stay in Trieste was nothing if not violent, and great cruelty continued to dominate his life. Furthermore, at least one of Globocnik's senior killers, Franz Stangl, who had been in charge of his largest killing center, Treblinka, was assigned to oversee the construction of massive defenses that were to make up the *Führer's* "steel ring," similar to the anti-tank trench network that Globocnik had constructed around Belzec, south of Zamosc, during 1940 and some of 1941, using Jewish labor from Lublin and elsewhere. "His [Stangl's] next assignment was in Italy as a special supply officer of the Einsatz Poll, a strategic construction project in the Po Valley, involving some half a million Italian workers under German command."[11]

The Reich's defensive posture on the Adriatic, and Globocnik's transfer to this region, also reunited him with his old Carinthian crony, Friedrich Rainer, who had actually lobbied for this reunion. This formidable two decade-old duo was therefore back together again — Globocnik in Trieste, and Rainer in Trieste and Klagenfurt, where he had been since November 1941—the two cities of Globocnik's youth and early manhood. The third member of this Carinthian team, Reinhold von Mohrenschildt, was at this time based in Klagenfurt, where he worked primarily on demographic affairs dealing with Slovenes, the people who had forced his family to move away from the Austro-Slovene border soon after the end of the Great War. Globocnik and Rainer now had just 20 months of free rein left before both were captured together by the British. Although Rainer lived until some time around 1949, the year he was by some accounts executed by the Yugoslavs, for Globocnik the 20 months in Trieste were his last.[12] Maurice Williams has described this, their final reunion:

> [T]he Adriatic Coastland, consisting of seven Italian and Slovene districts, was placed under the civilian direction of Friedrich Rainer, who now administered three areas: Carinthia, the occupied territories of Carinthia and Carniola, and the new occupation zone. In the new region Rainer was joined by his old friend. The day after his appointment, Globocnik too received a new posting. Instead of going to Russia as planned Globocnik went to his native Trieste as Higher SS and Police Leader where he reported to Rainer as well as to the SS. The two friends had kept in close contact and had met frequently, (Rainer had even vacationed in Poland) but this occasion was the first time they had worked together for nearly four and a half years. This time their collaboration would last until May 1945....[13]

By coming to Trieste, Globocnik, although occupying the city's top police post as a Higher *SS-und Polizeiführer*, was a subordinate of Rainer's and reported to Karl Wolff, who became the military governor of northern Italy and plenipotentiary to Mussolini. Therefore, Globocnik was still under Himmler's tight control. Globocnik and Rainer were in frequent, often daily, contact, and coordinated not only their eventual bid to escape north, but also their daily political and administrative activities. Globocnik established in Klagenfurt a special liaison office headed by his other friend, von Mohrenschildt. Rainer's political mission was more complicated than Globocnik's, for he was in something of a bind: He was an Austrian wanting to re-establish Germanic power south of Carinthia, as far as the Adriatic coast, but was confronted by diplomatic pressures from Mussolini's Social Republic, and from Ante Pavelic's Croatia, both allies of Berlin, like Pierre Laval's Vichy France, and Rumania's Ion Antonescu, and Wolodymyr Kubiiovych the fascist Ukrainian Nationalist in the General Gouvernement. Europe's "little führers" were men whose time was rapidly running out, as was Globocnik's and Rainer's.[14]

In September 1943 Adolf Hitler appointed Friedrich Rainer High Commissioner of the Operation Zone Adriatic Coastland (OZAK). For the next year and a half Rainer, who was also *Gauleiter* of nearby Carinthia and Chief of the occupied territories of Upper Carniola (presently the north-western part of Slovenia), ruled this region as the *Führer's* deputy.[15]

Williams says that although Rainer may not have been the initiator of
these southern Germanization policies, which included expulsions or resettling of Slovenes along the lines Globocnik had initiated in Zamosc Lands in
November 1942, Globocnik in this new region clearly backed such moves,
with initiatives like the stationing in Klagenfurt of von Mohrenschildt, a
senior planner of Poland's Zamosc Lands cleansing action.

> He inherited a number of institutions and practices set up to this end. There
> was an active deportation program in place and a busy officer of the *RKFDV*
> in Bled…. The Slovene language had been displaced as the language of school
> instruction. Rainer continued these efforts and extended them. Deportation of
> Slovenes began in April 1942 and was supplemented by efforts to re-populate
> the land with *Volksdeutsche* from Italy and Eastern Europe. Only the expand
> ing war coupled with vigorous partisan campaigns stopped the full imple
> mentation of the resettlement plans.[16]

The Slovene deportations had therefore commenced a full seven months
ahead of Globocnik's and von Mohrenschildt's Zamosc Lands expulsion
action. However, if Globocnik's Adriatic duties were intellectually and politically somewhat less demanding, they resulted in a great deal of brutality, for
he was in charge of what was designated as security. To him that meant capturing the Reich's real enemies, whose numbers were now expanding primarily through partisan activity, because opponents of fascism, following the
landing of the Allies, could now see the chance of winning out. Moreover,
the British and Americans began to supply both the Italian and Yugoslavian
partisans by land, sea, and air from bases in southern Italy. Globocnik was
also after anyone designated an enemy, and at the top of that list were Jews.
His other major task was to combat the growing problem of so-called bandits, Italians and Yugoslavs. Both tasks were far more difficult to effect because
he was not operating in an occupied country like Poland, but in what even
he himself referred to as a friendly state. In addition, he created a huge unproductive economic police force that numbered some 20,000 people, and
included Italians, Croats, and Slovenes. These were involved in enforcing
price controls and combating black marketeers. The force was unique to the
Adriatic Coastal Land Zone, with its rag-tag planned economy. The ordinary
police in the area objected to it because Globocnik was seen to be encroaching upon their area of activity, his bad old habit. There were even suspicions
that he had far more expansive plans, such as the takeover of the German army
in the region, and one German observer who traveled through Croatia in
August 1944 reported that Croatians suspected that Globocnik wished to

destroy their state.[17] Although these predictions never came true, they were similar to the suspicions that Lublin District Governor Ernst Zörner had about Globocnik, believing he was on the brink of launching an SS *coup d'etat* against him. If nothing else, these similar outlooks by nominal colleagues say a great deal about Globocnik's brash, indeed, threatening, administrative style. On 14 November 1944, Globocnik was awarded the Croatian Order of the Crown of King Zvonomir, First Class with Star and Sword, something that would no doubt have pleased him enormously. How times had changed! Only two decades earlier Globocnik had allegedly risked life and limb fighting Slavs to ensure these southern peoples did not encroach upon Austrian Carinthia. Now he was accepting Slavonic medals! All this he did in Trieste as he had in the Lublin District, though on nowhere near the same scale, in part because of the vastly more complicated ethnic and political situation in the north-western Balkans, but also because of the far smaller number of Jews potentially within his grasp. There was also the added factor that in Italy the relatively tiny Jewish community appears to have received greater assistance from the community at large than in Germany, Austria, or Poland. Furthermore, Italians, although often treated extremely harshly by Germans, both within and outside Italy, had not been accorded the same lowly racial classification as the Poles, though they were generally looked down upon. Hitler's rhetoric shows precisely that.

Globocnik is primarily remembered in the city of his birth for the La Risiera di San Sabba detention prison, transit camp, and killing center, all wrapped into one, just as his Lublin period is remembered most for the construction of the *Aktion Reinhardt* killing centers. One historian, Susan Zuccotti, has described La Risiera di San Sabba as follows:

> Tens of thousands of prisoners, Jews and non–Jews, Italians and Yugoslavs, passed through La Risiera. Survivors remember the clanking of cell doors opening and closing in the night, prisoners screaming as they marched through the corridors, executions in the courtyard accompanied by blaring music to cover the sound. They remember fierce dogs and ferocious Ukrainian guards. The crematorium, with a capacity of from fifty to seventy corpses a day, functioned regularly.... Estimates of deaths at La Risiera range from 3000 to 4500. The victims were usually partisans. Probably only about 50 were Jews.[18]

A key figure involved in the killings and cremations at San Sabba was Globocnik's *Aktion Reinhardt* gassing expert, Lorenz Hackenholt, referred to earlier. Another, and longer, account of the central role of La Risiera di San Sabba appears in a report for an American academic compiled by Gallan Fogar, secretary of Trieste's Resistance Archive. According to Fogar, the rice refinery had been built during the pre–1918 Austrian period, and was located in Trieste's industrial section of San Sabba, near the football stadium. That being the case, Globocnik may have recalled it from his boyhood days.

When Globocnik arrived, he came with the *Einsatz-Kommando Reinhardt* (EKR) that consisted of well in excess of 150 SS men, Austrians and Germans as well as Ukrainian and other auxiliaries who were split into three sections: EKR-1, based in Trieste in La Risiera di San Sabba; EKR-2, in Fiume; and EKR-3, in Udine.[19] The dreaded Christian Wirth was placed in control of these units held that post until the spring of 1944, when his place was taken by his former Lublin deputy, Gottlieb Hering. Hering, in turn, was later replaced by August Edward Dietrich Allers, who remained in charge until late April 1945. Allers had apparently been dispatched from Berlin by the Reich Chancellery, which had controlled *Aktion Reinhardt*, through Globocnik. Others in this wing of Globocnik's command structure were Franz Stangl, Kurt Franz, and Josef Oberhauser, with Oberhauser placed in charge of the La Risiera di San Sabba killing and detention center.

Globocnik's staff included his ever-loyal and ever-present pre-war pal, Ernst Lerch, as well as Wilhelm Gunter, Ludolf von Alvensleben, Gustav Hanelt, Werner Mundhenke, George Michalsen and Hermann Altman, all either from T4 of *Aktion Reinhardt, Sicherheitspolizei (Sipo)* or the *RSHA's* intelligence sections. Interestingly, he also had Cossack and Caucus auxiliaries, people who, along with Ukrainians, were destined to be recipients of population cleansing actions under *Generalplan Ost* if Globocnik had ever been stationed in the Soviet Union as initially intended. It appears that Globocnik had taken many more men from Lublin than he was permitted. This was a matter that had caused a dispute between him and his Lublin successor, Jakob Sporrenberg. It seems Globocnik had been allocated just 22 men, but took the greater part of his 450-member staff. Sporrenberg's superior, Wilhelm Koppe, who had succeeded Friedrich-Wilhelm Kruger in Krakow as the General Gouvernement's top SS police officer, claimed Globocnik had removed everything that hadn't been bolted down, including many vehicles. For him, the move to Trieste was more like shifting from one construction camp to another — the more men and equipment one took, the better. To this charge Globocnik countered with the expected claim that he had a task to undertake in Trieste and the work in Lublin had been largely completed, an argument that has a ring of truth about it, even if it is untrue. The Sporrenberg argument was that the removal of so many "experts," that is, the *Aktion Reinhardt* men, had created problems, so the work in Lublin had not been completed, which is a valid contention. That work had been made more difficult because most of the experienced killers were denied to Sporrenberg. The procedure adopted in Trieste under its new Higher *SS-und Polizeiführer* was to dispatch Jews by train to Auschwitz-Birkenau as had been done to over a thousand Poles from Zamosc from December 1942 to February 1943. Between October 1943 and 1 November 1944, 13 such northbound trains left Trieste, and subsequent research suggests that 1,074 people were involved, with 999 never returning to their homes.[20]

The EKR transformed the Risiera into a police detention camp (Polizeischaft Lager). The crematorium was promptly built by the "specialist" Erwin Lambert; plus cells, 1.2 meters wide, by 2 meters, and 2 meters high.... Prisoners already condemned to death, or in some case for further questioning were held in these cells. But these cells were insufficient. Thus many newly arrived prisoners were placed in large rooms located in one of the other buildings of the Risiera. Seven or eight thousand persons arrived at the Risiera during the period October 1943, to April 1945.[21]

According to Gallan Fogar, the estimated 7,000 to 8,000 figure emerged from investigations by the prosecutors in a trial of the camp directors that took place in Trieste between February and April 1976, following investigations which had commenced six years earlier. Even so, some Italians and Slavs insisted this was an underestimate, with figures of 10,000 and 15,000 being mentioned, showing once again that it is extraordinarily difficult to gain consensus on numbers of victims when dealing with Globocnik's killings, even when the numbers are relatively small, that is, well below the 1.5 million to two million range. Little wonder estimates differ so markedly on victim numbers for Globocnik's three major *Aktion Reinhardt* killing centers of Treblinka, Sobibor, and Belzec. La Risiera di San Sabba's internees and victims were partisans, hostages — men, women, and children — deserters from the Fascist side, or mere suspects. Tip-offs in the form of unsigned letters to the police could result in arrest, internment, and death in Germany, Austria, and occupied Poland. But not all internees remained there, for La Risiera di San Sabba was used as a dispatch center, with prisoners sent to *Lagers* in the Reich — Germany and Austria — and even to occupied Poland. Fogar recounts one particularly tragic case of a victim, a Mrs. Giannina Bordignor Sereni of Venice, being taken in with her husband and three sons: "She was Aryan and expected to be released. Unfortunately she requested the return of 30,000 Italian lire taken from her purse; she was promptly murdered."[22]

According to one witness, a Giovanni Wachsberger, a Jewish resident of Fiume who was held in La Risiera di San Sabba for about a year and was in charge of prison clothing, more than 2,000 garments that had been owned by murdered victims were acquired. Wachsberger was one of 200 witnesses heard during the 1970s investigation into La Risiera di San Sabba. Trieste was the Globocnikian Lublin District writ small, very small.

Mass executions, dozens at a time, took place two to three times a week, according to the testimony of many survivors. In some months there were even more. In addition, the SS killed as many as 10 prisoners every day by means of individual execution.[23]

Siegfried Pucher argues that La Risiera di San Sabba, which began operating on 1 October 1943 and was used until 30 April 1945, was an extermination camp for detained partisans; a deportation or transit center for political prisoners and Jews; a storage facility for stolen Jewish property; and also simply as a barracks. He says that this solid complex was known locally as the "German Barracks" between 1943 and May 1945. It was without doubt a precinct where incredibly cruel deeds were perpetrated, as they were at all the other Nazi concentration camps in the Reich, Poland, France, and wherever else the *Wehrmacht* reached and the SS followed. In it people were beaten to death, and there has even been recorded a case of a 13-year-old child being forced to collect the wood for his own cremation, which, although a single bestial act, is on a par with the murder by gassing and starvation of tens of thousands of Jewish adolescents and also large numbers of Polish children.[24]

EKR worked full-time on anti–Jewish operations, making its first arrests on 9 October 1943, less than a month after this unit's arrival. Much of the unit's work involved property confiscation both in and outside La Risiera di San Sabba, and determined attempts to acquire people's bank accounts, both named and unidentified, safety deposit boxes, and other forms of wealth storage. Unlike in the Lublin area, where victims were railed to killing centers, and those living within the district deported en masse, the Trieste assignment was complicated by the fact that there were witnesses who were, legally speaking, allies of the Reich. Globocnik's EKR thus had to work with greater care, and be cognizant of public awareness of activities that were covered up in Poland because its killing centers were hidden in out-of-the-way forests and, except for Majdanek concentration camp, well away from urban centers.

Treachery of a different kind also existed. Fogar reports a Trieste Jew acting as a spy for the murderous Franz Stangl in conducting manhunts. This traitor was, however, assassinated by the SS during the last days of the occupation. If such an individual existed, and there is no reason to doubt Fogar, it shows the lengths to which the EKR was prepared to go to fulfill its deadly mission of eliminating Jews.[25] But not all the blame is laid at the feet of Globocnik's T4 killers; Fogar sees some of it as belonging to what he called "collaborationists" both within the city and within Mussolini's Social Republic, which saw the emergence of an agency called the Inspectorate, which "operated in complete collaboration with the Gestapo (Office IV)." Civilian employees, interpreters, secretaries, and informers, who agreed to be hired by Globocnik and Rainer, were seen as also being culpable.

> Based on its [the Inspectorate's] information concerning the zone and individuals, this gravely damaged the Italian and Slav resistance and the Italian political and national policies of the area. Many died in the Risiera as a consequence of the actions of the Inspectorship, which was also directed against the Jews. It was a frightful disaster for the good name of Italy in this region.[26]

The trial to which Fogar refers also revealed that two methods of killing were used at La Risiera di San Sabba: suffocation by exhaust fumes from truck motors, and the use of a mallet ("mazza") to strike the condemned prisoner "at the nape of the neck." Lambert's crematorium, like those at Auschwitz-Birkenau, was destroyed as Globocnik's T4 killing team withdrew north to avoid capture by the British and local partisans. According to Siegfried Pucher, however, the crematorium was a garage into which engine fumes were passed, and he believes the number killed reached some 3,000 people.[27]

Crucial to Globocnik's 20 months in Trieste was his longstanding close association with Rainer, which was re-established with his transfer to the Adriatic city of his birth. According to Slovene historian Tone Ferenc, both these Carinthians, who had met on at least one occasion in Lublin — Globocnik also once traveled to Salzburg to visit Rainer in the company of his fiancée, Irmgard Rickheim — and no doubt exchanged ideas on Germanization and relations with Slavs, now returned to an earlier phase in their lives when they had worked to consolidate Austrian dominance in Carinthia and south of that province. Ferenc's investigations, although focusing primarily on their time in Trieste, also give an interesting glimpse into the significance of their earlier years together.

Ferenc, like the wartime London-based Polish researcher and German affairs expert Jozef Winiewicz, has highlighted the crucial importance of academic and other German activists who were linked to quasi-research and politically motivated institutes and cultural societies. Winiewicz focused in particular on the role of the important Kurt Lück and his pre-war, Poznan-based German historical society, the *Historische Gesellschaft für die Provinz Posen*. Ferenc, on the other hand, provides an assessment of several such research institutes based in Graz, Styria, and Klagenfurt, Carinthia, Austria's two main cities that lie adjacent a large concentration of Slavic people to the south in Slovenia. The situation during the 1920s and 1930s in Klagenfurt can be seen to be somewhat similar to that in wartime Lublin, which, like Klagenfurt, was situated on the edge of an expanse of Slavs, except in Lublin's case the peoples to the east were Poles, Russians, Belarusans and Ukrainians. Both Klagenfurt and Lublin, to Globocnik at least, had this in common, and with the exception of Rainer, probably only Globocnik realized and fully appreciated this demographic similarity. To him this was not so much a problem as a challenge. Both men were keen to get on with Germanizing lands beyond their immediate reach, beyond Lublin or beyond Klagenfurt. The creation of Yugoslavia after the Great War blocked a long held Germanic desire to have a permanent southern outlet to the Adriatic. One outcome of the uneasy inter-war unity of these southern Slavs had been a series of short lived border clashes between the Germanic Carinthians, with whom Globocnik and Rainer identified, and the most northerly of these Slavs, the Slovenes. Even after the Treaty of St. Germain of 1919 and the plebiscite of 1920, which ensured all of Carinthia remained inside Austria, this conflict continued. Once fighting had subsided, the ethnic rivalry over land and access took on a new form, namely ideological and propaganda campaigns which saw the emergence of influential personalities, with Globocnik and Rainer being just two associated political activists. Ferenc describes this phenomenon and highlights both these Nazis. Throughout these years German-Austrians were also active among the Germans living in Slovenia, across the border, in propagating the Nazi movement. This had begun to spread after the Nazis seized power in Germany, after 1933. Among those who brought Nazi literature, visited Nazi groups, and delivered courses, were Dr. Helmut Carstanjen and Anton Dorfmeister, who later became significant senior officials in Lower Styria.

> After the *Anschluss* the German minority in Slovenia came under the influence of new Nazi institutes in Graz and Klagenfurt (Celovec). Among the most important was the *Sudostdeutsches Institut*, founded in May 1938 under Dr Carstanjen's leadership in Graz, and the two provincial border offices (*Gaugrenzamt*) of the Nazi Party (NSDAP) in Graz and Klagenfurt (Celovec) established by decree on 2 February 1939 through the main NSDAP office. The Graz office was headed by Dorfmeister while the one in Klagenfurt came under Alois Maier-Kaibitsch, a prominent participant in the so-called defensive battles in Carinthia after World War I, leader of the *Kartner Heimatbund* and the provincial organs of two other associations (*Deutsche Schubverein Sudmark* and *Volksbund für das Deutschtum im Ausland*), all directed against the nationally conscious Slovenes residing in Carinthia. During 1934–38 Maier-Kaibitsch, as a member of the Carinthian provincial government, supported the Nazi underground, especially Odilo Globocnik and Friedrich Rainer, so that by 1942, he was to rise to the rank of colonel of the SS. These Austrians (Carstanjen, Maier-Kaibitsch, and Dorfmeister) were the principal officials in Graz and Klagenfurt laying the foundations for the subsequent Nazi-directed Germanic occupation of northern Slovenia.[28]

These are revealing findings by Ferenc. He goes on to describe these influential Carinthians, and many others, and their links to the powerful Globocnik and Rainer. However, the crucial point missing from his otherwise enlightening exposition of Globocnik's association with men like Carstanjen, Maier-Kaibitsch, and Dorfmeister, to name just three, is that Globocnik had embarked in 1942–43, on his own, the Germanizing and settlement program across Poland's Zamosc Lands, just as Rainer had been doing on a smaller scale in Carinthia-Slovenia from late 1941, until Globocnik's arrival in Trieste in September 1943. It is difficult not to conclude that the origin of Globocnik's crucially important Lublin-based Research Center for Eastern Settlement, headed by Gustav Hanelt and Dr. Franz Stanglica, somehow lie in his pre-war association with these Carinthian ethnographic researchers and NSDAP ideologists. On the question of Globocnik's transfer from Lublin to Trieste and his activities in Lublin, Ferenc also has pertinent observations:

It is almost certain that it was Rainer's wish that Hitler and Himmler selected as Leader of the SS and Police in the [Adriatic Coastal Land] Zone the notorious *SS-Gruppenführer* and Lieutenant-General of Police, Odilo Globocnik, an Austrian of ill-repute who, after his recall from the Lublin district of Poland, had been appointed by Himmler as Higher Leader of the SS and Police for the central section of the German front in the Soviet Union. Hitler and Himmler complied with Rainer's wish, and Globocnik set up his office in Trieste on 13 September, a day after Rainer had seen Hitler and Himmler in East Prussia.[29]

Globocnik's association with Carstanjen, Maier-Kaibitsch and Dorfmeister may be significant in another way. Each member of this trio of southern Austrians is likely to have been fully conversant with the methods used by Austria's Empress Maria Theresa and her son Emperor Joseph II in the "re-Europeanization" of former Turkish or Ottoman-controlled lands across the Balkans following the Treaty of Passarowitz/Pozarevac of 1718. Emperor Joseph II had, in addition, settled Germans from the Palatinate upon the Zamosc Lands during the 1780s. Not insignificant, it would seem, is the argument referred to earlier, by the historian Friedrich Heer in his book *Der Glaube des Adolf Hitler, Anatomie einer politischen Religiosität*, that Hitler was influenced by Joseph II "as much as, if not more than, the Prussian Frederick the Great."[30] The whole area of the origin of Globocnik's Lublin-based Research Center for Eastern Settlement, which so interested Himmler, who had his own Berlin-based settlement research institutes, and the impact of Carstanjen, Maier-Kaibitsch, Dorfmeister and Karl Haushofer upon Globocnik has not been adequately researched. This area calls for further empirical investigation, as does Friedrich Heer's contention that Maria Theresa's and Emperor Joseph II's 18th century settlerist activities may have been significant influences upon Nazism, and therefore Globocnik.

Globocnik's other task, the fighting of partisans, also occupied a great deal of his time. Here he attempted to repeat what he had done in Lublin, that is, first eliminate resistance leaders as had occurred under Aktion A-B of September 1939 to June 1940 across Poland. However, the mountainous Istrian peninsula complicated this objective. To add to Globocnik's problems, the Italian and Slovenian resistance movements drew up an agreement of cooperation over border issues on 7 May 1944, something the Polish and Ukrainian partisans failed to do in the Zamosc Lands because both claimed this territory, as did Globocnik by launching his plan to settle German farmers upon it. In addition, the Ukrainian Nationalists had no incentive to come to a *modus vivendi* with the Poles, because they had a far stronger ally in Globocnik. Globocnik's chief of anti-guerrilla activities had at his disposal a police and a *Jager* (Hunter) battalion, but failed to achieve the success desired. These activities were further hindered by the fact that Rainer, the *Wehrmacht*'s General Kubler, and Globocnik did not operate in unison at all times.[31] But not everything hindered his suppression and annihilation apparatus that he transferred from Lublin to Trieste and set out to put in motion. Susan Zuccotti has claimed that Trieste presented Globocnik with one important advantage: The city had a noticeably more obvious anti–Semitic tradition than other parts of Italy. Whether or not this state of affairs was coaxed along by members of Globocnik's team is uncertain.

> …as the war fanned popular emotions, ugly anti-Semitic violence began to occur in Italy. By far the worst cases took place in Trieste, where Jewish shops had been vandalized and signs reading "No Jews allowed" had appeared in stores even before the war. Germans, Italians, Slavs and Jews lived side by side in Trieste and heartily disliked one another. About four per cent of the population was Jewish — much more than the national average — and Jews played a visible role at the highest levels of society. The city always had a stronger anti-Semitic element than the rest of Italy. Furthermore, Italians' tolerance and skepticism of government had never prevailed there. Trieste shared the Austrian tradition of taking laws seriously, and the laws sanctioned anti–Semitism.[32]

Gallan Fogar complained several times in his report about the fact that so many of the T4 killers were never brought to justice after the war, and he laid the blame for this omission across the board, from the Italian judicial system to the Allied Military governments, which he alleged had made Trieste a kind of "free zone," and to postwar Germany's reluctance to act.

Well within six months of Globocnik's arrival, unmistakable signs of the Allied presence on the continent were felt even in Trieste. In early February 1944, the city's oil refinery was attacked by the Royal Air Force. Airfields at Klagenfurt, Aviano, and Udine were also attacked from the air. Both Rainer and Globocnik were at last coming within reach of Allied air power.[33] But it was still to be a full 16 more months before these two Carinthians were compelled to make a bid to escape. Reports reaching the Allies from anti-Axis sources across northern Italy pointed to widespread retaliation and loss of life. According to a report carried in *The Times* of London, based on anti–Axis sources, German-occupied northern Italy saw 50,000 Italians killed, either in combat, murdered, or executed, by April 1944, in encounters between patriots and neo–Fascists.[34] Disorder was rife and spreading: "Seventy thousand Italians, of whom 10,000 are Jews, are said to have been deported to Poland; 250,000 were sent to work in Germany; and 50,000 are now in prison and concentration camps in Italy."[35]

Although these figures may be over-estimates, they were an assessment of totals across all of northern Italy, not just Trieste. Added to this carnage across the region was the issue of retaliatory killings, which occurred even in Trieste. For instance, *The Times* of London reported in late 1944 that prominence had been given in northern Italian newspapers to the Germans having executed 77 of Trieste's citizens as a reprisal for the shooting of seven German soldiers. The 77 were reported as having been hanged from trees on Trieste's main street, a repeat of what was common in Poland throughout the entire war.[36]

Throughout 1944, Globocnik continued his traditional maneuvers aimed at gaining greater power. Never satisfied with less power if more was possibly available, in April he stepped on Field Marshall Albrecht Kesselring's administrative toes by trying to take over all anti-partisan activities. Himmler intervened on Globocnik's side, but eventually a compromise was reached out under which the police leader was given control over these activities in a zone 30 kilometers from the Adriatic's shores. His chain of command was again made somewhat ambiguous, going from Himmler to Karl Wolff and Globocnik, who was also under the guidance of Rainer, with Rainer being responsible to Hitler. However, the agreement provided for control to revert to the army if or when the Adriatic coastal region was entered by Allied troops. Under such circumstances, full responsibility for military affairs was to swing across to Kesselring and the *Wehrmacht*. In May Globocnik declared Trieste a citadel or fortress, along the lines that the Reich had made of eastern German cities like Breslau and Königsberg, which were declared to be fortresses as the Red Army advanced toward Berlin. These developments came after 20 July 1944, the day of the attempted assassination of Hitler, after which the *Führer* increasingly turned toward a socialistic or people's approach to defense, with the *Wehrmacht*, from which the plot to kill him had sprung, being largely discredited in his eyes. This meant Globocnik acquired powers over supplies, and laid the basis of a general withdrawal by civilians from Trieste in the event of the city coming under siege. Nine months later, and two months before Kesselring was transferred to the Western Front, Globocnik gained control over the army and the National Socialist Party as well as all foreign units — Slavs, Italians, Cossacks — and other regional fighting units that originated, often with their families, from the Soviet Union.

Six days after the failed assassination attempt on Hitler, 26 July 1944, the *Führer* ordered the construction of a fall-back line of defense between Switzerland and Trieste — nothing was too vast for the mentally deteriorating Hitler — and Rainer made Globocnik his representative in charge of its construction. This mammoth project — far larger than anything attempted by Globocnik around Belzec during 1940 — required hundreds of thousands of workers and sparked a series of mass round-ups, street arrests, and the capture of potential workers in trains and cities, along the lines used across Poland during most of the war to acquire workers for the Reich. Franz Stangl was appointed liaison officer for this huge project, and was told to spare no effort to ensure that the gargantuan defensive structure was built. According to Siegfried Pucher, Stangl's superior also told him that "money was no problem."[37]

This resulted in the rather bizarre sight of Stangl appearing in various parts of northern Italy accompanied by an assistant carrying boxes of cash to hasten construction. One tangible benefit for Globocnik was that he was awarded a German Cross in silver for these efforts, even though the defensive line appears to have played only a minor role in the defense of northern Italy. Before May 1945, the month he fled to his former home city of Klagenfurt, Globocnik's headquarters were at Cividale del Fiuli, 70 kilometers northwest of Trieste, where he briefly stayed with his staffers. Field Marshall Loehr and his army were withdrawing from northern Yugoslavia toward Carinthia with an array of followers and anti-Communists, including royalist Chetniks, White Russians, Cossacks, Croats, Montenegrins, and Bosnians. The Yugoslav Army of National Liberation, led by the Stalinist, Josip Tito, had its eyes on southern Carinthia, which Globocnik as a teenager, in the early 1920s, had apparently fought to ensure remained Austrian and Germanic, not to become Slavic. Not surprisingly, this renewed southern Slav move to acquire this land was backed by the Soviet Radio Free Austria, in the same way that various Soviet radio stations in Eastern Europe had backed the acquisition of prewar eastern Poland so that Poland's various component eastern territories — Ukraine, Belarus, and Lithuania — could be incorporated into republics within the Soviet Union, which indeed happened.

XIX

Globocnik's Last Journey: May 1945

Although Globocnik's last 30 days at large may be impossible to reconstruct with absolute precision, Siegfried Pucher has nevertheless presented an interesting account of his movements.[1] (See Map 6.) Pucher says Globocnik was ordered on 1 May, by Army Group "E," to ensure Germans ceased fleeing north and to instead commence constructing a new defensive line so that the Reich could fight to the last man, as had been asked of German forces in Stalingrad in the winter of 1942–43. At the same time, Friedrich Rainer made some cursory moves to cobble together a defense of Carinthia. However, Globocnik seems to have ignored his orders, deciding instead to try to enter his home province of Carinthia via the Plocken Pass. The ever-loyal Ernst Lerch, among others, accompanied him, and they were both seen in Klagenfurt, Rainer's home base, where Globocnik addressed people in the market place. During his unconvincing pep talk, he claimed that the Austrian people now needed to repeat what had been done in 1915 when an Italian bid to cross the mountains into their region had been blocked. For the next fortnight or so, he camped either in the open or hid out with helpers in the Lake Wörther, or *Wörthersee*, region, an area just west of Klagenfurt, one he was thoroughly familiar with. It seems that Rainer and he met during this time. According to the British author and journalist Gitta Sereny, Globocnik hid out in Rainer's lakeside house during his last days of freedom.

Map 6. Globocnik's last journey, May 1945.

Globocnik had stayed at the Rainers' lakeside villa the last night before going into hiding. "When he said goodbye in the morning," said Ada [Rainer], "he said that it was for ever. He showed me a pillbox and said that he would have to take the capsule.

"I said 'My God, does Friedl [Friedrich Rainer] have one of those, too?' 'No, no,' he answered. 'For me, it's because of Poland. Friedl doesn't need it; he never did anything wrong.'" (I remember my surprise at this casual admission of "wrong." Had his best friend's wife known, after all, about the nature of the "wrong" in Poland?)[2]

Pucher says that Globconik's wife Lore (nee Peterschinegg), whom he married in October 1944, had revealed in 1964 that she saw her by then notorious husband for the last time in that city either on 5 or 6 May, and that he visited a man she knew to be living in Poertschach, on the lake's northern shore, some 15 kilometers west of the city. During these wanderings he told an acquaintance in Carinthian-style slang, "We finished off two million,"[3] no doubt referring to the number of Jews murdered in his three killing centers. Soon afterwards he moved west to the vicinity of another alpine lake, *Weissensee* (White Lake), in the Karavanken Alps, which lies 1,000m above sea level and 18 kilometers southwest of Spittal. He ended up in a shepherd's house (often erroneously referred to as a hut) that overlooked this beautiful deep turquoise body of water. With him in this seasonally utilized mountain house that day were Rainer, Lerch, Karl Hellesberger, Hermann Höfle, Georg Michalsen, and three women described as secretaries. Rainer, who had a lakeside residence at Klagenfurt, had seen his wife Ada for the last time to say goodbye, on 8 May. On that day Rainer was driven by his chauffeur to Mallnitz, where he hid out in a friend's mountain hut until toward the end of the month. Rainer eventually reached the *Weissensee* house on his own, not realizing that he was being hunted by a determined Englishman, a former London metropolitan policeman who had been involved in fighting behind German lines. Many of the mountain slopes in this southern part of Alpine Austria were studded with such out-of-the-way dwellings that were used by shepherds who cared for stock grazing on the high pastures during summer months. Some of these structures were relatively comfortable and well furnished, and equipped with bunks and stoves. The fact that so many senior SS men from Trieste were in the same Alpine house, known as Moeslacher-Alm, certainly suggests they had arranged to rendezvous there. This was a shrewd decision, for the lake is rich in fish, it can be reached from the eastern side, and the western side looks like Norwegian fjord country, where stone eagles and vultures live in the hard-to-reach rocky nooks. Whether this group of once powerful SS men, now fugitives, was awaiting a guide to direct them to another location we do not know. Pucher says that from the Weissensee lakeside area there existed two escape routes: The first was via South Tyrol into Italy and beyond; and the second to Kreuzberg, at the lake's western extremity, then south to Gitschtal, Hermagor, and, via Nassfeld, down to the northern Italian plain, and beyond. Globocnik had the advantage of being a fluent Italian speaker, and could, if well disguised, probably have remained in Italy for some time, even though it was now occupied by the Allies. From there he could, with assistance, have moved beyond Europe either to a South American country or somewhere in the Middle East, as did several senior SS men who had sinister pasts to hide.

The trans–Italian escape network, which involved murky Vatican or clerical links, appears to have remained in place for some years, for Franz Stangl, who had been captured by the Americans and later handed over to the Austrians and imprisoned, went this way. Stangl simply walked out of the prison and managed to escape to Italy with his Austrian colleague, Gustav Wagner. Wagner was apparently assisted by a Bishop Hudal and the Vatican network to escape, via Rome on a Red Cross passport, with an entrance visa to Syria. In 1948 Wagner arrived in Damascus, where he worked for three years as a mechanical engineer in a textile mill and was joined by his wife and family. Stangl, on the other hand, emigrated to Brazil in 1951, where he was given an engineering job and after 1959 worked at a Volkswagon factory, using his own name.[4] If these lower ranking SS men managed to disguise themselves and arrange fleeing overseas, it seems reasonable to conclude that Globocnik and Rainer, at least, were making similar moves.

However, Globocnik used neither route, ending up instead, in the early hours of the morning of 31 May, in captivity at nearby Paternion, in the Drau Valley, just 18 kilometers southeast of Spittal, where members of a British regiment, the Queen's Own Fourth Hussars, had based themselves earlier that month. The Hussars had begun arriving at Paternion on 11 May, and by month's end most were either in this town or were billeted nearby, with the senior officers camping in and around Foscari-Widmann Schloss.

But the above is not the last word on Globocnik's final month at large, for Lerch and Michalsen, soon after being captured by these Hussars with Globocnik on 31 May, were separately interrogated, allowing the British to compile a retraced path.[5] Although both men had blatantly lied to the British about their wartime records, their separate interrogations provided what was probably a roughly accurate account of their, Globocnik's, and even Rainer's movements, since the British could cross-check each account.

Their accounts revealed that the staffs of the *Oberster Kommissar, BdS,* and *BdO* left Trieste by road on 30 April heading north for Klagenfurt. For Globocnik, who left the next day, this was in all likelihood the same path he and his family had taken after the Great War when they departed Trieste to settle permanently in Klagenfurt.

> The [Globocnik] convoy arrived at Arta near Tolmezzo [50 kilometers north of Udine] the same day, having passed the BdS convoy at Ospedaletto, north of Tricesimo. Some vehicles were strafed on the road and casualties inflicted. The convoy of the HSS & PF staged at Arta where dispositions for the defence of the Austro-Italian frontier was made [on 2 May].[6]

The next day Globocnik's staff proceeded to Hermagor, across the border in Austria, 20 kilometers west of Villach. There they were billeted in a camp. On 4 May Globocnik detached his close staffers to send them back to Moggio, 15 kilometers east of Tolmezzo and just south of the Austro-Italian border. The reason for this retracing of steps was that Globocnik claimed he wanted his men to assist an *SS-Brigadeführer* Harmel to defend the frontier at that point. But the events of 5 May were far more complicated, and during them Globocnik moved to the Klagenfurt area which he knew so well.

> On orders from Globocnik, Lerch proceed to Poertschach [15 kilometers west of Klagenfurt] to contact *Gauleiter* Rainer but failed to do so. Later Globocnik himself arrived in Poertschach for a conference with Rainer. According to Lerch, amongst others *Landesbauernführer* Huber and *Gauhauptmann* Natmessnig were present at the conference. Details of this conference were unknown to the source. After the conference Globocnik ordered Lerch to proceed to Adelsberg (Postumia) to establish contact with elements of 7 SS Mtn Div "Prince Eugen" and return to Globocnik in Hermagor with a report on the situation. Lerch was then to proceed to Neusach [on the northern shore of Weissensee] where Globocnik intended to establish Central HQ of all German Forces in Kaernten. A WT Station had already been installed there. Lerch's further orders were to wait for Globocnik until May 20 1945. The following alternatives were envisaged:
> i) Resistance to the Yugoslavs.
> ii) Retreat into the Alpine Redoubt.
> iii) Dispersal and retirement into hiding with peasants.
> The same day top-secret documents were burnt in the RAD Camp at Hermagor.[7]

Nothing here is markedly inconsistent with the earlier account of Globocnik's movements. It seems that he was simply alone or at least away from Lerch, from at least the end of the first week in May until after 20 May, about a fortnight. Meeting his wife, who was soon pregnant, and spending time around *Wörthersee* and Klagenfurt may have been what he did, in the full knowledge that his days were at long last numbered. Apart from having the ever-present thought of a war crimes trial and execution at the forefront of his mind, these days might have been extremely pleasant and exhilarating.

Lerch claims to have had his own brief misadventures. He said that on 6 May he left Poertschach by car for Adelsperg, but was captured by Yugoslav troops near Lubljana. But he said he managed to escape after 10 hours in captivity, and hitchhiked in German vehicles to Arnoldstein, where he spent the night. Whether this escape claim is true or not cannot be confirmed, but it matters little. Michalsen reported having seen Globocnik at Hermagor, from where, Michalsen claimed, Globocnik had moved back into Italy, to Moggio, allegedly to speak to *SS-Brigadeführer* Harmel. His staff, on the other hand, headed back into Austria once again and Lerch, Michalsen, Höfle, and *SS-Oberscharführer* Hellentscherger drove to Neusach, where they eventually discarded their weapons and, with rations, moved to Moeslacher-Alm, the house overlooking the huge and beautiful southern Austrian mountain lake, *Weissensee*. Two of Globocnik's female employees, *Frauleins* Espernheim and Ziranka, arrived on 10 May. The six-strong group now rested, and on 13 May an *SS-Oberscharführer* Kummerer arrived seeking shelter, a request that was denied him because he was short of rations. Kummerer was told instead to go to the Moeslacher-Alm farmstead. This was a fateful decision, because Kummerer was eventually captured by the British, and the group's decision to ostracize him provided him with a good reason to alert the British to its whereabouts.

The next day was 14 May; "Lerch wrote a letter to the British Military Authorities proposing a rendezvous between himself and a British Officer for the purpose of negotiating the surrender of the Party. He went to Boden (Map. ITALY 1:50,000 Sheet 4 D II 525880) where, to pass it [on], he handed the letter to a peasant with the request to the British Authorities at Hermagor."[8]

Furthermore, Lerch claimed to have accidentally met Rainer while out walking. After a brief chat, Rainer ordered him to return to the Moeslacher-Alm, and the two arranged to meet again in 10 days — on 24 or 25 May — at the same place. Even a whistle signal was arranged to ensure this next meeting was safely carried out. Globocnik reached Moeslacher-Alm on 20 May exhausted and ill. Nine days later, Lerch again tried to pass a letter to the British at Baden. On the same day, he met Rainer at their pre-arranged spot, and on 30 May Rainer arrived at the hut. According to Michalsen, Rainer and Globocnik had a private meeting and decided to surrender the next day. This surrender, however, did not take place, if indeed it was planned, for just before sunrise on 31 May those inside the hut were stunned to hear the yells of members of a British military unit ordering them to move outside with all hands up. Strangely, this fate may not have been as unwelcome as may appear, for the fugitives were apparently far more fearful of falling into the hands of Yugoslav Communist partisans, followers of Tito. The British interrogation report says as much: "Both sources [Lerch and Michalsen] stated that their main reason for hiding in the mountains was fear of falling into Partisan hands and expressed their willingness to assist in rounding up of other Germans still at large."[9]

Nevertheless, in the light of Globocnik's behavior between capture and shortly before noon, namely his persistent claim that he was a Klagenfurt merchant, using the name König, it is difficult to believe Michalsen's assertion that Globocnik intended surrendering to the British. False identification papers had been prepared for Globocnik in Trieste. Before describing Globocnik's fate, it will be helpful to consider briefly the fate of his Lublin successor, Jakob Sporrenberg, who also fell into British hands in 1945.

Jakob Sporrenberg Captured in Oslo

Sporrenberg was a former *SD* officer who saw service in Russia and had considerable trouble getting along with the few Globocnik staffers — the

Globocnikians — who remained behind in Lublin, even if only briefly. He had particular problems with the sinister Christian Wirth and his assistant, Höfle. However, Sporrenberg's period as Lublin District's *SS-und Polizeiführer* was relatively brief, with Lublin destined to be occupied by the Soviet Red Army in July 1944. Sporrenberg and several of his staffers were re-deployed to Norway, where the British captured them, at war's end. Because these men had held senior posts, they were naturally interrogated, and the British soon began learning of Globocnik's horror years in Lublin. Sporrenberg was two years older than Globocnik, and like his predecessor a Catholic, but a Reich German, a Rhinelander. He had organized the NSDAP in his hometown, joined the *Hitler Jugend* in 1930, and moved from the SA to the SS, where his advancement was rapid. He had served as a member of the *Reichstag*, and by 1933 was already a *Brigadeführer*. In 1943 he was assigned to the staff of General von dem Bach-Zelewski in Minsk, Belarus, to fight partisans, which may explain why he succeeded Globocnik in Lublin District, where Globocnik had left behind a major partisan problem because of his Zamosc Lands expulsions. Moreover, Lublin District by late 1943 was experiencing such strife not only across the Zamosc Lands. One outcome of Sporrenberg's interrogations by the British was that he was removed from Oslo and transferred to the Kensington Cages in London for further questioning, a measure of his perceived value.

> *SS-Gruppenführer* Sporrenberg was transferred to this Center from PWIS Detachment (Norway), where it was found that his political career warranted closer investigation. He was therefore subjected to a series of interrogations by War Crimes Interrogation Unit at London District and his participation in a number of major War Crimes committed in Poland and Soviet Union was established.[10]

The British had thus captured the top and a succeeding echelon of Lublin's two wartime SS administrative groups; the first, which included Globocnik, in Moeslacher-Alm, a high mountain shepherd's house in southern Austria, and the second in Oslo, Norway.

Interestingly, neither Lerch, Höfle, nor Michalsen ever attracted anywhere near as much interest as Sporrenberg, even though they were by far the more culpable and knowledgeable about Lublin's main organizer of mass murderer, Globocnik. Clearly all those in the Moeslacher-Alm should also have been transferred to the Kensington Cages, something that unfortunately never happened. Their British interrogators and their superiors appear to have instead believed that rank was synonymous with power. But they were wrong. Lerch, Höfle, and Michalsen, not to mention Rainer, were in fact far more significant captives. Even so, Sporrenberg's interrogation had at least meant gaining some insight into events of the months immediately after Globocnik's departure. Undoubtedly the most horrific single event to be uncovered was the so-called *Aktion Erntefest*, the massacre of more than 40,000 Jews and some Polish prisoners-of-war in just 14 hours, at Majdanek concentration camp, and at the Poniatowa and Trawniki work camps near Lublin. These were the last survivors in the huge network of Globocnik's labor and other camps surrounding Lublin.

XX

Globocnik's Capture and Death

Death was something that came increasingly to dominate Globocnik's daily activities from November 1939 to May 1945, when he died aged just 41. We can confidently say that had he died on the eve of war's outbreak, when a 35-year-old, some two million people, or the population of a sizeable American or European city, would have had a far greater chance of surviving Europe's most destructive war, made more destructive because of Globocnik. Clearly, such a statement is a terrible indictment of any human being, and one can, thankfully, only say it of a small number. But in Globocnik's case it is only too true. He was an extraordinarily evil and destructive individual, one who fully deserved the title of Germanic Margrave, so aptly applied by Jozef Winiewicz in his London writings about the Nazi occupation of Poland. Globocnik was such a major genocidal killer that it is not entirely surprising that the one documented bid to kill him was an assassination attempt that was apparently carried out not by Jews, or Poles, or Ukrainians for that matter, but by Germans, by people for whom he was allegedly destroying so many others. It is easy to forget that many of the Germans and probably even Austrians stationed in Lublin understandably and rightly feared Globocnik, and many undoubtedly also came to hate him. The report of this alleged attempt on his life was carried in a Polish Underground newspaper, *Samo Obronia*, (*Self Defense*) in July 1943, shortly before he was permanently transferred out of Lublin to become a Higher SS and police chief in the city of his birth, Trieste, and its surroundings, the Adriatic Coastal Land Zone, and just over a month after his breakdown. The report appeared in this underground newspaper's regular section, "The Week in the Country," and the brief reference read: "The attempt on the life of Globocnik did not succeed. Killed were the chauffeur and an accompanying SS-man. Globocnik experienced a nervous breakdown and for several days did not leave his house. An investigation showed that the assassination was carried out by Germans. Seven Gestapo officers were arrested."[1]

If this report is correct, then it is ironic indeed that a man who had so deliberately become Himmler's main harbinger of death was so obviously incapable of personally confronting it himself when it arrived at his front doorstep. But because this Polish claim that alleges an assassination attempt, and by Germans at that, was reported in no other Polish Underground newspaper, it may be that the editors of *Samo Obronia* were in error. The only other conclusion one can draw is that *Samo Obronia* got a scoop that no other underground newspaper was able to, or ever did, follow up. Although an unlikely event, it cannot be entirely discounted. However, this is only the first in a long line of claims about Globocnik's demise. News traveled slowly, but it traveled, even in wartime, for on 31 August 1943, a brief reference to what was probably this same alleged assassination attempt appeared in a London newspaper. In this article, whether by design or simply bad guesswork, it was the Poles, not the Germans, who were credited not only for the attempt, but also with actually succeeding in getting their man. The tiny article, a filler in newspaper parlance, read: "Nazi *Gauleiter* Executed.— Gen. Glovocnik [sic], Vienna's first *Gauleiter* has been executed by Polish guerrillas for murdering Poles."[2]

The above conjecture is further complicated by the fact that a documented claim exists alleging that the Polish Underground's intelligence had reported an attempt on Globocnik's life being made around 20 July 1943. However, this report, unlike the one carried in the London *Daily Telegraph* of 31 August 1943, also alleged that Globocnik's chauffeur was killed and that an adjutant was badly wounded, but it failed to refer to Germans being arrested.[3] Globocnik was responsible for the deaths of many tens of thousands of Poles, maybe even as many as 100,000, but he was also responsible for up to 20 times more Jewish lives, and a substantial number of these victims were children, including infants, some no doubt less than six months old. Polish Underground sources may also have learned of Globocnik's mental breakdown of May 1943, when Professor Pfannenstiel was brought in to minister him. Gossip spread from Germans to Poles (Polish telephonists were notorious for listening in on conversations), and eventually to the editor of *Samo Obronia*. Along the way conjecture probably occurred about the causes of the breakdown. It appears that no one could actually imagine the nerves of the cast-iron Odilo Globocnik breaking. The cause of his ailment was therefore attributed to something or someone else. And why not an assassination attempt? If nothing else, it was colorful. The two best known English-language biographical publications on Hitler's Germany, Robert Wistrich's *Who's Who in Nazi Germany*, and Louis Snyder's *Encyclopedia of the Third Reich*, give somewhat different accounts of his death. Wistrich, for instance, wrote:

> At the end of the war, Globocnik succeeded in evading arrest by returning to his native country in the mountains south of Klagenfurt. He was eventually tracked down and, according to some accounts, arrested on 31 May 1945 by a British patrol at Weissensee, Carinthia, committing suicide by swallowing a cyanide capsule a few minutes after being apprehended. According to another version, Globocnik was hunted down and killed by partisans or by a Jewish vengeance squad in June 1945.[4]

Snyder, on the other hand, wrote: "Arrested in Austria by Allied troops in *early* [emphasis added] May 1945, he committed suicide."[5] Although Wistrich is careful not to opt for either explanation, he dates the death at May 31, not earlier in that month. But another writer, Andre Brissaud, put Globocnik's death in another month. In a brief biographical section, Brissaud wrote: "He committed suicide in April 1945."[6] Alexander Donat, editor of a book on Globocnik's Treblinka death camps, wrote: "He [Globocnik] was captured by British troops in Carinthia, Austria, and committed suicide by taking poison in Weissensee, Austria, on May 21, 1945,"[7] 10 days too early. This date, May 21, was also accepted by Dressen and Riess, referred to earlier. They wrote: "On 21 May 1945, after capture by British troops, killed himself in Kärnten."[8]

However, the editors of *The Third Reich Almanac*, James Taylor and Warren Shaw, were far more cautious by simply claiming: "Globocnik committed suicide on his arrest by Allied troops in 1945,"[9] with no month, no location, and no hint of whether the troops were British, American, Soviet, or Polish for that matter. An American historian of the Jewish Holocaust, Raul Hilberg, includes a surprisingly brief biographical entry for Globocnik in one of his publications. After listing Globocnik's name and position, SS and police leader, Lublin, there is just the single word, "suicide," followed by the year, 1945.[10] The German-Canadian historian, Ruth Bettina Birn, in her specialist study of all of Himmler's higher SS and police leaders, said: "Globocnik was captured in the Alps by British troops in 1945. Once his identity was discovered on 31 May 1945 he took his own life."[11] It is possible that Wistrich's reference to a Jewish vengeance squad was taken from an account published by the one-time Jerusalem-based BBC correspondent, Michael Elkins, who describes the undercover activities of the Jewish reprisal squad, DIN (Hebrew for vengeance and judgement): "And so, among others in those days, the men of DIN hunted down and killed: SS Lieutenant General Odilo Globocnik: higher SS and police leader at Lublin; supervised the *Einsatz Reinhardt* massacres throughout Poland, 1942–43."[12]

Elkins, who listed 14 other wanted war criminals, including Globocnik's immediate superior in the General Gouvernement, Friedrich-Wilhelm Kruger, provided no evidence for his claims on their fate. On the contrary, he said that DIN was such a clandestine Jewish group that he had undertaken not to disclose the identity of his sources, who were, presumably, former DIN members. This is an unfortunate and thoroughly unsatisfactory, even if honorable, state of affairs, leaving no room for open and constructive discussion, analysis, or debate. The door has been slammed shut. Elkins credited the DIN groups with at least 100 successful revenge assassinations of war criminals who underwent summary justice during these confused postwar months. However, as will be seen, Globocnik was not one of those to fall victim to DIN, even if there is no doubt that such a group actually existed. "In those two months of the 'first hunting season' the small bands of Jewish avengers roaming through Germany tracked down and executed more than a hundred men who had for years committed or commanded mass murder. They then gathered together again, called by the leaders of DIN to Alt-Ausee, in the Austrian Alps...."[13]

Similarly off-target was Edward Crankshaw's description of Globocnik's fate. This English writer and journalist who also wrote on Soviet affairs, in part because he had been a specially assigned representative at the British embassy in Russia during the war, saw Globocnik first and foremost as a conspiratorial creature, which is quite true, and even claimed he was "a handsome brute in a coarse and heavy way," which few are likely to have agreed with.

> He had to be conspiratorial because he was required to double-cross [Hans] Frank. But he was one of those born conspirators and racketeers who can function as well when they are drunk as when they are sober. Globocnik was almost always drunk. It would be a pleasure to be able to believe that he was sober when, five years later, he met his death at the hands of Yugoslav partisans in Istria. But he was probably drunk then too.[14]

Crankshaw's colorful description and emphasis on drunkenness is somewhat overdone. Although other writers do raise Globocnik's tendency toward heavy drinking, their emphasis is nowhere near as pronounced as Crankshaw's. The fact of the matter is that he was not "almost always drunk." Nor does any other writer give Yugoslav partisans the credit for having killed this dedicated destroyer of human life. It is likely that Crankshaw has simply confused Globocnik with his senior *Action Reinhardt* staffer, the violent and vicious Christian Wirth, who, although at least as evil, was not even an Austrian. He had been a highly competent Stuttgart detective and police officer. It is also noteworthy that Globocnik's wartime former fiancée, Irmgard Rickheim, was quizzed several times by the author on the question of his alleged drunkenness, and she conceded he enjoyed having a drink, and sometimes was known even to be slightly tipsy, particularly at the end of one of his legendary and extravagant Lublin parties where the best French champagne flowed, cigarettes were in abundance, and food was available in festive quantities. But she insisted he was not a drunk, and he was certainly not permanently drunk as some allege. In other words, not everything about even this evil man was undesirable. He most certainly was not in a drunken stupor while being gunned down by Yugoslav partisans. Crankshaw is simply wrong on both counts.

Clearly the more one searches for the truth about Globocnik's death, the more confusion and contradictions one encounters, in the same way that occurs when attempting to establish if he bombed and killed the Jewish Viennese jeweler. For example, Gerald Reitlinger, in his large and in many ways pioneering study of the Jewish Holocaust wrote that Globocnik "[t]ook poison in Karavanken Alps, June 6th, 1945, to avoid arrest by a British patrol."[15] Elsewhere, Reitlinger varied this incorrect claim slightly by writing that Globocnik's fate was "suicide in Carinthia alleged, May 1945."[16]

Reitlinger alleged that the act of suicide was to thwart capture, which, as will be shown below, is quite incorrect, since Globocnik had already been in captivity for several hours before his death. Scanning the writings of about half a dozen extremely competent and successful English-language authors reveals a surprising number of differences about the time, place, reason for, and even manner, of Globocnik's death.

Understandably, this confusion could have prompted some to think that perhaps Globocnik, like Adolf Eichmann and several other leading Nazis, including Richard Glücks, Heinrich "Gestapo" Müller, and Martin Bormann, had slipped through the not-so-secure net cast by the Allies and Soviets across Europe just before and after the conclusion of the war. The London and Tel Aviv-based Wiener Library felt compelled, in 1961, to address this question in the case of some of these notorious war criminals. In a brief report the editors of that library's bulletin describe the fate of 17 war criminals, including Odilo Globocnik. The report read, concerning Globocnik:

> SS Lieut-Gen. As police chief in Lublin from the end of 1939 to August 1943, he was responsible for carrying out "Action Reinhardt," the mass gassing and shooting of nearly three million Jews. In spite of recent rumors about his capture in Argentina, it is certain that he committed suicide in May 1945, under British arrest.[17]

These rumors prompted even the Austrian government to contact the British Foreign Office soon after, seeking more definite evidence that their one-time citizen was in fact dead. Another wanted war criminal mentioned in the Wiener Library Bulletin was Globocnik's senior camp commandant,

Christian Wirth. The bulletin claimed he had died in Istria in May 1944. Interestingly, as mentioned above, Elkins credited the killing of Wirth to the Jewish DIN vengeance group, which he claimed was created after the war, contradicting the May 1944 date.[18] The *Wiener Library Bulletin*'s editors said they had been prompted to report on the 17 selected criminals because ever since the capture of Eichmann in Argentina by Israeli undercover agents in May 1960, they had received inquiries on the whereabouts of other key Jewish Holocaust criminals. They consequently wrote: "In many cases, e.g. in that of Martin Bormann, the evidence seemed inconclusive. Now some definite data have become available as a result of investigations made by the West German Federal Agency for the Prosecution of Nazi Criminals."[19]

The agency in question is otherwise named the Central Office of Land Judicial Authorities for the Investigation of National-Socialist Crimes, or the Central Office of the Regional Administrations of Justice, and is based in Ludwigsburg, near Stuttgart. Its director during 1987, Willi Dressen, when asked of Globocnik's fate, retorted quite confidently that Globocnik was dead, and had been since 1945.[20] This office was created following a meeting of West German *Lander* (state) ministers and senators in October 1958, and was federally funded, first from Bonn, and after German reunification from Berlin.

> In pursuance of the administrative agreement reached by the Ministers and Senators of Justice, the terms of reference of the Central Office were — to begin with — confined to investigating Nazi killings for which the scene of the crime did not provide any jurisdiction within federal territory and which had moreover been committed against civilians during World War II beyond the ambit of military actions. The main targets were the crimes of murder and manslaughter carried out by the operational units of Security Police and Security Service men as well as those perpetrated in concentration and labor camps or in the ghettos.[21]

Clearly, Globocnik would probably have been tried by an Israeli court had he survived the war but evaded a trial by a Polish or another Allied tribunal. We can also confidently predict that had Israeli agents captured him, his trial would have been as widely reported and publicized as that of Adolf Eichmann's. But that was not to be, and this, in part, explains why so little has been written about him, according to Israeli historian Yisrael Gutman.[22]

Despite the contradictions surrounding Globocnik's fate, it was clear to the first generation of postwar historians of Nazi crimes of genocide and of the Jewish Holocaust in particular, as well as those investigating the less popular topic of Nazi ethnic cleansing and resettlement policies, that Globocnik had not survived the war. Whether he died in April, May, or June 1945, and regardless of which Allied power's troops captured him, and precisely where he died, all were aware that Globocnik had died by his own hand toward the end of the war.

For the purposes of this investigation the key documents and sources which conclusively support this are:

  I. The official history of the British Regiment whose men captured Globocnik;
  II. That regiment's field diaries and related contemporary battlefield documents;
  III. Major Kenneth Hedley's statement, and a later statement to the British Foreign Office;
  IV. Dr. Morris Leigh's 1965 statement to the British Foreign Office;
  V. A letter to the author from the regiment's commanding officer during May 1945, Brigadier Guy Wheeler, referred to here as *The Guy Wheeler Report*. Wheeler was to also provide a statement to the British Foreign Office in January 1965.
  VI. Major Alexander Ramsay's handwritten account of Globocnik's capture and death, referred to here as *The Ramsay Report*; and
  VII. Historian Gitta Sereny's account in the *Independent* (London).

Each of these is separately set out so the reader has as complete a description as possible of Globocnik's capture and death. Together these sources show as conclusively as is now possible that Globocnik committed suicide while in the hands of the British military. The contents and details of each of these crucial sources, separately presented and elaborated upon, show that Globocnik's fate was an ignominious one.

Globocnik's Capture and Death: The Seven Accounts

I. The Official Regimental History

It is ironic indeed that the British soldiers who captured Globocnik were either members of, or were directly associated with, the famous cavalry regiment in which Britain's wartime prime minister, Winston Churchill, once served: the Queen's Own Fourth Hussars. This regiment's official historian, David Scott Daniell, therefore understandably refers to the colonel of the regiment, Churchill, as "the most famous Fourth Hussar of all," which he no doubt was. Daniell introduced his brief account of the capture of Globocnik, whose name he spelled throughout as "Glovocnik," because that was the way contemporary regimental documents recorded it, by pointing out that the regiment did not return to the United Kingdom until two and a half years after the Third Reich surrendered in May 1945, also the month of Globocnik's death. Writes Daniell on the expansion of regimental duties: "Soldiers have become policemen, administrators and welfare organizers, in all of which roles the British soldier is singularly proficient."[23]

During May 1945, the regiment had moved from northern Italy into southern Austria, southern Carinthia, the region adjacent to northern Yugoslavia, or more precisely, Slovenia, where its men encountered a range of problems and had to undertake duties far removed from soldiering and managing violence. As the soldiers went about their new tasks, they made their headquarters and "B" Squadron base at Paternion, "a quiet village in the Drava valley, dominated by an ancient castle which made an impressive Officers' mess."[24]

Other squadrons were detached, with one taking over a factory that had been used to hold Russian slave workers, while another was required to oversee prisoners-of-war at a place called Molzbichl, in which an entire SS division was later interned. The regiment's men soon encountered what Daniell called the "flotsam of war": thousands of Hungarians, Cossacks, Italians, Russians, and Yugoslavs, all fleeing their homes from Soviet and Yugoslav or Tito-led partisans. There were also Italians and other liberated Eastern, that is, Polish and Ukrainian, slave laborers. Although these were generally no danger to the British, among this wave of refugees there were Nazis in disguise.

The regimental headquarters were promptly established in Paternion's police station, and policing was immediately launched. This work included establishing roadblocks so that all passing through the region could be processed in a more-or-less orderly manner. However, it was quickly realized that those most sought, that is *Gauleiters*, SS divisional commanders, and senior party officials were probably hiding in the mountains, above the valley, so the regiment's senior planners moved to launch searches away from the highways and provincial roads.

This was big game hunting of the best sort and Lt. W.K. Hedley, the Provost Sgt.— Sgt Sowler — and a band of picked men were formed into the Regimental Intelligence Squad, and went hunting. They were indefatigable, and on receipt of information that suspicious persons had been seen upon the snowline, they would set off and be away for several days, climbing and stalking their quarry. The best bag of all was achieved on 30th May. A big party was being held in the castle when information was brought that some suspected Nazi leaders were hiding in a certain mountain hut. At midnight the hunting party set off, five officers and a dozen men, under Hedley. They were full of hope and determination, encouraged to some degree perhaps by the festivities. They climbed hard for four-and-a-half hours using only one hurricane lamp, and, approaching with the greatest caution, they surrounded the mountain hut. It was dramatic, and very successful. The inmates of the hut were taken by surprise. In spite of the revolvers they had, they were captured and taken down to Regimental HQ. Then it was discovered what a splendid night's work it had been. The leaders were Dr. Rainer and *Gruppenführer der SS* Glovocnik, the ex–SS commander in Trieste. Both were on the list of war criminals. Glovocnik was notorious for innumerable brutish deeds, and his wife had been as brutal. Both men denied their identity, and tried to bluff their way out, but in vain. When Glovocnik realized that there was no escape he bit on a phial of prussic acid. As well as the two prime criminals the bag included three *SS-Sturmbannführers*, two *Kreisleiters*, one *Oberscharführer* and two German women. Hedley and his efficient squad combed the mountains with the greatest perseverance and skill and captured in all 18 very important Nazi criminals and 15 minor ones. As well as the two women caught with Rainer and Glovocnik, a girl was caught who had been the secretary to the SS staff in Trieste. One party was found with a million and a half Lire in their possession....[25]

It is interesting that Daniell fails to mention a key player in Globocnik's apprehension, Major Alexander Ramsay, who at the time was with the regiment, though not a member.

II. Regimental Diary and Field Reports

The "War Diary or Intelligence Summary" (Army Form C.2118) of the Queen's Own Fourth Hussars for May 1945 showed that "C" Squadron moved from the River Po to Padua, the birth place of the architect of Zamosc, Bernado Morando, on 2 May. The same day a congratulatory message was received from Prime Minister Churchill, the colonel to the regiment. The next day saw the squadron reaching Albano, near Padua, and three days later the wheeled vehicles of "A" and "B" Squadrons also reached Padua, with the tracked vehicles arriving on 7 May. Headquarters and "B" Squadrons reached the small southern Austrian township of Paternion, which lies between Villach and Spittal, at 1400 on May 11. A prisoner-of-war camp was established the next day at Molzbichl, and on 14 May work began on a regimental rest camp on *Weissensee*. "C" and "A" Squadrons caught up on 21 and 26 May, respectively, and the regiment came under the command of the 78th Division on 27 May. The entries for 29, 30, and 31 May read as follows:

> **29, 1000.** KUHWEIDE and friend came to Schloss at PATERNION and reported that *KREISLEITER* and the *Gaurichter* HUGO HERZOG and another man were hiding in a hut on WIEDERSCHWING Peak at MR C640885. K reported that 5 of his men armed with pistols had surrounded the hut and would shoot the men concerned if they attempted to go away. A 4th Hussars' Party was immediately organized and finally consisted of Lt.W.K. Hedley and Sjt Sowler, Regtl Provost Sjt armed with tommy guns. They were accompanied by K and friend. On reaching the top of WIEDERSCHWING from the direction of RIED C692908 K's friend went ahead to the hut which was slightly below the summit. Sjt SOWLER went to the back of the house and Lt. Hedley entered through the front and both men, though armed, surrendered without a struggle. The papers taken from both these men are attached. The second man proved to be *Kreis Propaganda Leiter* FRIEDRICH PLÖB. They were arrested at approximately 1500 hrs and subsequently conveyed to the prison at PATERNION where they were held until turned over to Captain WILLETT 78 Div Provost Staff.
>
> **1800.** E reported that 2 SS men were hiding at STOCKENBOI No.34 MR C573902 disguised as agricultural workers.

2300. These two men were apprehended and gave their names as SIEG-FRIED KUMMERER; ? SCHUTZ.

30, 1500. Both men were interrogated and KUMMERER admitted to being a Corporal in the SS with approximately 6 years service. He had served two periods at DACHAU and protested that he took no active part in any "Atrocity duties" at the camp. SCHUTZ was released.

2200. KUMMERER volunteered a statement to the effect that one *SS-Gruppenführer* and 3 *SS-Sturmbannführer* and one other SS man and two women were hiding in a hut on the MOSLACHER ALM [sic] MR 5693. An expedition comprising two officers Special Force (Major Ramsay and Lt. Birkett) and three officers (Major Quarmby, Capt G.P. Wheeler and Lt. W.K. Hedley) and 12 Ors 4th Hussars was therefore organized to go to this to which KUMMERER was willing to guide the party.

31, 0230. The expedition arrived C570901.

0430. The expedition arrived at the hut.

0500. Hut surrounded.

0510. The door in front was opened by Major Ramsay who had entered through a loft window and the back was forced by Major Quarmby and Lt. Hedley, 4 men were found in the front of the house. Interrogation began at once and all men except the *Gauleiter* and *SS-Sturmbannführer* LERCH denied any knowledge of the SS. The women were allowed to remain in the hut, but arrangements are in hand (1430 hrs 31 May) to arrest them. DR RAINER, LERCH, three unidentified suspects and a fourth man who gave references in KLAGENFURT were brought down to the prison at PATERNION.

0715. SCHUTZ re-arrested on accusation of KUMMERER.

1130. Man who was suspected of being GLOVOCNIK was trapped into acknowledging his name *by a slight movement of the head* when Major RAMSAY shouted his name across the courtyard. He was ordered into arrest and poisoned himself with Prussic acid while walking 150yds between the courtyard at PATERNION and the prison. Capt. M.M. Leigh, RAMC attempted to revive him but was unsuccessful. It was considered that GLOVOCNIK had this poison concealed in his mouth from the moment in which the first alarm was raised at the hut as he consistently refused all form of refreshment.

1200. Three suspects on viewing the body of GLOVOCNIK confessed their identities as: *Sturmbannführer der SS* MICHALSON [sic]; *SS-Sturmbannführer* HÖFLE; *Oberscharführer* KARL HELLESBERGER SS in TRIESTE.

1245. All eight prisoners as listed in Appx "A" were removed by Captain WILLETT of 78 Div Provost Coy., leaving only SCHUTZ in detention and under further investigation.

APPENDIX "A"

1. *Gauleiter* and *SS-Obergruppenführer* DR. FRIEDRICH RAINER.
2. *Gruppenführer der SS* in TRIESTE GLOVOCNIK.
3. *Sturmbannführer der SS* MICHALSON. [sic]
4. *Sturmbannführer* ERNST LERCH SS in TRIESTE.
5. *SS-Sturmbannführer* HÖFLE.
6. *Oberscharführer* KARL HELLESBERGER *SS* in TRIESTE.
7. *Kreisleiter* & *Gaurichter* HERZOG.
8. *Kreis Propaganda Leiter* PLÖB.[26]

III. Kenneth Hedley's Malayan and Foreign Office Statements

In 1948 Globocnik's widow, Lore, who had been the *Gauführerin BdM* of Carinthia, a senior party official in her own right, applied to the Austrian authorities for a pension. Kenneth Hedley, now a major, was contacted in Malaya, where he was in command of the Fourth Hussar's "C" Squadron, and was requested to provide details of Globocnik's death in support of her application.[27] In a signed statement sent to the civil liaison officer, Spittal, Kärnten, Austria, Major Hedley said Globocnik was captured by troops under his command in a hut overlooking the *Weissensee* at 4 A.M. on 31 May 1945.

> He committed suicide, by poisoning at about 1130 hours the same day outside the small prison, 100 yards west of the schloss at Paternion, when he had been positively identified. He was certified as dead by Captain M.M. Leigh (sometime RAMC) who made every attempt to revive him. His body was seen by Dr. Friedrich Rainer — sometime *Gauleiter* of Carinthia and the following members of his staff. *SS-Sturmbannführers*, Lerch, Höfle, Michaelson [sic] and *SS-Oberscharführer* Hellesberger. He was buried in the presence of Captain G.P.M.C. Wheeler, 4th Queen's Own Hussars by members of the Regimental Police.... I personally saw Globocnik die from the effects of the poison.[28]

Late in 1964, concern developed in some quarters in Austria with claims that Globocnik, like so many other senior level SS men, had actually survived the war without having been brought to book for tormenting and murdering many hundreds of thousands of people, especially in the East. One outcome of this was that the Austrian embassy in London, no doubt on orders from its foreign ministry, contacted the British Government for details about the fate of their former Carinthian citizen. This led to the British Foreign Office contacting Hedley, Dr. Leigh, and Brigadier Wheeler. Hedley, who had taken greater interest in Globocnik's fate than the others, probably because he better appreciated Globocnik's crimes and with Ramsay had actually identified him, thereby prompting Globocnik to take his life, replied with a two-page statement containing a great deal of familiar information. Hedley said, as the only Hussar officer who spoke German fluently, he was detailed to deal with matters which could affect the local population. He initially saw this as a drab task but it became exciting when he learned that Rainer was believed to be in the district, "around whom a *Werewolf* Resistance Group was forming." Hedley arrested a number of SS men and locked them up in Paternion, where they received minimum rations and water "to loosen their tongues." The ploy worked, because one deprived SS man agreed to speak. He revealed that *SS-Obergruppenführer* Globocnik and some staffers were hiding in a hut above the *Weissensee*. The man in question knew of this because he had been acting as a food courier to the hide-away. As Wheeler has written, "At about 8.00 P.M. on the 30th May (1945) Lieutenant Hedley received information from an SS deserter on the staff of the *Gauleiter*, that the *Gauleiter* and some other important SS officers were hiding temporarily in a mountain hut...."[29]

A party of troops was organized to capture the inhabitants after dark. The group broke in and arrested all the fugitives. Rainer was quickly identified because he had a dueling scar on his cheek, according to the circulated description that Hedley possessed. "His presence tended to distract attention from the others in the hut, approximately seven men and three women,"[30] observed Wheeler. Hedley said he then handed over to another fluent German speaker, Major Ramsay of the Parachute Regiment, since Hedley had returned to Paternion to get more vehicles. Interestingly, Rainer was searched and found to possess "a metal phial containing a suicide capsule as issued to all senior members of the Nazi hierarchy."[31]

> Little attention was, at the time, attached to a similar empty phial found on the floor of one of the rooms. The SS informer had identified all the prisoners by name and gave details of their duties in Trieste. With one exception they were all locked up. The exception stated he was "a poor merchant from Klagenfurt frightened of the possible Yugoslav invasion." He had almost convinced Major Ramsay of his innocence, was walking up and down in the castle yard, very coolly, escorted by the regimental provost sergeant until his Klagenfurt references could be checked.
>
> The informer insisted he was Globocnik. Major Ramsay and I decided that he (Ramsay) should sharply shout out the name Globocnik while I watched the captive's reaction very closely.
>
> When the name was called Globocnik's step never faltered, but his head moved fractionally.
>
> I shouted to him (in German) "you have given yourself away, you moved your head very slightly" and ordered Sowler to add him to the gang in the lock-up.
>
> I then started to go to my room to have a bath only to hear shouts of "he's dead, he's dying."
>
> I ran downstairs to find Globocnik lying on the ground between the castle yard and the lock-up. He had held his suicide capsule under his tongue continually since his arrest and until using it about 11.25.
>
> We had noticed at the time that he refused any form of food or drink.
>
> Captain M. M. Leigh RAMC, the regimental medical officer, was quickly on the scene and he gave Globocnik two inoculations in the arm and one in the heart, but to no avail. As soon as they saw his corpse Lerch, Höfle, Michalsen and Hellesberger who had denied their identities admitted who they were and identified the corpse as their former commanding officer Globocnik. Rainer also identified the corpse as Globocnik.
>
> Globocnik was subsequently buried by the regimental police in the presence of Captain G.P.M.C. Wheeler.[32]

An interesting aside to these matters is that during the 1980s Michael Tregenza, while conducting initial inquiries into *Aktion Reinhardt* in various

London archives, contacted Hedley and was asked by the former Hussar to attempt to arrange some publicity about the May 1945 British capture of Globocnik. Tregenza made several efforts to promote Hedley's story to a number of London newspapers, but for a variety of reasons none were interested. Tregenza then focused his research in Ludwigsburg, reading and assessing thousands of documents about most of Globocnik's top staffers, after which he settled in Lublin to continue his extensive and impressive research.

IV. Dr. Morris Leigh's Statement to the Foreign Office

Like Hedley, Leigh was also contacted in 1964 because of the Austrian Government's inquiries into Globocnik's postwar fate. In response, Leigh wrote a letter on 7 January 1965 setting out his knowledge of the case. The letter says in part:

> I confirm that I attended the man believed to be Globocnik on 31st May 1945. When I reached him he was deeply comatose, suffering from cyanide poisoning; there were broken pieces of the glass phial in his mouth. He died within a minute or two.... I do not remember having certified Globocnik's death, although it seems highly probable that I must have signed some document to that effect; but I confirm Major Hedley's statement in par. 3 that "his death was established by Captain M. M. Leigh," i.e. I pronounced life extinct. I do recall that Globocnik was a big, heavily built man. I am, of course, quite unable to confirm Major Hedley's statement in par 2 that "his identity had been established." All I can state with certainty is that the man described as Globocnik by Major Hedley died in my presence.... It may be of interest to you that an unsigned account of this incident was published in "IV Hussars Journal," 1950: pp. 27–30. Considerable background detail is given. The account is written in the first person, and I am sure it must have been written by Major Hedley.[33]

V. The Guy Wheeler Report: May 1990, and Wheeler's Statement to the Foreign Office

Between the late 1940s and about 1960, Brigadier Guy Wheeler (Ret.), who in the concluding stages of the war served as regimental adjutant of the Fourth Hussars, received no fewer than seven requests for information on Globocnik's fate. In each case the inquirer explained that he or she was "researching for a book or a newspaper article (one claimed his article was for *The Times* of London) or a serial in a monthly journal."[34] These explanations prompted Wheeler to write in 1990:

> Not all the seekers after truth were English-speaking and not one book, article, serial etc was ever published to my knowledge and my letters to the alleged authors were never answered. The reason for this, I believe, after some research of my own, is that their real intention was to discover what knowledge Globocnik had

of the SS hoard of treasure alleged to have been hidden in that area. Certainly Globocnik would have made an excellent janitor for it, a little quiet murdering of some of the few who knew its whereabouts — if, indeed, it ever existed — would have been a holiday to one who was accustomed to murdering by the thousand.[35]

These deceitful inquiries and Wheeler's personal involvement in the capture of a mass killer like Globocnik near Paternion understandably prompted Wheeler to make his own inquiries about this major SS criminal. By about the mid–1950s, Wheeler knew more about Globocnik than even most experts on the SS and the Holocaust in the West did.

In setting out the details of Globocnik's capture and fate on 31 May 1945, Wheeler's report first gave brief introductory comments on the key players, namely, Lieutenant (later Major) W.K. Hedley; Major Alexander Ramsay; Captain Morris Leigh; and Captain Peter Quarmby, MC.

Kenneth Hedley, who in 1990 was living in Eire, was a fluent German speaker appointed assistant adjutant and intelligence officer in the regimental headquarters, which were established in the castle and hamlet of Paternion, on the main road which follows the valley of the river Drau, between Spittal and Villach.

Alexander Ramsay was an ex–SOE operative in at least the latter part of the war. He was the senior Intelligence Corps officer attached to HQ 78th Infantry Division, stationed at Spittal, and was temporarily attached to the Hussars Regimental Headquarters. Ramsay was responsible for organizing the search for senior SS officers believed to be hiding in the mountainous country along the Austrian-Italian border. Wheeler writes:

> At the request of Divisional HQ, Lieutenant Hedley was put under command of Major Ramsay. I was Regimental Adjutant at the time and, to help Lieutenant Hedley, ordered the Provost Sergeant — Sgt Sowler — and six of his Regimental Police — Cpl Halstead and Lcpls Lee, Oswald and three others — to work under his command when necessary. As Kenneth Hedley was my Assistant Adjutant I maintained an interest in what he was doing."[36]

Captain Morris Leigh was the regimental surgeon during the period.

Captain Peter Quarmby, MC, was an officer of the South African Armoured Car Regiment on temporary attachment to the Regiment.

Brigadier Wheeler described Globocnik's ignominious end as follows:

> At about 8.00 P.M. on the 30th May 1945, Lieutenant Hedley received information from an SS deserter on the staff of the *Gauleiter* [Rainer] that the *Gauleiter* and some other important SS officers were hiding temporarily in a mountain hut overlooking the Wöthersee [sic] — one of the lakes in the mountains just south of Paternion.

At the same time a celebratory party was in progress in the RHQ Mess, but it was decided to go out at once. Major Ramsay and another officer from the Intelligence Section of 78th Division, whose name I cannot remember, [it was probably Birkett] were in the Mess and joined with Lieutenant Hedley and Captain Quarmby, Sgt Sowler and six Regimental Police. With the Commanding Officer away on leave in England, responsibility for the approval of this Regimental operation fell to me; so I went as well.

We drove out on the track to the lake. To avoid the noise of our vehicle alarming our quarry, we dismounted a mile or so back from where a steep and narrow path led up the hillside from the track. It took about four hours to get from the vehicles to the hut. We moved slowly and as quietly as we could and arrived at the hut just before dawn. It stood in the middle of a small clearing on the hillside. We surrounded it, keeping under cover of the trees all round it and taking up firing positions in case of trouble. We waited for the light to improve. We saw that the hut was really two huts — one bigger than the other — built back to back, each with its own door on opposite sides of each other.

A man came out of the small hut, wearing civilian clothes; relieved himself, looking around, and went back into the hut, closing the door behind him. We decided that the time for action had come and that we would kick in both doors at once; Major Ramsay and two Policemen would deal with the small hut, Lieutenant Hedley, Sgt Sowler and two more Policemen with the large one.

Both parties were immediately successful. The doors were kicked in and all the occupants were ordered out, to stand in a line, half-naked, with their hands on their heads, shivering; it was a chilly morning. Rainer was encouraged out of the small hut by Lcpl Lees' boot and complained that he, as the *Gauleiter*, should be treated with more respect. He was offered a bullet in the back of his neck as an alternative and made no further complaint.

In addition to Rainer there were six other officers of the SS and three female 'secretaries', also a civilian who claimed to be from Villach and that he had been conscripted by Rainer to accompany the party because he knew the area very well. With the exception of the other civilian, all were armed with pistols and some light SMCs.

We made them clean out the huts and carry everything they had, in a sullen, scared single file, down the steep track to the road. Our transport had moved up to the junction with the track, so we piled them into the back of a truck, with two Regimental Police to keep them company, and drove to the Schloss. There they dismounted and, still under guard of the police, sat on their belongings to await interrogation at the Schloss or transport to Spittal and Divisional Headquarters. To their surprise, since it seems they had expected to be shot, they were offered some coffee; which all except the civilian accepted.

As the operation was concluded I returned to my office in the RHQ building — the village school — to attend to more routine regimental affairs, while Major Ramsay reported the success of the operation to Divisional HQ. After he had telephoned his message, he returned to the courtyard of the Schloss to start an interrogation of the prisoners. I learned later that he had tricked the civilian from Villach into revealing himself as *Obergruppenführer* Globocnik. While Lieutenant Hedley had kept Globocnik in casual conversation, Ramsay, who had suspected the civilian to be lying about his identity, standing a short space behind him, suddenly called his name. Globocnik half turned, then realizing that he had betrayed himself, bit on the poison phial which he had concealed in his mouth some time beforehand — and was probably the reason he refused the coffee — collapsed and, despite the best efforts of our regimental surgeon, died very quickly.

We received no orders on the disposal of the corpse, so, after it had been identified and there appeared to be no further use for it, I ordered Sgt. Sowler to bury it in a grave, dug for that purpose by the Regimental Police, in one of the small fields lying on both sides of a path leading from behind the RHG building. This was done and the turf replaced to conceal the grave. I said I thought that would be inappropriate in this case. Sgt. Sowler asked whether a cross should be put on the grave. I said I thought that would be inappropriate in this case.

As far as Globocnik is concerned that is the end of the story. Rainer, in due course, was tried and hanged; at which, I expect, he complained at the lack of respect ... let me assure you that Globocnik was buried in the dirty shirt and trousers he was wearing when we took him, with nothing in his pockets. I am not sure with whom he conversed during the short period of his captivity, but he had certainly almost convinced Lieutenant Hedley — the only other German speaker than Major Ramsay in the group — that he was harmless, innocent and of no importance and Ramsay himself was nearly of the same mind: so he could hardly have been acquainting them with the location of any hoard.[37]

Finally, it must be emphasized that Wheeler was a successful officer and a man whose integrity and honesty are beyond question, in the words of Major Hedley. Wheeler was the third member of the group involved in the capture of Globocnik who was contacted by the British Foreign Office in 1964 to provide information to the Austrian Government.

Together with a Captain Ramsay of SAS, who had been working in Austria during the war, I accompanied Hedley on the night expedition to the mountain hut above the *Weissensee*, where the former *Gauleiter* of Carinthia and his staff, together with Globocnik, were captured at dawn on May 31st 1945.

On first interrogations all those captured admitted their identity, except Globocnik, who claimed to be an engineer seized on Rainer's orders and brought up to the hut to advise on fortifying the area. The fact that he was sharing the small private room at the back of the hut with Rainer himself made us doubt this story. The whole party was brought down to the Schloss Paternion escorted by Hedley and the Regimental Policemen. They were all thoroughly cowed and gave no trouble. On arrival at the Schloss I went to my office in Regimental Headquarters (in the village school) and neither witnessed nor assisted in what followed.

I was informed that Globocnik, on being recognized by Captain Ramsay from photographs, had been challenged with his identity and had promptly committed suicide by biting on a cyanide capsule, which he had concealed in his mouth. In relation to this it was remembered that when after capture all the prisoners were offered breakfast, they all ate except Globocnik, who excused himself saying he felt unwell.... I was *not* at the burial but ordered the Provost Sergeant to bury the body anywhere outside hallowed ground. I was shown the grave after completion of the burial; it was entirely unmarked. It lay in a meadow outside the track leading north out of the center of the village. It so happens that I drove through Paternion, for the first time since 1945, in October last year, and did drive down the track to see if I could identify the spot; it seemed to have been built over but I could not be sure and I was in a hurry and could not stop. If required I could probably again find the place but might well require the assistance of members of the Regimental Police who buried the body. This might be the only way of finally establishing the body as Globocnik. He was, of course, searched thoroughly on capture — when he was wearing civilian clothes — and no other means of identifying him were found then.[38]

VI. The Ramsay Report[39]

This report is Alexander Ramsay's handwritten personal account of the capture of Globocnik and of his longtime party colleague, Dr. Friedrich Rainer, near *Weissensee*, above Paternion. Unfortunately, it is not dated, so we are not sure if Ramsay wrote it immediately after this important capture, some time afterwards, or well after the event. On the last page is a notation that reads: "Major Ramsay, Personal Documents," which was either written by his Austrian-born wife or longtime friend, Arthur Radley, who held the report and made it available to the author after consulting Sir Peter Wilkinson, who was his and Ramsay's commanding officer in the Balkans and Italy in the later stages of the war. Radley believed that the report was written very shortly after Globocnik had been captured and killed himself; perhaps the next day, 1 June 1945, or at least during that first month of peace.

Because Ramsay was such a key player in the capture and identification of Globocnik, and an industrious as well as highly experienced man of war, some detail about this British soldier is in order. Ramsay (1912–75) was the son of a professor and attended Jesus College, Oxford, where he read German and French. After graduating he held various positions, including that of salesman for Permutit, a firm supplying water-softening agents. He subsequently joined the London Metropolitan Police. Simon Withers provided further details in a letter to the author:

> He volunteered for the Army and was posted to the parachute regiment, where he was one of the first people to train at Ringway (now Manchester Airport). In 1942 he went with the 1st Army to North Africa where he was posted to No. 2 Parachute Regiment as its intelligence officer. He landed in southern Italy at Taranto in 1944. In Spring 1944 he joined No.6. Special Forces Clowder Mission under Lieutenant-Colonel Peter Wilkinson. He then held the rank of Captain.
>
> Captain Ramsay was seconded back to the Parachute Regiment for a drop in Greece in the summer of 1944 and then returned to Clowder Mission. He was then seconded to No. 1 Special Force to command Operation Herring,

which was to drop Italian partisans north of the River Po in anticipation of the 8th Army moving north. (He himself was not dropped owing to pilot error and thereby missed a certain DSO).

In May 1945 he was in Austria with No. 6 Special Force, now known as "No. 6 Special Force Staff section." In the course of his duties he was ordered to help 5 Corp (8ᵗʰ Army) in rounding up senior Nazis. His main task was to find *Gauleiter* Rainer, the governor of the province of Kärnten (Carinthia).[40]

Ramsay also served in Norway in April 1940, according to the office of The SOE Adviser, Foreign and Commonwealth Office:

He joined SOE on 28 May 1944, and after training went to an operational pool in Cairo. From August to September 1944 he was in Yugoslavia. He returned to UK for further training and was posted to Bari on 17.3.45. On 28.3.45 he led Operation HERRING. This was a Special Air Service operation in which a team of 200 were dropped into the Ferrara area to harass enemy transport and communications during his withdrawal towards the River Po.[41]

Of Ramsay, his commanding officer, Lieutenant-Colonel (later Sir) Peter Wilkinson wrote:

From December 1943 until the end of the War I commanded a small unit known as No. 6 Special Force (CLOWDER Mission) whose task was the penetration of Austria from Yugoslavia and north-east Italy. Major Ramsay was one of my officers and was with me when we entered Klagenfurt on 8 May with the Advance Guard of the British V Corps. It was, I think, as a member of No. 6 Special Force that he took part in the arrest of Globocnik, but I cannot be sure of this for, by then, I had returned to Rome, having been transferred to other duties.[42]

Ironically, therefore, Ramsay, in May 1945, was not actually looking for Globocnik. The former London Metropolitan policeman, who had been a paratrooper and fighter behind enemy lines in the Balkans, Italy, and North Africa, was in fact on the trail of Rainer. Not surprisingly therefore he began his report, "Events leading to the capture of ex–*Gauleiter* Rainer (Kärnten)," as follows: "Information that Rainer was in the mountains south-west of Spittal was originally provided by one Rudolf Durr of [Stockenboi] and laid at HQ V Corp on 22nd May. No.6 Special Force was given the task of following up the clues."[43]

Durr had brought to headquarters a Major Kuhweide of the Brandenburg Regiment. Kuhweide, who was living in the Stockenboi area, had volunteered to help find the *Gauleiter* and his SS bodyguard, which was estimated at numbering up to a dozen men. Apparently Kuhweide had been fighting Yugoslav partisans, but had failed to receive any orders, so decided to settle down, and when the British arrived opted to "buy his freedom." Ramsay stressed that no promises were made in return. However, the decision to co-opt this German officer proved a wise one, because the end result was the capture of Rainer and Globocnik. Ramsay also arranged for the use of two agents "who were introduced into the same area on 23 May, and two more on 27 May." By late May, therefore, the former London policeman had a sizeable team of informants and undercover operatives on the lookout for Rainer. These agents can be expected to have quizzed Austrians who may have known the identity of their prey. Rainer, after all, was not a complete unknown in the area being canvassed, so Ramsay's chances of making contact were better than even. But that was not all:

> Active pursuit of Rainer began on night of 23/24 May when a force approximating 2 platoons was put under the command of a Special Force office and moved up to the area of [left blank in original] to search the lead mines where it was reported there might be stocks of food and even the *Gauleiter*. This expedition was fruitless except in so far as the arrest of two minor Nazis in the area and the interrogation of various others produced information confirming that local sentiment was favorable to "*Wehrwolf*" activity. Small stocks of food were discovered and larger ones heard of.[44]

Between 23 and 27 May the 4th Hussars continued to send patrols into areas where Rainer was believed to be hiding, while Kuhweide and his men operated independently. On the morning of 28–29 May, on the basis of information Kuhweide had obtained, the Hussars sent a small expedition to apprehend a *Kreisleiter* Herzog and a few followers who were hiding out in a hut. These people were captured but they gave little information to the British.

> Meanwhile a report given to 68 Field Security Section [Army Intelligence] Villach somewhat revived the hope that Rainer might still be available in the area. It was said that the *Gauleiter* had been seen on the morning of 30 May at the Gasthause Cavaliar in company of two other men in local costume and moved off in the direction of the [left blank in original]. There were three *Alumhutten* [mountain pasture huts] in the mountains behind [left blank in original] where Rainer and his party might reasonably be supposed to be staying.[45]

Ramsay next had a stroke of good luck. Out of the blue, the captured Herzog declared he was ready to make a statement, and was further interrogated by the Special Forces officers. The information he supplied included advising that *SS-Gruppenführer* Globocnik, with three SS majors, an NCO, and two female employees, all recently returned from Trieste, had taken refuge in the Moeslacher-Alm. They were armed and had an adequate food supply to remain free for some time. Since this was one of the three mountain huts mentioned, it was decided to dispatch immediately a party of volunteers to confirm Herzog's revelation. Ramsay said those who went included 16 officers and other ranks of 4th Hussars and two officers from Special Forces Staff Section, a total of 18 men. The party left by motor vehicles for the *Weissensee* at 2 A.M. on 31 May, and took Herzog along.

The hut was 1,200 feet above the level of the lake, so the party parked its vehicles and went by foot for a further 90 minutes.

> Arrival in the vicinity of the hut was made unobserved and positions taken up covering the building and approaches. A recce up to the house established that it was occupied and it was decided that, as no alarm had been raised, an immediate investigation could be carried out without undue risk. Accordingly groups were detailed to each door and an entry was forced at 0510 hours.
>
> Surprise was complete and the occupants who were precisely as described by the SS sergeant (with one important exception) were paraded outside the house, and two of them carrying weapons, disarmed. A quick interrogation was carried out to establish identity when it was discovered that the additional person was the ex–*Gauleiter* who had arrived on the previous afternoon. He was quietly marched down to the transport and taken to Paternion by 4 Hussars. Further interrogation led to only two men "coming clean" (an SS major and sergeant). Globocnik posing as an engineer in hiding from partisans told a very plausible story, and had clearly thought out his cover very carefully. The whole party was marched off (less the two women members who were brought down in the afternoon) at 0815 hours and taken to HQ 4th Hussars in Paternion.
>
> Globocnik was left by himself for some time. He had not up to this time been challenged with his true identity. He betrayed himself by half answering a summons shouted in his real name, and was thereupon told that we knew who he was. Still protesting innocence he was marched away, but he had gone only some 150 yards when he collapsed and quietly died from hydrocyanic poisoning. It is almost certain that the glass ampoule was under his tongue from the time of his early morning arise as all prisoners were searched for poison, and one ampoule discovered on *SS-Sturmbannführer* Lerch.
>
> Rainer later confirmed that the dead man was in fact Globocnik.
>
> At 1230 hours all the prisoners were handed over to Provost Office, 78 Division for disposal through 88 Field Security Section.[46]

Globocnik had obviously prepared himself for the eventuality of being captured, for "the fourth man [Globocnik] gave references in Klagenfurt."[47]

VII. The Gitta Sereny Account[48]

Hungarian-born author Gitta Sereny, although writing in a London newspaper nearly half a century after Globocnik's death, was not merely presenting a sensational exposé of a war criminal. By the 1970s Sereny had become a leading expert on the Jewish Holocaust, and is author of the book *Into the Darkness*, based on lengthy interviews with, and the transcripts of the trial of, Franz Stangl, a senior member of Globocnik's *Aktion Reinhardt* killing team. Stangl had been commandant of the Treblinka killing center and, as outlined above, in 1940 had been a police superintendent of the euthanasia program at *Schloss* Hartheim. He had also been at the Sobibor killing center, and left the Lublin District with Globocnik in September 1943, to be placed in charge of *Einsatz* Poll, a defensive construction project along northern Italy's Po River Valley, which involved about half a million Italian workers. Stangl was arrested in Brazil in 1967 and was tried for co-responsibility in the murder of some 700,000 Jews at Treblinka, and was sentenced to life imprisonment on 22 October 1970. Sereny's account of Globocnik's fate appeared in the Sunday magazine of the London newspaper, *The Independent*, in 1992. Sereny was moved to undertake extensive research on Globocnik's fate because a Californian had alleged that both Globocnik and Himmler's Gestapo Chief Heinrich Müller, who had evaded capture in 1945, like Stangl, and had never been found, had been pardoned and hidden by the British and United States Governments.[49] Although Sereny established the documents sent to her from California were forgeries, she was nevertheless curious enough to inquire into Globocnik's fate, so she read the Fourth Hussar's records at PRO, Kew, which she said provided "a detailed account of Globocnik's capture and suicide in Carinthia, in the mountains of central Austria, on 31 May."[50] This has been set out in Section II, Regimental Diary and Field Reports, above, with her account quoting that day's entries for 1130 and 1200 hours.

> So this was the account prepared within days of the incident—surely that was definitive? And yet, wasn't calling out a name a rather banal way of "trapping someone?" Might not anyone hearing a sudden shout respond with "a slight movement of the head?" There were no independent witnesses who knew him, only members of his own staff. Could there have been a misidentification—or perhaps a conspiracy by his own men?[51]

In addition, Sereny met several people in southern Austria to discuss the reported death. Among them was former *Sturmbannführer* Ernst Lerch, who confirmed to her that Globocnik had died at Paternion. Sereny's search also led to Ken Hedley, Brigadier Guy Wheeler, and Ted Birkett, an intelligence officer who participated in the Moeslacher-Alm raid of 30–31 May, and who was then living in London. From what she learned during the Hedley interview, Sereny concluded that it was a young sergeant from an SS mountain unit, one Siegfried Kummerer, who told the British that Globocnik was up on the mountain with his staff and his long-time loyal Carinthian pal, Rainer. Kummerer claimed he could lead the British to him. Kummerer, she said, was the man who urged the British not to release the prisoner claiming to be a merchant, for that man was Odilo Globocnik, who had apparently almost convinced his captors of his innocence with his fake identity. That was how close Globocnik had come to being freed.

So they [the British] decided to set a little trap: Ramsay would go up to a little balcony and shout Globocnik's name, while Hedley and Birkett watched
the reaction. And sure enough. When Ramsay shouted the name in "parade
ground tones," the prisoner — "though he didn't falter in his stride, I'll give him
that," said Hedley — fractionally moved his head.

"I told him: 'You've given yourself away — you moved your head; you're
Globocnik," Hedley said. "And I told the sergeant to lock him up with the others, and went up to have a bath." Birkett and the Company Sergeant Sowler
walked the prisoner out through an archway and up the path. Almost at the
lock-up, Birkett was just behind him when he saw him "hit his mouth with
his right hand. He immediately collapsed on the ground."[52]

Ramsay, who carried a camera, took several photographs of the other
prisoners standing by Globocnik's body as it lay on the ground. Although this
was the ignominious end of "the worst man in the world," as Ramsay is reputed
to have dubbed this mass killer of Lublin on a caption of one photograph,
and later continued to refer to him thus, the story has an unexpected finale.

Globocnik's wife, *Gauführerin BdM* Lore, was also arrested, though not
at the same time and place as her notorious killer husband of less than one
year. According to the British security intelligence report covering the period
16 to 31 July 1945, Lore was one of four important individuals caught by 88
FS Section, 78 Division, in the Spittal and Lienz regions. Although probably
unaware of it at that time, she was already pregnant and gave birth, while in
Wolfsberg detention camp, to a son she named Peter, in January 1946. Sereny
reports that she met and spoke at length with Peter Globocnik during her
investigations into his father's fate and death.[53] Peter, naturally, never knew
his father. His mother, who died in 1974, would hardly speak of him. As
Peter grew up he devoured any information he could find, but there was no
one he could really ask about his father; the only Carinthian still around and
known to have been with him in Poland and to have remained at liberty, Ernst
Lerch, had always refused to see the son of the man to whom he had been so
loyal in crime and conspiracy[54]

In captivity, the British secretly eavesdropped on conversations Rainer
had with Dr. Siegfried Uiberreither, Steiermack's former *Gauleiter* and *Reich-
statthealter*. Of Globocnik's passing, Rainer said:

> Globocnik's suicide is a classical example: he accepted the responsibility of his
> actions. But why did the *Führer* do it? He could have exculpated Kaltenbrun-
> ner, just as Himmler could have exculpated the SS. Why did they choose sui-
> cide? Were they frightened of Bolshevism, or did their nerves fail them? Perhaps
> Himmler was offended because the Allies did not treat him as would have
> befitted his rank, though, like Jesus, he should have overcome such personal
> feelings.[55]

Hermann Höfle (bald man) and Georg Michalsen standing by the body of Odilo Globocnik. (Courtesy Gitta Sereny, London)

This was certainly a novel, and somewhat bizarre, way of viewing the passing of the *Reichsführer-SS*, Rainer's long-time ideological superior, the *Führer*, and their most loyal and obedient "Eastern" *Gruppenführer* who had begun to Germanize the entire East, a central desire of the NSDAP's leadership. Whatever else one can say of Rainer's strange interpretation of the suicides of these three men, he cannot be charged with having been gratuitous or disingenuous. After all, he could easily have followed their path. We know Rainer had a cyanide phial, but he chose to live in captivity until a bitter end that was not of his making. Mystery surrounds when and how he died, but we can be quite certain that his death was brought about by those heading the newly emerged Peoples' Democracy of Yugoslavia, the large nation of the southern Slavs, peoples he had engaged in battle for many of his Carinthian years and during much of Hitler's war. Rainer was handed over by the Allies to representatives of the southern Slavs after having given evidence at Nuremberg, and his wife and many children never saw him again. Earlier Globocnik's pregnant wife, Lore, had also said goodbye to her husband for the last time. Globocnik's and Rainer's fates were thus to be that their offspring were left without fathers, a fate that both, and most especially Globocnik, had so viciously inflicted upon so many others.

"Be not deceived; God is not mocked: for whatsoever a man soweth, that shall he also reap."

[Galatians 6: 7]

Notes

Introduction

1. Little has been written in the English-speaking world about the formal links — collaboration — between German civilian occupation forces, senior SS men, including Odilo Globocnik, and members of the pivotal pro-Berlin fascist Organization of Ukrainian Nationalists (OUN) that operated throughout the war within occupied Poland. The numbers of these activists were markedly augmented after September 1939 when several tens of thousand fled from eastern Poland, following its occupation by the Soviet Union. For the best critical assessments available on this largely unknown aspect of wartime Poland, see: Wiktor Poliszcuk, *Dowodny Zbrodni OUN i UPA: Integralny nacjonalizm ukrainski jako odmiana faszyzmu*, vol. 2, *Dzialalnosc ukrainskich struktur nacjonalistycznych w latach, 1920–1999* (Toronto: self-published, 2000); Czeslaw Partacz, *Kwestia Ukrainiska w Polityce Polskiego Rzadu na Uchodzstwie i Jego Ekspozytur w Kraju, 1939–1945* (Koszalin: Wydawnictwo Uczelniane Politechniki Koszalinskiej, 2001); Wasyl Veryha, ed., *Die Korrespondez des Ukrainischen Hauptausschusses in Krakau-Lemberg mit den deutschen Behorden in den Jahren 1939–1944* [The Correspondence of the Ukrainian Central Committee in Cracow and Liviv with the German Authorities], Edmonton and Toronto: Canadian Institute of Ukrainian Studies Press, University of Alberta, 2000); Tadeusz Piotrowski, *Poland's Holocaust: Ethnic Strife, Collaboration with Occupying Forces and Genocide in the Second Republic, 1918–1947* (Jefferson, NC: McFarland & Co., 1998). The Gestapo-created and financed Ukrainian Central Committee, based in Krakow during most of the war and headed by a former Polish citizen of part Polish, part Ukrainian ancestry, Wolodymyr Kubiiovych, sought in April 1941 German assistance to expel all Poles and all Jews from much of southeastern Poland — including a large part of Globocnik's Lublin District — so that a purely ethnic Ukrainian enclave could be established there and across the lands covering the foothills of

the Carpathian Mountains, or south-central Poland. OUN propaganda referred to these targeted lands as *Zakerzons'kyi Kraj*, meaning lands "beyond the Curzon Line," west of the Bug River, which formed the eastern boundary of Globocnik's district, meaning the Ukrainians were claiming much of the Globocnik-controlled territory.

2. Although no Polish historian has written Globocnik's biography, thus putting Polish historians and their academies on a par with their colleagues in the West in this regard, these four historians produced some important studies which future scholars investigating Globocnik, his involvement in the Jewish Holocaust (i.e., *Aktion Reinhardt*), and his launching of Hitler's long-term Pan-German Eastern expulsionist and settlerist plan aimed at deporting all Slavs into Western Siberia (i.e., *Generalplan Ost*), will be unable to ignore. For instance, Mankowski, in July 1980, published in *Palesta*, No. 7 "The Responsibility of the Chief of SS and Police in the Lublin Distrikt for the Deportation Action in the Zamosc Lands." In 1994 Mankowski published in *Studia Historiae Oeconomicae* (Poznan) Vol. 21, "Odilo Globocnik und Die Endlösung Der Judenfrage." Both these specific accounts and assessments are in addition to his study of the Lublin Distrikt under Nazi occupation, *Miedzy Wisla a Bugiem 1939–1944: Studium o polityce okupanta i postawach spoleczenstwa*. Lublin. Wydawnictwo Lubelskie, 1982, among others. Piotrowski's, *Misja Odyla Globocnika* ... a pioneering 1949 work that focused specifically on Globocnik's criminality vis-a-vis robbing his Jewish victims, is referred to extensively in this biography and more fully in note 1, chapter 1, below. In the case of Madajczyk, in addition to several major general studies of the wartime occupation of Poland, there is his pivotal two-volume documentary collection on the demographic or ethnic cleansing of Polish

peasant farmers and their families from the Zamosc Lands, which also saw Globocnik and the virtually forgotten Reinhold von Mohrenschildt launching *Generalplan Ost* for Hitler and Himmler and; *Zamojszczyzna — Sonderlaboratorium SS: Zbior dokumentow polskich i niemieckich z okresu okupacji hitlerowskiej*. Warsaw: Ludowa Spoldzielnia Wydawnicza, 1979. This two-volume collection carries all available German and Polish documents and Madajczyk followed it with another documentary collection, in German, on Hitler's *Generalplan Ost*. Eisenbach's two major works relevant to this bloody period are *Hitlerowska polityka zaglady Zydow* (Warsaw: 1961); and his 1962 44-page pathfinding article in *Polish Western Affairs* (Poznan) "Operation Reinhard: Mass Extermination of the Jewish Population in Poland." A reading of these publications gives one a far better insight into long term National Socialist thinking and planning vis-a-vis Poland with respect to the Jews and ethnic Poles and Globocnik's central role in the fate of both peoples than Western publications released during the same years, which fail to adequately highlight Globocnik and carry virtually no references to the crucial Zamosc Lands expulsion and *Generalplan Ost*.

3. Rudolf Höss, *Commandant of Auschwitz: The Authentic Confessions of a Mass Murderer* (London & Sydney: Pan Books, 1982), p. 258. The paucity of readily available information about Globocnik in the English-speaking world is well demonstrated by the fact that for several postwar decades Höss's five-page pen sketch in this book was all that was readily available to the general reader about him. Höss's work was first published in English in 1959. Louis Snyder's valuable *Encyclopedia of the Third Reich* (London: Blandford, 1976), carries a 112-word entry on Globocnik, while Robert Wistrich's *Who's Who in Nazi Germany* (London: Weidenfeld & Nicolson, 1982), has a 468-word entry.

Although both refer to Globocnik's involvement in *Aktion Reinhardt,* neither makes reference to his role as a population cleanser and initiator of *Generalplan Ost.*

Chapter I

1. Carinthian historian Siegfried J. Pucher published the first biography of Globocnik in 1997, 52 years after Globocnik's death. This brief but excellent pioneering work, *Odilo Globocnik — Kämpfer für den "Anschluss," Vollstrecker des Holocaust* (Klagenfurt: Drava Verlag, 1997), is derived from his academic thesis. In the introduction to that thesis, Pucher writes: "This work should not and cannot be regarded as the final biography about Odilo Globocnik. It is an attempt to reconstruct Globocnik's private and political career in order to show the qualities that helped his rise within the National Socialistic system and the SS." Prior to the publication of this thesis only two studies of Globocnik existed. One was a privately compiled collection of letters and other primary sources by the little-known but dogged Israeli researcher, Tuviah Friedmann, a one-time Globocnik slave worker. This study, *Himmlers Teufels — General SS- und Polizeiführer Globocnik in Lublin und Ein Bericht über die Judenvernichtung im General-Gouvernement in Polen 1941—1944,* focused only on Globocnik's role in the exploitation and murder of at least 1.5 million Jews. Polish lawyer and historian and later editor of Dr. Hans Frank's wartime office diary, Stanislaw Piotrowski, wrote *Misja Odyla Globocnika: Sprawozdania o Wynikach Finansowych Zaglady Zydow w Polsce [The Mission of Odilo Globocnik: A Report on the Financial Outcome of the Extermination of Poland's Jews]* (Warsaw: Panstwowy Instytut Wydawniczy, 1949). Piotrowski's monograph is a 59-page

commentary on a small number of primary source documents, and focuses on Globocnik's role in the plunder of his Jewish victims; it forms the basis of a separate section in this study. By the end of the 20th century therefore, just one biography, in German, existed, along with two rather specialized and brief monographs, both of which ignored Globocnik's early life and later role as a violent and inhuman suppressor of ethnic Poles, and his two other demographic missions, namely the expulsion of all ethnic Poles from prewar Polish lands, and likewise in the case of other Slavs, into Western Siberia, so as to settle Germans in their place. None of these three accounts, however, were available in English at the time of publication of this study. This is surprising in light of the fact that so many Jewish Holocaust survivors opted to live in British Commonwealth nations and in the United States of America.

2. When Pol Pot, leader of the genocidal Khmer Rouge, died "peacefully in his bed" on 15 April 1998, it was international news. *Newsweek* (Australian edition, 28 April 1998, p. 62) carried a four-page account of his career and death, claiming he was responsible "for the deaths of more than one million of his countrymen." Globocnik easily exceeded Pot's enormous figure. David Chandler, author of *Brother No 1: A Political Biography of Pol Pot,* wrote in *The Australian* (Sydney), 17 April 1998, p. 13: "...about 1.8 million people — or one Cambodian in four — had died of overwork, starvation, mistreated illnesses or execution," a phrase that well describes how Globocnik's Jewish, Polish, and other victims died. Interestingly, Globocnik's death on 31 May 1945 resulted in just one brief radio report broadcast in Vienna, a city he briefly governed as *Gauleiter* in 1938–39. The 1.5 million deaths for which Globocnik is responsible is a minimum. English historian Robin O'Neil, who researched the

fate of the Jews of Galicia, with most there dying in Belzec, confirmed in a March 9, 2002, email that he finally settled on the figure of no fewer than 600,000 perishing in that killing center. "The most reliable research for Treblinka is that of Dr Helmut Krausnick whose findings were accepted at post war trials of not less than 700,000. Sobibor had no less than 250,00 and Majdanek in excess of 100,000. This minimalist total of 1.65 million does not take into account all the shooting actions — and there were many — under Globocnik. Nor does it include the tens of thousands of Poles who died because of his police and the Soviet prisoners of war who perished in the network of temporary holding camps," O'Neil says. Despite all this, which would indicate that Globocnik was responsible for the deaths of some two million people, most of them Jews, I have estimated the minimum of 1.5 million Jews, to avoid the accusation of having exaggerated. (See note 5, chapter 7, for Polish historian Janina Kielbon's treatment of this ongoing debate about the number of Globocnik's Jewish victims, and the aggregates for his three "Terminal Stations").

3. Rusinow Dennison, *Italy's Austrian Heritage, 1919–1946* (Oxford: Clarendon Press, 1969), p. 307.

4. Robert Wistrich, *Who's Who in Nazi Germany* (London: Weidenfeld & Nicolson, 1982), p. 94. Wistrich's erroneous claim that Globocnik had Croatian ancestry has spread. For example, Yatzak Zucherman ("Antek") in his work, *A Surplus of Memory: Chronicle of the Warsaw Ghetto Uprising* (Berkeley: University of California Press, 1993), p. 176, writes: "Odilo Globocnik (1904–45). Born in Trieste into an Austro-Croat family."

5. Susan Zuccotti, *The Italians and the Holocaust: Persecution, Rescue and Survival* (New York: Basic Books, 1987), p. 311.

6. Peter Black, "Odilo Globocnik —

Himmlers Vorposten im Osten," in *Die SS: Elite unter dem Totenkopf: 30 Lebenslaeufe,* ed. Ronald Smelser and Enrico Syring (Paderborn: Schoeningh, 2000), p. 290.

7. Fogar Gallan, Report to Prof. Henry Howard, Los Angeles, 25 June 1990 (Copy in possession of author.)

8. U.S. Office of Strategic Services, Research & Analysis Branch, Biographical Report. National Archives and Records Administration, Washington, D.C. RG 153, Records of Judge Advocate General, V. 100–380–1. U.S. War Crimes Office, 14 March 1945. Another American intelligence report, which is untitled and dated 8 May 1943, says: "Globocnik is an Austrian Nazi of Slavonic antecedents." (11935 226/19/0161). This report appears to have been prepared in London, probably in the U.S. embassy, and it at least appears to have utilized wartime information gleaned from Polish Exile Government sources in London.

9. Bernard Newman, *Danger Spots of Europe* (London: The Right Book Club, 1939), p. 319.

10. Ibid, pp. 319–20.

11. Fran Zwitter, "The Slovenes and the Habsburg Monarchy." *Austrian History Yearbook*, vol. 3, 1967, p. 160.

12. Ibid., p. 159.

13. The *Yorkshire Post* (Leeds), 23 June 1938, "The New Austria in Ferment." From a Correspondent.

14. Siegfried J. Pucher, *Odilo Globocnik — Kämpfer für den "Anschluss," Vollstrecker des Holocaust* (Klagenfurt: Drava Verlag, 1997), p. 17.

15. Ales Brecelj, letter to Erwin Lerner, 2 February 1997, p. 2.

16. "Ales Brecelj," *Primorsi slovenski biografski leksikon*, vol. 19 Biographical Encyclopedia of Slovenian Littoral, 1993, p. 588.

17. Arthur J. May, *The Passing of the Hapsburg Monarchy, 1914–1918*, vol. 1 (Philadelphia: University of Pennsylvania Press, 1968), p. 172.

18. Thomas M. Barker, *The Slovene Minority of Carinthia* (Boulder: East European Monographs, 1984), pp. 87–88. On the question of *Umgangssprache* with respect to Carinthian Slovenes, Barker writes: "The pre-World War I Austrian sources proceeded on the subjective basis and counted as German all those persons who profess German as the language of everyday intercourse (*Umgangssprache*). It is doubtful that the official sources accurately reflect the total number of Slovenes. There are three reasons for this: 1) many native speakers were pro-German and would wish to be classified as German, thus exercising the *Bekenntnisprinzip* ("principle of profession"), upon which German authors vehemently insist; 2) a number of other speakers of Slovene might be "persuaded" by their German or semi-Germanized patrons to make the same declaration; and 3) certain German census takers might on their own account list the waverers or even Slovene nationalists as German." (p.86)

19. Pucher, p. 18.

20. Black, op. cit. "Odilo Globocnik," p. 292.

21. George L. Mosse, *The Crisis of German Ideology: Intellectual Origins of the Third Reich* (London: Wiedenfeld & Nicolson, 1970). See especially Part I, pp. 13–145.

22. Bruce F. Pauley, "The Austrian Nazi Party before 1938: Some Recent Revelations," in Fred Parkinson, ed., *Conquering the Past: Austrian Nazism, Yesterday and Today* (Detroit: Wayne State University Press, 1989), p. 35.

23. Ibid., p. 36.

24. Max Runhof (aka Cichotski), Statement to Wiesbaden Court, Abt. V/SK. Vol. 12. 15 September 1961, p. 5. (Internal or office numbers: 2501 & 2121).

25. Michael Burleigh, "Saving Money, Spending Lives: Psychiatry, Society and the 'Euthanasia' Programme," in *Confronting the Nazi Past: New Debates on Modern German History*, ed. Michael Burleigh (London: Collins & Brown, 1996), p. 109.

26. The U.S. Office of Strategic Services, Research & Analysis Branch, Biographical Report referred to in note 8 above says, "Nazi ideologies seem to prevail in his whole family." (RG 153. Records of Judge Advocate General V. 100–380–1.)

27. Pucher, p. 19.

28. C. Earl Edmondson, *The Heimwehr and Austrian Politics* (Athens: University of Georgia Press, 1976), p. 20.

29. Pucher, p. 19.

30. Edmondson, pp. 23–24.

31. Oron J. Hale, *The Captive Press in the Third Reich* (Princeton: Princeton University Press, 1964), p. 17.

32. Pucher, *Odilo Globocnik*, p. 19. Contemporaries of Globocnik's whom Pucher questioned on this point gave differing answers. One whom Pucher simply cites as "H.H.," and who knew Globocnik well, said: "The time scale does not fit!" Pucher's footnote (3) on this page reads: "According to the KLA from 23 August 1995 Globocnik's name does not appear in the completely preserved lists of persons awarded the Cross of Kaernten." It is likely that Globocnik embellished his involvement. He certainly did this by referring to himself as an engineer in later life whereas he was a trained construction manager or building site supervisor.

33. Warner Warmbrunn, *The Dutch Under German Occupation, 1940–1945* (Stanford University Press, Stanford: 1963), p. 30. Rauter's jurisdictional roles were to be emulated by Himmler in the case of Globocnik in Poland's Lublin region, with the proviso that Globocnik's powers extended much further, since he headed *Aktion Reinhardt*, controlled a large economic empire, and was given the honor of launching Generalplan Ost by clearing the Zamosc Lands of ethnic Poles so that Germans could be settled in their place. The author is grateful to Dr. Berndt Rieger for infor-

mation about Rauter's involvement in conflict across Carinthia.

34. "Lublin," in *Encyclopaedia Judaica*, vol. 7 (Keter Publishing House Ltd., Jerusalem: 1971), p. 622.

35. Pucher, *Odilo Globocnik*, pp. 22–23. The German journalistic team, Dieter Wagner and Gerhard Tomkowitz, in their study of the crucial week that saw Germany take over Austria, *Ein Volk, Ein Reich, Ein Führer: The Nazi Annexation of Austria, 1938*, refer to Globocnik, at page 94, as a "timber merchant," not as a builder, engineer, or in any other occupation directly linked with Carinthia's heavy construction sector. When Globocnik was attempting to disguise his true identity from his British captors at war's end, historian Gitta Sereny reports that he claimed to be a merchant, suggesting he may, well before the war, have been a builder and also traded in new and used building materials, as a sideline to earn extra cash.

36. Henry Ashby Turner, Jr., *Hitler's Thirty Days to Power: January 1933* (Bloomsbury, London: 1996.)

37. Black, "Odilo Globocnik," p. 293.

Chapter II

1. Alfred Elste, *Kärntens braune Elite* (Hermagoras, Klagenfurt: 1997), p. 106.

2. Pucher, p. 26.

3. Ibid., pp. 26–27.

4. *Völkischer Beobachter* (Munich), 21 April 1938.

5. "Brecelj, Ales," p. 588.

6. Stanislaw Piotrowski, *Misja Odyla Globocnika*, p. 8.

7. Walter Tschuppik, *The Quislings, Hitler's Trojan Horses* (Hutchinson & Co., London: n.d.), pp. 15–16.

8. David A. Hackett, *The Buchenwald Report* (Westview Press, Boulder: 1995), pp. 15–19.

9. Pucher, p. 28.

10. Ibid.

11. Eugen Kogon, *The Theory and Practice of Hell: The German Concentration Camps and the System Behind Them* (Berkeley, 1975) New York: p. 176. The remarks about Globocnik by Kogon continued: "I hope that some day there will be an exhaustive documentation of the awful fate that the Nazis prepared for the Jews of Eastern Europe. It is likely to be one of the ghastliest records in the history of the world." The documentation which Kogon so hoped for was realized with the huge body of histories published in the half century after 1945. Inexplicably, however, Globocnik failed to attract a biography over those years, and most especially in the English-speaking world. Moreover, when American academic Daniel Jonah Goldhagen released his highly acclaimed and controversial study in 1997, *Hitler's Willing Executions: Ordinary Germans and the Holocaust*, which one reviewer called "a monumental achievement", Globocnik rated just three mentions in the index. Why Goldhagen excluded Austrians, especially Carinthians, in the title of his study remains another mystery, with so many of Globocnik's Lublin collaborators hailing from there, not from Germany.

12. Ibid., p. 1.

13. Jurgen Gehl, *Austria, Germany and the Anschluss* (Oxford University Press, London: 1963), pp. 147–148.

14. Ibid., p. 148.

15. See especially: Maurice Williams, "Delusions of Grandeur: The Austrian National Socialists," *Canadian Journal of History/Annales Canadiennes d'Histoire* Vol. 14, No. 3 (December 1979), pp. 417–463; and also his "The Aftermath of Anschluss: Disillusioned Germans or Budding Austrian Patriots?" *Austria History Yearbook*, 14 (1978): pp. 129–144.

16. Williams, "Delusions of Grandeur," p. 433.

17. Stephen Koch, *Stalin, Willi Münzenberg and the Seduction of the Intellectuals* (HarperCollins, London: 1995).

18. Radomir Luza, *Austro-German Relations in the Anschluss Era* (Princeton University Press, Princeton: 1975), p. 34.

19. Martin Fuchs, *Showdown in Vienna* (G.P. Putnam's Sons, New York: 1939), pp. vii and 48. Interestingly, another member of the Committee of Seven was one Professor Oswald Menghin, "…who was Rector for a year of the Vienna University, where he lectured on the prehistoric period," archaeology and related issues, an interest of Globocnik's, and one that played a part in his decision to attempt to Germanize Poland's Zamosc Lands region. Wartime archeological work conducted in this region by Germans and drawn to Globocnik's attention apparently convinced him that evidence had been found of early or pre-historic Germanic settlements. As will be seen below, this, along with Globocnik's attraction to and links with Germany's famous geopolitical academic, Karl Haushofer, and his use of longtime SS-men Gustav Hanelt and Dr. Franz Stanglica in Lublin to create a Research Center for Eastern Settlement, were other crucial milestones in his secret intentions to become the Reich's premier eastern colonizer, hand in hand with Heinrich Himmler, of course. By late 1943, when Globocnik left Lublin, he had emerged as one the Reich's main, if not the main, mass murderers, easily outstripping Auschwitz-Birkenau's commandant, Rudolf Höss, even though Globocnik had hardly begun fulfilling his other desired mission of expelling millions of Slavs from the lands between Poland and the eastern perimeter of European Russia, namely the Ural Mountains.

20. Maurice Williams, "Captain Josef Leopold: Austro-Nazi and Austro-Nationalist?" In *Conquering the Past: Austrian Nazism, Yesterday and Today*, ed. Fred Parkinson (Wayne State University Press, Detroit: 1989), pp. 57–68.

21. Luza, p. 29.

22. Williams, "Delusions of Grandeur," pp. 430–431.

23. The *Daily Herald* (London), 15 May 1938.

24. Charles Wighton, *Heydrich — Hitler's Most Evil Henchman* (Odhams Press, London: 1962) p. 152.

25. Gordon Brook-Shepherd, *The Anschluss* (Macmillan, London: 1963), p. 100.

26. Jonathan Petropoulos, *The Faustian Bargain: The Art World in Nazi Germany* (Allan Lane, Penguin, London: 2000), p. 170.

27. Ibid., p. 176.

28. Ibid., p. 175.

29. Luza, pp. 34–35.

30. Peter R. Black, *Ernst Kaltenbrunner: Ideological Soldier of the Third Reich* (Princeton University Press, Princeton: 1984), p. 81.

31. William Rubinstein, *The Myth of Rescue: Why the Democracies Could Not Have Saved More Jews from the Nazis* (Routledge, London: 1997), pp. 39–40.

32. Luza, p. 35.

33. Quoted by Petropoulos, *The Faustian Bargain*, pp. 189–190, from: Mühlmann, Kajetan, and Gustav Barthel; *Krakow: Capital of the General Gouvernement in Poland* (1940). Petropoulos makes the interesting point that the Mühlmann-Barthel publication should be seen as "part of a larger Nazi literature on the region [Poland], which included Dagobert Frey's, *Krakau* (1941), where he 'refused to identify Krakow as a Polish city', and Karl Baedeker's guide to the General Gouvernement, which announced Krakow and Lublin were now '*Judenfrei*'.") It was Globocnik, who was headquartered in Lublin, as head of the SS and the Police, and who carried out the demographic cleansing of Lublin and its environs of Jews, by extermination, and of the Zamosc Lands of ethnic Poles as a *first* step to implementing the top-secret *Generalplan Ost*, which envisaged the removal of all Slavs from Poland, Ukraine, Belarus and Russia, up

to the forested western slopes of the Ural Mountain chain.

34. John Lukacs, *The Hitler of History* (Knopf, New York: 1998), p. 63.

Chapter III

1. Anna M. Cienciala, *Poland and the Western Powers, 1938–1939* (Routledge & Kegan Paul, London: 1968), p. 30.

2. Anthony P. Adamthwaite, *The Making of the Second World War* (Allen & Unwin, London: 1977), pp. 31–32.

3. Paul Schmidt, *Hitler's Interpreter: The Secret History of German Diplomacy, 1935–45* (William Heinemann, London: 1950), p. 80.

4. "The Programmed *Anschluss*," Part 3, "The Final Act, 1934–38," in *Austria Today* (Hofburg, Vienna: Verlags-Gesmblt., 1988), p. 28.

5. F.L. Carsten, *The First Austrian Republic, 1918–1938: A Study Based on British and Austrian Documents* (Aldershot, Hants, England, and Brookfield, VT: Gower/Maurice Temple Smith, 1986), pp. 276–277.

6. *Wiener Library Bulletin*, Vol. 9, no. 3–4, 1955, p. 24.

7. Gordon Brook-Shepherd, *Dollfuss* (Greenwood Press, Westport, CT: 1978), p. 197.

8. Dieter Wagner and Gerhard Tomkowitz, *Ein Volk, Ein Reich, Ein Führer: The Nazi Annexation of Austria, 1938* (Longman, Bristol: 1971), pp. 22–23.

9. Ibid., pp. 32–33.

10. Ibid., p. 57.

11. Ibid., pp. 58–59.

12. Ibid., p. 76.

13. "The Programmed *Anschluss*," p. 30.

14. Wagner and Tomkowitz, *Ein Volk*, p. 94.

15. Ibid., pp. 93–94.

16. Ibid., p. 111.

17. Ibid., p. 117.

18. "The Programmed *Anschluss*," pp. 30–31.

19. Wagner and Tomkowitz, p. 137.

20. Ibid., p. 140.

21. Ibid., p. 158.

22. Ibid., p. 158.

23. Paul Hoffman, *The Viennese Splendor, Twilight and Exile* (New York: Doubleday, 1988), p. 229.

24. Wagner and Tomkowitz, p. 166.

25. Ibid., p. 192.

26. Ibid., pp. 173–174.

27. Ibid., p. 207.

28. Ibid., p. 225.

Chapter IV

1. Williams, "Delusions of Grandeur," pp. 417–18.

2. Bruce F. Pauley, *Hitler and the Forgotten Nazis: A History of Austrian National Socialism* (University of North Carolina, Chapel Hill: 1981), p. 219.

3. Pucher, 44–45.

4. *The Times* (London), 25 May 1938.

5. The U.S. Office of Strategic Services, Biographical Report. (Odilo Globocnik), p.1

6. Pucher, pp. 46–47.

7. Evan Burr Bukey, *Hitler's Austria: Popular Sentiment in the Nazi Era, 1938–1945* (University of North Carolina Press, Chapel Hill: 2000), p. 57. Frauenfeld's career had several unusual subsequent turns. He firstly became a member of the German *Reichstag*. During the war he was Generalkommissar for Crimea, where he envisaged the settlement of Volga Germans who had long been settled in Russia, some South Tyroleans, and German Russians — probably Menonites — who had settled in the United States and Canada during the 1920s. This settlerist ideology was not far removed from Globocnik's work out of Lublin, which was launched with

his Carinthian friend, Reinhold von Mohrenschildt, involving the forcible removal of all ethnic Poles so as to settle Germans in their villages and homes as part of *Generalplan Ost*. Frauenfeld, in 1953, allegedly made a bid to topple the German Bonn Government.

8. Ibid., p. 57.

9. The *Catholic Herald* (London), 3 March 1939.

10. The *Daily Herald* (London), 13 June 1938.

11. Robin O'Neil, *The Belzec Death Camp and the Origins of Jewish Genocide in Galicia* (Hebrew and Jewish Department, University College, London: 2002), Chapter IV. 4.2: "*SS-Brigadeführer* Odilo Lothar Ludovicus Globocnik."

12. Saul Friedlander, *Nazi Germany and the Jews: The Years of Persecution, 1933–39*, vol. I (Weidenfeld & Nicolson, London: 1997), p. 245.

13. Pucher, p. 53.

14. The *Daily Telegraph* (London), 14 June 1938.

15. The *Daily Telegraph* (London), 30 June 1938.

16. The *Manchester Guardian,* 13 June 1938.

17. The *Times* (London), 27 June 1938.

18. Bukey, p. 137.

19. Ibid., p. 146.

20. The *Daily Telegraph* (London), 26 July 1938.

21. Globocnik SS file. This is a press cutting with the name of newspaper from which it originates handwritten in but in an indecipherable manner. It is, however, a Berlin publication with the word "*Berliner*" and the page and date, 19 June 1938, p. 15, shown. The headline is: "*Gauleiter* Globotschnik über Kampf über Sieg der Bewegung. Das Opfer war nicht vergebens. Grossfundgebung der NSDAP — Wien zum 5. Jahrestag des Parteiverbots." ["*Gauleiter* Globocnik on the Struggle for Victory of the Movement. Sacrifice was not in

Vain. Vienna on the fifth anniversary of the prohibition of the Party."]

22. The *Yorkshire Post* (Leeds), 23 June 1938. "The New Austria in Ferment — Competition Within the Nazi Party." From a Correspondent.

23. Ibid.

24. Ibid.

25. The *Daily Telegraph* (London), 15 July 1938.

26. Konrad Heiden, *Der Führer: Hitler's Rise to Power* (Victor Gollancz, London: 1944), p. 223.

27. Irmgard Rickheim, interview by author.

28. James Taylor and Warren Shaw, *The Third Reich Almanac* (New York: World Almanac, 1987), p. 297.

29. Globocnik SS File; *Stellungnahme.* 4 March 1941.

30. Pucher, p. 61.

31. Karl R. Stadler, *Austria* (Ernest Benn, London: 1971), p. 152.

32. Pucher, pp. 62–63.

33. Globocnik SS File, AR/740/24 January 1940. Rudolf Brandt to Globocnik.

34. Globocnik SS File, Gl/Ri 31 December 1940. Globocnik to Müller.

35. Globocnik SS File, Arl 740/44; 3 January 1941. Globocnik to Himmler.

36. Globocnik SS File, AR/740/24, RF/V; 20 February 1941. "Ihr" to Schwartz.

37. Globocnik SS File, Fl/Ri, 3 March 1941; Globocnik to Schwartz.

38. Globocnik SS File, Gl/Ri undated but received 7 March 1941. Globocnik to Wolff.

39. Globocnik SS File, 19 June 1941. Schwartz to Himmler.

40. The *Catholic Herald* (London), 3 March 1939.

41. David Irving, *Hess: The Missing Years, 1941–1945* (Grafton Books, London: 1989), p. 74.

42. Ibid.

43. The *Daily Mail* (London), 23 February 1939.

44. Reinhard Pohanka, *Pflichterfüller:*

Hitlers Helfer in der Ostmark (Picus Verlag, Vienna: 1997), p. 71. The author is grateful to Dr. Rieger for this source.

45. Joseph Poprzeczny, and Carolyn Simmonds, "Origins of Nazi Plans for Eastern Settlement and Extermination," in, *Power and Freedom in Modern Politics* (University of Western Australia Press, Perth Western Australia: 2002), pp. 189–208. This essay surveys the influence upon Nazism and the SS of an earlier generation of German propagandists and writers such as Adolf Bartels, Heinrich von Class, Max Sering, Friedrich von Schwerin, and the 19th century Gottingen Orientalist, Paul de Lagarde. In addition the impact of Otto Ammon, Alfred Ploetz, Wilhelm Schallmayer and Alexander Tille, are cursorily considered as the founding fathers of the Hitler-Himmler-Heydrich Globocnik exterminationist policy codenamed *Aktion Reinhardt.*

46. Globocnik SS File, *Neue Zürcher Zeitung*, 2 February 1939.

47. Globocnik SS File, 4 February 1939, *SS-Gruppenführer* Wolff to *SS-Gruppenführer* Schmitt.

48. Globocnik SS File, 23 December 1939, Zl. 4653/38, Globocnik to Himmler.

49. Globocnik SS File; 10 October 1939, Globocnik to Himmler.

50. Czeslaw Madajczyk, *Polityka III Rzeszy w Okupowanej Polsce*, Vol. 1 (Panstwowe Wydanictwo Naukowe, Warszawa: 1970), p. 119. "Wkrotce potem za spekulacje obca waluta osadzony zostal na rok w wiezieniu i zdegradowany z pulkownika SS do stopnia prostego czlonka SS." (Madajczyk says Globocnik was "jailed for a year and was demoted from the rank of SS colonel to simply being an SS member.") This claim is difficult to reconcile with the fact that Globocnik had left Vienna by early February 1939 and appears to have reached Lublin by 9 November the same year. If the claim was correct, Globocnik could not have taken up his Lublin

SS post until early 1940 and would have had no military training, milestones in his career that are both well documented in his SS file.)

Chapter V

1. Jozef Winiewicz, *German Withdrawal in the East: A Study of Vital German and Polish Statistics* (Polish Research Center, London: 1942), p. 2.

2. Hervert Feis, *Churchill, Roosevelt, Stalin: The War They Waged and the Peace They Sought* (Princeton University Press. Princeton, NJ: 1959), p. 30.

3. Clarification of the "Secret Supplementary Protocol" of 23 August 1939. (Translated document found at Woodrow Wilson International Center for Scholars archive, as part of the Cold War International History Project.) ("Payment of the sum of 31.5 million German marks will be made as follows: one-eighth, i.e., 3,937,500 German marks, in deliveries of nonferrous metals over a three month period beginning from the day of signing of the present Protocol, and the remaining seven eighths, i.e., 27,562,500 German marks, in gold through deduction from German payments of gold that the German side has to make before 11 February 1942, based on an exchange of letters between the People's Commissar of Foreign Trade of the USSR. A.I. Mikoyan and the Chairman of the German Economic Delegation Mr Schnurre that took place in conjunction with the signing of the 'Agreement of 10 January 1941, on Mutual Deliveries of Commodities for the Second Treaty Period according to the Economic Agreement of 11 February 1940, between the USSR and Germany.'"

4. Louis P. Lochner, *What About Germany?* (Hodder and Stoughton, London: 1943), p. 13.

5. Ibid.

6. Ibid.

7. William Shirer, *The Rise and Fall of the Third Reich* (Pan Books. London: 1960), p. 759.

8. Ibid.

9. Joachim Ribbentrop, *The Ribbentrop Memoirs* (Weidenfeld & Nicolson, London: 1954), p. 129.

10. Zygmunt J. Gasiorowski, "The Russian Overture to Germany of December 1924," *The Journal of Modern History*, 30 no. 2 (June 1958), p. 99.

11. Rudolf Heberle, *From Democracy to Nazism: A Regional Case Study on Political Parties in Germany* (Howard Fertig, New York: 1976), p. 7.

12. Erich Stockhorst, *Fünftausend Köpfe: Wer war was im Dritten Reich* (Blick and Bild Verlag), p. 156. Another essential, indeed, gripping, text that helps us understand the background against which Globocnik was operating in his bid to take over executive power of the entire General Gouvernement through implementation of SS demographic policies is Larry Vern Thompson's doctoral dissertation, *Nazi Administrative Conflict: The Struggle for Executive Power in the General Government of Poland, 1939–1943* (Madison: University of Wisconsin, 1967), as well as Thompson's equally insightful essay, "Friedrich-Wilhelm Krueger: Höherer SS-und Polizeiführer Ost," in Ronald Smelser and Enrico Syring, ed., *Die SS: Elite unter dem Totenkopf: 30 Lebenslaeufe* (Paderborn: Schoeningh, 2000), pp. 320–331.

13. "Lublin," *Encyclopedia of Jewish Communities in Poland*, vol. 5. (Yad Vashem, Jerusalem: 1957), pp. 13–38.

14. Governor Ernst Zörner was followed, temporarily (until 28 May 1943), by Ludwig Fischer, and the latter was replaced by Himmler's brother-in-law Richard Wendler, the man who coined the term the "Globocnikians."

15. Robin O'Neil, *The Belzec Death Camp*, Chapter IV, 4.1, "The SS District Lublin."

16. Victor Klemperer, *I Shall Bear Witness — The Diaries of Victor Klemperer, 1933–41* (Weidenfeld & Nicolson, London: 1998), p. 217.

17. Bogdan Musial, *Deutsche Zivilverwaltung und Judenverfolgung im Generalgouvernement* (Wiesbaden: Harrassowitz, 1999), p. 201. The author is grateful to Dr. Berndt Rieger for this source.

18. Peter Black, "Rehearsal for 'Reinhard'?: Odilo Globocnik and the Lublin Selbstschutz," *Central European History*, 25, no. 2 (1992), pp. 204–226.

19. PRO/WO 208/46739.

20. Michael Tregenza, "Christian Wirth: Inspekteur der SS-Sonderkommanos '*Aktion Reinhardt*'," *Zeszyty Majdanka* (Lublin) 15 (1993), pp. 7–57.

21. PRO/WO 208/46739.

22. Simon Wiesenthal, *Justice Not Vengeance* (Wiedenfeld & Nicolson, London: 1989), p. 279.

23. PRO/WO 204/13006 50885, p. 2.

24. Ibid., pp. 2–3.

25. Janina Kielbon, *Migracje Ludnosci w Dystrykcie Lubelskim w Latach 1939–1944* (Panstwowe Museum na Majdanku, Lublin: 1995), p. 127.

26. Dr. Berndt Rieger, interview by the author. Ongoing contact and communication since 2000.

27. Wiesenthal, p. 280.

28. Ibid., p. 281.

29. Ibid.

30. Winifried R. Garscha and Claudia Kuretsidis-Haider, "War Crime Trials in Austria" (paper presented at the 21st Annual Conference of the German Studies Association, Washington, 25–28 September 1997.)

31. Ibid.

32. Ibid. It remains a mystery to this day why two of Globocnik's closest wartime and pre-war associates, both of whom served in the SS with Globocnik in Lublin, Ernst Lerch and Reinhold von Mohrenschildt, did not face at least long jail sentences. Their ability to have lived out their lives in Carinthia without being

incarcerated for long terms must one day be satisfactorily explained.

33. Wagner and Tomkowitz, p. 58.

34. 208 AR-Z 74/60 Georg Michalsen. Vol. 49.

35. Otto Strasser, *Hitler and I.* (Jonathan Cape, London: 1940), p. 85.

36. Georg Michalsen, 208 AR-Z 74/60, Vol. 49.

37. Wiesenthal, p. 275.

38. PRO/WO 208/4673 166970. (Sporrenberg interrogation)

39. Ibid. Johann Wendelinius Cornelius Offermann, who was 66 years old in 1974, was tried after the war and "received a five-year term for complicity in the Lublin murders ... [but] had his sentence suspended." (See: *The Times* of London, 27 February 1974.) Offermann was interrogated, after capture in Norway, at Akershus Prison, Oslo. He should not be confused with SS-Hauptsturmführer Hans Offermann who was employed in Globocnik's personnel department.

40. Piotrowski, *Misja Odyla*, pp. 56–57.

41. Ibid., p. 57.

42. Jozef Marszalek, *Majdanek: The Concentration Camp in Lublin* (Interpress, Warsaw: 1986), p. 130.

43. O'Neil, *The Belzec Death Camp*, Chapter IX, "*Erntefest*' (Harvest Festival), SS investigations and transfer to Italy."

44. PRO/WO 208/4673 166970. (Sporrenberg interrogation).

45. Höss, p. 260.

46. Wiesenthal, p. 274.

47. Richard Breitman, *Report on the Investigative Records Repository File of Hermann Julius Höfle*, Washington, D.C.: National Archives and Research Administration, 2001.

48. Czeslaw Madajczyk, ed. *Zamojszczyzna — Sonderlaboratorium SS: Zbior dokumentow polskich i niemieckich z okresu okupacji hitlerowskiej*, Vol. 1 (Warszawa, Ludowa Spoldzielnia Wydawnicza: 1979), p. 189.

49. Runhof Statement to Wiesbaden Court.

50. Ibid.

51. Ibid.

52. *Samo Obronia*, 23 July 1943. (Polish Underground Study Trust, London.)

53. Runhof, Statement to Wiesbaden Court.

54. Oberhauser Bd 8. 208 AR-Z 252/59: Archives of the Central Office of Land Judicial Authorities for the Investigation of National-Socialist Crimes, Ludwigsburg, German Federal Republic. (Zentrale Stelle der Landesjustizverwaltungen). First Georg Wippern Statement, 27 October 1962.

55. Jozef Kasperek, *Kronika Wydarzen w Lublinie w okresie okupacji hitlerowskiej* (Wydawnictwo Lubelskie, Lublin: 1989), p. 151. Kasperek says this was reported both in *Dziennik Polski* (London) No. 602, 26 June 1942, and *Nowy Glos Lubelski* No. 128, 5 June 1942.

56. See Chapter XX: "Globocnik's Capture and Death."

57. Oberhauser Bd 8. 208 AR-Z 252/59: First Georg Wippern Statement. 27 October 1962.

58. Willi Dressen and Volker Riess, *Those Were the Days: The Holocaust as Seen by the Perpetrators and Bystanders* (Hamish Hamilton, London: 1988), p. 229.

59. Oberhauser Bd 8. 208 AR-Z 252/59: Second Georg Wippern Statement, 1 December 1962.

60. Ibid.

61. Ibid.

62. Tregenza, "Christian Wirth," p. 35.

63. Wagner and Tomkowitz, p. 137.

64. *Volksdeutsche Mittelstelle* (Racial Assistance Office). An office charged with caring for the welfare of Germans settled abroad. The assumption was that all Germans who lived in other countries were biologically linked with the pure Nordics of the Third Reich. *VoMi* was one of the five key divisions of the SS. Its chief was *SS-Obergruppenführer* (General) Werner Lorenz. Later it was combined with the *Rasse-und Siedlung-*

shauptamt, the Central Office for Race and Resettlement, to form the *Reichskommissariat für die Festigung des Deutschen Volkstums* (the Reich Office for the Consolidation of German Nationhood). [RKFDV] See: Snyder, Louis. *Encyclopedia of the Third Reich*. (Blandford, London: 1976), p. 364.

65. Wistrich, pp. 196–197.

66. PRO/WO 208/4673 166970. (Offermann Interrogation).

67. Madajczyk, *Zamojszczyzna — Sonderlaboratorium SS*, 1, pp. 182–190. See especially Clause II of this expulsion order.

68. 502 AR 420/1962 Vol. 4. Leaf 798–800. Bundesarchiv Ludwigsburg, Germany. (The author is grateful to Dr. Berndt Rieger for this source.)

69. Joseph B. Schechtman, *European Population Transfers, 1939–1945* (Oxford University Press, New York: 1946), p. 28.

70. In 1897 just 3.9 per cent of Estonia's population was classified as being German. By 1931 this figure had declined to 1.7 per cent, or 18,319 of 1,115,000. Until the agrarian reforms of 1919, 600 families of old German lineage owned about half the arable land of Estonia. Even in 1919 Germans played a key role in this newly independent nation's trade and industrial sectors.

71. For Mohrenschildt ancestral details see: *Genealogisches Handbuch des Adels* (C.A. Starke, Limburg an der Lahn: 1998), Adelslexikon vol. 9, p. 132, and Hasso von Wedel, *Die Estländische Ritterschaft vornehmlich zwischen 1710 und 1783: Das erste Jahrhundert russischer Herrschaft* (Ost-Europa Verlag, Konigsberg: 1935), p. 43. (The author is grateful to Dr. Berndt Rieger for this information by letter, 16 December 2000.)

72. PRO/HW 16/32, British decyphered Telex from *SS-Hauptsturmführer* Horn of the Ost Ministry to *SS-Hauptsturmführer* Reinhold von Mohrenschildt. (Klagenfurt) 5 December 1943. (The author is grateful to

Stephen Tyas for locating and providing this document.)

73. Details of these SS Italian raids were provided by Dr. Berndt Rieger by letter to the author 19 December 2000.

74. Dr. Rieger's investigations disclosed that the Mohrenschildt family was gossiped about in Wolfsberg, Carinthia, not only because of Reinhold's SS and wartime record, but also because many believed that he was related to an American citizen, George de Mohrenschildt, who gave evidence before the Warren Commission in 1964 that inquired into the assassination of President John F. Kennedy. De Mohrenschildt, a Texas oilman and footloose entrepreneur, had known Kennedy's assassin, Lee Harvey Oswald, and much earlier knew President Kennedy's wife's family, and even taught the young Jacqueline Bouvier horse riding. De Mohrenschildt told the commission he had remained a Polish citizen even after settling in the United States in 1938, where he was commonly referred to as Baron. He claimed his family was of Swedish and German ethnic origin, that it hailed from Czarist Russia, and that he and a cousin named Maydell had made a film in 1941 in the United States about the wartime Polish anti-German Underground. The relationship with Reinhold appears to have been, if not distant, then not publicized. De Mohrenschildt, although inspiring many unfounded conspiracy theories, appears to have been a mysterious individual who may have had links to some intelligence service earlier in his life. Such theories were undoubtedly fueled by the fact that he apparently committed suicide in 1977 on learning that he was to be subpoenaed by the House of Representatives Select Committee on Assassinations. Certain Congressmen therefore belatedly believed, among other things, that his unorthodox past warranted closer investigation. That committee's relevant report concluded: "This probe seemed justified in view of the

controversy that continues to surround the relationship [of de Mohrenschildt and Oswald], and the additional speculation that was caused by the apparent suicide of de Mohrenschildt in 1977 on the day he was contacted by both an investigator from the committee and a writer about Oswald." See also: *Jacqueline Bouvier: An Intimate Memoir*, by John Davies (John Wiley & Sons, New York: 1996), pp. 63, 75, 92.

75. PRO/WO 204/13006. (Joint Report on Michalsen and Lerch interrogations.)

76. PRO/WO 208/4673 XC68198.

77. Michael Tregenza, The *"Disappearance" of* SS-Hauptscharführer *Lorenz Hackenholt. A Report on the 1959–63 West German Police Search for Lorenz Hackenholt, the Gas Chamber Expert of the* Aktion Reinhardt *Extermination Camps* (n.d.), p. 12; (Copy provided to author by Michael Tregenza in February 2002). (Robert Wistrich, in *Who's Who in Nazi Germany*, reports that Hackenholt's Berlin superior, Viktor Brack, during 1941 "prepared to set up mobile gassing vans in Riga and Minsk to exterminate Jews defined as 'unsuitable for work,' "suggesting that a link existed between Belzec and these two northern centers, via Brack, who was based in Hitler's Chancellery.)

78. Ibid., p. 19.

79. Ibid., p. 20.

80. Michael Tregenza, *Report on the Archaeological Investigations at the Site of the Former Nazi Extermination Camp in Belzec, Poland, 1997–98* (Lublin: N.P., 1998), p.7.

81. Madajczyk, *Zamojszczyzna — Sonderlaboratorium SS*, pp. 289–291.

82. PRO/WO 309/374 XC14298, p. 6.

83. Globocnik's staff list was drawn up and provided by Michael Tregenza, Lublin, Poland, December 1997.

84. Tuviah Friedmann, *Himmlers Teufels — General SS-und Polizeiführer Globocnik in Lublin und Ein Bericht über*

die Judenvernichtung im General-Gouvernement in Polen 1941–1944 (Documentaten — Sammlung zusammengestellt u. herausgegeben). T. Friedmann, Direktor der Dokumentation in Haifa, P.O.B. 4950, Israel. April 1977. (Sequential page numbers not given). Dr. Stanglica may have been far more of an enthusiast and fanatic for Germanization of the Lublin region than even Globocnik and Hanelt, if, indeed, that was possible. One Polish historian, Janina Kielbon, writes of Stanglica as one "who specifically interested himself in the 'history of Germanness in Lublin.'" Kielbon's assessment should not be ignored. Stanglica, jointly with Hanelt, sought to Germanize both Lublin and Zamosc, as well as all surrounding villages, according to Kielbon. The Hanelt-Stanglica team was crucial in the Himmler-Globocnik-von Mohrenschildt bid to Germanize the Lublin District as a first step, followed by the entire General Gouvernement and then the so-called East.

85. Höss, p. 262.

86. PRO/ WO 208/4673 166970 (Offermann Interrogation).

87. Black, "Rehearsal for 'Reinhard'?" p. 208.

88. Waldemar Tuszynski, "Policyjny i Wojskowy Aparat Okupaczynjy na Lubelszczysnie (Organizacja, sily i niektore dzialania"), *Zeszyty Majdanka* (Lublin: 1969), vol. 3, p. 51.

89. Michael Tregenza, interview by the author, Lublin, Poland, December 1997. Tregenza provided a copy of an extract of Rheindorf's birth certificate which shows his date of birth as 11 June 1896; father: Adolf Hubert; mother: Antoine (formerly Keussen), all of 91 Grove Lane, Handsworth. The Registration District is West Bromwich, and the sub-district is Handsworth in the County of Stafford.

90. Walter Huppenkothen, Affidavit, Nuremberg Case VIII. Creutz Document Book, Document No. 22. 24 November 1947.

91. Bronislaw Wroblewski, "Struktura Wiezienia i Jego Funkcje," in Zygmunt Mankowski, ed., *Hitlerowski Wiezienie na Zamku 1939–1944* (Wydawnictwo Lubelskie, Lublin: 1988), pp. 34–35.

92. Zygmunt Mankowski, ed., *Hitlerowskie wiezienie na Zamku w Lublinie 1939–1944* (Wydawnictwo Lubelskie, Lublin: 1988), p. 367.

93. Robin O'Neil, "The Supporting Cadres in 'Aktion Reinhardt.'" Privately circulated essay.

Chapter VI

1. Wiktor Sukiennicki, *East Central Europe During World War I: From Foreign Domination to National Independence* (East European Monographs, Boulder: 1984), p. 119.

2. Kielbon, *Migracje Ludnosci*, p. 130.

3. *Völkischer Beobachter* (Munich), 8 February 1939.

4. Quentin Reynolds, Ephraim Katz, and Zwi Aldouby, *Minister of Death: The Adolf Eichmann Story* (Cassell & Co., London: 1960), p. 97.

5. Robert Cecil, *The Myth of the Master Race: Alfred Rosenberg and Nazi Ideology* (B.T. Batsford, London: 1972), p. 183.

6. Zygmunt Mankowski, *Miedzy Wisla a Bugiem 1939–1944: Studium o polityce okupanta i postawach spoleczenstwa* (Wydawnictwo Lubelskie, Lublin: 1982), pp. 98–99.

7. Ibid.

8. Ibid., p. 99.

9. Ibid.

10. Quoted in Jacob Apenszlak, *et al.*, eds., *The Black Book of Polish Jewry* (Roy Publishers, New York: 1943), p. 92.

11. Zygmunt Klukowski, *Dziennik z Lat Okupacji* (Lubelska Spoldzielnia Wydawnicza, Lublin: 1958), p. 81. Janina Kielbon, in her book, *Migracje*

Ludnosci ... writes on page 130, where she footnotes Dr. Klukowski's 7 December 1939 diary entry, "The news [of the proposed reserve] was even broadcast on British radio."

12. Zygmunt Klukowski, *Diary from the Years of Occupation, 1939–44* (University of Illinois Press, Urbana and Chicago: 1993), p. 47. The italicized phrase as shown in the 1958 Polish edition of the Diary is "...ktora rzekomo ma byc przeznaczona na osiedlenie sie Zydow," which may also be translated, "which is supposed to be designated as a settlement area for Jews," so perhaps the emphasis on it being for only a certain period was not implied by Dr. Klukowski.

13. Quoted in Apenszlak, p. 92.

14. Christopher R. Browning, "Nazi Ghettoization Policy in Poland: 1939–41," *Journal of Central European History*, 19 (1986), p. 346.

15. Ibid., p. 346.

16. Ibid., p. 347.

17. Quoted in Apenszlak, p. 93.

18. Philip Friedman, "The Lublin Reservation and the Madagascar Plan: Two Aspects of Nazi Jewish Policy During the Second World War," in *Roads to Extinction: Essays on the Holocaust*, ed. A.J. Friedman (Jewish Publication Society, Philadelphia: 1980).

19. Ibid., p. 163.

20. William D. Rubinstein, *The Myth of Rescue: Why the Democracies Could Not Have Saved More Jews from the Nazis* (Routledge, London and New York: 1997), p. 16.

21. Friedman, p. 159.

22. Francis Aldor, *Germany's "Death Space": The Polish Tragedy—Nazi Theory Has Evolved the Concept of "Lebensraum" (Living Space)—Nazi Practice Has Realized the Fact of "Todesraum" (Death Space)* 2 Mount Row, London W.1. (n.d.) self-published, p. 160.

23. Ibid., pp. 162–163.

24. Gordon Craig, *Germany 1866–1945* (Clarendon Press, Oxford: 1978), p. 748.

25. Gerald Reitlinger, *House Built on Sand: The Conflicts of German Policy in Russia, 1939–1945* (Weidenfeld & Nicolson, London: 1960). Craig claims his source is Ch. XVII, p. 637, but Reitlinger's book only has 12 chapters and goes no further than page 459.

26. Christian Gerlach, "The Wannsee Conference, the Fate of German Jews, and Hitler's Decision in Principle to Exterminate all European Jews," *The Journal of Modern History*, 70 (December 1998), pp. 811–812.

27. Friedman, p. 153.

28. See pp. 266–269 of Isaiah Trunk's *Judenrat: The Jewish Councils in Eastern Europe Under Nazi Occupation* (Macmillan, New York: 1972), for a detailed elaboration of how Globocnik ensured his police units gained control over Jewish affairs in the face of Governor Zörner's attempts to retain the powers to do so. This was done after May 1941 with the crucial assistance of Reinhard Heydrich, who oversaw the launching of the so-called Final Solution.

29. Ibid., p. 266.

30. Ibid., p. 267.

31. Ibid., p. 268.

32. Ibid.

33. Ibid., p. 269. Isaiah Trunk cites as his source for this crucial early move in Jewish affairs by Heydrich, via Globocnik, which soon after led to the "Final Solution," Tatiana Berenstein's article in the bulletin of the Warsaw-based Jewish Institute of History. See: Tatiana Berenstein, "Spory administratcji z SS w GG," [*sic*] *Biuletyn Zydowski Instytut Historyczny* No. 53 (1965), pp. 33–79.

Chapter VII

1. Wistrich, p. 303.

2. See especially, J. Hermand, *Old Dreams of a New Reich: Völkisch Utopias and National Socialism* (Indiana University Press, Bloomington and Indianapolis: 1988).

3. Ian Kershaw, *Hitler: 1936–2945, Nemesis* (Penguin Books, London: 2000), p. 483.

4. Christian Gerlach, "Failure of Plans for an SS Extermination Camp in Mogilev, Belarussia," *Holocaust and Genocide Studies* 11, no. 1 (Spring, 1997): pp. 60–61.

5. Polish historian Janina Kielbon, an expert on the demographic impact of Globocnik upon the entire Lublin District, draws attention in *Migracje Ludnosci...* (p. 175) to the differences between estimates of those murdered in his various Jewish killing centers. When dealing with this debate, one should note that no one acted as a census taker at the gates of each of the killing centers. There will therefore always be dispute about the exact numbers who perished in each of those centers. That said, it is noteworthy that Kielbon states that the numbers were: Belzec, 600,000; Sobibor, 250,000; and 120,000 in Majdanek. She fails to give an estimate for Treblinka, because it was situated outside Lublin District, the focus of her inquiry. Kielbon, however, points out that another Polish historian, Jozef Marszalek, in his study, "*Stan bandan nad stratami osobowymi ludnosci zydowskiej Polski oraz nad liczba ofiar obozow zaglady w okupowanej Polsce.*" *Dzieje Najnowsze*, 26, no. 2 (1994), pp. 33–40, states that Belzec was the venue for 500,000 victims, Sobibor, 150,000, and Majdanek, 80,000, with Treblinka having 775,000. Even on Marszalek's estimates the total reaches 1,405,000. Gerald Fleming accepts that the totals were: Belzec, about 600,000; Sobibor, 250,000, and Treblinka, 700,000, or 1.55 million, without the inclusion of Majdanek. See pages 63–64 of Gerald Fleming's, *Hitler and the Final Solution* (Berkeley: Univ. of California Press, 1984).

6. Michael Tregenza (Lublin) to Professor Maurice Williams (Kelowna,

British Columbia)— 27 January 1997; letter in the author's possession. Interestingly, in light of the chapter —"Himmler and Globus: A Double-cross?"— in his reply to Williams's comment, in which the latter claimed Globocnik may well have been a "front man" for both Oswald Pohl and Christian Wirth, Tregenza wrote: "Regarding your comment about Globocnik being a 'front man' while Pohl and Wirth had the real power — I couldn't agree more. It's still not generally known how close Wirth was to Himmler...."

7. Ibid.

8. Jochen von Lang and Claus Sibyll, eds. *Eichmann Interrogated: Transcript from the Archives of the Israeli Police* (Farrar, Straus & Giroux, New York: 1983), pp. 74–75.

9. Ibid., p. 75.

10. Ibid., pp. 90–91.

11. Gerald Fleming, *Hitler and the Final Solution* (University of California Press, Berkeley: 1984), p. 63.

12. Runhof, Statement to Wiesbaden Court.

13. Gerlach, *The Wannsee Conference*, p. 800.

14. Höss, p. 262.

15. Ibid., pp. 259–260. Höss's reference to Oldenburg is an error. One of Globocnik's main contact men or overseers within Hitler's Chancellery was in fact SA-*Oberführer* Werner Blankenburg.

16. Helmut Krausnick and Martin Broszat, *Anatomy of the SS State* (Paladin, London: 1970), pp. 120.

17. Oswald Pohl, Affidavit Document NO — 2714 (Office of Chief Counsel for War Crimes), United States of America. The Pohl statement's reference to Globocnik being a lieutenant-general is correct if using British equivalents of the rank of SS-*Gruppenführer*. The American equivalent, however, is major-general.

18. Viktor Hermann Brack, Statement, Nuremberg Document NO-426. p. 6.

19. Ibid.

20. Willi Dressen and Volker Riess, p. 229.

21. Warmbrunn, p. 30.

22. Dressen and Riess, p. 239.

23. Tregenza, "Christian Wirth," p. 27.

24. Gitta Sereny, *Into That Darkness: An Examination of Conscience* (Vintage, New York: 1983), p. 102.

25. Ibid., p. 102.

26. Ibid., p. 103.

27. Ibid.

28. Ibid., p. 109.

29. Ibid., p. 110.

30. Louis de Jong, "Sobibor," *Encounter Magazine* (London) 51, no. 6 (December 1978), p. 21.

31. Michael Tregenza, "Belzec Death Camp," *Wiener Library Bulletin*, 30, nos. 41/42, 1977, p. 15.

32. Ibid.

33. Louis P. Lochner, p. 13.

34. See especially Czeslaw Madajczyk's "Generalplan Ost," *Polish Western Affairs* (Poznan). 3 (1962): 391–442, ed., *Die Okkupationspolitik Nazideutschlands in Polen, 1939–1945* (East Berlin, Akademie-Berlag: 1987); and *Vom Generalplan Ost zum Generalsiedlungsplan* (Munich, Saur: 1994).

35. Tregenza, "Belzec Death Camp," p. 16.

36. Lang and Sibyll, p. 75.

37. Tregenza, "Belzec Death Camp," p. 15.

38. Wistrich, p. 92.

39. *Wiener Library Bulletin*; (London), 9, nos. 3–4, (1955), p. 22.

40. Pierre Joffroy, *A Spy for God: The Ordeal of Kurt Gerstein* (Collins, London: 1971), pp. 163–164.

41. Ibid., p. 146.

42. Ibid., pp. 147–148. Article 139 reads, "Whosoever has knowledge of criminal intentions and fails to inform the authorities or the person threatened shall be punished." According to Joffroy, the Bishop of Munster, who protested at the euthanasia program, invoked these

lines. Joffroy adds: "One may wonder why it is cited here — whether this relic of ancient laws was deliberately inserted as a trap to catch the signatory if the Final Solution were to be cancelled."

43. Poprzeczny and Simmonds, "Origins of Nazi Plans," pp. 189–208.

44. Madajczyk, *Zamojszczyzna — Sonderlaboratorium SS*, vol. 1, pp. 190–196.

45. Michael Thad Allen, "The Banality of Evil Reconsidered: SS Mid-Level Managers of Extermination Through Work," *Central European History* 30, no. 2, (1997), p. 288.

46. Czeslaw Madajczyk, *Deportations in the Zamosc Region in 1942 and 1943 in the Light of German Documents* (Acta Poloniae Historica, Warsaw: 1958), p. 75.

47. Janusz Wnuk, *Dzieci Polskie Oskarzaja*, 2d ed. (Wydawnictwo Lubelski, Lublin: 1975), p. 328. Wnuk's source for this table is given as: "Archiwum Gownej Komisej Badania Zbrodnej Hitlerowskich, akta 718z. Wykaz powyzszy zostal dolaczony przez swiadka Janine Suchodolska w czasie jej przesluchania."

48. Karel Fremund and Vaclav Kral, *Lesson from History: Documents Concerning Nazi Policies for Germanization and Extermination in Czechoslovakia* (Prague: Orbis, 1962), p. 114.

49. Ibid., p. 116.

50. Ibid.

51. Ibid.

52. Ibid.

53. Janusz Gumkowski and Kazimierz Leszczynski, *Poland Under Nazi Occupation* (Polonia Publishing House, Warsaw: 1961), pp. 12–13.

54. Madajczyk, *Zamojszczyzna — Sonderlaboratorium SS*, vol. 1, pp. 289–293.

55. Madajczyk, *Deportations in the Zamosc Region*, p. 103.

56. Ibid., p. 103.

57. Jerzy Markiewicz, *Paprocie Zakwitly Krwia Partyzantow* (Wydawnictwo Lubelski, Lublin: 1987), pp. 16.

58. Madajczyk, *Deportations in the Zamosc Region*, p. 103.

59. The *Times* (London), 26 September 1942.

60. Hermann Alois Krumey, Testimony, 27 May 1961. (The Nizkor Project), Nanaimo. Vancouver Island, British Columbia. Canada.

Chapter VIII

1. Black, "Rehearsal for 'Reinhard'?" p. 205.

2. Rickhelm, interview.

3. The author met Mrs. Jadwiga Stachurska (1900–1997) in Lublin in 1987. As an 18-year-old, she was assigned to teach in the village of Skierbieszow, 17km northeast of Zamosc. Her assignment was part of a broader on-going educational policy launched by the Austrians.

4. Wiktor Sukiennicki, pp. 138–172.

Chapter IX

1. W.J. Rose, *Poland* (Harmondsworth: Penguin, 1939), p. 152.

2. Jozef Winiewicz, "The Quest for German Blood: Policy of Germanization in Poland," in *Polish Studies and Sketches* (London: Polish Ministry of Information, 1943), p. 55.

3. Josef Winiewicz, *German Failures in Poland: Natural Obstacles to Nazi Population Policy* (Polish Research Center, London: 1942), p. 3.

Chapter X

1. Ian Kershaw, *Hitler: 1936–1945, Nemesis* (Penguin, London: 2000), p. 319.

2. Czeslaw Pilichowski, ed. *Obozy*

hitlerowski na ziemiach polskich 1939–1945: Informator Encyklopedyczny. (Panstwowe Wydawnictwo Naukowe, Warsaw: 1979), p. 662.

3. Ibid, entry 493. On Hitler's "Racial War" see Heinz Höhne; *The Order of the Death's Head: The Story of Hitler's SS* (Secker & Warburg, London: 1969), especially Chapter 12, "Racial Policy in the East." Höhne writes: "Like Himmler, Globocnik, the future mass murderer of Jews, was captivated by the prospect of vast racial biological experiments...."

4. *The Wiener Library Bulletin* (London), 19 (1965), p. 26. This and the subsequent extract were contained in the second of seven volumes of stenciled reports left among the documents of the Polish Ministry of the Interior in London. Possession of these documents shows the sophisticated level of intelligence gathering attained by that underground.

5. Ibid.

6. Pilichowski, entry 105.

7. Ibid., entry 5637

8. Ibid., entry 5390.

9. Ibid., entries 2546, 5007, 1644, 3903.

10. Ibid., entries: 2736–2738.

11. Ibid., entries 4593, 3865.

12. Ibid., entries 3595, 5039.

13. Ibid., entries 2431–2452.

14. Ibid., entries 1447, 4278.

15. Ibid., entries 2015, 19, 3827, 1245, 5788.

16. Ibid., entries 5841, 5859, 2757, 4798.

17. Ibid., entries 5785, 4201.

18. Louis de Jong, "Sobibor". *Encounter* (London), 51, no. 6 (December 1978): p. 20.

19. David Irving, *Hitler's War, 1939–1942* (Macmillan, London: 1977), p. 391.

20. Ibid., p. 391.

21. Ibid., pp. 391–392. Also see: Christian Gerlach's "The Wannsee Conference, the Fate of German Jews, and Hitler's Decision in Principle to Exterminate all European Jews," *The Journal of Modern History*, 70 (December 1998): 759–812.

22. Ibid., pp. 392–393. Irving's most celebrated encounter with an historian came early in 2000, following his decision to launch a libel action in an English court against the American academic, Deborah Lipstadt — and her publisher, Penguin Books — who wrote in her book, *Denying the Holocaust: The Growing Assault on Truth and Memory,* (New York: Free Press, 1993), p. 181.

Irving is one of the most dangerous spokespersons for Holocaust denial. Familiar with historical evidence, he bends it until it conforms to his ideological leanings and political agenda. A man who is convinced that Britain's great decline was accelerated by its decision to go to war with Germany, he is most facile at taking accurate information and shaping it to confirm his conclusions.

Irving's internationally publicized action was unsuccessful, with British Judge Charles Gray handing down his decision on 11 April 2000. Judge Gray said, *inter alia:*

Over the past 15 years or so, Irving appears to have become more active politically than was previously the case. He speaks regularly at political or quasi-political meetings in Germany, the United States, Canada and the New World. The content of his speeches and interviews often displays a distinctly pro-Nazi and anti-Jewish bias. He makes surprising and often unfounded assertions about the Nazi regime which tend to exonerate the Nazis for the appalling atrocities which they inflicted on the Jews. He is content to mix with neo-fascists and appears to share many of their racist and anti-semitic prejudices. The picture of Irving which emerges from the evidence of his extra-curricular activities reveal him to be a right-wing pro-Nazi polemicist.

Irving's view of the Anglo-German conflict that became World War II in some ways resembles that of William "Lord Haw Haw" Joyce's fears and warnings before his departure from England for Germany in 1939, where he worked as a Berlin Radio broadcaster. It also has some similarities with Rudolf Hess's outlook, which prompted Hitler's deputy to secretly fly to Great Britain just before the invasion of the Soviet Union, where *Generalplan Ost* was to be primarily applied, in a bid to avoid a continuance of fighting between the British and Germans. For an expansion of these points see: "The Man who Admires Hitler", by Joseph Poprzeczny, *The Sunday Times* (Perth), 28 March 1993. Irving was chaperoned, during his 1986 Western Australian visit, by members of Australia's right-wing lobby group, the League of Rights, many of whose members are Holocaust deniers. *The Sunday Times* article was an assessment of Irving's views expressed during a 1986 interview with the author in Perth, Western Australia. Irving attempted to revisit Australia during 1992, but was prevented from doing so by the Keating Labor Government, which refused his entry, a decision Irving challenged unsuccessfully in the Australian Federal Court in 1993. Notwithstanding all this, it would be quite unfair to portray Irving as in any way being sympathetic to Globocnik. During Irving's 1986 Perth interview, the author briefly alluded to Globocnik. **Question:** "Where does Globocnik fit into all this?" **Irving:** "Odilo Globocnik was born in Trieste.

A strange character of Austrian nationality who became an SS officer. He figures in the *Anschluss* with Austria as a little-known character during the famous telephone conversations Göring conducted from Berlin. Globocnik sometimes surfaced in the [German] embassy in Vienna talking with Göring, who had no idea at that time who he was. Later on Globocnik became one of the most brutal SS commanders, personally in charge of the liquidation measures in Poland, referred to as Globus by his pals, and was very, very close to Heinrich Himmler." **Question:** "Do you know anything about Globocnik's role in the resettlement of the Zamosc region of the Polish peasants?" **Irving:** "It's the kind of thing he would have been involved in. I don't know anything specific except this came within Himmler's aegis as Reichscommissar for the Reinforcement of Germandom."
23. Irving, *Hitler's War*, p. 392.
24. Constantine Simonov, *The Lublin Extermination Camp* (Foreign Language Publishing House, Moscow: 1944).
25. Jon Bridgeman, *The End of the Holocaust: The Liberation of the Eastern Camps* (B.T. Batsford, London: 1990), pp. 21–22.
26. Tadeusz Mencel, *Majdanek, 1941–1944* (Wydawnictwo Lubelski, Lublin, 1991), p. 510.
27. Marszalek, *Majdanek*, p. 22.
28. Globocnik SS File. The untitled file card that carries this information states beside the dates "1.9.—17.9.43" the following: "SS and *Polizeiführer* with duties as the main representative of the Reich for the Wolynian resettlement. Duties to be in charge of constructing the Wolynian resettlements. Duties in charge of constucting SS-Police Strongpoints in the new eastern territories; Reich Commissioner for the Strengthening of Germandom and in charge of Reinhardt."
29. Marszalek, p. 53.
30. Pilichowski, entries 2628 and 2629.

31. Marek Jan Chodakiewicz, *Accommodation and Resistance: A Polish County During the Second World War and its Aftermath, 1939–1947*, Ph.D. diss. (Columbia University, New York: 2000). See Chapter III, "The Polish Majority Under Nazi Rule."

32. Pilichowski, entry. 2634.

33. Ibid., entry 2633.

34. Ibid., entry 2632.

35. Ibid., entry 2630.

36. Mark Lewis, and Jacob Frank, *Himmler's Jewish Tailor: The Story of Holocaust Survivor Jacob Frank* (Syracuse University Press, Syracuse: 2000), p. xvii. The references to the earlier writers are to: Konnilyn Feig, *Hitler's Death Camps: The Sanity of Madness*. (Holmes & Meier, New York: 1981); Daniel Goldhagen, *Hitler's Willing Executioners: Ordinary Germans and the Holocaust*. (Abacus, London: 1997); and Leni Yahil, *The Holocaust: The Fate of European Jewry, 1932–1945* (New York: Oxford University Press, 1990).

37. Ibid., pp. xiv–xv.

38. Pilichowski, entry 2631.

39. Isaiah Trunk, *Judenrat: The Jewish Councils in Eastern Europe Under Nazi Occupation* (Macmillan, New York: 1972), p. 121.

40. Apenszlak, pp. 95–96.

41. "Lublin," *Encyclopedia of Jewish Communities in Poland*, pp. 13–38.

42. Pilichowski, entry 2447.

43. Ibid., entries 497, 1287, 1411, 1982, 4642, 4974, 5016, 5133, 5144, 5632.

44. Ibid., entries 186, 2158, 3190, 3887, and Kielbon, p. 156.

45. Mankowski, *Hitlerowskie Wiezienie*, p. 367.

46. PRO/WO 208/4673 166970, p. 13.

47. Alina Galan, "Pod Zegarem," in *Hitlerowskie Wiezienie na Zamku w Lublinie, 1939–1944*, ed. Zygmunt Mankowski (Wydawnictwo Lubelskie, Lublin: 1988), pp. 53–60, and Pilichowski, *Obozy hitlerowski*, entry 2449.

48. Pilichowski, entry 113.

49. Edward Dziadosz and Jozef Marszalek, "Wiezienia i Obozy w Dystrykcie Lubelskim," *Zeszyty Majdanka* (Lublin), 3 (1969), p. 119.

50. Pilichowski, entries 5631, 5788, 5789.

51. Ibid., entries 5132, 2170.

52. Ibid., entry 3905.

53. Ibid., entries 3, 961, 2170, 2201, 4469, 5788.

54. Ibid., entries 205, 210, 1398, 4973.

55. Kielbon, *Migracje Ludnosci*, p. 203.

56. Ibid., p. 203.

Chapter XI

1. Lewis and Frank, *Himmler's Jewish Tailor*; Mark Roseman, "Long Train to Lublin," commentary, BBC-Radio 4, 25 January 2002. See also Roseman's *The Past in Hiding: Memory and Survival in Nazi Germany* (Penguin Books, London: 2000).

2. Lewis and Frank, pp. 29–30.

3. Ibid., p. 31.

4. Ibid., p. 32.

5. Ibid., p. 35–36.

6. Ibid., p. 36.

7. Ibid., pp. 47–48.

8. Ibid., p. 147.

9. Ibid., p. 119.

10. Ibid., p. 192.

11. Ibid., p. 255.

12. Ibid., 215.

13. Ibid., 228.

14. Jozef Smiech "Ciag," "The Resettlement of Skierbieszow," in *Wydawnictwo Materialow do Dziejow Zmojszczyzny w Latach Wojny 1939–1944*, ed. Zygmunt Klukowski, vol. 1, (Zamosc, 1945), pp. 121–124.

15. Ibid., p. 121.

16. Zygmunt Klukowski, *German Crimes in the Zamosc Region* [*Glowna Komisja z Badania Zbrodnie Hitlerowskie*], vol. 2, (Warsaw: 1949), pp. 73–74.

17. Jan Grygiel, *Zwiazek Walki Zbrojnej Armia Krajowa w Obwodzie Zamojskim 1939–1944* (Panstwowe Wydawnictwo Naukowe, Warsaw: 1985), p. 85.

18. Ibid., pp. 79–81.

19. Martin Middlebrook, *The Peenemünde Raid: The Night of 17–18 August 1943* (Penguin Books, London: 1988), p. 30. Although we cannot be certain, it is likely that these peasant farmers came predominantly from Bilgoraj country, since so many villages within it were depopulated during the summer months of 1943.

20. Krepinska learned quite by accident, while still in Auschwitz-Birkenau, that her husband had died sometime early in 1943. While walking to work with a group of female prisoners, they passed a work team of Polish male prisoners walking in the opposite direction. In that work team was another expelled Skierbieszow resident, Czeslaw Szywera, who had been a longtime friend of her husband's. As the two groups passed each other, Szywera called out to Krepinska: "Wladek is no longer with us — he died." Szywera's fate is unknown. However, he had served as a personal aide in the Polish Army to Stefan Taraszkiewicz, who at the time was a schoolteacher in Skierbieszow. After Poland's defeat in September and October, 1939, both men had simply returned to their village homes. Soon after, however, Taraszkiewicz, who originally hailed from Nowy Sacz, was arrested by German authorities and was never seen again. His arrest and probable killing were in all likelihood part of *Aktion A-B*, which was undertaken by Globocnik and designed to eliminate educated Poles seen as likely leaders of a Polish resistance movement. This mass elimination of trained military personnel — teachers and military officers were deemed to be intellectuals — meant that the Zamosc Lands' resistance movement that sprang into action in December 1942 was markedly handicapped, because untrained men were required to become resistance fighters and they had to learn the required military skills as they went along.

21. Marszalek, *Majdanek*, p. 61.

22. Klukowski, *German Crimes*, p. 179.

23. Ibid., p. 79.

24. Danuta Czech, *Auschwitz Chronicle: 1939–1945, from the Archives of the Auschwitz Memorial and the German Federal Archives* (I. B. Tauris, London and New York: 1990), pp. 284–85.

25. Ibid., p. 285.

26. Ibid., p. 310.

27. Ibid., p. 286.

28. Ibid., p. 323.

29. Ibid. See also: Anna Zieba, "Wirtschaftshof Babitz" Podoboz Przy Majatku Dworski Babice, *Zeszyty Oswiecimski* (Wydnanictwo Panstwowego Museum w Oswiecimiu), No. 11, 1969, pp. 69–82, and Danuta Czech, "Konzentrationslager Auschwitz — A Historical Outline," in *Auschwitz Nazi Extermination Camp* (Interpress, Warsaw: 1985), pp. 15–44.

30. Czech, *Auschwitz Chronicle*, p. 809.

31. Michael Thad Allen, *The Business of Genocide: The SS, Slave Labor, and the Concentration Camps* (Chapel Hill: University of North Carolina Press, 2002). See Chapter IV. Professor Allen kindly provided the author a copy of a draft of his findings prior to publication.

32. Czech, p. 693. The source from which Czech obtained this information was a Polish Underground handwritten document which listed the names of all the women destined for Ebingen A.C. in Lorraine. Krepinska's name is on it, as are the names of two of her friends — Ela Roszkiewicz (55116) and Helena Noga (29853). *Archiwum Panstwowego Muzeum w Oswiecimiu: Materialy Ruchu Oporu*, Vol. VIIId, pp. 71–75, 89ff., list of names.

33. Ibid., Kazimierz Smolen, director of Panstwowe Muzeum Oswiecim Brzezinka (Auschwitz), letter to the author, 28 May 1987.

34. The woman who acted as Zofia Krepinska's guardian on the train journey between Zamosc and Pilawa was Rozalia Paslik, who in December 1942 was 48 years old. The two children she was accompanying were Wladyslaw Paslik (10) and his brother Stanislaw (7). Rozalia Paslik was instructed by a German official in Zamosc to take care of Zofia. As the June 1992 interview with Mrs. Kowalska reveals, Mrs. Paslik did this admirably. Mrs. Paslik's documented expulsion number was 413, and her two namesakes, either her children or grandchildren—probably the latter—were 414 and 415 respectively, while Zofia was 416. *Der Chef der Sicherheits-polizei und des S.D. Umwandererzentralstelle—Posen Dienststelle—Litzmannstadt (Lodz)*; "Zweigstelle—Zamosc inspectlisten von evakuiersten Polen aus der Kreisen Hrubieszow-Zamosc, 1096/78 (5843)"; National Archives, Lublin.

35. Mrs. Stanislawa Kowalska, interviewed on behalf of the author by John and Zofia Rurka (nee Krepinska), Gdansk, Poland, June 1992.

36. Zofia Weclawik, interviewed on behalf of the author by John and Zofia Rurka (nee Krepinska), Ozorkow, Poland, June 1992.

Chapter XII

1. I have opted for the spelling "*Aktion Reinhardt*" when referring to the Globocnik-led campaign of dispossession and extermination of the Jews of Europe within his three killing centers. There remains considerable confusion over whether this Hitler and Himmler-initiated genocide should be written this way, or as "*Aktion Reinhard*," that is, without the "t." I included the "t" because that is the spelling shown in Stanislaw Piotrowski's pioneering book, *Misja Odyla Globocnika*, when he quoted (p. 91) Himmler's letter of 30 Novem-

ber 1943, to Globocnik, then in Trieste, about this genocide and robbing. I accept that the name was taken from Fritz Reinhardt, a Reich Finance Ministry official, not from SS-*Gruppenführer* Reinhard Heydrich, as so many contend. Professor Ian Kershaw says of Fritz Reinhardt that he "hinted at the regime's interest in the material outcome of the mass murder of around 1.75 million Jews (mainly from Poland).... Mistakenly, SS-men involved in the 'Action' attributed the name to Reinhard Heydrich." In other words, there were precise bureaucratically devised code words for these mass killings and robbing and a more popularly utilized one that was used by certain SS men in and around Lublin after Heydrich's assassination in Prague, with the former seemingly being correct, since Himmler used it in private correspondence to Globocnik 18 months *after* Heydrich's death. Despite this, the subsequent more popularly used form without the "t" has survived and continues being used extensively in historical writings, with many historians opting to use it in preference to the original code word. As well as these two different spellings, historians describe this campaign of Globocnik's as Aktion, Action, or Operation *Reinhardt* or *Reinhard*. Irrespective of these additional variants, it is the same robbing and killing that Globocnik headed which is being referred to.

2. PRO/WO 309/374 XC 14298, p. 6.

3. Höss, Commandant of Auschwitz, p. 259.

4. PRO/WO 309/374 XC 14298, p. 6.

5. Tregenza, "Christian Wirth," p. 31.

6. Ibid., p. 32

7. PRO/WO 309/374 XC 14298, pp. 6–7.

8. Ibid., p. 7.

9. Ibid.

10. Oswald Pohl, Affidavit Docu-

ment NO — 2714. (Office of Chief Counsel for War Crimes). United States of America. The Pohl statement's reference to Globocnik being a lieutenant-general is correct if using British equivalents of the rank of *SS-Gruppenführer*. The American equivalent, however, is major-general.

11. PRO/WO 309/521 XC167205, (96), sheet four.

12. PRO/WO 309/521 XC167205, (96), sheets four and five.

13. PRO/WO 309/521 XC167205, (96), sheet nine.

14. Tregenza, Christian Wirth, p. 18.

15. Ibid., p. 19.

16. Ibid., p. 35.

17. Ibid., p. 30.

18. *Trial of the Major War Criminals before the International Military Tribunal, Nuremberg, 14 November 1945–1 October 1946* (Nuremberg, IMT: 1947–1949). Document No. NO-2614, Morgen Interrogation, 7 August 1946.

19. Max Runhof (aka Cichotski) Statement to Wiesbaden Court.

20. Ibid.

21. Ibid.

22. Quoted by Tregenza Christian Wirth, p. 34; see ff. 147 in Tregenza. Statement by Wilhelm Pfannenstiel, 9 November 1959, in Marburg/Lahn.

23. Yisrael Gutman and Avital Saf, eds, "The Nazi Concentration Camps: Structure and Aims, the Image of the Prisoner, the Jews in the Camps," *Proceedings of the Fourth Yad Vashem International Historical Conference, January 1980* (Jerusalem: Yad Vashem, 1984), p. 35.

24. Joseph Marcus, *Social and Political History of the Jews of Poland, 1919–1939* (Mouton de Gruyter, New York: 1983), p. 256.

25. Artur Eisenbach, "Operation Reinhard: Mass Extermination of the Jewish Population in Poland," *Polish Western Affairs* (Poznan), 3, no. 1 (1962): pp. 102–103.

Chapter XIII

1. Piotrowski, *Misja Odyla Globocnika*, pp. 77–110.

2. Ibid., p. 7.

3. Ibid., pp. 18–19.

4. Ibid., p. 103. Regarding the Lublin link with Krakow, it is perhaps significant that General Governor Dr. Hans Frank went out of his way to meet Georg Wippern, who at the time of the governor's visit to Lublin, was in hospital.

5. Ibid., pp. 104–108.

6. Ibid., p. 28.

7. Ibid., p. 29.

8. Ibid., p. 27.

9. Ibid., pp. 37–38.

10. Ibid., pp. 45–46.

11. Ibid., p. 49.

Chapter XIV

1. Globocnik SS File. Globocnik to Wolff, 28 January 1941.

2. Marian Pawlowski, "Sobieszyn — Wies z Tradycjami," in *Wies a Regionalizm*, ed. Alexander Kociszewski, *et al.* (Krajowego Osrodka Dokumentacji Regionalnych Towarzystw Kultury, No. 20, Ciechanow: 1997), pp. 55–58.

3. Alexander Donat, ed. *The Death Camp Treblinka: A Documentary* (Holocaust Library, New York: 1979), p. 271.

4. Rickheim, interview.

5. Irmgard Rickheim, letter to author, 15 April 1998.

6. British author and journalist Gitta Sereny had written: "Lore, a dark-haired beauty whom Globocnik married in October 1944, was, on her paternal side, of Jewish descent (would anyone understand the psychology of that marriage, I wondered)." See: "The Sins of their Fathers," The *Times* (London), 14 May 2001.

7. Werner T. Angress and Bradley F. Smith, "Diaries of Heinrich Himmler's

Early Years," *Journal of Modern History.*
31 (1959), pp. 218–219.
  8. Ibid., p. 219.
  9. Ibid.
  10. All the letters, notes and memoranda referred to are held in Globocnik's SS File.

Chapter XV

  1. Michael Thad Allen, *The Business of Genocide.* See Chapter IV.
  2. Ibid.
  3. Wistrich, p. 235.
  4. Höss, pp. 260–61.
  5. Ibid., pp. 247–253.

Chapter XVI

  1. Kielbon, p. 128.
  2. Aldor, p. 212.
  3. Ibid., p. 213.
  4. Ibid., p. 215
  5. Kielbon, p. 29.
  6. Ibid., pp. 134–135.
  7. Ibid., p. 202.
  8. "Lublin," *Encyclopedia of Jewish Communities in Poland*, pp. 13–38.
  9. Kielbon, p. 152.
  10. Wnuk, p. 328.
  11. Kielbon, p. 85.
  12. Marszalek, pp. 140–141. Gassing in fact commenced prior to October 1942, according to Marszalek. He says that before the concrete gas chambers had been completed, "exploiting Auschwitz experience with the use of that [Zyklon B] gas for killing Soviet prisoners of war, gassing was begun in a makeshift chamber." Large quantities of Zyklon B had been ordered prior to that.
  13. Kielbon, p. 203.
  14. Ibid., pp. 175–176. Kielbon's quote is from Eisenbach's book *Przesiedlenia ludnosci zydowskiej w okresie II wojny swiatowej* (Poznan: N.P., 1966), p. 281.
  15. Ibid.

  16. Ibid., p. 203.

Chapter XVIII

  1. Mencel, p. 509.
  2. Globocnik SS file. The brief entry on the relevant pro forma document reads: SS-u.Pol.F.Lublin mit erweiterten Aufträgen als Hauptregierungsvertreter des Reiches bei der Wohlhynienumsiedl. Beauftr.f.d.Errichtung d.Reiches b.d. Wohlhynienumsiedl., Beauftr.f.d. Errichtung v.Stützpunkten im neuem Ostraum. RK 'f.d.Fest. dt. Volkst. u. Sond.Auftr. Reinhardt.
  3. Globocnik SS File; Gl/Go Tgb. Nr. 291/43. 27 October 1943. Globocnik to von Herff.
  4. Rusinow, especially Chapter XIII, where the nature and complexities of German-Italian jurisdictional powers in both zones are considered.
  5. Pucher, p. 124.
  6. Wladyslaw Anders, *An Army in Exile: The Story of the Second Polish Corps* (The Battery Press, Nashville: 1981), and Harvey Sarner, *General Anders and the Soldiers of the Second Polish Corps* (Brunswick Press, Cathedral City, CA: 1997).
  7. Rusinow, p. 301.
  8. The *Times* (London), 12 September 1943, p. 3.
  9. Ibid.
  10. Ibid. It is worth noting that Germany, in September 1943, was still a formidable fighting entity, something military historians generally readily recognize. W.G.F. Jackson's study, *"Overlord": Normandy 1944* (Davis-Poynter, London: 1978), p. 119, for instance, states: "The two elements of German military capability which mattered most to Eisenhower were Luftwaffe fighter strength and the number of German mobile divisions which could reach his lodgment area [at Normandy] in the first three months after his landing. Allied Intelligence reports on both aspects of

Germany military capability were depressing, in spite of the weight of bombs dropped so far in the Combined Bomber Offensive. The German aircraft industry had been concentrating on fighter production and the Luftwaffe's strength was still rising. It had 4700 front line aircraft in July 1943 and 6700 in January 1944; and there seemed to be no major eastward drift in German air strength in spite of German military disasters in Russia. New bomber production was certainly going mainly to the East, but fighter production was shared equally between East and West (figures from *Grand Strategy*, vol. 5, page 287). The Luftwaffe remained a power to be reckoned with and was still inflicting uncomfortably heavy losses on the American day and British night bombers attacking targets in Germany.")

11. Wistrich, p. 296.

12. Maurice Williams, "Friedrich Rainer e Odilo Globocnik. L'amicizia insolita e i ruoli sinistri di due nazisti tipici." ["Typical Nazis, An Unusual Friendship, and Sinister Roles: Friedrich Rainer and Odilo Globocnik, Nazi Comrades."] Istituto Regionale per la Storia del Movimento di Liberazione Nel Friuli — Venezia Giulia. 25 (June 1997), p. 172. Professor Williams's research shows that in February 1947, Rainer was handed over by the British to the Yugoslavs to be placed on trial before a military court with 13 others. Of these 14 captives, Rainer and 11 others were found guilty and sentenced to death. "When and how he finally died remains a mystery, although solid evidence confirms him collaborating with the Yugoslavs until 1949," writes Williams. The extradition of Rainer by the Yugoslavs suggests that Globocnik could have expected similar treatment, that is, eventual handing over to the Poles for trial in Warsaw or, even more likely, in Lublin, and in all probability a public hanging within the confines of Majdanek concentration camp, on that city's out-

skirts, or perhaps on the site of one of the hidden killing centers, his "terminal stations": Treblinka, Sobibor or Belzec. However, there may have also been pressure in Poland for him to be hanged in Zamosc, on the site of the *UWZ* transit camp on the outskirts of Zamosc's historic market place, which he and Himmler found so aesthetically pleasing.

13. Ibid., pp. 162–163. Globocnik's obsession with creating the so-called Germanic SS and police strongpoints as the basic building blocks of expansive *Generalplan Ost*, the Final Solution of the Slavic Problem, had meant consideration was given to transferring Höfle out of Lublin, which was too far west for such a crucial venture, possibly to Kharhov in Ukraine. Consideration was also given to dispatching Globocnik during 1943, as opposition mounted against him, especially from German civil government officials based in Lublin. He would have been sent to what Pucher refers to as Middle Russia, probably the lands across northern Ukraine or beyond, even though these were as yet not conquered by the *Wehrmacht*. Moreover, his murderous adjutant, Hermann Höfle, was seen as a likely candidate to head the planned SS and police strongpoints around Tiflis, Georgia.

14. Maurice Williams, "The Nazis, German Nationalism, and Ethnic Diversity: The Adriatic Coastland Under Friedrich Rainer," *Slovene Studies*, 17, nos. 1–2 (1995), p. 3. Here Williams has made a detailed study of the two policies Rainer adopted in this ethnically diverse northern Adriatic region: his initial nationalistic one of wanting to Germanize segments of the population; and, after the fortunes of war had turned against the Reich in 1943, a reversal during which time he sought to accommodate the region's various ethnic desires. In the latter phase Rainer referred to the methods used during the Germanizing period as "inefficient" and "politically obsolete". (See p. 12). Williams sees the

intellectually formidable Rainer as "a remarkable official and an uncommon personality who became an important survivor of and witness to the Third Reich's collapse. Tried in Ljubljana and supposedly executed by the Yugoslavs in the summer of 1947, Rainer in fact lived and worked for his captors until 1949 and possibly later. He wrote hundreds of pages of history, political analysis, and personality assessments."

15. Rusinow, pp. 302–03.
16. Williams, "The Nazis, German Nationalism, and Ethnic Diversity," pp. 10–11.
17. Pucher, p. 127.
18. Zuccotti, p. 185.
19. Pucher claims that a fourth office existed outside the zone, based at Mestre. As for the three which came under Wirth's control, they were located at Trieste, Fiume-Susaka, and Udine.
20. Zuccotti, p. 311. Most Italian Jews, who numbered about 50,000 in 1933, and probably about 45,000 in September 1943, when Badoglio pulled Italy out of the war, lived in Northern Italy, Italy's economically more advanced regions. Of these, some 7,500 were deported to Auschwitz-Birkenau and other killing centers, with some 6,900 being killed. About 38,000 survived the war. These figures must, however, be set alongside those of the Lublin District, where Globocnik oversaw the killing of between 1.5 and two million Jews, most of them from Poland, and an unknown number of non-Jewish Poles, probably in excess of 100,000, with several thousand of these also dying in the *Aktion Reinhardt* killing centers.
21. Fogar, p. 2. Pucher's research has shown that 22 trains carrying Jews and political prisoners had been dispatched northward during the Globocnik era.
22. Ibid., p. 3.
23. Ibid.
24. Pucher, p. 132.
25. The story of this notorious informer is well known. Susan Zuccotti

even names the treacherous miscreant, saying he was Graziadio Mauro Grini, the son of a tailor whose mother was blind. Zuccotti reports that he claimed his treachery was motivated by a desire to save his family, whereas others alleged he was paid 7,000 Lire per victim. Grini is alleged to have betrayed several hundred people from Trieste, Venice, and Milan. However, Zuccotti doubts if the number was so high.

26. Fogar, p. 7.
27. Pucher, p. 133.
28. Tone Ferenc, "The Austrians and Slovenia during the Second World War," in *Conquering the Past: Austrian Nazism Yesterday and Today*, ed. Fred Parkinson (Wayne State University Press, Detroit: 1989), pp. 208–209.
29. Ibid., p. 218.
30. Quoted in John Lukacs, *The Hitler of History* (Knopf, New York: 1998), p. 63.
31. Pucher, p. 135.
32. Zuccotti, p. 59.
33. The *Times* (London), 3 February 1944, p. 3.
34. Ibid., 12 April 1944, p. 3.
35. Ibid.
36. Ibid., 29 September 1944, p. 3.
37. Pucher, p. 88.

Chapter XIX

1. Pucher, pp. 89–90.
2. Sereny, "The Sins of their Fathers," p. 4.
3. Elste, p. 179. Gitta Sereny, in "The Sins of their Fathers," has written: "...if tried, he [Globocnik] would have been held responsible for the death by shooting and gassing of a least two million men, women and children."
4. Wistrich, p. 296. Gustav Wagner, a Viennese who joined the NSDAP in 1931, and later the SS, was involved in the secret euthanasia killing program that developed into Globocnik's Lublin

T-4 or *Aktion Reinhardt* killing team. He helped build Sobibor killing center, becoming its second-in-command. Like the other Globocnikians, this sadist went to Italy in 1943 and, although captured by the Americans in 1945, bluffed his way out of captivity, like Ernst Lerch and Hermann Höfle. For a time he worked as a builder in Gratz, and teamed up with Stangl to reach Syria and Brazil via Rome. Although Stangl was extradited to West Germany in 1967, extradition requests for Wagner by Israel, Poland, and Austria were all turned down, and in 1978 Brazil's supreme court did likewise to a West German request.

5. PRO/ WO 204/13006.
6. Ibid., p. 4.
7. Ibid.
8. Ibid., p. 5.
9. Ibid., p. 6. Interestingly, Brigadier Guy Wheeler, in his letter of 5 January 1965 to the British Foreign Office, which was seeking to establish Globocnik's fate on behalf of the Austrian Government, wrote: "On first interrogation all those captured admitted their identity, except Globocnik, who claimed to be an engineer seized on Rainer's orders and brought up to the hut to advise on fortifying the area. The fact that he was sharing the small private room at the back of the hut with Rainer himself made us doubt this story."
10. PRO WO 208/4673 166970.

Chapter XX

1. *Samo Obronia*; 23 July 1943. Polish Underground Study Trust, London.
2. *Daily Telegraph* (London), 31 August 1943.
3. Jozef Kasparek, in *Kronika Wydarzen w Lublinie w okresie okupacji hitlerowskiej*, refers to the assassination attempt and gives as its source "Delegatura Rzadu RP na Kraj" (The Republic of Poland's Government Delegate in the Country), Centralne Archiwum KC PZPR w Warszawie, sygn. 202/III.
4. Wistrich, p. 95.
5. Louis Snyder, *Encyclopedia of the Third Reich* (Blandford, London: 1976), p. 117.
6. Andre Brissaud, *The Nazi Secret Service* (Corgi Books, London: 1975), p. 254.
7. Donat, p. 272.
8. Dressen and Riess, p. 293.
9. James Taylor and Warren Shaw, *The Third Reich Almanac* (World Almanac, New York: 1987), p. 134.
10. Raul Hilberg, *The Destruction of the Jews*, rev. ed. (Holmes & Meier, New York: 1985), p. 1,087.
11. Ruth Bettina Birn, *Die höheren SS-und Polizeiführer: Himmlers Vertreter im Reich und in den besetzten Gebieten* (Düsseldorf: Droste-Verl, 1986), p. 334.
12. Michael Elkins, *Forged in Fury* (Corgi Books, London: 1982), p. 199.
13. Ibid., p. 200.
14. Edward Crankshaw, *Gestapo: Instrument of Tyranny* (Greenhill Books, London: 1990), p. 185.
15. Gerald Reitlinger, *The Final Solution* (Sphere Books, London: 1971), p. 556.
16. Gerald Reitlinger, *The SS: Alibi of a Nation 1933–1945* (Arms and Armour, London: 1981), p. 465.
17. "Most of these SS Chiefs are Dead: Bonn Investigation Results," *The Wiener Library Bulletin*, 15, no. 2 (1961), p. 24.
18. Elkins, p. 200.
19. "Most of these SS Chiefs are Dead," p. 24.
20. Willi Dressen, interview with author, Ludwigsburg, Germany, March 1987.
21. Adalbert Ruckerl, *The Investigation of Nazi Crimes 1945–1978, A Documentation* (C.F. Müller, Heidelberg, Karlsruhe: 1979) p. 49.
22. Ysrael Gutman, interview with author, Jerusalem, February 1987.
23. David Scott Daniell, *Fourth Hussars: The Story of a British Cavalry Regi-*

ment (Aldershot, Gale and Polden, Hampshire: 1959). The account of Globocnik's capture and death is on pages 387–390.

24. Ibid.

25. Ibid.

26. PRO/WO 170/4622 117350. Gitta Sereny has provided background on Kummerer, who was the crucial informant who led to the capture of Rainer and Globocnik. "Twenty-five year old *SS-Unterscharführer* Siegfried Kummerer's record ... was not quite as innocuous as he told his captors. A member of Carinthia's illegal Hitler Youth in the 1930s, when Globocnik was one of the top men in the movement there, he served after the *Anschluss* as a guard at Dachau and Mauthausen. After a brief period of combat in an SS mountain division in Finland, he was transferred for 'special training' to Lublin — Globocnik's command — and then, yet again, under Globocnik, to Italy." See "A Nazi Hunter Run to Earth," *The Independent*, 19 July 1992

27. PRO/WO 170/7112 1087. Lore Globocnik is referred to in this source which is the 88 F. S. Section 78 Division, Security Intelligence Report — Austria — no. 6. Period from 16 July to 31 July 1945. Area Covered: Bezirk of Spittal, Bezirk of Liensz, 23–31 July. Her arrest report is No. 88/GFR/34.

28. Major W.K. Hedley, statement to Civil Liaison Officer, Spittal, 16 January 1949, which was sent by Peter R. Black, then of the United States Department of Justice, Washington D.C., to Zygmunt Mankowski, University of Marie Curie-Sklodowskiej, Lublin, with Zygmunt providing a copy to the author in May 1987.

29. Brigadier Guy Wheeler, letter to author, 9 May 1990. See also PRO/FO 371–179969. (Wheeler letter of 5 January 1964 to Foreign Office).

30. Ibid. It is entirely possible that the queries that hung over Globocnik from his period as *Gauleiter* of Vienna could have prompted some of these inquiries, that is, the belief that he was in possession of a fortune.

31. Ibid.

32. PRO/FO 371–179969. Hedley letter, 4 January 1965.

33. PRO/FO 371–179969. Leigh letter, 7 January 1965

34. Wheeler letter.

35. Ibid.

36. Ibid.

37. Ibid.

38. Ibid.

39. PRO/WO 170/4622 117350. This document reports that at 0510 "The door [of the mountain hut] was opened by Major Ramsay who had entered through a loft window and the door at the back was forced by Major Quarmby and Lt. Hedley..." *The Ramsay Report* was provided to the author by former SOE agent, Arthur Radley, of Holland Park Avenue, London. Sir Peter Wilkinson was Alexander Ramsay's commanding officer for a time in the final stages of the war in southern Europe (in Yugoslavia). Ramsay and Radley were close wartime and postwar friends. After the war Ramsay became the British Government's liaison official within Radio Free Europe, an America-financed radio service created to combat Soviet Communism. Ramsay married an Austrian and lived in Germany and Austria, where he died. Shortly before his death he gave Radley the report, no doubt because he realized its longer-term historical importance. This is the first time this report has been published.

40. Simon Withers, letter to author, 6 August 1994, based on his interview of Arthur Radley, in London.

41. Gervase Cowell, letter, SOE Adviser Room 3/976, OAB, 28 May 1991, to Carolyn Poprzeczny.

42. Sir Peter Wilkinson, letter to author, 22 June 1994. For details on SOE's efforts to penetrate southern Austria, including Sir Peter Wilkinson's and Captain Alfgar Hesketh-Pritchard's

roles, see Patrick Howarth, *Underground: The Men and Women of SOE* (Arrow Books, London: 1990).

43. Alexander Ramsay, *The Ramsay Report: Events leading to the capture of ex-Gauleiter Rainer (Kärnten)*. (Copy of Ramsay's handwritten document in the author's possession.)

44. Ibid.

45. Ibid.

46. Ibid.

47. PRO/WO 170/4622 117350.

48. Sereny, "A Nazi Hunter Run to Earth," pp. 10–14.

49. For Sereny's analysis of the fake documents sent to her, see her articles "A Nazi Hunter Run to Earth" and "Spin Time for Hitler," *The Observer (The Review)*, 21 April 1996. Also see Chapter 9 ("The Great Globocnik Hunt") in Sereny's *The Healing Wound: Experiences and Reflections on Germany, 1938–2001* (W.W. Norton: New York, 2001).

50. Sereny, "A Nazi Hunter Run to Earth," p. 11.

51. Ibid.

52. Ibid., p. 14.

53. Ibid., p. 12. In "The Sins of Their Fathers," Sereny returned to describing Peter Globocnik, and his response to his father's legacy. She wrote: "She [Lore Globocnik] rarely talked to him [Peter] about his father and never about Poland, He said: 'I don't know what to feel. Of course, I have read books about the genocide of the Jews. I got mountains of pamphlets and things sent to see, anonymously, by the radical right, all full of so-called 'proof' that the gassings in Poland never happened. Who was I to believe? If I believed the stuff they sent, then, obviously, I'd be siding with a strident minority whom I don't really empathize with. But if I believe the others … then, well, you understand don't you, he was, after all, my father.'"

54. Ibid.

55. PRO/WO 204—11505 XC5441. (1 SC/CSDIC/X 3).

Works Cited

Adamthwaite, Anthony P. *The Making of the Second World War*. London: Allen & Unwin, 1977.

Aldor, Francis. *Germany's "Death Space": The Polish Tragedy—Nazi Theory Has Evolved the Concept of "Lebensraum" (Living Space)—Nazi Practice Has Realized the Fact of "Todesraum" (Death Space)*. London: self-published, n.d.

Allen, Michael Thad. "The Banality of Evil Reconsidered: SS Mid-Level Managers of Extermination through Work." *Central European History* 30, no. 2 (1997): 253–294.

_____. *The Business of Genocide: The SS, Slave Labor, and the Concentration Camps*. Chapel Hill: University of North Carolina Press, 2002.

Anders, Wladyslaw. *An Army in Exile: The Story of the Second Polish Corps*. Nashville: Battery Press, 1981.

Angress, Werner T., and Bradley F. Smith. "Diaries of Heinrich Himmler's Early Years." *Journal of Modern History*, 31 (1959): 206–224.

Anonymous Polish Partisan. "Wysiedle-nie Skierbieszow 27 Listopada [*sic*] 1942." In *Zamojszczyzna—Sonderlaboratorium SS*, vol. 1., ed. Czeslaw Madajczyk. Warsaw: Ludowa Spoldzielnia Wydawnicza, 1979.

Apenszlak, Jacob, *et al.*, eds. *The Black Book of Polish Jewry*. New York: Roy Publishers, 1943.

Barker, Thomas M. *The Slovene Minority of Carinthia*. Boulder: East European Monographs, 1984.

Berenstein, Tatiana. "Spory administratcji z SS w GG." [*sic*] *Biuletyn Zydowski Instytut Historyczny* No. 53 (1965): 33–79.

Bettina Birn, Ruth. *Die höheren SS-und Polizeiführer: Himmlers Vertreter im Reich und in den besetzten Gebieten*. Düsseldorf: Droste-Verl., 1986.

Black, Peter. *Ernst Kaltenbrunner: Ideological Soldier of the Third Reich*. Princeton: Princeton University Press, 1984.

_____. "Odilo Globocnik—Himmlers Vorposten im Osten." In *Die SS: Elite unter dem Totenkopft: 30 Lebenslaeuft*. Ed. Ronald Smelser and Enrico Syring

(Paderborn: Schoeningh, 2000): 289–304.

_____. "Rehearsal for 'Reinhard'?: Odilo Globocnik and the Lublin _Selbstschutz._" _Central European History_ 25, no. 2 (1992): 204–226.

"Brecelj, Ales." _Primorsi slovenski biografski leksikon,_ vol. 19. Gorica (Gorizia): N.p., 1993: 587–589.

Breitman, Richard. _The Architect of Genocide: Himmler and the Final Solution._ New York: Knopf, 1991.

_____. _Report on the Investigative Records Repository File of Hermann Julius Höfle._ Washington: National Archives and Research Administration, 2001.

Bridgeman, Jon. _The End of the Holocaust: The Liberation of the Eastern Camps._ London: B.T. Batsford, 1990.

Brissaud, Andre. _The Nazi Secret Service._ London: Corgi Books, 1975.

Brook-Shepherd, Gordon. _The Anschluss._ London: Macmillan, 1963.

_____. _Dollfuss._ Westport, CT: Greenwood Press, 1978.

Browning, Christopher R. "Nazi Ghettoization Policy in Poland: 1939–41." _Journal of Central European History,_ 19 (1986): 343–368.

Bukey, Evan Burr. _Hitler's Austria: Popular Sentiment in the Nazi Era, 1938–1945._ Chapel Hill: University of North Carolina Press, 2000.

Burleigh, Michael. "Saving Money, Spending Lives: Psychiatry, Society and the 'Euthanasia' Programme." _Confronting the Nazi Past: New Debates on Modern German History,_ ed. Michael Burleigh. London: Collins & Brown, 1996.

Butler, J.R.M., ed. _Grand Strategy: History of the Second World War._ Vol. 5. London: HMSO, 1956.

Carsten, F.L. _The First Austrian Republic, 1918–1938: A Study Based on British and Austrian Documents._ Aldershot, Hants, England and Brookfield, VT: Gower/Maurice Temple Smith, 1986.

Cecil, Robert. _The Myth of the Master Race: Alfred Rosenberg and Nazi Ideology._ London: B.T. Batsford, 1972.

Chandler, David. "A Tyrant from the Shadows." _The Australian_ (Sydney), 17 April 1998, p. 13.

Chodakiewicz, Marek Jan. _Accommodation and Resistance: A Polish County During the Second World War and its Aftermath, 1939–1947._ Ph.D. diss. New York: Columbia University, 2000.

Cienciala, Anna M. _Poland and the Western Powers, 1938–1939._ London: Routledge & Kegan Paul, 1968.

Craig, Gordon. _Germany, 1866–1945._ Oxford: Clarendon Press, 1978.

Crankshaw, Edward. _Gestapo: Instrument of Tyranny._ London: Greenhill Books, 1990.

Czech, Danuta. _Auschwitz Chronicle: 1939–1945, from the Archives of the Auschwitz Memorial and the German Federal Archives._ London and New York: I.B. Tauris, 1990.

_____. "Konzentrationslager Auschwitz: A Historical Outline." _Auschwitz Nazi Extermination Camp._ Warsaw: Interpress, 1985: 15–44.

Daniell, David Scott. _Fourth Hussars: The Story of a British Cavalry Regiment._ Hampshire: Aldershot, Gale and Polden, 1959.

Davies, John. _Jacqueline Bouvier: An Intimate Memoir._ New York: John Wiley & Sons, 1996.

de Jong, Louis. "Sobibor." _Encounter_ (London) 51, no. 6 (December 1978): 20–28.

Donat, Alexander, ed. _The Death Camp Treblinka: A Documentary._ New York: Holocaust Library, 1979.

Dressen, Willi, and Volker Riess. _Those Were the Days: The Holocaust as Seen by the Perpetrators and Bystanders._ London: Hamish Hamilton, 1988.

Dziadosz, Edward, and Jozef Marszalek. "Wiezienia i Obozy w Dystrykcie Lubelskim." _Zeszyty Majdanka_ (Lublin) 3 (1969): 54–129.

Edmondson, C. Earl. *The Heimwehr and Austrian Politics.* Athens: University of Georgia Press, 1976.

Eisenbach, Artur. *Hitlerowska polityka zaglady Zydow.* Warsaw: Ksiazka and Wiedza, 1961.

_____. "Operation Reinhard: Mass Extermination of the Jewish Population in Poland." *Polish Western Affairs* (Poznan) 3, no. 1 (1962): 30–124.

_____. *Przesiedlenia ludnosci zydowskiej w okresie II wojny swiatowej.* Poznan: N.p., 1966.

Elkins, Michael. *Forged in Fury.* London: Corgi Books, 1982.

Elste, Alfred. *Kärntens braune Elite.* Klagenfurt: Hermagoras, 1997.

Feig, Konnilyn. *Hitler's Death Camps: The Sanity of Madness.* New York: Holmes & Meier, 1981.

Feis, Herbert. *Churchill, Roosevelt, Stalin: The War They Waged and the Peace They Sought.* Princeton: Princeton University Press, 1959.

Ferenc, Tone. "The Austrians and Slovenia during the Second World War." *Conquering the Past: Austrian Nazism Yesterday and Today,* ed. Fred Parkinson. Detroit: Wayne State University Press, 1989: 207–223.

Fleming, Gerald. *Hitler and the Final Solution.* Berkeley: University of California Press, 1984.

Fogar, Gallan. Report to Prof. Henry Howard of Los Angeles, 25 June 1990. (Copy in possession of author.)

Fremund, Karel, and Vaclav Kral. *Lesson from History: Documents Concerning Nazi Policies for Germanisation and Extermination in Czechoslovakia.* Prague: Orbis, 1962.

Friedlander, Saul. *Nazi Germany and the Jews: The Years of Persecution, 1933–1939.* Vol. 1. London: Weidenfeld & Nicolson, 1997.

Friedman, Philip. "The Lublin Reservation and the Madagascar Plan: Two Aspects of Nazi Jewish Policy during the Second World War." *Roads to Extinction: Essays on the Holocaust,* ed.

A.J. Friedman. Philadelphia: Jewish Publication Society, 1980.

Friedmann, Tuviah. *Himmlers Teufels—General SS-und Polizeiführer—Globocnik in Lublin und Ein Bericht über die Judenvernichtung im General-Gouvernement in Polen 1941–1944.* T. Friedmann (Director, Institute of Documentation, Haifa, P.O.B. 4950, Israel), April 1977.

Fuchs, Martin. *Showdown in Vienna.* New York: G.P. Putnam's Sons, 1939.

Galan, Alina. "Pod Zegarem." *Hitlerowskie Wiezienie na Zamku w Lublinie, 1939–1944,* ed. Zygmunt Mankowski. Lublin: Wydawnictwo Lubelskie, 1988: 53–60.

Garscha, Winfried R., and Claudia Kuretsidis-Haider. "War Crime Trials in Austria." Paper presented at the 21st Annual Conference of the German Studies Association, Washington, D.C., 25–28 September 1997.

Gasiorowski, Zygmunt J. "The Russian Overture to Germany of December 1924." *The Journal of Modern History,* 30, no. 2 (June 1958): 99–117.

Gehl, Jurgen. *Austria, Germany and the Anschluss.* London: Oxford University Press, 1963.

Genealogisches Handbuch des Adels. Limburg an der Lahn: C.A. Starke, 1998.

Gerlach, Christian. "Failure of Plans for an SS Extermination Camp in Mogilev, Belorussia." *Holocaust and Genocide Studies* 11, no. 1 (Spring 1997): 60–78.

_____. "The Wannsee Conference, the Fate of German Jews, and Hitler's Decision in Principle to Exterminate All European Jews." *The Journal of Modern History,* 70 (December 1998): 759–812.

Goldhagen, Daniel Jonah. *Hitler's Willing Executioners: Ordinary Germans and the Holocaust.* London: Abacus, 1997.

Grygiel, Jan. *Zwiazek Walki Zbrojnej Armia Krajowa w Obwodzie Zamojskim 1939–1944.* Warsaw: Panstwowe Wydawnictwo Naukowe, 1985.

Gumkowski, Janusz, and Kazimierz Leszczynski. *Poland Under Nazi Occupation*. Warsaw: Polonia Publishing House, 1961.

Gutman, Yisrael, and Avital Saf, eds. "The Nazi Concentration Camps: Structure and Aims, the Image of the Prisoner, the Jews in the Camps." *Proceedings of the Fourth Yad Vashem International Historical Conference, January 1980*. Jerusalem: Yad Vashem, 1984.

Hackett, David A., ed. *The Buchenwald Report*. Boulder: Westview Press, 1995.

Hale, Oron J. *The Captive Press in the Third Reich*. Princeton: Princeton University Press, 1964.

Heberle, Rudolf. *From Democracy to Nazism: A Regional Case Study on Political Parties in Germany*. New York: Howard Fertig, 1976.

Heiden, Konrad. *Der Führer: Hitler's Rise to Power*. London: Victor Gollancz, 1944.

Hermand, J. *Old Dreams of a New Reich: Völkisch Utopias and National Socialism*. Bloomington and Indianapolis: Indiana University Press, 1988.

Hilberg, Raul. *The Destruction of the Jews*. Rev. ed. New York: Holmes & Meier, 1985.

Höss, Rudolf. *Commandant of Auschwitz: The Authentic Confessions of a Mass Murderer*. London and Sydney: Pan Books, 1982.

Hoffman, Paul. *The Viennese Splendor, Twilight and Exile*. New York: Doubleday, 1988.

Hohne, Heinz. *The Order of the Death's Head: The Story of Hitler's SS*. London: Secker & Warburg, 1969.

Howarth, Patrick. *Underground: The Men and Women of SOE*. London: Arrow Books, 1990.

Irving, David. *Hess: The Missing Years, 1941–1945*. London: Grafton Books, 1989.

_____. *Hitler's War, 1939–1942*. London: Macmillan, 1977.

Jackson, W.G.F. *"Overlord": Normandy 1944*. London: Davis-Poynter, 1978.

Joffroy, Pierre. *A Spy for God: The Ordeal of Kurt Gerstein*. London: Collins, 1971.

Kasperek, Jozef. *Kronika Wydarzen w Lublinie w okresie okupacji hitlerowskiej*. Lublin: Wydawnictwo Lubelskie, 1989.

Kershaw, Ian. *Hitler: 1889–1936, Hubris*. London: Penguin, 1998.

_____. *Hitler: 1936–1945, Nemesis*. London: Penguin, 2000.

Kielbon, Janina. *Migracje Ludnosci w Dystrykcie Lubelskim w Latach 1939–1944*. Lublin: Panstwowe Museum na Majdanku, 1995.

Klemperer, Victor. *I Shall Bear Witness—The Diaries of Victor Klemperer, 1933–41*. London: Weidenfeld & Nicolson, 1998.

Klukowski, Zygmunt. *Diary from the Years of Occupation, 1939–44*. Urbana and Chicago: University of Illinois Press, 1993.

_____. *Dziennik z Lat Okupacji*. Lublin: Lubelska Spoldzielnia Wydawnicza, 1958.

_____. *German Crimes in the Zamosc Region* [*Wydawnictwo Glowna Komisja Badania Zbrodnie Niemieckich w Polsce*]. Vol. 2. Warsaw: 1949.

Koch, Stephen. *Stalin, Willi Münzenberg and the Seduction of the Intellectuals*. London: HarperCollins, 1995.

Kogon, Eugen. *The Theory and Practice of Hell: The German Concentration Camps and the System Behind Them*. New York: Berkeley, 1975.

Krausnick, Helmut, and Martin Broszat. *Anatomy of the SS State*. London: Paladin, 1970.

Lang, Jochen von, and Claus Sibyll, eds. *Eichmann Interrogated: Transcript from the Archives of the Israeli Police*. New York: Farrar, Straus & Giroux, 1983.

Lewis, Mark, and Jacob Frank. *Himmler's Jewish Tailor: The Story of Holocaust Survivor Jacob Frank*. Syracuse: Syracuse University Press, 2000.

Lipstadt, Deborah. *Denying the Holocaust: The Growing Assault on Truth and Memory.* New York: Free Press, 1993.

Lochner, Louis P. *What About Germany?* London: Hodder and Stoughton, 1943.

"Lublin." *Encyclopaedia Judaica,* Vol. 7. Jerusalem: Keter Publishing House, 1971.

"Lublin." *Encyclopedia of Jewish Communities, Poland.* Vol. 7. Jerusalem: Yad Vashem, 1999.

Lukacs, John. *The Hitler of History.* New York: Knopf, 1998.

Luza, Radomir. *Austro-German Relations in the Anschluss Era.* Princeton: Princeton University Press, 1975.

Madajczyk, Czeslaw. *Deportations in the Zamosc Region in 1942 and 1943 in the Light of German Documents.* Warsaw: Acta Poloniae Historica, 1958.

_____. *Vom Generalplan Ost zum Generalsiedlungsplan.* Munich: Saur, 1994.

_____. "Generalplan Ost." *Polish Western Affairs* (Poznan) 3 (1962): 391–442.

_____, ed. *Die Okkupationspolitik Nazideutschlands in Polen, 1939–1945.* East Berlin: Akademie-Verlag, 1987.

_____. *Polityka III Rzeszy w Okupowanej Polsce.* Vol. 1. Warsaw: Panstwowe Wydanictwo Naukowe, 1970.

_____, ed. *Zamojszczyzna—Sonderlaboratorium SS: Zbior dokumentow polskich i niemieckich z okresu okupacji hitlerowskiej.* Warsaw: Ludowa Spoldzielnia Wydawnicza, 1979.

Mankowski, Zygmunt, ed. *Hitlerowskie Wiezienie na Zamku w Lublinie, 1939–1944.* Lublin: Wydawnictwo Lubelskie, 1988.

_____. *Miedzy Wisla a Bugiem 1939–1944: Studium o polityce okupanta i postawach spoleczenstwa.* Lublin: Wydawnictwo Lubelskie, 1982.

_____. "Odilo Globocnik und Die Endlösung Der Judenfrage." *Studia Historiae Oeconomicae* (Poznan) 21 (1994): 147–155.

_____. "The Responsibility of the Chief of SS and Police in the Lublin Distrikt for the Deportation Action in the Zamosc Lands." *Palesta* (The Organ of the Main Council of Lawyers) No. 7 (July 1980): 89–100.

Marcus, Joseph. *Social and Political History of the Jews of Poland, 1919–1939.* New York: Mouton de Gruyter, 1983.

Markiewicz, Jerzy. *Paprocie Zakwitly Krwia Partyzantow.* Lublin: Wydawnictwo Lubelskie, 1987.

Marszalek, Jozef. *Majdanek: The Concentration Camp in Lublin.* Warsaw: Interpress, 1986.

_____. "Stan bandan nad stratami osobowymi ludnosci zydowskiej Polski oraz nad liczba ofiar obozow zaglady w okupowanej Polsce." *Dzieje Najnowsze,* 26, no. 2 (1994): 33–40.

May, Arthur J. *The Passing of the Hapsburg Monarchy, 1914–1918.* Vol. 1. Philadelphia: University of Pennsylvania Press, 1968.

Mencel, Tadeusz. *Majdanek, 1941–1944.* Lublin: Wydawnictwo Lubelskie, 1991.

Middlebrook, Martin. *The Peenemünde Raid: The Night of 17–18 August 1943.* London: Penguin, 1988.

Mosse, George L. *The Crisis of German Ideology: Intellectual Origins of the Third Reich.* London: Weidenfeld & Nicolson, 1970.

"Most of these SS Chiefs are Dead: Bonn Investigation Results." *Wiener Library Bulletin* 15, no. 2 (1961): 24.

Musial, Bogdan. *Deutsche Zivilverwaltung und Judenverfolgung im Generalgouvernement.* Wiesbaden: Harrassowitz, 1999.

Newman, Bernard. *Danger Spots of Europe.* London: The Right Book Club, 1939.

O'Neil, Robin. *The Belzec Death Camp and the Origins of Jewish Genocide in Galicia.* London: Hebrew and Jewish Dept., University College, 2002.

_____. "The Supporting Cadres in 'Aktion Reinhardt.'" (Privately circulated essay.)

Padfield, Peter. *Himmler Reichsführer SS.* London: Macmillan, 1990.

Parkinson, Fred, ed. *Conquering the Past: Austrian Nazism, Yesterday and Today.* Detroit: Wayne State University Press, 1989.

Partacz, Czeslaw. *Kwestia Ukrainiska w Polityce Polskiego Rzadu na Uchodzstwie i Jego Ekspozytur w Kraju, 1939–1945.* Koszalin: Wydawnictwo Uczelniane Politechniki Koszalinskiej, 2001.

Pauley, Bruce F. "The Austrian Nazi Party before 1938: Some Recent Revelations." *Conquering the Past: Austrian Nazism, Yesterday and Today,* ed. Fred Parkinson. Detroit: Wayne State University Press, 1989.

_____. *Hitler and the Forgotten Nazis: A History of Austrian National Socialism.* Chapel Hill: University of North Carolina Press, 1981.

Pawlowski, Marian. "Sobieszyn — Wies z Tradycjami." *Wies a Regionalizm.* Ed. Alexsander Kociszewski, *et al.* Ciechanow: Krajowego Osrodka Dokumentacji Regionalnych Towarzystw Kultury, No. 20, 1997.

Petropoulos, Jonathan. *The Faustian Bargain: The Art World in Nazi Germany.* London: Allen Lane, Penguin, 2000.

Pilichowski, Czeslaw, ed. *Obozy hitlerowski na ziemiach polskich 1939–1945: Informator encyklopedyczny.* Glowna Komisja Badania Zbrodni Hitlerowskich w Polsce. Warsaw: Panstwowe Wydawnictwo Naukowe, 1979.

Piotrowski, Stanislaw. *Misja Odyla Globocnika: Sprawozdania o Wynikach Finansowych Zaglady Zydow w Polsce.* Warsaw: Panstwowy Instytut Wydawniczy, 1949.

Piotrowski, Tadeusz. *Poland's Holocaust: Ethnic Strife, Collaboration with Occupying Forces and Genocide in the Second Republic, 1918–1947.* Jefferson, NC: McFarland & Co., 1998.

Pohanka, Reinhard. *Pflichterfüller:* *Hitlers Helfer in der Ostmark.* Vienna: Picus Verlag, 1997.

Poliszczuk, Wiktor. *Dowody Zbrodnie OUN i UPA: Integralny nacjonalizm ukrainski jako odmiana faszyzmu.* Vol. 2: *Dzialalnosc ukrainskich struktur nacjonalistycznych w latach, 1920–1999.* [Evidence of OUN and UPA Crimes: Ukranian Integral Nationalism as a Form of Fascism. The Activities of Ukranian Nationalist Structures in the Years 1920–1999, vol. 2) Toronto: self-published. 2000.

Poprzeczny, Joseph. "The Man who Admires Hitler." *The Sunday Times* (Perth), 28 March 1993.

_____, and Carolyn Simmonds. "Origins of Nazi Plans for Eastern Settlement and Extermination." In *Power and Freedom in Modern Politics.* Perth, Western Australia: University of Western Australia Press, 2002.

"The Programmed *Anschluss.*" Part 3: "The Final Act, 1934–38." In *Austria Today.* Hofburg, Vienna: Verlags-GesmbH., 1988: 16–32.

Pucher, Siegfried J. *Odilo Globocnik — Kämpfer für den "Anschluss," Vollstrecker des Holocaust.* Klagenfurt: Drava Verlag, 1997.

Reitlinger, Gerald. *The Final Solution.* London: Sphere Books, 1971.

_____. *House Built on Sand: The Conflicts of German Policy in Russia, 1939–1945.* London: Weidenfeld & Nicolson, 1960.

_____. *The SS: Alibi of a Nation 1933–1945.* London: Arms and Armour, 1981.

Reynolds, Quentin, Ephraim Katz, and Zwi Aldouby. *Minister of Death: The Adolf Eichmann Story.* London: Cassell & Co., 1960.

Ribbentrop, Joachim. *The Ribbentrop Memoirs.* London: Weidenfeld & Nicolson, 1954.

Rose, W.J. *Poland.* Harmondsworth: Penguin, 1939.

Roseman, Mark. "Long Train to Lublin." Commentary, BBC-Radio 4. 25 January 2002.

_____. *The Past in Hiding: Memory and Survival in Nazi Germany.* London: Penguin, 2000.

Rubinstein, William D. *The Myth of Rescue: Why the Democracies Could Not Have Saved More Jews from the Nazis.* London and New York: Routledge, 1997.

Ruckerl, Adalbert. *The Investigation of Nazi Crimes, 1945–1978, a Documentation.* Heidelberg, Karlsruhe: C.F. Müller, 1979.

Rusinow, Dennison. *Italy's Austrian Heritage, 1919–1946.* Oxford: Clarendon Press, 1969.

Sarner, Harvey. *General Anders and the Soldiers of the Second Polish Corps.* Cathedral City, CA: Brunswick Press, 1997.

Schechtman, Joseph B. *European Population Transfers, 1939–1945.* New York: Oxford University Press, 1946.

Schmidt, Paul. *Hitler's Interpreter: The Secret History of German Diplomacy, 1935–45.* London: William Heinemann, 1950.

Sereny, Gitta. *The Healing Wound: Experiences and Reflections on Germany, 1938–2001.* New York: W.W. Norton, 2001.

_____. *Into that Darkness: An Examination of Conscience.* New York: Vintage, 1983.

_____. "A Nazi Hunter Run to Earth." *The Independent* (London) 19 July 1992.

_____. "The Sins of Their Fathers." *The Times* (London) 14 May 2001.

_____. "Spin Time for Hitler." *The Observer (The Review)* (London) 21 April 1996.

Shirer, William. *The Rise and Fall of the Third Reich.* London: Pan Books, 1960.

Simonov, Constantine. *The Lublin Extermination Camp.* Moscow: Foreign Language Publishing House, 1944.

Smiech, Jozef ("Ciag"). "The Resettlement of Skierbieszow." *Wydawnictwo*

Materialow do Dziejow Zamojszczyzny w Latach Wojny 1939–1944, ed. Zygmunt Klukowski, Vol. 1, 121–124. Zamosc: Lubeska Spoldzielnia Wydawnicz, 1945.

Snyder, Louis. *Encyclopedia of the Third Reich.* London: Blandford, 1976.

Stadler, Karl R. *Austria.* London: Ernest Benn, 1971.

Stockhorst, Erich. *Fünftausend Köpfe: Wer war was im Dritten Reich.* Bretton: Blick and Bild Verlag, 2000.

Strasser, Otto. *Hitler and I.* London: Jonathan Cape, 1940.

Sukiennicki, Wiktor. *East Central Europe During World War I: From Foreign Domination to National Independence.* Boulder: East European Monographs, 1984.

Taylor, James, and Warren Shaw. *The Third Reich Almanac.* New York: World Almanac, 1987.

Thompson, Larry Vern. "Friedrich-Wilhelm Krueger: Höherer SS-und Polizeiführer Ost." In *Die SS: Elite unter dem Totenkopf: 30 Lebenslaeufe.* Ed. Ronald Smelser and Enrico Syring. Paderborn: Schoeningh, 2000: 320-331.

_____. *Nazi Administrative Conflict: The Struggle for Executive Power in the General Government of Poland, 1939–1943.* Ph.D. diss. Madison: University of Wisconsin, 1967.

Tregenza, Michael. "Belzec Death Camp." *Wiener Library Bulletin* (London) 30, nos. 41/42 (1977): 8–25.

_____. "Christian Wirth: Inspekteur der SS-Sonderkommandos 'Aktion Reinhardt.'" *Zeszyty Majdanka* (Lublin) 15 (1993): 7–58.

_____. *The "Disappearance" of SS-Hauptscharführer Lorenz Hackenholt. A Report on the 1959–63 West German Police Search for Lorenz Hackenholt, the Gas Chamber Expert of the Aktion Reinhardt Extermination Camps.* The Mazal Library. Retrieved from: http://www.mazal.org/archive/documents/Tregenza/Tregenza01.htm

_____. *Report on the Archaeological Inves-tigations at the Site of the Former Nazi Extermination Camp in Belzec, Poland, 1997–98.* Lublin: N.p., 1998.

Trunk, Isaiah. *Judenrat: The Jewish Coun-cils in Eastern Europe Under Nazi Occu-pation.* New York: Macmillan, 1972.

Tschuppik, Walter. *The Quislings, Hitler's Trojan Horses.* London: Hutchinson & Co., n.d.

Turner, Henry Ashby, Jr. *Hitler's Thirty Days to Power: January 1933.* London: Bloomsbury, 1996.

Tuszynski, Waldemar. "Policyjny i Wojskowy Aparat Okupaczynjy na Lubelszczyznie (Organizacja, sily i niektore dzialania)." *Zeszyty Majdanka* (Lublin) 3 (1969): 21–51.

Veryha, Wasyl, ed. *Die Korrespondenz des Ukrainischen Hauptausschusses in Krakau-Lemberg mit den deutschen Behorden in den Jahren 1939–1944.* [The Correspondence of the Ukrain-ian Central Committee in Cracow and Lviv with the German Authorities]. Edmonton and Toronto: Canadian Institute of Ukrainian Studies Press, University of Alberta, 2000.

Wagner, Dieter, and Gerhard Tom-kowitz. *Ein Volk, Ein Reich, Ein Führer: The Nazi Annexation of Aus-tria, 1938.* Bristol: Longman, 1971.

Warmbrunn, Werner. *The Dutch under German Occupation, 1940–1945.* Stan-ford: Stanford University Press, 1963.

Wedel, Hasso von. *Die Estlandische Rit-terschaft vornehmlich zwischen 1710 und 1783: Das erste Jahrhundert russis-cher Herrschaft.* Konigsberg: Ost-Europa, 1935.

Wiener Library Bulletin (London). Vols. 9 (1955); 19 (1965); 30 (1977).

Wiesenthal, Simon. *Justice not Vengeance.* London: Weidenfeld & Nicolson, 1989.

Wighton, Charles. *Heydrich — Hitler's Most Evil Henchman.* London: Odhams Press, 1962.

Williams, Maurice. "The Aftermath of *Anschluss*: Disillusioned Germans or Budding Austrian Patriots?" *Austrian History Yearbook* 14 (1978): 129–144.

_____. "Another Final Solution: Friedrich Rainer, Carinthian Slovenes, and the Carinthian Question." Paper presented at the American Association for the Advancement of Slavic Stud-ies, St. Louis, Missouri, 19 November 1999.

_____. "Captain Josef Leopold: Austro-Nazi and Austro-Nationalist?" In *Conquering the Past: Austrian Nazism, Yesterday and Today,* ed. Fred Parkin-son. Detroit: Wayne State University Press, 1989: pp. 57-71.

_____. "Delusions of Grandeur: The Austrian National Socialists." *Cana-dian Journal of History/Annales Cana-diennes d'Histoire* 14, no. 3 (December 1979): 417–436.

_____. "Friedrich Rainer e Odilo Globocnik. L'amicizia insolita e i ruoli sinistri di due nazisti tipici." ["Typi-cal Nazis, an Unusual Friendship, and Sinister Roles: Friedrich Rainer and Odilo Globocnik, Nazi Comrades."] Istituto Regionale per la Storia del Movimento di Liberazione Nel Friuli — Venezia Giulia. 25 (June 1997): 141–175.

_____. "Friedrich Rainer, National Socialism, and Postwar Europe: The Historical World of an Austrian Nazi." *Austrian History Yearbook* 30 (1999).

_____. "The Nazis, German National-ism, and Ethnic Diversity: The Adri-atic Coastland Under Friedrich Rainer." *Slovene Studies,* 17, nos. 1–2 (1995): 3–23.

Winiewicz, Jozef. *German Failures in Poland: Natural Obstacles to Nazi Pop-ulation Policy.* London: Polish Research Center, 1942.

_____. *German Withdrawal in the East: A Study of Vital German and Polish Statistics.* London: Polish Research Center, 1942.

_____. "The Quest for German Blood: Policy of Germanization in Poland."

In *Polish Studies and Sketches*. London: Polish Ministry of Information, 1943.

Wistrich, Robert. *Who's Who in Nazi Germany*. London: Weidenfeld & Nicolson, 1982.

Wnuk, Janusz. *Dzieci Polskie Oskarzaja*. 2d ed. Lublin: Wydawnictwo Lubelskie, 1975.

Wroblewski, Bronislaw. "Struktura Wiezienia i Jego Funkcje." *Hitlerowskie Wiezienie na Zamku 1939–1944*. Ed. Zygmunt Mankowski. Lublin: Wydawnictwo Lubelskie, 1988.

Yahil, Leni. *The Holocaust: The Fate of European Jewry, 1932–1945*. New York: Oxford University Press, 1990.

Zieba, Anna. "'Wirtschaftshof Babitz' Podoboz Przy Majatku Dworski Babice," *Zeszyty Oswiecimski* (Wydnanictwo Panstwowego Museum w Oswiecimiu) No. 11, 1969: 69–82.

Zuccotti, Susan. *The Italians and the Holocaust: Persecution, Rescue and Survival*. New York: Basic Books, 1987.

Zucherman, Yatzak. *A Surplus of Memory: Chronicle of the Warsaw Ghetto Uprising*. Berkeley: University of California Press, 1993.

Zwitter, Fran. "The Slovenes and the Habsburg Monarchy." *Austrian History Yearbook*, Vol. 3 (1967): 159–188.

Primary Sources

Newspapers

The Catholic Herald (London), 3 March 1939.

The Daily Herald (London), 15 May 1938; 13 June 1938.

The Daily Mail (London), 23 February 1939.

The Daily Telegraph (London), 14 June 1938; 30 June 1938; 15 July 1938; 26 July 1938; 31 August 1943.

The Manchester Guardian, 13 June 1938.

Samo Obronia, 23 July 1943. (Polish Underground Study Trust, London.)

The Times (London), 25 May 1938; 27 June 1938; 26 September 1942; 12 September 1943; 3 February 1944; 12 April 1944; 29 September 1944; 27 February 1974.

Völkischer Beobachter (Munich), 21 April 1938; 8 February 1939.

The Yorkshire Post (Leeds), 23 June 1938.

Documentary Sources

Brack, Viktor Hermann. Statement. Nuremberg Document NO-426.

Der Chef der Sicherheits-polizei und des S.D. Umwandererzentralstelle — Posen Dienststelle — Litzmannstadt (Lodz). "Zweigstelle — Zamosc inspectlisten von evakuiersten Polen aus der Kreisen Hrubieszow-Zamosc, 1096/78 (5843)." National Archives, Lublin, Poland.

PRO/FO 371–179969.
PRO/WO 170/4622 1165.
PRO/WO 170/7112 1087.
PRO/WO 170/4622 117350.
PRO/WO 204/13006 50885.
PRO/WO 204/13006.
PRO/WO 204–11505 XC5441. (1 SC/CSDIC/X 3).
PRO/WO 208/46739.
PRO/WO 208/4673 166970.
PRO/WO 208/4673 XC68198.
PRO/WO 309/374 XC 14298.
PRO/WO 309/521 XC167205.
PRO/HW 16/32.

Globocnik, Odilo. SS File. Berlin Document Center, U.S. Mission, Berlin. This documentary collection is now held by the German Federal Archive service, with microfilmed copies in the U.S. National Archive and Records Administration, Washington, D.C.

Hedley, W.K. (Major). Statement to Civil Liaison Officer. Spittal, 16 January 1949.

Huppenkothen, Walter. Affidavit, Nuremberg Case VIII. Creutz Document Book, Document No. 22. 24 November 1947.

Krumey, Hermann. Testimony. 27 May 1961. (The Nizkor Project). Nanaimo, Vancouver Island, British Columbia, Canada.

Oberhauser Bd. 8. 208 AR-Z 252/59. Archives of the Central Office of Land Judicial Authorities for the Investigation of National-Socialist Crimes, Ludwigsburg, German Federal Republic. Zentrale Stelle der Landesjustizverwaltungen.

502 AR 420/1962, vol. 4, leaves 798–800.

Michalsen, George. 208 AR-Z 74/60: Michalsen, Bd. 1.

Runhof [aka Cichotski], Max. Statement to Wiesbaden Court, Abt. V/SK. Vol. 12. 15 September 1961. (Internal or office numbers: 2501 & 2121).

Trial of the Major War Criminals before the International Military Tribunal, Nuremberg. 42 vols. Nuremberg: IMT, 1947–49.

U.S. Office of Strategic Services, Research & Analysis Branch, Biographical Report. National Archives and Records Administration, Washington, D.C. RG 153, Records of Judge Advocate General, V. 100–380–1. U.S. War Crimes Office, 14 March 1945.

Interviews

Dressen, Willi. Interview by author. Ludwigsburg, Germany, March 1987.

Gutman, Yisrael. Interview by author. Jerusalem, February 1987.

Kowalska, Stanislawa, Mrs. Interview for the author by John and Zofia Rurka (nee Krepinska). Gdansk, Poland, June 1992.

Rickheim, Irmgard. Interview by author. First interview in May 1998; ongoing contact.

Rieger, Berndt, Dr. Interview by author. First interview in 2000; ongoing contact.

Tregenza, Michael. Interview by author. Lublin, Poland, December 1997.

Weclawik, Zofia. Interview for the author by John and Zofia Rurka (nee Krepinska). Ozorkow, Poland, June 1992.

Personal Narrative

Ramsay, Alexander. *The Ramsay Report: Events Leading to the Capture of ex-Gauleiter Rainer (Kärnten).* Copy of Ramsay's handwritten document in the author's possession.

Index